COMPLEXITY AND PLANNING

New Directions in Planning Theory

Series Editors
Professor Gert de Roo, Department of Planning and Environment
University of Groningen, The Netherlands
Professor Jean Hillier, School of Global Studies, Social Science and Planning,
RMIT University, Melbourne.
Dr Joris Van Wezemael, Geography Unit, Department of Geosciences,
University of Fribourg, Switzerland

Ashgate's series, New Directions in Planning Theory, develops and disseminates theories and conceptual understandings of spatial and physical planning which address such challenges as uncertainty, diversity and incommensurability.

Planning theories range across a wide spectrum, from questions of explanation and understanding, to normative or predictive questions of how planners should act and what future places should look like.

These theories include procedural theories of planning. While these have traditionally been dominated by ideas about rationality, in addition to this, the series opens up to other perspectives and also welcomes theoretical contributions on substantive aspects of planning.

Other theories to be included in the series may be concerned with questions of epistemology or ontology; with issues of knowledge, power, politics, subjectivation; with social and/or environmental justice; with issues of morals and ethics.

Planning theories have been, and continue to be, influenced by other intellectual fields, which often imbue planning theories with awareness of and sensitivity to the multiple dimensions of planning practices. The series editors particularly encourage inter- and trans-disciplinary ideas and conceptualisations.

Complexity and Planning
Systems, Assemblages and Simulations

Edited by

GERT DE ROO
University of Groningen, The Netherlands

JEAN HILLIER
RMIT University, Australia

JORIS VAN WEZEMAEL
University of Fribourg, Switzerland

Routledge
Taylor & Francis Group

LONDON AND NEW YORK

First published 2012 by Ashgate Publishing

Published 2016 by Routledge
2 Park Square, Milton Park, Abingdon, Oxon OX14 4RN
711 Third Avenue, New York, NY 10017, USA

First issued in paperback 2017

Routledge is an imprint of the Taylor & Francis Group, an informa business

Copyright © 2012 Gert De Roo, Jean Hillier and Joris Van Wezemael

Gert De Roo, Jean Hillier and Joris Van Wezemael have asserted their right under the Copyright, Designs and Patents Act, 1988, to be identified as the editors of this work.

All rights reserved. No part of this book may be reprinted or reproduced or utilised in any form or by any electronic, mechanical, or other means, now known or hereafter invented, including photocopying and recording, or in any information storage or retrieval system, without permission in writing from the publishers.

Notice:
Product or corporate names may be trademarks or registered trademarks, and are used only for identification and explanation without intent to infringe.

British Library Cataloguing in Publication Data
Complexity and Planning: Systems, Assemblages and Simulations. –
    (New Directions in Planning Theory)
    1. City planning. 2. City planning – Simulation methods. 3. Public spaces – Planning.
    4. Public spaces – Planning – Simulation methods.
    I. Series II. Roo, Gert de. III. Hillier, Jean. IV. Wezemael, Joris Van.
    307.1'216–dc23

Library of Congress Cataloging-in-Publication Data
Roo, Gert de.
    Complexity and Planning: Systems, Assemblages and Simulations / by Gert De Roo,
    Jean Hillier, and Joris Van Wezemael.
        p.   cm. – (New Directions in Planning Theory)
    Includes bibliographical references and index.
    1. City planning – Philosophy. 2. City planning – Social aspects. I. Hillier, Jean.
    II. Wezemael, Joris Van. III. Title.
    HT166.R655 2012
    307.1'216–dc23   2012010057

ISBN 13: 978-1-138-10958-2 (pbk)
ISBN 13: 978-1-4094-0347-0 (hbk)

Contents

List of Figures

List of Tables

Notes on Contributors

Arwin van Buuren is Associate Professor at the Department of Public Administration, Erasmus University Rotterdam. His research activities focus on the domain of water and climate governance. He is especially interested in the way in which complex governance processes are organized and how the relation between knowledge and governance can be optimized.

David Byrne is Professor in the School of Applied Social Sciences at the Durham University. Byrne's research interests include case base methods, complexity theory, postindustrial social structures, privatization of welfare systems, quantitative methods and urban systems.

Karen S. Christensen is Associate Professor of City and Regional Planning at the College of Environmental Design, University of California, Berkeley. Karen Christensen has taught in the Department of City and Regional Planning since 1982 in the areas of housing policy, program planning and evaluation, organization and politics of planning, and implementation, among others. Karen Christensen is a research associate in the Institute of Urban and Regional Development. Her specializations are Intergovernmental Relations, Evaluation, Housing Policy, Organizational Theory and Planning Theory.

Andrew Crooks is Assistant Professor at the Department of Computational Social Science, George Mason University. Since completion of his PhD and before joining George Mason University, Andrew held the position of 'GLA Economics Research Fellow in Urban Systems' at the Centre for Advanced Spatial Analysis (CASA), University College London, where he continued to develop geographical explicit agent-based models along with exploring and developing various other GIS applications and models focused around London.

Gert de Roo is Professor in Planning, Head of the Department of Spatial Planning and Environment at the Faculty of Spatial Sciences, University of Groningen. He is President of the Association of European Schools of Planning (AESOP) (2011-2015). His research interest is on decision making concerning interventions within the physical environment. Gert de Roo's work bridges contemporary planning theory and the complexity sciences, making use of concepts such as 'degrees of complexity' (static complexity), 'non-linear rationales' (dynamic complexity), transition management, robust-dynamic interplay of spatial and spatial economic models representing complex systems, and more. Since 2005 Gert de Roo is coordinator of the AESOP working group on complexity and planning. He is editor of *A Planner's Encounter with Complexity*, the volume previous to this book.

Oswald Devisch is lecturer and researcher at the PHL-University College, Belgium, since 2006 where he explores themes such as coproduction, new media, private planning, urban games. Oswald Devisch is by origin a civil-engineer architect and urban designer. He studied at the Catholic University of Leuven, Belgium and at the Bartlett School of Architecture, London. He obtained a doctoral degree at the Technical University of Eindhoven, the Netherlands, on spatial simulation models.

Jurian Edelenbos is Professor at the Department of Public Administration, Erasmus University Rotterdam. In November 2000 he finished his PhD thesis on process-management of interactive governance about spatial development. From 2001 till 2003 he worked as a Research Fellow in the field of Multiple Land Use, Complex Decision-Making and Public-Private Partnership at the Department of Public Administration, Erasmus University Rotterdam.

Lasse Gerrits is Associate Professor in Public Administration at the Erasmus University Rotterdam, research group Governance of Complex Systems. He studied Policy and Management of Complex Spatial Developments and was a researcher at TNO Built Environment and Geosciences. He received his Doctor's degree in 2008. His current research focuses on the complexity of the process of decision-making in metropolitan governance, urban planning and transport and infrastructure. The projects are approached from the perspective of complexity theory.

Jean Hillier is Associate Dean in the School of Global Studies, Social Science and Planning at the RMIT University, Melbourne. Hillier is Discipline Head of Environment, Planning and Sustainability. Hillier's research interests include questions of social justice, social exclusion and ethics and citizen participation in government decision-making and in planning theory. She is interested in decision making and in issues of institutional transformation. Her work explores ideas of complex adaptive systems and resilience with regard to both spatial areas and planning systems. Hillier is editor of the international journal *Planning Theory*.

René Kemp is Professorial fellow at UNU-MERIT and Professor of Innovation and Sustainable Development at ICIS, Maastricht University. He obtained his PhD in Economics from Maastricht University in 1995. Kemp's expertise is in Eco-innovation, Sustainability transitions, Policy analysis, Science-policy interactions and Governance for sustainable development. His book *Environmental Policy and Technical Change* received great acclaim. His expertise covers various sectors, in particular industry, mobility, energy and waste.

Derk Loorbach is director of the Dutch Research Institute for Transitions (DRIFT) and Associate Professor at the Faculty of Social Science, both at Erasmus

University Rotterdam. Derk Loorbach was amongst the first researchers to develop the concept and approach of transition management. He started his professional career working as researcher for the International Centre for Integrative Studies (ICIS), Maastricht University. Within his research, he focuses on the development of transition management in theory and practice through his PhD-research and diverse consultancy projects in this area.

Valeria Monno is Assistant Professor in Urban and Regional Planning at the Polytechnic of Bari (Italy). Her research has recently focused on the theoretical challenges emerging in participatory formal and informal environmental and urban policy-making processes to collaborative planning in order to expand its transformative potentials.

Sibout Nooteboom is Associate Professor at the Department of Public Administration, Erasmus University Rotterdam and Senior Policy Advisor at the Ministry of Internal Affairs, the Netherlands. His areas of interests are learning, leading and professionalizing in complex policy systems, the organization of civil services to facilitate emergence, cooperation in area-based development and cooperation between ministries, between public and private sector and between layers of government.

Juval Portugali is Professor in Geography at the Department of Geography and the Human Environment, Tel Aviv University. He is Head of the ESLab (Environmental Simulation Laboratory), the Porter School of Environmental Studies. His specializations are Cognitive Geography, theories of self-organization in relation to cognitive maps, urbanism, agent-based modelling, socio-spatial change, spatial and regional archaeology. His current research focuses on inter-representation networks and the construction of cognitive maps and on the city as a self-organizing system.

Jan Rotmans is Professor in transitions and transition management at the Erasmus University Rotterdam. He is also the scientific director of DRIFT (Dutch Research Institute For Transitions), which he established in September 2004. Jan Rotmans is one of the founding fathers of Integrated Assessment and an expert in the field of integrated modelling, scenario-analysis, indicator-development and uncertainty analysis and management. He is scientific director of the Dutch Network on System Innovations: Transitions to a Sustainable Society (KSI).

Geert Teisman is Professor in Public Administration at the Erasmus University Rotterdam. He achieved degrees in transport and sociology. His PhD thesis concerned the phenomena of complex decision making especially in the field of urban development, transport en environmental affairs. Since 2000 he is Professor in Complex Decision Making and Process Management at the Erasmus University. Furthermore he practices several functions on the edge of scientific research and practical applications. Geert Teisman is member of the executive board of Netlipse, a European knowledge exchange network in the field of infrastructure project management.

Peter Trummer is Professor and Head of the Institute of Urban Design & Urban Planning at the University of Innsbruck. He was formerly employed as a Professor at the Academy of Fine Arts Vienna and is the former head of the Berlage Institute's Associative Design Research Program. This program investigated the potential of designing new site-specific housing environments by applying associative design to all scales of a design process to increase its relevance to the architectural discipline. Peter Trummer lectures and publishes internationally and his research focuses on population thinking in architecture; in particular, how city life, urban planning policies, economic desires, and population growth may be better integrated into the design of living environments.

Paul M. Torrens is Associate Professor in the Department of Geography, University of Maryland and Director of its Geosimulation Laboratory. Paul Torrens is also an Affiliate in the University's Center for Social Dynamics and Complexity, as well as the GeoDa Center for Geospatial Analysis and Computation. His research is focused on Geographic Information Science and development of geosimulation and geocomputation tools, applied modelling of complex urban systems, and new emerging cyberspaces. His work earned him a CAREER Award from the US National Science Foundation in 2007 and he was awarded the Presidential Early Career Award for Scientists and Engineers by President George W. Bush in 2008. The Presidential Early Career Award is the highest honour that the US government bestows upon young scientists; Torrens is the first geographer to receive the Award.

Joris E. Van Wezemael is Associate Professor at the Socio-spatial complexity lab, University of Fribourg; and Pensimo Management Ltd, Switzerland. Before he was director of the Centre of Research on Architecture, Society & the Built Environment at ETH Zurich. His teaching and research interests are focused on economic and political geography and on planning. His main research interest lies in the analysis of spatial decision-making and social complexity. Research projects comprise policy analysis and studies on decision making in economic contexts. In theoretical respects he developed an action-theory based approach for spatial decision making analysis. More recently complexity thinking and its potential to move beyond anthropocentric and essentialist traditions of spatial decision making analysis constitutes a major focus of interest.

Cathy Wilkinson is a doctoral candidate at the Stockholm Resilience Centre in Sweden. Cathy's PhD research will critically explore the application of resilience science and an ecosystem services approach to metropolitan spatial planning and governance. It seeks to identify ways in which cross-scale coordination between earth system ecosystem governance and metropolitan scale urban governance can be improved to deliver social-ecological resilience. It draws on empirical work with government agencies across Europe (particularly Sweden) and in Melbourne, Australia. Cathy Wilkinson was the Executive Director Strategy Development for the Victorian Department of Sustainability and Environment until 2005 where she led the development and implementation of Melbourne's most recent metropolitan plan, Melbourne 2030.

Preface

Complexity and Planning: Systems, Assemblages and Simulations is the second book on complexity and planning in the Ashgate series 'New Directions in Planning Theory'. As the first book on complexity and planning, *A Planner's Encounter with Complexity*, it is a product that emerged out of AESOP's working group on Complexity and Planning. AESOP is the Association of European Schools of Planning, and supports working groups to come together several times a year. The working group on Complexity and Planning has been in existence since 2005, holding its first meeting in Vienna. This second book shows an evolution from pure curiosity about complexity (the first book) to in-depth engagement with specific topics, such as adaptivity, resilience and self-organization. These are new notions to planning, worth exploring 'in depth'. 'In-depth analysis' was, in fact, the working title of this second volume.

The moment the book was completed, we felt 'systems, assemblages and simulations' would be a more suitable title reflecting the book's content. Spatial planners create bridges between 'what is' and 'what could be', 'what should be' and 'what is desired'. The authors in the volume *Complexity and Planning: Systems, Assemblages and Simulations* approach this challenge by exploring the productivity of combining spatial planning traditions with thinking about complexity. Systems, assemblages and simulations are the abstractions which relate a 'complex' world full of autonomous change and the human desire to interfere.

Complexity thinking has become an increasingly important theoretical perspective within planning related fields. In recent years have we witnessed an intensification of the engagement of planning researchers with complexity theories. In this volume the various authors tap into the potential of the ontological shift from simple, fixed or static systems to complex adaptive systems. In doing so the authors reap benefits from the cross-fertilization of diverse fields within planning thought – from communicative approaches to modelling and simulation – with the intellectual diversity offered in complexity thinking.

The result is an invitation for theorists and modellers of planning to reach beyond an analysis–synthesis mode of thinking and embrace an associate–creativity mechanism. The philosophical consequences are to consider not just realism and relativism as important perspectives, but also idealism and relationalism. In bridging planning theory and complexity thinking this book explores the possibilities and consequences of idealism and relationalism as powerful additional perspectives within spatial planning.

While the first volume is very much about exploring the whereabouts of complexity and planning, this second volume is concerned with identifying new routes of interest to planning theory. The various authors in this volume point to the possibility of a 'crisis' in what has become planning's major theoretical and practical debates, suggesting the 'end' of the dominance of the communicative paradigm for planning. This watershed has to be passed and can be, the authors argue, if we are willing to engage the potentialities embedded within the complexity sciences. These could result in trajectories emerging out of contemporary planning debates towards issues which relate to time, non-linearity, development and progress. These trajectories are explored in this volume, oriented towards understanding the emergence of dynamic change.

Complexity and Planning - Systems, Assemblages & Simulations is the result of a process that took substantially more time than expected. Series of discussions were needed among the editors and between editors and authors, convincing authors to develop specific issues or to explore an entirely different perspective. With respect to the latter, while realist and relativist perspectives are common to planning theorists and practicing planners, a relationalist perspective is not, which is crucial when engaging with complexity. A project like this volume needs time to allow its content to emerge and mature. Having done so, we feel that the book makes a clear statement: relationalism is at least as important a perspective for spatial planning as realism and relativism. As are also issues of time, non-linearity, emergence, adaptivity, self-organization and co-evolution. Taking a relationalist perspective to planning demands a whole new set of concepts for which the complexity sciences prove to be a wonderful source.

We thank all our authors for participating in this volume with both faith and patience. Many thanks also to the people at Ashgate, in particular our publisher Val Rose, who was always reassuring about quality being more important than speed of production. A warm thanks also to Willem Dijkstra for the cover design and to Tamara Kaspers for reshaping the various authors' figures proposed into a coherent whole.

We hope this book will be appreciated by the spatial planning community as a source of inspiration for exploration of new routes to theoretical insights which will help us better to understand our emergent, non-linear, complex world, so full of surprises.

Gert de Roo
Groningen

Jean Hillier
Melbourne

Joris Van Wezemael
Zurich

Chapter 1

Complexity and Spatial Planning: Introducing Systems, Assemblages and Simulations

Gert de Roo, Jean Hillier and Joris Van Wezemael[1]

1.1 What about planning in a fuzzy, fluid world?

Proposing interventions within the urban space is like putting your head into a lion's mouth. It is the spatial planner's job to create a bridge between 'what is' and 'what could be' (or in normative terms: 'what should be'). The 'what is' represents issues such as traffic congestion, appreciation of more space, the need for cheap housing, tensions between stakeholders, the call for public safety, undesirable urban landscapes, and much more. These difficulties are seen by the public and the media (not to mention the opposition within the political arena) preferably in black or white, or requiring a yes or no answer, therefore assuming these can be tackled easily.

Every planner knows from experience that even out of fairly straightforward planning issues, fuzzy and fluid moments emerge that are full of uncertainties and could easily result in legislative jungles, bureaucratic nightmares and confusing power relations. Moreover, a growing number of planning issues are not straightforward at all, being overly complicated throughout the various stages of the planning process, with no-one being able (anymore) to grasp all of the aspects of any one project. This is caused by increasing internal and external complexities. Both space and time, being points of reference in planning and the issues it deals with, also add to the complexities. With regard to space and place, this constrains as well as implies a difference, and it injects a notion of distribution (Craviolini, Van Wezemael, Wirth, 2011). This distribution, as Thrift (1999) argues, accounts for much of what happens in the world. With regard to time, so ignored by planners

1   Gert de Roo is Professor in Planning and heads the Department of Spatial Planning and Environment at the Faculty of Spatial Sciences, University of Groningen. Jean Hillier is Associate Dean in the School of Global Studies, Social Science and Planning at the RMIT University, Melbourne. She is also Discipline Head of Environment, Planning and Sustainability. Joris E. Van Wezemael is Associate Professor at the Geography Unit of the University of Freiburg, Switzerland.

(De Roo, 2010b), it produces an order of concomitance with distinct and emerging properties, as well as non-linear change.

There is also the issue of contextual dynamics in spatial planning, which is becoming increasingly relevant as a result of a rapidly changing environment, but also because of changing societal opinions (what matters today was not an issue five years ago, and might no longer be an issue, say, five years from now). Experienced planning practitioners therefore take a humble position while playing the game called spatial development. This 'game' is by no means an academic fun park, where everything goes as planned, where moves can be well explained and always have a happy ending. On the contrary, it is a very serious 'game' full of pitfalls and with rules that are still barely understood.

Most of the issues that matter within the realm of spatial planning are not easily defined, if a definition is possible at all. This ambiguity continues to increase due to the growing complexities of our society and the dynamics of urban life. Thus, the control that remains is seen by some as a mere illusion. The response often seen attempts to reduce the project into smaller parts that are better understood. This does not mean, however, that the project as a whole is understood, let alone controlled. What are the consequences for spatial planning if nothing is any longer what it seems and everything is in flux? Are we meant to be thinking outside the box, finding alternative means to grasp reality, celebrating story lines, discourses and metaphors and conducting proper situation analyses, taking account of a more dynamic perspective on the reality we are in? Planners must find ways to engage in the development of futures-to-come; however, they are doing a bad job if these worlds cannot be related to an understanding of the here and now, and how it evolves. Thus, neither adhering to a 'positivists' reality nor merely plunging into a sea of social constructs will do the job.

One promising approach to moving beyond the 'facts-versus-stories' contradiction is to identify the theoretical ideas that appreciate dynamics, flows and uncertainty, and to carefully consider possible bridges and linkages between these theoretical ideas and both planning theory and practice. The complexity sciences offer such a perspective for understanding and dealing with dynamics, flows and uncertainty, and much more. This volume is the second concerned with issues of complexity in the Ashgate series, *New Directions in Planning Theory*. The first volume, edited by Gert de Roo and Elisabete Silva (2010), highlighted the variety of meanings that complexity possesses as a concept in planning theory and practice. As such, the volume represented the 'planner's first encounters with complexity' (De Roo and Silva, 2010: 10). In this second volume we hope to make a substantial step forward, with authors who have tried to delve further into the mechanisms of complexity, superimposing these on spatial planning and decision-making in order to make sense of their planning practices and experiences in a dynamic world that time and again generates states that are far from equilibrium.

In support of this more in-depth analysis that will discuss complexity and planning from a systems perspective, an assemblage perspective and a simulations perspective, this introduction presents the philosophical context of the volume as a whole. This context is intended to be a common ground, a rough framework, from which the discipline of spatial planning and the complexity sciences – and their intertwining – can be understood (see Section 1.2). Our 'common ground' opens up a number of established pathways for thinking about the world, for making sense of it. It is a toolbox for navigation that will – hopefully – be helpful to the reader of this volume. This common ground is outlined in terms of four different perspectives on reality that are partly complementary and allow for different entry points into a planner's engagement with complexity – representing his/her (theoretical) background and harvesting different perspectives.

We feel that it would not be wise to begin a volume on planning and complexity with a proclamation of 'one coherent world'; rather, the openness and indeed the ambiguity of our framework reflects key insights from complexity thinking (see below). More precisely, we welcome lines of thought that can be related to realism, idealism, relativism and relationalism as a reference for considering the various ways in which spatial planning and the complexity sciences can be understood, as a reference to proposed linkages between spatial planning and complexity, and as a reference for positioning the various contributions in this book.

However, we will not make use of these philosophical perspectives as ready-made 'boxes' in which we place the contributions – this would be an injustice to most of the authors. Rather, we use these perspectives as a means to navigate through the sea of ideas and approaches created by the interaction and thinking of planning and complexity together. In planning theory, reference is frequently made to realism, critical realism and relativism. We believe these issues are of value but constrain the debate. In positioning complexity within the realm of planning theory we strongly feel that relationalism (valuing is relation-dependent – referring to various 'degrees of ...' in planning and complexity) and idealism (making reference to time) are also relevant if we are to understand our world, which is a non-linear world that is out of equilibrium.

Our contribution to the debate on planning theory is to examine relationalism and idealism, which is desirable in relating the complexity sciences to planning theory and being able to benefit from the complexity sciences within planning theory. We will also briefly outline the nature of 'complexity'. Complexity is a term within the complexity sciences that represents a materially identifiable mechanism and also acts as a metaphorical umbrella and conceptual framework for a variety of understandings and debates. The introduction then presents some of the more prominent streams of thought that constitute various complexity theories and actual and possible bridges between them. A guide to the volume's structure will then be provided to assist readers in navigating its contents.

1.2 It's all mind-stuff

Since Immanuel Kant (2003 [1781]) it is widely accepted that the mind is the centre of our self-understanding, as well as our understanding of others and the universe that surrounds us. Or, as Arthur Eddington (1928) stated, 'The stuff of the world is mind-stuff.' The mind mirrors all that comes to us, either through the senses or through our reasoning, and it allows us to construct a perceived and logical reality that we reflect upon and challenge continuously, and through which we deconstruct, reconsider and adapt to our latest insights (a process that usually takes place within the subconscious).

This does not mean there is clarity about how the mind constructs one or many realities and how these constructed realities condition our movements, choices and responses to the outside world. Nor should the notion of 'mind-stuff' be misread as a claim for mere social constructivism. However, while rejecting a perspective that reduces the world to what the mind (or an interaction of various minds) makes of it, we wish to point out that spatial planning needs to be able to develop alternative futures which relate people, places, discourses, and more, in varying ways. The alternative futures produced on this basis (ideas, story lines, draft plans, etc.) can and should then be discussed, debated and evaluated. Our starting point should help us consider the variety of modes in which the materiality of humanity or the spatiality of the social, political and economic realms can be approached.

There are various ideas, by and large from philosophers and psychologists, about how to conceptualize the way we understand the reality of which we are part. These various ideas represent differences in opinion as to what triggers the mind most and how this influences our understanding. We take the view that the various opinions and ideas do matter and are valid in some way, as they represent a variety of routes to understanding. We take it as important to consider not just one but the variety of routes to understanding reality, ideally in combination with each other, as we believe this is also what our mind does.

The routes that we propose to consider are realism, idealism, relativism and relationalism. We see these as partly complementary in understanding the outside world, and we consider them relevant to a reflection upon the discipline of spatial planning, the complexity sciences and the way these two possibly relate. These routes represent four different strategies of argumentation about how reality is given, perceived and understood, and how reality features identities or images of social and physical environments that are appreciated by the many. We will outline the four perspectives in order to construct a frame of reference that helps us to recombine two streams of thought: the discipline of spatial planning and the complexity sciences.

Realism and critical realism

From a traditional realist perspective, an object has an intrinsic meaning which is apparent to us in the encounter with it. Taking this to its extreme, one could say there is just one 'true' reality. As such, the world can be understood through a subject-object relationship. The understanding focuses by and large on the object (entity) and its causal interactions with its environment. Through cause and effect relationships the object unveils its 'given' quality, and this quality is represented by functionalities relating to the object that explain how 'it' works through internal mechanisms and how we can make use of these mechanisms. The validity of the observation is tested by repetitive measures and repeat results, and if done correctly, predictability regarding future developments becomes possible. Within spatial planning, this realist perspective has led to a strong focus on goals-and-means relationships, conceiving of the planner as the 'expert' in these relationships, and laying ground for some planners to believe they could create the world single-handedly.

Such a realist perspective and its object orientation considers that the subject is able to become aware of an outside world through its interactions with what is physically 'real'. These interactions with the material world (the physical as well as the social) lead us to experiences from which we learn and from which we gain understanding of this outside world. As a result of this process of interaction we gain knowledge upon which we base our choices while responding to the outside world. The contribution by Byrne in this volume is particularly helpful in this respect.

The traditional realist stance has been criticized in many ways, giving rise to a revision in the form of so-called critical realism (Sayer, 1984; Yeung, 1997). This strand of reasoning considers that humans are limited in interpreting all that comes through the senses. Full objectivity is therefore an illusion. The best we humans can do is to continuously critically assess our interpretations of what is given and what we think is given. This is sometimes referred to as 'representative realism', as there is an interpretive step between the object and the observer. Despite the acceptance of an interpretative phase between the object and the observer, causality is considered to be the main route to understanding reality.

Today we increasingly acknowledge that the result of this subject-object encounter is a biased view, which is a 'functional' reality. Causality, or as the explanation of events taking place as a result of action (cause) and reaction (effect) between objects (or functions or messages or ...), is also no longer an outspoken representative of this functional reality, as we have to consider remote causal ('causa remota' or indirect causality) relationships in addition to direct causal relationships ('causa proxima'). With regard to the complexity sciences we must also acknowledge non-linear causalities and causalities that are self-referential. Despite the growing ambiguity regarding causality, planning theory has always been very strongly related to this critical realist perspective on reality. In planning theory this is represented by the functional, instrumental or technical rationale as the driving force behind planning and decision-making.

Finally, recent contributions to planning theory (Van Wezemael, 2008, 2010; see also the contributions by Monno, Trummer and Hillier and Van Wezemael in this volume) have introduced Deleuzian/Delandian thought and with it a 'neo-realist' approach. It argues that a belief in the autonomous existence of the world offers insights into the genesis of form that provide a way out of essentialist or rationalist views. It can therefore be considered as a form of relationalism (see below).

Idealism

As the second of the four perspectives on reality, we propose idealism. It contrasts with traditional realism insofar as it does not build on the idea of an absolute existence but on ideas per se. Ideas, abstractions and imaginings are products that our mind is very capable of constructing. Through ideas we are able to deviate from our ideas of the 'real' as a mere reflection of the realist's 'given', and to reflect upon it from a virtual distance, without this having to become a metaphysical exercise (in this respect idealism is an appreciated precondition of relationalism and vice versa). This enables us to think through how a reality could be in an imaginary or virtual way (imagined reality), which could lead to the ideal in contrast to the real. This is what planners and decision-makers do: they compose and suggest a desired outcome (the ideal) to tackle the difficulties we face today.

Schopenhauer (2000 [1851]) defined the ideal as 'mental pictures' out of which we deduct 'subjective knowledge'. For Schopenhauer, the 'ideal' is synonymous with 'ideas in a subject's mind', raising considerations regarding the relationship between our ideas and the reality that surrounds us. The ideal is therefore a representation of the images we produce in our head, with the world being nothing but a representation – consciously perceived and reasoned and unconsciously grasped – based on mental pictures we are able to produce. In its extreme, the consequence is that our awareness of the 'real' remains restricted to our own consciousness. Taking a less extreme position, it is reasonable to say that above all we are aware of anything through mental representations, from which we deduce the message about something happening out there. What precisely is happening out there remains, for the mind, a mental construct about which we are able to communicate with others and which, in return, colours our mental construct again as it links in intersubjectively with others (relativism, see below).

Models, for example, are tools designed to help us obtain a better grip on reality, proposing representations of the 'real'. Models are simplifications 'replacing reality with its representation' (Batty, 2005: 515). Building a fruitful representation is, on the one hand, about simplifying the 'real' (realism, see above) and, on the other hand, about constructing mind frames for considering the various components of the model and how these components (might) interrelate.

Idealism is not, however, so much about how the world 'is' but how it 'could be'. It refers to a capacity of our minds to compose 'another' world, however much related to the 'real', it can propose different 'reals-to-come'. In this imagined realm we can play with 'reality'. This allows us to imagine, for example, desired, extreme or 'worst-case' realities which differ from what we consider to be the actual 'real'.

However, from the perspective of idealism, the 'real' as the offspring of realism is also no more than just an idea. The importance of idealism is therefore to acknowledge that we can move beyond what we perceive as 'real', whatever the 'real' is, to deconstruct and reconstruct this 'real', proposing a different content to a form, an alternative function for a structure, or various scenarios for a process and so on. As such, we humans are able to give an alternative, aberrant meaning to an object, situation, story, discourse, etc., which puts these into a different perspective and might alter the use we put them to and the way we see them in relation to other objects, stories or the environment of which they are part (or which they generate). This process is called *creativity*.

It is not an easy process as we humans are constrained by dogmas, doctrines and paradigms; ideas that have proven themselves worthwhile (at least for some period of time). Nevertheless, this process of creativity means that we are able to superimpose an imagined world in which we are able to replace our image of the 'real' world with alternative ones. And this leads to conclusions regarding our image of the 'real' world and to actions with regard to how to deal with it or, more precisely, how to improve it.

This idealism is of interest to planners as it leads to a possible and virtual reality that can represent a desired future world into which we want to transform the reality of today, with all its problems, difficulties and mistakes. Spatial planners no longer believe that a utopian world can be created, as we have more or less abandoned blueprint planning. Nevertheless, and perhaps even more so, we still need directions to spatial developments in the sense of alternative futures. The complexity sciences allow the production of many images, allowing us to see the world differently, such as fractals as a metaphor for flows and repetitions of reality on various scales, and bifurcations representing thresholds in evolutionary processes. Understanding idealism as allowing us to focus on a world to come, also allows us to address the temporal dimension in which transformations of structures and functions, of objects and the way we see them, of situations and the way we appreciate them, all alter. Through idealism we can touch upon the relevance of development and progress for planners, emphasizing trajectories in time. As such, we are able to progress towards a desirable world or set of worlds that we are capable of imagining and to which spatial planners want to contribute.

Relativism

While idealism stands in opposition to traditional realism, our third perspective in the framework offers many points of passage to idealism. Relativism takes the position that the world is to be understood through interacting subjects sharing ideas, values and opinions regarding the outside world. From this perspective, our reality is a construct strongly fed by intersubjective relationships and this often entails a social-constructivist approach. Subjects share their ideas, values and emotions regarding the objects they encounter, leading to a common understanding and to shared values regarding the world out there. This touches upon the world of symbols and language.

However, it also implicitly means that a subject-object relationship (see realism) is somehow still desired, at least to have experience of a material world, being the frame of reference to which all subjects relate, with language (in a broad sense, including diverse sets of code systems) as representing the material world.

One important consequence is the need for a subject-object interaction to be located somewhere within a relativist world perspective.

In the struggle to understand the 'complex' mechanisms in our physical and social environments, and when finding ways to construct appropriate mental frameworks which enhance the way we interfere with 'reality', relativistic reflections and confrontations are both prominent and crucial. Relativism is a perspective that is increasingly appreciated within the theoretical debate in planning and for many it works as an alternative to realism and the criticism that accompanies it.

Traditional realism and the world of facts and figures have their charm, but their limitations are becoming increasingly obvious. While realism is one main driver in seeking evidence and gaining certainty, we have to acknowledge uncertainty and ambiguity as *part* of reality. From a planning theory perspective, we no longer see the world solely from a critical realist perspective but from a relativist perspective as well. While a critical realist view of the world remains dominant, a shift took place in planning theory in the early 1990s, known as the communicative turn in planning, which has led to the adoption of various perspectives relating to a relativist view of reality. This means that the intersubjective (or social-constructivist) perspective is appreciated as at least complementary to the object-oriented perspective.

In this respect, one solution to dealing with uncertainty could be the appreciation of stories and story lines about the 'real' in order to find common ground. Stories are helpful in reasoning about and imagining how reality 'is', how it works and how it could work. While it is impossible to grasp every detail of reality, stories support us in imagining how reality 'can be seen'. 'How reality can be seen' and 'how reality might work' become a means of understanding reality, which is an attractive way of negotiating about possibilities and likelihoods regarding the 'real' without necessarily having to understand the real in all its details.

The outcome of such a trajectory could be a discourse that combines and connects various individual opinions and values into a shared vision, which then becomes the point of reference for an entire group with regard to their actions, behaviour and attitude. The downside to this is that consensus about how to see reality could very well deviate from what is 'real' beyond intersubjective discourses and in the end could be entirely unrelated to the facts. Nevertheless, shared values result in agreements about how to see and how to deal with the world that surrounds us. As such we can speak of an 'agreed reality'. In spatial planning this idea of an agreed reality is embedded within the notions of a communicative rationale, participative planning, communicative action and collaborative planning.

While realism builds on the idea of certainty, relativism is, in a way, able to deal with uncertainty, which, however, comes at a price, as it is a mode of thinking where the natural and technological worlds are fully absorbed by the social world ('interpretation'; see Van Wezemael in this volume). Some planning theorists therefore take both perspectives as extreme and opposing visions, and focus on a world between them, where both certain and uncertain realities can be found side by side. Some point out that this creates a duality between an object-oriented and an intersubjective perspective on reality (De Roo and Porter, 2007; Portugali, 2000; Zuidema, 2011). Despite this duality, the world will present us with a variety of situations that differ in degrees of certainty and uncertainty. Some take this differentiation as a means to categorize planning issues according to which approaches, techniques and tools can best be used. This differentiation, considering the world in terms of 'degrees of ...' (see also De Roo, 2003) and contingency, brings us to another perspective, namely relationalism.

Relationalism

Finally, we propose relationalism, which is not yet widely accepted as a frame of reference in spatial planning. We view relationalism as entailing an understanding of our world as one in which objects, situations, values, ideas and behaviour acquire meaning in their relationship to other objects, situations, values, ideas and behaviour. Relationalism does not refer to a reality that is 'black and white', provides 'yes and no' answers, or 'zero and one' solutions. Nor is it a reality in which agreement about how to see reality prevails. Rather, relationalism embraces a world with infinite shades of grey, produced on the basis of relationships. These infinite shades of grey can be seen as a metaphor for the endless number of situations with which spatial planners, for example, are confronted.

With regard to spatial planning, relationalism presents us with an elegant alternative or addition to realist and relativist modes of reasoning. A 'one true world' perspective could result in treating all planning situations alike, making use of generic rules. From a relativist perspective, all these situations could very well be dealt with individually, agreeing with stakeholders about how to see the particular case and how to act accordingly. The alternative offered by a relational perspective is to consider how each situation is produced on the basis of specific relationships, how it relates to other, comparable situations, how they are generated and how they are treated and dealt with.

Comparing planning situations could result in categories that differ, for example, in terms of certainty and uncertainty, or the simplicity-complexity-chaos spectrum, which could lead to a differentiation in approach. For some situations, the most straightforward ones, generic rules will suffice, while others are so specific, unique and highly embedded within the local context that an area-specific strategy is needed (as proposed by De Roo, 2003). With regard to spatial planning, most issues are found somewhere between the two alternatives (certainty and simplicity versus uncertainty and chaos), in the fuzzy middle where certainty and uncertainty are found side by side (De Roo and Porter, 2007). Taking the position that situations differ but are comparable, and therefore connect, results in a reality that is considered contingent.

A contingent reality is of interest in understanding planning situations as it leads to a differentiation of reality (and therefore of planning situations) into various 'degrees'. These degrees are helpful with respect to how to act, as this varies from category to category. On the one hand, these varying degrees by which we can categorize planning situations can be deduced from reality through various criteria (realism). On the other hand, the varying degrees can also be the product of what is perceived and valued by subjects in their interactions with others (relativism). In both ways, entities, issues, situations and events acquire meaning through their relationship to other entities, issues, situations and events (see the contributions by De Roo, Monno and Van Wezemael in this volume). Our actions with regard to a specific situation depend largely on how this situation relates to other situations, their specifics (internal) and their contextual setting (externally). This is what we consider crucial in our reflections on planning and complexity, using phrases such as 'degrees of a mix of spatial functions', 'degrees of interaction' and 'degrees of complexity'.

A contingent reality includes a causal world in which both time and space are related, and by comparing situational change in time and space we are able to see development (earlier-later relationship; see Weinert, 2006). As such, it helps us to understand historical events by putting them in the dimensions of time and space. However, this relational perspective is not just about comparing (relating) physical or material events. Through a relational perspective, intersubjective phenomena such as power relations also acquire meaning and guide our actions, behaviour and attitude.

A second strand that can be considered relational thought refers to assemblage thinking (as proposed for planning by Van Wezemael, 2008). In his definition of relationalism, Kaipayil (2009) states that the identity of an entity is defined by its relations. These relations include the entity's intra-relations (relations between its constitutive elements) and inter-relations (relations with other entities). Assemblage thinking emphasizes that every relation has a localized rather than a transcendent motive. Thus, individuals and society, in other words the subject and the social, are empirically inseparable and 'strictly simultaneous and con-substantial' (Massumi, 2002: 68). Relations, however, remain 'exterior', in the sense that component parts are not solely constituted by the very relations to other parts in the whole (Deleuze and Parnet, 2002). Insofar as relationalism claims that everything that exists is relational, it may be considered as a form of neo-realism, as mentioned above. Furthermore, a relationalist would agree that the world is (being) constructed – however, not (solely) in a social (constructivist) way.

When creating alternative story lines or trying to think 'outside the box' in our daily life, professional or otherwise, we relate things, avoiding the common and the obvious – thereby unveiling novel, emergent properties of the planning situation and possibly alternative ways of actualizing sets of solutions (idealism, see above). This comparing, relating or re-relating of situations takes place in various ways. What we often do is compare by metaphor and analogy. Nietzsche (2000) was very much aware of the power of metaphors, as he saw 'truth' as being the result of the repetitive use of metaphors. Lakoff and Johnson (1980) convincingly state that metaphors structure our perceptions and understanding. We are very willing to share metaphors and analogies with others if we feel that there is a common understanding. For example the 'butterfly effect', presented by Lorenz (1963, 1972) to explain 'sensitive dependence on initial conditions' (De Roo, this volume), is appreciated as a means to understand the concept of chaos. As another example, in this volume Hillier refers to the Baroque and the Romantic eras when discussing two ways of considering the interaction between spatial planning and the complexity sciences. It is a kind of understanding that does not make use of an *analysis-synthesis* approach but an *association-creativity* mechanism. It refers to our ability to combine various independent attributes (objects, events, meanings, interactions, stories) into something meaningful, which is a creative process shared with and understood by others.

1.3 Mechanisms of understanding complexity and planning

The 'isms' here are proposed as a frame of reference for the various contributions in this book. These isms consider structure ('it') and function (the 'meaning' given to 'it') in various ways: realism, as 'it' 'is'; idealism as 'it' 'can be seen'; relativism, as 'it' 'is agreed upon'; relationalism by putting 'it' 'in relation to other(s)'. This frame of reference is considered desirable in the context of this book: relating two theoretical story lines representing the discipline of spatial planning and the complexity sciences, respectively, which at first sight have little in common. Nevertheless, it is strongly felt that relating the two fields of theory can be beneficial to both and will add to the debate within each of the two domains of thought.

Mechanisms of understanding

In the above sections we touched upon realism and the object-oriented view and discussed relativism and intersubjective interaction as a means to understand reality. The object-oriented view is very much related to evidence-based research, with a strong focus on analysing reality. Intersubjective interaction, in contrast, is the source of story lines and discourses. This can also be subject to analysis, if we want to know how interactions lead to a common understanding. Common understanding itself, being a product of intersubjective interaction, is by and large argumentative, and research that relates to it is also by and large argumentative research. Both evidence and arguments present an understanding of the reality at stake, together representing a synthesis (a meaning to a 'whole') of the analysis (of the parts, the whole and the context, as 'it' is and how it is 'seen') that has taken place.

The *analysis-synthesis* mechanism is a traditional means of gaining knowledge which is very familiar to us all. Analysis means deconstructing the whole into (understandable) parts, through which we can obtain an idea of how these interrelate and from which we can deduce a meaning to understand the whole. Less common is the *association-creativity* mechanism. This mechanism places less emphasis on the real in successive parts, wholes and contexts, and more on their interrelationship in terms of which they should be understood, becoming functional and meaningful. The association-creativity mechanism adds a second strategy, which is key for planners as we must be able to explore virtual 'becomings' and map out future trajectories. In this respect we can take as the lead the potential of the mind to evaluate what comes to the mind through the senses – such as the successive parts, wholes and contexts and their interactions – and to turn these into understandings of the 'real'. Re-relating components of planning situations, in the sense of creating novel ideas, but also in the sense of exploring how a relational change of component parts can also affect the ways and direction in which the planning situation may evolve, thus finds an analogy in the mind with regard to its ability to form associations and constructs. These associations and constructs are welcomed as representations of reality as long as these 'work', and they should be multiplied in order to explore futures-to-come. By 'work' we mean as long as these representations support a reasoned and therefore logical succession of 'situations' encountered, 'actions' taken and the resulting 'consequences'. This latter perspective is related to relationalism in our framework.

This association can be seen as a straightforward synthesis, associating the parts of the 'real' into a 'whole' that is grasped by understanding how the individual parts 'work'. The power of our mind to associate is almost limitless (although never far from what is perceived as 'real'), as associations can also result in 'alternative', 'proposed', 'desired' and 'future' realities (and, yes, also in 'undesired' or 'negative' realities). This means that through our associating capacities we are able to imagine alternatives to the 'real', which can help us – as spatial planners, for example – to imagine a future worth aiming for (idealism). This imagining, however, touches upon a mechanism that supports our associating capacities, that is, creativity. This means we are not only capable of associating structures (and their parts and interactions) in various ways but also of superimposing alternative functions (meanings) on them.

While the *analysis-synthesis* mechanism brings us knowledge of the 'real', the here and now, and therefore 'being', *associative creativity* brings us understanding of the virtual, a possible future, a future 'becoming', from which we can deduce what is possible. This is what spatial planners do: they build a bridge between the 'real' and the possible while guiding processes of transformation within our living environment.

Confronting spatial planning and the complexity sciences

This frame of reference constituted by the four isms and their mechanisms for understanding are – we believe – of importance when considering the conditions – and an understanding of these – under which the discipline of spatial planning and the complexity sciences are complementary and willing to learn from each other, such that both move forward. At stake is the impetus that the complexity sciences can give to the discipline of spatial planning, but here we also discuss how the complexity sciences could benefit from lessons learned within the discipline of spatial planning.

This comparison and sharing of theories, concepts, ideas and understandings between two different theoretical fields, related to very different backgrounds within science, does not come easily. We are not discussing an evolutionary path within a discipline, or referring to a paradigm or paradigm shift that a discipline might be undergoing (although it might eventually, as a spin-off from what we are discussing here). We are not discussing two related disciplines or what they might have in common (e.g., comparing spatial planning with organizational theory). We are doing none of things. What we are doing is something entirely different.

We consider planning theory to be a theory about rationalized choice and decision-making relating to interventions within our living environment. The rationale is the abstraction and the living environment, including its actors and factors, is its material object. We consider the complexity sciences to work differently, as they primarily seek a universal mechanism or abstraction that has meaning within various disciplines which investigate a material object or objects which relate to the world around us. It does not, therefore, ignore the material world, but its main aim is to seek abstractions that could support the *various disciplines* which focus on a material or informational object.

The complexity sciences are therefore part of what we would call the 'general sciences', presenting us with theories, concepts and ideas that cut across the various scientific disciplines and are helpful in forming a bridge between these disciplines as they offer a form of universal understanding. Mathematics is a general science of this type, supporting the various science disciplines in understanding our world in quantitative terms. General systems theory (Bertalanffy, 1968) is another example from the general sciences, explaining the (material) world in terms of nodes and interactions.

Systems theory is very well embedded within planning theory debate. Class I systems are called 'closed systems' (Kauffman, 1995; De Roo, 2010b). They represent a controlled world with complete information about its factors and actors and how these interact. Blueprint planning is considered to be its equal within the world of spatial planning. Scenario planning could be seen as representing Class II systems. This class of systems refers to so-called 'feedback mechanisms', through which semi-open systems correct themselves as a result of circular techniques that assess what is happening and what is meant to happen. This leaves us Class III systems. In the world of spatial planning, these emerge as open networks in which actors interact formally and informally in temporal settings, depending very much on the context. These systems classes taken together can be seen from a relational perspective as representing the world in terms of nodes, and their interaction, as seen in the here and now, in terms of their 'being'.

Since the 1980s, a fourth class of systems has been proposed (Holland, 1998; Kauffman, 1995; Waldrop, 1993; Wolfram, 1984; De Roo, 2010b), namely 'complex adaptive systems', which evolve through time and are both robust and flexible, and hence able to adapt to changing conditions, which in turn leads to these systems being able to evolve through time. The contributions by Gerrits and Teisman and by Van Buuren, Nooteboom and Teisman in this volume point out how planning theory can both learn from and experiment with a range of concepts from complex adaptive systems theory. We believe these complex adaptive systems also have representatives in the world of spatial planning. A good example is the city (see Wilkinson, this volume), or forms of it, as a system that has evolved over time from, say, a local marketplace for rural products into a metropolitan nucleus in which the local and the global meet. While the essence of the idea of a settlement has remained, its structure and functions have changed. This brings us to the relational question about how these complex adaptive systems relate to Class I, II and III systems.

With these complex adaptive systems we touch upon the complexity sciences and all they entail: emergence, adaptivity, co-evolution, self-organization and non-linearity. All these new notions emphasize the issue of time, and with it 'becoming'. While it was sufficient in the case of Class I, II and III systems to focus on an *analysis-synthesis* mechanism of understanding, this is not true for Class IV systems. *Associative creativity* is also needed to imagine 'becoming'.

Spatial planning is one of the disciplines that has for some time been ignorant of these complexity-related developments that are emerging elsewhere in science. De Roo and Silva (2010) propose relating spatial planning and the complexity sciences by following the same line of reasoning as with systems theory in the past, therefore appreciating the progression that systems thinking demonstrates with Class IV systems, the complex adaptive systems.

The whole issue regarding complex adaptive systems is just beginning to affect mainstream thinking within the discipline of spatial planning, with the exception of the modellers, who are far ahead of all spatial planners but so far little understood (and who are sometimes not very interested in 'cultural' aspects, discourses, subjectivities and other more 'qualitative' planning issues). In this book we discuss the importance of the complexity sciences, and the lessons we can deduce from it should spur spatial planners to rethink their conceptions of reality and reconnect these with issues in both planning theory and practice. This is easier said than done, however, as spatial planning also touches upon the social sciences and their specific characteristics.

Social complexity

While the issue of complexity and complex adaptive systems is quite manifest in disciplines such as physics, chemistry, biology, ecology and economics, it is still not much appreciated within the wider social sciences. However, in all the social sciences we do see a growing awareness of the complexity sciences and complex adaptive systems – however slow, as forging the relationship between the social and the complexity sciences is not so easy – bringing notions of social complexity to the fore.

As we consider the complexity sciences to be general sciences, they must have consequences and an applicability in the social sciences. How to see this is however quite another issue. The key concepts of the complexity sciences such as complex systems behaviours (including adaptivity, emergence, non-linearity) are interpreted in various ways, often missing the point of non-linearity, emergence and adaptivity, sometimes implying – not only for social scientists – a deterministic worldview and in fact a form of 'traditional realism' (as outlined above): a 'knowable reality'.

Although physical scientists struggle with notions of fundamental uncertainty, it also seems to be difficult for social scientists to move beyond all too simple notions of 'nature's objectivity' towards 'society's relativism'. Certainly, the social world cannot be reduced as easily (if at all) to a singular representation of the world. Understanding the social world solely through a realist perspective would result in a limited understanding, not just because we humans are limited in time, money and energy, or in terms of absorbing all signals that reach us through the senses; it would also make the world 'meaningless'.

This is in itself nothing new. However, with regard to precisely this issue, the complexity sciences are a source rather than a threat. Currently, the rise of 'complexity thinking' within the social sciences is predominantly a trajectory that evolves through metaphors. However, a growing number of scholars believe that there is more to complexity, seeking ways to move away from a metaphorical perspective towards conceptions, ideas and proposals which connect to the 'real', that is, to the social world and the world of planners. We believe that this volume provides evidence of this, and significantly advances complexity thinking in planning.

We are limited in our ability to perceive all that is going on between the multiple interacting actors and factors, as each individual actor is by and large a black box in terms of choices, decision-making, actions and behaviour. Taking only a realist perspective ignores a reality that is interpretable in multiple ways. It therefore ignores a relativist perspective, which is greatly valued in spatial planning and resulted in a communicative turn in planning during the 1990s.

It also brought us the duality of an object orientation versus an intersubjective orientation. This duality must also be acknowledged within the complexity sciences, but this is yet to happen (an exception is Portugali, 2000, see also this volume). In this respect, the current volume is clearly breaking new ground. It acknowledges that humans function as associating bodies that are able to extract from this multi-interpretable world an image that we rely upon when taking action and that feeds our behaviour (relationalism). This partly explains why 'social complexity' is facing difficulties in gaining ground as both a relevant and obvious perspective.

The social world is a world full of multiplicity and plurality. It is a world grasped by modellers who make use of multiple agents with their varying sets of rules, ideas and behaviour (relationalism). It is also a world to be understood through mechanisms of agreement, choice and opinions (relativism). And it is a world in which actors are able to respond to ideas of complexity, projecting these ideas upon the world and including them in processes of decision-making, which could lead to a self-fulfilling prophecy: we are willing to see our ideas and hopes in reality, ignoring opposing alternatives. This is what we call a social paradox. This is perhaps a somewhat negative explanation of what we have seen as one of the fabulous possibilities of the mind, through which we can imagine and construct various realities, including those we desire and believe are worthwhile to attain (idealism). How to view this social paradox with regard to the complexity sciences is one of the challenges of this book.

In the struggle to identify the additional value of complexity thinking to the social sciences, we see an excessive use of metaphors (idealism). Nevertheless, this struggle has led to proposals that should be taken seriously. Within spatial planning, for example, the notion of 'adaptive planning' has been proposed. In spatial planning, and more widely in the organizational sciences, 'transition management' has been introduced as a response to non-linear change (See De Roo and Rotmans, Loorbach and Kemp in this volume). This underlines the importance of an idealist perspective at this stage of relating the discipline of spatial planning to the complexity sciences.

However, are we able to move convincingly beyond metaphor to touch upon the 'real' in a material sense? Consider the idea that the complexity sciences represent a universal mechanism, a world that is more or less continuously out of balance and quite often far from any form of equilibrium. Moreover, bear in mind that complex adaptive systems are very real within this out-of-equilibrium world. Add to this the idea that systems in balance or at equilibrium are basically dead systems – what would that mean for our social world? This question is addressed from different perspectives in this book.

We wish to emphasize that it is not a one-way relationship, with the social sciences and with them the discipline of spatial planning, only being inspired by the complexity sciences. There is a mutual benefit, for example with regard to the issue of influencing what is seen within the complexity sciences as autonomous behaviour. The complexity sciences lack the idea of influencing (or intervening in, as is common in the world of planning) the behaviour of complex adaptive systems, focusing on those affected by it. By contrast, spatial planning is able to generate various strategies that support institutional intervention.

Another point of reference with respect to mutual benefit is the possibility of differentiation. In the complexity sciences, issues, situations or events are either seen as representatives of complex adaptive behaviour or not. In the latter case, they are seen as being linear, static or 'dead'. There is little debate about how to differentiate within the group of complex adaptive systems. In the social sciences and certainly *within* spatial planning, detailed strategies are proposed to differentiate situations, translating them into categories of planning issues on the basis of which we determine our actions and from which we deduce possible consequences. We must conclude that in the social sciences and in spatial planning a relational perspective is appreciated, in contrast to the complexity sciences. However, bridges between relational approaches and the complexity sciences are increasingly being built, for example by assemblage thinkers, contingency and post-contingency theory, actor-network theory and systems thinking. This, in turn, may inform the complexity sciences.

Therefore, what can be said about positioning the complexity sciences not only within a realist world but also in a relative, relational and ideal world? In an obvious and – we believe – unavoidable shift, the complexity sciences will encounter the magnificent struggle that the social sciences have been engaged in for decades. The struggle is about grasping the human factor, multi-interpretable as it is.

1.4 The emergence of the complexity sciences

Most authors in this volume make reference to the rise of complexity sciences, as a means to explain its characteristics, its whereabouts and its consequences to planning. Having mentioned Kant and Schopenhauer and framing our storyline on the basis of our four 'isms' we also have constructed our introduction to the complexity sciences, particularly referencing to philosophical framework.

The complexity sciences referred to and illustrated in this volume represent recent interpretations of ideas that have evolved since the concept of the differential was introduced into infinitesimal calculus in the late seventeenth century and since the work of mathematicians and philosophers such as Spinoza (1632-1677), Leibniz (1646-1716) and Riemann (1826-1866).

Spinoza and Leibniz's work led to the development of new theories of relations and relational space (see Duffy, 2004, 2007; Plotnitsky, 2007), in which 'something finite consists of an infinity under a certain relation' (Duffy, 2004: 203). Riemann, in turn, further developed some of the key mathematical and philosophical aspects of the notion of topological space. He furthered Gauss's revolutionary idea that a surface is a space in itself and that, rather than the features of the curvature of a plane being determined by the geometry of the space within which the plane is projected, the geometry of the surface conceived as a space is – in itself – intrinsic to that surface. Riemann's differential geometry thus enabled the analysis of n-dimensional multiplicities, which are very important to complexity thinking, as they allow for a conception of immanence as opposed to essences (Van Wezemael, 2008), and lay the ground for the explanatory power of relations.

In addition, n-dimensional multiplicities ease alternative story lines and futures-to-come as discussed above with regard to idealism. They do so because they should be viewed as a space of potentiality, which, according to Agamben (1998), has its own consistency. Potentiality does not always immediately disappear into actuality, meaning that constitutively it is also the potentiality not to do or be, so that the alternative consistently continues to exist alongside an actualization of, say, one specific spatial strategy, one participation practice or one particular change in the flow of traffic. The aim of seeking one solution without abandoning its alternative also calls for communicative action and thus for a relativist perspective.

Additional challenges to Newtonian-Cartesian ideas came from Clausius's (1865) Second Law of Thermodynamics – when an isolated system reaches maximum entropy (disorder) it is in equilibrium – and from the development of quantum mechanics by Poincaré, who claimed that 'prediction becomes impossible' (1914) if one attempts to determine the properties of complex functions in a plane.

As Hillier indicates (this volume), Poincaré attended seminars with the physicist Einstein, the philosopher Bergson, the artist Picasso and the psychoanalyst Freud, at a time in the early twentieth century when linearity and certainty were strongly challenged, also under the influence of the American pragmatists Peirce, Dewey and James and their views on experience and experiment. Perhaps the complexity sciences could have become dominant as a way of thinking and acting a century ago had the First World War not intervened. When this was followed by the Great Depression of the late 1920s and 1930s, the Second World War and the need for rebuilding nations, both physically and economically, the demand may have been for theories and practices with directional certainty rather than those of exploration and uncertainty. This historical contingency may in itself illustrate a basic notion of complexity. In Deleuze's words 'we do not know in advance which way a line is going to turn' (1987: 137), which calls for politics or planning as active experimentation.

Moreover, the concept of cybernetics emerged through US Army research in the Second World War, while operations research developed in the UK to address naval and air force strategies in multidimensional circumstances of uncertainty. Such ideas were also influential in strategic management and organizational studies in the 1940s and 1950s, led by Simon's (1947, 1962, 1969) interest in computational complexity.

From the 1960s, Hillier (this volume) suggests, complexity thinking tended to bifurcate into two streams relating to system dynamics and narrative approaches respectively. Prigogine is important with regard to dynamic systems. He identified dissipative structures within the world of physics, as such greatly contributing to grounding the idea of a world out of equilibrium (see De Roo in this volume). While a world in equilibrium is to be considered static, fixed or 'dead', a world out of equilibrium is one that allows for change, development and progress. Proposing a world 'far from equilibrium' was a major contribution to the idea of dynamic systems.

Although this and the previous volumes on complexity and planning are meant to contribute to building a bridge between the two different worlds of spatial planning and the complexity sciences, the very beginning of the narrative approaches to complexity lies within the discipline of spatial planning, at least to some extent. In 1972 Rittel, an urban planner at the University of California, Berkeley, proposed the concept of 'tame' and 'wicked' problems (see De Roo, Rotmans, Loorbach and Kemp, Wilkinson and Byrne in this volume; Vasishth, 2008; Rittel, 1972; Rittel and Webber, 1973). De Roo (this volume) reasons as follows: while the planning community made a communicative turn, more or less ignoring Rittel's reflections regarding the critique of the technical or functional rationale in planning, his concept of 'wicked problems' is very much appreciated within the complexity sciences, and is referred to today in various disciplines of science (Conklin, 2005; DeGrace and Stahl, 1990).

Wicked problems represent a category of issues that are essentially unique, impossible to define (no definite formulation), connected to a wider field of problems and unsolvable in the sense that these end with a clear and straightforward solution. Wicked problems were seen by Ackoff (1974) as 'messes', as problems interacting with other problems with which they are interrelated (see also Grunau and Schönwand, 2010, previous volume). These wicked, messy, fluid, fuzzy (De Roo and Porter, 2007) or complex problems share the characteristics which led us to become interested in the complexity sciences in the first place. These are also those from which spatial planning is likely to benefit, possibly progressing towards a new turn in planning, away from the communicative aspects and embracing a non-linear understanding of planning (see De Roo, this volume and De Roo, 2010b).

Whereas system dynamics is often associated with a realist perspective and narrative approaches with a relativist or relationalist view, the contributions in this volume indicate that this is by no means always the case. Nevertheless, theories and practices associated with system dynamics have tended to focus on mathematics and computational modelling, whilst narrative accounts of 'social complexity' have tended to focus on qualitative, often ethnographic, research.

Note that these are only tendencies and that several of the philosophical ideas which have strongly influenced narrative approaches are firmly grounded in mathematics and physics. Differences between the two epistemological streams of complexity theories are bridged – if indeed they were ever separate – by authors such as Plotnitsky (1994, 2002, 2003), Martin and Sunley (2007), Bergmann et al. (2009), Cilliers and Preiser (2010) and Gaffney (2010). 'In the broad canvas of social change, an approach drawing on complexity is potentially powerful' (Fowler, 2008: 10).

Furthermore, there is a historical continuity, demonstrated in the work of Deleuze (1988, 1993, 1994 especially), between, for instance, Leibniz, Spinoza and Riemann, Poincaré and Bergson. Deleuze uses mathematics to challenge the modern reduction of differential calculus to set theory, and he reintroduces infinitesimal to calculus in his construction of a relational, differential metaphysics of logic (1994).

Recognition is gradually building that practitioners such as professional planners are attempting to cope with a 'heterogeneous, yet interactive space of relationships (Relationality), where differences, similarities and interactions are all found, but each becomes more or less critical at different conceptual, historical or cultural junctures' (Plotnitsky, 2007: 178). Philosophy, mathematics, physical science and spatial planning practices are, from the perspective of this volume, all means of attempting to keep chaos at bay, or at least at the border.

All recent and ongoing research on cities as complex adaptive systems, from Nicolis and Prigogine's original contribution in 1977, to indicative work by Batty (1969, 1994, 2005), Portugali (2000, 2008), Booher and Innes (2006, 2010) and De Roo and Silva (2010), deals with spatio-temporal dynamics (becoming) rather than some static configuration of space (being). As we indicate below, many of the contributions to this volume continue to develop such work.

'The ontological shift from simple, fixed or static systems to complex adaptive systems opens new paths to knowledge and understanding yet incorporates much current knowledge; it validates novel research methods; and theories founded in this approach will generate radically different solutions to policy problems' (Harrison, 2006: 2). The complexity sciences bring together philosophy and science in a suite of theories and practices, ranging from computational probability modelling in a predominantly realist perspective to strategies of adaptive navigation which necessarily introduce the need to relate things differently (relationalism), create alternative potentialities (e.g. in the form of creative mental pictures, idealism) and evaluate them on a communicative plane (relativism). Even in contingent situations such as those faced by planning practitioners, indeterminism does not imply that plans should not attempt to effect change for the better. The challenge for planning theorists and practitioners, we argue, lies not so much in debating the relevance of the complexity sciences but in working with them to suggest new practices and tools to increase the effectiveness of spatial planning.

1.6 Structure of the volume

The volume is divided into four parts. In Part I we commence with theoretical reflections on complexity and planning in order to identify and understand the basic relationship between complexity theories and planning theory and practice. Part II builds on the first, considering complex systems behaviour as a new but exciting path for planning theory. The authors take a systems understanding of reality and make use of ideas and proposals suggested within the realm of systems thinking to form a bridge between the complexity sciences and spatial planning. In doing so it becomes clear that, alongside a realist and relativist perspective, a relational perspective is unavoidable. The authors in Part III have made a relational attitude prominent, exploring complex assemblages of creativity and transformation. The volume ends with Part IV, representing the richness that modelling has generated with regard to complexity and planning, simulating non-linear connections between the 'real' and the 'ideal'.

Part I – Theoretical Reflections: Bridging Complexity and Planning

In order to contextualize the theoretical observations of authors in this volume, the first three papers consider historical and philosophical approaches to planning. In other words, what is already being addressed by planning theory with regard to complexity, and what philosophical conditions are we touching upon? If we look at historical developments within the planning theoretical debate, can we identify aspects that relate to or incorporate complexity? In this introductory chapter we have made a point about the desire to supplement philosophical perspectives common to planning, namely realism and relativism, with two more perspectives, namely idealism and relationalism. The philosophical angle on complexity and planning brings into focus several more issues of relevance. For example, what do post-modernism, pragmatism, post-structuralism and deconstructivism, etc., tell us about complexity and planning? Will complexity solve the philosophical dilemmas that we attempt to address within current planning debates?

We should also be aware of the importance of thought and theories that cut across disciplines, particularly systems theory and assemblage theory, which affect many disciplines. How do the various disciplines consider the issue of complexity? What are the key issues that link complexity to the specific disciplines? How is complexity incorporated? And what effect does this have on how we understand and deal with reality? The complexity sciences not only transcend but also connect the different academic disciplines, including planning, focusing as they do on the various aspects of our world. These contextual aspects of the issues of complexity and planning, as outlined in Chapter 2 by *Jean Hillier*, provide the reader with a contextual focus for approaching other chapters and their explorations of and questions about how complexity and spatial planning might relate to each other.

The chapters in Part I, beginning with Hillier, thus take a broad perspective on complexity theories; a perspective that reaches out to current spatial planning debates. In this respect we appreciate a line of reasoning that began with *Karen Christensen* (1985), who introduced complexity as a phenomenon that could help construct a view of planning that has to cope with a reality that differentiates 'degrees of complexity' (see also De Roo, 2010b and this volume). Using the degree of complexity as a criterion, in Chapter 3 Christensen attempts to deal with issues of certainty and uncertainty. In this attempt she very much takes a relational approach (see above), proposing a contingency between an intergovernmental system and multiple agencies and their shared governance responsibilities, a means of expressing the effectiveness of planning actions. In response to a problem, she demonstrates how one agency makes changes that prompt another agency to make its own changes, which then ripple through the complex system in 'hyper-partisan mutual adjustment' (after Lindblom, 1965). The process spawns more agencies. Such a proliferation of agencies also enables some to tailor projects to special needs, thereby propelling the larger system into a diverse array, a pseudo-market for previously non-market goods. Christensen indicates how 'savvy' planners make use of the profusion of complexity as building blocks and tools to create new combinations and solutions (after Webber, 1978).

Joris Van Wezemael (Chapter 4) elaborates on the contribution of assemblage theory to the 'planning-and-complexity' tradition in the line of Christensen. In the context of our framework, he explores the spaces between realism and relativism. By introducing 'degrees of freedom' with regard to spaces of possibility in planning decision-making, he also offers a 'relational' way out of some of the dilemmas that arise with Christensen's suggestion of 'degrees of complexity'.

Part II – Complex Systems and Planning: between the Real and the Relative

Complex systems can be found between order and chaos, where the world is never in balance. Nevertheless, there is some form of knowable 'reality'. 'This is possible because, in addition to the inevitable and continuous presence of chaos, a certain amount of order results from developments in the direction of stability and equilibrium' (De Roo, 2001: 133). Research in various disciplines has revealed that complex systems tend to gravitate towards an area of complexity between order and chaos, never reaching the ultimate state of chaos, but evolving as 'coherent structures that propagated, grew, split apart, and recombined in a wonderfully complex way' (Waldrop, 1992: 226). To a greater or lesser extent, these complex systems are stable, robust and predictable. There is, however, also a degree of uncertainty, resulting in a situation that allows the system to optimize 'the benefits of stability while retaining a capacity of change' (Phelan 1995: 6). In these circumstances, complex systems are capable of co-evolution as they adjust through the adaptation of opposing contextual interferences.

The chapters in Part II explore various aspects of complex systems as defined above. Chapters 5 and 6, by *Portugali* and *De Roo* respectively, are very much a bridge between the first two parts. Both underline the *relational* perspective on planning and complexity, embracing systems theory as the backbone to exploring evolutions of the two trajectories of planning and complexity, slowly merging together. Portugali (Chapter 5) is known for his explicit understanding of cities as complex adaptive systems and for his concern with the dual perspective that planners must take into account when considering reality. This duality involves an object-oriented perspective and an intersubjective perspective on planning, which must be bridged. The duality strongly relates to the opposition between quantitative analytical science and qualitative descriptive science, and to that of the logical deductive method versus the critical constructivist method. This bridging should have consequences, according to Portugali, who proposes a cognitive approach to cities.

In Chapter 6, De Roo follows more or less the same line of reasoning as Portugali, acknowledging the evolutionary path followed by planning thought, including its ups and downs, the various crises, with perhaps a 'communicative' crisis to come, and a likely progression towards a non-linear understanding. In the volume that precedes this book, De Roo introduced ideas that are developed further here, proposing a non-linear outline to spatial planning. In the previous volume he emphasized the importance of time to planning theory, an aspect that has thus far been ignored, while in complexity sciences the issue of time is crucial and fundamental. In his contribution to this volume he adds to this the significance of being 'out of equilibrium' in relation to spatial planning, and the relevance of this when planners want to give meaning to development, progress and change. De Roo presents a taxonomy of planning rationales, taking a relational perspective as a bridge between the 'real' and the 'relative', relating contemporary planning theory to notions such as complexity (static versus dynamic complexity), co-evolution, transition, adaptivity, being out of equilibrium and non-linearity. This results in an outline of a non-linear approach to planning called adaptive planning.

While De Roo points to various non-linear possibilities for transformation and change, in Chapter 7, *Rotmans, Loorbach and Kemp* focus on one in particular, the transition and its consequences for planning and decision-making, in other words, transition management. They consider transition as a radical, structural change within society, affected by internal and external factors such as economic, cultural, technological and institutional change. Through a process of co-evolution, a social and/or spatial system is able to successfully adjust to change and might arrive at a higher level of complexity. The authors take a *relational* as well as a *relativist* perspective – relational since the social system relates to its contextual flow while progressing, and relative since Rotmans, Loorbach and Kemp consider it important for this progression to take a more sustainable direction. It is the task of planners to influence this direction. In support of this, Rotmans, Loorbach and Kemp propose management principles that are not predetermined but reflexive.

In Chapter 8, *Lasse Gerrits and Geert Teisman* examine the issue of co-evolution as an explanation for developments at the edge of planning. In planning theory there is a certain anthropocentric emphasis on human planners and decision-makers. There is, however, an extensive amount of empirical evidence indicating that spatial developments are often heavily influenced – for better or for worse by events and process dynamics beyond the reach and imagination of planners and decision-makers, who are only parts of relational processes in which physical subsystems develop their own self-organizing capacity. In other words, Gerrits and Teisman address one problem of a *relativist* stance, in which ideas are developed on an intersubjective basis that cannot, however, be implemented, as 'planning takes place in a complex social and physical world that is constantly changing', as the authors state. The systems perspective proposed in the chapter helps to 'synchronize' the *relativist/idealist* production of planning goals and tactics with the 'real' of self-organizing planning objects. Consequently, spatial development is viewed as the result of intertwined, co-evolutionary action.

In Chapter 9, *Arwin Van Buuren, Sibout Nooteboom and Geert Teisman* apply some core concepts from theories on complex adaptive systems to understand the 'normality' of implementation problems in planning. The authors perceive government as a complex governance system that is composed of many interrelated networks in which a whole variety of values and interests must be dealt with. They criticize the widespread assumption that government systems can be easily adjusted to new external demands, highlighting *relational* dynamics that give rise to autopoietic behaviour around vested interests and routines.

The authors indicate patterns of path dependency, negative feedback and self-organization as the main explanations for planners' resistance to paradigm shifts. They present an example of water governance systems, where traditional solutions for dealing with sea-level rise or increasing water discharges in large rivers are perceived to be no longer sufficient by climate experts. The governance system that deals with water must therefore move to a new dynamic equilibrium that fits the new climate system and climate effects. The authors apply the concepts of 'change events', 'positive feedback' and 'adaptive self-organization', and elaborate on the extent to which these change-creating elements are at work in the case studies and whether they can push governance systems to a new system state.

In her contribution (Chapter 10), *Catherine Wilkinson* reflects on a decade-long experiment of applying a complexity approach to strategic spatial planning on a metropolitan scale in Melbourne, Australia. In particular, she highlights the catalysts for the experiment, key communicative breakthroughs in translating scientific concepts into practice, and the implications of a complexity approach for the development of *Melbourne 2030*, Melbourne's most recent metropolitan strategy. In her chapter, the author takes a *relative* stand, mapping out the space of a metaphorical use of complexity that allows for the generation of alternative (shared) story lines (ideas) and thus new modes of planning practice. At the same time, the Melbourne case nicely illustrates how 'relativist' controversies about 'what the world is like' challenge the way planners synchronize their strategies with the experienced or imagined 'real'. Following this line of reasoning, Wilkinson concludes by exploring the consequences for spatial governance that are implied by a complexity approach.

David Byrne considers complex systems within the social and physical environments and with regard to planning and decision-making. In Chapter 11, he elaborates on the position that interventions take with regard to influencing the physical environment and asks what kind of qualities these interventions would have, if we consider the behaviour of phenomena in a complex system environment to be related to contextual processes that are more or less autonomous. Byrne is critical of the relativist position and questions the planner's knowledge and imagination with regard to their relationship to the 'real': if 'we are going to plan we are going to have to plan on the basis of valid knowledge claims'. Following this line of reasoning, the author criticizes a take on sustainability that focuses on actions in relation to any single system, as the traditional negative-feedback tools of control are not sufficient to shape the future trajectories of these systems taken together. Concluding, Byrne takes an *ideal* stand, advocating a collectively imagined transformation towards a desirable and sustainable future that goes beyond the restoration of existing equilibria.

Part II – Assemblage and a Relational Attitude to Planning

In this part, the authors specifically engage with the hybrid nature of entities and the non-linearity of relations. In other words, they consider a complexity that is produced by sustained heterogeneity. This sustained heterogeneity conditions planning and decision-making and it frames planners' contributions and their *degrees of freedom*. This view on complexity owes a debt to precursors in assemblage thinking such as Gilles Deleuze. Rather than an *analytical* stand, the power of making *associations* (see end of Section 2 in this chapter), arrangements and assemblies (assemblage) is emphasized as a means to understanding our reality. Clearly, the authors take a *relational* perspective on planning and decision-making.

When entities connect and preserve their heterogeneity, they change 'what they can do' as an assemblage, or as Latour (2005) puts it: they change the 'script'. The power of scripts is well known to practical planners: decision-making processes fundamentally change when modes of representation are altered, for example, from narratives to plans or spreadsheets (Law and Mol, 2002), or when people are grouped around different issues in civic participation (Hillier and Van Wezemael, 2007).

Since a script does not 'have form', it belongs to a virtual rather than an actual field of reality. Each script displays a field of potential becoming (or a manifold), which, as DeLanda (2002) argues, can be conceptualized using Riemann's 'degrees of freedom'. In 'becoming-actual', when form is generated ('morpho-genesis'), we can rethink planners' decision-making on the basis of studies of intensive processes that work in far-from-equilibrium conditions. Here, matter and energy as such are not passive but creative (DeLanda, Protevi and Thanem, 2004).

The contributions in this part can be related to what Cilliers calls a 'critical understanding of complexity' (Cilliers, 2005: 257). The ideal type of a 'Baroque' or narrative approach to complexity (Kwa, 2002; Law and Mol, 2002; Hillier, this volume) and the emerging assemblage approaches in spatial planning confront us with the limits of our understanding and show us why complex problems are so 'wicked' (see Rittel, 1972; Conklin, 2005; Davies, 2003; and De Roo, Wilkinson and Byrne in this volume). Systems boundaries are 'folded-in', this is why 'one is never quite sure whether one is dealing with the inside or outside of the system' (Cilliers, 2002: 82). Complexity theories in Part III regard 'actants' as being in turbulent motion, highlighting the boundaries of presumed systems that become blurred in a Baroque perspective, and the creative or destructive potential that emerges from connections in hybrid entities. Accordingly, planning is challenged to rethink Callon and Law's (2004: 5) question: 'how can we produce order by managing these multiple fluxes and flows?'

In Chapter 12, *Valeria Monno* discusses the concept of complex *relationality* at the core of recent argumentative/collaborative thinking in spatial planning. She describes the code underlying such thinking and, specifically, its point of view about time and space, knowledge, agents and the 'proper' processes through which they can manage their relationships in order to discover new ways of living together. Monno argues that such a code, rather than helping to manage complexity and free up creative energies, as theorized, seems in actuality to facilitate processes of control, repetition and exclusion. She contrasts such a perspective with a Deleuzian-inspired understanding of relational complexity as an emergent and volatile assemblage of trajectories and metamorphic agents, and concludes that such a view is crucial to tracing and learning about the contextual and dynamic features of complex relational situations by taking into account the many injustices and power games that emerge in the making of cities.

In Chapter 13, *Jean Hillier and Joris Van Wezemael* then consider an empirical case of participatory strategic planning in the North-East of England, in which multiple relational 'strategies' were mobilized with regard to urban regeneration. The authors trace community-involvement strategies and indicate that 'front-loading' in regeneration planning largely failed in this case. In asking why this failure occurred and what might generate a more inclusive, democratic involvement of citizens, the authors adopt a Deleuzian framework, distinguishing between assemblage and *agencement* (agency), to ask how, why and with what implications, relations between actants might gather sufficient instruments, power, etc. to generate *agencement* and eventuate change rather than simply remaining as assemblages.

In Chapter 14, *Peter Trummer* examines issues relating to urban design and complex systems. He adopts Manuel DeLanda's (2006) view that 'urban centers and living creatures must be seen as different dynamical systems operating far from equilibrium, that is, traversed by more or less intense flows of matter-energy that provoke their unique metamorphoses'. Trummer conceptualizes the shift from typological thinking to population thinking in fields such as biology, and experiments with its analogies in urban design. More precisely, the author introduces a *relational* perspective and challenges essentialist worldviews that rely heavily on conceptions such as typologies. The author develops an *associative* protocol that allows for a structure that might range from a manufacturing component to the scale of an urban neighbourhood.

In Chapter 15 *Sibout Nooteboom and Jurian Edelenbos* argue that second-order governance systems and interdependencies are visible within embedded physical, economic and social layers. The authors consider responses to interdependencies by individual actors and by institutions and organizations as exemplifying adaptive networks. In their analysis they highlight a number of *relational* aspects, including co-evolution and connectivity, as important in the explanation of strategic behaviour in planning decision-making processes and institutional capacity within a changing environment.

The authors are concerned with the correspondence between the relational complexity of the environment to be governed and the relational complexity of the governance system as proposed in the rule of 'requisite variety' (Ashby, 1974). They argue that in order to be effective, diversity in the environment should be handled by a governance system that reflects the diversity of the spatial, economic and physical system itself, while also adding something specific to it. They tackle the tensions that can emerge from a cleavage between a *relativist* perspective and the 'real' of physical and social environments. The authors describe *ideal* typical social systems that emerge from the 'official' governance system and co-evolve with it. They reveal that such systems also indirectly co-evolve with, and therefore influence, wider societal and technological change. They are led by the 'strange' attractors created by the wisdom of the crowd. At some point, wider agreement is possible about which 'abstract' futures are desirable. Adaptive networks seek this point and use it to energize the social system, creating a psychological (i.e. shared social) tension between it and the current circumstances in society and governance. The authors also indicate how existing theories, such as those of 'creative tension' or 'communities of practice', offer possible tools to that end.

Part IV – Simulating between the Real and the Ideal

Progressing from Part III to Part IV, we make a transition from the virtual perception of space and its *relational* attitude towards virtual realities to the presentation of the *ideal*, captured in digital modelling. Models are tools designed to help us to gain a better grip on reality. Models are simplifications, 'replacing reality with its representation' (Batty, 2005: 515). Nevertheless, it is important to consider, on the one hand, processes that simplify the 'real' and, on the other, processes for constructing mind frames concerned with understanding the various components of the model and how these components might interrelate. In this respect, models bridge the *real* and the *relative*. Therefore the chapters in this part contribute both to modelling the *real* and to critical reflection on the question of what it is we are modelling.

Conventional science builds on models through simplification to obtain certainty and predictability. The models used for this purpose are supposed to work within predefined conditions. Irrelevant or minor details are put aside while emphasizing what is considered essential. However, part of the story about complex systems concerns the importance of minor details, which have a major effect in dynamic processes. Some modelling proposals focus on the effects of minor details, how they interact and co-evolve into an emerging process, ultimately resulting in an understanding of a system's robustness. In other words, models are used to understand the life and death of systems, resulting in conditions under which systems either remain stable or are susceptible to sudden change (also known as 'tipping points').

Where conventional science makes use of scenarios, we take this further, using various simulation techniques. From these considerations a number of instruments can be derived, such as agent-based modelling, cellular automata and autopoiesis. These instruments differ slightly from each other. Agent-based modelling refers to processes resulting in macro-level effects due to minor changes in the behaviour of interacting nodes (actors) at the system's micro-level. Modelling based on cellular automata takes processes of spatial diffusion as the route to identifying and understanding guiding principles for spatial change. Autopoiesis emphasizes the self-organization, self-creation and self-perpetuation of systems, as a result of a fundamental complementarity between structure and function. As such, autopoiesis refers to the dynamics of non-equilibrium systems, taking the flow of interactions as the organizational dimension of an open system as the factor responsible for stability and change.

Modellers were the very first among planners to acknowledge the importance of the complexity sciences and its notion of time and change to planning. The three contributions in Part IV therefore represent a long tradition and an activity within planning that is still very much alive and progressing. The latest insights are presented, showing a struggle to move away from 'presupposed preknowledge', as Devisch calls it, towards tools that, according to Crooks, are 'more a mind set than a technology'.

In the opening chapter of this part, *Oswald Devisch* (Chapter 16) explores the lessons that planners can learn from the rapid growth of virtual realities ('models' reflecting the 'real' world), building on considerations from complexity thinking and complex systems. Devisch explains how such developments will enhance planners' understanding of how to intervene in complex physical environments.

In Chapter 17, *Andrew Crooks* elaborates on the benefits of agent-based computer modelling for understanding the effects of social relations, taking conceptions from complexity thinking as cornerstones. This understanding supports initiatives and decision-making with regard to planning interventions within the social and physical environment to enhance the local quality of life.

Finally, in Chapter 18, *Paul Torrens* argues that urban modelling is at an important stage in its development. The pace of urbanization and city growth, and the ever-increasing rate of adaptation of urban phenomena have, to some extent, accelerated beyond the abilities of modelling methodology to remain practically relevant and diagnostically useful. In response, agent-based models may serve as the next generation of urban-simulation methodology, but in order to do so they must prove themselves able to engage with urban theory on all scales – small, large and in-between. In other words, they must be *relational*. Torrens focuses on the concept of geosimulation, as well as on efforts to build innovative forms of dataware in support of dynamic urban modelling, using space-time Geographic Information Systems and information visualization.

Overall, the chapters in this volume build a strong argument about how planning and complexity are intrinsically interrelated. They offer a broad perspective for thinking complexity and planning together and should facilitate a better understanding of processes with regard to the physical and social worlds with which planning interacts. Planes for mutual learning between the complexity sciences and spatial planning are depicted by the spatiality that generates planning situations as hybrid entities, the need for imagined and different futures-to-come and to set up alternatives with regard to 'realities' as perceived by different societal groups, the need for verbal and non-verbal representations of these realities and the very materiality of the human and the non-human component parts of any 'planning assemblage'. Were they to engage with the perspectives illustrated in this volume, planners would perhaps be able to recognize planning realities as complex systems and understand those realities and the conditions under which stability persists and change occurs. They might also begin to recognize multiple *relational* approaches to dynamic complexity that enhance their understandings of and facilitate working with the contingencies of place, time and 'actant' behaviours.

References

Ackoff, R.L. (1974) *Redesigning the Future, A Systems Approach to Societal Problems*, John Wiley & Sons, New York/London.

Ashby, W.R. (1956) *An Introduction to Cybernetics*, Chapman & Hall, London.

Batty, M. (1969) A Review of the Theory Pertaining to Spatial Organisation. In I. Masser (ed), *The Use of Models in Planning*, Dept. Of Civic Design, University of Liverpool, Liverpool, pp. 1-27.

Batty, M. (2005) *Cities and Complexity: Understanding Cities with Cellular Automata, Agent-based Models, and Fractals*, MIT Press, Cambridge (US).

Batty, M., P. Longley (1994) *Fractal Cities: a geometry of form and function*, Academic Press, Oxford.

Bergmann L., Sheppard E., P. Plummer (2009) Capitalism Beyond Harmonious Equilibrium: Mathematics as if Human Agency Mattered, *Environment and Planning A*, 41, pp. 265-283.

Bertalanffy, L. von (1968) *General System Theory: Foundations, Development, Applications*, George Braziller, New York.

Booher, D., J. Innes (2006) Complexity and Adaptive Policy Systems: CALFED As an Emergent Form of Governance for Sustainable Management of Contested Resources, Proceedings of the 50th Annual Meeting of the ISSS, http://journals.isss.org/index.php/proceedings50th/article/viewfile/295/68 [accessed 22/12/2008].

Booher, D., J. Innes (2010) *Planning with Complexity*, Routledge, New York.

Byrne, D. (1998) *Complexity Theory and the Social Sciences – An Introduction*, Routledge, London.

Christensen, K.S. (1985) Coping with Uncertainty in Planning, *Journal of the American Planning Association*, Winter, pp. 63-73.

Christensen, K.S. with R. Sadik, M. Lim and R. Weiner (2000) The Challenge of Affordable Housing in 21st Century California: Constraints and Opportunities in the Nonprofit Housing Sector. Institute of Urban and Regional Development, University of California at Berkeley, Berkeley.

Cilliers, P. (1998) *Complexity and Postmodernism*, Routledge, London.

Cilliers, P. (2005) Knowing Complex Systems. In K. Richardson (Ed.) *Managing Organizational Complexity: Philosophy, Theory And Application*, Information Age Publishing, Greenwich, pp. 7-19.

Cilliers, P., R. Preiser (Eds.) (2010) *Complexity, Difference and Identity*, Springer-Verlag, Heidelberg.

Clemens, Jnr.,W. (2001) Complexity Theory as a Tool For Understanding and Coping With Ethnic Conflict and Development Issues in Post-Soviet Eurasia, *International Journal of Peace Studies*, 6, 2, on line.

Conklin, J. (2005) *Dialogue Mapping: Building Shared Understanding of Wicked Problems*, Wiley, New York/London.

Craviolini, C., Van Wezemael, J., Wirth, F. (2011) The Spatiality of Control. Intertwining ICT and Physical Space in Social Protest. Special Issue on

'Online and Offline Social Movements: Critical Perspectives', *Journal of Critical Studies in Business and Society*, (4/2011), in print

Davies, L. (2003) *Conflict and Chaos*, Routledge, London.

DeGrace, P., and L.H. Stahl (1990) *Wicked Problems, Righteous Solutions*, Yourdon Press, Prentice Hall.

DeLanda, M. (2002) *Intensive Science and Virtual Philosophy*, Continuum, London.

DeLanda, M. (2006) Associativity Neighborhood Models Madrid, in: Projecting the City Beyond Mapping – Special issue Architecture Biennale Venice 2006, The Berlage Institute Postgraduate Laboratory of Architecture, Rotterdam (pp. 20-32).

DeLanda, M., J. Protevi, T. Thanem (2004) Deleuzian Interrogations: A Conversation with Manuel DeLanda, John Protevi and Torkild Thanem, *Tamara Journal of Critical Postmodern Organization Science*, pp. 65-101.

DeLanda, M. (no date) 'Deleuze and the Open-Ended Becoming of the World', available online at: [http://www.cddc.vt.edu/host/delanda/pages/becoming. htm], accessed 28 September 2006.

Deleuze, G., (1988) [1970] *Spinoza: Practical Philosophy*, (trans. Hurley, R.), City Light Books, San Francisco.

Deleuze, G., (1993) [1988] *The Fold: Leibniz and the baroque*, (trans. Conley T.), Athlone Press, London.

Deleuze, G. (1994) [1968] *Difference and Repetition*, (trans. Patton, P.), Athlone, London.

De Roo, G. (2001) Planning per se, planning per saldo – Over conflicten, complexiteit en besluitvorming in de milieuplanning, Sdu Uitgevers, Den Haag, its English version is from (2003) *Environmental Planning in the Netherlands – Too good to be true: From Command-and-Control Planning to Shared Governance*, Ashgate, Aldershot.

De Roo, G. (2003) *Environmental Planning in The Netherlands: Too Good to be True – From Command-and-Control Planning to Shared Governance*, Ashgate, Aldershot.

De Roo, G. and Porter, G. (2007) *Fuzzy Planning – The Role of Actors in a Fuzzy Governance Environment*, Ashgate, Aldershot.

De Roo, G. (2010a) Planning and Complexity: An Introduction. In G. De Roo and E. Silva (eds) *A Planner's Encounter with Complexity*, Ashgate, Farnham, pp. 1-18.

De Roo, G. (2010b) Being or Becoming? That is the Question! Confronting Complexity with Contemporary Planning Theory. In G. De Roo and E. Silva (eds) *A Planner's Encounter with Complexity*, Ashgate, Farnham, pp. 29-38.

De Roo, G. and E.A. Silva (eds) (2010) *A Planner's Encounter with Complexity*, Ashgate, Farnham.

Duffy, S. (2004) Schizo-math: the Logic of Different-Ciation and the Philosophy of Difference, *Angelaki*, 9, 3, pp. 199-215.

Duffy, S. (2007) The Ethical View of Affective Life: The Transformation of Relations in Spinoza's Metaphysics. In B. Bolt, F. Colman, G. Jones and A. Woodward (Eds.) *Sensorium: Aesthetics, Art, Life*, Cambridge Scholars Publishing, Newcastle, pp. 194-207.

Eddington, A. (1928) *The Nature of the Physical World*, Macmillan, London.

Fowler, A. (2008) Connecting the dots: complexity thinking and social development, *The Broker*, 7, pp. 10-15.

Gaffney, P. (ed.) (2010) *The Force of the Virtual*, University of Minnesota Press, Minneapolis.

Grunau, J.P, W.L. Schönwandt (2010) Dealing with Society's 'Big Messes', in G. de Roo and E.A. Silva (eds) *A Planner's Encounter with Complexity*, Ashgate, Farnham, pp. 41-62.

Harrison, N. (2006) Thinking about the World we Make. In N. Harrison (ed), *Complexity in World Politics: Concepts and Methods of a New Paradigm*, SUNY Press, Albany, pp. 1-24.

Hillier, J. (2010) Introduction to Part 3: conceptual challenges for spatial planning in complexity. In J. Hillier and P. Healey (eds) *The Ashgate Research Companion to Planning Theory: Conceptual Challenges for Spatial Planning*, Ashgate, Farnham, pp. 367-398.

Hillier, J., P. Healey (2008) *Critical Essays in Planning Theory*, Ashgate Series Volume 3, Ashgate, Aldershot.

Hillier, J. and J.E. Van Wezemeal (2007) Civic engagement in a complex world, paper presented at the XXI Aesop conference at Naples, July 2007.

Holland, J. (1998) *Emergence: From Chaos to Order*, Addison-Wesley, New York.

Kaipayil, J. (2009) *Relationalism. A Theory of Being*. JIP Publications, Bangalore.

Kant, I. (2003 [1781]) *The Critique of Pure Reason* [Kritik der reinen Vernunft], Project Gutenberg Literary Archive Foundation, Oxford, MS.

Kauffman, S. (1995) *At Home in the Universe*, Oxford University Press, New York.

Kwa, Ch. (2002) Romantic and Baroque: Conceptions of Complex Wholes in the Sciences. In J. Law and A. Mol (eds.), *Complexities: Social Studies of Knowledge Practices*, Duke University Press, Durham, NC, pp. 23-52.

Lakoff, G. and M. Johnson (1980) *Metaphors we Live By*, University of Chicago Press, Chicago.

Latour, B. (2005) *Reassembling the Social: An Introduction to Actor-Network Theory*, Oxford University Press, Oxford.

Latour, B. (1999) *Pandora's Hope – Essays on the Reality of Science Studies*, Harvard University Press, Cambridge.

Law, J. (2004) *After Method: Mess in Social Science Research*, Routledge, London.

Law, J., A. Mol (eds.) (2002) *Complexities: Social Studies of Knowledge Practices*, Duke University Press, Durham.

Lindblom, Ch.E. (1965) *The Intelligence of Democracy: Decision-making through Mutual Adjustment*, Free Press, New York.

Lorenz, E.N. (1963) Deterministic Nonperiodic Flow, *Journal of the Atmospheric Sciences*, 20, 2, pp. 130–141.

Lorenz, E.N. (1972) *Predictability: Does the Flap of a Butterfly's Wings in Brazil set off a Tornado in Texas?* Paper presented to the American Association for the Advancement of Science, Washington, D.C.

Martin, R., P. Sunley (2007) Complexity thinking and evolutionary economic geography, *Journal of Economic Geography*, 7, pp. 573-601.

Mitleton-Kelly, E. (2003) *Complex Systems and Evolutionary Perspectives on Organisations*, Elsevier, Amsterdam.

Nicolis G., I. Prigogine (1977) *Self-Organization in Nonequilibrium Systems*, Wiley, New York.

Nietzsche, F. (2000) On Truth and Lie in an Extra-Moral Sense, in Cazeaux, C. (ed.), *The Continental Aesthetics Reader*, Routledge, London, pp. 53-60.

Phelam, S.E. (1995) From Chaos to Complexity in Strategic Planning, Paper presented at the 55th Annual Meeting of the Academy of Management, Vancouver, Canada, August 6-9.

Plotnitsky, A. (1994) *Complementarity: Anti-epistemology after Bohr and Derrida*, Duke University Press, Durham.

Plotnitsky, A. (2002) *The Knowable and the Unknowable: Modern Science, Nonclassical Thought and the 'Two Cultures'*, University of Michigan Press, Ann Arbor.

Plotnitsky, A. (2003) Algebras, Geometries and Topologies of the Fold: Deleuze, Derrida and Quasi-mathematical Thinking (with Leibniz and Mallarmé). In P. Patton and J. Protevi (Eds.), *Between Deleuze and Derrida*, Continuum, London, pp. 98-119.

Plotnitsky, A. (2007) 'The Shadow of the "People to Come"': chaos, brain and thought in Gilles Deleuze and Félix Guattari's What is Philosophy?. In B. Bolt, F. Colman, G. Jones and A. Woodward (eds) *Sensorium: Aesthetics, Art, Life*, Cambridge Scholars Publishing, Newcastle, pp. 166-193.

Poincaré, H. (1914) [1908] *Science and Method*, Flammarion, Paris.

Portugali, J. (2000) *Self-Organisation and the City*, Springer, Heidelberg.

Portugali, J. (2008) Learning from Paradoxes about Prediction and Planning in Self-Organizing Cities, *Planning Theory*, 7, 3, pp. 248-262.

Prigogine, I. (1996) *The End of Certainty: Time, Chaos, and the New Laws of Nature*, The Free Press, New York.

Ramalingam, B., Jones, H., Toussaint R., J. Young (2008) Exploring the Science of Complexity: Ideas and Implications for Development and Humanitarian Efforts, Working Paper 285, ODI, London.

Rittel, H. (1972) On the Planning Crisis: Systems Analysis of the 'First and Second Generations', *Bedriftsokonomen*, 8, pp. 390-396.

Rittel, H., M. Webber (1973) Dilemmas in a General Theory of Planning, *Policy Sciences*, 4, pp 155-169.

Sayer, A. (1984) *Method in Social Science, a Realist Approach*, Hutchinson, London.

Schopenhauer, A. (2000) [1851] *Sketch of a History of the Doctrine of the Ideal and the Real, in Part I of Parerga and Paralipomena*. E.F.J. Payne translation. Oxford: Clarendon Press.

Simon, H. (1947) *Administrative Behaviour*, Macmillan, New York.

Simon, H. (1962) Architecture of Complexity, *Proceedings of the American Philosophical Society*, 106, pp. 467-482.

Simon, H. (1969) *The Sciences of the Artificial*, MIT Press, Cambridge, MA.

Trummer, P. (2006) Associativity Neighbourhood Models Madrid, in: Projecting the City Beyond Mapping – Special issue Architecture Biennale Venice 2006, The Berlage Institute Postgraduate Laboratory of Architecture, Rotterdam (pp. 20-32).

Van Wezemael, J.E. (2008) The Contribution of Assemblage Theory and Minor Politics for Democratic Network Governance, *Planning Theory*, 7, 165-185.

Vasishth, A. (2008) A Scale-hierarchic Ecosystem Approach to Integrative Ecological Planning, *Progress in Planning*, 70, pp. 99-132.

Verma, N. (1998) *Similarities, Connections and Systems – The Search for a New Rationality for Planning and Management*, Lexington Books, New York.

Wagenaar, H. (2005) Stadswijken, complexiteit en burgerbestuur [Neighbourhoods, complexity and local participatory policymaking], Nederlands Studiecentrum Criminaliteit en Rechtshandhaving, Universiteit Leiden en XPIN, Leiden en Den Haag.

Waldrop, M.M. (1992) *Complexity: The Emerging Science at the Edge of Order and Chaos*, Penguin Books, London.

Webber, M.M. (1978) A Difference Paradigm for Planning. In R. Burchell and G. Sternlieb (Eds.), *Planning Theory in the 1980s*, Center for Urban Policy Research, Rutgers University. New Brunswick.

Webster, C., L. Wai-Chung Lai (2003) *Property Rights, Planning and Markets: Managing Spontaneous Cities*, Edward Elgar Publishing, London.

Weinert, F. (2006) Relationism and Relativity. In H. Breger, J. Herbst and S. Erdner (eds.) Conference Reader VIII, *Einheit in der Vielfalt*, International Leibniz Congress, Hannover, pp 1138.

Wolfram, S. (1984) 'Universality and Complexity in Cellular Automata', *Physica D*, No. 10, January, pp. 1-35.

Yeung, H.W. (1997) Critical realism and realist research in human geography: A method or a philosophy in search of a method?, *Progress in Human Geography*, 21, 1, pp. 51-74.

Zuidema, C. (2011) Stimulating local environmental policy; on Adopting a post-contingency approach towards governance and decentralization in environmental policy, PhD thesis, University of Groningen, Groningen.

PART I
Theoretical Reflections Bridging Complexity and Planning

Chapter 2

Baroque Complexity: 'If Things were Simple, Word Would Have Gotten Round'[1]

Jean Hillier[2]

2.1 Introduction

Town and country planning practitioners and academics have traditionally singularised both 'town' and 'country'. In images, plans and texts, 'they have fashioned an ordered and unifiable whole out of what is often a disordered, spontaneous, even intractable multiplicity of places, practices and people' (Robbins, 1998: 37). In this chapter I engage in what must inevitably be an over-simplification of an introduction to complexity theories and their potential relevance for planning theory and practice.

I previously had little idea of the 'complexity' of the issue and how many trees have been sacrificed in writing about complexity. Although there is a plethora of published material on complexity across a wide disciplinary range, there nevertheless appears to be little agreement on whether there is *a* theory or several theories of complexity and what this or these theories are. It appears that several, very different, schools of thought have developed,[3] variously described as hard or soft (Richardson and Cilliers, 2001), computational, scientific, mathematical or critical (Cilliers, 2005), logico-scientific or narrative (Bruner, 1986), ecological (Smith and Jenks, 2005), romantic or baroque (Law, 2003d; 2004b), these last two being the terms I adopt in this chapter.

In this introduction I suggest several definitions of complexity, before offering an extremely reductionist evolutionary account of complexity thinking. I refer to what I understand as two key readings or trajectories of complexity theories, which I refer to as the romantic and the baroque. I then gloss several 'keywords' or metaphors of complexity thinking before comparing romantic and baroque approaches with examples of UK Evidence Based Policy Making and the CALFED process in the US. I conclude with some indeterminate implications for planning theory and praxis. Although my chapter is in a traditionally linear format, at odds with the nature of complexity which I describe, its intent is 'to make a space, define outlines, sketch contours' (Mol and Law, 2002: 7). I also recognise that the chapter is a mere inscription device, performing (hopefully) clarification

---

2 Jean Hillier is Professor and Associate Dean in the School of Global Studies, Social Science and Planning at the RMIT University, Melbourne.

1 Derrida, 1988: 119.

3 See Richardson and Cilliers (2001) for more detail.

and connection, and I fully accept that the content is inextricably connected to my 'hinterland' (Law, 2004a) or lifeworld 'baggage'; my philosophical preferences, my ideology, my choice of reading etc. The chapter is thus offered as an assemblage, 'a tentative and hesitant unfolding, that is at most only very partially under any form of deliberate control' (Law, 2004a: 41-42). As such, it inevitably generates presences, manifest absences and Otherness, for which I apologise.

Some definitions

I begin by distinguishing between the words complex, complicated and complexity. 'Complex' and 'complicated' are often used interchangeably to indicate something which includes several elements plaited or folded together and which thus becomes far from simple, difficult to comprehend, not easily disentangled or analysed (Alhadeff-Jones, 2008). 'Complexity', in contrast, focuses on 'the dynamical properties and structural transformation of non-linear, 'far-from equilibrium' systems' (Martin and Sunley, 2007: 575). For example,

> There is complexity if things relate but don't add up, if events occur but not within the processes of linear time, and if phenomena share a space but cannot be mapped in terms of a single set of three-dimensional coordinates (Mol and Law, 2002: 1).

> the study of complex adaptive ('vital') matter that shows ordering but which remains 'on the edge of chaos' (Urry, 2005a: 1).

> a system that is comprised of a large number of entities that display a high level of nonlinear interactivity (Richardson and Cilliers, 2001: 8).

> the interdisciplinary understanding of reality as composed of open systems with emergent properties and transformational potential (Byrne, 2005: 97).

> an accretion of ideas, a rhetorical hybrid … representing a shift towards understanding the properties of the interaction of systems as more than the sum of their parts. This is, then, the idea of a science of holistic *emergent* order; a science of qualities as much as of quantities, a science of 'the potential for emergent order in complex and unpredictable phenomena' (Goodwin, 1997: 112), a more open science which asserts 'the primacy of processes over events, of relationships over entities and of development over structure' (Ingold, 1990: 2009) (Thrift, 1999: 33, emphasis in original).

> it is usually recognised that complexity includes a variety of branches, among them chaos theory, cellular automata, fractal theory, neural networks etc (Suteanu, 2005: 115).

Complexity is complex! Social theorists have adopted/adapted the language of complexity from the natural sciences, such as physics, chemistry and biology. Definitions of complexity are context-dependent. Complexity thinking is multidisciplinary; concerned with relationships and processes of unpredictable movement or emergence where there is a tension between structure/order and a lack of structure/chaos. As Clark (2005: 166) suggests, complexity theory enables acknowledgement of 'the unmanageability of the contemporary world whilst also holding open the possibility that novel forms of organisation or structuring might emerge spontaneously out of a sea of dense and disorderly interaction'.

Cilliers (2005: 257) summarises 'the view from complexity' as follows:

- Complex systems are open systems.
- They operate under conditions not at equilibrium.
- Complex systems consist of many components. The components themselves are often simple (or can be treated as such).
- The output of components is a function of their inputs. At least some of these functions must be non-linear.
- The state of the system is determined by the values of the inputs and outputs.
- Interactions are defined by actual input–output relations and they are dynamic (the strength of the interactions change over time).
- Components on average interact with many others. There are often multiple routes possible between components, mediated in different ways.
- Some sequences of interaction will provide feedback routes, whether long or short.
- Complex systems display behaviour that results from the *interaction* between components and not from characteristics inherent to the components themselves. This is sometimes called emergence.
- Asymmetrical structure (temporal, spatial and functional organisation) is developed, maintained and adapted in complex systems through internal dynamic processes. Structure is maintained even though the components themselves are exchanged or renewed.
- Complex systems display behaviour over a divergent range of timescales. This is necessary in order for the system to cope with its environment. It must adapt to changes in the environment quickly, but it can only sustain itself if at least part of the system changes at a slower rate than changes in the environment. This part can be seen as the 'memory' of the system.
- More than one description of a complex system is possible. Different descriptions will decompose the system in different ways. Different descriptions may also have different degrees of complexity.

Cilliers (2005: 258) suggests that

since different descriptions of a complex system decompose the system in different ways, the knowledge gained by any description is always relative to the perspective from which the description was made. This does not imply that any description is as good as any other. It is merely the result of the fact that only a limited number of characteristics of the system can be taken into account by *any* specific description. Although there is no a priori procedure for deciding which description is correct, some descriptions will deliver more interesting results than others.

He indicates, in particular, differences between 'a more strictly mathematical and computational view' (romantic complexity), derived largely from cybernetics, systems and chaos theory, and a more narrative-based, 'critical understanding of complexity' (baroque complexity), which 'argues that complexity theory does not provide us with exact tools to solve our complex problems' (Cilliers, 2005: 257) but confronts us with the limits of our understanding and shows us why complex problems are so wicked.

To aid comprehensibility of what follows, I have adapted Snowden and Stanbridge's (2004: 144) 'landscape' (Figure 2.1).

I readily admit the ironic nature of my diagram. It is a reductionist approach and I am all too aware of its incompleteness; the impossibility of including everything. My figure is fractional. Its orderings can only be indeterminate: 'they are partially connected, benevolently or viciously, with any other orderings, orderings that cannot be grasped from any one place, from within any one ordering' (Law, 2003a: 7).

In (C in Figure 2.1) , an ordered system, relationships between cause and effect can be discovered. A desired outcome or end state is identified, the current situation is analysed and a series of steps is prescribed to achieve the given outcome. (e.g. McLoughlin's 1969 systems theory in planning.)

In an ordered system where emphasis is placed on heuristics, (D in Figure 2.1), processes are incremental (Lindblom, 1959; 1979), rational (Faludi, 1973) and involve mixed scanning (Etzioni, 1967).

In an unordered system, desired end states are not given and essentially cannot be predicted (Portugali, 2008). In seeking favourable outcomes, (A in Figure 2.1), facilitators manage negotiations by applying certain 'rules of play'. (For example, Byrne, 1997, 1998; Innes and Booher, 1999a; 1999b; Booher and Innes, 2002 – although Innes and Booher's work straddles the boundary between A and B above, as I elaborate below.) Portugali's (2000, 2008) view of cities and planning as complex, self-organising systems, advocates use of planning rules concerning the relations between urban elements (see, especially, Alfasi and Portugali, 2007).

In an unordered system, with emphasis on heuristics, (B in Figure 2.1), which Smith and Jenks term ecological complexity (2005: 147), issues of participation and communication are important. Space and time are performative. Outcomes are unpredictable and emergent (Hillier, 2005; 2007a).

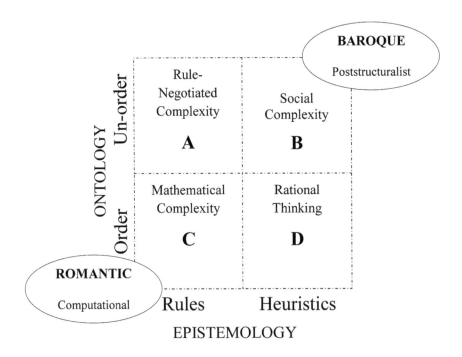

Figure 2.1   Snowden and Stanbridge's 'landscape' and the Romantic and Baroque

Source: Adapted from Snowden and Stanbridge (2004: 144)

2.2 Complexity theories in evolution

At the end of the 19th/beginning of the 20th Centuries, aleatory circumstances provided a window of opportunity for thinking relationally. Henri Poincaré, a mathematician and physicist, famous for his use of non-Euclidean geometry (1892-1909) and for describing the Hallmark of Chaos as sensitive dependence on initial conditions in which 'prediction becomes impossible' (1914); Albert Einstein's 1905 theory of relativity and Henri Bergson's ideas about durée (temporality and relational time) (1896, 1907, 1921), were all published. Also influential were the American pragmatists Charles Sanders Peirce, John Dewey and William James and the anarchist Piotr Kropotkin (who lived in France), whilst it is known that Einstein corresponded with Sigmund Freud (Novotny, 2005) and that Picasso read Bergson's work and attended seminars by Einstein, Bergson and Poincaré, which had a bearing on the development of Cubism. John Urry (2005b: 240-243) traces complexity thinking back to Marx and Engels' (1848) Communist Party Manifesto, which included the phrase 'all that is solid melts into air'.

There are far more connections and foldings together of thinkers and scholars than I have outlined here. I do not propose to engage debates about how ideas (such as relativity, relationality etc) travel and flow (see Latour, 1987; Thrift, 1999; Law, 2003b). Suffice it to say that in the post-World War II period, as mainframe computing systems were becoming more widespread, scholars such as Ilya Prigogine (1955),[4] studying chemical reactions and thermodynamics, and the US Rand Corporation's systems modelling for policy decision-making, identified the importance of connections and networks of flow. Cybernetics and operations research, investigating adaptive networks of relations, together with developments in neural networks, artificial intelligence and cognitive sciences, were increasingly applied to organisational decision making in the 1940s and 1950s by scholars such as Herbert Simon (1947, 1958, 1962), known in planning fields for his 'satisficing' ideas.

System Dynamics

Since the 1970s, complexity thinking has tended to follow two different paths, which are generally regarded as epistemologically antagonistic to each other. The first was largely based on 'system dynamics'. Mandelbrot's (1975) work on fractals indicated that 'if different points of view produce different results, this is not a problem to solve, but an opportunity to use' (Suteanu, 2005: 116). He went on to develop mathematical methods of extracting the relations which connect the different views and in so doing demonstrated the importance of regarding a problem from multiple perspectives, with multiple possible results. Meanwhile, Prigogine (1968, 1980) was concentrating on open and chance-governed non-linear systems evolution (Kwa, 2002). His seminal volume, written with Isabelle Stengers (1984), has paved the way for subsequent thinking on complex systems including issues of far-from-equilibrium conditions, autopoiesis, irreversibility, path dependency and energised interaction (Kwa, 2002; Smith and Jenks, 2005).

Chaos theory (Gleick, 1987) provided a theoretical lens through which to describe behaviour of systems which depend so sensitively on precise conditions that they are effectively unpredictable, but which can have highly significant impacts. Consideration of identity, difference and relationality also 'emerged' in organisational management (especially in the work of the Santa Fe Institute in the USA) where 'emergence' became a prominent element of research, fostered by scholars such as Waldrop (1993) and Lewin (1993). This aspect of complexity theorisation has continued to develop, spurred by the Report of the Gulbenkian Commission (Wallerstein, 1996) on which Prigogine sat, the journal *Emergence* (now *E:CO*) founded in 1999 by Jeffrey Goldstein, and the Complexity Research Programme at the LSE (http://is.lse.ac.uk/complexity).

With regard to strategic spatial planning, Brian McLoughlin's (1969) systems approach was based in complexity theory, cybernetics and operations research.

---

4   Who had been influenced by Bergson's work early in his career (Prigogine, 1977).

McLoughlin's attempt to construct a holistic, and also dynamic, model of evolving urban systems envisaged planning practitioners as 'steering' the system towards equilibrium, with urban development plans as critical ordering devices. In addition, since the late 1960s, Mike Batty (eg 1969, 1994, 2005) has been modelling urban systems, paving the way for scholars such as Cletus Moobela (2005) and Angelique Chettiparamb (2006, 2007).

The above developments, centred on emergence, belong to what I term (following John Law and others) romantic complexity. Whilst complex adaptive systems (CAS) based research is rapidly becoming highly significant in organisational management (see, for example, Richardson, 2005; Tsoukas, 2005; Meek et al, 2007), it has, as yet, few adherents in spatial planning or policy studies research, with the notable exceptions of authors such as Judith Innes and David Booher (see below), Cletus Moobela (2005) and David Byrne (1998, 2002, 2005). Such research views complexity as institutional complexity. It involves investigation of sophisticated multi-levels of coordination and authority, geared to producing dynamic, adaptive functioning and performance (Knorr Cetina, 2005: 214).

Narrative Approaches

The second path which complexity theories have taken is variously known as narrative, soft, critical or baroque (Bruner, 1986, Richardson and Cilliers, 2001; Cilliers, 2005). This trajectory can be traced from Henri Bergson (or even from Leibnitz and Spinoza). We can trace psychoanalytical trajectories through Sigmund Freud, Melanie Klein and Jacques Lacan and into French social theory (notably Gilles Deleuze, Félix Guattari, Michel Foucault, Michel Callon, Bruno Latour, Jacques Derrida, Michel Serres and others). In Germany, the work of the Frankfurt School and early Jürgen Habermas also displayed significant influences, both from these sources (Habermas, 1971; 1979) and from systems theory (Habermas, 1976; Habermas and Luhmann, 1971).

These scholars acknowledged the subjectivity of knowledge and argue that there is no objective way to determine any 'correct' meaning. This insight resonated with ideas in cybernetics of actants as cybernetic systems, able to adapt to changes in their environments. Researchers, such as Gregory Bateson (1972) wrote of 'not arriving at a place but following a path of continual questioning assumptions and values' (McWhinney, 2005: 34). The path is non-linear; a spiral of connection and contradiction. Bateson applied his thinking to urban planning, stressing the importance of practitioners practising flexibility as 'uncommitted potentiality for change' (Bateson, 1972: 505). Bateson had a profound influence on the work of Deleuze and Guattari (especially their *A Thousand Plateaus*, 1987).

Manuel Castells' (1996) material on the network society has popularised the concept of networks significantly. In planning, Patsy Healey's (1997) *Collaborative Planning* drew planning theorists' and practitioners' attention to the importance of relationality and connections, building on, amongst other influences, the work of Habermas and Giddens' structuration theory. Healey (2000, 2004, 2006, 2007) provides probably the key texts on institutional relational conceptions of strategic spatial planning. See, for instance, Healey's definition of spatial planning as:

> self-conscious collective efforts to re-imagine a city, urban region or wider territory and to translate the result into priorities for area investment, conservation measures, strategic infrastructure investments and principles of land use regulation. The term 'spatial' brings into focus the 'where of things', whether static or in movement; the protection of special 'places' and sites; the interrelations between different activities and networks in an area; and significant intersections and nodes in an area which are physically co-located (Healey, 2007: 3)

Most planning academics are familiar with the work of Michel Foucault and his subsequent influence on planning theory (via the concepts of discourse, governmentality and so on) and on actor network theory and geography (concepts of relational materiality, performativity, heterogeneity). As 'a machine for waging war on Euclideanism' (Law, 2003c: 4), fixed categories (such as human/ non-human) are dissolved in radical relationality (Law, 2003b) of stronger and weaker associations. As Thrift (1999: 57) comments 'actor-network theory has become contingency incarnate; the gaps and uncertainties having become almost as important as the networks'.[5]

Whilst recognising the immense contribution of Jacques Derrida (especially in *Limited Inc*, 1988) in arguing for the irreducibility of meaning – that meaning and knowledge are always contingent and contextual (Cilliers, 2005) – and his influence on geographical thought (eg Massey, 2005, and the 2005 RGS/IBG conference session devoted to Derrida), his work has yet had relatively little influence on planning theory.

> I personally turn to the work of Gilles Deleuze, a French philosopher whose early writing ([1969] 2004) engages significantly with that of Bergson and of Freud. Deleuze's close friendship with Michel Foucault fostered his development of Foucault's notions of: agonism and a lack of commensurability between actors (Deleuze, 1981; Foucault, 1994); non-representation (Foucault, 1989: 260): 'the very being of that which is represented is now going to fall outside representation itself', in geography (see, for instance, Thrift, 1996) and in planning (Hillier, 2007a); chance and unpredictability (Deleuze, 1990; 2003; Foucault, 2004: 31): 'l'art de gouverner et le traitement de l'aléatoire'[6].

Deleuze teamed up with Félix Guattari, a practising psychoanalyst who had studied with Jacques Lacan, to produce a geophilosophy of space, which I find of immense

---

5   See the work of John Law, Annemarie Mol and John Urry in particular.
6   The art of governance and the regulation of chance.

potential significance to planning theory and practice (Hillier, 2007a).[7] As Protevi (nd: 4) remarks, 'Deleuze was a "sensitive" who picked up currents in the air, and thought through, with Guattari, what a chaos/complexity approach to what a complex econo-psycho-politics might look like'. Since my 'keywords' below rely heavily on Deleuzean thought, I do not expand further on his work at this point.

A 'Necessary Encounter'

With regard to strategic spatial planning, Karen Christensen's (1985, 1999) matrix of means, ends and uncertainty has become fundamental to development of many complexity analyses of spatial planning practice. David Byrne (2003) has suggested that there should be a 'necessary encounter' between planning and complexity theories; one which has been facilitated by authors including Juval Portugali (2000, 2008) and Gert de Roo (2007).

Making links between romantic and baroque notions of complexity lies the work of philosopher Manuel deLanda (1997, 2002) and social scientist Isabelle Stengers (1997, 2000, 2004). Both authors are concerned with investigating non-metaphorical relations between scientific and social-philosophical thought. For them, complexity science provides 'a source of insight into the nature of virtual multiplicities' (Mackenzie, 2005: 52). DeLanda, for instance, takes Poincaré's and Prigogine's concept of phase space to render the behaviour of a process in time more intelligible. Phase space[8] trades off time for space. Phase space is Thrift's (1999) 'space of possibility', identifying some patterns where previously only disorder was perceived. DeLanda offers a non-essentialist theory of multiplicity based on Deleuzean ideas, which he applies to issues of governance and the city (deLanda, 2006).

Stengers (1997, 2000) adds a political dimension to complexity thinking. She distinguishes between the invention of complex objects and their mobilisation and

---

7   For simplicity, in this chapter I reduce Deleuze and Guattari to Deleuze, an oversimplification of a complex relationship, for which I apologise to Félix Guattari.

8   There are five steps in constructing a phase space portrait of a system:

- Identify important impacts of a system's behaviour; its degrees of freedom.
- Model a space with as many dimensions as degrees of freedom of the system.
- Each state of the system can then be represented as a single point, with as many values as dimensions. For example, with one degree of freedom, there is one dimension and one value (eg body temperature).
- The changing states of a system trace a line, or trajectory, through fractal phase space. Eg with an increase in body temperature the line rises, but in complex phase spaces the trajectory explores all permutations throughout the space.
- In closed systems, trajectory equations can be solved and patterns emerge. In open systems some patterns may still be identified even though equations cannot be solved. (taken from Protevi, nd: 1-2). Cities are open systems.

the 'problem posed in the future it creates' (Stengers, 2000: 67) by becoming other than anticipated.[9]

- DeLanda and Stengers teach us that:
- generalisable solutions pertain only to unproblematic (usually highly reductionist) aspects of situations (Mackenzie, 2005);
- experimental practice is a way of posing relevant questions (Mackenzie, 2005);
- expect the unexpected.

As Plummer and Sheppard (2006, 2007), Martin and Sunley (2007) and Bergmann et al (2009) demonstrate, dialogues are taking place and resonances emerging. Eric Sheppard (2008) presents an excellent comparative summary of DeLanda's thinking on assemblages, Prigogine on complexity and David Harvey's relational aesthetics, which I reproduce below (Table 2.1, Source: Sheppard, 2008: 2607).

Table 2.1   Parallels between relational dialectics, assemblages and complexity

Attributes	A. Relational dialectics (after Harvey, 1996)	B. Assemblages (after DeLanda, 2006)	C. Complexity (after Prigogine, 1996)
Relational ontology	Entities have no stable, essential, characteristics, but are constituted through the 'internal' relations through which they are connected	An assemblage is a whole, whose properties emerge through interactions among components	Objects are relationally constituted
Heterogenety	All entities are heterogeneous, possessing internal contradictions	Its components are heterogeneous, at all scales	Objects and systems are heterogeneous (at all scales)

---

9   On this point see also Rabinow (2003) following a Foucauldian approach, Latour (1987, 1999) and in planning, Healey (2005, 2008).

Attributes	A. Relational dialectics (after Harvey, 1996)	B. Assemblages (after DeLanda, 2006)	C. Complexity (after Prigogine, 1996)
Relational causality	Subject/object, cause/effect are interchangeable, parts and wholes are mutually constitutive	Assemblages at one scale emerge from relations between smaller scale components; components can be unplugged from assemblages, because their existence is not entirely determined by their relations, yet they are also internally related	Local/global and short term/long term are mutually constitutive
Socionature	Society and 'nature' are inseparable, dialectically related	Assemblages are socionatural, with agency operating in all domains; components play roles that vary from material to expressive in nature	Systems are socionatural, with agency operating in all domains
Change	Change is a characteristic of all 'systems'; it is stasis and 'permanence' that require explanation; transformative behavior is an emergent feature of the heterogeneities and contradictions within and between entities	Immanent processes of emergence are driven by repetition and difference	The system spends large amounts of time in motion, far from equilibrium; change is path dependent and potentially transformative
Space-time	Space – time is contingent and relational, and contained within socionatural processes	Components shape assemblages through mechanisms of territorialisation (reinforcing homogeneity/ identity) and deterritorialisation (undermining homogeneity/ identity)	Time is unidirectional and spatiotemporality is an emergent relational feature

Attributes	A. Relational dialectics (after Harvey, 1996)	B. Assemblages (after DeLanda, 2006)	C. Complexity (after Prigogine, 1996)
Open endedness	Dialectical inquiry works with concepts and abstractions that are always subject to revision, and necessarily incorporates ethical and political choices given the always present possibility of the emergence of other possible worlds	The relations of an assemblage are not logically necessary but contingently obligatory, and must be revealed empirically	The future is uncertain: minor events can have large and lasting effects

With regard to planning theory, I believe that the work of Judith Innes links the two 'arms' of complexity thinking. I come to this conclusion from looking at the reference material on which Innes and Booher base their thinking. They cite texts from the romantic, computational side of complexity theory: (eg Prigogine and Stengers, 1984; Nicolis and Prigogine, 1989; Lewin, 1993; Waldrop, 1993; Axelrod, 1997; Axelrod and Cohen, 1999; Argyris, 1995; Argyris and Schön, 1974) and explore the implications of complex adaptive systems thinking to underpin their empirical practice and analysis of collaborative planning (Innes and Booher, 1999a, 1999c; Booher and Innes, 2002; 2006). Theirs is a rule-based practice of consensus-building through collaborative dialogue: 'a practical view of what it takes to make robust choices about the future in a real world situation, taking into account diverse views and multiple knowledges and understandings' (Innes, 2004: 9). They recognise, however, the emergent or immanent character of consensus-building processes (Innes and Booher, 2003) and that any agreements reached may be 'more like punctuation marks in an ongoing deliberative process than they are the final end product' (Innes, 2004: 8-9).

I turn now to brief explanation of some of what I regard as the key terms in baroque complexity theory. Many of the terms are also found in romantic complexity approaches, but their meanings and performativities tend to differ.

2.3 Towards a conceptual vocabulary of baroque complexity

Gandy (2005: 40) writes that, 'the contemporary city needs a conceptual vocabulary that can give expression to the unknown, the unknowable and what is yet to come'. In this spirit I offer a non-metric dozen keywords: a fragment – 'more than one and less than many' (Mol and Law, 2002: 11). I concur with John Law's (2004a) view of lists, that they are potentially endless, or otherwise reductionist, imposing clarity and rigor where all is vague and indistinct. The terms below should all be regarded as an assemblage in which 'the elements put together are not fixed in shape, do not belong to a larger pre-given list but are constructed at least in part as they are entangled together' (Law, 2004a: 42). I make no claims to inclusiveness. There are more absences than presences in this particular, limited performance. As mentioned above, my understanding is highly influenced by Deleuzean thinking. Connections between terms are multiple.

Multiplicity

Multiplicity concerns coexistences at a single moment (Mol and Law, 2002: 8). Academics in the social sciences are now used to the idea that humans are composites of multiple subjectivities. Deleuze extends this concept to non-humans. A lap-top computer, for instance, is a box containing a multiplicity of parts, each with their own specific constituents, histories and networks. (For example, a single wire coated in plastic, comprises plasticisers, fillers, colour pigments, copper alloy wire, petroleum hydrocarbons, salt and so on which originate from around the world, sourced and assembled by workers, probably in the South, working and living in networks of their own.)

Space, then, can be regarded as a multiplicity which brings together characteristics of externality, simultaneity, contiguity or juxtaposition and qualitative and quantitative differentiations (Bergson, 1988: 206; Grosz, 2001: 113). As Grosz (2001: 114) describes, 'space is discontinuous, infinitely divisible, static and always actual. Space in short is the milieu of things, matter, identities, substances, entities that are real, comparable and calculable'. Planning practice itself is a complex institution, whose multiple outcomes are often unpredictable. Truths are multiple. Planning is the art (or science) of spatial manipulation. It is a mediator between multiple representations of the 'good' in the continuous process of space-becoming or spacing.

Connection

Deleuze and Guattari (1983, 1987) use the connection 'and' rather than the static 'is'/'is-not'. Identity/difference thus becomes identity *and* difference, self *and* other. Each 'one' is actually a multiplicity of others. No wonder Deleuze said that he stammered 'and, and, and' (Deleuze and Parnet, 2002: 9) when contemplating multiplicity. This is relational thinking; connections within and between multiplicities.

The phenomena with which planning struggles have become 'less about territorial boundaries and states and more about connection and flow' (Law and Urry, 2003: 10). The performativity of entities (human and non-human) has widespread time-space impacts due to the multiplicities of connections across various networks leading to emergent, often unanticipated outcomes. The connections between actions and emergent effects are non-linear, occurring through an irreversibility of time (Urry, 2005b: 238; Urry, 2004).

Fluid, relational networks

Relations imply social practices. They are therefore vital to the active constitution of existence. It is the contingent 'circumstances, actions, and passions' (Deleuze and Parnet, 2002: 56) of life which provide for the specific forms of relations between different terms. Relations are endowed with a positive reality as they are not derived from the terms or entities themselves. In other words, Deleuze challenges the fundamental ontological assumptions of an essentialist theory of relations. Relations are not subordinated to the essence of things. Rather, they come into being via practice. Moreover, if relations between entities alter, there is no necessity that the entities themselves change.[10]

Relations are thus 'effects of the activities and practices of individuals who are different yet nevertheless interacting' (Hayden, 1995: 286). Relations as practices inevitably involve plays of power and politics. It may be useful to map the interrelations between, for example, a network of actors/actants, highlighting different forms of power, such as instrumental legislative power or economic power. Following Foucault's notion of power as a capillary process, Deleuze suggests that power works on and through subjects via the relations produced within the various contexts. We may then begin to deconstruct or unfold the complex interactions we have mapped, affording greater understanding of what is happening and of potential impacts.

Relations/connections require mediators. As Deleuze (1995) explains, mediators can be people or things (books, plans, money etc). There are clear links to actor network theory.

Relational networks of connected elements are inherently unstable and fluid. Society performs by recording, channelling and regulating the flow of energies through such networks (Thrift, 1996: 285). Network boundaries are indeterminate and frequently challenged, transgressed and/or extended as new connections occur and old ones rupture. 'Neither boundaries nor relations mark the difference between one place and another. Instead, sometimes boundaries come and go, allow leakage or disappear altogether, while relations transform themselves without fracture. Sometimes, then, social space behaves like a fluid' (Mol and Law, 1994: 643, cited in Urry, 2003: 41).

Networks are increasingly 'light', institutionally (Knorr Cetina, 2005): informal, non-rational, non-bureaucratic and lightly-regulated, thus creating opportunities for flexibility and adaptability in varying contexts. As Knorr Cetina (2003) indicates, there are often several temporal dimensions at play simultaneously in network or meshwork multiplicities of rich and diverse layers and flows of entities and practices.

Based on Deleuzean ideas and recent work in fluid dynamics, authors such as Sheller (2004) and Law (2004a) challenge the concept of networks as being

---

10   For this reason, Deleuze's ideas have been described as non-relational (see Hallward, 2000).

representations of lines between fixed points, which thereby reify presence and absence. Sheller (2004: 47) suggests replacing networks as a concept with that of 'gel or goo': 'whereas a network implies clean nodes and ties ... a gel is suggestive of the softer, more blurred boundaries of social interaction'. People and places are not stationary nodes in a network but 'flexible constellations of identities-on-the-move' (Sheller, 2004: 49). The idea of a gel or viscous liquid implies fluidity, slipperiness, instability, movement and transformation in form which, nevertheless, has the capacity for momentary stabilisation.

Immanence/emergence

Immanence refers to creativity; the quality of an action which proceeds from the spontaneity essential to the living subject or agent. 'We will say of pure immanence that it is a LIFE' (Deleuze, 2001: 27, emphasis in original). Immanence, in which new properties emerge, can occur autopoietically without need of external intervention or 'top-down' imposition (Clark, 2005: 168; DeLanda, 2002: 28). Immanence is both unpredictable, with no necessary proportionality between cause and effect (Urry, 2003: 24), and irreversible, 'full of unexpected and irreversible time-space movements, often away from points of equilibrium' (Law and Urry, 2003: 9). The multiple cocktail effects of air and water pollution exemplify immanence whereby individual elements, connected in new relationships, may interact and develop different collective properties not implicit within their singular components.

Emergence is the appearance of behaviour that could not be anticipated simply from knowledge of the elements of a system. Emergence is concerned with the many local, micro interactions which generate macro or large-scale entropic transformation. (For more depth see Waldrop, 1993; Holland, 1995; 1998.)

Deleuze terms such behaviour as 'becoming'. Becoming is linked rather to the unpredictable, indeterminate, never-accomplished actualisation of virtualities.[11] Becoming entails an openness to the new instead of pre-formism of the expected (Grosz, 1999). The most that can be done is to anticipate or map possible becomings. These anticipations could then be collaboratively discussed by all stakeholders and, if deemed undesirable, planned interventions could occur, noting, however, the inevitably uncertain outcomes of such interventions.

Lines/trajectories

A space of flows is a space of lines rather than of points. Moreover, points are not fixed (Cartesian-style) but lie on the intersections of many lines. 'We looked for foci of unification, nodes of totalisation, and processes of subjectification in arrangements, and they were always relative' (Deleuze, 1995: 86). The aim is thus to follow and disentangle lines, which are themselves in constant flux, bifurcating

---

11   Deleuze uses the term 'virtual' to indicate potentiality. Potentiality is more indefinite than possibility. Potentialities cannot be fully realised or 'actualised'.

and changing dimensions. The issue for planning becomes to conceive of and plan lines or trajectories rather than a final point (Rajchman, 2000: 100).

Deleuze distinguishes between two different forms of line. Firstly there are broad molar lines of rigid sedimentarity. Molar lines tend to map the official organisation of institutions and lives (eg life-stages: school, job, retirement). The second lines are molecular lines of supple segmentivity which 'trace out little modifications … they sketch out rises and falls' (Deleuze and Parnet, 2002: 124) along which occur processes of desire, affective attachments and all kinds of becomings. The two forms of line are closely entangled, as Deleuze and Guattari (1987: 260) describe: 'every society, but also every individual, is, therefore, composed of both segmentarities at once: the one molar, the other molecular. These are distinguished by the fact that they don't have the same terms, the same relations, the same nature or the same type of multiplicity. They are inseparable by virtue of the fact that they co-exist, the one leading into the other … always in presupposition to the other'.

Deleuze also identifies a third kind of line; the line of flight. This is a line without segments along which structures constituted in terms of molar or molecular lines break down and/or become transformed. It is a crack or rupture of the other lines and a flight from what has been and what is towards a destination which is unknown. It marks a threshold of lowered resistance to something ('you can no longer stand what you put up with before', Deleuze and Parnet, 2002: 126), a change in desire or the intensity of desire, a new anxiety and so on. Often political, lines of flight may be born out of resistance, but they can be positively creative. 'It's along this line of flight that things come to pass, becomings evolve, revolutions take shape' (Deleuze, 1995: 45). Deleuze is far more interested in the middle of lines than their beginning or end-points: the 'and' rather than the 'is'. Transformation starts in the middle, in between, in the margins, where there is the need for 'more to come' (Law, 2003a: 2); where there is endless transformation: 'of continual movements to find some kind of stable place. That never find a stable place. Of continuing incompleteness. Of continuing. Of incompletenesses' (Law, 2003a: 2). Transformation occurs through cracking, rupturing, and more importantly, through folding.

Folding

The French noun for fold '*le pli*' has a philosophical lineage in a family of words such as com*pli*cation, im*pli*cation, multi*pli*cation, re*pli*cation, suggesting that multiples are folded in complex ways rather than simply added on. Similarly, to ex*pli*cate is to unfold or explain, while something *pli*ant is foldable. Folding brings new connections as once-distant entities are now juxtaposed. It generates new energies as folds are never pre-formed or given. They have no transcendent rules or final solutions. Folds literally com*pli*cate. They express a multi*pli*city.

In folding there are always potential elements of chance (Foucault, 2004; Massey, 2005) due to the very multiplicity of trajectories which traverse and bump up against each other. Suburban neighbours, each with their own, multiple trajectories, thrown together by chance, inhabit adjacent houses (Massey, 2005: 111). Massey links such aleatoriness to the political. There is an undecidable contingency which possibilises the opening up of the political. Households (perhaps of different ethnicities, or perhaps groups of students and aged persons) may find themselves folded together, living adjacent to each other, sharing the same space differently. Political responses may occur.

Assemblages

An assemblage is an entity constructed from heterogeneous parts. It can refer to atoms, ecosystems, social human and non-human entities, from a subjective state of cognition and experience to 'objective relations, a material structure-like formation, a describable product of emergent social conditions; a configuration of relationships among diverse sites and things' (Marcus and Saka, 2006: 102, cited in Hillier, 2007a: 61). What is particularly important about an assemblage is the relations (especially the power or force relations) between the heterogeneous parts or elements. Relational interaction and connectivity are vital. A city (Deleuze and Guattari, 1986), a planning system or a plan are assemblages.

Diversity/fragmentation/fractionality

These terms are linked to heterogeneous multiplicity. The idea of partial connection; of 'more than one but less than many' (Strathern, 1991) outlined above, or 'that which is separate but which is also joined' (Law, 2003b: 8). For example, a city comprises heterogeneous multiplicities of actants, places, representations, meanings and identities.

Diversity, fragmentation and fractionality should not be confused with pluralism. Pluralism implies a series of separate, unrelated or parallel entities which happen to coexist. Fractionality implies that the diverse entities 'support, undermine, and in general interfere with one another in complex and uncertain ways' (Law, 2003a: 5).

Lack/openness/undecidability

The conceptualisation of incompleteness and the lack comes from psychoanalysis (Freud, Lacan) and Nietzschean philosophy (Nietzsche, Foucault), joined in the work of Deleuze and Guattari. Projects are unfinished, decisions are undecidable. There are always alternatives: decisions which could have been otherwise. There is also always a gap or lack between an object and its representation, a goal and its achievement.

We can never fully understand complex systems because we can never understand all their complexity (Cilliers, 2005). They are open systems and so we cannot comprehend their complete environments. We thus inevitably reduce their complexity, or simplify what we describe or try to explain. There is always a remainder, or outside, which is excluded but which interacts with what is included in non-linear and unpredictable ways.

Contingency

'The future of reality is always at risk in a sea of uncertainty' (Law, 2004a: 29). Representations, perceptions, events are contextually contingent (Thrift, 1996, 1999). Outcomes connect to the hinterlands of the multiplicity of actants whose trajectories are folded together and the contingencies of time and place. Contexts are never closed in that there is a 'margin of play' (Derrida, 1988: 151) for strategies, rhetorics, ethics and politics as actants' lines or trajectories connect.

Time-space

Complexity theory 'depends on emergent properties arising out of excitable spatial orders over time' (Thrift, 1999: 32). From Bergson and Prigogine, Deleuze drew the idea of rhythms and difference-producing repetition. Something repeated can never be *exactly* identical to that which went before (the clock-time is different, the weather has varied slightly and so on). This is difference-in-itself. Repetition thus becomes open and 'new senses of sense become possible built on the new frames of anticipation and forms of memory that can show up and be touched in and by events now' (Thrift, 2004: 188).

Time becomes other than a linear process. The past is yet to be determined as we overwrite or restructure the past. It is a virtuality of the present and future. Futures are unforeseeable with the implication that we cannot completely know or plan who we are or what we may become. Future cities are 'those invented, imagined, "constructed" relations or passageways between this unforeseen future and this indeterminate past in our being, through which we respond to the necessity, in what is happening to us, of some event – of some "actualization" of some virtual future' (Rajchman, 1998: 109). Planning's role is to make the virtual intelligible. Time is integral to the spatial (Massey, 2005).

Space is a verb; to take place. It is a process of action or happening. As Grosz (2001: 117-118) suggests, 'this kind of space can no longer be considered static, infinitely extended ... regular, amenable to gridding, to co-ordinates, to geometric division. ... It is not an existing, God-given space, the Cartesian space of numerical division, but an unfolding space, defined, as time is, by the arc of movement and thus a space open to becoming, by which I mean becoming other than itself, other than what it has been'. Think, for example, of sand on a beach, flowing into drifts and dunes. Let us then regard space not as a container or passive receptacle, but as change, a moment of immanent becoming. Bulldozing sand dunes to give sea views for prime residential development will be ephemeral as sand will blow across the flattened surface creating new entities of drifts and mounds.

Space-time is *pli*ant. As such, planning attempts to perform a kind of controlled folding. However, plans rarely eventualise exactly as anticipated because space is a virtuality, in continuous transformation, which makes the constellation of what are apparently stable forces slide. Planning may be said to pass between the folds, floating on the surface of a plane of immanence, eluding its own actualisation. Spaces may resist intended folding whilst unanticipated folding occurs elsewhere. Space and time are 'beyond any fixed formulation, no longer guaranteed by the a priori, or by the universalisms of science' (Grosz, 2001: 95).

Deleuze and Guattari distinguish between two main different spaces. Smooth and striated spaces can be physical (as in cities), or mental (psychological). Smooth space is seemingly undifferentiated space (eg felt cloth), in contrast to striated space (woven cloth) which is regular, ordered and closed. Smooth space may be regarded as composed chaos; a 'complex web of divisions, bifurcations, knots and confluences' (Serres, 2000: 51). In striated space, relationships are linear cause and effect and the observer has a god's-eye view, able to see the order of things by deterministic laws. Smooth space consists of points as relays between lines; striated space consists of lines between points (Deleuze and Guattari, 1987: 480-481). Table 2.2 summarises the various qualities of smooth and striated space.

Table 2.2   Qualities of smooth and striated space

Smooth Space	Striated Space
nomadic space of movement	sedentary space
space of war machine	space instituted by state apparatus
constantly transversed into striated space	constantly reversed into smooth space
felt: entanglement	woven space: warp and woof
infinite, open and unlimited	fixed, limited
continuous variation	back and forth
'barbarian'	imperial
close-range/micro-vision	long-distance/macro-vision
multiple perspective	central perspective
points of reference immanent	points of reference transcendent
abstract line: wandering, irregular	concrete line: bounded, constant, regular
line without beginning or end	line of fixed orientation
matter variable	matter gridded and organised
smooth space of Go	striated space of Chess
thought space	Ideology

Source: Adapted from Bonta (1999)

Striated space is fixed. It 'bounds, structures, frames and locates action; and practices of discipline, regulation, subjection take place inside these spaces' (Osborne and Rose, 2004: 218). Moreover, time is detached from space. Yet, as Osborne and Rose indicate, striated space always fails – it is lacking. There is a constitutive outside or lack: people rebel, plans go awry, things change. 'Striated spatialisation, precisely because it aspires to a certain rigour or rigidity, is vulnerable to forces that would turn its lines into points, open up its intervals, redistribute its surfaces' (Osborne and Rose, 2004: 218).

Striated space tends to be associated with the State: 'one of the fundamental tasks of the State is to striate the space' (Deleuze and Guattari, 1987: 479) (eg, in the UK, through the Office of the Deputy Prime Minister or the Home Office), whilst smooth space is created by 'war machines' along lines of flight (eg anti-wind farm lobbies, civil liberties organisations). Both spaces, nevertheless, cannot be completely actualised. The lack remains, opening up opportunities for the counter form of space.

Smooth and striated space should not be regarded as mutually exclusive, but rather 'intermixtures which constantly make use of elements of each other' (Osborne and Rose, 2004: 211). Forces at work within space are constantly attempting to striate it whilst in the course of striation other forces are smoothing. The two presuppose each other in an agonistic relation. As Bogard (2000: 290-291) writes, 'smooth(ing) society has rough spots. ... [R]oughness is just part of smoothing, both its condition and its effect'. If we think of a 'classic' smooth physical space, such as the Antarctic icecap, it actually contains many localised striations.

Whilst smooth space is the fluid space of flight and becoming, and striated space is controlled, the former should not necessarily be regarded as positive and the latter negative. Smooth space is uncontrollable by definition and disappears as it becomes overcoded and over-regulated.

Space, is then, as Massey (2005) proposes:

- the product of interrelations, constituted through interactions;
- the sphere of coexisting heterogeneity and open-ended configurations within multiplicities;
- multiplicity and space are co-constitutive;
- always under construction; a fluid product of relations-between;
- co-implicated with time.

2.4 The Romantic and the Baroque

Following Kwa (2002), Law (2003d, 2004b) offers the romantic and the baroque as two ideal sensibilities for imagining complexity (Table 2.3), although he recognises such a list as being inevitably romantic: 'it characterises the baroque by making it explicit and abstracting it' (2003d: 10). After outlining characteristics of the romantic and baroque below, I offer two brief examples of romantic and baroque practices in relation to spatial planning.

Table 2.3   Qualities of Romantic and Baroque sensibilities

Romantic	Baroque
looking up	looking down
complexity emergent	complexity within
complexity big	complexity small
holism	non-coherence
making explicit	accepting implicit
homogeneity	heterogeneity
abstraction	specificity, sensuousness
centering view	no overview

Source: Law, 2003d: 9-10.

Romantic complexity is characterised by holistic views of the world, 'seeking to bring conceptual unity to what otherwise would not easily be put together' (Kwa, 2002: 23). McLoughlin's (1969) systems approach to planning attempted to integrate all the relevant heterogeneous fragments of complex systems into a single higher level entity or system, such as a city. A romantic gaze looks upwards; an explanatory overview of a situation which can lend itself to mathematical modelling using indicators which define a finite set of dimensions. It depicts society as an organism (Kwa, 2002: 26).

Romantic complexity favours structural metaphors, such as the self-correcting cybernetic machine (Kwa, 2002: 46). There are fixed sets of natural laws by which entities can be 'known'. As such, criteria can be delineated and measured to enable modelling and prediction of system attributes and patterns.

Law's (2003d, 2004b) excellent description of formalist romantic complexity thinking demonstrates how the romantic notion of identifying a number of different elements and then indicating how they are connected to produce a new, complex reality incorporates several important underlying assumptions. These assumptions include:

- that the emergent is a reality in its own right; 'there is connection; the connection produces something that is emergent; that which emerges is a whole; it is real; it is a reality that is *qualitatively different* from its component parts; and it can only be grasped if we look at the whole' (Law, 2003d: 2, emphasis in original);
- a formalist attempt to render the emergent explicit (2003d: 2);
- to render the relations between different elements explicit, they are made homogeneous – often either algebraically or through translation to

expenditure or cost (2003d: 3);
- abstraction from material reality (2003d: 3);
- centralised modelling and control. Overviews are necessary: 'look up so you can look down' (2003d: 4). Homogenisation to measurements of cost, for example, permits overview and comparison.

In contrast, baroque complexity looks downwards, to the individual fragments or elements and how they connect and interrelate or reciprocally refer (Kwa, 2002: 29). One may thereby discover the many fragmented, heterogeneous worlds which comprise a multiplicity. A baroque view depicts an organism as a society (Kwa, 2002: 26).

Baroque complexity sees individual actants in turbulent, unstable motion. Although there may well be some higher order level (eg a city), it is impossible to describe and explain it fully from a baroque viewpoint. As Kwa (2002; 46, emphasis in original) comments, 'it is easier to say what it is *not*'. If patterns may be discerned, they tend to be short-lived and never exactly repeated. Individuals act in multiple networks simultaneously, contingent on context. Representations are similarly contingent on the hinterland 'baggage' of those representing and perceiving: 'contextualised through and through' (Cilliers, 2002: 80).

Law's (2003d, 2004b) conceptualisation of baroque complexity is founded in Deleuze's (1993) work on Leibniz' (1998) 'ponds within the ponds'. Baroque complexity looks down within formalism and the 'big picture' to discover complex detail. Law's characteristics of baroque complexity include:

- 'it is in the specific and the concrete that complexity is located' (Law, 2003d: 6);
- It discovers heterogeneity: 'the holistic environment of romantic complexity has been turned into a set of endlessly unassimilable and materially heterogeneous elements' (2003d: 7);
- The baroque allows the discovery of potentially everything: 'wherever we look everything is already present if we just look hard enough' (2003d: 8). There are theoretically no limits;
- There are no natural, pre-given boundaries (2003d: 9).

However, as we are aware (from Lacan, Deleuze et al), we will never discover everything and there are always limits and boundaries to what we know and make explicit. As Cilliers (2001, 2002) explains: 'the very notion of 'system' presupposes the existence of a boundary to the system' (2002: 81). These boundaries are often constructions imposed by theorists and/or practitioners in order to reduce complexity and to render the 'system' more manageable. What baroque complexity suggests is that a boundary comprises those elements of a system that interact directly with the outside of a system (its environment). If the system is constituted through its interrelated elements, then all the elements will be close to the boundary. The boundary is 'folded in' and 'one is never quite sure whether one is dealing with the inside or the outside of the system' (Cilliers, 2002: 82). The boundary exists, but it is impossible to specify.

The boundary constitutes the system rather than confines it. Moreover, 'by differentiating the system from the environment, and simultaneously allowing for the transcending of the boundary, the system can be and become' (Cilliers, 2002: 82-83). Cilliers (2001, 2002) offers the example of the eardrum as a performative boundary which is permeable by sound[12]. The boundary is therefore an interface which participates in constituting the system. As such, Cilliers (2001) suggests that we should follow the deconstructionists, such as Derrida, and be concerned with difference and margins rather than centres and cores. Baroque complexity denies the possibility of a coherent system or overview of a network.

Evidence Based Policy Making: A Romantic Example

Drawing on Parsons (2002) and Davoudi (2006), I offer the brief example of Evidence Based Policy Making (EBPM) in the UK to demonstrate the workings of romantic complexity in practice. EBPM may be traced back to Geoff Mulgan's (then a leading Labour policy advisor) romantic understanding of complexity as involving the discernment of 'big pictures' and their control through top-down steering: 'human systems are neither so unknowable that we are unable to act, nor so self-organising that we have no need to' (Mulgan, 1997: 189, cited in Parsons, 2002: 9).

The underlying assumptions of the UK government's approach to EBPM (Cabinet Office, 1999a, 1999b, 2001; National Audit Office, 2001) are that 'hard facts' and patterns exist which can support policy decisions. Policy would thus be instrumentally driven by evidence rather than political ideology.[13] EBPM conceptualises reality as 'a territory *capable* of being "mapped" and "occupied"' (Parsons, 2002: 3, emphasis in original). Policy should be based on knowledge of 'what works and why'. 'Reliable answers' to such questions demand that policy makers are 'able to measure the size of the effect of A on B' (Parsons, 2002: 3), thus assuming determinable causes and effects. 'Measurement' tends to imply quantitative methodologies. The UK government has imposed 'indicators' to measure just about everything relating to public sector performance. What EBPM is effectively saying is that the government does not trust individual actants to perform in a 'correct' manner and in order to avoid unpredictable immanence or emergence, which may not be in its (or other actants') best interests, it will attempt to impose predictive control.

---

12   Although I personally find this example limited as only sound can penetrate and only in one direction. I prefer the idea of boundaries as permeable and transgressable in multiple ways.

13   Of course, as Law (2004a) and others indicate, political ideology both drives the method which constructs and gathers the "facts' and influences their interpretation and the direction of policy-steering.

EBPM exemplifies some of the problems which may be associated with romantic complexity. Firstly, measurement of 'evidence' as such inevitably does injustice to complexity. In the processes of methodological selection, indicator construction and enumeration, boundaries are drawn. '[W]hat counts as evidence is what is available' (Davoudi, 2006: 20). Certain elements are inevitably foregrounded, others are excluded and the political aspects of evidence-construction are ignored.

Moreover, 'predictive modelling requires a commitment to determinist explanation' (Wynne, 2005: 76). As Mol (2002: 237) suggests, 'conditions become fixed in the process', which obscures the issue of how they might have been shaped differently. Conditions and their measurement become normalised, in Foucauldian terms. Individual elements tend to be homogenised and measured in cost-effectiveness terms.

There is a danger that romantic complexity can lead to positivism where it is uncritically appropriated. As Law (2003b: 3) poignantly states, with regard to UK defence procurement policy, 'it is not very important to think about the safety of individual aircraft (or pilots) but rather of the overall effectiveness (including cost-effectiveness) of air power as a whole. *Individual* losses don't matter so much any more. What's important is "bangs pre buck"'. Such sentiments are readily transferable to UK government policies on health care, education, social work, urban regeneration and so on.

EBPM leads to a particular deterministic conception of policy-making as technicised and path-dependent. A baroque interpretation of path-dependency, however, would be very different; suggesting that paths can take new directions, can overlap, bifurcate, network, flow or collide (Smith and Jenks, 2005: 146), but perhaps this non-linear unpredictability is exactly what the UK government is afraid of.

Academics, in particular, should be asking questions about what is being bracketed in the romantic reductionism of EBPM; what imagined world is being affirmed, with what implications and for whom.

Complex Assemblages: A Baroque Example

The expression, complex adaptive system (CAS), emerged in the 1980s with the work of the Santa Fe Institute in the US attempting to understand the commonalities connecting artificial, natural and human systems. Duit and Galaz (2008) and Jones (2003) identify several key traits of CAS:

- CAS consists of agents (such as humans, ants, starlings etc) assumed to follow certain behaviours, including swarming;
- There is no central control directing agent behaviour, which is self-organising (autopoietic), acting on locally available information;
- Such co-evolutionary, adaptive processes generate temporary, unstable equilibria which, in turn, give rise to
- Emergent behavioural patterns with limited predictability;

- CAS does not respond to change in a continuous or linear manner. Instead, CAS continues in much-the-same-way until it reaches a 'tipping point' when resilience ceases and large-scale changes (crises) occur (eg Coaffee and Murakami Wood, 2009);
- CAS comprises interconnected elements across multiple time-spaces whose interactions are often poorly understood, resulting in 'surprises';
- There are no neutral observers of CAS. Anyone observing affects the system;
- There is no 'objective reality' which can describe CAS;
- Definitions of CAS are inevitably arbitrary, since interconnectivity and adaptive transformation is pervasive. (Adapted from Hillier, 2010.)

There is an important difference, however, between a complex system and a complex *adaptive* system: a complex system can be simply chaotic and not necessarily self-organising, whereas a CAS is, by necessity, self-organising or autopoietic.

Cities are complex, non-linear systems of networks whose future behaviour is essentially unpredictable. David Booher and Judith Innes (2006) have applied selected aspects of CAS interactions to analysis of the CALFED process in the San Francisco Bay-Delta area of the US. CALFED involved 25 State and Federal agencies and 35 major stakeholders in adaptive management of the complex network of water systems and the demands of water supply and quality in the area. CAS features studied comprised agents, interactions, non-linearity, openness, unpredictability and emergence, adaptation and autopoiesis (self-reorganisation). The authors conclude that CALFED's success was due largely to its functioning as a CAS.

Booher and Innes regard several elements as of particular importance to this success. For instance, CALFED was structured as independent networked clusters of agencies and stakeholder groups rather than as an imposed top-down hierarchy. Boundaries were open rather than closed. Procedures were not predetermined, but developed interactively. Leadership was generative rather than directive. Intelligence and control were distributed among the agencies in a collaborative process in which the 'manager' acted as a mediator who guided interactions and provided opportunities. There was extensive public/stakeholder involvement in developing intelligence and decision-making. Decisions were made through processes of interest-based negotiation.

Processes were non-linear, with actions taking place often simultaneously and fluidly, as actants became aware of different issues and the relationships between them. CALFED did not seek legislative adoption of a plan, although there was an understanding between the actants to implement decisions. Booher and Innes suggest that such informality avoids actants having to make politically difficult formal commitments. CALFED operated in what the authors term a 'shadow system': in the shadow of traditional governance.

Regarding systems of governance (such as CALFED) as CAS offers the possibility of developing new, more appropriate, processes for coping with complexity and uncertainty. Booher and Innes conclude that CALFED exemplifies such a 'self-guiding system, its agents trying in a turbulent context to create their own shared path to the future' (2006: 20).

I doubt whether systems of governance in other geographical areas have the potential to be as self-organising as CALFED. In England, at least, I regard cities and planning as being too centrally regulated to offer scope for self-organisation. I, therefore, prefer to think of cities and spatial planning systems as complex assemblages rather than CAS, as strictly defined.

2.5 Conclusions: Some Implications for Planning Practice

There is no such thing as complexity *theory*; rather a range of complexity *theories*, or different theorisations of complexity. Distinctions are situational. I believe that ideas, things and forces exist in dynamic interrelationality. In other words, to varying degrees, everything is connected to everything else. In such context, I also believe that there are roles for both romantic and baroque theorisations of complexity. 'Science is a necessary condition for understanding the world, but not a sufficient one' (Isabelle Stengers, 2005: 37ff, cited in Shaviro, 2007: 7).

Scholars are increasingly realising that romantic and baroque approaches are 'no more than an emergent permanence', whose nature and properties are 'shaped through their relations with other ontologies and epistemologies' (Sheppard, 2008: 2610). As such, Eric Sheppard argues that there is much potential benefit for researchers exploring these relationalities: an 'and ... and ... and' (Deleuze and Parnet, 2002: 9) approach rather than an 'either/or' across the multiplicity of complexity-referential theories.

Whilst I recognise and accept the strengths of romantic theorisations, my own research leans towards a poststructuralist baroque approach. In summary, a baroque complexity approach to understanding and planning the city would argue that actants (humans and non-humans) 'do not *naturally* live anywhere in particular' (Callon and Law, 2004: 3, emphasis added) as there is no transcendent context in which beings, things or events naturally arrange or order themselves. Planning practice has traditionally been concerned with order and control: 'of putting to rights. ... Of aims and objectives. Of goals and milestones. Of strategic plans. Of that which has no tension because it has achieved its aim. Or of that which has tension only because it has not yet been achieved' (Law, 2003a: 2).

If planning theory and practice can become 'open to potentiality', then I think they can make a difference. So, what would becoming open to potentiality entail?

For me, it would be admitting 'I don't know', aiming for 'insights, not answers' (Suteanu, 2005: 125), acknowledging a limited capability to make predictions. I would propose a break-down of the silo mentality between government departments and between sections within strategic planning (such as transport, housing and so on) in local authorities. A local plan could then operate as 'the collection of bifurcating, divergent and muddled lines' (Deleuze and Parnet, 1987: ix) which would constitute the plan as a multiplicity, passing between the 'points' (sections/departments) and carrying them along. Production of a local plan would be a collaborative, pragmatic process with lines of becoming connecting with the lines of other multiplicities in unpredictable ways.

Spatial planning as emergent, immanent or becoming would begin from the general as instituted in a particular situation, such as a local authority preparing its new local strategic plan. It would force apart transcendent thinking, converting constraints into opportunities, and invent new trajectories, new responses and unheard-of futures (Massumi, 1993: 101). There would be no specific predesignated end point, but it would produce 'strategies' (Massumi, 1993) as pragmatic guidelines for future movement which would be collaboratively agreed and reworked as required. 'Strategy should be emergent and subject to continuing reassessments and alterations' (Santa Fe Center for Emergent Strategies, cited in Thrift, 1999: 46).

I should like spatial planning practice to pay attention to the connectivity of human and non-human networks or assemblages and especially to the ways in which different realities of time and space interrelate or clash (see Hillier, 2005, 2007a, 2007b). Planning is the art of 'bringing into line the significance of the irretrievable, indeterminate, and excessive qualities of everyday life with an immanent, creative and pragmatic project for future social explication' (Thrift and Dewsbury, 2000: 428). Planning practice is a performative (Dewsbury, 2000) folding of time-space: 'every move ... is an untimely moment redistributing what has gone before while opening up what may yet come' (Deleuze, 1991: 96).

Planning is a virtual practice. Rajchman (1998: 117) regards the virtual city as the city that holds together the most, and most complicated, 'different possible worlds', allowing them to exist together along a constructed plane with no need of a pre-established harmony. A virtual city, like a virtual plan, is agonistic; it allows insurgencies and encounters.

Virtual planning is not concerned with setting out all possibilities in advance. A plan should always be incomplete so as to be able to respond to the 'unforeseen moments in what happens in us and to us that open up onto new histories, new paths in the 'complication' of our ways of being' (Rajchman, 2000: 61). A virtual plan constitutes a space whose rules can themselves be altered through what happens in it. It could allow a great number of points lying at the intersections of many entangled lines with a host of complex connections made from them. For me, the role of a plan is not to predict but to 'remain attentive to the unknown knocking at the door' (Deleuze, 1994). A plan is about connections: 'and'.

'To make connections one needs not knowledge or certainty, but rather a trust that something may come out, though one is not yet completely sure what' (Rajchman, 2000: 7). A 'belief of the future, in the future' (Deleuze, 1994: 6). However, this is not to suggest abdicating responsibility for trying to prepare for a 'better' future than the present, even if transcendent notions of 'the good' are destabilised and dissolved. Deleuze and Guattari (1987: 483) write of an 'anexact yet rigorous' practice which is 'open and connectable in all of its dimensions' (Deleuze and Guattari, 1987: 12); a continuous exchange of striated and smooth space.

Planning practice could perform a space in which representations are unsettled and destabilised. Spatial planning practice and its practitioners need to be self-reflexive; to recognise the performativity of our descriptions and representations and how representation reflects our hinterlands to include and exclude selectively. Although identities and spaces are fluid, they nevertheless require partial fixing in some manner if differential subject positions and social relations are to exist. Such partial fixing takes place round nodal or passage points in the form of temporary, hegemonic relations (eg the outcome of public consultation, the adoption of a local plan, a development assessment decision). In traditional forms of planning practice temporary and partial fixations have tended to perpetuate for many years turning into reified rigidities rather than the non-closures called for by Healey (1997, 2004). Spatial planning policy-making could become a performative process which mobilises complex, heterogeneous understandings to temporarily fix the meanings of dynamic entities. It could seek out in particular, understandings from the interstices, those 'cracks' and liminal spaces in which lines of flight appear.

How will 'planning' cope with the dissolution of fixed categories. Many people will not be comfortable trying to come to terms with baroque thinking. Law (2003b) identifies two possibilities: *either* treat it as an irreducible impasse, either giving up – going home or allowing 'anything goes' – or ignoring it and continuing as before, *or* explore the empirical, ethical and theoretical implications of acting differently. I include 'ethical' here because we, as academics and practitioners, are neither free-floating, neutral, objective nor independent. Spatial planning is a creative experiment which generates change and creative points of resistance. Planning can never be actualised completely. It has schizophrenic effects, beneficial for some entities and disadvantageous to others, which cannot entirely be anticipated. 'We only have limited access to a complex world and when we are dealing with the limits of our understanding, we are dealing with ethics' (Cilliers, 2005: 261). Impossible as it may be to act responsibly (see Derrida, 1995), I believe there is a moral requirement to ask key questions at critical/nodal points, such as what versions of the complex are being enacted? (Law, 2003d); which 'realities' and whose 'realities' do we want to help make more real and which less real, and why? (Law and Urry, 2003); how do we want to interfere? (Law and Urry, 2003); what realities are we interfering with and what might emerge?

There can be no end-point. Baroque thinking has been heavily criticised as being flaccid, modest, vague and weak. I would suggest, however, that it offers much of value in helping us, as spatial planning researchers and practitioners, 'to grasp the world in its becoming, with its complexities, yet without reducing it to the coordinates of a reality we are already disposed to know how to measure' (Elden, 2008: 2649).

References

Alfasi, N. and Portugali, J. (2007) 'Planning rules for a self-planned city', *Planning Theory*, 6(2), pp. 164-182.

Alhadeff-Jones, M. (2008) 'Three generations of complexity theories: nuances and ambiguities', *Educational Philosophy and Theory*, 40(1), pp. 66-82.

Argyris, C. and Schön, D. (1974) *Theory in Practice*, Jossey Bass, San Francisco.

Argyris, C. (1995) *Knowledge for Action*, Jossey Bass, San Francisco.

Axelrod, R. (1997) *The Complexity of Cooperation*, Princeton University Press, Princeton.

Axelrod, R. and Cohen, M. (1999) *Harnessing Complexity: Organizational Implications of a Scientific Frontier*, Free Press, New York.

Bateson, G. (1972) *Steps to an Ecology of Mind*, Jason Aronson Inc., Northvale.

Batty, M. (1969) 'A review of the theory pertaining to spatial organisation', in Masser, I. (ed.) *The Use of Models in Planning, Dept. Of Civic Design*, University of Liverpool, Liverpool, pp. 1-27.

Batty, M. (2005) *Cities and Complexity: Understanding Cities with Cellular Automata, Agent-based Models, and Fractals*, MIT Press, Cambridge.

Batty, M. and Longley, P. (1994) *Fractal Cities: a geometry of form and function*, Academic Press, Oxford.

Bergmann, L., Sheppard, E. and Plummer, P. (2009) 'Capitalism beyond harmonious equilibrium: mathematics as if human agency mattered', *Environment and Planning A*, 41, pp. 265-283.

Bergson, H. (1921) *Durée et Simultanéité a propos de la théorie d'Einstein*, F. Alcan, Paris.

Bergson, H. (1975) [1907] *Creative Evolution* (trans. A. Mitchell), Greenwood Press, Westport (US).

Bergson, H. (1988) [1896] *Matter and Memory* (trans. N. Paul and W. Palmer), Allen & Unwin, London.

Bogard, W. (2000) 'Smoothing machines and the constitution of society', *Cultural Studies*, 14(2), pp. 269-294.

Bonta, M. (1999) 'The Smooth and the Striated: reactions of a "geographer"', http://www.artsci.su.edu/fai/Faculty/Professors/Protevi/DG/ATP14.html [accessed 06/02/2004]

Booher, D. and Innes, J. (2002) 'Network power in collaborative planning', *Journal of Planning Education and Research*, 21, pp. 221-236.

Booher, D. and Innes, J. (2006) 'Complexity and adaptive policy systems. CALFED as an emergent form of governance for sustainable management of contested resources', Proceedings of the 50th Annual Meeting of the ISSS, http://journals.isss.org/index.php/proceedings50th/article/viewFile/295/68 [accessed 22/12/2008].

Bruner, J. (1986) *Actual Minds, Possible Worlds*, Harvard University Press, Cambridge (US).

Byrne, D. (1997) 'Chaotic places or complex places: cities in a post-industrial age', in Westwood, S. and Williams, J. (eds) *Imagining Cities: Scripts, Signs, Memory*, Routledge, London, pp. 50-70.

Byrne, D. (1998) *Complexity Theory and the Social Sciences*, Routledge, London.

Byrne, D. (2002) *Interpreting Quantitative Data*, Sage, London.

Byrne, D. (2003) 'Complexity theory and planning theory: a necessary encounter', *Planning Theory*, 2(3), pp. 171-178.

Byrne, D. (2005) 'Complexity, configurations and cases', *Theory, Culture and Society*, 22(5), pp. 95-111.

Cabinet Office (1999a) *Modernising Government,* (Cmnd 4310), The Cabinet Office, London.

Cabinet Office (1999b) *Professional Policymaking in the 21st Century*, The Cabinet Office, London.

Cabinet Office (2001) *Better Policy-Making*, Centre for Management & Policy Studies, London.

Callon, M. and Law, J. (2004) 'Guest editorial', *Environment & Planning D, Society and Space*, 22, pp. 3-11.

Castells, M. (1996) *The Rise of the Network Society,* Blackwell, Oxford.

Chettiparamb, A. (2006) 'Metaphors in complexity theory and planning', *Planning Theory*, 5, pp. 71-91.

Chettiparamb, A. (2007) 'Re-conceptualising public participation in planning: a view through autopoiesis', *Planning Theory*, 6(3), pp. 263-281.

Christensen, K. (1985) 'Coping with uncertainty in planning', *Journal of the American Planning Association*, 51, pp. 63-73.

Christensen, K. (1999) *Cities and Complexity*, Sage, Thousand Oaks.

Cilliers, P. (2001) 'Boundaries, hierarchies and networks in complex systems', *International Journal of Innovation Management*, 5(2), pp. 135-147.

Cilliers, P. (2002) 'Why we cannot know complex things completely', *Emergence*, 4(1/2), pp. 77-84.

Cilliers, P. (2005) 'Complexity, deconstruction and relativism', *Theory, Culture and Society*, 22(5), pp. 255-267.

Clark, N. (2005) 'Ex-orbitant globality', *Theory, Culture and Society*, 22(5), pp. 165-185.

Coaffee, J. and Murakami Wood, D. (2009) *The Everyday Resilience of the City*, Palgrave Macmillan, Basingstoke.

Davoudi, S. (2006) 'Evidence-based planning: rhetoric and reality', disP 165(2), http://www.nsl.ethz.ch/index.php/de/content/download/1277/7708/file/ [accessed 12/12/2008].

De Roo, G. (2007) 'Understanding fuzziness in planning', in De Roo G. and Porter G. (eds) *Fuzzy Planning: The Role of Actors in a Fuzzy Governance Environment*, Ashgate, Aldershot, pp. 115-129.

DeLanda, M. (1997) *A Thousand Years of Nonlinear History*, Swerve, New York.

DeLanda, M. (2002) *Intensive Science and Virtual Philosophy*, Continuum, London.

DeLanda, M. (2006) *A New Philosophy of Society*, Continuum, London.

Deleuze, G. (1981) Cours de Gilles Deleuze, cours du 28/04/1981, session 1, ref: 16A, *La voix de Gilles Deleuze*, http://www.univ-paris8.fr/deleuze/article/php3?id_article=47 [accessed 07/03/2007].

Deleuze, G. (1986) [1983] *Cinema 1: the movement-image* (trans. Tomlinson, H.), University of Minnesota Press, Minneapolis (US).

Deleuze, G. (1990) [1969] *The Logic of Sense* (trans. Lester, M. and Stivale, C.), Athlone, London.

Deleuze, G. (1991) [1960] *Bergsonism* (trans. Tomlinson, H. and Habberjam, B.), Zone Books, New York.

Deleuze, G. (1993) [1988] *The Fold: Leibniz and the Baroque* (trans. T. Conley), Athlone Press, London.

Deleuze, G. (1994) [1968] *Difference and Repetition* (trans. Patton P.), Athlone Press, London.

Deleuze, G. (1995) [1990] *Negotiations* (trans. M. Joughin), Columbia University Press, New York.

Deleuze, G. (2001) [essays 1965, 1972, 1995] *Pure Immanence* (trans. A. Boyman) Zone Books, New York.

Deleuze, G. (2003) [1981] *Francis Bacon: The Logic of Sensation* (trans. Smith, D.W.) Continuum, London.

Deleuze, G. (2004) [1969] *The Logic of Sense* (trans. M. Lester & C. Stivale), Continuum, London.

Deleuze, G. and Guattari, F. (1983) [1972] *Anti-Oedipus* (trans. R. Hurley, M. Seem and H. Lane), University of Minnesota Press, Minneapolis (US).

Deleuze, G. and Guattari, F. (1987) [1980] *A Thousand Plateaus: capitalism and schizophrenia* (trans. Massumi B.) Athlone Press, London.

Deleuze, G. and Parnet, C. (1987) [1977] *Dialogues* (trans. H. Tomlinson & B. Habberjam), Columbia University Press, New York.

Deleuze, G. and Parnet, C. (2002) *Dialogues II,* Continuum, London.

Derrida, J. (1988) *Limited Inc* (trans. S. Weber), Northwestern University Press, Evanston Ill.

Derrida, J. (1995) [1990] *The Gift of Death* (trans. D. Wills), University of Chicago Press, Chicago.

Dewsbury, J.D. (2000) 'Performativity and the event: enacting a philosophy of difference', *Environment & Planning D, Society & Space,* 18, pp. 473-496.

Duit, A. and Galaz, V. (2008) 'Governance and complexity – emerging issues for governance theory', *Governance: an International Journal of Policy, Administration and Institutions*, 21(3), pp. 311-335.

Einstein, A. (1905) 'On the electrodynamics of moving bodies', *Annalen der Physik*, 17, pp. 891-921 (in German).

Elden, S. (2008) 'Dialectics and the measure of the world', *Environment and Planning A*, 40, pp. 2641-2651.

Etzioni, A. (1967) 'Mixed scanning: a third approach to decision making', *Public Administration Review,* 27, pp. 387-392.

Faludi, A. (1973) *Planning Theory*, Pergamon, Oxford.

Foucault, M. (1989) [1966] *The Order of Things*, Routledge, London.

Foucault, M. (1994) 'Le sujet et le pouvoir', in Rabinow, P. (ed) *Dits et Ecrits, Vol 3*, Gallimard, Paris, pp. 222-243.

Foucault, M. (2004) *Sécurité, Territoire, Population: cours au Collège de France, 1977-1978*, Gallimard/Seuil, Paris.

Gandy M. (2005) 'Cyborg urbanisation: complexity and monstrosity in the contemporary city', *International Journal of Urban and Regional Research*, 29(1), pp. 26-49.

Gleick, J. (1987) *Chaos*, Viking, New York.

Goodwin, B. (1997) 'Community, creativity and society', *Soundings*, 5, pp. 111-123.

Grosz, E. (1999) 'Thinking the new: of futures yet unthought', in Grosz, E. (ed) *Becomings*, Cornell University Press, Ithaca, pp. 15-28.

Grosz, E. (2001) *Architecture from the Outside*, MIT Press, Cambridge.

Habermas, J. (1971) [1968] *Knowledge and Human Interests* (trans. J. Shapiro), Beacon Press, Boston.

Habermas, J. (1976) [1973] *Legitimation Crisis* (trans. T. McCarthy), Polity Press, Cambridge.

Habermas, J. (1979) [1976] *Communication and the Evolution of Society* (trans. T. McCarthy), Heinemann, London.

Habermas, J. and Luhmann, N. (1971) *Theorie der Gesellschaft oder Sozialtechnologie?* Suhrkamp Verlag, Frankfurt-am-Main.

Hallward, P. (2000) 'The limits of individuation, or how to distinguish Deleuze and Foucault', *Angelaki*, 5(2), pp. 93-111.

Hayden, P. (1995) 'From relations to practice in the empiricism of Gilles Deleuze', *Man and World*, 28, pp. 283-302.

Healey, P. (1997) *Collaborative Planning*, Macmillan, Basingstoke (2nd edition, 2006).

Healey, P. (2000) 'Planning in relational space and time', in Bridge, G. and Watson S. (eds) *A Companion to the City*, Blackwell, Oxford, pp. 517-530.

Healey, P. (2004) 'The treatment of space and place in the new strategic spatial planning in Europe', *International Journal of Urban and Regional Research*, 28(1), pp. 45-67.

Healey, P. (2005) 'Network complexity and the imaginative power of strategic spatial planning' in Albrechts, L. and Mandelbaum, S. (eds) *The Network Society: The New Context for Planning*, Routledge, London, pp. 146-160.

Healey, P. (2006) 'Relational complexity and the imaginative power of strategic spatial planning', *European Planning Studies*, 14(4), pp. 525-546.

Healey, P. (2007) *Urban Complexity and Spatial Strategies: A Relational Planning for our Times*, Routledge, London.

Healey, P. (2008) 'Making choices that matter: the practical art of situated strategic judgment in spatial strategy-making', in Van den Broeck, J., Moulaert, F. and Oosterlynck, S. (eds) *Empowering the Planning Fields: Ethics, Creativity and Action*, Acco, Leuven, pp. 23-41.

Hillier, J. (2005) Straddling the Post-Structuralist Abyss: Between Transcendence and Immanence? *Planning Theory*, 4(3), pp. 271-299.

Hillier, J. (2007a) *Stretching Beyond the Horizon: A Multiplanar Theory of Spatial Planning and Governance*, Ashgate, Aldershot.

Hillier, J. (2007b) 'Multiethnicity and the Negotiation of Place', in Neill W. and Schwedler H-U., (eds) *Migration and Cultural Inclusion in the European City*, Palgrave Macmillan, London, pp. 74-87.

Hillier, J. (2010) 'Introduction to Part Two – Conceptual Challenges for Spatial Planning Theory', in Hillier, J. and Healey, P. (eds) *Ashgate Research Companion to Planning Theory: Conceptual Challenges for Spatial Planning*, Ashgate, Farnham (forthcoming).

Holland, J. (1995) *Hidden Order: How Adaptation Builds Complexity*, Addison-Wesley, Redwood City.

Holland, J. (1998) *Emergence: From Chaos to Order*, Addison-Wesley, Redwood City.

Ingold, T. (1990) 'An anthropologist looks at biology', *Man* (NS), 25, pp. 208-229.

Innes, J. (2004) 'Consensus building: clarification for the critics', *Planning Theory*, 3(1), pp. 5-20.

Innes, J. and Booher, D. (1999a) 'Consensus building and complex adaptive systems: a framework for evaluating collaborative planning', *Journal of the American Planning Association*, 65(4), pp. 412-423.

Innes, J. and Booher, D. (1999b) 'Consensus building as role playing and bricolage: toward a theory of collaborative planning', *Journal of the American Planning Association*, 66(1), pp. 9-26.

Innes, J. and Booher, D. (1999c) 'Metropolitan development as a complex system: a new approach to sustainability', *Economic Development Quarterly*, 13(2), pp. 141-156.

Innes, J. and Booher, D. (2003) 'Collaborative policymaking: governance through dialogue', in Hajer, M. and Wagenaar, H. (eds) *Deliberative Policy Analysis: Understanding Governance in the Network Society*, Cambridge University Press, Cambridge, pp. 33-59.

Jones, W. (2003) *Complex Adaptive Systems*. http://crinfo.beyondintractability.org/essay/ complex_adaptive_systems/ [accessed 05/02/2009].

Knorr Cetina, K. (2003) 'From pipes to scopes', *Distinktion*, 7, pp. 7-23.

Knorr Cetina, K. (2005) 'Complex global microstructures', *Theory, Culture & Society*, 22(5), pp. 213-234.

Kwa, C. (2002) 'Romantic and Baroque conceptions of complex wholes in the sciences', in Law, J. and Mol, A. (eds) *Complexities: Social Studies of Knowledge Practices*, Duke University Press, Durham (US), pp. 23-52.

Latour, B. (1987) *Science in Action,* Harvard University Press, Cambridge (US).

Latour, B. (1999) *Pandora's Hope,* Harvard University Press, Cambridge (US).

Law, J. (2003a) [1999] 'Heterogeneities', Centre for Science Studies, Lancaster University. http://www.comp.lancs.ac.uk/sociology/papers/Law-Heterogeneities.pdf [accessed 31/05/2004].

Law, J. (2003b) [2000] 'Networks, Relations, Cyborgs: on the social study of technology', Centre for Science Studies, Lancaster University. http://www. comp.lancs.ac.uk/ sociology/papers/Law-Networks-Relations-Cyborgs.pdf [accessed 31/05/2004].

Law, J. (2003c) [1997] 'Topology and the naming of complexity', Centre for Science Studies, Lancaster University. http://www.comp.lancs.ac.uk/ sociology/papers/Law-Topology-and-Complexity.pdf [accessed 31/05/2004].

Law, J. (2003d) 'And if the global were small and noncoherent? Method, complexity and the baroque', http://www.comp.lancs.ac.uk/sociology/papers/ Law-And-If-the-Global-Were-Small.pdf [accessed 31/05/2004].

Law, J. (2004a) *After Method: Mess in Social Science Research*, Routledge, Abingdon.

Law, J. (2004b) 'And if the global were small and noncoherent? Method, complexity and the baroque', *Environment & Planning D, Society and Space*, 22, pp. 13-26.

Law, J. and Urry J. (2003) [2002] 'Enacting the social', Centre for Science Studies, Lancaster University. http://www.comp.lancs.ac.uk/sociology/papers/ Law-Urry-Enacting-the-Social.pdf [accessed 31/05/2004] [also published in *Economy and Society*, (2004) 33(3), pp. 390-410].

Leibniz, G. (1998) [1714] *Philosophical Texts* (trans. Francks R. and Woolhouse R.S.) Oxford University Press, New York.

Lewin, R. (1993) *Complexity: Life on the Edge of Chaos*, Dent, London.

Lindblom, C. (1959) 'The science of muddling through', *Public Administration Review*, 19, pp. 79-88.

Lindblom, C. (1979) 'Still muddling, not yet through', *Public Administration Review*, 39, pp. 517-526.

Mackenzie, A. (2005) 'The problem of the attractor', *Theory, Culture and Society*, 22(5), pp. 45-65.

Mandelbrot, B. (1975) *Les Objets Fractals,* Masson, Paris.

Marcus, G. and Saka, E. (2006) 'Assemblage', *Theory, Culture, Society*, 23(2-3), pp. 101-106.

Martin, R. and Sunley, P. (2007) 'Complexity thinking and evolutionary economic geography', *Journal of Economic Geography*, 7, pp. 573-601.

Marx, K. and Engels, F. (1967) [1848] *The Communist Manifesto,* Penguin, Harmondsworth.

Massey, D. (2005) *For Space*, Sage, London.

Massumi, B. (1993) *A User's Guide to 'Capitalism and Schizophrenia'*, MIT Press, Cambridge (US).

McLoughlin, J.B. (1969) *Urban and Regional Planning: A Systems Approach*, Faber & Faber, London.

McWhinney, W. (2005) 'The white horse: a reformulation of Bateson's typology of learning', *Cybernetics and Human Knowing*, 12(1-2), pp. 22-35.

Meek, J., de Ladurantey, J. and Newell, W. (2007) 'Complex systems, governance and policy administration consequences', *Emergence*, 9(1/2), pp. 24-36.

Mol, A. (2002) 'Cutting surgeons, walking patients: some complexities involved in comparing', in Law, J. and Mol, A. (eds) *Complexities*, Duke University Press, Durham (US), pp. 218-257.

Mol, A. and Law, J. (1994) 'Regions, networks and fluids: anaemia and social topology', *Social Studies of Science*, 24, pp. 641-671.

Mol, A. and Law, J. (2002) 'Complexities: an introduction', in Law, J. and Mol, A. (eds) *Complexities*, Duke University Press, Durham (US), pp. 1-22.

Moobela, C. (2005) 'From worst slum to best example of regeneration: complexity in the regeneration of Hulme, Manchester', *Emergence*, 7(1), pp. 29-42.

Mulgan, G. (1997) *Connexity: How to Live in a Connected World,* Chatto & Windus, London.

National Audit Office (2001) Modern Policy-Making: ensuring policies deliver value for money. Report by the Comptroller and Auditor General, HC 289 Session 2001-2, November 2001, National Audit Office, London.

Nicolis, G. and Prigogine, I. (1989) *Exploring Complexity*, Freeman, New York.

Novotny, H. (2005) 'The increase of complexity and its reduction', *Theory, Culture & Society, 22*(5), pp. 15-31.

Osborne, T. and Rose, N. (2004) 'Spatial phenomenotechnics: making space with Charles Booth and Patrick Geddes', *Environment & Planning D, Society & Space,* 22, pp. 209-228.

Parsons, W. (2002) 'From muddling through to muddling up: Evidence Based Policy Making and the Modernisation of British government', paper presented to Political Studies Association Conference, Conference Proceedings, http:// psa.ac.uk/cps/2002/ parsons.pdf. [accessed August 2005].

Poincaré, H. (1914) [1908] *Science and Method,* Flammarion, Paris.

Poincaré, H. (1993) *New Methods of Celestial Mechanics,* [1982, vol. 1; 1892, vol 2; 1899, vol 3. Book 2: 1905, vol 1; 1907, vol 2.1; 1909, vol 2.2; 1911, vol 3] American Institute of Physics, New York.

Portugali, J. (2000) *Self-Organization and the City*, Springer, Heidelberg.

Portugali, J. (2008) 'Learning from paradoxes about prediction and planning in self-organizing cities', *Planning Theory*, 7(3), pp. 248-262.

Plummer, P. and Sheppard, E. (2006) 'Geography matters: agency, structures and dynamics', *Journal of Economic Geography*, 6, pp. 619-637.

Plummer, P. and Sheppard, E. (2007) 'A methodology for evaluating regional political economy', in Fingelton, B. (ed.) *New Directions in Economic Geography*, Edward Elgar, Cheltenham, pp. 250-276.

Prigogine, I. (1955) *Introduction to Thermodynamics of Irreversible Processes*, Thomas, Springfield.

Prigogine, I. (1977) *Ilya Prigogine – Autobiography,* http://nobelprize.org/ chemistry/ laureates/1977/prigogine-autobio.html [accessed 14/11/2005].

Prigogine, I. (1980) *From Being to Becoming: Time and Complexity in the Physical Sciences*, WH Freeman, San Francisco.

Prigogine, I. (1997) *The End of Certainty*, The Free Press, New York.

Prigogine, I. and Lefevre, R. (1968) 'Symmetry-breaking instabilities in dissipative systems, II', *Journal of Chemical Physics*, 48, pp. 1695-1700.

Prigogine, I. and Stengers, I. (1984) [1979] *Order out of Chaos*, Bantam, New York.

Protevi, J. (nd) 'Some remarks on the philosophical significance of complexity theory', http://www.artsci.lsu.edu/fai/Faculty/Professors/Protevi/Postmodernity/complexity.htm. [accessed 23/09/2005].

Rabinow, P. (2003) *Anthropos Today: Reflections on Modern Equipment*, Princeton University Press, Princeton.

Rajchman, J. (1998) *Constructions*, MIT Press, Cambridge (US).

Rajchman, J. (2000) *The Deleuze Connections*, MIT Press, Cambridge (US).

Richardson, K. and Cilliers, P. (2001) 'What is complexity science? A view from different directions', *Emergence,* 3(1), pp. 5-23.

Richardson, K. (ed.) (2005) *Managing Organizational Complexity*, Information Age Publishing, Greenwich (US).

Robbins, E. (1998) 'Thinking the city multiple', *Harvard Architecture Review,* 10, pp. 36-45.

Serres, M. (2000) *The Birth of Physics* (trans. D. Webb), University of Manchester Press, Manchester.

Shaviro, S. (2007) 'Deleuze's encounter with Whitehead', http://www.shaviro.com/ Othertexts/DeleuzeWhitehead.pdf [accessed 20/04/2008].

Sheller, M. (2004) 'Mobile publics: beyond the network perspective', *Environment & Planning D, Society and Space*, 22, pp. 39-52.

Sheppard, E. (2008) 'Geographic dialectics?', *Environment and Planning A*, 40, pp. 2603-2612.

Simon, H. (1947) *Administrative Behaviour*, MacMillan, New York.

Simon, H. (1962) 'Architecture of complexity', *Proceedings of the American Philosophical Society*, 106, pp. 467-482.

Simon, H. and Newell, A. (1958) 'Heuristic problem solving: the next advance in operations research', *Operations Research*, 6, pp. 1-10.

Smith, J. and Jenks, C. (2005) 'Complexity, ecology and the materiality of information', *Theory, Culture & Society*, 22(5), pp. 141-163.

Snowden, D. and Stanbridge, P. (2004) 'The landscape of management: creating the context for understanding social complexity', *E:CO*, 6(1-2), pp. 140-148.

Stengers, I. (1997) *Power and Invention: Situating Science,* Theory out of Bounds, Vol 10, University of Minnesota Press, Minneapolis.

Stengers, I. (2000) *The Invention of Modern Science,* Theory out of Bounds, Vol 19, University of Minnesota Press, Minneapolis.

Stengers, I. (2004) 'The challenge of complexity: unfolding the ethics of science. In memoriam Ilya Prigogine', *E:CO,* 6(1-2), pp. 92-99.

Stengers, I. (2005) 'Whitehead's account of the sixth day', *Configurations*, 13(1), pp. 35-55.

Strathern, M. (1991) *Partial Connections*, Rowman & Littlefield, Savage.

Suteanu, C. (2005) 'Complexity, science and the public: the geography of a new interpretation', *Theory, Culture & Society*, 22(5), pp. 113-140.

Thrift, N. (1996) *Spatial Formations*, Sage, London.

Thrift, N. (1999) 'The place of complexity', *Theory, Culture & Society*, 16(3), pp. 31-70.

Thrift, N. (2004a) 'Remembering the technological unconscious by foregrounding knowledges of position', *Environment & Planning D, Society & Space*, 22, pp. 175-190.

Thrift, N. and Dewsbury, J.D. (2000) 'Dead geographies – and how to make them live', *Environment & Planning D, Society & Space*, 18, pp. 411-432.

Tsoukas, H. (2005) *Complex Knowledge*, Oxford University Press, Oxford.

Urry, J. (2003) *Global Complexity*, Polity, Cambridge.

Urry, J. (2004) 'Connections' *Environment & Planning D, Society & Space*, 22, pp. 27-37.

Urry, J. (2005a) 'The complexity turn', *Theory, Culture & Society*, 22(5), pp. 1-14.

Urry, J. (2005b) 'The complexities of the global', *Theory, Culture & Society*, 22(5), pp. 235-254.

Waldrop, M. (1993) *Complexity*, Viking, London.

Wallerstein, D. (1996) *Open the Social Sciences: Report of the Gulbenkian Commission on the Restructuring of the Social Sciences*, Stanford University Press, Stanford.

Wynne, B. (2005) 'Reflexing complexity', *Theory, Culture & Society*, 22(5), pp. 67-94.

Chapter 3

Planning in Complexity

Karen S. Christensen[1]

3.1 Intergovernmental system's importance for planning

Planners operate in a complicated arena that arises from numerous sources including economic, social, political, and natural. Furthermore, human-made factors interact with natural factors, creating sustainability and other issues. This chapter focuses on some important factors humans create: government and non-profit agencies. The world of governance is made up of myriad of these government parts and their interactions. They constitute a complex intergovernmental system within which and through which planning operates (Christensen, 1999).

Planners often have worked in practice settings of multiple, overlapping agencies with different goals. But today the intergovernmental system is growing increasingly fragmented and thus more challenging. As planners become aware of complex multi-organizational systems, they grapple with burgeoning new constraints and opportunities. Further, information technology and globalization speed the multiplicative interactions.

Planners need to understand the complex intergovernmental system and its dynamics to be effective. The complexity of the system is also important because an underlying assumption of the normative task of planning is that it should make the planning situation more simple, clear, ordered and rational – in short not complex.

Complexity means "a state of being composed of two or more parts, not simple" (Webster, 1956). For purposes of this chapter, and its role in this book, complexity refers to a complex, robust, flexible system that is self-organizing, evolving, and adapting.

This chapter examines the case of complexity of the U.S. intergovernmental system. It finds that the U.S. intergovernmental system is indeed complex, self-organizing, adapting and highly interdependent. But the U.S. intergovernmental system's structural conditions to ensure local scale and fragmentation prevent the system from developing features that promote efficiency and effectiveness.

Planning means a deliberate process of devising a set of actions to change the future course of events for some value laden public purpose. Thus planning entails

---

1   Karen S. Christensen is Associate Professor of City and Regional Planning at the College of Environmental Design, University of California, Berkeley, US.

agency. Agency means "faculty or state of acting or exerting power" (Webster, 1956) and connotes the power or ability to do something.

The central question is, then, whether it is possible to plan – to have agency – in the US complex intergovernmental system. If so, how? Axelrod and Cohen lay out how to harness complexity, an "approach to designing interventions in a complex world, as … city planners must do" (2000: 159). Their approach does not simplify complexity, but rather takes advantage of it.

Similarly Alexander finds that "planning in [complex, multi-organizational systems] usually involves some institutional transformation or change to enable action in this changing and uncertain context… [such systems'] interdependence, one of the complexity dimensions of [complex, multi-organizational systems], limits the feasibility of autonomous action". Thus planning in such systems "always involves multiple interdependent actors." (2009: 518). Accordingly plans can be characterized "as means of interaction and influence among organizations rather than as mechanisms of control over a complex multi-organizational environment" (Kaza and Hopkins, 2009: 491). Within the context of the U.S. intergovernmental system, then, there are multiple levels of planning agents: first, the individual planner, second, the organization (government, non-profit or for-profit), third, the inter-organizational network. Alexander (2009) and Kaza and Hopkins (2009) find that planning occurs at the third level, through organizations interacting.

The following examination of planning in the U.S. complex intergovernmental system[2] discusses seven processes within that dynamic system which contribute to the system's elaboration. The discussion concludes with ways planners plan within and through the complex intergovernmental system.

3.2 Processes of elaboration in US intergovernmental system

The U.S. intergovernmental system develops and elaborates through seven processes and from interactions among them.

Structural Divisions

The first source of these dynamic processes is structural. The founding fathers designed the U.S. government system to be divided and multiple on purpose. Sometimes this historical fact shocks planners and planning students as they assume the government system should be rational and efficient. But the founding fathers were not concerned with efficiency. Rather they wanted to protect against tyranny. They had fled the tyranny of the king and the tyranny of state religion. They espoused

---

2   The following discussion examines complexity and planning in the U.S. intergovernmental system. Nevertheless it is generally relevant to any complex country or collection of them, such as the European Union, or a complex country in transition to a more complex economy in the midst of transforming intergovernmental and global markets.

freedom of thought, speech, and religion. In effect they promoted diversity or at least tolerance of diversity. In this way they were antithetical to efficiency.

In particular the founding fathers sought to protect against tyranny by dividing power. They established checks and balances among governmental powers and functions. Thus one branch of government could counteract or restrain excessive actions of another.

The federal structure of two governments having sovereignty over the same place constitutes an especially sophisticated division of powers. One government could check the excesses or abuses of the other. Indeed they would come to check each other on different issues and provide mitigation and buffers for extreme political leanings or shifts of the political pendulum. In particular this territorial division of power protects not only against the tyranny of a potential despot, but also against the tyranny of the majority, for example a local majority legislating local policies of racial segregation. The federal structure in effect constitutes redundancy in government (Landau, 1973), providing insurance against extreme measures. The two levels having authority at the same time also provides opportunities for tradeoffs and political cover and intricate compromises.

For all of its strengths the federal division of power contributes directly to the convolution of the US governmental system. Not only do legislative bodies, courts and administrative agencies create and interpret government policies, but also these multiple government units operate at multiple levels. This structural fragmentation creates a source of variation in governance and governmental policies which in turn contributes to the intergovernmental system's adaptability.

A century after the constitution of the U.S. government, events led to further structural divisions of power and accordingly to further fragmentation of government. The period from approximately 1880-1910 was an era of immense growth, industrialization, expansion of the country, waves of immigration, urbanization, and land speculation. Concomitantly, it was the Gilded Age, the age of the robber barons, and as it offered opportunities for vast fortunes to be made, it was also a period of notable graft and corruption. Thus, during this same period of social and political movements such as the anarchist and progressive movements and the origins of modern city planning, came the good government movement.

The good government movement sought to end graft and corruption in city government both by separating politics from government, and by dividing local government authorities. The movement attempted to replace politics with professional and scientifically managed government instituted through professional City Managers and civil service systems. The movement divided local authorities by instituting independent commissions, with appointed commissioners with staggered terms, and separate elected officials for various governmental functions. The movement led to different reforms in different cities.

The City and County of San Francisco illustrates local government structure as reformed by the good government movement. See the City and County organization chart (Figure 3.1).

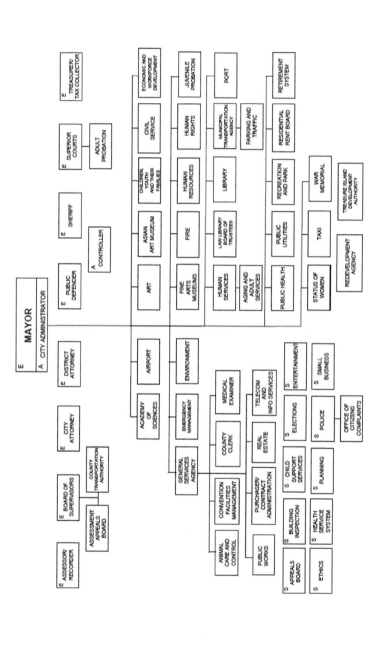

Figure 3.1 City and County of San Francisco Organization Chart, with A = Appointed by Major and confirmed by Board of Supervisors / E = Elected / S = Shared – appointed by various elected officials

The various offices near the top of the chart show separate, elected officials and their functions, e.g. District Attorney, Sheriff. A number of important boards and commissions are shown as independent (without lines connecting them to the Chief Administrative Officer), such as the Planning Commission and the Redevelopment Agency.

These structural divisions of U.S. government, both the initial federal design and the reforms instigated by the good government movement, were expressly intended to divide government powers and thus effectively created fragmentation in government.

System Evolution

Originally the powers and responsibilities of the two levels in the US federal structure appeared to be mutually exclusive. The two levels of power were understood to be separate and autonomous. In reality some responsibilities were always shared, for example waterways (Elazar, 1962; Grodzins, 1966).

Strong centralizing forces, notably civil war, industrialization, world wars and the Great Depression, shaped the intergovernmental system's evolution to increased influence of the national level. The tendencies toward centralization and specialization continue in the present as electronic connectivity and globalization propel the processes forward. Meanwhile the tendencies toward centralization and specialization play out in the U.S. federal structure of multiple, divided powers and the ongoing U.S. culture and ideology of local home rule and states rights.

In such a system, it is unseemly for the national government (called the federal government in the U.S.) to act directly in domestic policy. Even in extreme economic need, such as the great depression or the current economic crisis, the national government works through state and local government. The American Recovery and Reinvestment Act of 2009 includes national tax relief and unemployment benefits, but works primarily through investments channeled through state and local government.

Conventionally if the national government wanted to act, but do so in a politically acceptable way, it worked indirectly through state and local government, offering persuasive incentives. Frequently the national government would offer states or localities funding to do what the national government wanted, sometimes through competitive, discretionary grants, sometimes through formula allocation of funding to states and localities. Sometimes the funding conditions focused closely on nationally desired outcomes, whereas other grants provided scope for more local preference or innovation. Another approach to using state and local governments as instruments of national policy was to pass legislation, such as the Clean Water Act, asking states to create plans for specified national goals, such as clean water. Such legislation included the provision that the respective national (federal) agency would prepare the plan for the state if the state failed to do so itself.

Accordingly the complex US federal government structure generates an array of splintered, fragmented authorities and policies among national, state, regional

– areawide, county and city levels. The U.S. 2007 Census of governments finds 89,527 governments of which 89,476 were local governments.

Despite the system's tendency toward devolution, some parts operate at the national level. Some government activities, especially in the international arena, such as defense and formal international relations, are exclusively national. Other major investments, such as national parks, and regulations, such as internal revenue, are national, but have state counterparts.

This caveat suggests another example, the National Environmental Protection Act and its provision for Environmental Impact Statements. States followed suit, for example with the California Environmental Quality Act, and its provision for Environmental Impact Reports. These planning efforts to anticipate environmental consequences of proposed projects and mitigate or avoid environmental damage before acting entail multiple planning phases, including scoping and drafting the anticipated environmental consequences, inviting comments and holding public hearings. Accordingly these processes involve multiple actors at multiple levels.

Interest Group Liberalism

The third process within the U.S. intergovernmental system which contributes to the system's elaboration comes from interest group liberalism. That process is the development of policies and programs for the pluralist political purposes of responding to interest groups (Lowi, 1969). Each program was designed to address a particular issue according to its own interest group specific technologies and constituencies. For example, the U.S. interstate highway system was developed after WW II to link the U.S. roadway transportation system and thus to facilitate military movement and promote economic growth. The highway system responded to the auto and gas (oil) constituencies and contributed to the housing building boom and suburbanization.

In addition, each program was an intergovernmental issue as well. As noted above, if the national government wanted to accomplish something, it could not simply do so directly. Instead, the politically expedient, culturally and ideologically appropriate way for the national government to accomplish something is to work indirectly through state and local government.

Thus the U.S. complex intergovernmental system has multiple agencies at different levels pursuing the same general goal, such as better transportation, linked together into specialized policy networks, termed sectors (Christensen, 1999: 66-88). Many different sectors pursue a gamut of public goals. Furthermore, for policy and political purposes, sets of non-profit agencies are also linked to the sectors. In addition these agencies interact with otherwise unrelated agencies serving the same neighborhood. Thus every city has a wide array of government and non-government agencies interacting – negotiating, coordinating – as they deliver their sector's services.

Examining cases in Europe Healey refers to similar interactive processes as "relational" geography and complexities of governance. Planning as "mobilization operates through all kinds of webs of relations, that connect the organisations and procedures of formal government with informal governance arenas and networks..." (2007: 269).

In the U.S. there is no overarching plan or control guiding the system and no prospect for coordinating policy at any particular level, such as the city. Even a strong mayor with a coherent policy cannot direct the programs in his city. Even at the national level, with enormous resources such as the economic stimulus package, a national plan interacts with the complex intergovernmental system. For example to carry out the economic stimulus plan, the American Recovery and Reinvestment Act of 2009, planners pluck "shovel ready" projects from Transportation Improvement Plans which were created through intergovernmental planning at the metropolitan level.

In the U.S. the extent of the national (federal) role in each sector varies according to the importance or urgency of the issue or publicly perceived need, the salience of states rights and local home rule, and the political climate of the time. Thus, for example, in the 1960s, with urban riots seizing national attention and marches on Washington demanding civil rights, national legislation was both feasible and necessary. In contrast, in the early 1990s, with a conservative Republican Congress calling for a Contract for America reducing and decentralizing government, legislation "ending Welfare as we know it" came in the form of a block grant to each state to reform welfare as it saw fit. Thus the program to reduce and reform welfare was not a single, coherent national reform, but rather a decentralized, fragmented array of state initiatives.

Correcting Premature Programs

The fourth process that elaborates the complex U.S. intergovernmental system is correcting premature programs. Each new program (created through the interest group liberalism process described above) is adopted as if it is proven reliable and effective. Accordingly it is institutionalized in new rules and procedures and new organizations. But because the new program is basically untested, founded on social and political assumptions and situated in multifaceted institutional and cultural settings, implementing the program frequently leads to surprising, sometimes unfortunate results. These in turn can prompt media attention and political pressure.

In response to such stress, agencies search for a way to correct the premature program with a new, presumably effective program. Each new program iteration is adopted as if it is certain, with new regulations and often new agencies as well. The U.S. Department of Housing and Urban Development, for example, has tried centralization, decentralization, devolution to the states, subsidies to for-profit developers, housing vouchers for low income households, and reliance on nonprofit housing developers. Chisholm (1989) describes the convolution of multiple government agencies and associated nonprofit and for-profit organizations in multiple counties in the San Francisco Bay Area transportation sector, and

Agranoff and Rinkle (1986) describe similarly multifaceted intergovernmental decision-making in the human services sector.

Partisan Mutual Adjustment

The fifth process that elaborates the complex U.S. intergovernmental system is interactions and adjustments among the multiple agencies in the system. Something in one part of the system affects another, which in turn reacts and adjusts, thus affecting others in spiraling partisan mutual adjustment (Lindblom, 1965). So, for example, a constituency may require further service, correcting an error or oversight in a premature program, as discussed above. The newly revised program thus, for example, now requires that its grantee agencies provide support services to formerly homeless people. So the non-profit service providers add that support service, and do so by subcontracting with other non-profit organizations. The latter then seek an adjustment in their duties from their primary funding agency, the county mental health agency, which in turn negotiates with the state department of mental health, which in its turn negotiates with the National Institute of Mental Health. The National Institute of Mental Health then makes changes in its regulations for all its grantees, affecting all fifty states. This chain of reactions continues, and it interacts with spiraling partisan mutual adjustments playing out in other policy arenas.

This simple example of how a single requirement creates spiraling interactions illustrates "partisan mutual adjustment" (Lindblom, 1965). The process is partisan because each agency acts in its own interests, pursing its interpretation of its goal and its own organizational survival. For example, the nonprofit housing provider in the example above wants to get the grant to help serve homeless people. The adjustment is mutual among the various agencies, as the non-profit social service provider adjusts both to the non-profit housing provider and to its funder in the County Mental Health agency, while the nonprofit housing provider and the County Mental Health agency adjust to the non-profit social service provider.

Correcting Negative Side Effects

The sixth process that elaborates the complex U.S. intergovernmental system occurs when something peripheral impacts an element in the system as an inadvertent side effect. For example, the 1986 major tax reform focused on simplifying taxes, eliminating tax loopholes and rationalizing taxes. Just before the tax reform was to be voted on, someone noticed that it would have destructive consequences for housing production. Consequently experts on the tax code, who had little knowledge of housing, and less on the production of affordable housing, further modified the tax code to address the housing production problem. Thus the tax code experts invented Low Income Housing Tax Credits.

(In essence, state Low Income Housing Tax Credit Allocation Committees give tax credits to non-profit housing developers, who syndicate the housing project and sell the tax credits to private investors. The non-profit housing developers use the net proceeds to finance the low income housing.)

This was supposedly a tax solution to a tax problem. But de facto it became an affordable housing "program" fabricated outside of the housing sector. Accordingly, the Low Income Housing Tax Credits program was administered outside of the housing sector, by the Treasury Department. Tax reform was enacted (entirely politically logically) in an era of conservative, anti-Washington ideology. Accordingly the Treasury Department devolved its administration to state finance agencies. Each state developed its own rules of how the tax credits would work. California's Tax Credit Allocation Committee allocates the credits by various criteria including requirements for very low income residents, by geographic area, and for the first decade of the program, by lottery.

Because the Low Income Housing (LIH) Tax Credits program was designed as a tax maneuver, it was cumbersome and complicated to use as a tool for funding affordable housing. But because the affordable housing sector was then and continues to be severely underfunded, nonprofit housing developers try to use whatever funding sources they can find. If the nonprofit housing developers are large, strong and relatively well-funded, they have their own, internal LIH tax credit expertise. Smaller, less well-funded nonprofit housing developers have to depend on contracting out to consultants and lawyers who specialize in the intricacies of assembling tax credit funding.

Thus maneuvering to correct a negative side effect of tax reform with a tax manipulation created further complications in the intergovernmental system. This example shows how correcting an inadvertent side effect can generate convoluted repercussions. In this case the tax credit spawned fifty new branches of, or entirely new, state finance agencies, Tax Credit Allocation Committees, specialized consultants and lawyers, and various affordable housing intermediaries.

This process illustrates the adapting, evolving, flexible nature of the US. complex intergovernmental system. But the process is constrained in ways that make the system inefficient.

Reducing government increases non-profit agencies

The seventh process that elaborates the complex U.S. intergovernmental system arose from efforts to streamline, simplify and do away with government (e.g. the Contract for America, and the popular book, Reinventing Government, Osborne and Gaebler, 1992). This exercise to reduce government ironically generated a surge of non-profit agencies. This development nominally replaced government programs with non-profit volunteers, and thus supposedly did away with government. Reformers also believed that these non-profit organizations would be closer to the people they were trying to serve and more responsive than government agencies. In addition, the non-profits were expected to tap private charitable donations for resources.

In some cases government workers left government, became private consultants and contracted with the government to provide the same services they had previously provided inside the government.

The more prevalent consequence of the neoliberal, reduce government policy was the emergence of many non-profit agencies to provide needed services that private, for-profit firms could not provide. In the housing sector, for example, many non-profit housing developers developed affordable housing. They did so by piecing together multiple grants (typically nine different funding sources for a single project). Almost all the grants came directly or indirectly through the federal government (Christensen, with Sadik, Lim and Weiner, 2000). Likewise, a large network of human services non-profit agencies has developed, heavily dependent on government funding. Thus the effort to reduce government generated a large number of agencies dependent on government funding.

A study of San Francisco non-profits (Silverman et al., 2009) found more than 7,000 registered non-profits, more than 4,000 of which had annual revenues of more than $25,000. Most were public charities, which provided a wide range of services: art and culture, education, environment, health, human services. While San Francisco has more non-profits per capita than the state of California and other regions in the state, it still illustrates the trend of growth in non-profits.

Funding agencies require their grantees to follow prescribed conditions on the use of funds and to report progress regularly. These "strings" on the use of funds constrain the grantees' ability to be flexible and "responsive". Further, as the typical non-profit housing developer depends on nine different sources of funding, each with a different set of requirements and conditions, the difficulties amplify. Moreover as the non-profits are effectively governed by their funding agencies, they become arms of the government.

In the affordable housing sector this growth of convoluted funding arrangements for growing numbers of non-profit agencies brought about a cadre of intermediaries to serve them by providing financial support and technical assistance (Christensen, with Sadik, Lim and Weiner, 2000; the Urban Institute, 1994; Keyes, Schwartz, Vidal and Bratt, 1996).

Thus the neoliberal policy of reducing government has ironically led to a surge of non-profit agencies dependent on government funding, constrained by conditions on their funding, and supported by consultants and intermediaries.

In sum, the complex US intergovernmental system developed from its original, purposeful structural divisions, which have become more overlapping and interactive over time. The system elaborates through processes of interest group liberalism. (Lowi), correcting premature programs and partisan mutual adjustment (Lindblom, 1965). Processes of correcting peripheral side effects create further complications in the intergovernmental system. Finally, policies attempting to reduce government ironically engender nonprofit agencies as arms of government, and various support agencies, thus further elaborating the intergovernmental system.

3.3 Assessment of this complexity

Benefits of Complexity

Academics, planners and politicians have grappled with this complex, intergovernmental system, trying to understand it, work with it and occasionally reform it. Some extol the values of a complex, intergovernmental system.

Charles Tiebout (1956) describes how households could "vote with their feet" and choose from a large array of local governments the local government with their preferred bundle of goods and services for the tax dollar they chose to pay. Thus fragmented local governments provide choice (for those who have adequate income and are not subject to discrimination). As a consequence of the costs of the different desirable bundles of goods and locations, the localities become specialized by fine gradations of income and demographics (Perin, 1977). The composite result is that the poor and disadvantaged become concentrated in some localities which are thus further burdened by being unable to raise taxes sufficient to provide the services they need.

With many local governments and many special purpose agencies, many with elected boards of directors, fragmented local governance offers many opportunities for popular representation. This results in the benefits of "multiple cracks", that is multiple opportunities of public access to decision makers. If one representative is unresponsive, a citizen can look for a preferred response from another representative. Moreover, many governments also provide more opportunities for minorities to be elected and have voices in democratic governments.

A large metropolis, like the San Francisco Bay Area, may have a hundred local cities and one hundred and eight special purpose districts. As a whole, it thus contains multiple cracks, multiple representatives, as noted above, and accordingly multiple decision makers and thus multiple checks. Like not putting all your eggs in one basket, such a complex system protects against large errors. Even huge infrastructure investments are decided upon by multiple decision-makers and are redundant (Landau, 1973).

Costs of Complexity

The proliferating agencies duplicate simple administrative activities. Moreover in their search for funding each must waste time and energy on multiple applications, reports, and tailor efforts to various, sometimes conflicting funding conditions. Collectively their efforts are staggering and elicit a large cadre of intermediaries to serve them in the intricate piecing together of funding. Thus the complex intergovernmental system causes the expenditure of considerable time and energy as well as money.

The fragmentation of agencies makes it difficult to address important planning problems that cross jurisdictional and specialization boundaries. For example, it is difficult to address the significant interactive effects of transportation and land use, and their interaction with energy, and the transportation – land use- energy interaction with the environment and climate change.

The fragmented government and non-profit agencies' functions and authorities make it impossible to hold anyone accountable for outcomes. Accordingly, it is impossible to have oversight and comprehensive planning. Thus it seems the complex, intergovernmental system itself encourages the avoidance of hard public problems. It is difficult to plan wisely.

Furthermore the complex intergovernmental system produces some outcomes that most consider unfair and unjust. The "market of local governments" creates specialized localities with fine gradations of income and demographics. This market effect concentrates poor and disadvantaged households in certain communities. In turn such localities have concentrations of bad housing conditions, low tax bases and bad schools.

3.4 Planning in this complexity

Planners plan in the midst of this complexity. The agencies, their networks and their intricate interactions constitute the medium of planning. Planning takes its effect through the actions of planning agencies and of other government and non-profit agencies and the interactions among them. Planners' ability to work within and through this complex intergovernmental system influences planning effectiveness. Planners' facility varies from passivity to pro-active engagement.

Approaches to Taming the Complexity

One way of managing the complexity in order to be able to plan within the system is to simplify the planning task either by ignoring the complexity or establishing routine roles and procedures for coping with it. Some planners are unaware of the complexity of the intergovernmental system and its influence on planning processes and outcomes. As described by Baum (1983) such planners do not understand what happens to their plans and feel inept. Other planners can see the system's operations and complain it is "so political" but may feel it is inappropriate to take an active role in that system. Such passive planners are not able to be effective.

As Forester noted in the simpler planning department setting (1983), some planners rely on following the rules to deal with conflict. Similarly, some planners function in the midst of the complex intergovernmental system by following prescribed routines. Such planners are able to do so because their tasks are specialized and structured within a larger, interconnected set of tasks, comparable to a bureaucracy. For example, a planner might specialize in Geographic Information Science (GIS) analysis within a large city planning department. The GIS planner's projects would have other planners working on them as well, interacting with other agencies in the complex intergovernmental system. Thompson (1969) explains that such "boundary spanners" protect the routine core technology, buffering it from the uncertainty of the larger system.

Alexander (2009) argues that institutions must change to enable action in a complex intergovernmental system. For example, the Federal Housing Administration (FHA), within the US Department of Housing and Urban Development (HUD) follows a routine set of procedures to provide mortgage insurance for housing developments. When stress came in the form of an external requirement for conducting Environmental Impact Statements, the FHA administrators resisted the imposition, disruption and delay of its core technology. They argued "time is money!" in housing development. The "boundary spanners" and FHA administrators eventually resolved the issue by conducting Environmental Impact Statements concurrently with other reviews. They managed to adjust to change, providing the required Environmental Impact Statements while maintaining their routine timetable.

Some planners rely on prescribed procedures for planning in the complex intergovernmental system. Some institutions have developed to facilitate such intergovernmental planning, for examples, the Metropolitan Planning Organization (MPO) for dealing with transportation planning, the Council of Government (COG) for planning with many local governments in a metropolitan area, and the Environmental Impact Assessment (EIA) process for planning to deal with environmental impacts of projects affecting multiple interests and governmental agencies. Each of these institutions offers prescribed procedures to identify and address the different concerns of different cities, special purpose agencies and interests in these intergovernmental arenas. This description is not meant to imply that the intergovernmental planning tasks are simple. Rather the institutions have developed routine processes to take the complexity into account.

Planners Engaged with the Intergovernmental System

A different approach to the complex intergovernmental system is to engage with it directly. As argued elsewhere (Christensen, 1993), planners can actively analyze planning practice settings and carry out savvy planning. Merely examining the actors, their interests, and the incentives and constraints they act within can suggest constructive planning strategies and options. Kaza and Hopkins (2009) and Alexander (2009) argue that plans show intentions in complex, multi-organizational systems, entail institutional interdependence and usually require some institutional change to be implemented.

The proliferation of agencies and programs described above enables some agencies to tailor projects and programs to special needs. This process makes some planners entrepreneurs, as they both help the special need constituency and create a niche for themselves. Similarly a group develops special expertise, and helps non-profit agencies while creating a niche for itself as an intermediary. For example the Low Income Housing Tax Credit consultants, discussed above, responded to the needs of the non-profit housing developers and thereby created a niche for themselves. Such specialization propels the larger system into a diverse array, a pseudo-market for previously non-market goods. Planners in such roles find ways to work with the complex intergovernmental system to provide a specialized service, thus working within and contributing to the system's proliferation.

Some planners engage in stakeholder analysis and consensus building. Fisher and Ury (1981) explain the process which planners use both formally and informally to arrive at planning solutions in complicated intergovernmental situations. A growing literature documents processes, cases and outcomes (Susskind et al., 1999; Scholz and Stiftel, 2005; Ozawa, 1991; Connick and Innes, 2003; Innes and Booher, 2010). This approach pro-actively addresses multiple stakeholders, interests, values, and ways of knowing to fashion a solution that tries to deal with the constellation of issues in a particular situation. For example the joint California-Federal (Cal-Fed, 1994) program was a collaborative among 35 state and federal agencies along with key stakeholders, such as environmentalists and farmers that ended policy stalemate around the management of much of California's water and developed innovative ways to use water for multiple, conflicting purposes.

Some planners embrace the complex intergovernmental system because it provides not only the "multiple cracks" mentioned above, but also multiple levers and action channels to achieve planning goals. Savvy planners can make constructive use the profusion of actors, networks and practice settings as building blocks and tools to create new combinations. Policy interventions in one part of the complex intergovernmental system can have impacts in other parts of the system. For example by directing housing to cities with salaried workers, Mexico's mortgage financing program effectively furthers regional development, favoring manufacturing cities in the north (Monkkonen, 2010).

Webber (1978) encourages planners to find ways to expand choice and develop policies that encourage difference in order to encourage argumentation and evolutionary variation. In effect he promotes encouraging profusion to generate increased responsiveness to diversity. Similarly Fisher and Ury (1981) encourage those negotiating to explore many differences in order to generate creative win-win solutions. Axelrod and Cohen have taken these principles further into a framework for using the complex adaptive system approach to generate action. For example they write: "build networks of reciprocal interaction that foster trust and cooperation…to provide the basis of social capital" (2000, 156).

Some planners have made self-serving use of the convoluted system. For example, some funding agencies present themselves as cautiously prudent and at the same time highly productive. First, they spread their risk by spreading their resources, giving a bit of money to a number of non-profit affordable housing projects, rather than fully funding a few projects. Second, they claim that they are leveraging their funds, generating a large number of new housing units with many small grants. Many funding agencies follow this practice, from a mayor's office of housing, using hotel tax funds, to a city redevelopment agency, using tax increment financing funds, to another city agency using Community Development

Block Grant funds, to low income housing tax credit, and so on. The various funding agencies engage in mutual leveraging.

While the funding agencies accrue the benefits of reducing risk and leveraging their funds, they impose substantial costs on the non-profit housing developers. The non-profit housing developers must engage in piecemeal funding of their projects, as noted above, typically applying for nine different sources of funds and accordingly complying with nine different sets of regulations, constraints and conditions and nine reporting requirements.

3.5 Conclusion

In sum, planners practice in a complex, intergovernmental system. The intergovernmental system has the key features of a complex adaptive system (Innes and Booher, 2010: 32): Agents: individual agents, connected by networks, Interactions: agents interact dynamically, exchanging information, Nonlinearity: interactions are nonlinear, iterative, recursive and self-referential, Systems behavior: system is open, system's behavior determined by interactions not by components, Robustness and Adaptation: capacity to maintain viability and evolve. The U.S. intergovernmental system, purposely structured to be complex, evolved through processes of federal program development, interest group liberalism, partisan mutual adjustment, correcting negative side effects and expanding roles for non-profit organizations.

The system's fragmentation constrains its evolution, however, by preventing it from developing mechanisms that promote efficiency and effectiveness. The proliferating agencies create costly administrative burdens as non-profit housing developers and service providers seek funding from multiple sources and comply with multiple conditions and reporting requirements. More significantly, the fragmentation of agencies makes it difficult to address important planning problems that cross jurisdictional and specialization boundaries and impossible to hold anyone accountable for outcomes or to conduct comprehensive planning.

Planners can and do work within this complex system to achieve their goals and be effective planners. They can reduce difficulty and uncertainty in a particular situation with a particular set of actors at a specific time and place; they can arrive at consensus, "get to yes" and build social and political capital for the future. Nevertheless, they cannot conduct planning in a conventional way and make their planning situation simple, clear, ordered and rational. Furthermore, their planning situation exists within the complex intergovernmental system, subject to the processes discussed above. Accordingly their agreed upon solution will need to adjust and change over time.

Moreover, these effective planners will attempt to address the inter-relatedness of the various factors in their situation. Thus they become re-engaged with the complex intergovernmental system.

References

Alexander, E.R. (2009) "Symposium discussion: Planning in complexity – institutional design implications", *Journal of Planning Education and Research*, 28: 518-524.

Axelrod, R.M. and Cohen, M.D. (2000) *Harnessing Complexity: Organizational Implications of a Scientific Frontier*, Basic Books, New York.

Baum, H. (1983) *Planners and Public Expectations*, Schenkman, Cambridge (US).

CALFED Bay-Delta Program, (1996) *Phase I progress report: CALFED Bay Delta Program*, Sacramento (US).

Chisholm, D. (1989) *Coordination Without Hierarchy: Informal Structures in Multiorganizational Systems*, University of California Press, Berkeley.

Christensen, K. (1993) "Teaching Savvy", *Journal of Planning Education and Research*, 12: 202-212.

Christensen, K. (1999) *Cities and Complexity: Making Intergovernmental Decisions*, Sage, Thousand Oaks.

Christensen, K, with Sadik, R., Lim, M. and Weiner, R. (2000) 'The challenge of affordable housing in 21st century California: Constraints and opportunities in the nonprofit housing sector' *Working Paper*, 2000-04, Institute of Urban and Regional Development, University of California, Berkeley (US).

Connick, S. and Innes, J. (2003) "Outcomes of collaborative water policy making: Applying complexity thinking to evaluation", *Journal of Environmental Planning and Management*, 46: 177-197.

Elazar. D.J. (1962) *The American Partnership*, University of Chicago Press, Chicago.

Fisher, R and Ury, W. (1981) *Getting to Yes: Negotiating agreement without giving in*, Houghton Mifflin, Boston.

Forester, J. (1983) "Planning in the face of power", *Journal of the American Planning Association*, 48(1): 67-80.

Grodzins, M. (1966) *The American System*, Rand McNally, Chicago.

Healey, P. (2007) *Urban Complexity and Spatial Strategies: Towards Relational Planning for our Times*, Routledge, London.

Innes, J.E. and Booher, D.E. (2010) *Planning with Complexity: An Introduction to Collaborative Rational for Public Policy*, Routledge, Oxford.

Kaza, N. and Hopkins, L. (2009) "In what circumstances should plans be public?", *Journal of Planning Education and Research*, 28: 491-502.

Keyes, L.C., Schwartz, A., Vidal, A.C. and Bratt, R.G. (1996) "Networks and nonprofits: Opportunities and challenges in an era of federal devolution", *Housing Policy Debate*, 7(2): 201-29.

Landau, M. (1973) "Federalism, redundancy, and system reliability", *Publius*, 3(2): 173-196.

Lindblom, C.E. (1965) *The Intelligence of Democracy: Decision-making Through Mutual Adjustment*, Free Press, New York.

Lowi, T. (1969) *The End of Liberalism,* Norton, New York.

Monkkonen, P. (2010) *The Housing Transition in Mexico: Local Impacts of National Policy,* Dissertation filed in completion of the PhD in City and Regional Planning at the University of California, Berkeley.

Osborne, D., and Gaebler, T. (1992) *Reinventing Government: How the Entrepreneurial Spirit is Transforming the Public Sector,* Penguin, New York.

Ozawa, C. (1991) *Recasting Science: Consensual Procedures in Public Policy Making,* Westview Press, Boulder.

Perin, C. (1977) *Everything in its Place,* Princeton University Press, Princeton.

Silverman, C., A. Martinez, J. Rogers, G. Waddell, L. Morin-Calderon (2009) *San Francisco's Nonprofit Sector: A Regional Nonprofit Sector Report,* Institute for Nonprofit Management, University of San Francisco, San Francisco.

Scholz, J.T. and Stiftel, B. (2005) *Adaptive governance and water conflict: New institutions for collaborative planning,* Resources for the Future, Washington D.C.

Susskind, S., McKearnan, S. and Thomas-Larner, J. (Eds.) (1999) *The Consensus Building Handbook: A Comprehensive Guide to Reaching Agreement,* Sage Publications, Thousand Oaks.

Thompson, J.D. (1967) *Organizations in Action,* McGraw-Hill, New York.

Tiebout, C. (1956) "A pure theory of local expenditure", *Journal of Political Economy,* 64(5): 416-424.

The Urban Institute (1994) *Status and Prospects of the Nonprofit Housing Sector,* U.S. Department of Housing and Urban Development, Washington D.C.

Webber, M.M. (1978) "A difference paradigm for planning", in R. Burchell and G. Sternlieb (Eds.) *Planning theory in the 1980s,* Center for Urban Policy Research, Rutgers University, New Brunswick.

Webster-Merriam (1956) *Webster's New Collegiate Dictionary,* Merriam, Springfield.

Chapter 4

Transformative Practice as an Exploration of Possibility Spaces

Joris E. Van Wezemael[1]

Ever tried. Ever failed. No matter. Try again. Fail again. Fail Better. (Samuel Beckett, 1983)

Spatial planning theory has quite some time ago reacted to the 'discovery of complexity' (Stengers, 2000), not least by putting communicative approaches and participatory methods at centre stage (Forester, 1999; Healey, 1996). Accordingly, planning cultivated both a stance that recognised the planner as an active participant – a trend watcher, enabler, advocate, transition manager, mediator – and a positive reception of the fluidity and the openness of the world. As De Roo (2003, 2009) has shown Karen Christensen's (1985) suggestion to classify planning issues according to their 'degree of complexity' is a promising way to develop strategies for planning to cope with uncertainty and complexity. In her conception moving from low towards higher degrees of complexity is seen as moving through a continuum from a technical rationale towards a communicative rationale and a more intersubjective understanding of reality. However, the bulk of planning problems are in the 'shades of grey' (De Roo, 2009) between one ideal type situation where we can apply a technical rationale and another one where we search for order in chaos. In the light of the work of Hillier (2005, 2007), Karadimitriou (2010), Innes and Booher (1999a, 1999b), De Roo (2009) and Van Wezemael (2010a) in planning and with the conceptual foundation of Deleuze (1990, 1994), Deleuze and Guattari (1987), and DeLanda (2002, 2006a) I would like to take Christensen's productive work further.

In this chapter I aim at:

1. relating Christensen's degrees of complexity to the conception of degrees of freedom to generate a continuum of problem conditions in which generative processes vary in intensity
2. introducing possibility spaces to planning research to conceptualise the planner as an active explorer of those spaces

1   Joris E. Van Wezemael is professor in Geography, Socio-Spatial Complexity Lab, University of Fribourg, Switzerland.

In order to do this I will challenge some aspects of Christensen's degrees of complexity, which include the role of communicative rationality and language in relation to complexity. Furthermore I want to point out the empirical and also the practical value of complexity thinking.

The proposed conception has been developed mainly in the course of empirical research (Van Wezemael and Loepfe, 2009). As an entry point into the discussion I will borrow John Urry's argument that complexity is not placed on the plane of interpretation, meanings or linguistic structures, but on the plane of a relational materiality and a *realistic constructivism* (Urry, 2005). This is not just an academic question since the relation of the physical world and a linguistic/symbolic reality is crucial for planning practice. The first section of the chapter outlines key characteristics of present planning conditions and highlights the relevance of project-orientation (Siebel, Ibert and Mayer, 1999) and governance-modes of decision-making. Then I will outline the core of Christensen's argument with regard to the aim of this chapter, followed by a critical acclaim. This lays ground for the conception of complexity as a property of reality in the sense of Urry's (2005) *complexity turn*. I will introduce a number of key conceptions from complexity thinking, which provide the basis to use degrees of freedom as a mediator between Christensen's work and the proposition of spaces of possibilities in planning and planning theory. An empirical case of an urban extension project allows me to illustrate the practicability of the concept. In the conclusion I will wrap up my argument and discuss the role of the planner in the light of the proposed conception.

4.1 Planning conditions today

I think that many authors today agree that places, neighbourhoods or cities are not objectively given, identifiable and integrated economic or social systems. Rather, they are emergent entities, generated by the intertwining of physical, mental, relational networks – each with their own temporality, scale and reach (Amin, 2004; Healey, 2006). They are materially perceived as significant, but also as relatively fluid compositions (Hillier, 2007). These processes that eventually generate places (see below) are changing; in recent years it has become increasingly clear that they are not bound solely or even primarily to spatial proximity or historical concentration (Eisinger and Schneider, 2003; Schmid, 2007). For instance the term globalisation means that the size of a place cannot be known in advance (Van Wezemael and Loepfe, 2009). Technically speaking a planning perimeter can no longer be deduced from zoning or administrative territories, but it must be experimentally explored in a process of scaling up and down in order to perform the 'right' size of the site, as will be showed in the empirical illustration. This challenges the strategies and the self-image of planners. Strategies to cope with uncertainty highlight the active and interactive role of planners and subsequently lead concrete planning projects away from a sequential (techno-rational) model of gathering the relevant (objective) knowledge first and then applying it to the situation. In fact the appreciation of communicative rationality in addition to technical rationality legitimates variable, and varying (Ibert, 2007), and active roles (Albrechts, 1999; Healey, 2003) of planners in present planning situations which include multiple stakeholders from various government agencies, firms and so on. However, this does not mean that a communicative rationale is the only way to conceptualise transformative practice in the light of complexity (Karadimitriou, 2010).

It should be clear now that the up-valuation of communicative practices does not only stem from planning theorists, rather it also points at the fact that relevant resources in planning processes are increasingly distributed among diverse agents (subjects, groups, organisations, networks): procedural competence, authority, investment capital, key positions in networked power (Innes and Booher, 2002). As empirical research (Van Wezemael and Loepfe, 2009) and evolutionary perspectives on planning processes (see Gerrits and Teisman in this volume) indicate agents often engage in negotiation processes *only after having failed* in trying to proceed single-handedly. They do so because they cannot reach their goal on their own, and because the uncertainties with regard to the activities of other agents are too big (Jessop, 2006). The changed role of the planner, the impact on the organisation of planning projects (ad-hoc organisations, governance procedures), and resource interdependence refer to the emergence of heterarchic modes of governance which on several scales complement and intertwine with the ideal typical state-hierarchical regulation and market-based efficiency. This has been discussed broadly in the context of governance decision-making (see Healey, 2005; Jessop, 2006). Resource interdependence can, as I will show below, be viewed as a *virtual diagram* (Deleuze and Guattari, 1987) that is actualised in an individual way in concrete situations (DeLanda, 2006a). I will also argue on the basis of the conception of exploring possibility spaces that the negotiating process can be viewed as a *trial-and-error process*, which step-by-step generates a collective agent that by 'adding' agents grows by incremental drift. In such negotiating processes roles are newly defined, tasks have to be explored, goals are not yet set (Scholl 1995; Siebel, Ibert and Mayer, 1999). Uncertainties with regard to goals, procedures and agents are a key characteristic of these constellations. Another product of changed processes that create places (and also planning situations) refers to the constitution of temporary ad-hoc organisations in concrete planning projects, which can be described as (temporary) project environments (Van Wezemael, 2008a). As a consequence of the changing planning problems authors such as Scholl (1995) demand that organisational forms of planning should be designed in accordance with the job at hand and not the other way round. I believe that my argument here is in line with Christensen (1985) as she urged planners to tailor their styles to problem conditions ten years earlier (see below). In the next sections I turn to the conception of complexity and the connection to complex systems.

Christensen's approach to introduce complexity as a phenomenon in planning has laid ground for a very productive discussion (De Roo, 2009). Her work defines a starting point that could help us to construct a view on planning that must cope with a reality comprising various degrees of complexity (De Roo, 2009). However we should note that for Christensen uncertainty and complexity are bound to what people know and how they agree:

> If people agree on what they want and how to achieve it, then certainty prevails and planning is rational application of knowledge. If they agree on what they want but do not know how to achieve it, then planning becomes a learning process; if they do not agree on what they want but do know how to achieve alternatives, then planning becomes a bargaining process; if they agree on neither means nor ends, then planning becomes part of the search for order in chaos. Each prototype situation suggests a particular range of planning styles. Planners should tailor their styles to problem conditions. By acting contingently they can use reason to cope with uncertainty. (Christensen, 1985, 63).

The very core of Christensen's argument is the proposition to classify planning issues according to their 'degree of complexity'. As De Roo (2009: 27) explains (emphasis added) ".when moving along the spectrum from a technical rationale towards a communicative rationale, the view of the world becomes less object-oriented and *our understanding of reality becomes more intersubjective.* And, indeed, it is also considered a move from orderly towards chaotic and uncertain situations, in other words, an increase in complexity."

From this I define two challenges which I want to tackle in this chapter:

1. The mentioned continuum is defined between two poles which refer to incommensurable worldviews (or ontologies): on the one hand there is an object oriented, means-to-ends fitting, positivist world, governed by technical rationality in which certainty prevails; on the other hand there is a social constructivist one, which is oriented towards an interactional, communicative definition of the real, which is relativist (not: relationalist[2]) in the sense that no certainty about 'one reality' can exist because multiple stakeholder bring in multiple truths and so on. How coherent is the idea to position real planning issues in a continuum that, in the end, is defined by two conflicting worldviews?

---

2   Piaget's theory of relationalism (Kitchener, 1985) states that it is the set of relations that is primary and the relata – the individuals – that is secondary. In the line of thinking of Delanda (who opposes a postmodern relativism, see DeLanda, Protevi and Thanem (2006)) individuals as assemblages emerge on the basis of exterior relations (Van Wezemael, 2010, 2008b). Thus, one key contribution of the anti-essentialist assemblage theory is the notion that the opposition lies not between individualism and holism (or structuralism) since they both are placed on the same bi-polar field (see Latour, 2005) on micro-versus-macro. Rather, the counterplayer of both individualism (in the sense of micro-perspectives) and holism (in the sense of macro-perspectives) is relationalism (in the sense of Deleuze's and Guattari's assemblages of enunciation or Delanda's (2006) (social) assemblages).

2. As a side effect of the continuum in which Christensen parallels an increase in degrees of complexity with communicative rationality, she eventually places complexity on the plane of humans interpreting reality. I will discuss this issue in depth in the next section.

4.2 The interpretative plane of complexity and the cost at which the world is made open

I believe that it is worth taking some time at this point to reflect a bit more on the 'continuum' of the degrees of complexity and the polarisation of ideal type rationalities, to discuss the way complexity has been approached. This is important because the relation of the physical environment and a linguistic/symbolic reality is crucial for theorising planning, and it will be paramount for the decision of where we can move from here and also how to get there.

The 'communicative' strategy of dealing with a more interactive conception of the planner or researcher in order to allow for a worldview that acknowledges fluidity, complexity and uncertainty is common not just in planning but among many branches of social and cultural sciences: the fluidity, uncertainty and complexity of the world has been brought to the fore by placing it on a symbolic/ linguistic plane. This strategy includes approaches which sail under the flag of late modernism and partly also post-structuralism[3] (Arbor and Hirt, 2003; Doel, 2000; Doel and Matless, 1992). In planning theory, the most influential approaches are referred to as communicative or collaborative (Forester, 1999; Healey, 1996) and they are still attracting the attention of many planning theorists at the beginning of the 21st Century (Allmendinger and Tewdwr-Jones, 2002). But, as I would like to point out, both communicative rationality (Habermas, 1981) and postmodern approaches have – as a side effect of the linguistic turn – reinforced a perspective where almost everything is related to hermeneutic, linguistic or sociological constructions (Srnicek, 2007: 300).

The outlined recognition of the open and complex nature of social life in the symbolic/linguistic dimension (Urry, 2005) has been criticised recently with an explicit regard to complexity (DeLanda, 1998, 2006a, 2006b; Latour, 2005; Latour and Weibel, 2005; Srnicek, 2007; Tormey, 2006; Van Wezemael, 2008b). I want to use this critique in order to move a step forward with the conceptions of degrees of complexity by mooting what I call the key question for planning theory in the face of complexity: is complexity *a property of reality* or a *property of humans interpreting reality*?[4]

---

3 Mind exceptions such as Hillier (2005).

4 This question should not be conceived in an absolute manner as it, to some degree, can be viewed also as a matter of choice: we can see an issue straight forward, complex and even from a chaotic perspective.

Sure, the so-called linguistic turn helped to acknowledge the active involvement of the observer of society and the open, complex nature of social life as the focus of analysis and also of planning decision-making. Wider social sciences have reconciled themselves with the idea of observers as active participants in the research of social reality, giving them a central and pivotal role. This perspective, however, provides a *second order representation* by reading all instances of human/non-human relations as somehow culturally determined (Hinchcliffe, 2003; Hacking, 1999). This eventually enables a social constructivist (in a broad sense!) approach to planning issues. Reality is now exposed to the interpretation of the 'active human participant'. This means that the 'realities' of the objects of study are inevitably substituted by the analyst's interpretations of the objects (or are even equated with deeper linguistic structures). This effectively vaporised the relational materiality of social structures into conceptual, idealistic constructions.

With other words, almost unperceived by many, for most social scientists and many contemporary planning approaches a sort of linguistic idealism[5] has become a predominant paradigm that has accepted the fortification of the symbolic/ linguistic dimension (and also an anthropomorphic view of the world). As a consequence the term 'construction' is not used in the sense in which e.g. Foucault (1995) talks of the construction of soldier bodies through drill and discipline, but to the way our minds 'construct' the world of appearances via linguistic categories. (DeLanda, Protevi and Thanem, 2006). This consequently reinforces a modernist essentialist perception of matter as inert, passive and docile, which again conflicts with what we learn from complex adaptive systems or generally speaking, from what DeLanda calls 'intensive science' (DeLanda, 2002).

Thus, the material world is 'exposed' to interpretation, to meaning, to word games, substituting the 'realities' of the objects of research with intersubjective interpretations. We have thus made the world open and complex at the expense of giving up its objectivity (DeLanda, 1998). In other words, the world becomes open only through human intervention. This, in turn, overestimates the capacity of human action – and of planner's interventions – as it is cut off from the relations of forces that govern hybrid and non-human systems.

Maybe this point is hard to accept for some since social constructivism is (or was) supposed to be an antidote to the essentialist assumption of general categories: by showing that general categories are mere stereotypes it should block the move towards their reification. But by coupling the idea that perception is intrinsically linguistic with the ontological assumption that only the contents of experience really exist, the position leads directly to a form of social essentialism. (DeLanda, 2006a: 45-46). Furthermore, as Latour has pointed out, accepting a

---

5   Delanda (DeLanda, Protevi and Thanem, 2006) argues that within linguistic idealism metaphors become foundational but that, detached from that ontology, they are useful devices; but nonetheless they could not be expected to do the theoretical work that necessitates deeper topological isomorphisms such as the sharing among processes of universal singularities (see below).

social constructivist approach inevitably leads to a mode of thinking where the natural and technological world is fully absorbed by the social world. Latour has referred to this as the social turn (Latour, 2005).

I believe that answering the above question in the sense that complexity is a property of reality, and taking all the consequences of this decision, can move us a step forward from here. In the following section I will elaborate some more on the term complexity, introduce three key concepts and then connect the degrees of complexity that is well received in planning to the notion of degrees of freedom in order to introduce the idea of *possibility spaces* and the way they are structured.

The radicalism of contemporary approaches to social complexity, such as assemblage theory (DeLanda, 2006a, 2006b) or also actor-network theory (Latour, 1987, 2005), lies in the recognition of complexity *as a property of reality* and not as a property of humans interpreting reality (Urry, 2005).[6] However, this radicalism can also be related as a transition from 'complexity' to 'complex systems' (see below).

I identify, as the *Leitmotiv* of complexity sciences, the notion that every observable order, including every spatial setting or social ensemble, is a product of interactions of elements. An individual, therefore, is viewed as a process, which brings temporality right into the core of the conception; the term 'individual' refers to all semi-stable entities (as long as they have consistency, see Watson, 2009; Guattari, 1984) with the capacity to affect. Families, institutional organisations, cities, nation states are all real entities that are the product of specific historical processes and whatever degree of identity they have, it must be accounted for via the processes which created them and those that maintain or change their identity (DeLanda, 2006a). Studies on the basis of complexity theory therefore focus on the dynamics of non-equilibrium and on multiple futures, historical path dependency and intrinsic uncertainty. Complex adaptive systems are described by interaction, non-linearity, instability, self-organisation and unpredictability. Here a given cause or event generates a potential, which still has to be transformed into possibilities by means of generative processes (DeLanda, 2002)

With other words, complexity thinking asks less what a thing is, but how it has come into being and *what it can do*. It sets up the challenge to recognise complex and dynamic phenomena such as urban areas as intertwined systems with human and non-human, material and expressive components.

At this point, I think it is helpful to introduce some key conceptions from complexity thinking in order to further develop the argument. They will also allow me to follow some helpful Deleuzian-inspired conceptions in order to unfold the idea of possibility spaces.

---

6   For key differences between Latourian and Deleuzian approaches see Palmas (2007).

Non-ergodic systems

The time path of an ergodic system is not sensitive to initial conditions; their dynamics are predictable. They consequently display a tendency for convergence and states of equilibrium. For planning this means that an understanding, for instance of urban areas as systems in equilibrium, introduces an a-political task for planning, which is: reconstituting their equilibrium. The city as a place of difference, but also characteristics such as innovation, competition, or conflict (see Lefebvre, 1991; Lambooy, 2002; Schumpeter, 1935) are opposed to an orientation towards a natural equilibrium. This is why I suggest to view planning settings, places, regions and their path dependencies as non-ergodic systems, whose dynamics are not predictable in the long run: exogeneous shocks shape their dynamics, initial conditions are constitutive for their long-term development (see also Wilkinson in this Volume).

Phase transitions

Phase transitions mark qualitative transitions which may appear abruptly and imply a sort of threshold of a dynamic system (Durlauf, 2005). If it reaches this threshold the relations between system's components change in a qualitative way, which generates new qualities on the next 'higher level' of emergence (see below). Sometimes such phase transitions are also referred to as tipping points. Take as an example the tilting of the residential market in a neighbourhood at a certain share of a population group (Lichtenberger, 1998; Müller-Ibold, 1996; Van Wezemael and Odermatt, 2000). At this point it is helpful to point out the non-linear dynamics of complex systems (see Table 4.1). As a direct consequence of non-linear relations cause and effect are not proportionally related.

Table 4.1   Characteristics of linear and non-linear relations according to Law and Urry (2004)

Linearity
• large changes in causes produce large changes in effects • same causes always produce same effects • *proportionality between 'causes' and 'effects'*
Non-Linearity
• small causes can produce large effects and vice versa • same cause can produce qualitatively different kinds of effect in specific circumstances *(no necessary proportionality between 'causes' and 'effects')* • individual and statistic levels of analysis are not equivalent • system effects do not result from the simple addition of individual components

Emergence

Emergence describes the effect that is generated from the interaction of elements, but it should also be understood as a form of self-organisation, which refers to the spontaneous generation of structures on the basis of changing relations and the co-evolution of component parts (DeLanda, 2006a, 2006b). It thus addresses competition and conflict between elements. Issues such as innovation, surprise and novelty come to the fore. One can talk about emergence on any resultant level, but mind that 'level' refers to the relation of an assemblage of component parts to those parts only.

Cities, neighbourhoods, or places are generated by the intertwining of physical and mental, relational networks which include components as diverse as construction elements, relations to temporally and spatially distant places, political discourse and contestation, regulations, economic accumulations, architectural expression, and so on.

According to the Conant-Ashby theorem (every good regulator of a system must have a model of that system; see Conant and Ashby (1970)) the controller becomes a model of the controlled and thus disposes of a comparable amount of degrees of freedom as those of the system itself. In his 'law of indispensable/ requisite variety' Ashby (1956) states that any effective control system must be as complex as the system it controls. From this we can formulate the suggestion that such modes of governance tend to fail, which display too low degrees of freedom if compared with the space of possibilities of the planning problem. What is a degree of freedom? In mathematical terms, degrees of freedom are the dimensions of a phase space;[7] they are a property of a system. In physical systems we can think of the number of coordinates that we need in order to describe the system.[8] The degree of complexity is to be understood as an emergent property of a system.

Degrees of freedom are immanent as they are generated on the basis of the relations of component parts of a system. For planning theory this means that shifting degrees of freedom on the basis of changing relations in assemblages can be used in order to deal with changing degrees of openness and uncertainty in planning conditions without the need to refer to contradictory worldviews. Degrees

---

7   A phase space – a concept widely used in mathematics and physics – is a space in which all possible states of a system are represented. Think of a multidimensional space in which every degree of freedom or parameter of the system is represented as an axis. In order to construct a phase space of a system one must determine the number of significant ways in which the system can change. As Srnicek (2007) states, in social systems, the number of relevant changes is vast and so the theorist must make explicit their choices/limitations. Each relevant factor is then mathematically described as a dimension of the constructed space (visually, this quickly becomes impossible to imagine, but mathematically it can be worked out). Each point within the space defined by these dimensions therefore represents a particular possible state of the system.

8   When describing mechanical devices such as hinges or a bicycle their degree of freedom informs us about the movements that this device can perform.

of freedom generally refer to a space of possibilities, which is structured by a set of singularities (see below).[9] It is crucial to note that a space of possibilities is not amorphous but structured, given that the capacities of an assemblage are merely possible when not exercised. This is also evident since different assemblages exhibit different sets of capacities (DeLanda, 2006a: 29).

The continuum between technical and communicative rationality can now be understood as a trial-and-error process during which the planner (usually a collective whose components are not restricted to persons) experimentially (by interfering) explores the space of possibilities of a planning situation and adjusts the degrees of freedom of its intervention. The collective actor thus grows by incremental drift as relations are added or altered.

In order to be clear in this important point let me explain what I count as an 'agent': it encompasses anything that modifies a state of affairs by making a difference. The two questions to ask about any agent are simply the following: 'Does it make a difference in the course of some other agent's action or not?' (Latour, 2005).

For planning research after the complexity turn this means that we have to examine everything, including infrastructures, remote places, discourses, decision-support instruments[10] etc. and ask if and how they affect other agents. If one cannot remove them without consequences from a course of action, then they are part of the collective actor (Latour, 2005). Materiality thus enters the stage again without being absorbed by a social pole or mediated by a plane of interpretation or reduced to docile matter[11]. Here I want to point out that discourse and debate are not set apart from the relations of other elements. Historical formations of series of texts generate linguistic assemblages and should never be considered as any more than

---

9   The conception of degrees of freedom can also be used in order to conceptualise human action. We gain more degrees of freedom (1) the greater the constraints the subject level can exercise over 'autonomic' sub-systems; (2) the more one's 'subject position' allows one to negotiate social constraints embedded in institutions and free-floating or 'peer pressure' systems (e.g., gender and race constraints); and (3) the more money one has (in some places gender and race constraints are being replaced by economic constraints), since then, to complete the system, you can move to places where economic power mitigates race and gender constraints, etc. (DeLanda, Protevi and Thanem, 2006).

10   They include the models, images and so on: Van Wezemael (2010b) observed the relevance of technologies of representation such as architectural models, plans, renderings, but also spreadsheets and tables, and images. They play an important role in the coordination of collective action as they translate ideas, information and authority (Latour, 2005; Callon, 1986). They point out that decision-making processes include much more than the people involved! In the Brünnen case representations are used in order to synthesise complex aspects of the urban texture, simulate urban futures, and of course to convince other agents of the desirability of distinct developments (Söderström, 2000).

11   See as an illustration Latour's conception of the groom in his article ,Where are the missing masses?' (Latour, 1992).

component parts entering into exterior relations with other component parts of an assemblage (DeLanda, 2006a: 45; Sarasin, 2009: 15).

Planning becomes an experimental exploration of possibility spaces, during which the generative processes that generate both the planning conditions as well as the collective actor intertwine. I have shown elsewhere (Van Wezemael, 2010a: 298) that modes of decision-making in planning approach their degrees of freedom to those of the possibility spaces of the problem via an experimental trial-and-error process. This is also to say that over time the problem determines the complexity of the collective actor and thus the planning mode in the sense of Christensen (see above).

Spaces of possibilities

Spaces of possibilities as a crucial conceptual element are still underdeveloped in my argument. Here I will draw on some work of Deleuze (1994) and Deleuze and Guattari (1987). For me the key credit of Deleuze for urban governance lies precisely in his deeper insight that nothing can be understood if it is reduced to the properties that it displays at any given moment. Here I argue that Deleuze introduces a realist ontology which I roughly map out in Table 4.2.

Table 4.2   A realist ontology

Virtual	Intensive	Actual
Virtual continuum formed by multiplicities	Fields of individuation/ morphogenesis	Extensities and qualities
Progressive differentiation		

Source: draft of the author on the basis of Deleuze (1994)

Thus we have to complement the plane of the actual (extensities and qualities) with a virtual plane (virtual continuum formed by multiplicities) and a generative field (the 'intensive'; field of individuation/morphogenesis), which incorporates tendencies of change and becoming as well as its potential properties. An individual, viewed as a process and thus as an assemblage in the sense of a statistical product of lower-scale connections of an assemblage, displays emergent properties. However, its properties are not 'given'. When not exercised they are merely possible. Real assemblages consist of a field of actualities (exercised properties), a possibility space, which refers to the virtual, containing potential properties, and a generative field: the intensive, individuating level (DeLanda, 2002: 143; Deleuze, 1994: 173).

The virtual is necessarily structured since different assemblages exhibit different sets of capacities, and here possibility spaces come into play. We can address the virtual by means of unactualised tendencies ('singularities') and unactualised capacities to affect and be affected ('affects') (DeLanda, 2002: 62). Singularities are virtual, but they are individuated in assemblages, and so they are vital to the operation of those assemblages (Deleuze and Guattari, 1987: 100). Since no individual – which refers to every constellation with an identity (see above) – is ever (ontologically) independent from its environment, every individual must be viewed as an open system through which matter, information and energy passes. Therefore, all individuals need certain singularities in order to maintain their identity; those singularities, however, are not transcendent types (see also Trummer in this volume) – rather they are generated on the basis of the relations that give rise to the system itself. In other words they are immanent. This means that every assemblage as a historical individual must be understood not only on the basis of its actual relations, but also with regard to a space of possibilities (e.g. its tendencies of becoming) that is structured by singularities (see Table 4.2).

Thus, we can say that a space of possibilities is structured by a map of relations between forces, which can be addressed as a map of intensity. This map refers to a set of invariances (or 'universal' singularities) that structure the space of possibilities associated with the assemblage (see empirical illustration, below). It is not a copy of the actual, but it constructs a real-to-come, or a becoming. Actualisations are (temporary) solutions which are generated by processes of individuation; therefore real (not actual) problems are defined by singularities and maintain certain autonomy from their particular solutions. The empirical illustration below will discuss resource interdependency in planning situations as a virtual invariance (that is nonetheless generated on the basis of specific relations in the respective assemblages) that allows for many (temporal) actualisations.

Empirical Illustration

I will illustrate transformative practice as an exploration of possibility spaces with a case study from the field of project-oriented planning.[12] It traces an urban extension project in the west of the Swiss Capital Bern in an area called Brünnen

The data were retrieved from a series of workshops with main protagonists of the recently accomplished project which includes a shopping and leisure centre designed by Daniel Libeskind, and a group of experts from consultancy firms, universities and planning offices as discussants. Furthermore original data including plans, reports, presentations, and images were analysed, and additional interviews were conducted. The workshops were recorded and analysed with the help of the content analysis support software atlas.ti.

Planning in the Brünnen area has a history of 40 years of trial-and-error. However, it is not only a history of failure, but also one of repeated reconfiguration

---

12   The example forms part of a series of empirical studies on the invariances in project oriented planning in Switzerland. For an overview see Van Wezemael & Loepfe (2009).

of place-making. I will summarise the first two decades' series of events and then focus on the period after 1994 on which the case study focused.

The top-down designed so-called 'approximative masterplan Brünnen' from 1972 suggested an urban extension with dwelling space for 20,000 people (see Figure 4.1). However, it coincided with a recession in the course of the oil crisis and the urbanisation turned into a trend of suburbanisation. The plan therefore ended in the archives. Then, in 1978, a redimensioned version was pushed ahead, however it was turned down at a popular vote. Later, the conception of a partial encroachment of the northern part while permanently protecting the south of the area from being developed was agreed on in a 1991 popular vote. However, the property market crash in the early 1990s produced no investor.

The possibilities for development were additionally narrowed because of very high costs for noise protection (a motorway has to be covered). Covering the motorway is precondition in order to meet legal standards for noise protection. In connection with the bankruptcy of two landowners/investors, which were supposed to cover the high infrastructure costs, the chances of a realisation of the project dwindled away.

The pressure on the city of Bern and the Federal State, which both held a substantial amount of shares of those real estate companies on the basis of a social housing scheme, was increased since the bankruptcy was about to develop into a political scandal, too: in 1994 the federal state threw 'good money' after 'bad money' in the sense that it invested massively into real estate companies, which where thus saved from bankruptcy; without that money the economic fundament for the now realised project would have been lost. However, the reason for this intervention was a political one, which is only loosely related to the project in question.

The housing scheme that lay ground for the federal office holding shares of those real estate companies was being consulted in parliament in those days, and due to a newly constituted conservative majority it was at risk of being cancelled. According to the Federal Office of Housing, writing off a large sum would have meant the political end of this law. The money thus was basically paid in order to avoid a political headline that would have possibly abolished the federal office of housing (the office is proposed for closing periodically). Mind that at the time of the investment nobody believed in the success of the Bern-Brünnen development.

The outline of the process between 1972 and 1994 highlights the sensitivity of both the internal dynamics and the direction of the trajectories to external shock. Furthermore, the encounter of processes that are previously independent and unconnected (e.g. oil crisis and masterplan, the property market crisis and a newly established conservative majority in parliament) generates thresholds in the dynamic of the processes and emergent properties. The unfolding of the process can be traced in a genealogical sense, which points out that individuals are assembled from 'disparate' elements; it has no pretended essence and it cannot be predicted (Sarasin, 2009: 301).

The 1994 standoff generated a high degree of uncertainty which again produced a series of activities which involved public authorities, real estate companies,

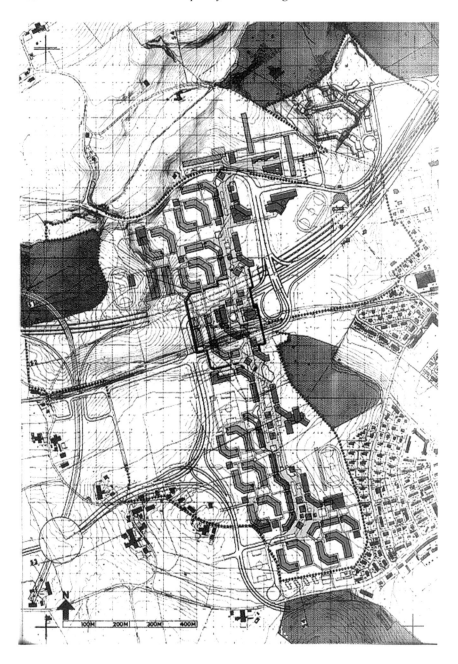

Figure 4.1   Approximative Masterplan Brünnen

Source: Archiv Stadtplanungsamt Bern

some experts on economy as well as architects and planners in the surroundings of the city. In such a phase of increased uncertainty the number of agents and their heterogeneity grows very rapidly – and their relations transform the space of possibility not least by enhancing its degrees of freedom. This generated the capacity to allow for creative ideas and alternative interpretations of the becoming of the place. It is at this point that we can trace a phase transition which marks a discrete change in both the dynamics and the direction of the process. Up to now every solution contained the strategy of keeping the cover for the motorway small because its high costs were obviously the limiting factor for the area's development. Now an engineer who had been working on the project before, suggested an alternative way to finance the infrastructure not by minimising its cost but by enlarging it in order that more commercial floorspace was created. This plan also included a reduction of dwelling space. This strategy introduced a change in the relations of a whole range of component parts of the Brünnen assemblage and it generated a possibility space where the roles of key elements could be altered. The creation of more attractive conditions for investors re-established a development in the Brünnen area. The changing relations of forces generated new relations between previous actors, discourses and places and they also introduced new ones. A local real estate developer introduced the idea of having a supra-regional leisure and shopping centre built. In connection with new narratives, changing economic potentials and the possibility of finally attracting a viable investor, the relations within public authorities as well as their relations with economic organisations but also with the discourse regarding what kind of place Brünnen ought to become changed rapidly. They started negotiating with a private investor, which again altered many exterior relations of component parts.

We can see how the collective actor in a trial-and-error process incrementally grows by drift and adds other agents – whether people, organisations and firms, or a piece of infrastructure. The concrete motorway cover – at the same time the fundament of the commercial floor space – started to play a relevant material role as a calculative element in the 'yield'-assemblage with commercial developers and investors as well as an element in the political/planning assemblage that is being generated by relations of forces which concern noise protection. On the basis of its relations the motorway cover generated sets of options in both assemblages which simply did not exist before. Thus the material element 'concrete slab' becomes a full-blown actor in the sense of Latour – or a relevant part of the collective actor that grows by incremental drift during its exploration of possibility spaces. In either way it possesses capacities to affect others.

Whereas area development became possible again – a well-heeled investor agreed to pay for the entire noise-protection infrastructure – the previous housing development was restricted. The sensitivity of non-ergodic systems to external shocks and the subsequent unpredictability can be illustrated very well here – and they do not only affect the 'drifting' collective actor, but also the direction, nature and the goal of the process. The degree of uncertainty has decreased immediately as the well-heeled investor agreed. The lines of actualisation changed and, again, the collective actor changed. Specific relations between the developer, public authorities and the new private investor are manifested. The relation of material, economic and political/planning elements generated a dynamic that reconfigured procedures as well as the discursive summoning up of elements (Amin, 2004) and the ex-ante framing of the project. The hitherto conception of the place as a residential area has been destabilised by the altered actual relations as well as a newly structured space of possibilities. The conception changes now towards a development area with mixed use and a leisure and shopping centre with a supra-regional relevance. It was exactly its relation to other places that generated the place. The empirical case nicely illustrates the performative character of place-making (Healey, 2004). The Brünnen case (see Figure 4.2) shows how various issues, things, sites and actors are made an element of the project, and the scaling-up of the place on the basis of the relations of these component parts is also being performed by a range of representations. In sum they generate a new place that has hardly anything in common with the original conception (see Figure 4.1).

4.3 Conclusion

I have started from Christensen's degrees of complexity that are well received in planning theory and I used the conception of degrees of freedom as a modulator in order to generate a continuum of problem conditions in which generative processes vary in intensity. This cleared the ground for the introduction of possibility spaces, which allow for dealing with properties of complex adaptive systems and conceptualising the planner as an active explorer of those spaces. The Brünnen case study has illustrated the empirical and also the practical value of complexity thinking in planning.

Both my theoretical argument and the case study point out that the complexity-turn calls for a conception of planning as an active, creative and experimental exploration of trajectories in heterogeneous assemblages and thus asks what they can do, which introduces an orientation towards the future and the notion of becoming. The question of 'what might happen if...' (Hillier, 2007) can be approached on the basis of an exploration of possibility spaces. A communicative rationale in order to conceptualise transformative practice therefore seems limited in the light of complexity since historical formations of series of texts generate linguistic assemblages that should be considered as component parts entering into exterior relations with other (non-linguistic) component parts of an assemblage. The conception of a collective actor creates a space for linguistic series within the outlined approach.

In our case study we can clearly show that modes of decision-making in planning approach their degrees of freedom to those of the possibility spaces of the problem via experimental trial-and-error processes. In the sense that the controller (planner as a collective) tends to become a model of the controlled (requisite variety in the Conant-Ashby theorem, see above); hence, over time the problem determines the complexity of the collective actor and thus the planning mode. Taking into account generative processes puts planning problems and the experimentally generated response into an intrinsic relationship. The planning process becomes readable as a repeatedly and experimentally generated response to changed relations in spatial development. Via trial and error the space of possibilities and thus the virtual structure of the problem are explored.

Furthermore, the case study displays both overlapping and sequential phases of temporary stability and instability, of differing degrees of complexity, which are separated by transitions at which relations between components change in a qualitative way. Although the mode of planning was adopted in a seemingly accidental way, it also displays invariant properties with regard to the transformations of planning conditions. In the Brünnen case we can address on invariance as the interdependence of resources: resources such as procedural capacities, know-how, investment capital, social and cultural capital, discretionary power and more are distributed across a number of actors with different goals. We can conceptualise resource interdependence as a virtual diagram that is generated by the relations of all components that give rise to a governance process and to which they give an answer. Resource interdependencies can be viewed as an invariant with regard to the actualisation of a population of project-oriented planning settings. Certainly, every governance process displays its own individual properties and spatio-temporal dynamics. But they also remain individual answers to the universal problem of resource interdependency that generates the trial-and-error process that I introduced in order to describe the mode of negotiating in project-oriented planning.

References

Albrechts, L. (1999) 'Planners as Catalysts and Initiators of Change. The New Structure Plan for Flanders', *European Planning Studies*, 7(5), pp. 587-604.

Allmendinger, P. and Tewdwr-Jones, M. (2002) *Planning Futures: New Directions for Planning Theory*, Psychology Press, London.

Amin, A. (2004) "Region Unbound: Towards a New Politics of Place", *Geografisker Annaler*, 86(B), pp. 33-44.

Arbor, A. and Hirt, S. (2003) "Measuring Postmodernism: Placing Urban Planning in the Context of a Broader Cultural Values Tradition", Paper presented at the 2003 Distinguished Faculty and Student Symposium: Crossing Disciplinary Boundaries in the Urban and Regional Context.

Ashby, W.R. (1956) *An Introduction to Cybernetics*, Chapman and Hall, London.

Beckett, S. (1983) *Worstward Ho*, Grove Press, New York

Callon, M. (1986) 'Some Elements of a Sociology of Translation: Domestication of the Scallops and the Fishermen of St Brieuc Bay', *Power, Action and Belief: A New Sociology of Knowledge*, 32, pp. 196-233.

Christensen, K.S. (1985) 'Coping with Uncertainty in Planning', *Journal of the American Planning Association*, 51(1), pp. 63-73.

Conant, R.C. and Ashby, W.R. (1970) 'Every Good Regulator of a System Must be a Model of that System', *International Journal of Systems Science*, 1(2), pp. 89-97.

DeLanda, M. (1998) 'Deleuze and the open-ended Becoming of the world', http://www. diss.sense.uni-konstanz.de/virtulitaet/delanda.htm

DeLanda, M., (2002) *Intensive Science and Virtual Philosophy*, Continuum, London.

DeLanda, M. (2006a) *A New Philosophy of Society. Assemblage Theory and Social Complexity*, Continuum, London.

DeLanda, M. (2006b) 'Deleuzian Social Ontology and Assemblage Theory', in Fugslang, M. and Meier Sorensen, B (eds) *Deleuze Connections*, Edinburgh University Press, Edinburgh, pp. 250-266.

DeLanda, M., Protevi, J. and Thanem, T. (2006) 'Deleuzian Interrogations: A Conversation with Manuel DaLanda, John Protevi and Torkild Thanem' *Journal of Critical Postmodern Organisation Science*, http://www.tamarajournal.com.

Deleuze, G. (1990) *The Logic of Sense* (trans. Mark Lester and Charles Stivale, orig. 1969), Columbia University Press, New York.

Deleuze, G. (1994) *Difference and Repetition*, Continuum, London.

Deleuze, G. and Guattari, F. (1987) *A Thousand Plateaus. Capitalism and Schizophrenia*, University of Minnesota Press, Minneapolis.

De Roo, G. (2003) *Environmental Planning in the Netherlands: Too Good to be True. From Command and Control Planning to Shared Governance*, Ashgate, Aldershot.

De Roo, G. (2009) 'Being or Becoming? That is the Question! Confronting Complexity with Contemporary Planning Theory', in De Roo, G. and Silva, E.A. (eds) *A Planner's Encounter with Complexity*, Ashgate, Farnham, pp. 19-39.

Doel, M.A. (2000) 'Un-glunking geography: spatial science after Dr Seuss and Gilles Deleuze', in Crang, M. and Thrift, N. (eds) *In Thinking Space*, Routledge, London, pp. 117-135.

Doel, M.A. and Matless, D. (1992) 'Geography and postmodernism', *Environment and Planning D: Society and Space*, 10(1), pp. 1-4.

Durlauf, S.N. (2005) "Complexity and Empirical Economics", *The Economic Journal*, 115, pp. 225-243.

Eisinger, A. and Schneider, M. (2003) *Stadtland Schweiz*, Birkhäuser, Springer, Basel.

Forester, J. (1999) *The Deliberate Practitioner*, MIT Press, Cambridge (US).

Foucault, M. (1995) *Discipline and Punish*, Knopf Doubleday Publishing Group, New York.

Guattari, F. (1984) *Molecular Revolution: Psychiatry and Politics*, Penguin, London.

Habermas, J. (1981) *Theorie des kommunikativen Handelns*, Suhrkamp, Frankfurt.

Hacking, I. (1999) *The Social Construction of What?,* Harvard University Press, Harvard.

Healey, P. (1996) 'The communicative turn in planning theory and its implications for spatial strategy formations', *EBP,* 23(2), pp. 217-234.

Healey, P. (2003) *Creativity and Governance. An Institutionalist Perspective,* unpublished manuscript.

Healey, P. (2004) 'Relational complexity and the imaginative power of strategic spatial planning', *European planning studies,* 14(4), pp. 525-546.

Healey, P. (2006) *Urban Complexity and Spatial Strategies: Towards a Relational Planning for our Times,* Routledge, London.

Hillier, J. (2005) 'Straddling the Post-structuralist Abyss: Between Transcendence and Immanence?', *Planning Theory,* 4(3), pp. 271-299.

Hillier, J. (2007) *Stretching Beyond the Horizon : A Multiplanar Theory of Spatial Planning and Governance,* Ashgate, Aldershot.

Hinchcliffe, S. (2003) 'Inhabiting: Landscapes and Natures', in Anderson, K. (eds) *The Handbook of Cultural Geography,* Sage, London, pp. 207.

Ibert, O. (2007) 'Towards a Geography of knowledge-Creation: The Ambivalences between "Knowledge as an Object" and "Knowing in Practice"', *Regional Studies,* pp. 103-114.

Innes, J. and Booher, D. (1999a) 'Consensus Building and Complex Adaptive Systems: A Framework for Evaluating Collaborative Planning', *Journal of the American Planning Association,* 65(4), pp. 412-423.

Innes, J. and Booher, D. (1999b) 'Consensus Building as Role Planning and Bricolage: Toward a Theory of Collaboratory Planning', *Journal of the American Planning Association,* 65(1), pp. 9-26.

Innes, J. and Booher, D. (2002) "Network Power in Collaborative Planning", *Journal of Planning Education and Research,* 21, pp. 221-236.

Jessop, B. (2006) *The Governance of Complexity and the Complexity of Governance: Preliminary Remarks on some Problems and Limits of Economic Guidance.*

Karadimitriou, N. (2010) 'Cybernetic Spatial Planning: Steering, Managing or Just Letting Go?', in Hillier, J. and Healey, P. (eds) *Conceptual Challenges for Planning Theory,* Ashgate, Aldershot.

Kitchener, R. (1985) 'Holistic Structuralism, Elementarism and Piaget's Theory of "Relationalism"', *Human Development,* 28, pp. 281-294.

Lambooy, J.G. (2002) 'Knowledge and urban economic development: an evolutionary perspective', *Urban Studies,* 39(5-6), pp. 1019.

Latour, B. (1987) *Science In Action: How to Follow Scientists and Engineers Through Society,* Harvard University Press, Cambridge (US).

Latour, B. (1992) 'Where are the missing masses? The sociology of a few mundane artifacts', *Shaping technology/building society: Studies in Sociotechnical Change*: 225–258.

Latour, B. (2005) *Reassembling the Social,* Oxford University Press, New York.

Latour, B. and Weibel, P. (2005) *Making Things Public: Atmospheres of Democracy*, MIT Press, Cambridge (US).

Law, J. and Urry, J. (2004) 'Enacting the Social', *Economy and Society*, 33(3), pp. 390-410.

Lefebvre, H. (1991) *The Production of Space*, Blackwell Publishing, Oxford.

Lichtenberger, E. (1998) *Stadtgeographie–Begriffe, Konzepte, Modelle, Prozesse, Bd. 1*, Teubner, Leipzig.

Müller-Ibold, K. (1996) *Einführung in die Stadtplanung*, Kohlhammer, Stuttgart.

Palmas, K. (2007) *Deleuze and DeLanda: A New Ontology, A New Political Economy?*, in paper presented 29 January 2007 at the Economic Sociology Seminar Series, The Department of Sociology, London School of Economics & Political Sciences, London.

Sarasin, P. (2009) *Darwin und Foucault*, Suhrkamp, Frankfurt/M (G).

Schmid, C. (2007) 'Die Wiederentdeckung des Städtischen in der Schweiz', in V. Lampugnani, M., Keller, T.K. and Buser, B. (eds) *Städtische Dichte*, Verlag NZZ, Zürich (CH)

Scholl, B. (1995) *Aktionsplanung: Zur Behandlung komplexer Schwerpunktaufgaben in der Raumplanung*, vdf Hochschulverlag, Zürich (CH).

Schumpeter, J. (1935) *Théorie de l'évolution économique*, Dalloz, Paris.

Siebel, W., Ibert, O. and Mayer, H. (1999) 'Projektorientierte Planung – ein neues Paradigma?', *Informationen zur Raumentwicklung*, 3/4, pp. 163-172.

Söderström, O. (2000) *Des images pour agir: le visuel en urbanisme*, Payot, Lausanne.

Srnicek, N. (2007) *Assemblage Theory, Complexity and Contentious Politics. The Political Ontology of Gilles Deleuze.* Unpublished master's thesis, University of Western Ontario.

Stengers, I. (2000) *The Invention of Modern Science*, University of Minnesota Press, Minneapolis.

Tormey, S. (2006) '"Not in my Name": Deleuze, Zapatismo and the Critique of Representation', *Parliamentary Affairs*, 1, pp. 138-154.

Urry, J. (2005) Complexity. Special Issue of Theory, *Culture and Society*, 22

Van Wezemael, J.E. (2010) 'Urban Governance and Social Complexity', in De Roo, G. and Silva, E.A. (eds) *A Planner's Encounter With Complexity*, Ashgate, Aldershot.

Van Wezemael, J.E. (2008a) 'Knowledge creation in urban development praxis', in Baum, S. and Yigitganlar, T. (eds) *Knowledge-based urban development*, Idea, Hershley, pp. 1-20.

Van Wezemael, J.E. (2008b) 'The Contribution of Assemblage Theory and Minor Politics for Democratic Network Governance', *Planning Theory*, 7(2), pp. 165-185.

Van Wezemael, J.E. (2010a) 'Modulation of Singularities – a Complexity Approach to Planning Competitions', in Hillier, J. and Healey, P. (eds) *Conceptual Challenges for Planing Theory*, Ashgate, Aldershot, pp. 273-290.

Van Wezemael, J.E. (2010b) 'Zwischen Stadtplanung und Arealentwicklung', *Standort-Zeitschrift für angewandte Geographie*, pp. 1–6.

Van Wezemael, J.E. and Loepfe, M. (2009) 'Veränderte Prozesse der Entscheidungsfindung in der Raumentwicklung', *Geographica Helvetica*, 64(2), pp. 106-118.

Van Wezemael, J.E. and Odermatt, A. (2000) 'Verändert die Marktmiete die residentielle Segregation? Die Marktmiete aus sozial- und wirtschaftsgeographischer Sicht', *Geographica Helvetica*, 4(55), pp. 251-261.

Watson, J. (2009) *Guattari's Diagrammatic Thought*, Continuum, New-York.

PART II
Complex Systems and Planning, in between the Real and the Relative

Chapter 5

Complexity Theories of Cities: First, Second or Third Culture of Planning?[1]

Juval Portugali[2]

In two recent studies (Portugali, 2006; Portugali, 2011) I describe the study of cities in the last 60 years in terms of a conjunction between Snow's (1964) thesis about *The Two Cultures* (of science) and Kuhn's thesis about *The Structure of Scientific Revolutions* (Kuhn, 1962); that is, as a pendulum that is moving between two poles that roughly correspond to Snow's two cultures when the moves from one pole to the other take the form of what Kuhn has termed "paradigm shifts" and what students of complexity call *phase transition*. At one pole, we see scholars that approach the city from the perspective of the sciences with their scientific methods, attempting to develop *a science of cities*, while at the other, studies that approach cities from the perspective of the humanities and social philosophy with hermeneutics as their major methodological tool.

The central thesis in the above studies is that complexity theory has the potential to bridge this gap. In that article the emphasis was on human geography and on cities; in the present paper the emphasis is on planning – urban, regional and environmental planning. More specifically, in what follows I show that similarly to cities the history of planning can be interpreted in terms of Snow's two cultures (§ 5.1). Next I explore the current and potential relations between complexity theory and planning (§ 5.2). Finally, I explicate hitherto implicit links between complexity theories and social theory oriented urbanism and planning (§ 5.3). The chapter concludes with a suggestion to reformulate planning theory.

5.1 The two cultures of planning

The Snow-Kuhn conjunction

On May 7, 1959 the British scientist and novelist C. P. Snow delivered the Rade Lecture in the Senate house, Cambridge with the title *The Two Cultures*. The

---

1   This chapter is based on a concise compilation of Chaps. 1, 12, 15 in Portugali (2011).

2   Juval Portugali is Professor of Human Geography at the Department of Geography and the Human Environment, Tel-Aviv University. He is Head of the ESLab (Environmental Simulation Laboratory) at the Tel-Aviv University.

central thesis of his talk was that the breakdown of communication between the "two cultures" – the culture of the sciences and the culture of the humanities and "literary intellectuals" – is a major hindrance to solving the world problems. A few years later he reiterated and elaborated his thesis in a short monograph entitled *The Two Cultures and a Second Look* (Snow, 1964).

Snow's thesis is interesting because while his observation about the gap between the sciences and humanities was not a new revelation – as he himself was the first to admit (Yee, 1993), the influence of his *two cultures* was tremendous. To my mind the reason for the strong impact was due to his suggestion to look at science and scientific differences not from the point of view of logic but from the perspective of cultures. Scientists, he implied, are not just logical-thinking entities, as it is common to portray them and as they often tend portray themselves, but first and foremost human beings that similarly to humans in general tend to conform with the cultures to which they belong – a view that appears also in another influential work – *The Structure of Scientific Revolutions* by Kuhn (1962).

Kuhn, "was deeply impressed by Snow's thesis" (Andresen, 1999), and he "constituted his theory about scientific revolutions as a version of the 'two cultures'" (Westman, 1994). Kuhn added to Snow's cultural interpretation of science the notion that science evolves not linearly and gradually, but by means of revolutions – a view that reminds one of the notion of "punctuated equilibrium" (Gould 1980) and of course of complexity theory's central notions such as *bifurcation, phase transition* and *self-organization* (see below).

Prior to Snow and Kuhn, studies about the philosophy of science centered on the question of the appropriate scientific method. The controversy between the logical positivism's notion of *verification* and Karl Popper's principle of *falsification* as formulated by him in his *The Logic of Scientific Discovery* (Popper, 1959), is a famous example. Snow's and Kuhn's theses have added the view that cultures play a central role in science and research. As noted in the above article (Portugali, 2006), cultures come into existence spontaneously, by means of self organization, by emphasizing common values, norms and material goods shared by their members and by emphasizing and often exaggerating the differences between their common elements and those of other groups. Cultures survive by the process of *cultural reproduction* – the process that routinely and daily produces and reproduces the common (often exaggerated) elements that unite the group's members as well as the differences between them and other groups (Giddens, 1997).

Snow's and Kuhn's perception of scientific communities in terms of cultures implies that scientists are no exception in this respect – they are first and foremost human beings and as such tend to form cultural groups by emphasizing and often exaggerating the common elements that unite them and those that separate them from other groups, by forming stereotypes of themselves and of the others and so on.

The two cultures of cities

During the first half of the 20th century, "quantitative" and "qualitative" studies of cities developed in parallel: On the one hand we see "soft" humanistic studies such as Mumford's *The City in History* (Mumford, 1961), or Wirth's "Urbanism as a way of life" (Wirth, 1938), or the notion of *regional geography* as developed in urban geography, while on the other, quantitative studies such as Auerbach's inductive study of the size distribution of cities (Auerbach, 1913), Christaller's (Christaller, 1933/1966) and Lösch's (Lösch, 1954) central place theories, spatial interaction models and the like.

In the 1950s we see a split – a *quantitative revolution*. It was a revolution not because the proponents of this move invented the scientific approach to cities but because as part of their effort to convey their quantitative message they have strongly criticized and even de-legitimized the scientific validity of what they have described as descriptive, non-analytical and therefore non-scientific approaches. This criticism entailed an almost unbridgeable gap between the quantitative vs. the descriptive studies – very much in line with Snow's two cultures.

The quantitative paradigm dominated the field of urban research during most of the 1950s and 1960s just to be replaced, in the early 1970s, by social theory oriented urban studies. As in the days of the quantitative revolution here too, this move took the form of a "revolution" when proponents of the new paradigm started to strongly criticize the positivistic-quantitative approach. They did so from two main points of view: from a Structuralist Marxist perspective and from a phenomenological idealistic perspective. The result of this second revolution was that the gap between the two cultures of urban studies further widened with all the ingredients indicated by Snow and by cultures in general: a breakdown of communication, emphasis and exaggeration of differences between the cultures, stereotypic images of the other and a process of cultural reproduction that reinforces and safeguards the differences.

In the last two decades we see two parallel developments: The social theory oriented Structuralist, Marxist and Humanistic (SMH) urban studies have adopted postmodern, poststructuralist and deconstruction approaches, while the quantitative urban sciences were strongly influenced by theories of complexity and self-organization.

Utopian planning – The first hermeneutic culture of planning

Similarly to cities, one can describe the history of planning in terms of a pendulum that is moving between two poles that correspond to Snow's two cultures: a qualitative descriptive *study* of city/urban/regional/environmental planning, versus a quantitative analytic *science* of (city/urban/regional/environmental) planning or *regional science* as it is often called. In the first half of the 20th century the domain of planning was dominated by the hermeneutic-descriptive culture of planning. Peter Hall (1975/2002) has described the style of planning during these years as *utopian planning*. By that he meant that influential planners such as Howard and Corbusier directed their energies to produce future visions, i.e. utopias, of cities. The notion of "utopia" often comes with a negative connotation (specifically in Marxist thought) something unrealistic; yet this was not the case with utopian planning. Some of its utopias, such as the "garden city" or the concept of 'green belt' became rather influential and have shaped the form and structure of 20th century cities.

The 'rational comprehensive' as the first scientific culture of planning

As just noted, the first quantitative-analytic-scientific culture of cities has developed in the 1950s and 1960s. Hand in hand with this development emerged also the "rational comprehensive" culture of planning, when the division of labour between the two is in line with Faludi's distinction between *theory of planning* and *theory in planning* (Faludi, 1973a; Faludi, 1973b). The science of cities was to supply the theory in planning with an insight about the development and structure of the city and the way it should scientifically and rationally be, whereas 'the rational comprehensive' was the favourable planning theory, that is, the planning procedure which will enable to plan and implement the good city in an efficient and rational way.

As illustrated in some details by Camhis the rational comprehensive planning theory and practice was an attempt to apply the so-called *scientific method* to the domain of planning (Camhis, 1979). At the basis of both was the positivist mechanistic logical-deductive scientific method. During the 1950s and 1960s planning has been transformed from intellectual-humanistic and somewhat utopian endeavour into a formal scientific university discipline that similarly to other such disciplines (engineering, economics…) produces researchers, theoreticians as well as practitioners. As with the scientific culture of cities so with the scientific culture of planning, by the end 1960s and early 1970s came the disillusionment from both the first scientific culture of cities and its associated first scientific culture of planning. In *Self-Organization and the City* (Portugali, 2000) we've referred to this process of disillusionment as the "first planning dilemma" and described it in the following words:

> it became evident that "rational comprehensive planning" [...] is an irrational assumption, that planning is a political, incremental [...] and essentially 'non-scientific' and non-technical process; it became apparent that [...] [the] spectacular scientific instruments we've developed fail to tame the city, the metropolis, the megalopolis, the environment [...], that beautiful scientific instruments such as the gravity, interaction, or entropy maximization models [...] can hardly scratch the complexity of the urban scenario, and that so are the 'rent bid curves' of [...] urban land use theory, and the 'factorial ecology' of Chicago's 'urban ecology' and the 'location triangle' of [...] industrial location theory, and the hexagonal geometrical landscapes of [...] 'central place theory'.

> All this scientific – mathematical arsenal seemed "incapable of saying anything of depth and profundity about [the real problem of society and][...] when we do say something, it appears trite and rather indecorous.

In retrospect it can be observed that the doubts about the rationality of the rational comprehensive started already in the end 1950s and early 1960s – during the high days of the first science of planning – when students of planning such as Lindblom (1959) or Davidoff (1965) started to question the approach. Theirs, however, was a "constructive criticism from within"; the aim of Lindblom with his *incremental planning* and Davidoff's with his *advocacy planning* was not to altogether reject the *raison d'être* of the rational-comprehensive approach to planning but rather to correct and improve it. Thus, Lindblom added to the rational comprehensive a politically more realistic twist, and Davidoff a more democratic one. This is evident, to my mind, from the fact that their papers appeared as chapters in Faludi's (1973) *A Reader in Planning Theory* – Lindblom in Part II entitled "Toward a comprehensive planning" while Davidoff in Part IV on "Bureaucrats, advocates, innovators". The all out attack on the first science of planning came at a later stage, in the early 1970s, when scholars such as David Harvey and Manuel Castells started to criticize it from a structuralist-Marxist standpoint and others from a phenomenological-idealistic standpoint. Unlike Lindblom's and Davidoff's critisizms, they criticized its very foundations.

SMH planning as the second hermeneutic culture of planning

The above disillusionment from the first science of cities and planning was one of the forces behind the "qualitative revolution" of the early 1970s that took place in the domains of urban studies, urban geography and urban and regional planning; a revolution that was dominated by social theory oriented approaches, in particular by *structuralist-Marxist and humanistic* (SMH) critical views on urbanism and planning (Portugali, 2000). Two lines of thought emerged out of the SMH approaches with respect to a "theory of the city" and a "planning theory of the city". One was the humanistic approach whose central message was *awareness*: humanistic studies of cities, so it was believed, will expose the significance of cities to the subjectivity and individuality of people, will distinguish between *place and placelessness* (Relph, 1976) as well as between "place cities" and "placelessness cities". The cumulative effect of this discourse about the qualitative aspects of cities and landscapes will eventually enter the awareness planners and architects when they are practically working in and on cities.

The Marxist-structuralist stand was to altogether reject the distinction between theory in planning and theory of planning as ideological false consciousness, with the implication that both the rational comprehensive planning theory and the above naive humanistic stand, are but part of the superstructure – integral element in the overall socio-spatial structure of the modern capitalistic city. As a consequence, any genuine change in planning is conditioned by a total transformation – a revolution – in the structure of society. Despite their good will, claimed Marxist critics, the planners are structurally doomed to play to the hands of the politicians, the ruling classes and the multi-nationals that control *the system*.

No one can deny the important contribution of the SMH criticism of planning and the deep insight gained by the SMH approaches. On the other hand, however, it entailed a dilemma, as it was not accompanied by any practical suggestion to the practice of planning. In *Self-Organization and the City* (Portugali, ibid.) we've termed this situation the second planning dilemma and described it as follows:

> ... what are you to do with the SMH insight when as a planner you have to make a decision about urban renewal, or road networks; what would you say? Start talking about base and superstructure? The labour-process? How this beautiful theoretical insight becomes praxis? Gradually it became evident that SMH planning discourse and research is remote from reality and social relevance even more than positivism. Thus, since the mid 80s, we hear once again the very same question: "how can we account ..."; but this time not only for the coexistence of great scientific achievements, on the one hand, and the failure to apply them to society, on the other hand, but also "how can we account for the failure of the alternatives".

The catch of the kitsch

The result was a kind of a split in the domain of planning by which the practice of planning is dominated by the rational comprehensive approach while the theory of, and discourse on, planning by SMH planning approaches. This general state of dissonance between theory and practice and the inability of modernist SMH planning approaches to practically guide action, was one of the grounds upon which the postmodern view of cities and planning originated. As with postmodernism in general, so with respect to urbanism and planning, postmodern urbanism and planning have transformed the above dissonance and disillusionment from modernist ideologists, to an ideological platform.

On the face of it the new vision of postmodernism sounds highly desirable and creative: an ever-changing reality, ever changing and ever moving city. However, the reality of the postmodern condition shows that there is a catch here – *the catch of the kitsch*: The most prominent example is in architecture and the urban landscape: Indeed the postmodern architectural style started with free and creative quotations from the ancient past and from futurist visions of buildings and architecture but very quickly it turned into a uniform style – into a kind of neo-conservatism – into the very opposite of what postmodernism advocated for. This dissonance between the decided intentions and the daily praxis forms the deadlock of postmodernist city of the 1990s and the first aspect of what we have described (Portugali, ibid.) as the third planning dilemma:

You can't tame, plan, engineer, the environment, since you are trapped in its chaos, and you cannot participate in its chaotic play since you are trapped in its structure, fashion and style.

Planning in Crisis? is a recent book by Schönwandt in which he responds to the title of his book in the affirmative, suggesting that urban planning and design are in crisis as a consequence of a growing gap between theory and practice (Schönwandt, 2008) – very similar to what I've referred to above as the three planning dilemmas.

Planning and the new urban reality

While postmodernism had immediate effect on architecture and urban design, its impact on city and urban planning started to be felt at a later stage when postmodernism was interpreted as a phenomenon of late capitalism associated with technological changes, on the one hand and the social, economic and political processes of globalization, multi culturalism, the decline of the welfare state and the rise of civil society, on the other. Of specific influence here were the studies by authors such as David Harvey (Harvey, 1989) *The Condition of Postmodernity: An Enquiry into the Origins of Cultural Change*, or Castells (Castells, 1996) *The Rise of the Network Society*.

These interpretations acted as an impetus to the emergence of several responses that currently dominate discourse in the domain of planning, namely, the communicative approach (Healey, 2007), strategic urban planning, governance and the New Urbanism. While the first two respond mainly to social changes of the last decades (globalization, civil society, etc) and are thus more related to the process of planning and planning policies, New Urbanism is more related to urban design and architecture and the physical structure of cities.

5.2 Complexity theories of cities: first, second or third culture of planning?

And what about complexity theories and more specifically complexity theories of cities (CTC)? What do they have to say about urbanism and planning in the 21st Century? On the one hand, the reality of 21st century – of highly connected global society, major and fast changes in world society – almost invites looking at it from the perspective of complexity theory. And indeed, some of the aspects of 21st society and cities are often described in terms taken from the language of complexity theories and CTC: A most prominent example is Castells' (1996) *The Rise of the Network Society* and his notions of *space of flow* and *information city* (Castells, 1989). A more recent example is Healey's book *Urban Complexity and Spatial Strategy* (Healey, 2007). However, both Castells and Healey are using the notions "complexity" and "network" literally without the theoretical formalism and meaning added to it by complexity theory. In fact, in Healey's book there is not even a single reference to complexity theory.

My view is that CTC have a lot to say about the 21st city and can suggest interesting insight to the current discourse and debate of planning. The fact is, however, that so far it has said very little about the 21st century city and its specific properties and close to nothing about planning. Most researchers in the domain of CTC preferred and still prefer to focus on rather traditional, conservative and somewhat anachronistic urban issues: central place theory, land use, rank-size distributions of cities, national systems of cities and the like – issues that were dominant in the 1950s and 1960s. However, in order to see the wider implications of CTC to cities and planning we have first to shortly introduce them.

Complexity theory – a concise introduction

In the last three decades we see the emergence of a whole domain of studies that is commonly referred to as *complexity theory*. The notion complexity theory is an umbrella name to a set of theories that refer to systems that are open in the sense that they exchange matter and information with their environment and complex in the sense that their parts form a complex network with complex feedback and feedforward loops. Such systems commonly exhibit phenomena of chaos and fractal structure, abrupt phase transitions from chaos to order and visa versa, emerging new properties, and all these spontaneously, that is to say, by means of *self-organization* (Portugali, 2011).

Several Complexity and Self-Organization theories have been suggested since the emergence of this paradigm in the 1960s. They differ in their mathematical formalism and also in the properties and processes they emphasize: Based on the latter we can identify two types of theories (Figure 5.1): comprehensive complexity theories and emergence complexity theories.

Comprehensive complexity theories are the founding theories, namely, Prigogine's theory of *dissipative structures* (Nicolis and Prigogine, 1977; Prigogine and Stengers, 1984), Haken's theory of *synergetics* (Haken, 1983; Haken, 1987) and to some extent also Bak's *self-organized criticality* (Bak and Chen, 1991). They are "comprehensive" in the sense that they refer to all stages of the evolution of such systems: the bottom-up process of *emergence* that brings complex systems into a global ordered state and the process of *steady state* that keeps them is a structurally stable state. Of the latter, Haken's *synergetics* is the most comprehensive one due to its emphasis on circular causality, that is to say, the feedback process by which the system enslaves the parts that brought it into being in the first place.

Emergence complexity theories limit their focus of interest to the process of emergence, that is, the bottom-up process by which local interaction between the parts gives rise to a global structure. These theories tend to ignore the conditions and dynamics of the steady state stage that keeps the system in a structurally stable

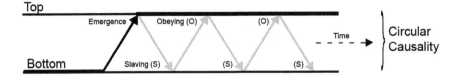

Figure 5.1   Comprehensive complexity theories (*top*) follow the long-
term evolution of complex systems: the bottom-up process of
emergence, the steady state and the top-down impact of the
global system on the local parts of the system. Emergence
complexity theories (*bottom*), per contra, focus only on the
bottom-up part of the above process

Source: Portuali 2011, Figure 4.2

state for long periods. Mandelbrot's theory of fractals is of this nature and so are
cellular automata, agent base and network simulation models.

Complexity theories of cities (CTC)

Most theories of complexity have been applied to cities with the implication that
there now exists a research domain that I suggested calling *CTC – complexity
theories of cities* (Portugali, 2011). However, while probably all complexity
theories have been applied to the domain of cities, the kind of theories that
seems to be most dominant in current CTC are the emergence theories with agent
base (AB) and cellular automata (CA) urban simulation models being the most
dominant ones.

In two recent studies (Portugali, 2000, 2011) an attempt has been made not
just to *apply* but rather to *adapt* complexity theory to cities. That is, to take into
consideration not only the similarities but also the differences between cities and
material systems such as the Bénard cells or the LASER. The most important
property that differentiates between material complex systems and cities is that
cities are *dual complex, self-organizing systems*: In the case of the LASER, for
instance, the parts (atoms, molecules...) are simple systems and complexity is a
property of the global system only. In the case of cities, the city as a whole is
a complex system and also each of its elementary parts – the urban agents – is

a complex system too. More specifically, urban agents (e.g. individual humans, households, firms...) are cognitively and physically complex and this property must be taken into consideration when studying cities and when simulating their dynamics. From here follows a need for a cognitive approach to cities and urban simulation modelling (Portugali, 2004, 2011).

Potentially speaking, CTC have two messages to deliver to planning theory and practice in the age of postmodernity and globalization; the first is quantitative and the second qualitative. According to the first, CTC is seen as the second scientific culture of cities that similarly to the first culture, attempts to transform the study of cities and city planning into a science. According to the second, CTC indeed originated in the "hard" sciences and are thus genuinely "hard" scientific theories, but at the same time they share many properties with the "soft", hermeneutic, social theory oriented approaches. This dual nature has the potential to make CTC a bridge between the two cultures of cities and the two cultures of planning. Let me elaborate.

CTC: the quantitative message

How is CTC related to the above moving pendulum between the two cultures of planning? On the face of it the answer is apparent: complexity theory originated in the sciences, was applied to cities by scientists – physicists such as Peter Allen, student of Prigogine (Allen, 1981), and Wolfgang Weidlich, a colleague of Haken (Weidlich, 1994), – and was enthusiastically adopted by "quantitative" students of urbanism. It is therefore not surprising that so far the main message delivered by CTC to planning is essentially quantitative and can be formulated as follows:

Indeed world society is becoming connected, society is becoming a "network society" (Castells, 1996) but the factors and forces that made our cities and system of cities more complex than ever before also provide us with the key to the solution: The last two decades have witnessed a dramatic progress in information and communication technologies. These technological changes indeed changed society but at the same time opened new possibilities. In the domain of cities and planning these new technologies created new potentials we urbanists and planners never had before: GISs that can easily control and process huge amounts of information, virtual reality (VR) software that allow us to build virtual cities and regions and move in them in real time, cell-phones combined with GPS not only increase communication but also allow real-time monitoring of pedestrian and car movements in urban areas, and finally the new sophisticated urban simulation models (USMs) backed as they are by the theory of complexity allow us to study the dynamics of cities as complex systems.

Each of the above systems is by itself a strong planning tool and if we combine them together into an integrative comprehensive system we get a planning support system (PSS) and/or decision support system (DSS) that is more than the sum of its elementary parts. This is, in fact, the idea behind the DSSs and PSSs that are currently advocated as the state-of-the-art of the new, second science of planning (Brail and Klosterman, 2001; Brail, 2006).

A standard PSS is a three-part system composed of a set of simulation models – usually agent based (AB) and/or cellular automata (CA) – a Geographical Information System (GIS) and a set of 2D, 3D and VR visualization devices (to which one can add a monitoring system based on GPS, etc). The AB/CA simulation models are assumed to enable the planners to simulate future scenarios representing current trends, and also to envision the impact of various plans and policies; the GIS provides the data base for such scenarios, the monitoring system provides real time information and feedback, while the visualization systems provide the means to practically see the results. A case in point is a planning support system (called *O'Jerusalem*) that was specifically designed to deal with the planning of, and legal controversies over, the wall that is being planned and built between the Israeli and Palestinian parts of Jerusalem (Portugali et al, 2009).

The enthusiasm currently surrounding PSS is reminiscent of the excitement that followed the appearance in the 1950s and 1960s of the rational comprehensive planning and its arsenal of quantitative planning tools. "This is an exciting time for simulation modeling and visualization tools in planning and public policy," writes Brail (2006) and continues: "Planning support systems (PSS) have moved from concept to application. Is this future so bright … ?"

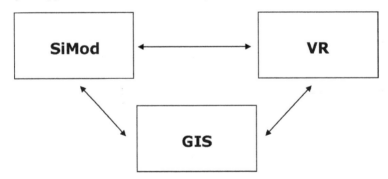

Figure 5.2   A typical Planning Support System (PSS) is composed of three components: A set of urban simulation models. GIS and a visualization device such as virtual reality (VR).

Source: Portgali 2011, Figure 12.1

CTC: the qualitative message

But there is another message complexity theory has for planning and it goes like this: Indeed complexity theory originated in the sciences and CTC is therefore a science of cities, but complexity theory is a new kind of science referring to systems and phenomena never explicitly studied before – open, complex, far from equilibrium systems that exhibit phenomena such as chaos, fractal structure, non-causality, non-linearity self-organization and the like. Such systems are *qualitatively* different from the systems studies by the first, scientific culture of cities. The latter, as noted, treated cities as simple, closed, entropic, equilibrium-tending, linear systems. In a recent article (Portugali, 2008) I've suggested calling the latter *classical* theories of cities and the first complex or non-classical theories of cities (a distinction that echoes the terminology in physics).

Classical systems are in principle simple, closed, predictable and causal. They might be highly complicated, but still simple in the sense that given all initial conditions, one can establish causal relations between their parts and predict their future state. Wrong prediction in such systems is the result of insufficient data or information about initial conditions. Complex systems are in principle unpredictable – given all initial conditions the future is still unpredictable. This is due to the property on nonlinearity, which in its turn is the result of the property of complexity. In what follow I illustrate the first by the story of "the butterfly effect of Tel-Aviv balconies", and the second, by studying the lessons of several planning paradoxes.

The butterfly effect of Tel Aviv balconies and its implications

From its early days in the early 1920s the city of Tel Aviv has been a city of many balconies. People used to spend long hours sitting on their balconies, especially on summer evenings and nights. One day, probably at the end 1950s, an un-known resident of Tel Aviv decided to enlarge his/her apartment by closing the balcony and making it a "half-room." He/she made a small plan, hired a builder and implemented the plan. One of the neighbours liked idea and did the same. A process of innovation diffusion started – very much in line with Hägerstrand's theory (Hägerstrand, 1967) – and before long the vast majority of balconies in the whole country was closed (Figure 5.3, right). At this stage, the municipalities decided to intervene and started to tax all balconies as if they are a regular room. In response, developers started to build buildings with closed balconies (Figure 5.3 center). For several years no balconies were built in Tel Aviv and other Israeli cities. But then, with the arrival of postmodern architecture, balconies became fashionable and architects started to apply for permits to build balconies – not to seat on them, as in the past, but as a decorative element. Equipped with their past planning experience and the wish not to lag behind the advancing (post)modern style, the city planners gave architects and developers permits to build open balconies but in a way that would not allow them to be closed as in the past. The result is the "jumping balconies" so typical nowadays in Israel's urban landscape (Figure 5.3).

A comparative empirical study on "urban pattern recognition," which took place in the early 1990s at Tel Aviv University and involved cities from Europe, America and East Asia, found that the most prototypical architectural patterns in the cityscape of Israel are one: the closed balcony, and two: the jumping balcony (Reuven-Zafrir, Not published).

Figure 5.3   Tel Aviv Balconies

Source: Portgali, 2011, Figure 15.1

The story of Tel Aviv balconies illustrates three aspects of the relations between CTC and planning. The first aspect concerns the property of non-linearity by which the planned action of a single person might have a much stronger and significant impact on the urban landscape than the plans of architects and official planners. The second aspect concerns the planning implications of the specific nature of cities as dual complex self-organized systems. Applied to planning, cities as dual complex systems imply that each urban agent is a planner at certain scale and that planning is a basic cognitive capability of humans (Portugali, 2011 and further bibliography there). From these two properties follows a new view on the dynamics of cities: The common view is to see the city as a complex system that comes into being out of the interaction between its many agents, and planning as an external force acting on the system – say, by means of new planning policies. From what has been said above follows a new view according to which each agent is a planner – be it a single individual, a firm or the city's planning team – and the city comes into being out of the interaction between the many agents *and their plans*. Similarly to small-scale urban agents/planners, the official planners are participants in the overall urban game.

Forms of planning

One outcome from the above is a twofold distinction between forms of planning: On the one hand, a distinction between top-down, *global planning* versus bottom-up, *local planning*. The first refers to a planning process executed by professionals – city planners, architects, engineers, etc. – that tend to deal with the city as a whole, while the second to planning acts executed by non-professionals (individuals, firms…) that tend to act locally by virtue of the fact that planning is a basic human capability (Portugali, ibid). On the other hand, a distinction between *mechanistic* or *engineered* or *entropic planning* versus *self-organized planning* can be recognized. The first refers to a relatively simple "closed system" planning process, closed in the sense that it is, or rather should be, fully controlled. The second refers to a relatively complex "open system" planning process, which like other open and complex systems exhibits phenomena of non-linearity, chaos, bifurcation and self-organization. The planning of a bridge or a building is an example of the first form of planning, while a city plan is an example of the second.

The above forms of planning are related to each other in the following way: On the one hand, there are certain planning activities that unless they are fully (or almost fully) controlled they would not be attempted at all. In other words, unless one can create a closed system for them one would not attempt to implement them. For example, one would not build a bridge or a building unless one can "close the system", at least temporarily, and thus have full control on the outcome, namely, that the bridge will not collapse. On the other hand, in a self-organized planning system such a requirement doesn't exist, for instance, when making a city plan. In the latter case once the city plan is completed and implemented, the story just begins – it triggers a complex and unpredictable dynamics that no one fully controls. This is true with respect to master plans, development plans and other forms of large-scale city planning, but it is also true for the global effect and role of small-scale plans implemented in the city: the effect of a new building or a bridge on the urban system as a whole is neither predictable nor controllable. Similarly to large-scale plans, they become participants in the urban self-organized planning game.

The co-existence of global and local forms of planning sheds new light on the notion of "public participation in planning". The latter is based on an implicit assumption that there exists only one form of planning – global planning, and, as a consequence, on a sharp dichotomy between the planners and the planned. Public participation is the outcome of a common view among planners that in order for planning to be more democratic and just, planners have to give more say to people, above and beyond the say given them via the standard political process.

The fact that global and local planning co-exist and interact in the dynamics of cities, and that in many cases local planning can be more dominant and effective in the overall urban process than global planning, implies that it must be perceived not as a reactive force, but an important source for planning ideas and initiatives. The role of public participation and planning democracy are thus not just to be more generous to the people affected by the planning, but also to allow the huge amount of planning energy to go bottom-up.

Planning paradoxes and the limits of prediction

AB and CA simulation models are presently suggested as a means to simulate cities as complex self-organizing systems and as means to predict future urban scenarios. This is their main role in the context of PSS, as we have just seen.

But there is a problem here that can be described as the *prediction paradox* of self-organizing systems, in general, and of cities in particular. There are three interrelated facets for this paradox. First, the nonlinearities that typify cities imply that one cannot establish predictive cause-effect relationships between some of the variables. Second, many of the triggers for change in complex systems have the nature of mutations. As such, they are unpredictable, not because of lack of data, but because of their very nature. Third, unlike closed systems, in complex systems, the observer, with his/her actions and predictions, is part of the system. In such a situation, predictions are essentially feed-forward loops in the system, important factors that affect the system and its future evolution with some interesting implications that include *self-fulfilling* and *self-falsifying* or *self-defeating* predictions.

The above findings are taken from the summary to a recent paper "Learning from paradoxes about prediction and planning in self-organizing cities" (Portugali, 2008). The paper employs the ancient methodology of paradoxes as means to show that predictions in the context of cities often lead to paradoxes that are the result of the complexity of cities. This is illustrated by studying in some details several imaginary and real planning scenarios.

From the above follows a twofold question: what is the role of urban simulation models and what is the role of planning in the unpredictable urban situation that is implied by CTC? Firstly, when using urban simulation models we have to be aware that "the map is not the territory," namely, that our models are not one-to-one representations of reality but tools that allow us to study some aspects of it. While such tools cannot predict the evolution of cities they can still give us some indications as to the probabilities of the city evolving along certain courses if its current structure and current conditions remain the same. Given the fact that once self-organized, cities tend to be in a steady state and that these steady state periods are relatively long, such information is significant to the various urban agents acting in the city as top-down professional or bottom-up latent planners.

Furthermore: urban simulation models can be useful devices for what has been described as an "Artificial planning experience" (Portugali, 2000). According to this view the aim of these models is not to predict the future but rather to enable planners and decision makers to artificially experience a certain planning phenomenon is a relatively short period of time. An urban simulation model can thus be seen as a heuristic planning tool with which the planner can play, learn the various facets of the situation, acquire (artificial) experience and understanding and as a consequence be in a better position to take decisions intuitively. The rationale behind this suggestion is the distinction between "explanation" and "understanding". If explanation is a process, which seeks to identify the laws and common denominators for a multiplicity of phenomena, than, understanding is a process that seeks to expose their variability and uniqueness. If explanation is gained by analysis then understanding is gain by experience. In other words, we see urban simulation models as planning simulators that similarly to flight or driving simulators can artificially improve (though not replace) experience.

As for the second part of the question that concerns the role and meaning of planning in an un-predictable reality – I'll respond to it bellow at the end of § 5.3. In order to do so, however, we have first to explore the relations between CTC and social theory oriented urban theories.

5.3 CTC and social theory oriented urban theory and planning

As noted above, proponents of CTC are sympathetic with the first science of cities and implicitly or explicitly regard themselves as belonging to the first culture of cities and planning as the new, more sophisticated, science of cities and urban planning. What they often fail to see, however, is that CTC has two significant interfaces with the second culture of cities, namely, with SMH (structuralist Marxist and humanistic) and Postmodern cities. Firstly, similarly to social theory oriented urbanism CTC is critical of classical urbanism and planning. Secondly and related to the above, CTC perceive the urban process in a way similar to social theory oriented urban studies.

Implicit criticism

CTC never explicitly criticised classical urbanism and yet the criticism is there, implicit in the very logic of CTC: Classical theories of cities and planning assume that cities are essentially closed systems and that as such tend toward a state of equilibrium (e.g. the classical location theories of Thünen, Weber, Christaller and Lösch and their followers) and maximum entropy (e.g. Allen Wilson's family of entropy maximization models – Wilson, 1970). CTC per contra assume that cities are essentially open systems and as such are in a "far from equilibrium condition", "on the edge of chaos", and thus tend toward *negative entropy* or *negentropy* – a term suggested to indicate a process that is the exact opposite of entropy (Schrödinger, 1946). Furthermore, classical urbanism and planning theory pre-supposes that cities are essentially predictable and as such controllable and planable (e.g. the rational comprehensive planning approach); CTC as we've just seen implies the exact opposite.

Needless to stress that the above criticism has yet to be fully elaborated and spelled out; its essence, however, is apparent. It is also apparent that by overlooking this criticism proponents of CTC often tend to treat "their" complex, self-organizing cities as if they were classical systems – in the case of PSS, for instance.

As we've seen above, social theory oriented urban studies and planning are critical of classical urbanism for applying to cities positivism – the quantitative scientific method that was originally developed for the study of matter and mechanistic phenomena. They claim that the human domain is fundamentally different from the domain of nature and as a consequence the application of the scientific approach to the study of cities and the practice of planning leads to reductionism; in the human domain they suggest, the "soft" hermeneutic approaches are therefore more appropriate. Marxists further claim that positivism with its rational comprehensive planning approaches is not just inappropriate approach mistakenly applied to the human domain but an ideological false consciousness that obscures people's view from their real state of existence in an unjust capitalist social structure.

CTC agree with social theory oriented urban studies that the human-urban domain is different and that therefore applying the classical approaches to the human domain of cities leads to reductionism and misconception of the urban process, and, that the specific structure of society and the city must be taken into consideration when studying cities. But they agree on the above for a different reason: the complexity of the system. Classical urban theorists and planners have treated the city as simple and classical and yet it is complex and non-classical. In fact, as implied by Batty (Batty, 2008), the message was on the wall already in the 1960s – for example, in the writing of Jane Jacobs (Jacobs, 1961) and Christopher Alexander (Alexander, 1965) who have perceived cities as complex systems several years before formal complexity theory came to the fore. But classical urbanists failed or rather were not able to respond to these new ideas because they were part of, and enslaved by, the first culture of cities.

Similarities

In several previous studies I've indicated the similarities between complexity theory and social theory (Portugali, 1985; Portugali, 2006); here is a short summary. As noted above, the various complexity theories have originated in the sciences – in the study of matter. However, one of the interesting aspects of these theories is that they have found properties in matter hitherto assigned to the organic and human domains, including history, evolution, irreversibility, nonlinearity (Portugali, 1985). It is therefore not surprising that several of the basic notions of complexity can be related to parallel notions that originated in the domain of social theory.

Thus, both complexity theory and social theory are essentially systemic and even holistic. Complexity theory rejects atomism, and social theory refuses to conceptualize society in terms of essentially independent disciplines (economics, sociology, politics etc.). Furthermore, both theoretical domains tend to conceptualize "development" and "evolution" in terms of abrupt changes rather then a smooth progression and in both we therefore find an emphasis on structural changes. In social theory the common term for an abrupt change is (social/political/cultural) "revolution", while in the language of complexity theory one tends to speak about "bifurcations" and "phase transitions" (Gould and Eldredge coined the term *punctuated equilibrium* suggesting that biological evolution too proceeds as a sequence of abrupt changes – see Gould, 1980). The complexity theory's notion of "steady state" is similar to social theory's notions of "epoch", "period" or "mode of production". The last is similar to synergetics' notion of "order parameter", while synergetics' notions of "enslavement" and "circular causality" as conceptualized by Haken (1983), are close to social theory's notions of "social reproduction" and "socio-spatial reproduction" as conceptualized by Lefebvre (Lefebvre, 1995) or Giddens (Giddens, 1984). In a similar way postmodernism's and post-structuralism's recent emphasis on viewing reality as ever changing and transforming is close to the social theory's notion of "a far from equilibrium condition" which is the basic characteristic of complexity theory. The latter similarity is to my mind one of the reason for the general popularity, among postmodern and deconstruction writers, of complexity theory's notions such as "chaos" and "butterfly effect".

The self-organization of communicative planning

The above similarities provided the basis for my claim that complexity theory can provide a link between space and place, that is, between the two cultures of cities (Portugali, 2006). Can the same be said about the two cultures of city planning? Put in other words: Communicative and strategic planning approaches that currently dominate planning discourse are seen as the planning counterpart of the critical urban studies and as a response to the postmodern urban condition of globalization, the decline of the welfare state and the rise of strong civil society. Can there be links between CTC and social theory oriented planning similar to the links discussed above?

The answer to my mind is positive: In his book *A Sociological Theory of Communication: The Self-Organization of the Knowledge-Based Society*, Loet Leydesdorff (Leydesdorff, 2001) makes an explicit link between Giddens' theory of structuration (Giddens, 1984), Luhman's perception of society as a self-organizing system and Habermas' communicative action (Habermas, 1984; Habermas, 1987; Habermas, 1990). In line with this view I suggest similar relations between self-organization and communicative planning, namely, that complexity and self-organization theories provide a theory to the way communicative planning discourse is evolving.

Some indications that this is indeed the case emerge from our recent study (Portugali and Alfasi, 2008) on planning discourse analysis, in which we show that planning discourse evolves by means of self-organization as a synergetic inter-representation network (SIRN).[3] This theoretical-empirical study followed closely, by means of participatory observation, the discourse of a small planning team that was assigned to plan the city of Beer Sheva, Israel. What is striking about this case study is that the planning team conducted its activities in line with the rational planning approach and yet, despite their intentions the real process of planning evolved as a self-organized SIRN process. What this study indicates is that discourse is central to planning, including to the rational comprehensive approach, that planning discourse evolves by means of self-organization and that there exist

_____

3   SIRN is a complexity theory derived approach developed by Portugali and Haken to deal with cognitive mapping, on the one hand, and urban dynamics on the other (Haken and Portugali, 1996; Portugali, 1996; Portugali, 2002).

an interesting potential (that has yet to be elaborated and realized) of linking complexity/self-organization theory with the communicative planning approach.

The ethical dimension of CTC

But the potential link between complexity theories oriented planning and social theory oriented planning goes beyond self-organized communicative planning. The latter commences with an ethical message suggesting that this form of planning implies a more democratic and just planning process and practice. This is so since it gives a central role to the various NGOs that compose civil society. The idea is that these organizations are genuine representatives of society so that their active participation in the planning discourse gives a stronger say to sections of society hitherto not represented. Communicative planning is not specific about the planning framework within which the communicative discourse should take place. From recent studies it seems that strategic planning is regarded as the favourable approach for this purpose. Central to the strategic planning approach is the determination of the future *vision of a city* as the locomotive that carry the planning process. According to communicative planning the active participation of the various civil society organizations in the discourse that determines the urban vision will lead to a more democratic and just planning.

Complexity theory originated in the sciences with no explicit ethical message and as a consequence CTC commonly come with a self-image of a scientific and thus objective and ethically neutral approaches. My claim is that the extension of the theory to the human domain and to cities does enfold an implicit ethical message that I'll try to explicate. The latter follows from our observation that each urban agent is a planner at a certain scale and that due to nonlinearities the planning actions and ideas of single individuals can be as influential as plans and actions of the city's planning team. In other words, from the point of view of CTC there is no qualitative difference between large-scale formal planning institutions such as governmental or municipal planning bodies, medium-size planning organizations such as NGOs and small-scale, un-official, planners such as firms, households and individuals. From here follows one of the two major challenge of a complexity theory derived planning: to design a planning system that does not discriminate between small-scale un-official local planner and large-scale official planners. The other challenge, as we've seen above, is to design a planning system that is not based on predictions.

Can there be a planning system that is not dependent on prediction and at the same time allows planning ideas and actions to flow bottom-up, in other words, a planning approach that will be tuned with, and reflect, the city as a complex self-organizing system? Such an approach was never attempted in the past for two reasons. Firstly, because mainstream discourse on cities and their planning perceived cities as simple systems and secondly, because the discourse on cities was dominated, as noted, by Faludi's (1973) distinction between theory of planning and theory in planning; the question of the appropriate planning system was not considered a general theoretical issue but rather a specific question related to one country or the other (Portugali, 2011). A first and preliminary attempt at a self-organized planning system was suggested in *Self-Organization and the City* (Portugali, 2000, Chap. 11) and was further developed by Alfasi and Portugali (2007) and in Portugali (2011, Chap. 16).

5.4 Concluding notes: toward a reformulation of planning theory

Let us re-iterate the question: What have complexity theory and CTC to say about urbanism and planning in the 21st Century? First, as we've seen they suggest a new set of tools: urban simulation models, decision support systems and planning support systems. Second, they suggest that mathematical formalism is not automatically alien to critical science and social theory. Third they suggest a new insight on the problematic of planning in the 21st century – on what Schönwandt (2008) has recently termed 'planning crisis' (see also De Roo, this Volume). The new insight is this: according to the prevailing view the current problematics of planning theory is the result of the dramatic changes that mark the last three decades, namely, globalization, the decline of the welfare nation state, the rise of a stronger civil society, in short, of the new postmodern condition. The latter has made the city and its planning complex to the extent that the good old planning approaches do not function properly and new ones (communicative and/ or strategic planning, etc.) should replace them.

From CTC follows that cities and their planning were always complex – from the very emergence of civilization and urban society some 5,500 years ago. What the new era of globalization did was to expose and bring to the fore this complexity; it created a situation that the complexity of cities can no longer be ignored. The story of Tel Aviv balconies took place in the 1950s-1960s. And more of these planning paradoxes were always present in the cities. In fact the shortcomings of the prevailing planning theory and its approaches were apparent already at the end 1960s and early 1970 and provided one of the impetuses to the emergence of critical urban theory and planning.

What then is the source of the current problems of planning? From complexity theory and CTC follow that for several decades planning theory, discourse and practice have treated cities and planning as simple systems and yet they are not – they have always been and still are complex systems. In order to overcome the crisis planning theory has to treat cities as such. When this is done three theoretical tasks and domains of research come to the fore: to understand the dynamics of cities as complex self-organizing systems, to formulate a planning process appropriate for cities as such, and, to formulate a planning system that will be tuned with the city as a complex self-organizing system. Planning theory has traditionally dealt with the first and the second tasks, but not with the third. From what has been said above thus follows a need to re-structure planning theory as illustrated in

Figure 5.4, that is, to add to it a third domain of research that will deal with the appropriate structure of the planning system.

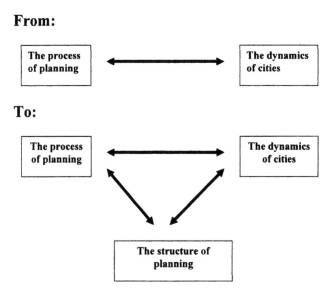

From:

To:

Figure 5.4   A suggestion to re-structure planning theory

Source: Portugali 2011, Figure 15.2

References

Alexander, C. (1965) A city is not a tree, *Architectural forum* (April-May), pp. 58-62.

Alfasi, N. and J. Portugali (2007) Planning rules for a self-planned city, *Planning theory* 6(2), pp. 164-182.

Allen, P. (1981) The evolutionary paradigm of dissipative structures, The Evolutionary Vision. E. Jantch, Westview Press, Boulder, pp. 25-71.

Auerbach, F. (1913) Das gesetz der Bevolkerungskoncentration [The law regarding conceptration of population], *Petermanns Geographische Mitteilungen*, 59: 74-76.

Bak, P. and K. Chen (1991) Self-organized criticality, *Scientific American*, 28, pp. 26-33.

Batty, M. (2008) The Size, Scale, and Shape of Cities, *Science*, 319(5864, 8 February), pp. 769-771.

Brail, R.K. (2006) Planning support systems evolving: When the rubber hits the road. Complex Artificial Environments, in: J. Portugali (ed.), *Complex Artificial Environments*, Proceedings, Springer, Heidelberg, pp. 307-317.

Brail, R.K. and R.E. Klosterman (Eds.) (2001) *Planning Support Systems*, ESRI Press, New York.

Camhis, M. (1979) *Planning Theory and Philosophy*, Tavistok Publications, London.

Castells, M. (1989) *The Informational City: Information Technology, Economic Restructuring, and the Urban-Regional Process*, Blackwell, Oxford.

Castells, M. (1996) *The Rise of the Network Society*, Blackwell, Malden.

Christaller, W. (1933/1966) *Central Places in Southern Germany*, Prentice Hall, Englewood Cliffs.

Davidoff, P. (1965) Advocacy and pluralism in planning, in A. Faludi (ed.) *A Reader in Planning Theory*, Pergamon, Oxford, pp. 277-296.

Faludi, A. (1973a) *Planning Theory*, Pergamon, Oxford.

Faludi, A. (Ed.) (1973b) *A Reader in Planning Theory*, Pergamon, Oxford.

Giddens, A. (1984) *The Constitution of Society: Outline of the Theory of Structuration*, University of California Press, Berkeley.

Giddens, A. (1997) *Sociology*, Polity, London.

Gould, S. (1980) *The Panda's Thumb*, Norton, New York.

Habermas, J. (1984) The Theory of Communicative Action, Vol. 1: Reason and the Rationalization of Society, Heinemann, London.

Habermas, J. (1987) The Theory of Communicative Action, Vol. 2: Lifeworld and System:

A Critique of Functionalist Reason, Beacon, Boston.

Habermas, J. (1990) *Moral Consciousness and Communicative Action*, Polity, Cambridge.

Hägerstrand, T. (1967) *Innovation Diffusion as a Spatial Process*, University of Chicago Press, Chicago.

Haken, H. (1983) *Synergetics, An Introduction*, Springer, Heidelberg.

Haken, H. (1987) *Advanced Synergetics: An Introduction* (2nd print), Springer, Berlin.

Haken, H. and J. Portugali (1996) Synergetics, Inter-representation networks and cognitive maps, in: J. Portugali, *The Construction of Cognitive Maps*, Kluwer, Dordrecht, pp. 45-67.

Hall, P. (1975/2002) *Urban and Regional Planning*, Routledge, London.

Harvey, D. (1989) *The Condition of Postmodernity: An Enquiry into the Origins of Cultural Change*, Blackwell, Cambridge.

Healey, P. (2007) *Urban Complexity and Spatial Strategy: Towards a Relational Planning of Our Times*, London, Routledge.

Jacobs, J. (1961) *The Death and Life of Great American Cities*, Penguin, London.

Kuhn, T. (1962) *The Structure of Scientific Revolutions*, Univ. of Chicago Press, Chicago.

Lefebvre, H. (1995) *The Production of Space*, Blackwell, Oxford.

Leydesdorff, L. (2001) *A Sociological Theory of Communication: The Self-Organization of the Knowledge-Based Society*, Universal Publishers, Boca Raton.

Lindblom, C.E. (1959) The science of 'muddling through', *Public Administration Review*, 19, pp. 79-88.

Lösch, A. (1954) *The Economics of Location*, Yale University Press, New Haven.

Mumford, L. (1961) *The City in History: Its Origins, Its Transformations, and Its Prospects*, Harcourt Inc, San Diego.

Nicolis, G. and I. Prigogine (1977) *Self-Organization in Nonequilibrium Systems: From Dissipative Structures to Order Through Fluctuations*, Wiley, New York.

Popper, K. (1959) *The Logic of Scientific Discovery*, Hutchinson, Fayetteville.

Portugali, J. (1985) Parallel currents in the natural and social Sciences, *Geoforum*, 16(2), pp. 93-98.

Portugali, J. (1996) Inter-representation networks and cognitive maps, in: J. Portugali (ed.) *The Construction of Cognitive Maps*, Kluwer, Dordrecht, pp. 11-43.

Portugali, J. (2000) *Self-Organization and the City*, Springer, Heidelberg.

Portugali, J. (2002) The seven basic propositions of SIRN (Synergetic Inter-Representation Networks), *Nonlinear Phenomena in Complex Systems*, 5(4), pp. 428-444.

Portugali, J. (2004) Toward a cognitive approach to urban modelling, *Environment and Planning B: Planning and Design*, 31, pp. 589-613.

Portugali, J. (2006) Complexity theory as a link between space and place, *Environment and Planning A*, 38, pp. 647-664.

Portugali, J. (2008) Learning from paradoxes about prediction and planning in self-organizing cities, *Planning Theory*, 7(3), pp. 248-262.

Portugali, J. (2011) *Complexity, Cognition and the City*, Springer, Heidelberg.

Portugali, J. and N. Alfasi (2008) An approach to planning discourse analysis, *Urban Studies*, 45(2), pp. 251-272.

Portugali, J. Ros, A. Gonen, D. Oz, S. (2009) O'Jerusalem: A decision support system for Jerusalem, in: H. Lin and M. Batty (eds.), *Virtual Geographic Environments*, Science Press, Beijing.

Prigogine, I. and Stengers, I. (1984) *Order Out of Chaos*, Bantam, New York.

Relph, E. (1976) *Place and Placelessness*, Pion, London.

Reuven-Zafrir, O. (Not published) Urban pattern recognition, Tel Aviv University, Tel Aviv.

Schonwandt, W.L. (2008) *Planning in Crisis? Theoretical Orientations for Architecture and Planning*, Ashgate, Aldershot.

Schrödinger, E. (1946) *What is Life?*, Macmillan, London.

Snow (1964) *The Two Cultures and a Second Look*, Cambridge University Press, Cambridge.

Weidlich, W. (1994) Synergetic modeling concepts for sociodynamics with application to collective political opinion formation, *Journal of Mathematical Sociology*, 1(4), pp. 267-291.

Westman, R. (1994) Two culture or one? A second look at Kuhn's *The Copernican Revolution*, *Isis*, 85, pp. 79-115.

Wilson, A.G. (1970) *Entropy in Urban and Regional Modelling*, Pion, London.

Wirth (1938) Urbanism as a way of life, *American Journal of Sociology*, XLIV,
     pp. 1-24.
Yee, D. (1993) A book review of The two cultures by C.P. Snow, http://
     dannyreviews.com /h/The_Two_Cultures.html

Chapter 6

Spatial Planning, Complexity and a World 'Out of Equilibrium': Outline of a Non-linear Approach to Planning

Gert de Roo[1]

Some believe that planning theory is encountering its third crisis, with growing criticism of the one-sidedness of communicative and collaborative planning. If the planning community agrees that this is indeed the case, could the complexity sciences present us with a way out of this crisis, showing us a new route to take our theoretical debate forward? A small but growing number of planners strongly believe that they add value to the planners' theoretical debate and substantially enhance our understanding of our physical and social environment. This is the basic message of *A Planner's Encounter with Complexity*, the book that precedes this volume.

In this contribution I identify links between planning theory and the complexity sciences. These must be captured in a coherent outline if both story lines are to become mutually beneficial. In essence, planning theory helps us to differentiate between situations, issues or cases, an aspect that is not yet touched upon by the complexity sciences. However, they do underline the importance of time and all its implications, which, strangely enough, has been a non-issue in spatial planning. In this contribution I will work towards such an outline for spatial planning that combines both time and differentiation. This outline also proposes a way out in the event of a third crisis in planning theory.

6.1 In concurrence with systems thinking

> Under the seeming disorder of the old city, wherever the old city is working successfully, is a marvelous order for maintaining the safety of the streets and

1   Gert de Roo is Professor of Spatial Planning. He is head of the Department of Spatial Planning and Environment, Faculty of Spatial Sciences at the University of Groningen in the Netherlands. He is President (elect) of the Association of European Schools of Planning (AESOP) (2011-2015) and has been the coordinator of AESOP's Planning and Complexity thematic group since 2005. De Roo is also the editor of *A Planner's Encounter with Complexity*, the book preceding this volume.

the freedom of the city. It is a complex order. [...] This order is all composed
of movement and change, and although it is life not art, we may fancifully call
it the art form of the city. (Jane Jacobs, The Death and Life of Great American
Cities, pp. 60-61.)

How can we bridge urban order and disorder, complexity and chaos in an abstract
and theoretical sense? In my view, this would involve bridging the gap between the
discipline of spatial planning and the complexity sciences, and a logical step would
be to apply systems thinking. The disciplines of spatial planning, decision-making,
and organization and management traditionally relate their progress to steps
acknowledged within systems thinking (Gharajedaghi, 2005; West Churchman,
1984). Systems thinking, being representative of the 'general sciences', cuts
across the various disciplines of science (Boulding, 1956; Checkland, 1991;
Kramer and De Smit, 1991; Von Bertalanffy, 1968) and, hence, also touches upon
the discipline of spatial planning (Chadwick, 1971, McLoughlin, 1969). Various
periods are acknowledged within planning theory to coincide with a particular
class of systems, recognized within systems thinking.

The first crisis in the theory of planning arose during the 1960s, with growing
criticism of blueprint planning and the underlying technical rationale. Heavily
influenced by logical positivism and the mathematical simplicity of a Newtonian
worldview, actions proposed with a view to intervening in the physical environment
were considered to be definite and final. The physical world would bend to our
(i.e. the planners') will. Class 1 systems (Kauffman, 1993) express this kind of
thinking, being the so-called 'closed systems'. These closed systems represent
a fixed or static reality consisting of nodes and their interactions, without any
interaction with an outside world. Closed systems exclude contextual interference,
as if there is nothing more beyond the whole and its parts. In physics and chemistry,
excluding the context and focusing entirely on the parts of the whole in order to
understand the whole as an entity has been extremely successful. It is therefore not
surprising that this is seen as an appropriate route for the social sciences, including
the discipline of spatial planning.

The most profound proposal to emerge in this period was the 'rational choice'
approach of Meyerson and Banfield (1955). It comprises a number of steps,
including 'considering all alternatives open to the decision-maker', 'identifying
and evaluating all consequences' and 'selecting the preferable alternative in
terms of its most valued ends'. In this sense, 'technical-rationality is a positivist
epistemology of practice' (Usher et al. 1997, p. 143). While the notions 'all' and
'ends' are true representations of a technical rationale underlying the actions of
planners, the idea of 'alternatives' is not. A technical-rational view of the world
takes account of the existence of only one true reality. Given the facts as they come
to us here and now, we should be able to deduce what the future will bring. If this
future is not to our liking, the planner will intervene accordingly. Why, then, this
reference to 'alternatives'?

From a logical-positivist perspective, alternatives indicate an imperfect world in which all the facts that are needed to comprehend the future are not available. One could distinguish between theory and practice, stating that, given enough time, money and energy, all facts will come to us eventually. For some time, this proposal solved the first crisis in planning theory: the fall of the technical rationale (Schön, 1983), acknowledging its boundedness (Simon, 1957). Alternatives were seen as the practical solution to this imperfect world. In spatial planning, so-called scenario planning was proposed as a solution. Scenario planning had its counterpart in systems thinking, since it was based on semi-open feedback systems, also known as Class II systems. During the 1960s, internal evaluation loops became popular and were designed to alter direction if the results did not match the facts. The initial set of conditions of nodes and their interactions would change accordingly. During the 1980s, this approach also became less popular (Alexander, 1984, 1986). The second crisis in planning theory was in the making.

In various European countries, institutional settings have undergone radical change since the 1980s and 1990s, representing a shift from a coordinative government to shared governance. Aside from facts, values mattered too. These values proved to be very much dependent on opinions, ideas, understandings and perceptions, which vary between actors (Innes, 1995, 1996; Forester, 1993), and there can be quite a number of actors involved in planning processes. The consequences were far-reaching. Constructivism and post-positivism replaced neo-positivism. A realist perspective had to make way for critical-realist and relativist perspectives on reality (See Chapter 1), and the technical rationale was set aside to make way for communicative approaches. The communicative rationale, with its focus on values rather than facts, became a major driver in seeking consensus in the various processes of planning.

This communicative turn (Healey, 1992) brought the concept of open networks into planning. These networks are Class III systems in systems thinking. According to Kauffman (1993), they do not have 'predictable patterns of stability'. Every actor is basically a black box, from which we cannot predict with certainty any of their actions. Also, planning processes are no longer such that they can be reduced to one actor. The communicative approach to planning therefore takes uncertainty as its starting point. Planners seek a negotiated or 'agreed' certainty rather than facts contributing to certainty. In this respect, I regard it as the opposite to the technical-rationale perspective on planning.

The communicative rationale, being an extreme perspective on planning, might offer a very clear and straightforward idea about what it stands for, however, as with the technical rationale at the other extreme of planning, it is above all an ideal-type constellation, and criticism is therefore around the corner. For example, the idea of stakeholders all having more or less the same amount of power to optimally negotiate about differences in their desires, interests and responsibilities, and in relation to ideas about tackling the issue, is under pressure from a reality full of power conflicts and mistrust. The ideal-type constellation might be in line with a Habermasian understanding of communicative rationality (an undistorted dialogue), but is increasingly regarded as somewhat naïve (Bengs, 2005; Harper and Stein, 2000; Huxley, 2000; McGuirk, 2001).

Another important criticism arising as a result of the strong commitment to a communicative perspective on spatial planning in the past twenty years concerns a shift away from content and an overwhelming emphasis on processes of planning and the interaction of stakeholders within these processes. This has resulted in a neglect of the content side of spatial planning (Imree, 1999). With this awareness, a third crisis in planning theory is just a few steps away (Alfasi and Portugali, 2007; Schönwandt, 2007).

6.2 A relational perspective on spatial planning: spectrum thinking

Thus far, this reflection on planning theory contains nothing new, including the link made with systems theory. The consequences of this form of reflection, however, have not yet been closely addressed within the planning community. One of the obvious consequences of seeing a sequence of related system classes in planning is an appreciation of a spectrum between the technical and communicative rationales (see Figure 6.1) representing the various planning issues, how these are perceived and how they might be dealt with (De Roo, 2003; Van der Valk, 1999). The position of a planning issue on the spectrum depends, for example, on its certainty-uncertainty ratio. Among other things, the spectrum is a representation of the degree of certainty and uncertainty relating to an issue in planning. The spectrum also magnifies a shift in the ratio between object orientation and intersubjective orientation. This is accompanied by a transformation from closed to open systems (read 'planning issues'), a shift from a reductionist focus on the parts of a whole towards an expansionist view that considers influences on the whole from its broader context and a subtle balancing of a (critical-) realist perspective and a relativist perspective.

The transformations occurring along the spectrum, moving from a technical towards a communicative rationale, provide us with a few basic insights that are important to planning and decision-making. For example, while seeking certainty in a planning process, attention should also be paid to coping with uncertainty (a statement that explicitly acknowledges uncertainty as a phenomenon within the realm of science!). A further insight is that a shift along the spectrum means a transition in the approach to the results of planning actions, namely from goal maximization to process optimization. Moreover, there is the insight relating to the differentiation of planning issues into at least three categories: simple and straightforward issues (with direct causality, no interference from the context, clear entity, etc.), complex issues (between the technical and communicative realms, where both certainty and uncertainty prevail) and very complex (some would prefer 'chaotic') issues (agreements on how to define the issue are needed, consensus among stakeholders is desired, and perceptions and values prevail over facts and figures) (see Figure 6.1). This should be regarded as a statement

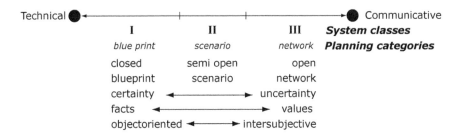

Figure 6.1   A rationality spectrum for spatial planning and its relation to Class I, II and III systems

that explicitly acknowledges differentiation between situations, issues and cases, meaning that, aside from a general or generic understanding of our reality, a specific understanding that acknowledges differences in a relational (see Chapter 1) and contingent way is a necessity. These few basic insights are not just important to planning in general, but are also crucial to the story line in this contribution and to the argument I wish to put forward.

It is logical to expect that a possible third crisis in planning theory (Schönwandt, 2007) will be dealt with by shifting attention to the 'fuzzy middle' between the technical and communicative rationales. In this fuzzy middle, both certainty and uncertainty prevail, an object-oriented perspective is as important as an intersubjective perspective and both facts and values matter (De Roo and Porter, 2007). This is a good move, one could say, since the majority of planning issues fall within this fuzzy middle. Moreover, for planners, this position is not entirely undiscovered or new, since scenario planning is also rooted in it.

This is not, however, the route I wish to take here, although I am by no means denying the importance of the 'fuzzy middle'. I would rather move on, following the progress made by systems thinking.

6.3 Complex adaptive systems and spatial planning

In addition to Class I, II and III systems, there is also a systems Class IV, the systems class of complex adaptive systems (Kauffman, 1993; Wolfram, 2002). I am rather confident about the impact that this system class will have on planning thought and on planning actions. The impact could be tremendous, since it embraces time and non-linear behaviour. It underlines the idea of differentiation between planning situations even further.

The becoming

The first three system classes might differ in terms of their openness to the contexts of systems, but the attributes on the basis of which the system exists (nodes and interactions) are considered to remain the same. These three classes implicitly represent systems with a definite problem or case formulation, as these are considered to be more or less fixed or static entities or situations. I am referring to their 'being'. This means that the planning issue, case or situation at hand is considered to be an 'it', present in the here and now. It is a perspective common to a Newtonian worldview and to what Kuhn called the 'normal' sciences (Kuhn, 1962). I challenge this static point of view here and elsewhere (see De Roo, 2010; De Roo and Rauws, 2012), despite the fact that this is a common and appreciated perspective within the realm of planning and decision-making.

The theoretical debate on planning and decision-making was and still is very much about the rationale underlying choices made (with regard to intervening in the physical environment). As such, choice or decision-making – likely to be the most essential aspect of planning – is by and large restricted to the here and now, to the 'being' at hand. One could conclude that most attention is focused on the precise moment at which a decision is to be made, with arguments referring to the here and now, while the 'becoming' (which is what we basically plan for, a fact that some of us tend to forget) is secondary, considered as not much more than the logical follow up of a linear extrapolation (technical rationale) and a commitment (communicative rationale) made operational to a decision.

Here, the criticism relates to the fact that planning theory has not paid attention to time. To ignore the issue of time is to ignore processes of change. With change being perhaps the only constant factor in the reality that surrounds us, it might be wise to reconsider the importance of time and change to planning theory and practice. Systems Class IV does just this: it incorporates time, presenting a world in flow, full of discontinuous change. Systems Class IV is therefore an example of phenomena reflected upon by what Funtowicz and Ravetz (1993) call 'post-normal' sciences. Systems Class IV presents the 'becoming' as a phenomenon that is far more essential than the 'being'.

Adaptive and self-organizing

These Class IV systems are known as 'complex adaptive systems' (Cilliers, 1998; Coveney and Highfield, 1991; Gros, 2008; Holland, 1998; Lewin, 1993; Mainzer, 1994; Waldrop, 1992). With these 'complex adaptive systems' we touch upon the complexity sciences and the central theme of this book: spatial planning and complexity. Contrary to Class I, II and III systems, complex adaptive systems are not fixed or static entities with given nodes and interaction. Complex adaptive systems are considered to be robust and flexible at the same time. Cities are a good example of complex adaptive systems (Allen, 1997; Batty, 2005; Portugali, 1999; Portugali et al., 2011), as cities are robust in the sense that they rarely disappear, whatever happens (Hiroshima's existence as a city was not ended by the atom bomb in 1945). Property rights are a crucial factor in a city's robustness (Webster and Lai, 2003; Webster 2010). At the same time, cities are very flexible in adapting to various global and local changes, such as industrialization, the phenomenal rise of motorized transport, the rural-to-urban demographic and the rapid rise of the communication age.

Complex adaptive systems therefore adapt to contextual change, as they are able to transform themselves through processes of self-organization. This keeps the system fit for change, which results in processes of co-evolution with its transforming contextual environment and its self-organizing abilities. Change and co-evolution, as representatives of change, are processes in time. These time-related processes do not shift from one entity or 'being' to another. There is something to say about the routes taken by these processes of co-evolution: they are not random but dependent on past events (history matters) and on the context. This is called 'path dependency' (Liebowitz and Margolis, 1995). There is also something to be said about the extent to which change takes place.

Wicked problems

Let us go back to 1972 and Rittel's remarkable reflections on the first crisis in planning (see also Rittel and Webber, 1973). Rittel discussed West Churchman's proposition (1967) regarding the difference between 'tamed' and 'wicked' problems when reflecting upon the difficulty of understanding and defining planning problems. From the perspective we take today, 'tamed' problems are those that can be understood as they 'are', and can be defined, controlled and solved. Rittel no longer believed in this type of problem (represented here as Class I systems, although 'static' or 'fixed' Class II and III systems could also apply), stating that 'all essential planning problems are wicked' (Rittel, 1972: 392).

Wicked problems have 'no definite formulation', as they are not and cannot be fully understood. In my own words, any specification of the problem corresponds to a specific selection of those properties that are considered likely representations of the problem (the problem is situational) emerging from the past and, since these properties come and go, there is no clear boundary or end to their domain. Others call them messy (Ackoff, 1974), fluid or fuzzy (De Roo and Porter, 2007). Responding to or solving these problems often reveals or creates additional problems, because of complex interdependencies between problem-related properties and their contexts. A 'wicked problem' is therefore unique and allows 'many explanations for the same discrepancy' (Rittel, 1972: 393) with no test available to determine which of these explanations is the best. Therefore, it is not possible to evaluate whether this has been done well or not. In Rittel's words: 'The wicked problem solver has no right to be wrong. He is responsible for what he is doing' (1972: 393). In my own words: the 'wicked problem' becomes ethical.

Rittel and West Churchman were both very much interested in planning, and it is remarkable to see how, in retrospect, they perceived the world at the end of the 1960s and in the early 1970s, and the way in which they regarded planning issues as 'wicked'. History shows us the route that the debate in planning has taken since then. On this route, we see planners acknowledging problems not as 'wicked' but as 'communicative'. Recently, planners have again begun to wonder about alternative routes to the future, as a response to the growing criticism of communicative and collaborative types of planning. Those looking into the complexity sciences, as I am, are now touching upon complex, adaptive phenomena labelled as 'wicked' by various authors from outside the discipline of planning (Davies, 2003; DeGrace and Stahl, 1990). In contrast to planners, these authors seem to have appreciated the considerations of Ritter and West Churchman's suggestion of 'wicked' problems in planning.

Rittel referred as well to 'tame problems', which are acknowledged by Prigogine (1996) as stable systems, those within which 'small changes in the initial conditions have minor consequences' (1996: 27). Rittel's 'wicked problems' are frequently regarded as synonymous with complex adaptive and unstable systems, as these have the same implications as Rittel's 'wicked problems'. There is slight twist, however. According to Prigogine with regard to these complex systems, small changes in the initial conditions 'will inevitably diverge exponentially over time' (1996: 27), with an unpredictable result given the conditions at the beginning. It is therefore unlikely that a method applied to a complex adaptive system will produce the same results twice. Furthermore, small variations between systems might eventually lead to substantial differences in their trajectory and could have major consequences in due course. In terms of causality, foreseeable and confined amplifications have a disproportionate result to future circumstances. To obtain an idea of how this could work out in an urban environment, let's see how 'Lola runs'.

6.4 Lola and Lorentz

Run Lola Run is a cult movie that convincingly shows how the world is full of coincidences.[2] The story of the movie translates rather well into Lorentz's story of the cyclone and the butterfly, which begins in the tropical jungle and ends catastrophically in the urban jungle. This metaphor (Lorentz, 1963) is one of the most popular in the complexity sciences. Lorentz's metaphor connects a tropical cyclone which suddenly hits the coast of North America with the butterfly and its apparently randomly flapping wings somewhere in the Amazon. This random flapping of wings at a particular location and at a sudden moment in time proves to be the trigger for a dramatic chain of events, as it creates the first pressure wave that ripples outward, going through a sequence of coincidences and culminating in an unstoppable natural disaster. Lorentz by no means wants to present the butterfly as having unprecedented powers. The butterfly is like all butterflies, but this particular one happens to be at the beginning of a series of events whereby, supported by the circumstances, a barely detectable movement evolves into a powerful phenomenon that cannot be ignored.

---

2   *Run Lola Run* is a German thriller (In German *Lola Rennt*, literally 'Lola Runs') released in 1998, written and directed by Tom Tykwer. The film won numerous awards.

Run Lola Run presents us with another route as it unfolds, this time in the urban jungle. I have to admit that the event that triggered this chain of events is less common than a butterfly flapping its wings. Lola's friend has left his bag, which contains a large sum of borrowed money, on the metro in Berlin. The friend panics and informs Lola that he is going to rob a nearby supermarket to settle his debt. Lola decides to intervene.

As Lola leaves her apartment in a hurry, she passes a punk with a dog. The dog growls at her, which makes her yell and run faster. Running through the streets of Berlin, she encounters, at various moments, all kinds of events and chance occurrences, which together result in her being too late to prevent the robbery. Instead she participates in it and is eventually shot.

The gods favour Lola and allow her to repeat the run once more. Being hardly any later than on the first occasion, she stumbles over the punk and his dog and hurts herself. As a result, she limps. Again she encounters various people and events on the streets of Berlin, only the time and place are slightly different. Although Lola arrives in time and manages to catch her friend's attention, he is distracted and run over by a passing ambulance. He dies.

Again, this is not a happy ending, and therefore the story unfolds a third time. Lola manages to escape from the punk and his dog by jumping over them both. This time, too, various events and chance meetings occur on the streets of Berlin, among them a tramp with a bag. While he had been there on the previous runs, he had been in a different place at different moments, and subsequently his presence was without consequences. This time, the tramp crosses the path of Lola's friend, who recognizes the bag as his own. The moment Lola arrives, her friend's troubles have fortunately disappeared. With this, the significance of her run seems to evaporate.

When we connect the principal characteristics of complex adaptive systems with the story line of this film, a scenario unfolds that is of interest in urban planning. Comparable to Lorentz's metaphor, small changes at the beginning (passing the punk and his dog) lead to various consequences at the 'end', some of them rather dramatic. The spatial functions and structures of Berlin condition the various shades, nuances and movements of what seem to be coincidences. These coincidences are nevertheless connected by invisible threads, which manifest themselves in a slightly different way when repeated, and hence create alternative situations with alternative responses, resulting in completely different and sometimes dramatic closing scenes.

Numerous causalities and interpretations can be related to Berlin's spatial structures and functions. Interwoven with these visible contours of the 'urban jungle' of Berlin is a diversity of comprehensive and less comprehensive sets of uses, symbols, rules, movements and actions. These movements, operations and actions do not depend solely on the existing structure and functions, but are products shaped partially through interaction with these structures and functions (contextual), partially through historical connections (path dependency), partially by cultural and social rules (referring to adaptive processes), and partially by choices made independently of all these factors (referring to processes of self-organization). Therefore, few causalities and interpretations in urban space are the direct result of urban structures and functions. They are affected by various shades, nuances and movements that depend on, but are not determined by, the way in which Berlin's space is set up and organized. Together, they produce manifestations of space to which we attribute qualities. These manifestations condition our decisions, operationalizations and action space. By and large we perceive the outcomes of all this as coincidences, which could lead to different and sometimes rather serious consequences.

6.5 Linear versus non-linear: a matter of perspective

Complexity sciences assume that development and progress cannot be expected in a world in which the Newtonian perspective of a never-ending cycle of repetition prevails. This Newtonian world is a reality in perfect equilibrium, where time has no role and the interactions of entities (nodes in a system) are fixed and determined, now and permanently. In such a Newtonian world, everything (nodes and their interactions in a system) remains more or less the same, isolated, 'tamed', closed and linear. This is the world to which the 'normal' sciences relate. There is no change, the isolated linear move from A to B has no effect apart from the move itself. The move is meaningless in a broader context. Therefore, in a state of equilibrium there cannot be any progress or development. Ecologists would say that such a system is nothing but a dead system (Lister, 2008).

Development becomes possible in a situation of disequilibrium where circumstances are 'complex', and certainty and predictability are replaced by emergence and non-linearity (see also Section 8 of this chapter). Given the initial conditions, there is no longer an unequivocal development that leads to an unequivocal outcome. By contrast, we are faced with an infinite number of possible routes, each resulting in a different outcome. A process that is repeated on the basis of the same initial conditions will not produce the same outcome, and, if it does, this is merely coincidental (Coveney and Highfield, 1995). There is diversity rather than coherence.

This diversity is the world to which 'post-normal' science relates. Diversity does not lead to the degeneration of the process. In physics, reference is made to increasing entropy in the case of degeneration (entropy: state of maximum disorder and unchanging events). In a complex world (non-linear and out of equilibrium) it may very well lead to an evolutionary process. Some call this 'extropy', presenting it as the opposite of entropy. This evolutionary process may even take on 'chaotic' forms. According to chaos theory (Gleick, 1987), a new order might emerge out of this 'chaos', a line of reasoning that is just one step away from the concept of a multilevel perspective (not seen here as hierarchical and linear with downward coordination, but as mutually interacting and mutually dependent), becoming an issue in spatial planning.

The 'complexity' of a complex adaptive system more or less stands for interactions (out of equilibrium) of systems (wholes) at the various levels, with subsystems at micro levels, neighbouring systems at meso level and hypersystems at macro level. These interactions represent the exchange of matter, energy and information – characteristics commonly referred to as dissipative. Complex systems are dissipative by nature (Prigogine, 1984). Therefore, without mutually related multilevel interactions complex adaptive systems cannot exist. One example is the complexity of traffic and infrastructure: politicians would frequently like to see wider roads to solve the problem of congestion. This is an obvious but simplistic thought which originates from linear thinking. Indeed, widening roads and adding more lanes will initially reduce congestion, but it also prompts those who used to travel by public transport to take the car instead, as the roads are now less busy. Due to these processes at the individual (micro) level, roads become congested again within a short period of time. Spatial planners are very much aware of these mechanisms (Papageorgiou et al., 2003).

Another example is demography, its effect on housing projects and the development of neighbourhoods. Planners were once considered to be the creators of urban space, who not only defined institutional conditions under which a function could be spatially allocated, but also defined future space. This meant physical transformation as the consequence of blueprints that included neatly designed neighbourhoods. From a multilevel perspective, this notion of the planner being the creator of space can be questioned as the planner is instrumental to demographic forces (Gober, 1992). The planner's world is not one to be created but one in a continuous flow – a world full of autonomous processes. Urban development is not only influenced by demography but also by technical, economic, institutional and many more factors. To put it in a slightly different perspective: the urban is where the local and the global meet, where the local adapts to the global, and where the global receives impulses from the local. This mechanism leads to an exchange of ideas and eventually to innovations.

In this complex environment I would propose the planner to become the party attempting to acknowledge the local benefits of the major forces triggering local urban responses, and attempting to prevent negative consequences that could impact on liveability at the local level. The planner does not do this by controlling, conditioning or restricting the use of urban space. He/she attempts to influence or manipulate, in a positive way, developments that are seen to affect the local as products of developments at higher levels. Rather than being the creator (within a technical realm) or mediator (from a communicative perspective), in this respect the planner can be acknowledged as a trend watcher and transition manager.

6.6 Positioning complexity

Waldrop (1992) discusses the result of computer-simulation research, from which it can be inferred that there is a continuum of simplicity, complexity and chaos.

His message tells us more. Our dynamic reality, including life itself, occurs at the edge of order and chaos, 'where the components of a system never quite lock into place, and yet never quite dissolve into turbulence either' (1992: 12) and in which a complex reality can be found that reflects 'the right balance of stability and fluidity' (1992: 308). This complex reality is what Weaver, one of the founding fathers of the complexity sciences, in 1948 introduced as 'problems of organized complexity' (See also Devisch in this Volume).

The logic between order and chaos

The message is that the world is never in balance but there is nevertheless a knowable reality. All functioning or living systems are either moving towards equilibrium or away from it. Such systems cohere with or adapt to the context's flow. Out-of-equilibrium situations might eventually lead to chaos, a situation that is not necessarily destructive or negative. This is possible because, in addition to the inevitable and continuous presence of chaos, a certain amount of order results from developments towards stability and equilibrium, albeit on a higher level (a definition of 'progress'). Simplicity and chaos are apparent opposites 'that, at second sight, should be considered more in terms of their complementarity', as Goudappel (1996: 76) concludes. The question that remains is how we should deal with this view of reality.

Dealing with it is not easy, as it very much contrasts with the elementary rules of logic and the ideas of the Enlightenment, ideas that we carry with us as if they were in our genes. For example, Aristotle's notions of logic, which most of us have considered to be self-evident, are no longer a foundation upon which we can build when considering the ideas of complexity. Aristotle's law of identity (a chair is a chair and definitely not a couch or a tree) is no longer valid, as reality is constantly changing, co-evolving from one state to another. Aristotle's law of noncontradiction ('A' cannot be the same as its opposite 'not-A') is no longer valid, since systems can be represented as orderly and chaotic at the same time, depending on the perspective taken. Aristotle's law of the excluded middle (It is either 'yes' or 'no', '1' or '0', black or white) is no longer valid as there are infinite shades of grey between black and white, and between order and chaos there are various complexities. For example, with regard to spatial planning we have pointed to the fuzzy middle between the technical and communicative rationales (De Roo and Porter, 2009). This fuzzy middle is probably more important for spatial planning than both of the extremes of the ideal type.

The 'complexity' of complex adaptive systems does not address a current state, an 'it' or a straightforward, well-defined entity that 'is'. Complex adaptive systems cannot be defined on the basis of a fixed 'it'. Nor can they be defined as an 'is', which would make such a system unchangeable and atemporal. The 'complexity' of complex adaptive systems expresses a system in motion as a consequence of a situation that is out of equilibrium. Rather than descending into a 'dead' situation or into chaos, complex adaptive systems show emergent behaviour and co-evolve, while maintaining a proper level of 'fitness', that is, the ability of a system to survive between extremes – between order and chaos, coherence and diversity.

Non-linearity and irreversibility

If complex adaptive systems are to flourish, the presence of a transient contextual environment with the constraints of irreversibility and non-linearity is essential (Coveney and Highfield, 1995). Both irreversibility and non-linearity are strongly related to time and change. Time is a carrier of the directions that developments take, and these directions are dependent on both the past and the context.

Irreversibility therefore contradicts a Newtonian world, an atemporal world in which movements of entities, sole objects or stand-alone situations do not distinguish directions in time. Nor can this be seen in a contemporary planners' world that focuses on decisions made in the here and now, without much awareness of their consequences.

Non-linearity is very much in contrast with linear systems or systems that progress exponentially. Non-linearity does not add up in the way '1 + 1' adds up to '2' (Coveney and Highfield, 1995). There is no immediate, straightforward and direct causal relationship between variables which would result in a change in one variable due to a causal relationship with another variable whose state has also just changed, whereby the degree to which change takes place is the outcome of a fixed ratio between the two.

A well-known example of non-linearity is the iterative process of population growth, with the outcome of growth at one stage serving as input for growth in the following stage, a process that endlessly repeats itself and results in a rather chaotic and discontinuous line of progression in the size of a population (Gleick, 1987). Another example is Lorentz's butterfly, discussed above. It is a metaphor referring to how a minor event in a complex world can survive and even take on massive proportions, being pushed forward and gaining energy in interactions within a context willing to connect and willing to expand. This is again the result of an iterative process, no longer within a system (a population growing and declining over time), but a system continuously connecting with similar systems, resulting in amplified and discontinuous behaviour (a movement originating from a butterfly's wing and evolving into a cyclone). In these examples, non-linearity presents itself as amplified and discontinuous.

Connectivity and potentiality

Irreversibility and non-linearity are necessary constraints on complex adaptive systems and result from interactions with their contextual environment. It must be possible for this contextual environment to become connected to the complex adaptive system. Moreover, the degree to which this connectivity takes place is a measure of a system's potential to 'go with the flow', adapting to its environment, continually seeking a best fit, optimizing its ability to survive and progress.

Between order and chaos there is a 'complex' world in which entities, objects and stand-alone situations as we traditionally see them (as fixed, static and unchangeable) are not the phenomena representing a world to come. They have proven not to be the drivers of progress and innovation. In a complex world, these traditional entities, objects and frozen situations are reduced to rare species, exceptions to the rule and of no interest in our quest to understand our changing world. What does interest us, amongst other things, are systems, subsystems and hypersystems evolving in close interaction with each other and becoming transient, due to a context in motion and to processes of self-organization between the parts. In addition to a multifaceted and multilevel understanding (not to be understood as a hierarchical, linear perspective) of interactions and exchange, a situational insight into reality emerges.

Situational and temporal assemblies

A situational understanding of reality entails a constellation of events that come together and become manifest at a particular time and place. From this manifestation in reality we assemble one particular and relational construct that we would call a 'situation', to which we can attribute qualities (see DeLanda, 1997; Deleuze and Guattari, 1987; Van Wezemael, 2010 and this volume). In other words, we see a situation becoming manifest. This manifestation of a dynamic situation allows us to identify a planning issue; we can propose actions to be taken and we can reflect upon imaginable consequences. This all results in a rather fundamental chain that most planners implicitly take into consideration: (1) a manifestation of a situation, (2) from which a planning issue is formulated, (3) on the basis of which a planner formulates actions, and (4) imagining the consequences of these actions after they have been implemented and translated into interventions within our physical environment. This idea of a situational understanding makes our reality quite temporal as well.

Assembling situations out of a multifaceted, pluriform and timely world (Deleuze and Guattari, 1987) not only touches on (critical) realism, but also addresses both relativism and relationalism (see also Chapter one). In assembling an understandable reality out of a manifestation which is multifaceted and pluriform in nature, a subjective and intersubjective touch is unavoidable in obtaining an impression of the reality that surrounds us. An assembly or arrangement is nothing but a proposition that refers to the way in which the various observed elements, events, happenings or systems seemingly relate to each other as constructs. This represents a 'situation' that is understood as such, becomes knowable and can be shared as a phenomenon among others who are or can also be made aware of it, and are willing to connect or relate to the 'situation'. The situational understanding of our reality is a consequence of considering the environment we live in as a complex adaptive system. This brings us to the essence of spatial planning.

6.7 Complexity and an outline for spatial planning

With Class IV systems and so-called complex adaptive systems, a range of new understandings have been presented that are as yet unknown in the contemporary debate in planning theory. They include co-evolution, self-organization, emergence and adaptivity, and represent conceptual insights that are to be taken seriously if we agree on the importance of time and non-linear processes as a consequence. While these insights are rather new to planning, some notions that describe phenomena representing the various aspects of complexity and complex adaptive systems are not.

Notions such as resilience, multilevel and situatedness have already enriched the language of planning. These are representative of recent shifts towards new insights in planning, borrowed from other disciplines or philosophical strands and appreciated by a growing number of people in the planning community. With the conceptualization of complexity, these notions could very well become stepping stones to an understanding that includes the principles relating to 'post-normal' science and to Class IV systems: non-linearity, irreversibility and connectivity with a transient context and processes of self-organization.

What once was can no longer be

Most of us will admit that our planning issues long ago ceased to be linear. The successes of the functionality approach within a 'singular' and direct causal world are long gone. Post-war planning, driven by a common interest in rebuilding Europe, was very effective in the past. However, roads, as connections between places and spaces, are no longer constructed entirely on the basis of the criterion of effectiveness. This would mean following a straight line between A and B, something that is now considered overly simplistic. Today, multiple criteria are used to identify an optimum route, including the possibilities for connecting various modes of transport into a multiple-use corridor. Routes no longer cross nature areas and landscapes because these are now protected. Furthermore, routes are restricted due to various environmental qualities being protected by law. Today, the idea that a route might also be taken because its users value it (the idea of observing and enjoying the environment while driving) is taken seriously by a growing number of infrastructure planners (Nijenhuis and Van Winden, 2007).

Most of the more strategic issues in spatial planning and projects representing development planning are far from linear, a statement that should not come as a total surprise to planners. Some time ago, Peter Hall (1980) demonstrated the non-linearity and irrationality of a series of planning disasters apparent throughout the world. Flyfbjerg et al. (2003) studied the reasons why these major projects got so out of hand, reducing the doctrine of control to realistic and therefore minimal proportions. Numerous planners consequently turned their back on projects that were 'too complex', focusing instead on the parts or the modules of which the projects were composed. However, this resulted in a narrow view – quite often too narrow, as we can see in various current projects that have got out of hand.

The Amsterdam North-South metro project is an excellent example (Soetenhorst, 2011). This project would supposedly cost 1.46 billion euros and was guaranteed not to harm the local environment. With an expected rise in costs of more than 100 percent (3.1 billion), a six-year delay, damage to historical sites and leading to the downfall of politicians and project managers, it is a perfect example of the many projects that spiral out of control, with no-one having an overview of the project as a whole.

Moving outside the box

In confronting the idea of 'situatedness', we must acknowledge that such projects do represent a 'situation', as they are a manifestation of various trajectories converging, including a dynamic assembly of a whole range of actors and factors. A clear image of such a situation will not be at all realistic, as it strongly depends on how those involved assemble the various components of a project into a 'whole'. Moreover, mechanisms of communication must ensure that the various actors continually acknowledge that they all still embrace the same understanding or specification of the project (situation) at hand. This is by no means an assurance that an overall view – let alone an in-depth understanding – will be maintained, as the project (being an institutional response to the 'situation') is in a constant state of discontinuous and non-linear change.

    The aim of this contribution is not to resolve this issue, since it is fundamentally impossible to find an ultimate and definitive solution. It cannot be solved using a technical rationale, as we have seen (amongst other things) that humans are limited in their ability to perceive the whole through its constituent and interacting parts. Relying on a communicative rationale, we are also unable to think through each and everyone's behaviour, desires, perceptions and interests regarding a project and/or its consequences. To add to these imperfections, the non-linearity of these projects makes it even harder to understand the whole.

    What awaits us is not the ultimate solution but an alternative solution (contrasting common approaches and outcomes), if we are willing to move forward in our thinking, abstractions and theories with regard to spatial planning and decision-making. What matters is how a project is seen, against an outline of planning that allows the project to be positioned in such a way that (1) the situational characteristics of the project can be distilled into (2) a planning issue, from which (3) planning actions can be deduced and (4) the consequences of these actions can be imagined.

    An alternative approach does not deliver a 'better' solution than traditional practices (resulting in appreciated 'ends'), but instead proposes a different type of solution that appreciates those issues that could not be successfully dealt with by traditional means. This is what happened for example with the introduction of the communicative rationale. The communicative rationale was an answer to failing technical-rationale approaches to projects that had gained in 'complexity'. These approaches did not function properly due to increasing numbers of stakeholders, who each had different interests and had (or wanted to have) a voice. The technical rationale proved to be unsuccessful in dealing with the actor-related uncertainty in these projects. However, the communicative rationale did not provide the ultimate answer through which all planning issues could be dealt with. Rather, it added substantially to the spectrum of possibilities and introduced appropriate methods and tools for a specific group of planning issues. This innovation also highlighted the limitations of the technical-rationale perspective, being particularly successful in planning issues that we would today call straightforward.

A frozen moment in time

In various publications I have proposed the spectrum between the extremes of the technical and communicative ideal types as the spectrum for spatial planning and decision-making on which planning issues can be positioned in order to identify approaches and actions, and from which the consequences of these actions can be imagined (see Figure 6.1). This spectrum is more then just a line, as can already be seen in De Roo (2003), where the spectrum carries a model of decision-making, and in De Roo and Porter (2006) with the spectrum being a contingency representing a dual mix of an object-oriented and an intersubjective-oriented approach to spatial planning and decision-making. The spectrum in Figure 6.1 presents three 'meta' approaches to planning: blueprint planning, scenario planning and network planning.

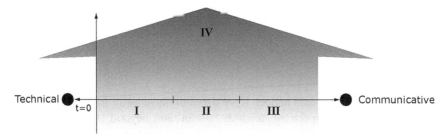

Figure 6.2   A possible relationships between system classes I, II and III (being) to system class IV (becoming) (De Roo, 2010)

In Chapter 2 of *A Planner's Encounter with Complexity*, the volume preceding this one, a proposal incorporating time is added to this spectrum of planning and decision-making (see also Figure 6.2). The result is the beginnings of a matrix (see Figure 6.6) that builds on the planning and decision-making spectrum. The importance of this matrix is that it positions the spectrum relative to time. The matrix thus reduces the spectrum to a moment in time, this moment being the 'here and now'. In other words, the spectrum can be found at 't = 0'.

From a temporal perspective, the planning and decision-making spectrum and its extremes (the technical and communicative rationales) is no longer atemporal but represents a 'snapshot' in time. This is precisely what the spectrum is about: it represents decisions as they are made in spatial planning, in the here and now.

Decisions made within a technical realm are driven by a rationale that takes the facts presented to us here and now as a 'true' representation of our reality, from which we can extrapolate the future to our liking. Logically, the result is a decision made in the 'here and now', at 't = 0'.

Decisions made within a communicative realm are driven by a rationale that prompts us to seek consensus amongst stakeholders with respect to their various interests and powers. Consensus-seeking is the main driver of decisions. Therefore, little attention is paid to trajectories representing the evolution of power relationships, balances of interest and perspectives, opinions and values through time, and how these might lead to alternative networks and alternative desires to intervene at a later stage. Reaching consensus in the here and now is already challenging enough.

Between the technical and communicative rationales we find the category of scenario planning. This particular approach to planning is intrinsically related to time, extrapolating a given past to an open future (Dammers, 2000). This extrapolation involves a linear technique, a technique that is not favoured by this contribution, which emphasizes the reality of non-linearity. However, scenario planning is also strongly related to the moment of decision-making, which is, again, in the here and now. Although scenario planning considers the time dimension far more than any other approach, scenarios also present arguments upon which we base our choice made in the 'here and now' and relating to issues that matter in the 'here and now'.

Pushing the boundaries

Let us imagine what would happen if we dared to move away from the planning and decision-making spectrum, towards 't = m' and beyond (see Figure 6.3), considering non-linearity as a major principle representing developments over time. We might obtain the following results. If we were to release a blueprint plan from its frozen condition, making it susceptible to time, we might see how, over time, our present reality bends towards the plan's proposals, ideally remaining the same as long as the plan remains valid. The result is a feed-forward loop in time, which affects a future reality, conditioning the future somehow by the plan, its proposals and commitment to act accordingly. These conditions interact with the future. This future, in due course – perhaps at 't = m' – will be reconsidered as input for a subsequent plan, which again will claim a future to come, and which is consequently again a feed-forward loop.

Releasing a network from its frozen state would result in emerging networks, a notion not entirely new to spatial planning (see Figure 6.3). Today this is quite a popular theme in the telecommunication sciences a.o. reflecting on phenomena such as Twitter and Facebook. Emerging networks not only represent interacting and consensus-seeking actors. They do show dynamic movements, not directed by anyone in particular, as they are the result of interplay between the various actors, parties and institutions (Taylor, 2003). Emerging networks are both dynamic and integrated entities, in a constant process of discontinuous change. This results in different settings for participating organizations (and their representatives) during the project, by and large to be distributed across the various stages through which the project progresses. It is unlikely, therefore, that an individual actor representing an organization will participate in the project from beginning to end.

What we see is by and large a process of self-organization that drives the evolution of these networks, with actors moving in and out of the formal and informal organizations participating in the project in question. This process of self-organization and self-regulation leads to frequently changing structures, dependencies and interactions, hence the emergence of a network. This network is often temporary, set up for a particular reason, which could be the development of a particular site, the construction of a railroad, or the renewal of a neighbourhood. Multiple parties are involved in all of these cases, and each one has some degree of power to act, invest or withdraw, and to appreciate and enjoy the benefits of any results. All these parties are needed to keep the project up and running. In other words, aside from the liberty to participate, there is a necessity to participate.

Public Private Partnerships (PPPs) are an example of cooperating networks, and open to ideas of emergence, adaptation and complexity (Klijn and Teisman, 2000; Van Assche and Verschraegen, 2008). PPP is considered a good alternative to one-sided and quite often ineffective initiatives by governments, sometimes even outside their fields of expertise (CPFI, 2008). Examples are the construction of roads, tunnels or development sites, the management of parks, industrial sites and ferry lines, and other activities such as waste collection and energy production. For several decades, PPP has been presented as an alternative approach, allowing more efficient activities to take place under the responsibility of experts. It has led to numerous positive examples. Beyond this, it has also led to surprising and sustainable innovations. For example, with regard to site constructions, not only the construction itself but also maintenance is now considered an important and financially viable activity of project developers. This innovation has led to results far more widely appreciated than the 'hit-and-run' strategies frequently employed in the past.

There is a dilemma, however. PPPs are very much organized around a contract between the partners. This contract is made at a particular moment in time, right at the beginning of the intervention, resulting in fixed conditions that are difficult to change during the later stages of the project. This finding sounds all too familiar. New approaches to PPP are now being considered (Wettenhall, 2008), to allow flexibility during the project period, making the project more adaptable to changing conditions, which are welcomed by and beneficial to all the parties involved.

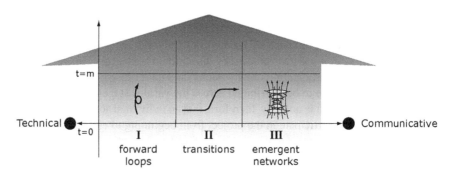

Figure 6.3   Positioning feed-forward loops, transitions and emergent networks in a taxonomy of planning rationales

Transitions

Scenario planning, the name we have used for the planning category in the middle of the spectrum between the technical and communicative rationales, makes direct references to 'time', allowing it to flow, but only in a linear manner, extrapolating the past and present into the future. Transcending scenario planning, as we previously transcended blueprint and network planning, would mean having to replace a linear idea of progression with a non-linear understanding of progression over time. I would consider transitions to be a good example of non-linear progression over time that could be of interest to spatial planning.

Transitions are non-linear movements or leaps from one stable level to another (Figure 6.4; see also Rotmans, Loorbach and Kemp in this volume; De Roo, 2010; Geels, 2005; Kemp, 1994; Rotmans, Kemp and Van Asselt, 2001). These transitions are likely to take place when the time is 'right'. This is the case when the system and its environment no longer have a proper optimal or appreciable fit, that is, the system and/or its environment are ready for change and have the potential to make the leap (rather than collapsing during the transition and reverting to the previous level of stability). This could also be the case when the contextual environment in which the system is embedded is no longer stable and an appreciated haven to which the system, in systems language, 'connects well'. In such a situation, the system can collapse, together with its increasingly unstable context, or can be pushed towards another level of stability, preferably a higher level. If a higher level is indeed reached, we are likely to perceive this as a development that has taken place.

Complex adaptive systems have the potential to co-evolve during a process of transition. With co-evolution, the system undergoing the transition might fundamentally transform in terms of its structure and function (see Figure 6.4A with the white circle transforming into a shaded square). This process of co-evolution is the result of the system adapting to a new context, the new environment embracing the system to allow a better fit between the system and its environment. During the process of co-evolution, stability decreases while the system's dynamics increase.

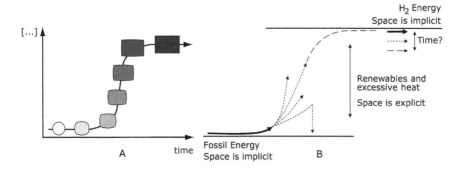

Figure 6.4   **The co-evolutionary process of a transition (A. De Roo, 2010), made explicit for the 'energy transition' between two stable levels, and its time-space relationship (B. De Roo, 2011)**

As soon as the system connects with a new contextual environment, stability increases again and the system's identity is likely to have changed radically due to the co-evolution of its structure and function.

Cities are good examples of systems that change over time in a structural and a functional sense. Cities were once nodes connecting trade routes and brought security, which was evident in physical entities such as bridges and defence structures. During the Industrial Revolution, cities became modes of production, providing space for industrial sites and a rapidly growing labour force. This marked the beginning of the functionally planned city, with neighbourhoods separated from other functions. Today we are willing to see cities as nodes again, this time linking the global and the local, fuelling creativity and knowledge. Moreover, the physical manifestations are no longer very clear, with a huge variety of communicative functions operating, to varying degrees, in the 'virtual' world.

Another example is energy, with the decline of the fossil-fuel era and the transition towards a new source of energy that is universally available (see Figure 6.4B). Various trajectories are drivers of change away from fossil-fuel consumption. One of these will be the depletion of oil and gas reserves in the next 30 to 40 years. Another is the CO_2 emissions that are released from fossil fuels, which affect our climate and the sea level. Geopolitics is also a reason for finding alternative sources of energy. Today we still remember the oil crisis of 1973, when oil was used as a political tool by OPEC countries to punish the US and European countries for supporting Israel in the Yom Kippur War. Today, European countries are very much aware of their dependency on Russian gas and the power relations that come with it. All these trajectories together represent what we today call an energy crisis. The set of trajectories constitute a strong motive for seeking alternatives, such as renewables, excessive heat networks, smart grids, seasonal thermal storage, and more. It is interesting to see how this relates to spatial planning. While fossil fuels were (and still are) available everywhere, it has hardly affected spatial design. The price of energy proved not to be the crucial criteria in people's strategy for deciding where to live in relation to their place of work. The time they were willing to spend commuting proves to be the decisive factor (Lyons and Chatterjee, 2008). In contrast to this, renewables, excessive heat networks and other alternative sources of energy are spatially constrained (Noorman and De Roo, 2010). This makes spatial planning rather relevant at a time of transition towards another level of stability, with energy (e.g., hydrogen, see Bockris, 1975; Rifkin, 2002) again being universally available (see Figure 6.4B).

'Transition' is a relatively new concept derived from the complexity sciences that could become instrumental to planning theory and practice. I am willing to say that it touches upon reality more realistically than scenarios and their linear assumptions. Transitions present a reality full of leaps and sudden change, causation being strongly relational (see Chapter 1). Causation is not a clearly defined straightforward action-reaction mechanism between two parts, as in a Newtonian world. The cause of the transition emerges out of the often fuzzy relationship between a system, its subsystems and the contextual environment to which the system is connected. The connectivity between system and context diminishes, affecting the system's relationship to its subsystems through self-organizing mechanisms, pushing the system into a process of co-evolution towards a better fit with a new contextual environment.

Representing fundamental change, due to processes of co-evolution, the progression of transitions are impossible to quantify a priori. At a meta level, a-priori quantifications are at best a guess, being markers of change, not directly and immediately linked to content and causalities. Stock market indexes are such meta markers of economic change. Nevertheless, transitions do follow a certain path in close relationship with the contextual environment, which would suggest a multilevel and path-dependent perspective for understanding the 'situation' to come. Understanding the path of a transition, means being willing to understand patterns of macro developments taking place. Moreover, we would want to investigate how these developments at the macro level influence potentially interesting initiatives at the micro level. Considering these conditions, we would propose that the role of a planner is that of trend watcher and transition manager, as suggested above.

Managers of change

As a transition manager, the planner acknowledges evolving processes. Clearly the planner 'in control' (within a technical, direct causal world) or the planner as the mediator (in a communicative realm with relative perceptions) would not do well under these evolving conditions. Rather than a 'controlled' or 'man-made' environment, and in contrast to an 'agreed' environment, the complex adaptive system brings to light a more or less autonomously evolving reality. In this respect, our reality is not a creation of human beings who are 'in control', nor is it an agreed reality. Am I questioning the notion of the planner creating entire neighbourhoods? No, but I would like to emphasize that the creation of neighbourhoods is not so much the product of a 'creator' but the result of planners responding or adapting to demographic change and to people's desire to live in a safe, pleasant and well-connected environment.

When should a change be regarded as autonomous, and when should it be regarded as induced (by people)? Thinking through the example of population change, we can see that autonomous flows of change (trends) at the macro level affect the micro level. The planner responds to these at the meso level, guiding processes of neighbourhood development. We also see individual responses to these autonomous flows at the micro level, and the resulting possibilities and constraints (induced by planners) at the meso level, with people making choices about where to live, taking account of the results or consequences of processes at higher levels. Thinking through processes that are either autonomous or induced relates to impossible debates such as 'nature versus nurture' and 'nature versus man'. I will not touch upon these debates here. What is important is the positioning of the planner not as a creator per se, but as a manager of change that comes to us in some form or another. The planner's task is to try to influence this change, embracing and emphasizing its positive spin-offs and trying to avoid or reduce its negative effects. This would be the task of the planner as a manager of change.

6.8 Out of equilibrium

A non-linear world is a 'post-normal' alternative to the reality commonly understood within planning, which I would argue is at least of additional value. I also consider a non-linear world to be more 'real' than a linear world. This might be so, but the main question is: do we have the means to grasp this non-linear world? Can we make it ours in such a way that it will enhance not only our understanding but also the techniques supporting our planning actions?

A non-linear reality assumes a world 'out of equilibrium', that is, a world in which there is flow, motion and the transfer of energy, matter and information. Taken together, these are the conditions of development and progress, and therefore the preconditions for change.

I began this contribution by considering change as the only constant in our reality. More specifically, non-linearity is seen as the characteristic representation of the path that progress takes. The complex adaptive system is presented as the carrier and manifestation of change. Being 'out of equilibrium' is its contextual mode.

Being 'out of equilibrium' implicitly means a desire to reach equilibrium. Equilibrium is not so much a state of 'balance' but a situation in which there is no flow of energy, maximum entropy. Biologists define this state as 'dead'. Such a state will not be reached unless the system is 'down' (communications and electronics), 'dead' (biology), 'broke' (economics), 'neutral' or 'fixed, frozen or static and a-temporal' (planning). A system that functions well will never reach a steady state at equilibrium.

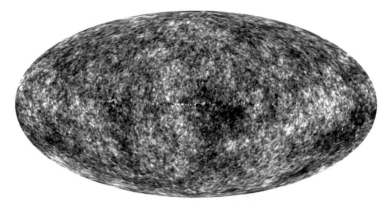

Figure 6.5   'The detailed, all-sky picture of the infant universe created from seven years of WMAP data. The image reveals 13.7 billion year old temperature fluctuations'.

Source: Quoted from: http://wmap.gsfc.nasa.gov/media/101080/. Credit: NASA / WMAP Science Team.

A properly functioning system is always ready for change, taking advantage of being between extremes which create bipolar conditions, being responsible for a 'potential difference' and a contextual flow with which the complex system interacts, engages and adapts to continuously. According to Pirsig (1991), arguing at a metaphysical level, this is all about 'the right balance between stability and fluidity', being the result of constant tension between static and dynamic quality, which he sees as the driving force of development.

The sea's tides cause the waves to which surfers adapt as they ride them. This metaphor is just one step away from the metaphor that some planners use to explain the discipline of planning to outsiders: 'playing billiards on a bouncing ship' (Goudappel, 1973). Most likely Goudappel was unaware of 'Sinai's Billiard', introduced by Sinai (1970), a mathematician, studying non-euclidean geometries and dynamical systems with elastic reflections, to show ideal gasses are maximally chaotic. Within the context of this Chapter we can consider Goudappel's remark a reference to 'out-of-equilibrium' situations in planning.

It is only within physics and mathematics that proposals have been made to quantify the various 'out-of-equilibrium' states. These proposals are restricted to singular environments and do not provide much inspiration for finding a meaningful way of expressing the possible states of a system in a plural environment. Various concepts such as 'Small World Theory' (also known as Milgram's experiment: Milgram, 1967), the 'Law of the Few' (Gladwell, 2000) and Ashby's 'Law of Requisite Variety' (Ashby, 1956) do give some insight in the system's conditions and relational behaviour with its environment. In general, 'out of equilibrium' can be seen as a contextual mode in which it is no longer accurate or valid to quantitatively explain new phenomena emerging from situations and systems.

What is important, however, is that the concept 'out of equilibrium' expresses unity/coherence versus diversity, a fundamental contrast that is apparent at every level of our existence. We could say that unity and diversity are fundamental and go back to the very beginning of the universe: the Big Bang did not result in a cosmos seamlessly and equally divided into matter and energy, but one showing differences (see Figure 6.5) within a whole called the 'universe'. This marks the very beginning (as far we can tell) of flows of matter and energy which, not only at the level of galactic entities but also at the human level, allow a world full of variety from which processes of extropy, processes of increased complexity and processes of development and progress emerge. This not only involves the flow of matter and energy but also that which (complex adaptive) systems exchange with their environment. This is known as dissipative inequality (Prigogine and Stengers, 1984), and is responsible for the dynamic behaviour of systems.

Not only physicists and astronomers, but also biologists and ecologists have given meaning to the idea of systems 'out of equilibrium'. In particular, Holling is known for his so-called panarchy model of adaptive cycles, with connectivity and potentiality (for connections to become meaningful) as the main variables (Gunderson and Holling, 2002; Holling et al., 1995). Would this model assist in enhancing planning? With respect to conservation planning, Lister (2008) showed a remarkable difference in attitude and result between a traditional and an adaptive perspective: the traditional focus of the conservation planner would be to manage nature reserves, not allowing any change to happen, despite this being associated with a decline in ecological variety, while a more dynamic approach would allow a forest fire, for example, to occur occasionally in order to increase the resilience of such reserves. Holling's model is particularly interesting for semi-closed systems, being in a 'near equilibrium' state. Therefore, the model is not a very likely representation of the heterogeneous, plural and multilayered social environments that most planners have to deal with.

Holling's proposal is quite a step forward in thinking through how a non-linear world, out of equilibrium, might be understood: In terms of connectivity and potentiality. Holling's proposal results in an endless loop similar to the trajectory of a Lorentz' system. This system is a well known example of a non-linear dynamic system's long-term behaviour, representing a chaotic flow (Strogatz, 2001). Holling's proposal framing an ecological system on the basis of connectedness and potentiality could be an example for spatial systems that are highly dynamic, open and out of equilibrium. It might give expression to the 'fitness' of a spatial system and the 'fit' with its environment. And it would allow the planner to address, in abstract terms, a heterogeneous, plural and multilayered social environment in a discontinuous flow. Such an adaptive model is not yet available.

The best I can come up with is adding to our model of non-linear rationality (Figure 6.3) 'out of equilibrium'. 'Out of equilibrium' is a variable which is crucial with relation to situations (in planning) in flow, transforming and co-evolving, while exchanging energy, matter and/or information. 'Out of equilibrium' as a variable gives expression to degrees in which situations or systems transform and co-evolve, distinguishing 'far from', 'near' and 'at equilibrium'. Figure 6.6 gives expression to this variable, additional to time and 'degrees of (static) complexity'. The result is a matrix representing the various modes a planning situation can be in, and each mode representing a specific situation, approach, action and likely consequences. Adding characteristics, conditions and criteria to the various modes would be a step towards non-linear understanding of planning and decision-making.

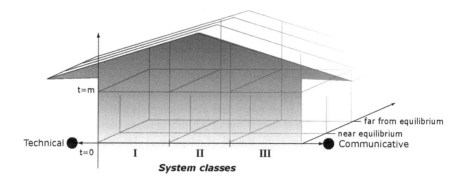

Figure 6.6   Adding to our model of non-linear rationality the notions 'near' and 'far from equilibrium', and the possibility space with regard to the variety of planning situations and their preferred approaches

Although it would be a very interesting route to follow to frame a complex adaptive system in relation to a world out of equilibrium, and the fitness of this relationship in terms of connectivity and potentiality, I would like to propose an alternative route. I would like to advocate the complex adaptive system itself. I aim to identify criteria that characterize the system throughout its life span, while going through the various transitions and moments of co-evolution. In particular, I am looking for criteria that could give a complex adaptive system an identity that strongly reflects its specific evolving and self-organizing qualities. If we were able to find such an identity, we could push the complex adaptive system beyond the metaphor, allowing it to become as 'real' as any other system that we use to represent reality. It would give the complex adaptive system a reference or markers to adhere to, in order to define it, but also support communication about it with others. Moreover, it would bring a critical assessment of the complex adaptive system within reach.

To arrive at such criteria, I take the position that they should make reference to a few very fundamental characteristics of the complex adaptive system mentioned earlier in this contribution. The duality of coherence and diversity is fundamental. Coherence expresses the 'order' to which the system connects, and diversity refers to 'chaos', being the other extreme to which the system relates. Both represent extremes between which the system is able to survive. Another fundamental characteristic addresses the potential of a complex adaptive system to maintain its structure and function (surviving, not disintegrating) while having the flexibility to adapt (through which structure and function co-evolve). This is due to another duality, which is to be robust and dynamic at the same time. These dualities represent contrasts that generate complexity. A complex adaptive system has a certain robustness that grounds dynamic behaviour, which could then become a driver of innovation, development and progress when there is a positive fit with its environmental context. An abstraction of this reasoning is illustrated in Figure 6.7A.

Figure 6.7 A presents the basic model. Figure 6.7B presents a complex adaptive system with a spatial economic identity. In line with the reasoning above, this spatial economic system with complex adaptive behaviour should be represented by criteria that express the system's robustness and dynamics, with both of these making reference to coherence and diversity. I propose the following notions as relevant in this respect: cohesion, compatibility, complementarity and competition.

Cohesion refers to the strength (or harmony) of internal relationships of the various parts, components or subsystems of the region. Social cohesion comprises notions that are frequently used with regard to spatial planning and urban renewal. Territorial cohesion is a concept which has often been used in the past ten years by the European Commission in its quest to find centripetal forces that could lead to a robust and unified conglomerate of nations (Faludi, 2007).

The compatibility of a spatial economic region refers to the interchangeability of economic functions. If an economic function disappears for whatever reason, a robust region would not collapse if that function could be relatively easily replaced by economic functions that were more or less congruent to it.

The concept of 'competing regions' is one that is well understood by politicians, economic geographers, spatial economists and spatial planners. Most regions have a strong desire to be competitive, as competition stands for innovation, development and progress. Competition can lead to 'differential fitness' and 'relative survival' (Lucas, site visite 2011). However, simply being competitive is ultimately rather destructive. Regions acting individually will have different effects than regions working together. A balance between competing and cooperating is desirable. Regions that are complementary to each other are likely to benefit when cooperating, as this might improve the collective fitness. At the same time, it allows the individual region to specialize, which could eventually lead to improvements of the 'integrated whole' of cooperating regions, due to mutually beneficial initiatives, actions and strategies.

A good illustration is the northern Netherlands, the region in which I am based, that is peripheral to the Randstad conurbation, the urban and economic core of the Netherlands. For decades, the northern Netherlands wanted to compete with the Randstad at the level of manufacturing industry and services. It also wanted its own sea port such as in Rotterdam, and an international airport such as in Amsterdam. All these desires proved to be extremely costly. In addition, the competitive urge made the region blind to other developments, such as the rise of the leisure industry, which would prosper in this region, known for its tranquillity, space and

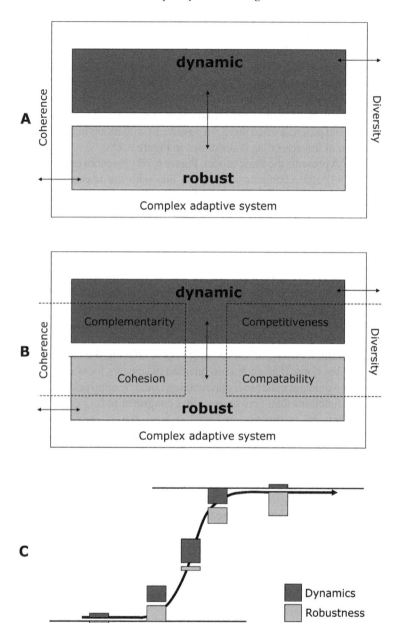

Figure 6.7   Model of (A) the complex adaptive system's main characteristics
with (B) indicators of spatial economic development conditioning
(framing) the system and (C) hypothetically positioned at the
various stages in a transition

nature. A leisure industry making reference to tranquillity, space and nature could very well make the region complementary to the Randstad region. It would also be less costly than fighting a losing battle (Hermans and De Roo, 2006).

One of the messages we can deduce from this complex adaptive understanding of spatial economic regions is that a competing region will also have to identify its complementary qualities in order to cooperate. The complex adaptive model also tells us that a region cannot compete and cooperate properly if there is no robustness in terms of cohesion and compatibility.

The challenge is thus twofold: first, to elaborate on this model and, second, to come up with more proposals to frame other complex adaptive systems within the realm of spatial planning. If the results are convincing and become part of a theoretical discourse, we might have a means of identifying the various complex systems within planning. Moreover, within planning we could acknowledge the beginning and end of systems, their rise and fall, and the processes of their emergence and co-evolution. Overall we would have an instrument that gives meaning to the complex adaptive behaviour of issues in planning, and we would have a tool from which we could develop a form of planning that would be adaptive to the world in which the planner wants to intervene. This kind of planning will be called 'adaptive planning' (Lister and Kay, 1999).

6.9 Adaptive planning

So what can be said about planning in a non-linear world? There is a serious danger in using metaphors and analogies, and copying ideas, concepts and models from other disciplines, hoping for links that might not even exist. We must be critical and cautious in our quest for a non-linear understanding of the world in support of planning actions and strategies. There is, however, much in favour of the quest. There might be a whole new world to discover, which will bring new perspectives to spatial planning and decision-making. Rather than the technical (means-end approaches) and communicative rationales (consensus through interaction), entirely different ontologies will emerge, with adaptivity as a likely possibility. An adaptive rationale, representing the non-linear mode of our environment, would or could result in adaptive planning.

This non-linear or adaptive rationale appreciates an 'in-between' world, continuously reaching out to its extremes while in motion. An adaptive rationale entails a balance between inert sustainability and destructive revolution, allowing dynamic spaces and places to evolve from robust environments. An adaptive rationale lies between inert collaborative actions and destructive competition looking to find a balance that is beneficial to all, allowing specialization and supporting innovation. This adaptive rationale leads to differential fitness and relative survival. All in all, adaptivity involves finding a balance between coherence and diversity, robustness and dynamics, and order and chaos. This balance is called 'fitness' or 'resilience'.

Clearly, these proposals for planning focus strongly on autonomous change (emergence) to which an issue or a situation (represented as a complex adaptive system) will adapt, fuelling internal self-organizing processes as well, resulting in the structural and functional co-evolution of the issue or situation (behaving as a complex adaptive system). Transitions, transition management and emergent networks are presented as examples of a form of planning that adapts to this idea of non-linearity and change. Understanding the mechanisms of change will support the planner's attempts to emphasize and benefit from the positive effects of autonomous change, and will allow the planner to take appropriate action to minimize the negative consequences. Hence the suggestion to regard planners as managers of change.

References

Ackoff, R.L. (1974) *Redesigning the Future, A Systems Approach to Societal Problems*, John Wiley and Sons, New York/London.

Alexander, E.R. (1984) After Rationalism, What? A review of responses to paradigm breakdown, *Journal of the American Planning Association*, pp. 62-69.

Alexander, E.R. (1986) *Approaches to Planning; Introducing Current Planning Theories, Concepts, and Issues*, Gordon and Breach Science Publishers, New York.

Alfasi, N. and Portugali, J. (2007) Planning Rules for a Self-Planned City, *Planning Theory*, 6 (2), pp. 164-182.

Allen, P.M. (1997) *Cities and Regions as Self-organizing Systems: Models of Complexity*, Gordon and Breach Science Publishers, Amsterdam.

Argyris, C., and Schön, D. (1978) *Organizational Learning: A Theory of Action Perspective*, Addison Wesley, Reading (US).

Ashby, W.R. (1956) *An Introduction to Cybernetics*, Chapman and Hall, London.

Batty, M. (2005) *Cities and Complexity; Understanding Cities with Cellular Automata, Agent-Based Models, and Fractals*, The MIT Press, Cambridge.

Bengs, C. (2005) Planning Theory for the Naïve?, *European Journal of Spatial Development*, 4, Debate and Miscellaneous.

Bockris, J (1975) *Energy, The Solar-Hydrogen Alternative*, Wiley, London.

Boulding, K.E. (1956) General System Theory - The Skeleton of Science, *General Systems I*, Vol. 2, pp. 197-208.

Byrne, D. (1998) *Complexity Theory and the Social Sciences: An Introduction*, Routledge, London.

Cilliers, P. (1998) *Complexity and Postmodernism: Understanding Complex Systems*, Routledge, London.

Chadwick, G. (1971) *A Systems View of Planning: Towards a Theory of the Urban and Regional Planning Process*, Pergamon Press, Oxford.

Checkland, P.B. (1991) From Optimizing to Learning: A Development of Systems Thinking for the 1990s, in: R.L. Flood and M.C. Jackson (eds.), *Critical Systems Thinking*, John Wiley and Sons, Chichester, pp. 59-75.

Christensen, K.S. (1985) 'Coping with Uncertainty in Planning', *Journal of the American Planning Association*, pp. 63-73.

Coveney, P., R. Highfield (1991) *Frontiers of Complexity, The Search for Order in a Chaotic World*, Faber and Faber Limited, London.

CPFI (2008) Op de goede weg en het juiste spoor [On the right direction and the right track], Commissie Private Financiering van Infrastructuur (CPFI), The Hague.

Dammers, E. (2000) *Leren van de toekomst, over de rol van scenario's bij strategische beleidsvorming* [Lessons from the future, about the role of scenarios within strategic policies], Eburon, Delft (NL).

Davies, L. (2003) *Conflict and Chaos*, Routledge, London.

DeGrace, P., and L.H. Stahl (1990) *Wicked Problems, Righteous Solutions*, Yourdon Press, Prentice Hall.

Deleuze, G., F. Guattari (1987) *A Thousand Plateaus: Capitalism and Schizophrenia*, University of Minnesota Press, Minneapolis and London.

De Roo, G. (2003) *Environmental Planning in the Netherlands - too Good to be True: From Command-and-Control Planning to Shared Governance*, Ashgate, Aldershot.

De Roo, G. (2010) Being or Becoming? That is the Question! Confronting Complexity with Contemporary Planning Theory, in G. de Roo and E.A. Silva (eds.), *A Planner's Encounter with Complexity*, Ashgate, Farnham, pp. 19-38.

De Roo, G. (2011) Derde generatie energielandschappen – Van energie naar exergie [Third generation energy landscapes – From energy to exergy], *Geografie* 20 (5), pp. 10-13.

De Roo, G. and G. Porter (2007) *Fuzzy Planning: The Role of Actors in a Fuzzy Governance Environment*, Ashgate, Farnham.

De Roo, G. and W.S. Rauws (2012) Positioning Planning in the World of Order and Chaos: On perspectives, behaviour and interventions in a non-linear environment. In: J. Portugali, H. Meyer, E. Stolk, E. Tan (eds) *Complexity Theories of Cities Have Come of Age: An Overview with Implications to Urban Planning and Design*, Springer, Heidelberg.

Emery, F.E. (ed.) *Systems Thinking*, Penguin Books, Harmondsworth.

Faludi, A. (1973) *Planning Theory*, Pergamon Press, Oxford.

Faludi, A. (ed.) (2007) *Territorial Cohesion and the European Model of Society*, Lincoln Institute of Land Policy, Cambridge.

Flood, R.L. and M.C. Jackson (eds.) *Critical Systems Thinking*, John Wiley and Sons, Chichester.

Flyvbjerg, B., N. Bruzelius, W. Rothengatter (2003) *Megaprojects and Risk: An Anatomy of Ambition*, Cambridge University Press, Cambridge.

Forester. J. (1993) *Critical Theory, Public Policy, and Planning Practice. Toward a Critical Pragmatism*, State University of New York Press, Albany.

Friedmann, J. (1987) *Planning in the Public Domain: From Knowledge to Action*, Princeton University Press, Princeton.

Friend, J.K., Jessop, N. (1969) *Local Government and Strategic Choice*, Pergamon, Oxford.

Funtowicz, S. and Ravetz, J. (1993) Science for the Post-Normal Age, *Futures* 25 (7), pp. 739-755.

Geels, F. (2005) *Technological Transitions and System Innovations: A Co-evolutionary and Socio-technical Analysis*, Edward Elgar, Cheltenham.

Gharajedaghi, J. (2005) *Systems Thinking: Managing Chaos and Complexity – A Platform for Designing Business Architecture*, Butterworth-Heinemann, Oxford.

Gladwell, M. (2000) *The Tipping Point*. Little, Brown, London.

Gleick, J. (1987) *Chaos, Making a New Science*, Viking, New York.

Gober, P. (1992) Urban Housing Demography, *Progress in Human Geography*, 16 (2), pp. 171-189.

Goudappel (1973) Handelen in Onzekerheid [Acting in Uncertainty], Phd Thesis, TU Eindhoven, Eindhoven (NL)

Gros, C. (2008) *Complex and Adaptive Dynamical Systems*, Springer Verlag, Heidelberg, London.

Gunderson, L.H., C.S. Holling (eds.) (2002) *Panarchy: Understanding Transformations in Human and Natural Systems*, Island Press, Washington, DC.

Hall, P. (1980) *Great Planning Disasters*, University of California Press, Berkeley, Los Angeles, London.

Harper, T. and Stein, S. (2000) Critiques of Communicative Planning: A Pragmatic Response, Paper presentation at the annual ACSP conference, Atlanta.

Healey, P. (1992) Planning through debate; The communicative turn in planning theory, *Town Planning Review* 63(2), pp. 143-162.

Hermans, E.W. and De Roo, G. (2006) Lila en de Planologie van de Contramal – De ruimtelijk-economische ontwikkeling van Noord-Nederland krijgt eigen kleur [Lilac and the Spatial Planning of the Contra Mould – The spatial economic development of North of the Netherlands gets its own colour], In Boekvorm, Assen (NL)

Holland, J. (1998) *Emergence: From Chaos to Order*, Addison-Wesley, New York.

Holling, C.S., Sanderson, S. (1996) Dynamics of (Dis)harmony in ecological and social systems, in: S. Hanna, C. Folke and K. Mäler (eds.) *Rights to Nature: Institutions for Humans and the Environment*, Island Press, Washington, DC, pp. 57-85.

Holling, C.S., D.W. Schindler, B.W. Walker, J. Roughgarden (1995) Biodiversity in the functioning of ecosystems: An ecological synthesis, in: C. Perrings, K.G. Maler, C. Folke, C.S. Holling, B.O. Jansson (eds.), *Biodiversity Loss: Economic and Ecological Issues*, Cambridge University Press, Cambridge, pp. 44-83.

Huxley, M.E. (2000) The Limits to Communicative Planning, *Journal of Planning Education and Research* 19 (4) (Summer), pp. 369-377.

Imrie, R. (1999) The implications of the 'New Managerialism' for planning in the millennium, in P. Allmendinger and M. Chapman (eds.) *Planning Beyond 2000*, John Wiley, New York, pp. 107-120.

Innes, J.E. (1995) Planning Theory's Emerging Paradigm: Communicative Action and Interactive Practice, *Journal of Planning Education and Research* 14 (3), pp. 183-189.

Innes, J.E. (1996) Planning through Consensus Building; A New View of the Comprehensive Planning Ideal, *Journal of the American Planning Association* 62 (4), pp. 460-472.

Jacobs, J. (1961) *The Death and Life of Great American Cities*, Random House, New York.

Kauffman, S.A. (1993) *The Origins of Order: Self Organization and Selection in Evolution*, University Press, New York.

Kauffman, S.A. (1995) *At Home in the Universe*, Oxford University Press, New York.

Kemp, R. (1994) Technology and the transition to environmental sustainability: the problem of technological regime shifts, *Futures*, 26, pp. 1023-1046.

Klijn, E.H. and G.R. Teisman, G. (2000) Governing public-private patnerships, in: S.P. Osborne, *Public Private Partnerships, Theory and practice in international perspective*, Taylor and Francis, London, p. 91.

Kramer, N.J.T.A., J. de Smit (1991) *Systeemdenken* [Systems thinking], Stefert Kroese, Leiden.

Kuhn, Th.S. (1962) *The Structure of Scientific Revolution*, University of Chicago Press, Chicago.

Latour, B. (1993) *We Have Never Been Modern*, Harvester Wheatsheaf, Hemel Hempstead.

Lewin, R. (1993) *Complexity: Life on the Edge of Chaos*, Phoenix, London.

Liebowitz, S.J., S.E. Margolis (1995) Path dependence, lock-in and history, *Journal of Law, Economics, and Organization* 11, pp. 205-226.

Lister, N.M.E. (2008) Bridging Science and Values – The Challenge of Biodiversity Conservation, in D. Waltner-Toews, J.J. Kay, N.M.E. Lister, *The Ecosystem Approach – Complexity, Uncertainty, and Managing for Sustainability*, Columbia University Press, New York, pp. 83-124.

Lister, N., Kay, J.J. (1999) Celebrating Diversity: Adaptive Planning and Biodiversity Conservation, in S. Bocking (ed.), *Biodiversity in Canada: An Introduction to Environmental Studies*, Broadview Press, Peterborough (CA), pp. 189–218.

Lorentz, E.N. (1963) 'Deterministic nonperiodic flow', *Journal of Atmospheric Sciences* 20, pp. 130-141.

Lucas, Ch. (site visite 2011) http://www.calresco.org/lucas/fitness.htm.

Luhmann, N. (1995) *Social Systems*, Stanford University Press, San Francisco.

Lyons, G., and Chatterjee, K. (2008) A Human Perspective on the Daily Commute: Costs, Benefits and Trade-offs, *Transport Reviews* 28 (2), pp. 181-198.

Mainzer, K. (1994) *Thinking in Comlexity – The Complex Dynamics of Matter, Mind and Mankind*, Springer-Verlag, Heidelberg, London.

McLoughlin, J.B. (1969) *Urban and Regional Planning: A Systems Approach*, Faber and Faber, London.

Meyerson, M., Banfield, E. (1955) *Politics, Planning and the Public Interest: The case of public housing in Chicago*, Free Press, New York.

Milgram, S. (1967) The Small World Problem, *Psychology Today* 1 (1) May, pp. 60-67.

Nijenhuis, W. and Van Winden, W. (2007) *De Diabolische Snelweg – Over de traditie van de mooie weg in het Nederlandse landschap en het verlangen naar de schitterende snelweg in de grote stad* [Diabolic Highway – About the tradition of beautiful roads in the Dutch landscape and the desire for the magnificent highway in the main city], Uitgeverij 010, Rotterdam.

Noorman, K.J., G. de Roo (2010) Energielandschappen, de 3de Generatie [Energy Landscapes, the Third Generation], In Boekvorm, Assen., Papageorgiou, M., Diakaki, Ch., Dininopoulou, V., Kotsialos, A., and Wang, Y. (2003) Review of Road Traffic Control Strategies, *Proceedings of the IEEE* 91 (12), December, pp. 2043-2067.

Portugali, J. (1999) *Self-organization and the City*, Springer-Verlag, Berlin.

Portugali, J., H. Meyer, E. Stolk, E. Tan (eds) (2012) *Complexity Theories of Cities Have Come of Age: An Overview with Implications to Urban Planning and Design*, Springer, Heidelberg.

Prigogine, I., Stengers, I. (1984) *Order out of Chaos*, New Science Press, Boulder.

Rauws, W.S., G. de Roo (2011) Exploring Transitions in the Peri-Urban Area', *Planning Theory and Practice* 12, pp. 269-284.

Rifkin, J. (2002) *The Hydrogen Economy*, Penguin Putnam Inc., New York.

Rittel, H. (1972) On the Planning Crisis: Systems Analysis of the 'First and Second Generation', *Bedriftsøkonomen* 8, pp. 390-396.

Rittel, H., M. Webber (1973) Dilemmas in a General Theory of Planning, *Policy Sciences* 4, pp. 155-169.

Rotmans, J., R. Kemp and M. van Asselt (2001) More Evolution Than Revolution: Transition Management in Public Policy. *Foresight* 3 (1), pp. 15-32.

Schön, D. (1983) *The Reflective Practitioner; How Professionals Think in Action*, Temple Smith, London.

Schönwandt, W.L. (2007) *Planning in Crisis? Theoretical Orientations for Architecture and Planning*, Ashgate, Aldershot.

Simon, H. (1957) *Models of Man, Social and Rational: Mathematical Essays on Rational Human Behavior in a Social Setting*, Wiley, New York.

Sinai, Ya.G. (1970) Dynamical Systems with Elastic Reflections, *Russian Math Surveys* 25, pp. 137–191.

Soetenhorst, B. (2011) *Het wonder van de Noord/Zuidlijn – Het drama van de Amsterdamse metro* [A miracle called the North/South connection – The disaster the Amsterdam metro is], Bert Bakker, Amsterdam.

Stogatz, S.H. (2001) *Nonlinear Dynamics and Chaos*, Perseus Books, Cambridge.

Taylor, M.C. (2003) *The Moment of Complexity: Emerging Network Culture*, The University of Chicago Press, Chicago.

Urry, J. (2003) *Global Complexity*, Polity Press, Cambridge.

Usher, R., I. Bryant and R. Johnston (1997) *Adult Education and the Postmodern Challenge – Learning Beyond the Limits*, Routledge, London.

Van Assche, K. and G. Verschraegen (2008) The Limits of Planning: Niklas Luhmann's Systems Theory and The Analysis of Planning and Planning Ambitions, *Planning Theory* 7, pp. 263-283.

Van der Valk, A. (1999) Willens en wetens: Planning en wetenschap tussen wens en werkelijkheid [Deliberately and Knowingly: Planning and science between wish and reality], Inaugural lecture, Wageningen Universiteit, Wageningen.

Van Wezemael, J.E. (2010) Urban Governance and Social Complexity, in: G. de Roo and E.A. Silva, *A Planner's Encounter with Complexity*, Ashgate, Farnham, pp. 283-308.

Von Bertalanffy, L. (1968) *General Systems Theory: Foundations, Development and Applications*, Braziller, New York.

Waldrop, M.M. (1992) *Complexity: The Emerging Science at the Edge of Order and Chaos*, Penguin Books, London.

Weaver, W. (1948) Science and Complexity, *American Scientist* 36, pp. 536-541.

Webster, C.J. (2010) Emergence, Spatial Order, Transaction Costs and Planning, in: G. de Roo and E.A. Silva, *A Planner's Encounter with Complexity*, Ashgate, Farnham, pp. 123-138.

Webster, C.J., L.W.C. Lai (2003) *Property Rights, Planning and Markets: Managing Spontaneous Cities*, Edward Elgar, Cheltenham.

West Churchman, C. (1967) Wicked Problems, *Management Science* 14 (4), Guest Editorial.

West Churchman, C. (1984) *The Systems Approach*, Delacorte Press, New York.

Wettenhall, R. (2008) Public-Private Mixes and Partnerships: A Search for Understanding, *The Asia Pacific Journal of Public Administration* 30 (2), pp. 119-138.

Wolfram, S. (2002) *A New Kind of Science*, Wolfram Media, Champaign Ill.

Chapter 7

Complexity and Transition Management

Jan Rotmans, Derk Loorbach and René Kemp[1]

This chapter presents transition management as a governance model for addressing 'persistent societal problems' and explores how it relates to spatial problems and planning. Transition management is based on key notions from complex systems theory and new forms of governance that are integrated into a new management paradigm. This management paradigm starts from complexity and uncertainty as means of leverage of societal innovation instead of obstacles that must be contained. This chapter deals with the theoretical grounding of the model of transition management, by discussing in more detail its theoretical roots in complex systems theory. Accordingly we explore the implications for transition management when applied in a spatial context, and illustrate this by the application of transition management in the CityPorts project in Rotterdam, the Netherlands.

7.1 Introduction

Our society faces a number of persistent problems whose symptoms are becoming more and more apparent. Persistent problems are complex because they are deeply embedded in our societal structures, uncertain due to the hardly reducible structural uncertainty they include, difficult to manage with a variety of actors with diverse interests involved and hard to grasp in the sense that they are difficult to interpret and ill-structured (Dirven, Rotmans and Verkaik, 2002). Persistent problems are the superlative form of what Rittel and Webber (1973) refer to as 'wicked problems' and can be observed at the level of sectors (e.g. energy provision, food production) or in spatial areas (e.g. regions, cities or large scale development areas). Persistent problems cannot be solved using only current policies (Ministry of Housing, Spatial planning and Environment, 2002; Social and Economic Council of the Netherlands, 2001). In order to combat system failures a restructuring of our societal systems is required: transitions. A transition is a radical, structural change

---

1   Jan Rotmans is Professor in transitions and transition management at the Erasmus University Rotterdam. He is also the scientific director of DRIFT (Dutch Research Institute For Transitions). Derk Loorbach is director of DRIFT and associate professor at the Faculty of Social Science, Erasmus University Rotterdam. René Kemp is Professorial fellow at UNU-MERIT and Professor of Innovation and Sustainable Development at ICIS, Maastricht University, the Netherlands.

of a societal (sub) system that is the result of a co-evolution of economic, cultural, technological, ecological and institutional developments at different scale-levels (Rotmans et al., 2001). A transition is characterized by fast and slow developments as a result of positive and negative feedback mechanisms and usually spans one or two generations (25-50 years). In a transition a societal system is successfully adjusted to changed internal and external circumstances and the system thus arrives at a higher order of organization and complexity (Rotmans, 2006). In 'transition language' we call the constellation that gives stability to a system the incumbent regime: a conglomerate of structure (institutional and physical setting), culture (prevailing perspective) and practices (rules, routines and habits). And we denote an emergent structure as a niche: a structure formed by a small group of niche agents that deviates from the regime and that might build up niche regimes that are able to break down the incumbent regime and ultimately establishing a new regime. This differs somewhat from the common definition of a niche as individual technologies, practices and actors outside or peripheral to the regime, as loci for radical innovation (Geels, 2005). Newcomers have not yet been moulded by the existing equilibrium and are therefore able to break through it, but for this they need to be shielded in a relatively protected environment, what we call a transition arena (Loorbach, 2007).

The very idea is that a better insight into the functioning of societal systems provides insight into the possibilities of directing these systems. We suggest using complex systems theory to study the dynamics of societal systems in order to derive a collection of basic guidelines that can be used to direct societal systems. Obviously, societal systems, because of their complexity, cannot be directed in command and control terms. We do however hypothesize that it is possible to use the understanding of transition dynamics to influence the direction and pace of a transition of a societal system into a more sustainable direction. The latter explicit normative orientation of sustainability is important, because historical transitions often did not lead to a more sustainable society (Rotmans, 2005). What is considered sustainable is dependent on time, place and participants. In other words, it is inherently ambiguous, uncertain and contested. However we argue that it is possible to facilitate a process of searching-and-learning within which various and competing options are experimented with, multiple images and pathways are pursued and strategies and behaviour are adapting to the evolving understanding of what is sustainable. Fostering sustainability transitions in such a way is what we call transition management (Rotmans et al., 2001).

So far, most research and applied work on transition management has been in the context of national and sectoral transitions. Increasingly however local and regional transitions have been emerging as new topic of interest. The concept of 'urban transitions' is being studied especially from an ecological or resilience perspective (e.g., Ernstson et al., 2010), there are some scientific debates emerging on the spatial dimensions of transitions (Hodson and Marvin, 2010) and more and more spatial transition programs are being set up. In this chapter we will therefore also reflect on the question whether spatial areas can also be viewed as complex systems facing persistent problems, and to what extent the transition management approach could be applied.

The structure of the chapter is as follows. First we delineate basic principles of complex systems theory. Second, we discuss how the complex systems and planning paradigms relate. Third, we 'delve' into the issue of managing complex adaptive systems, resulting in the formulation of core theoretical principles for transition management. The principles are instrumentalized in a framework of 'systemic instruments' and steps for managing societal systems in a reflexive manner, to be applied in practice. Finally we illustrate this briefly by means of the planning process for the Cityports area of Rotterdam, the Netherlands.

7.2 Complex systems theory

Complexity theory, otherwise known as complex systems theory, has its roots in the general systems theory that Von Bertalanffy (Von Bertalanffy, 1968) published since the 1930s. Systems theory is an interdisciplinary field of science that studies the nature of complex systems in society, nature, science and technology. It provides a framework by which a group of interrelated components that influence each other can be analysed. That can be a sector, branch, city, organism, or even a society. Systems theory evolved over the last century. The first generation, roughly from the beginning till the 1960s, focused on general systems theory and was somewhat deterministic, arising from cybernetics and control engineering. Topics like complexity, self-organization, emergence and adaptive systems came up in the 1940s and 1950s, but a niche phenomenon at that time. In the 1970s and 1980s integral systems theory became an important field, focusing on the integration of social, economic and ecological processes (Holling, 1978; Hordijk, 1985; Rotmans, 1990). During the 1970s and 1980s soft systems theory emerged, taking a qualitative approach rather than a quantitative approach, mostly applied to companies and organizations (Senge, 1990). In the 1990s complex systems theory was introduced, focusing on the co-evolutionary development of systems. The establishment of the Santa Fé institute in New Mexico in the US in the early 1980s functioned as incubator for a new research movement, which laid the basis for complex systems theory (Holland, 1995; Kauffman, 1993; 1995). Although the theory is far from mature, it has attracted a great deal of attention and has many applications in diverse research fields: in biology (Kauffman, 1995), economics (Arthur, Durlauf and Lane, 1997), ecology (Gunderson and Holling, 2002; Kay et al., 1999), public administration (Kickert, 1991; Teisman, 1992) and policy analysis (Geldof, 2002; Rotmans, 2003). Complex systems theory comes in different forms, but we take the developed understanding of the dynamic behaviour and patterns of change of complex systems as a starting point for our transition research. We especially make use of insights that relate to the cyclical periods of relatively long periods of equilibrium, order and stability interspersed with relatively short periods of instability and chaos complex systems run through.

Primary focus is on complex systems, which have the following characteristics, as
drawn from Prigogine and Stengers (1984), Holling (1987), Holland (1995) and
Kauffman (1995):

- Complex systems are open systems that interact with their environment.
  This takes place through a constant import and export of matter, energy and
  information across system boundaries. It is usually difficult to determine
  the boundaries of a complex system, which is often based on the observer's
  needs and prejudices rather than an intrinsic property of the system itself.
- Complex systems contain many, diverse components and interactions
  between components. These interactions are non-linear. There are no simple
  cause and effect relationships between components. A small stimulus may
  cause a large effect or no effect at all. On the other hand a big stimulus may
  cause a small effect.
- Complex systems contain feedback loops. Both negative (damping) and
  positive (amplifying) feedbacks are key ingredients of complex systems.
  The effects of a component's behaviour are fed back to it in such a way that
  the component itself is altered.
- Complex systems have a history. The history of a complex system is
  important and cannot be ignored. Prior states have an influence on present
  states that have an influence on future states. This creates path dependence,
  where current and future states depend on the path of previous states.
- Complex systems are nested and encompass various organizational levels.
  That means that the components of the systems are themselves complex
  systems. They have emergent properties, i.e. higher level structures arise
  from interaction between lower level components.
- Complex systems have multiple attractors. An attractor is a preferred
  steady system's state set to which a complex system evolves after a long
  enough time. So attractors describe the long-term behaviour of a complex
  system. Geometrically, an attractor can be a fixed point such as a target
  state, a curve, a manifold, or even a complicated set with chaotic behaviour
  known as a strange attractor.

Complex adaptive systems

Complex adaptive systems are special cases of complex systems. They are adaptive
in the sense that they have the capacity to change and learn from experience.
Formulated otherwise, they are able to respond to and adjust themselves to
changes in their environment. What makes a complex adaptive system special
is the set of constantly adapting nonlinear relationships. Examples of complex
adaptive systems are the stock market, ant colonies, living organisms, ecosystems,
cities, the human brain, business companies, political parties and communities.
Complex adaptive systems contain special objects, agents that interact with each
other and adapt themselves to other agents and changing conditions. This makes

why complex adaptive systems have unique features which are: co-evolution, emergence and self-organization.

In the biological or economic context co-evolution refers to mutual selection of two or more evolving populations (van den Bergh and Stagl, 2004). In the complex systems context, however, we speak of co-evolution if the interaction between different systems influences the dynamics of the individual systems, leading to irreversible patterns of change within each of the systems (Kemp, Rotmans and Loorbach, 2007). The irreversibility aspect distinguishes co-evolution from co-production which indicates mere interaction. Co-evolution means that a complex system co-evolves with its environment (which in turn consists of complex systems), referring to interdependencies and positive feedbacks between the complex system and its environment (Mitleton-Kelly, 2003). In such a co-evolutionary process both competition and cooperation have a role to play.

Emergence can be defined as the generation of novel and coherent structures, patterns and properties during the process of self-organization in complex systems (Goldstein, 1999). Behind the notion of emergence is the basic idea that there may be autonomous properties at a higher (macro) level that cannot be understood by reducing it to lower (micro) levels (Sawyer, 2005). We speak of emergent properties if a group of components has different properties showing deviant behavior at a higher scale level than the individual components at a lower scale level. De Haan (2006) distinguishes between three different types of emergence: discovery, mechanistic emergence and reflective emergence.

Self-organization is a process in which the internal organization of a complex system increases in complexity without being guided or managed by an outside source. This self-organization refers to the ability to develop a new system structure as a result of the system's internal constitution and not as a result of external management (Prigogine and Stengers, 1984). In essence, self-organization refers to systems that organize themselves without external direction of control. An example of self-organization is a network that autonomously built its structure as network devices detect each other's presence. Emergence and self-organization are related to each other but they are different. Self-organizing systems usually display emergence but not always. Self-organization exists without emergence and emergence without self-organization. But in complex, adaptive systems emergence and self-organization occur together.

Complex adaptive systems continuously adapt to their changing environment. Any kind of adaptation and all self-organization (see below) involves variation and selection internal to the system which may well be external to components of that system. Most of the time complex adaptive systems are in a period of dynamic equilibrium, with ongoing variation and selection, but with selection as predominating mechanism. External stimuli force the system to shift (across the chaotic edge) to a relatively short phase of instability and chaos (punctuated equilibria), where variation predominates. In societal systems, this non-linear shift between two fundamentally different system states is what is called a transition (Rotmans et al., 2001).

From a complex systems perspective, transitions are emergent phenomena that come about under specific conditions. The dominant system structure (regime) predetermines to some extent the possible development pathway (lock-in), while the external environment to the system (e.g. demography, economy, resource availability, political landscape and so on) gradually changes. This leads to increasing tension between the regime and its environment in terms of performance. Simultaneously, alternatives are being developed (niches) that mature over time and might make use of the increasing problems at the regime level. Whenever the pressure on the regime reaches a certain level and/or an alternative direction is found to be feasible or attractive enough, a threshold might be reached after which a reorganization phase is entered through which a new systemic structure is developed.

7.3 Complex systems and spatial transitions

Relating to the theme of this book, the question is whether spatial areas can be viewed as complex systems. Following the above mentioned characteristics of complex systems, this seems to be certainly the case, but even more so spatial systems seem to have additional properties that might even further complicate understanding and governance or planning. As Thrift writes, we

> can easily say that space complicates because it immediately injects a notion of distribution. For all the notion that we live in an infinite web of meaning, the fact is that this web is differentially distributed. Its elements do not crop up everywhere equally, however often deferred. Spatial distribution, by itself, can therefore begin to account for much of what happens in the world: from the start, the geographical world is a messy one, it does not cohere. On the whole geographers therefore tend to be wary of theories that ride roughshod over ambiguity and polarize complexities. (1999)

Also in spatial problems, a complexity and transition perspective seems to be worthwhile pursuing. Both because there are many examples of fundamental transformation in regions and cities (in terms of for example changing economies or demography), and because many areas are increasingly facing such transformations combined with the need to achieve more sustainable solutions at a larger scale. However, because of historically evolved routines, (infra-)structures, actor-networks, policy institutions and use of space (e.g. regimes), dealing with such challenges is complicated and the role of planning increasingly complex.

As for transitions in general, spatial transitions are equally uncertain, emergent, surprising and unmanageable through blueprint planning. It is clear that such changes include physical and technological changes, but more importantly they are about institutional and behavioural change. Urban or regional transitions can thus be defined as long term structural transformation processes in complex spatial systems. Over decades, a region or city itself can go through a transition (for example from industrial to service-based, from rural to urban, from unsustainable to sustainable). Such a transition is composed of different transitions at subsystem level (for example in mobility, energy, housing, consumption, or health-care). In going through such transitions, cities themselves are also part of broader regional, national systems for which they might form a place in which innovations and experiments take place.

A desire for spatial transitions to sustainability therefore implies planning strategies that open up innovation trajectories rather than predetermine them, that create the conditions for self-organization and surprise, rather than to manage these, and that offer stimulation, guidance and direction rather than to try and control through long-term plans. Urban transition management then is the search for ways to deal in a pro-active way with such semi-autonomous processes, guiding and accelerating social innovation while simultaneously developing new modes of governance and policy-making.

7.4 Managing complex, adaptive societal systems

What does complexity as described above then mean in terms of management? It means that we do not view complexity as a problem or obstacle, but rather as a means of leverage for management. Management in the context of complexity theory – means influencing the process of change of a complex, adaptive system from one state to another, through anticipation and adaptation management. Adaptive management consists of adjustments while the structure of a system is changing, while anticipative management means directing and guiding while taking the possible future behaviour of the system into account (see also Van der Brugge and Van Raak, 2007). Greater insight into the dynamics of a complex, adaptive system leads to improved insight into the feasibility of directing it. This results in an understanding of the limitations of and scope for the management of complex, adaptive systems and at the same time provides insight into the opportunities and conditions under which it is possible to steer such systems, with governance being part of the dynamics which are governed.

Based on theoretical knowledge and practical experience with complexity theory, we have developed a number of guidelines for management listed below (Rotmans and Loorbach, 2009):

- Management at the system level is important.
- The status (in terms of its performance) of the system determines the way it is managed.
- Objectives should be flexible and adjustable at the system level.[2]

---

2   Target-setting may be a short-term way to stimulate and focus effort to improve performance, but as their use in education and health care (two complex adaptive systems) has

- The timing of the intervention is crucial.[3]
- Managing a complex, adaptive system means using disequilibria rather than equilibria.
- Creating space for agents to build up alternative regimes is crucial for innovation.

Transition management is based on this conceptualization of 'governance of complexity' (Loorbach, 2010) and built around the management paradox that 'societal change is too complex to handle in terms of managing but still we have formulated a set of relatively simple rules how to influence societal change'. The rationale for handling this management paradox is that insight into societal complexity by taking a complex systems approach can help in fathoming the possibilities for influencing societal complexity. This logically connects content and process, which are explicitly linked in transition management: the complexity analysis of a societal system under observation also determines the opportunities for managing such a system (Loorbach, 2007: p. 86). Using analytical concepts such as multi-stage and multi-level (Rotmans et al., 2001) and multi-pattern (de Haan and Rotmans, 2008) provides opportunities for identifying patterns and mechanisms of transitional change. Once transitional patterns and mechanisms are identified, it is possible to determine process steps and instruments to anticipate and adapt to these patterns and mechanisms. Our approach is oriented towards reflexive planning: no deterministic, but reflexive rules.[4] We have formulated rules for managing societal change, but once we apply these rules in a process context we realize they need to be adjusted because the conditions and dynamics (content) will change as a result of applying these rules. Therefore learning, searching and experimenting are crucial in transition management. In that sense it has similarities with strategic niche management: experimenting with new technologies in an experimental space (Kemp, Schot and Hoogma, 1998).

7.5 Management principles of transition management

Here we briefly describe the practical focus of transition management based on the complex systems perspective. Exactly because small changes might evoke large

---

shown, there is a danger that they undermine general system performance (Chapman, 2002).

3   The aspect of interventions being 'time critical' is addressed in the book *Time strategies, innovation and environmental policy* (Sartorius and Zundel, 2005). Before problems become urgent, policy should stimulate the development and creation of technologies through window preparation and creation policies, to be able to act effectively at times of crisis when something needs to be done because of public demand.

4   By reflexive rules we mean rules that are adaptive, not by accident but because governance is part of the dynamics which are governed (Voss et al., 2006; Loorbach, 2007; Zeitlin, 2005).

scale systemic change when the system itself is close to a threshold (a take-off in transition terminology), transition management focuses on coordination and stimulation of the emerging innovations and alternative futures rather than on the mainstream or regime. The first principle is that of creating space for niches in so-called transition arenas. The notion of arena originates from that part of complexity theory that indicates that a small initial change in the system may have a great impact on the system in the long run. In systems terms we call this an emergent structure: an environment that offers some protection for a small group of agents. The self-organizing capacity of the system generates new, dissipative structures in the form of niches. A niche is a new structure, a small core of agents, that emerges within the system and that aligns itself with a new configuration.

The focus on frontrunners is a second key aspect of transition management. In complex system terms frontrunners are agents with the capacity to generate dissipative structures and operate within these deviant structures. They can only do that without being (directly) dependent on the structure, culture and practices of the regime. In the context of transition management we mean with frontrunners agents with peculiar competencies and qualities: creative minds, strategists and visionaries. In order to effectively create a new regime agents are needed at a certain distance from the dominant regime.

Another principle of transition management is guided variation and selection. This is rooted in the notions of diversity and coherence within complexity theory. Diversity is required to avoid rigidity within the system. Rigidity here means reduced diversity due to selection mechanisms which means that the system cannot respond flexibly to changes in its environment. Coherence refers to the level of interrelatedness among the entities of a complex system. In the equilibrium phase there is continuous variation and selection but when a regime settles this becomes the dominant selection environment and thus decreases the diversity. But a certain amount of diversity is required to explore a diversity of innovative options instead of looking for the optimal solution. Rather than selecting innovative options in a too early stage options are kept open in order to learn about the pros and cons of available options before making a selection. Through experimenting we can reduce some aspects of the high level of uncertainty so that it leads to better-informed decisions about variation and selection in the next round.

The principle of radical change in incremental steps is a paradox that is derived from complexity theory. Radical, structural change is needed to erode the existing deep structure (incumbent regime) of a system and ultimately dismantle it. Immediate radical change, however, would lead to maximal resistance from the deep structure, that cannot adjust to a too fast, radical change. In situations of complexity, rational planning solutions is known to produce bad results, as shown by planning fiasco's of the collectivisation of Russian agriculture, the compulsory villagization in Tanzania and the use of scientific forestry in Prussia (Scott, 2004). Abrupt forcing of the system would disrupt the system and would create a backlash in the system because of its resilience. Incremental change allows the system to adjust to the new circumstances and to build up new structures that align to the new configuration. Radical change in incremental steps implies that the system heads for a new direction towards new attractors, but in small steps.

Empowering niches is an important principle of transition management. With empowering we mean providing with resources, such as knowledge, finances, competences, lobby-mechanisms, exemption of rules and laws and space for experimenting (Avelino, 2007). An empowered niche may cluster with other empowered niches and emerge into a niche-regime. This arises from the notion of co-evolution in complexity science. Crucial is the co-evolution of a regime within the existing power structure and a niche-regime outside the power realm. Co-evolving regimes influence each other in an irreversible manner, with an unknown outcome. The niche-regime may take over the incumbent regime, but may also be absorbed and encapsulated by the incumbent regime.

Anticipation and adaptation Anticipating future trends and developments, taking account of weak signals and seeds of change acting as the harbingers of the future, is a key element of a pro-active, long-term strategy as transition management. This future orientation is accompanied by a strategy of adaptation, which means adjusting while the structure of the system is changing. This requires adequate insight into the dynamics of a complex system. Not in the sense that the future state of such a system is predictable, but there are periods when the system behaves in a relatively orderly manner and, to a limited extent, is predictable. But there are also periods in which the behaviour of the system is quite unpredictable. So although the degree of predictability is rather small, transitions do imply generic patterns that indicate the future pathway. Path dependency is an example of such a pattern.

The next section describes a framework for doing transition management in practice, using theoretical principles of complex systems theory.

7.6 Transition management: the framework

The challenge with transition management is to translate the above, relatively abstract management rules into a practical management framework without losing too much of the complexity involved and without becoming too prescriptive. We have attempted this by designating transition management as a cyclical process of development phases at various scale levels. In complex system terms transition management can be described in terms of the following steps (Loorbach, 2007; Loorbach and Rotmans, 2006): (i) stimulate niche development (emergence, variation) at the micro-level and try to interconnect niches with the same direction. In the transition management framework this is done by establishing and organizing a transition arena, a quasi-protected area for frontrunners (niche-players and change-inclined regime players); (ii) try to find new attractors for the system by developing a sustainability vision in terms of shared guiding principles for future development and derived pathways at the macro-level that can act as guidance for niche-development; (iii) try to stimulate the formation of niche-regimes by creating coalitions and new networks around the transition agenda (compass) and the different pathways; (iv) create diversity by setting out transition experiments that are related to specific pathways onto the vision; (v) select the most promising ones that can be scaled up to a higher level by learning from these experiments and develop an up scaling strategy; (vi) try to further modulation between the micro- and macro-level (co-evolution) by adjusting the vision, agenda and coalitions if necessary by monitoring and evaluating (analysing patterns and mechanisms) the transition management process, after which the cycle starts again. For the sake of simplicity we present the cycle of transition management as a sequence of steps, as presented in Figure 7.1. However, in practice there is no fixed sequence of steps in transition management and the steps can differ in weight per cycle. In practice the transition management activities are carried out partially and completely in sequence, in parallel and in a random sequence.

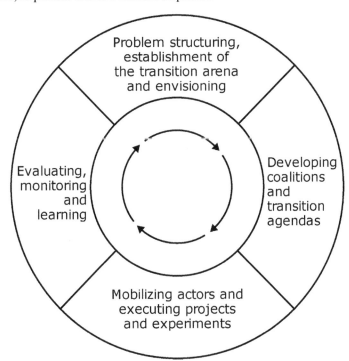

Figure 7.1   The transition management cycle

In effect transition management comes down to creating space for frontrunners (niche-players and inclined regime-players) in transition arenas, forming new coalitions around these arenas, driving the activities in a shared and desired direction and develop coalitions and networks into a movement that puts societal pressure on regular policy. In the transition management framework activities related to the content (integrated systems analysis, envisioning, agenda building and experiments) are linked to activities related to the process (network- and coalition building, executing experiments and process structuring). The preferred actors to be involved (based on the necessary competencies) and instruments (like scenarios, transition-agendas, monitoring instruments, etc.) are derived from this framework. The four activity clusters as depicted in Figure 7.1 are described in more detail below.

Integrated systems analysis and actor selection

An integrated systems analysis forms the basis of every transition management process, providing a common ground for a variety of actors and enough information for informed debates and discussions. Informed insight into the complexity of the system, its major defining subsystems, the dominant causal relations, feed-back loops, the roots and the nature of structural problems establish a baseline as well as conditions for discussing visions, strategies and actions in the future. At the same time, such a preliminary assessment yields knowledge about the main actors influencing the system in both a conservative and an innovative way and helps to guide the selection of participants for the transition arena.

Problem structuring and envisioning, establishment of a transition-arena

The transition-arena is best viewed as a virtual arena or network which is a legitimate experimental space in which the actors involved use social learning processes to acquire new knowledge and understanding that leads to a new perspective on a transition issue. Such a transition arena has to be supported by political actors or regime-powers, but not dictated by them, for example through the support of a minister or a director. In the transition arenas so far established, most started to involve some 15-20 frontrunners in the beginning (Loorbach and Rotmans, 2010). The transition arena develops a shared understanding of the persistency of a problem at the level of a societal system, the necessity of a transition or radical change and the definition of the challenge this poses. A key outcome is a new shared perspective and language to discuss the transition and the definition of a set of guiding principles for the envisaged transition.

The development of sustainability images, pathways and a transition agenda

Transition images are the 'translation' of the generic guiding principles or 'sustainability criteria' to specific concrete settings, sub-sectors or themes. These images must be appealing and imaginative so as to be supported by a broad range of actors and inspire and guide short term action. Transition images embrace multiple transition pathways to represent a variety of possible options. They include transition goals, which are qualitative rather than quantitative. Various transition pathways lead to a particular transition image (a sustainability vision comprises various transition images) and from various transition images a particular transition pathway may be derived. The transition images can be adjusted as a result of what has been learned by the players in transition experiments.

The initiation and execution of transition-experiments and the mobilization of actors

From the transition vision, images and pathways, transition-experiments can be derived which are either related to or combined with existing activities. Transition-experiments are high-risk experiments with a social learning objective that are supposed to contribute to the sustainability goals at the systems level and should fit within the transition pathways. It is important to formulate sound criteria for the selection of experiments and to make the experiments mutually coherent. Around and between these experiments all sorts of actors can be involved that will not engage regularly in debates about long-term issues: small business, consumers, citizens, local groups etc. Here as well the emphasis is on involving frontrunners.

(Reflexive) monitoring and evaluating the transition process

Continuous monitoring is a vital part of the search and learning process of transitions. We distinguish between monitoring the transition process itself, and monitoring transition management. Monitoring the transition process involves physical changes in the system in question, slowly changing macro-developments, fast niche-developments, seeds of change as well as movements of individual and collective actors at the regime level. Participatory monitoring involving the actors that are developing the policies themselves could help raise their awareness of the complexities involved as well as sensitize them to other possibilities and strategies for governance and thus become more reflexive.

In each of the above activity clusters, coalition and network formation is of vital importance combined with the systemic structuring and synthesizing of discussions. The transition arena is meant to stimulate the formation of new coalitions, partnerships and networks that together create a new way of thinking. Mostly, coalitions emerge around transition pathways or experiments, or around specific sub themes, where sub-arenas arise. The very idea behind transition management is to create a societal movement through new coalitions, partnerships and networks around arenas that allow for building up continuous pressure on the political and market arena to safeguard the long-term orientation and goals of the transition process.

In complexity terminology, the efforts of transition management in practice are to develop coordinating mechanisms that might accelerate and guide self-organizational and emergent dynamics. By creating shared values, meaning and language, indirect effects are achieved and indirect governance takes place. However, as is captured in the definition of self-organization, the level of control over these processes is very limited and also impacts can only very difficultly be attributed to the governing body. Table 7.1 summarizes how the instruments of transition management relate to the theoretical principles and the underlying complex system perspective.

Table 7.1   Linking complexity characteristics, theoretical principles of transition management and systemic instruments for transition management

Complexity Characteristics	Theoretical Principles TM	Systemic Instruments for TM
Emergence	creating space for niches	transition arena
dissipative structures	focus on frontrunners	transition arena and competence analysis
diversity and coherence	guided variation and selection	transition experiments and transition pathways
new attractors, punctuated equilibria	radical change in incremental steps	envisioning for sustainable futures
co-evolution	empowering niches	competence development
variation and selection	learning-by-doing and doing-by-learning	deepening, broadening, scaling up experiments
interactions, feedbacks	multi-level approach multi-domain approach	complex systems analysis
patterns, mechanisms	anticipation and adaptation	multi-pattern and multi-level analysis

7.7 Cityharbours

How the described transition management approach could lead to novel planning processes in practice can be illustrated by means of the redevelopment of a large industrial area (ca. 16,000 hectares) within the city boundaries of Rotterdam, the Netherlands. It is located on both banks of the River Meuse and largely used for harbour activities, but will transform in the next 25 years as harbour activities move outward to the sea. The city and the harbour started a joint program 4 years ago to facilitate this process with the aim of transforming the area into an urban area. It is the largest urban development area within the urbanized western part of the Netherlands and defined as a project of national importance. The first years however, the city and harbour were in a confrontation about who was in charge, what the strategy should be and where to start. They did create a vision for the area, which was to maintain the character of the harbour by allowing for harbour activities as long as possible, to accommodate some 15,000 houses and to improve accessibility of the area. Most stakeholders in the area and city officials involved however felt that this vision was too mediocre for such an historic and unique area and transition researchers were asked to help develop the project into a transition program.

This started by an envisioning process in which innovative stakeholders were involved at the strategic level to develop a more ambitious long-term perspective and multiple groups were formed at the tactical level, discussing specific parts of the area or specific sub-themes. Out of this process, a vision emerged of sustainable city harbours in which an innovative mix of living, working and recreation should develop. This vision 'Creating on the edge', emphasizes the need for experiment and innovation and the unique features of this area in terms of the interwovenness with the water, the availability of space and the urgency to ensure sustainable development of this area. Some of the guiding principles defined were energy self-sufficiency, closed material loops, living on and with water, new communities and clean mobility.

The vision explicitly positioned the area development as a transition process, requiring not only an inspiring vision and ambition, but also an innovative approach. It tied the economic development to sustainable innovation for the area and therefore makes a strong case to see the area development itself as booster for the regional economy and development. The area itself was presented as experiment zone and a lobby started to create as much space in terms of finance and regulation as possible. The process of developing the vision and following strategy involved over a hundred representatives from different city departments (economic, housing, mobility, social), from the harbour company, from local business and industry, from the research community and from NGO's. During this process, the discussion on the vision, the need for structural change and the requiring governance approach created enthusiasm and a new spirit. It also led to much political support for the project.

The over-all vision is now being translated to different areas on a lower level (Cityharbours is divided into five sub-areas), which all have their own specific characteristics and time-horizon upon which harbour activities will gradually disappear. One area in specific (Merwe-Vierhavens) has been designated as pilot zone, as here a lot of space will become available in 5 years. A number of concrete experiments are now almost through the development process and have started or will start in 2009. Some of the examples are:

- A floating city. May 2010, a first module opened of what could evolve into a floating city. The basic rationale is that increasing water levels in the river and of groundwater will necessity more innovative living concepts that are able to adapt to this. In the Cityharbours, thousands of people could possible live on water. The first experimental module will include education and office facilities, an entertainment centre, a hotel, a garden and some other functions.
- Clean Tech Delta. During 2009, a consortium of companies (like Van

Gansewinkel, Waste Incineration Rijnmond AVR, Arcadis, BP, Shell, IBM, Eneco) and other institutes (Rotterdam and Delft University, WWF, TNO) started a new joint institute in the area. The key focus of this institute will be sustainable innovation in the area of energy and water, whereby the philosophy is in the first place to actually experiment real life with innovations and learn for the implementation. It is hoped that this will create a physical space for new concepts developed around the globe to be actually built and tested in reality.

- Mobility over water. Key to the areas development is accessibility and clean mobility. Since the area is located on the river bank and much is expected of new housing concepts on water, a plan was developed for a new infrastructure of public transport over water. The first waterbus line has started late 2008 and is connecting the different areas with each other and with the inner city.
- Sustainable communities. In one of the areas, a small village in the midst of the harbour industry needs a large reconstruction the coming decade. The 1,500 houses are planned to be largely be replaced by more sustainable ones. A project has started to involve frontrunner consumers that search for an adventurous environment (close to harbour activities), are willing to accept some of the disadvantages that would normally block housing (noise, traffic), and want to develop their own houses. A consortium of construction experts in sustainable housing will take care of the design and construction and harbour and city are exploring ways to create symbiosis between harbour and living (sharing resources and facilities, exchanging waste-heat and so on). Facility sharing and industrial ecology are guiding principles here.

These are just some of the initiatives that came out of the transitioning process of the last three years. Key is that this type of participatory envisioning and planning process has produced a shared conception of the spatial development challenge, how it could be approached and what types of concrete innovations would be desirable. It has thus created coordination mechanisms that will facilitate and guide activities of spatial planners, architects, mobility managers, companies, researchers and so on, possibly for decades. Obviously it remains to be seen where this will all lead to, but by now it is safe to say that counterweight has been developed against the usual tendencies to develop the area in an ad-hoc manner. Too often spatial development is based on short-term gains, resulting in suboptimal pathways from the perspective of sustainability transitions. One of the examples of this counterweight has been the adoption by the city of sustainability criteria to which all developers that want to do something in the area need to subscribe and need to follow.

7.8 Conclusions

In this chapter we presented a transition management framework for addressing persistent societal problems that is grounded in complex systems theory. Variation and selection, emergence, co-evolution, attractors, diversity and coherence and interactions and feedbacks are key elements of transition management. The underlying premise is that a better understanding of the dynamics of complex, adaptive systems provides insight into the opportunities, limitations and conditions under which it is possible to influence such systems. This implies a strong link of content and process: the combination of analytic insights into systems complexity and understanding of the process of governance complexity is new and has resulted in a set of management principles which forms the basis for the management framework.

The management principles are far from deterministic, however, but rather reflexive: they evolve with transition processes thanks to mechanisms of evaluation, guiding the transition process towards sustainability. Applying these principles implies adjusting them to the new conditions and dynamics that will change as a result of applying these principles. As a form of reflexive governance, transition management understands itself to be part of the dynamics which are governed (Kemp and Loorbach, 2006). The concept of transition management and the derived framework is promising but needs to largely prove itself empirically. Elements of the concept have already been empirically tested in the many transition trajectories that are currently going on. More than that, the management framework itself has been the result of experiences within testing grounds and has evolved in the past couple of years. It is a great challenge to empirically validate the partly descriptive and partly prescriptive parts of transition management in such a manner that the framework can be further developed and used in a spatial context.

As the brief case description illustrates, the spatial dimension might add to the complexities involved in managing transitions, but it might also offer a fruitful source of inspiration for planning processes. A focus on frontrunners, on creating guiding principles and a new type of language, on portfolios of experiments and of reflexive monitoring might become part of the toolkit for spatial planning related to transitions to sustainability. Even though it is far too early to judge upon any success of the spatial transition approach, it can indeed be argued that contemporary complexities involved in spatial planning are increasingly asking for governance strategies that are explicitly based on a conceptualization of this complexity.

References

Arthur, W.B., Durlauf, S.N. and Lane, D.A. (1997) *The economy as an evolving complex system*, Addison-Weasly, Reading.

Ashby, W.R. (1958) 'Requisite variety and implications for control of complex systems', *Cybernetica*, 1, pp. 83-99.

Ayres, R.U., and Ayres, L. (1996) *Industrial ecology-towards closing the materials cycle*, Edward Elgar, Cheltenham.

Braungart, M. and McDonough, W. (2002) *Cradle to Cradle: remaking the way we make things*, North Point Press, New York.

Chapman, J. (2002) System Failure. Why governments must learn to think differently, DEMOS.

De Haan J. (2006) 'How Emergence Arises', *Ecological Complexity*, 3(4), pp. 293-301

De Haan, J. and Rotmans, J. (2008) 'Patterns in transitions', submitted to *Research Policy*.

De Vries, J., and Te R'ele, H. (2006) 'Playing with Hyenas: Renovating environmental product policy strategy', *Journal of Industrial Ecology*, 10(3), pp. 111-127.

Dirven, J., Rotmans, J. and Verkaik, A.P. (2002) *Samenleving in transitie: Een vernieuwend gezichtspunt* [Society in transition: A renewed point of view] Innovatienetwerk Agrocluster en Groene Ruimte, The Hague.

Ehrenfeld, J. (1997) 'Industrial ecology: a framework for product and process design', *Journal of Cleaner Production*, 5(1-2), pp. 87-96.

Ehrenfeld, J., and Gertler, N. (1997) 'Industrial ecology in practice: The evolution of interdependence at Kalundborg', *Journal of Industrial Ecology*, 1(1), pp. 67–80.

Energy Council of the Ministry of Housing, Spatial Planning and Environment (VROM) and VROM-council (2004) *Energy transition: Climate for new chances*, The Hague (NL).

Ernstson, H., Van der Leeuw, S., Redman, C.L., Meffert, D.J., Davis G., Alfsen, C. and Elmqvist, T. (2010) Urban Transitions: On Urban Resilience and Human-Dominated Ecosystems. AMBIO Published On-line first (DOI: 10.1007/ s13280-010-0081-9)

Geldof, G. (2002) *Omgaan met complexiteit bij integraal waterbeheer,* Universiteit Twente, Enschede.

Goldstein, J. (1999) 'Emergence as a construct: history and issues', *Emergence*, 1.

Green, K. and Randles, S. (2006) *Industrial ecology and spaces of innovation*, Edward Elgar, Cheltenham.

Gunderson, L.H. and C.S. Holling. (2002) *Understanding transformations in human and natural systems*, Island Press, Washington DC.

Green, D.G. (1994) 'Evolution in complex systems', in Stonier, R.J. and Xing Huo Ju (eds.) Complex Systems: mechanism of adaptation. IOS Press, Oxford.

Hodson, M. and Marvin, S. (2010) Can cities shape socio-technical transitions and how would we know if they were?, *Research Policy*, 39(4), pp. 477-485.

Holland, J.H. (1995) *Hidden order: How adaptation builds complexity*, Ulam Lectures Series, Helix Books/Perseus Books, Cambridge (US).

Holling. C.S. (ed.) (1978) *Adaptive environmental assessment and management.* John Wiley and Sons, London.

Hordijk, L. (1985) 'A model for evaluation of acid deposition', in Sydow, A., Thoma, M., Vichnevetsky, R. (eds.) *Systems Analysis and Simulation 1985 (II)*, Pergamon Press, Oxford, pp. 30-39.

Kauffman, S. (1993) *The origins of order*, Oxford University Press, Oxford.

Kauffman, S. (1995) *At home in the universe: The search for laws of complexity*, Oxford University Press, Oxford.

Kay, J., Regier, H., Boyle, M. and Francis, G. (1999) 'An ecosystem approach for sustainability: addressing the challenge of complexity', *Futures*, 31(7), pp. 721-742.

Kemp, R, Schot, J. and Hoogma, R. (1998) 'Regime shifts to sustainability through processes of niche formation: the approach of strategic niche management', *Technology analysis and strategic management*, 10, pp. 175-196.

Kemp, R. and D. Loorbach (2005). *Dutch policies to manage the transition to sustainable energy*, Jahrbuch Okologische Okonomik. J. Meyerhoff. Marburg, Metropolis Verlag. 4, pp. 123-151.

Kemp, R. and D. Loorbach (2006) 'Transition management: A reflexive governance approach', in J.P. Voss, D. Bauknecht and R. Kemp (eds.) *Reflexive Governance for Sustainable Development*, Edward Elgar, Cheltenham, pp. 103-130.

Kemp, R., Loorbach, D. and Rotmans, J. (2007) 'Transition management as a model for managing processes of co-evolution towards sustainable development', *The International Journal of Sustainable Development and World Ecology* (Special Issue on Co-evolution) 14, 1-15.

Kemp, R., Rotmans, J. and Loorbach, D. (2007) 'Assessing the Dutch Energy Transition Policy: How does it deal with dilemmas of managing transitions?', *Journal of Environmental Policy and Planning*, 9(3-4), pp. 315-331.

Kickert, W.J.M. (1991) *Complexiteit, zelfsturing en dynamiek. Over management van complexe netwerken bij de overheid.*, Erasmus Universiteit, Rotterdam.

Kooiman, J. (1993) *Modern governance: new government-society interactions*, Sage, London.

Korhonen, J. (2004). 'Industrial ecology in the strategic sustainable development model: strategic applications of industrial ecology', *Journal of Cleaner Production*, 12(8-10), pp. 809-823.

Loorbach, D. and Rotmans, J. (2010), The practice of transition management: Examples and lessons from four distinct cases, *Futures*, 42 (2010), pp. 237-246.

Loorbach, D. (2010) 'Transition management for sustainable development: A prescriptive, complexity-based governance framework', *Governance*, 23, pp. 161-183.

Loorbach, D. and Kemp, R. (2005). *Innovation policy for the Dutch energy transition: Operationalising transition management*. ERSA, Amsterdam.

Loorbach, D. and Rotmans, J. (2006) 'Managing transitions for sustainable development', in A.J. Wieczorek and X. Olsthoorn (eds.) *Industrial Transformation: disciplinary approaches towards transformation research*, Kluwer Academic Publishers, Dordrecht.

Loorbach, D. (2007) *Transition Management: new mode of governance for sustainable development*, International Books, Utrecht (NL).

Ministry of Economic Affairs (2004) *Innovation in energy policy. Energy transition: state of affairs and continuation*, The Hague.

Ministry of Housing, Spatial Planning and Environment (2002) 'A world and a will: working on sustainability', *Fourth National Environmental Plan*, The Hague.

Mitleton-Kelly, E. (2003) 'Ten principles of complexity and enabling infrastructures', in Mitleton-Kelly, E. (ed). *Complex systems and evolutionary perspectives of organizations: the application of complexity theory to organizations*, Elsevier, London, (2003), pp. 3-19.

Prigogine, I. and I Stengers. (1984) *Order out of chaos: man's new dialogue with nature*, C.O. New Science Library, Boulder (US).

Rittel, H. and Webber, M. (1973) 'Dilemmas in general theory of planning', *Policy Sciences* 4 (2), pp.155–159.

Rotmans, J. (1990) *IMAGE: an Integrated Model to Assess the Greenhouse Effect*. PhD-thesis, Kluwer Academic Publishers, Dordrecht.

Rotmans, J., Kemp, R. and van Asselt, M. (2001) 'More evolution than revolution: Transition management in public policy', *Foresight,* 03(01), p. 17.

Rotmans, J. (2003) *Transitiemanagement: Sleutel voor een duurzame samenleving*, Koninklijke Van Gorcum, Assen (NL).

Rotmans, J., D. Loorbach and R. van der Brugge (2005) *Transitiemanagement en duurzame ontwikkeling: Co-evolutionaire sturing in het licht van complexiteit*. Beleidswetenschap Juni.

Rotmans, J. (2006) *Societal Innovation: between dream and reality lies complexity*, RSM Erasmus University, Rotterdam.

Rotmans, J. and Kemp. R. (2008) 'Detour Ahead: a response to Shove and Walker about the perilous road of transition management', *Environment and Planning A*, pp. 1006-1012.

Rotmans, J. and Loorbach, D. (2009) 'Complexity and Transition Management', *Journal of Industrial Ecology*, 13, pp. 184-196.

Sartorius, C. and S. Zundel (eds) (2005) *Time Strategies, Innovation and Environmental Policy*, Edward Elgar, Cheltenham.

Sawyer, R.K. (2005) *Social emergence: societies as complex systems*, Cambridge University Press, Cambridge.

Scott, J.C. (1998) *Seeing like a state: How certain schemes to improve the human condition have failed*, Yale University Press, New Haven.

Social Economic Council (2001) *Ontwerpadvies Nationaal Milieubeleidsplan 4* [Preliminary Proposal National Environmental Policy Plan 4], The Hague.

Stacey, R.D. (1996) *Strategic Management and Organisational Dynamics*, Pitman, London.

Thrift, N. (1999) 'The Place of Complexity', *Theory, Culture and Society*, 16(3), pp. 31-69.

Van den Bergh, J. and Stagl, S. (2004) 'Coevolution of economic behaviour and institutions: towards a theory of institutional change', *Journal of Evolutionary Economics*, 13, pp. 289-317.

Van der Brugge, R. and Van Raak, R. (2007) 'Facing the adaptive management challenge: Insights from transition management', *Ecology and Society*, 12 (2), art. 33.

Von Bertalanffy, L. (1968) *General system theory: foundation, development and applications*, New York.

VROM-raad (2002) *Milieu en Economie: ontkoppeling door innovatie* [Environment and Economy: uncoupling through innovation], The Hague.

Zeitlin, J. (2005) 'Social Europe and Experimentalist Governance: Towards a New Constitutional Compromise', *European Governance Papers* No. C-05-04.

Chapter 8

Coevolutionary Planning Processes

Lasse Gerrits and Geert Teisman[1]

Planning and decision making over physical systems is often embedded in the implicit or explicit assumption that the human planner is in control over the object of planning. Considerable resources are spent on research and planning procedures in order to develop a comprehensive plan for an area. As long as the object of planning responds in predictable ways, there are no obvious reasons to challenge this assumption. But often, however, the results of planning are disappointing. Planner's actions then fail to generate the desired outcome but generate unfavourable side-effects instead.

Often, the unfavourable consequences are attributed to poor planning strategies. Implementation deficits, then, are starting point for a search into more powerful strategies. The planning and implementation of highways and railways is a classical example. A majority of such projects face cost overrun and delay and in the large majority of the cases the solution is sought in regulation, risk analysis, streamlining of procedures and so on. Much less attention is paid to the possibility that it is not the planning procedure itself but the characteristics of the object of planning that prevents planners from being successful. In the words of Flyvberg, Bruzelius and Rothengatter: "[...] most appraisals of megaprojects assume, or pretend to assume, that infrastructure policies and projects exist in a predictable Newtonian world of cause and effect where things go according to plan. In reality, the world of megaproject preparation and implementation is a highly risky one where things happen only with a certain probability and rarely turn out as originally intended." (2006: 6).

8.1 Planning port extensions

In this contribution we will start our complexity theory perspective on planning processes from this axiom: planning takes place in a complex social and physical world that is constantly changing, consequently distorting the intentions of planning initiatives. We will argue that planning objects are not lifeless, passive things that can be changed at will. A more realistic approach understands them as

1   Dr. Lasse Gerrits is associate professor in Public Administration and prof. Geert Teisman is Professor in Public Administration, both at the Erasmus University Rotterdam, research group Governance of Complex Systems.

living objects with self-organizing capacities. This means that planning successes are chiefly dependent on the ability to synchronize planning activities with the development of self-organizing planning objects. The concept of coevolution will help understanding the dynamics between planners and their environment and will open the way for new possibilities to improve planning effectiveness. Coevolution asks for a coevolutionary revision of planning processes, which is a fundamentally different planning ontology and different research epistemology.

First, one has to take a systemic point of departure to understand planning processes, as argued elsewhere in this book. Second, such an analysis should take into account that causation is complex and will change over time. It is complex in the sense that planning activities are not the single cause of change and the planning object not the final result. Planning implies mutual interaction between planner, planning object and planning context. Thirdly, it should convert the unicentric (Teisman, 1992) and anthropocentric perspective into a coevolutionary view on planning processes (Gerrits, 2008). These three points encompass a coevolutionary revision of planning processes. This chapter draws on empirical material about planning port extensions in Hamburg (Germany) presented elsewhere (Gerrits, 2008; 2010). The next section introduces this case study. The third section is dedicated to the introduction of the coevolutionary framework for planning that allows understanding the case study as it evolves. The conclusions are presented in the final section.

The case study concerns the plans to deepen the Unterelbe estuary near Hamburg (Germany; see Figure 8.1). This case study covers the period between 1996 and 2007 and follows the attempts of the planners to prepare a deepening operation in order to facilitate large ships and how the planners decides to deal with physical changes following that operation while at the same time preparing for another deepening. Data was collected through document analysis and interviews between 2004 and 2008. Document analysis covered 175 newspaper articles, policy documents and scientific publications published about this case. Twenty respondents were interviewed during semi-structured in-depth interviews. Full lists of the documents and respondents can be found in Gerrits (2008). Using the document analysis, a chronological series of events was reconstructed. The personal accounts of the respondents were then used to give meaning to the events and to retrieve events that had remained outside the public domain. These accounts were merged to form a single hybrid account of the case.

The Elbe is an important lifeline for Hamburg and the entire north-western region of Germany because it provides maritime access to one of Europe's largest ports and as such facilitates logistics, industries and jobs. The port authorities of Hamburg (HPA) constantly plan port extensions. European ports such as Hamburg, Antwerpen and Rotterdam are engaged in fierce competition over market share and extending the port is perceived as the main strategy to win this competition. The planning strategies employed by HPA include the planning of a motorway from east to west to improve turn-around of trucks (see Van Gils, Gerrits and Teisman, 2009) and the deepening of the Unterelbe (see Gerrits, 2008).

Figure 8.1   The Unterelbe between Hamburg and the North Sea.

Source: Gerrits, 2008.

The Unterelbe is approximately 100 kilometres long and connects the port of Hamburg with the North Sea. Its shallow depth compromises the number of ships that can reach the port. Cargo ships of the latest generation are considered too large to enter the port around the clock and they are obliged to wait until the high water level is high enough to safeguard the depth under the keel before the tide turns around. The port authorities are therefore eager to deepen the main channel in the estuary. The Unterelbe has been deepened several times between 1900 and 2007. After the deepening in 1980, the port authorities and the Senate of Hamburg planned another deepening operation that had to be completed somewhere between 1995 and 2000.

During the mid-1990s, the planning process is hampered by fierce resistance from many stakeholders such as environmental pressure groups and concerned citizens. The port authorities and the Senate are convinced that the extension of the port in general, and the deepening specifically, will benefit the region tremendously in terms of employment and prosperity. Opponents on the other hand argue that the extension adds marginally to economic growth and they fear that it comes at the cost of the environment, safety and quality of life. There is also opposition from the neighbouring federal states Niedersachsen and Schleswig-Holstein. They are afraid that any damage to the environment has to be compensates by them rather than by Hamburg, since the Unterelbe runs through their territory, as per the EU Habitat Directive (see Figure 8.1).

Fearing that public resistance would hamper the deepening operation, HPA and the Hamburg Senate try to shield the planning process away from the public eye and its pressures and try to speed up the process as much as possible. The obligatory environmental impact assessment (EIA) is delayed but the operation is approved in 1996, before the EIA is published. The assessment arrives in 1997 and by that time the port authorities have already advanced their planning. The EIA indicates that the deepening can be carried out without major unfavourable consequences for the environment but the opposition remarks that any other conclusion would be impossible given the fact that the planning is already well-advanced. A monitoring program will be established in order to monitor the effects of the deepening. While the EIA marks the start of the formal planning procedure, including the possibilities to object against the deepening, HPA announces that it will start to remove the first layer of 30 centimetres from the riverbed immediately, in what it calls a 'preparatory dredging' operation. The environmental pressures groups are infuriated because of this strategy. This rage extends to the other federal states, to local fishermen and to people living near the cities.

Where possible, HPA and the Senate try to settle the conflict through financial means. Fishermen receive compensation for the supposed decline in fishing grounds. Other objections are more difficult to deal with. Niedersachsen and Schleswig-Holstein are forced to cooperate in the end, partly because of pressure from the national level. Many pressure groups submit complaints during the formal planning procedure. However, the organization that is to judge these complaints, the Behörde Für Wirtschaft und Arbeit (BWA), is the same one that plans the deepening and the complaints are brushed aside. BWA decides that these groups are illegitimate parties and therefore the City of Hamburg is under no obligation to respond to them. The preparatory dredging operation goes ahead, followed by the actual deepening operation and a concluding ceremony on December 14, 1998. Ships with a draught of up to 12.80 metres are now able to call at the port without being dependent on the tide.

8.2 Pushing forward a new deepening

Much of the uproar fades away after the deepening operation. Niedersachsen senses that the growth in the cargo shipping will continue in the foreseeable future and plans the construction of a deep-sea terminal at Wilhelmshaven. The purpose of this terminal is to create additional capacity for the turnover of goods, especially for those ships that are too large to travel on the Elbe to Hamburg. This strategy is not favoured by the City of Hamburg. They fear that the construction of a new port relatively close to Hamburg will draw ships away from the city's port. Consequently, they start talking about another deepening operation that could accommodate the largest ships destined for the future Wilhelmshaven terminal before the construction of the latter is finished. The mayor of Hamburg manages to strike a deal with Niedersachsen that gives Niedersachsen its much-desired terminal because Hamburg promises to finance 20 percent of it in return for support for yet another deepening.

However, re-elections in the summer of 2001 mark a change in Hamburg, with the Christian Democratic Party (CDU) now heading the BWA and appointing Mr. Gunnar Uldall as its Senator. Uldall has been strongly against the agreement between Niedersachsen and Hamburg and one of his first measures is to announce that Hamburg will not take up its 20 percent share in the deep-sea terminal project. Instead, he aims to deepen the Elbe as soon as possible in order to secure a potential market share of the new terminal at Wilhelmshaven. He appoints a civil working group to investigate the possibility of conducting a new deepening operation. Although he says that Niedersachsen agrees with this move, Niedersachsen itself asserts that it has not granted permission. There is also fierce resistance from the environmental pressure groups. Uldall pushes ahead with his plans and aims for a quick decision.

The civil working group, however, is less confident about the feasibility. Its members are struggling with the compensation measures from the previous deepening. Although they have made suggestions on how to realize aquatic compensation, such as through the regeneration of secondary channels, putting these ideas into practice proves to be more complicated than expected. Compensation measures are therefore focused on the terrestrial dimension but this poses another range of problems. There are few spots along the banks of the Unterelbe where room can be found for such compensation. This is a problem because compensation for the previous deepening is mandatory and because it could even get more difficult if a new operation is carried out. In the end, the City of Hamburg argues that some of the observed physical changes to the Unterelbe cannot be contributed to the previous deepening operation anyway and should not be taken into account when debating compensation. In other words: compensation does not need to be as intensive as planned before. Despite all good intentions, compensation is deemed to be only a marginal success among the civil working groups and on April 4, 2002, Uldall announces that the City of Hamburg will deepen the Unterelbe once again, 3 years after the previous deepening. The civil working group releases a report in October 2002, stating that the deepening can be carried out without major unfavourable effects.

The planning of the new deepening goes ahead during the years that follow. HPA and BWA start to organize meetings in the region to provide information about the next deepening. Uldall urges to publish a preliminary monitoring report. Some argue that it is not yet possible to observe any physical changes because morphological changes to the riverbed take around 10 to 15 years to appear. However, a rapport is published and the fact that it shows that there were no changes so soon after the deepening is announced as evidence that the previous deepening was without unfavourable consequences.

Off-record, however, BAW acknowledges that the previous deepening caused an increase in the tidal range (the difference between ebb and flood). There are also some problems with sediment transport that may arise due to increased tidal velocity in the Unterelbe. The new dredging works are not expected to require considerable reallocation of sediments but the tidal currents in the Unterelbe may cross this point of departure. Artificial shoals in the mouth of the Unterelbe are considered as measures to slow down the tidal currents. A solution to social unrest is found in the establishment of a mediation process.

8.3 An unpleasant surprise

While the planners are working on securing a new deepening, they are suddenly faced with a major unfavourable physical change in the Unterelbe. Dredgers find that the amount of material dredged during maintenance operations in 2004 is considerably higher than during previous years (see Figure 8.2). Soundings confirm their observation, i.e. that the amount of sediments flowing in from the North Sea and accumulating in the harbour basin has suddenly increased from 4,5 million cubic metres to 9 million cubic metres per year. This comes as a major surprise to all actors involved in the deepening operation. A small increase had been predicted in the EIA but no one foresaw this large of an increase. It poses a major problem for all everyone in favour of a deepening. The first of these problems are escalating costs arising from an urgent need to intensify dredging to remove the sediments which are now obstructing navigation in the port. The second problem is the lack of space to dispose of the sediments. Having no more space available within the city, Hamburg needs to turn to its neighbours but following the many as described above, it does not gain any clearance to store the sediments within the two states. HPA therefore chooses to go back to an earlier solution: to take the sediments to the border of their territory, dump them in the Unterelbe, and hope that the tidal currents will then take the sediments to the North Sea. This doesn't happen, as it is the North Sea where the sediments come from in the first place. Consequently, HPA has to dredge the port over and over again in a vicious dredging cycle.

Although it is very complicated to assess how each individual measure has contributed to this change, there are a number of mechanisms that can explain this sudden increase of sedimentation. These are documented in great detail in Gerrits (2008). The sediment accumulation began prior to the most recent deepening and maintenance dredging operations have always been necessary. However, some policy makers acknowledge that the deepening operation has contributed to this development by altering the stable state of the Unterelbe in such a way as to disproportionately accelerate sedimentation in the port.

The incident marks a change within the homogeneous group of planners. At the one hand there are the people who favour a new deepening and who are deeply concerned about the incident as it could lead to further delays of the plans. They view the physical changes as a bad coincidence rather than a consequence of the deepening. At the other hand, there are people who start to think that the deepening of the Unterelbe, and continuous economic use of the river altogether, is not the best way for the future and the start pleading for a change of direction. However, they represent a minority view. But while the planners debate about the causes of the physical changes, there is ongoing pressure to do something about it – if only because the accumulation of sediments crosses the very reason of the deepening. The press in Hamburg is unanimous in their verdict. They state that the planners are blinded by their ambition to get a new deepening, consequently overlooking or underestimating the potential risks of using the Unterelbe for the needs of the port. They point at, among others, the monitoring program that was scheduled to

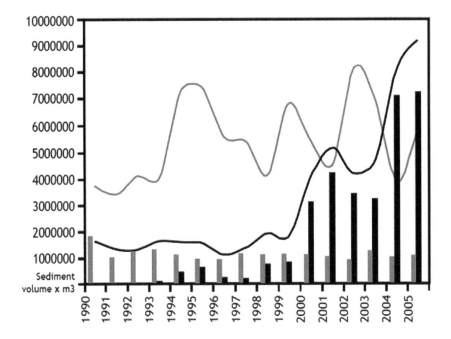

Figure 8.2   Sediment accumulation in the Unterelbe, 1990–2005. The total volume of sediments is indicated by the black line. The total volume comprises sediments that are processed locally, e.g. storage, remediation (grey columns), and sediments that are dumped at the territorial borders of the City of Hamburg (black columns). The grey line indicates the fresh water discharge at Neu Darchau

Source: Gerrits, 2008, adapted from Bundesanstalt für Wasserbau, 2005.

run for an additional 10 years before a new deepening would be considered. With hindsight, the very early publication of the monitoring report was a poor move.

At first sight, one could blame the proponents of the deepening of blindly following their ambitions and being ignorant to anything that could potentially delay or postpone a new deepening operation. This is certainly a popular image, judging by what the press writes. However, although there were some politicians who were certainly pushing forward with their case, there were also planners who were genuinely taken by surprise by the physical changes. One could then argue that the research for the deepening was faulty and that the inability to predict this change is down to the researchers' lack of knowledge.

However, this kind of thinking does not take into account the unpredictable and complex nature of physical systems. Even the most elaborate studies and models are able to capture this complexity fully (Gerrits and Moody, 2011). This is problematic because uncertainty over future developments does not allow for the clarity that is required to make an informed plan. As stated by Otter in the context of coastal zones planning: 'a fully deterministic approach [as required in the political and planning arena – LG] cannot handle the uncertainty related to the management of many environmental systems.' (2000: 110). One must always bear in mind that planners do not make decisions on passive physical systems. Systems such as the Unterelbe could respond dynamically and unpredictably to policy decisions, which could yield unfavourable results. One should move beyond the obvious explanations in order to understand the full complexity of decision making processes such as the one described here.

8.4 Towards a systemic understanding of planning processes

The analysis in this chapter uses a systemic approach to the issues in the case study because it is unhelpful to study the issues without context as it is precisely this context that is determining the course of events (cf. Gerrits, 2010). In other words: the first step in understanding how seemingly sound decisions can lead to adverse effects on physical systems is to understand that decisions and the actors who make these decisions are an integral part of the chain of causes and consequences that drives physical change (Hooke, 1999; Turner, 2000; Teisman, Van Buuren and Gerrits, 2010). There is growing interest within the natural sciences in understanding physical changes in coastal zones as features of system dynamics rather than regarding these coastal changes in isolation from their environment (cf. Turner, Lorenzoni, Beaumont, Bateman, Langford, and McDonald, 1998). However, the process of planning is still generally regarded as a black box from the perspective of the natural sciences. And while the dynamics of planning processes are the core subject areas in the planning, urban studies, public administration and so on, it is society and the physical systems of which too little is known. In those domains, it is the social and physical systems that are the black boxes.

A thorough understanding of the mutual relationships between planning processes in social systems and the development of physical systems has been lacking, as identified by among others Folke, 2006; Gual and Norgaard, 2010; Kallis and Norgaard, 2010; Kotchen and Young, 2007; and O'Sullivan, Manson, Messina, and Crawford, 2006. When two systems influence each other and develop because of this mutual influence, and when this influence is simultaneous, reciprocal and qualitatively altering the characteristics of the systems without a fixed final stage or end goal, this is called coevolution (Norgaard, 1994; Porter, 2006; Gerrits, 2008; Marshall, 2009). It combines two strands in literature: the systemic approach of complexity theory with the concept of coevolution (cf. Porter, 2006; Gerrits, 2008). The argument in this chapter assumes a social perspective on complexity and systems (cf. Byrne, 1998; 2005). Essentially, this means that it is accepted that the real world has systemic properties but that at the same time the boundaries of the systems are defined by the people who work with them, i.e.

they are not given but largely mental constructs based on real world observations (Flood and Jackson, 1991: Flood, 1999; Cilliers, 2001).

8.5 Coevolution

The concept of coevolution is rooted in evolutionary biology and was first coined by Ehrlich and Raven (1964), who observed that groups of organisms evolved through reciprocal selective interaction (Odum, 1971; Norgaard, 1984). Coevolution follows from evolution after Ehrlich and Raven observed that the evolution of an organism, butterflies in their case, can depend on the evolution of another related organism in a reciprocal way. While mutation can be explained by observing selection pressures from the environment on an organism, coevolution explains that this mutation in turn affects the environment of that organism. The explanatory value of coevolution for understanding change through time is therefore situated in the patterns of reciprocal selection that can arise between organisms. This proved to be of value in explaining biodiversity because coevolution adds to evolution that both organism or the entity and its environment are in flux because of reciprocal selection, i.e. the arrow of selection is bi-directional when it concerns one organism and one environment.

As with evolution, coevolution was originally restricted to the biological domain while the social scientific discourse was concerned exclusively with socio-cultural evolutionist theories (Norgaard, 1994). However, over time a growing number of accounts that regard socio-cultural change as a result of coevolution between a biological system with genetic mechanisms and a cultural system with non-genetic mechanisms emerged (Sanderson, 1990; Porter, 2006). This introduces the idea that, broadly speaking, biological and social systems can be considered to be intertwined in a coevolutionary relationship in which there is reciprocal selection between these seemingly incompatible systems.

8.6 Coevolution and planning

An explicit attempt to abandon the development of a physical or social system as a parallel or analogue one and to replace it with a coevolutionary perspective can be attributed to Norgaard (1984; 1994; Kallis and Norgaard, 2010). Norgaard's argument is that coevolution can explain how highly complex societies develop. From this perspective, coevolutionary development has been occurring for millennia as people attempt to use physical systems to their benefit. In doing this people engage in a pattern of feedback loops constituting reciprocal selection. In order to deal with the ensuing feedback from the physical system and aim for optimization of the use of a particular system (Norgaard uses agriculture and tropical rainforests as examples in his 1994 book), they are pushed to create increasingly individualized task specifications and more complex institutional and cultural contingencies. Thus, while ecosystems respond to anthropomorphic changes, social systems respond to the ensuing changes from the ecosystem, which the ecosystem then responds to with yet another set of changes. Over time, the complexity of this pattern renders it nearly impossible to attribute any particular development to a specific feedback loop as the two systems have become completely intertwined. The feedback loops act as selection pressures as they can have a determining impact on future possibilities for *both* the systems.

This, then, is the coevolutionary argument about social and physical complex adaptive systems in a nutshell. In other words: planning is about the coevolution between planners and the social system at the one hand and the object of planning, such as a physical system, at the other hand. Humans are able to select and manage the selection pressures deliberately, to a certain extent, but the degrees of freedom are limited (see also Van Wezemael in this book). This ability to act deliberately but constrained is important for the argument in this chapter. It is through this focus that the biological understanding of coevolution coincides with complex adaptive systems and human planning activities (Marshall, 2009; Gual and Norgaard, 2010; Kallis and Norgaard, 2010). Coevolution has been applied to a wide range of domains (cf. Lewin and Volberda, 2003), such as evolutionary economics (cf. Van den Bergh, 2004), organizational studies (cf. Porter, 2006), urban planning (cf. Marshall, 2009) and public administration (cf. Sementelli, 2007; Gerrits, 2008).

A theoretical framework that allows analysing planning processes as a coevolutionary process should take the following into account. First, isolating the object of planning from its environment does not explain the outcomes of the whole (Marshall, 2009). Changes in the planning object and planning context are driven by many variables and can only be contributed partially to planning activities (ibid.). Unintended effects of those activities still may occur as a result from an incorrect decision by the planner, but will more often than not be caused by a physical or social action elsewhere or by a combination of these factors as exemplified by the case study in this chapter.

Secondly, a systemic framework must take into account the mutual interaction between varieties of systems and between the elements within the systems. With circular causation, the interaction between the physical system and the social system is mutual, i.e. the physical system responds to the changes made by the planners and in turn creates a situation to which the planners are compelled to respond. Whether this response is deliberate and whether it results in adaptation is discussed later in this chapter.

Third, the complexity of causation does not stem only from the multiple causes and effects but also from erratic change. This means that the relationship between cause and effect could be altered through the occurrence of events or could lead to different developmental pathways if repeated elsewhere in time and/ or location, as explained elsewhere in this Volume. The outcome of an intended change may therefore be disproportional or adverse to the intent. This also holds true for unintended change or change that takes place outside the actors' influence. Although it is possible to understand complex non-linear change theoretically, in practice causality is probabilistic. Any change made to the physical system may or may not lead to the desired outcome and if repeated, could produce different results.

These approaches differ wildly in the applications but they share the ambition to deploy the mechanisms of (co)evolution to explain for the seemingly incremental and destination-free changes observed in those fields. That ambition requires defining three main items: [1] structure (what or who selects?), [2] content (what is selected?), and [3] process (how is the selection done?). These items will be discussed in the following section.

8.7 A coevolutionary framework for understanding planning processes

As to the question what or who selects, it appears from the literature that (co) evolution always concerns systems (cf. Levin, 1983; Lewin and Volberda, 2003; Kallis and Norgaard, 2010), such as ecosystems, populations, communities or organizational fields (cf. Okasha, 2003). The basic properties of systems have been explained elsewhere in this book. From evolutionary economics comes the understanding that the elements of such systems are of a diverse nature, such as a population with people with individual and mutually diverging preferences (Foster and Hölz, 2004) at different scales (i.e. nestedness).The idea that actors engaged in planning interact in complex systemic networks, rather than modernist hierarchies, is well-established by now (cf. Kickert, Klijn and Koppenjan, 1996; Healey, 2006; Klijn and Snellen, 2009). In addition to network theories of planning, complexity theory questions the anthropocentric approach of social network theories. There is an obvious difference between human agency and physical agency. The (often assumed) anthropocentric relationship between physical and social systems, which places planners in control of the physical system, is in complexity theory replaced by a complex pattern of interactions in which all actors are engaged in a pattern of actions and responses. The physical system is as much an actor in a planning process as are human planners (cf. Law, 1996).

Theoretically speaking, systems are connected to each other ad infinitum. However, people draw boundaries around systems in order to create a form of (projected) order. Such system boundaries are therefore subjective interventions in reality. Each planner will implicitly or explicitly define the physical system as soon as he is deciding what is included and excluded. In this case study, there was a clear tendency among planners during the early stages to use a narrow definition that centred on the main channel. Water was defined as a thing that could be utilized for shipping and that definition inevitably lead to the 'obvious' conclusion that dredging was necessary whereas the environmental pressure groups used a broader definition, perceiving the water system as environmental resource in a large ecosystem. It is therefore no surprise that they arrived at very different plans for the future.

System definitions define the scope of planning. Due to an incomplete definition of the physical system the authorities applied an approach vulnerable for unwanted responses. One could argue that the authorities were too short-sighted to be successful. If this insight is accepted the definitions actors use with respect to system and system boundaries become important elements for improving planning processes. In that respect it is important to note that these definitions can change over time, as shown in this case. Planners can stick to the existing definition, consequently displaying autopoietic behaviour that reinforces their beliefs but loosen their connections with reality (cf. Pel, 2009). They also can apply a more adaptive strategy by redefining the system and taking the context into account to include that what has been left out of the previous system analysis.

It is important to indicate that planners also define their own social system with people who they tend to include and those will be excluded. If actors are excluded but still take actions with respect to the planning object tensions will arise and planning failure can be underway. The case shows that the system of planners evolved over time with people changing their opinion about the planned deepening operation, consequently allowing themselves in and out of planning systems. The ambiguous stance of the federal states Niedersachsen and Schleswig-Holstein is example of how planners and policy makers can change their perceptions and thus change the constitution of the planning system. Consequently, the boundaries of systems (both physical and social systems) are porous and evolve along the system definitions of actors. This implies that the act of defining the system in relation to planning as an act of coevolution must be understood instead of simply attempting to arrive at a second-order boundary judgment (cf. Cilliers, 2001). It is understood that the agents' perception of what defines the system is decisive in determining what is included in the system, as it is from this perception that agents act accordingly. This leads to the next two questions from the previous section: what is being selected and how is it selected?

The answer to the question of what is being selected is basically that the selection concerns the future state of a complex adaptive system (physical or social or both). The adaptation to a certain incentive means a change in the systems' states but, following the processes of path-dependency and lock-in, this in turn means that certain future trajectories or sequences of systems' states become possible while others are relegated outside the range of what is feasible. This process applies to both physical and social systems. With regard to physical systems, it means that choices made by planners lead to changes within the physical system that rule out other possible directions for development. For example, the decision to deepen the Unterelbe denies it the possibility of silting up and meandering in a different lay-out. Conversely, a physical change such as the dramatic increase in sediment accumulation pushes planners (as part of the social system) into a reactive role as they face an unfavourable situation to which they have to respond regardless of their earlier intentions. Reciprocal selection therefore means that the future state of systems is mutually determined by selection pressures from *both systems*.

Reciprocal selection (rather than a general mutual influence) lies at the heart of coevolution. Originally, Norgaard (1984) stated that coevolution occurs when at least one feedback loop between systems changes. In his later work, he added that a change in feedback loops does not necessarily lead to a change in the state of systems as negative feedback loops can stabilize the current system's state. Arguably, this does cause mutual influence but not coevolution because of lack of change. Coevolution is therefore driven by positive feedback loops that become selection pressures because they provoke adaptation from the other system (Norgaard, 1994). That means that the characteristics of (positive or negative) feedback loops apply to the selection pressures. Reciprocal selection consists of three stages: variation, selection and retention. We will argue here that all three elements are in fact one continuous looping process that is not necessarily as sequential as the terms may indicate. In other words: variation, selection and retention are part of the same feedback loop (Foster and Hölz, 2004). Also, the selection process is not only mutual and causing qualitative change in all systems concerned but also simultaneous (Porter, 2006).

Starting with variation, Aldrich and Rueff (1999) note that there are two ways in which variety is created: intentionally and blindly. Intentional variety is driven by active attempts by agents to find their way through time when encountering problems, while blind variation occurs through events independent from people's behavior (Aldrich and Rueff, 1999). This points at the fact there is no clear separation between variation that is created intentionally and variation that is not. Blind variation cannot be separated from selections (intentionally or unintentionally) made by people because, although some actions can be without consequences, it is possible that actions lead to a multitude of changes and variations at a later point in time with complex causality obscuring the relationship between the two. The case study illustrates that actors struggle with determining the impact of their decisions. They argue that favourable outcomes are due to their decisions whereas unfavourable outcomes are attributed to chance or the unwanted actions of others. The discussions regarding the cause of the sudden sediment accumulation is an example of that. This ostensible absence of clear causation may give the impression that, while intentional selection is observable, certain variation cannot be related and is, therefore, blind. Complex causation could indeed create that impression but variation in the future can still be triggered by current selection, even when this variation is unintended, unobserved and unexpected – witness this case study. In other words, selection and variation are part of the same feedback loop that affects a complex adaptive system (Hrebiniak and Joyce, 1985). There are therefore two basic types of reciprocal selection in (coevolutionary) planning processes: visible and blind, each being real and exerting selection pressures on the systems.

Visible selection is a result of deliberate choices. People assess the current situation, define a desired state of the system and draw up a solution to change the current situation into the desired situation. Upon execution of the solution, the system concerned will move through the attractor basin towards a new (and desired) system state. For example, HPA and BAW aim to receive larger ships, they deem the current depth insufficient to achieve this aim and consequently make a plan for the deepening of the navigation channel that they execute. In other words: the choices made leads to a selection pressure on the system. This creates a renewed situation from which the actors can continue to work, i.e. it determines the variation available to actors at a later stage. Although a clear and intended change in the other system could occur, it is also possible that a certain action may lead to no changes or to unintended changes. The timeframe of these changes might be erratic, with results sometimes appearing immediately while there may be long delays in others cases. Due to the limited information capacity of actors, the consequence of a particular action may appear to be detached from it. Because this consequent action also results in changes to a situation and determines the variation available at a later stage, this is considered to be blind selection, i.e. variation that is seemingly detached from the act of selecting but that, in fact, is not. For example, changes to the sediment transport of the Unterelbe can be attributed to several decisions made by planners, but its exact causation is almost impossible to determine. However, it still pressures planners to act even though its cause is obscure and might, in fact, be a result of the decisions made by the same people.

The erratic nature of blind selection can be explained by processes known in complexity theory. Selection pressures as feedback loops can be positive or negative and can lead to the occurrence of change, punctuated equilibrium, hysteresis, path-dependency and lock-in effects, all of which render the result different in time and place from the initial intention. Because feedback loops can bring about proportional results (negative feedback) or disproportional results (positive feedback) it becomes difficult to gauge the future effect of a planning proposal. Maybe a change will take place as expected; maybe a change will trigger reinforcing or dampening mechanisms, consequently altering the expected outcome. Even more, complex systems do not always change instantly following pressures. Sometimes it takes the accumulation of multiple pressures before the system topples into a new stable state (Muradian, 2001). This also happened in the case of the Unterelbe. A history of anthropocentric changes built pressure on the physical system. The final dredging operation triggered a system shift from one equilibrium into the next one. The consequent efforts necessary to alter the new situation again exceed the initial efforts to get into that situation in the first place. This process of hysteresis means that once a system has arrived in a new equilibrium it becomes very hard to make that situation undone if it is an unfavourable situation (Hughes, Bellwood, Folke, Steneck, and Wilson, 2005; Scheffer, Carpenter, Foley, Folke, and Walker, 2001). Even more, the costs of changing the unfavourable situation exceed the benefits of staying in that situation. This is a classic example of lock-in and consequent path-dependency (Greener, 2002; Pierson, 2000).

The characteristics of complex systems mean that change following planning activities is highly erratic. The resulting situation defines the degree of freedom available to all actors. Planning as the act of selecting can therefore be blind because of the disposition of processes in complexity while still being reciprocal because of the mutual influence of systems to determine their future states. The nature of perceptible and blind reciprocal selection as part of coevolutionary processes raises the ostensible complexity and inherent uncertainty experienced by actors (Rammel, Hinterberger, and Bechtold, 2004).

Taken together, all selection pressures present a complex puzzle to the planners. They have to make decisions regarding the physical system but some demands, wishes and practical possibilities are not compatible. And although planners have increased their capacity for estimating future developments, there are no computational models that can predict the consequences of a certain planning proposal accurately (Gerrits and Moody, 2011).

8.8 Conclusions

Planning effectiveness is still also about rational and powerful planning schemes and project management approaches. These approaches, aiming for stability order and control, will continue to be needed now. Nevertheless, it is necessary to introduce more adaptive capacity in planning in order to move along with the dynamics of the environment. It can be argued that this is needed because a considerable part of planning disappointments is caused by the impact of external actions and events that emerge after the plan was adopted. This final section outlines the contours of a coevolutionary revision of planning processes, followed by lessons for practitioners.

From this research, it appears that the dominant way of thinking in planning focuses on the planners' ability to make visible selections regarding the future of the planning object, in this case the Unterelbe. However, planners are also subjected to blind selection stemming from earlier planning decisions that have adverse effects, accidental changes and events. The relationship between these decisions and the actual outcomes is obscured because of complex causation. The new situation is unfavourable to the planners, consequently forcing them to abandon their original plans and to deal with the new situation. This is partly because the relationship between plans, selections and actions from planners and subsequent outcomes is erratic. In other words: the outcomes do not evolve gradually following decisions from planner but instead show that results can emerge elsewhere in time because of the nature of feedback loops. Therefore, planners could face new situations relatively unexpectedly, especially when the new situation is unintended. It appears that selections and selection pressures of coevolving systems have a reciprocal quality insofar as the degree of freedom of the planners is limited by events and developments outside the direct, perceivable and intended control of those planners. The collection of possible future states of the systems can be compromised through adverse, unintended results and events. They can respond in different ways to such situations.

Lesson 1: If you are facing planning problems like cost overrun and delay, just try a more complex planning process

Effective planning implies the ability to take the dynamics of the planning object and the actors in the context affected or activated by the planning activities into account and to adjust the planning goals, the planning process and even the planning arrangement like the team, the type of planners and the procedures to the emerging external actions and events.

Based on this case and on many other cases (e.g. Teisman, 1992; Klijn, 1996; Koppenjan, 2003; Teisman, Van Buuren and Gerrits, 2009) the conclusion seems that planning success is often not generated by doing efficiently what is decided in advance, but much more by the ability of planners to adjust to changes in the environment of a planning activity. It is only through the adaptive capacities of a planner that a process of coevolution between his aims and the demands from events and actions in his context can emerge. And it is not the ability to stick to the planning targets and planning procedures, but much more the vitality of the coevolutionary process that is responsible for reaching mutually desired results. Such an approach was shown in the case study in this chapter. Following the societal resistance and physical problems, the authorities started to realize that the chosen route would not take them much closer to their ambitions to create a highly accessible port. First they applied a narrowly focussed approach that failed. Then they started a mediation process and started to rethink their system boundaries. They began to accept that the Unterelbe was not only an economic asset. It also had other functions to other stakeholders who were subsequently allowed a say in the planning process (albeit with reluctance from the planners). Although this alternative approach does not yield big changes, yet, it is significant that for the first time the port authorities developed a long-term vision for the region and for the first time listened to input from opponents. It means that there is potential to take a larger part of a complex social and physical system into account. In terms of management tools and prescription this leads to an important and probably counter-intuitive advice: if a planning process is facing growing resistance, delay and rising costs, opening up the original planning framework, bringing in more actors, taking into account more events and expanding the scope can help the process substantially. Making the planning content, process and arena more complex can help to find new ways of implementation.

Lesson 2: Planning is the combination of doing what is decided and adjusting to what is emerging

The application of a coevolutionary framework explicitly focuses on the empirical reality that planning processes are subject to patterns of reciprocal selection. Planners can be both architects of new stable states and victims of their own system boundary judgments at the same time. The planner is creating a process that initially really speeds up his own planning path. But at the same moment he is facing the possibility of becoming path dependent. If the environment in which he is laying out his planning route is changing, this path easily can become a dead end. The best advice then would be to burn his outdated and obsolete plan and to open his eyes for the new challenging environment and discovering what should be done here to achieve satisfactory results.

Thinking about planning in terms of coevolution means accepting that planning processes unfold in time without a clear definite end state (cf. Marshall, 2009). That means that each step that is taken is a goal in itself rather than one interim step towards a distant final state. Therefore, planning should focus on incremental changes that are dictated by the possibilities that are specific to a certain time and location. Often, planners aspire to make sweeping comprehensive plans that aim to alter a given situation profoundly (and supposedly for the better). However, the coevolutionary nature of planning processes shows that such ambitions are destined for failure because they fail to address the fact that evolution is, essentially, directionless in the long run.

Although coevolutionary planning processes ask planners to focus on the local space of possibilities, it does not mean that they should focus on a narrow planning scope. As shown in the case study, ignoring environmental factors can seriously hamper planning ambitions. Thus, planning as an coevolutionary act requires a wide scope that is local in time instead of a narrow scope that encompasses a considerable time span. We think that this is a crucial element for successful planning processes because again and again it has been proven that planners (like other humans) are not very good at making predictions. And any planning process that is far-reaching in time runs the severe risk of building on wrong assumptions about what will happen in the future and what will be considered favourable in that future.

Our analysis and reframing of planning processes as coevolution are not meant to mark the end of planning as it is generally known. There is still a role for planners in this erratic and complex world. We envision this role to be the one that recognizes and articulates the complexity of planning, as outlined in this chapter and elsewhere in this book, without falling back on grand (modernist) planning behaviour. Rather, the planner should focus on the complexity that is available and should work with that instead of attempting to shield off the planning process (as was tried unsuccessfully in this case study). Working with all stakeholders and being open to all (unsolicited) proposals and possible events, the planner tries working with the flow rather than against it. Indeed, this will be difficult in politically controversial settings such as the one in Hamburg in this case study, but we think that a good planner is someone who can explore the limits and possibilities of a given situation in such a way it reconciles ambitions with the current situation. Only then can we, to paraphrase Marshall (2009), keep the built future in our hands.

References

Aldrich, H.E. and Ruef, M. (1999) *Organizations Evolving*, Sage, London.

Byrne, D. (1998) *Complexity Theory and the Social Sciences*, Routledge, London, New York.

Byrne, D. (2005) Complexity, Configurations and Cases. *Theory, Culture and Society*, 22(5), pp. 95-111.

Edelenbos, J., Gerrits, L. and Gils, M.K.A. van (2008) The Coevolutionary Relation Between Dutch Mainport Policies and the Development of the Seaport Rotterdam, *Emergence: Complexity and Organization*, 10(2), pp. 49-60.

Cilliers, P. (2001) Boundaries, Hierarchies and Networks in Complex Systems. *International Journal of Innovation Management*, 5(2), pp. 35-147.

Edelenbos J. and Teisman G.R. (2008) Public Private Partnership: On the Edge of Project and Process Management, *Environment and Planning C*, April 2008, pp. 614-626.

Ehrlich, P.R. and Raven, P.H. (1964) Butterflies and Plants: A Study in Coevolution. *Evolution*, 18(4), pp. 586-608.

Folke, C. (2006). Resilience: The Emergence of a Perspective for Social-ecological Systems Analysis, *Global Environmental Change*, 16(1), pp. 253-267.

Foster, J. and Hölz, W. (eds.) (2004) *Applied Evolutionary Economics and Complex Systems*, Edward Elgar Publishing, Cheltenham.

Flood, R.L. (1999) *Rethinking the Fifth Discipline: Learning Within the Unknowable*, Routledge, London.

Flood, R.L., and Jackson, M.C. (1991) *Creative Problem Solving: Total Systems Intervention.* Chichester, John Wiley and Sons, Chichester.

Flyvbjerg, B., Bruzelius, N., Rothengatter, W. (2006) *Megaprojects and Risk. An Anatomy of Ambition*, Cambridge University Press, Cambridge.

Gerrits, L. (2008) The Gentle Art of Coevolution. A Complexity Theory Perspective on Decision Making over Estuaries in Germany, Belgium and the Netherlands. Rotterdam: Erasmus University, Rotterdam.

Gerrits, L., Marks, P.M. and Van Buuren, A. (2009) Coevolution: A Constant in Non-linear Thinking. In: Teisman, G.R., Van Buuren, A.W., Gerrits, L. (eds.) *Managing Complex Governance Systems*, Routledge, New York.

Gerrits, L. (2010) Public Decision-Making as Coevolution, *Emergence: Complexity and Organization*, 12(1), pp. 19-28.

Gerrits, L. and Moody, R.F.I. (2011) Envisaging Futures: Analyzing the use of Computational Models in Public Decision Making. In: K. Richardson and A. Tait (Eds.) *Applications in Complexity Science: Tools for Managing Complex Socio-Technical Systems*. Emergent Publications, Litchfield Park, pp. 1-10.

Greener, I. (2002) Theorising Path Dependency: How Does History Come to Matter in Organisations, and What Can We Do About it? The University of York, Heslington.

Gual, M.A. and Norgaard, R.B. (2010) Bridging Ecological and Social Systems Coevolution: A Review and a Proposal, *Ecological Economics*, 69(4), pp. 707-717.

Healey, P. (2006) *Urban Complexity and Spatial Strategies: Towards a Relational Planning for Our Times*, Routledge, New York.

Hooke, J.M. (1999) Decades of Change: Contributions of Geomorphology to Fluvial and Coastal Engineering and Management, *Geomorphology*, 31(4), pp. 373-389.

Hrebiniak, L.G. and Joyce, W.F. (1985) Organizational Adaptation: Strategic Choice and Environmental Determinism, *Administrative Science Quarterly*, 30(3), pp. 336-349.

Hughes, T.P., Bellwood, D.R., Folke, C., Steneck, R.S., and Wilson, J. (2005) New Paradigms for Supporting the Resilience of Marine Ecosystems, *Trends in Ecology and Evolution*, 20(7), pp. 380-386.

Kallis, G., and Norgaard, R.B. (2010) Coevolutionary Ecological Economics, *Ecological Economics*, 69(4), pp. 690-699.

Kickert, W., Klijn, E.H., Koppenjan, J. (1996) *Managing Governance Networks*, Sage, New York.

Klein, R.J.T., Smit, M.J., Goosen, H. and Hulsbergen, C.H. (1998) Resilience and Vulnerability: Coastal Dynamics or Dutch Dikes? *The Geographical Journal*, 164(3), pp. 259-268.

Klijn, E.H. (1996) *Regels en sturing in netwerken* [Rules and guiding in networks], Eburon, Delft.

Klijn, E.H., Snellen, I. (2009) Complexity theory and public administration: a critical appraisal, In: Teisman, G.R., Van Buuren, A.W., Gerrits, L. (eds.) *Managing Complex Governance Systems*, Routledge, New York, London, pp. 17-35.

Koppenjan, J.F.M. (2003) De moeizame aanloop naar publiek-private samenwerking. Negen totstandkomingsprocessen bij transportinfrastructuur [The problematic start towards a public private cooperation. Nine start up processes for transport infrastructure], *Beleidswetenschap*, 2, pp. 99-123.

Kotchen, M.J., and Young, O.R. (2007) Meeting the Challenges of the Anthropocene: Towards a Science of Coupled Human-biophysical Systems, *Global Environmental Change*, 17(2), pp. 149-151.

Law, J. (1996) Notes on the Theory of the Actor Network: Ordering, Strategy and Heterogeneity, Centre for Science Studies, Lancaster University, Vol. 11, Lancaster (UK).

Levin S.A. (1983) Some Approaches to the Modeling of Coevolutionary Interactions. In: M. Nitecki (eds.) *Coevolution*, University of Chicago Press, Chicago, pp. 21-65.

Nicholls, R.J. and Branson, J. (1998) Coastal Resilience and Planning for an Uncertain Future: an Introduction, *The Geographical Journal*, 164(3), pp. 255 - 258.

Marshall, S. (2009) *Cities, Design and Evolution*, Routledge, London, New York.

Muradian, R. (2001) Ecological Thresholds: a Survey, *Ecological Economics*, 38(1), pp. 7-24.

Norgaard, R.B. (1984) Coevolutionary Development Potential, *Land Economics*, 60(2), pp. 160-173.

Norgaard, R.B. (1994) *Development Betrayed: The End of Progress and a Coevolutionary Revisioning of the Future*, Routledge, London, New York.

Odum, E.P. (1971) *Fundamentals of Ecology*, W.B. Saunders Company, Philadelphia.

Okasha, S. (2003), Recent Work on the Levels of Selection Problem, *Human Nature Review*, 3, 349–356.

O'Sullivan, D., Manson, S.M., Messina, J.P. and Crawford, T.W. (2006) Space, Place and Complexity Science. *Environment and Planning A*, 38(4), pp. 611-617.

Otter, H.S. (2000) *Complex Adaptive Land Use Systems; an Interdisciplinary Approach with Agent-based Models*, Eburon, Delft.

Pel, B. (2009) The Complexity of Self-Organization; Boundary Judgments in Traffic Management, In: G.R. Teisman, A. van Buuren and L. Gerrits (Eds.) *Managing Complex Governance Systems; Dynamics, Self-Organization and Coevolution in Public Investments*, Routledge, London, pp. 116-133

Pierson, P. (2000) Increasing Returns, Path Dependence and the Study of Politics. American *Political Science Review*, 94(2), pp. 251-267.

Porter, T.B. (2006) Coevolution as a Research Framework for Organizations and the Natural Environment. *Organization and Environment*, 14(4), pp. 479-504.

Sanderson, S.K. (1990) *Social Evolutionism. A Critical History*. Blackwell, Cambridge.

Scheffer, M., Carpenter, S., Foley, J.A., Folke, C. and Walker, B. (2001) Catastrophic Shifts in Ecosystems, *Nature*, 413, pp. 591-596.

Sementelli, A. (2007) Distortions of Progress: Evolutionary Theories and Public Administration. *Administration and Society*, 39(6), pp. 740-760.

Teisman, G.R. (1992) Complexe besluitvorming. Een pluricentrisch perspectief op besluitvorming over ruimtelijke inversteringen, Katholieke Universiteit Brabant. The Hague (NL).

Teisman G.R., E.H. Klijn (2008) Complexity Theory and Public Management: An Introduction, *Public Management Review*, 10(3), (May), pp. 287-297.

Teisman G.R. (2008) Complexity and Management of Improvement Programmes: An Evolutionary Approach, *Public Management Review*, 10(3), (May), pp. 341-359.

Teisman, G.R., Buuren, M.W. van and Gerrits, L. (Eds.) (2009) *Managing complex governance systems. Dynamics, self-organisation and Coevolution in Public Investments*, Routledge, New York/London.

Turner, R.K. (2000) Integrating Natural and Socio-economic Science in Coastal Management. Journal of Marine Systems, 25(3-4), pp. 447-460.

Turner, R.K., Lorenzoni, I., Beaumont, N., Bateman, I.J., Langford, I.H. and McDonald, A.L. (1998) Coastal Management for Sustainable Development:

Analysing Environmental and Socio-economic Changes on the UK coast, *The Geographical Journal*, 164(3), pp. 269-281.

Van den Bergh, J.C.J.M. (2004) Evolutionary Thinking in Environmental Economics: Retrospect and Prospect. In: Foster, J. and Hölz, W. (eds.) *Applied Evolutionary Economics and Complex Systems*, Edward Elgar, Cheltenham, pp. 239-270.

Van Gils, M., Gerrits, L., Teisman, G.R. (2009) Non-linear Dynamics in Port Systems: Change Events at Work. In: Teisman, G.R., Van Buuren, A.W., Gerrits, L. *Managing Complex Governance Systems*, Routledge, New York.

Volberda, H.W. and Lewin, A.Y. (2003) Co-evolutionary Dynamics Within and Between Firms: From Evolution to Co-evolution. *Journal of Management Studies*, 40(8), pp. 2111-2136.

Chapter 9

Climate Adaptation in Complex Governance Systems: Governance Systems between Inertia and Adaptability

Arwin van Buuren, Sibout Nooteboom and Geert Teisman[1]

If climate change will occur in line with expectations of the International Panel on Climate Change (IPCC), some challenging problems have to be dealt with all over the world. Especially the deltas of our world are facing increased dangers of flooding. The Netherlands is one of the world's most developed and densely populated delta areas. The Netherlands and many other deltas have a long tradition of flooding protection measures and accompanying measures against dropping of the ground level and related salt water intrusion in the peat meadow areas and for increasing water discharges in large rivers. Some climate experts argue that these 'traditional' measures no longer will be sufficient and perceive existing governments' repertoire as inert: either the measures taken are not decisive enough, or they are only incremental improvements of existing measures which are no longer compatible with the challenges we face. If this is the case, the catastrophe theory, as one of the theories under the rubric of complexity theories, assumes that external tensions on the inert system will build up, even though this is neglected. At a certain moment, however, traditional responses no longer will work. A small variation in the weather system then can trigger unexpected system shocks leading to small or large catastrophes. What happened in the UK and along the Danube in the last decade can be seen as strong signals for what climate change can do to existing societies which are not able to adapt to changing conditions.

It is for these reasons that climate experts argue that the existing mitigation of climate change is not effective. More radical adaptation measures are necessary to reduce the vulnerability of our social-ecological systems (Folke et al., 2002; 2005). A policy agenda is not considered enough; many proposals are formulated to reform the governmental institutions to enhance their 'adaptive capacity'. Several reports, like the Dutch Second Delta report (Second Delta Committee, 2008), not only present an agenda of adaptation, they also question the ability of existing governance systems to develop adaptive policies and implementation

---

1   Arwin van Buuren and Sibout Nooteboom are both Associate Professor and Geert Teisman is Professor in Public Administration. All three are from the Department of Public Administration at the Erasmus University Rotterdam.

schemes. In the Delta report it is even suggested to centralize a substantial part of the existing formal decision-making authority of national, regional and local governments. It seems as if climate experts assume that government has to be reinvented in order to deal with the expected substantial climate changes. But is it realistic to reshape government based on one external threat or should climate policy and implementation schemes be reshaped in such a way that they fit in with existing governance practice?

9.1 Introduction

From national policy documents of the Dutch government, we can read that climate adaptation has high political and administrative priority. The National Water Vision, the National Spatial Planning Document and the Cabinet's Declaration all declare that climate change has to get high priority. The influential report of the Second Delta Committee (2008) underlines the necessity of action. Reports, however, are not always a good indication of real governance system change. When developers elaborate concrete investment projects, the idea of climate adaptation is not fully integrated (Mickwitz et al., 2009). Although a variety of policy instruments is available, like financial arrangements and spatial planning instruments, the planning practices will not change overnight (Van Buuren et al., 2012a).

In this chapter, we elaborate on the opportunities and difficulties with 'reinventing government'. In contrast to the sometimes technocratic view of scientists in climate research on the role of government, assuming that government systems can easily be adjusted to new external demands, we will apply a social science view in which government is perceived as a complex governance system, composed of many interrelated networks in which – beside climate adaptation – a whole variety of values and interests have to be dealt with. Governance systems can be compared with living organisms that are not, and cannot, be designed and engineered by someone in charge. What can be achieved is evolution to a system state of a higher, more cooperative or reflexive, order. This, however, is much more generated by mutual learning than by design.

From these theories we can understand the patterns of resistance against (radical) change in governance networks. *Path dependency (caused by hysteresis), negative feedback* and *autopoïetic self-organization* are perceived to be the stabilizing forces in governance systems, enabling effective implementation of any policy. They, however, also can lead to inertia and indecisiveness. As long as these forces prevent governance systems against hypes and shocks they can be labelled as stabilizing forces. If, however, these forces prevent governance systems from adjustment to serious threads, they must be labelled as inertia. We illustrate the working of these stabilizing forces with a case of climate adaptation in a Dutch peat meadow area (Section 9.3) in which necessary adaptation measures are not realized due to the dominance of these stabilizing forces preventing change.

At the same time, we elaborate the existence and working of *change events*, *positive feedback* and *adaptive self-organization* as abilities of learning in existing governance systems. In complexity theory it is assumed that these forces can push governance systems to a new system state. We will illustrate these phenomena in a successful adaptation case in which these forces support a transition towards a new – more climate proof situation (Section 9.3).

From this exercise we derive some principles of 'the governance of adaptation' based upon the understanding of the complex behaviour of social systems which try to help the governance system adapt ('adaptive networks'; Nooteboom and Marks, 2009). The main conclusion is that governance systems balance between a variety of values and interests. It seems to be more wise and realistic to achieve climate adaptation by an evolution of governance systems instead of a technocratic redesign. This creates high demands on the formulation of climate adaptation proposals. In order to have a large impact, they have to fit in with the demands of the existing governance system and its complex characteristics. At the end of this chapter we will present an adaptation strategy that fits in with the complexity, dynamics and demands of existing governance systems.

9.2 Complex adaptive systems, stable and dynamic

Our analysis builds upon complex adaptive system theory (Axelrod and Cohen, 1999; Duit and Galaz, 2008). Sherman and Schultz (1998, p. 17) define a complex adaptive system as a system: '… *composed of interacting 'agents' following rules, exchanging influence with their local and global environments and altering the very environment they are responding to by virtue of their simple action*' (in Chiva Gomez, 2003).

In the complex adaptive systems theory, governance systems, like any other system, are characterized by five elements. First of all, an adaptive system embraces an undefined set of interrelated agents or elements. These agents influence each other in mutual and multiple ways. At the same time, all agents are assumed to have relative autonomy. This means that each agent is capable to respond to external events and pressure in an individual way (Eidelson, 1997; Chiva Gomez, 2003).

Secondly, complex adaptive systems are nested, in the sense they have a hierarchy of embedded layers, which are, however, hard to define. The layers and subsystems co-evolve with each other. In that sense, governance systems are comparable with organisms in which there is some, but no straightforward, context – agent hierarchy and a large amount of mutual dependency. The whole (social) system is only adaptive when a critical mass of subsystems is prepared to respond in a synchronized adaptive way.

Thirdly, the external context can be of great importance for the evolution process. Adaptive system development depends upon the interaction between the composing agents and their surrounding systems (the exchange of energy). The interaction between a nested governance system and its context can be visualized as a set of negative and positive feedback loops. If an external event or pressure is seen as confirmation of existing patterns of actions agents and systems will react in terms of stability and repeat existing repertoires. If an event or pressure is seen as a threat that cannot be ignored, or as an advantage, the agent and system will look for new responses. The first reaction can minimize, and the second can amplify, the impact of external pressure on governance systems.

Fourthly, a complex system will normally develop in a non-linear pattern. The interactions between agents will be changing over time and this will create a whimsical pattern. It is almost impossible to predict the dynamics in interaction, because each agent can decide to change course.

Fifthly, the course of development of complex systems depends upon the initial conditions of each new step of action. Often the course will be guided by path dependency. Relatively small changes of conditions may generate a significant system leap.

Stabilizing forces in complex systems

In complex adaptive systems, change and dynamics are as normal as stability. There are different mechanisms that constitute and conserve system stability. Within complexity theory there are three explanations for stability (Stacey, 2003; Eidelson, 1997; Axelrod and Cohen, 1999; Cilliers, 1998). First of all, processes of *negative feedback* will dampen internal and external change initiatives. In the second place *autopoïetic (conservative) self-organization* is the normal effect of individual agents' conduct in the system. External pressures and events tend to be interpreted as a reason to go on with existing actions. It reinforces existing patterns and practices (Luhmann, 1995). And, finally, the amount of *hysteresis* makes it difficult for a system to change its path and thus causes path dependencies and even lock-in. Hysteresis can be seen as the amount of resistance of a system against change (Eidelson, 1997). A system with hysteresis exhibits path-dependence, or 'rate-independent memory' (Mielke and Roubicek, 2003). The output of such a system cannot be explained without taking into account the history of its input (the former state of the system). In order to predict the output, one must look at the path that the output followed before it reached its current value (cf. Eidelson, 1997).

Stable systems are in an equilibrium state, which may be a state of steady (autopoïetic) growth, and they are confronted with mechanisms which prevent them from being pushed to the edge of chaos. That implies that the extent to which they are able to adapt themselves proactively to changing circumstances, is low (Van Buuren et al. 2012b).

Adaptive forces in complex systems

There are also forces that may bring a system in a 'far from equilibrium' situation. Again we distinguish three explanations for change. First of all, processes of *positive feedback* can reinforce change initiatives. An event or stimulus is reinforced because it triggers events which reinforce the initial event, or it receives environmental signals which reward the sender of the stimulus, and thereby encourage repeating and intensifying the stimulus. Examples of patterns of positive feedback within social systems are vicious circles, self-fulfilling prophecies, bandwagon effects and chain reactions (Stacey, 2003).

Systems in states of instability do have a potential for *dissipative self-organization*. They have a certain degree of freedom to act and are open for the influence of energy, information and/or matter from their environment (Mathews et al. 1999). It is assumed in complexity theory that especially systems that are pushed to the edge of chaos, and open for external influences, do have the capacity to leave existing structures and to organize themselves into new structures. The system becomes open to influences from outside and generates the capacity to reorganize itself. Dissipative self-organization in governance systems is built-up from its constituting agents. Some of them first make innovative proposals that challenge the autopoïetic path of action. If the amount of agents that support these proposals will grow, a system leap becomes possible. Uhl Bien et al. (2007) call this adaptive leadership. A new pattern of action emerges, even though it would have been easier on the short term to stick to conservative self-organization. The question when the threshold of a critical mass is exceeded, and whether or not this is a point of no return in governance system leaps, however, still remains unanswered.

Thirdly, *external events* are crucial for system development. Trigger events (Dooley, 1997) can cause unexpected dynamics and overcome path dependencies. They bring a system out of its equilibrium, potentially far enough to display dissipative self-organization by which a new and higher level of order can be realized.

9.3 Governance networks as complex systems

Governance networks, the easier observable embedded components of governance systems at large, can be conceptualized as complex adaptive systems. They are composed of public agencies, private companies, interest groups, citizens and so on. These agents are at the one hand autonomous in persecuting their strategies and trying to maximize their ambitions. At the same time, they are mutually dependent due to the dispersion among them of necessary financial, juridical, organizational and political resources (Koppenjan and Klijn, 2004).

With this rough conceptualization in mind, we can give meaning to other elements of complex adaptive systems in the context of governance systems. Positive or negative feedback in governance processes can be seen as specific types of interaction between the actors in a governance network. Some actors do have ideas or ambitions, which they bring forward. These ideas can meet resistance from other actors who mobilize strategies to invalidate such ideas, but they can also trigger enthusiasm and a deliberative search towards enriching these ideas and developing them. A government agency which has a brilliant idea about restructuring a spatial area can find other agencies and governments which have compatible or even supplementary ideas. That would mean an important support for this original idea and can cause a self-reinforcing pattern of positive feedback.

Within governance networks, we can witness both patterns of autopoïetic (within contexts of internal procedures, fixed routines, closed interaction patterns etc.) and dissipative self-organization. This has much to do with the frames of reference, or attitudes, that actors have. Cognitive and social closedness (Schaap and Van Twist, 1997) is an important explanation of autopoïetic self-organization. Openness, on the other hand, is an impetus for dissipative self-organization (e.g. Nooteboom and Marks, 2009). Some governance systems are rather closed. Corporatist networks are good examples. However, there are also highly dynamic, temporary issue networks, which show many actors joining and resigning the network. These networks are open, maintaining many, varied relationships with their environment. They do have a range of strategies available with which they can respond to changing conditions. One-issue networks, loosely organized constellations of widely different actors, are oftentimes successful in realizing a new (temporary) order with regard to the societal and political opinion about a specific theme. A third type of networks operate more informally behind the scenes, trying to maintain openness and connectedness between organizations with contrasting short-term interests, in order to help them to jointly and individually adapt to changing circumstances (Nooteboom and Marks, 2009).

Path dependency in governance networks implies that actors cooperate or fight, being open or closed to each other, for historic reasons, simply because they have started to trust or distrust each other. Civil servants may act according to their expectation of how politicians will reward them, and be guided by past reward in similar situations (governance in the shadow of hierarchy; Scharpf, 1997). Change events can provoke important policy transitions. The flood disaster of 1953 in the Southern part of the Netherlands caused a policy window for an unparalleled program of sea surge barriers and dike improvement. The same holds true for the near river floods of 1993 and 1995 within central Netherlands. However, also less impressive events, like the termination of businesses or the unexpected moves of a political body can trigger a chain of events that gives a policy process a dynamic move.

Successful implementation of climate adaptation measures highly depends on the state of the complex governance system in which these measures have to be developed and applied (Boons et al., 2009; 2011). To implement adaptation measures within a highly inert system, much more effort is necessary than when they are developed within the context of a more dynamic system.

Governing principles in complex system approaches

Applying complex adaptive system theory to governance systems not only will have consequences for the analysis of stability and change, as indicated above, but also for the view on leadership. Traditionally, leadership is about one person and one single actor 'in charge'. We can refer to the books on the president of the United States, or the kings and emperors in the past. And even nowadays, there is still a huge fascination for leaders making the difference in business, banking or politics. In complex adaptive system theory, agents are important and in that sense leadership in the traditional multifocal way can be incorporated. However, when the focus is on system change, the concept of leadership will become more multiple. McKelvey (2008) describes how leadership can build adaptive tension into a social system that moves it to the edge of chaos, even a specific edge, with the precise aim of proactive adaptation and harmonic co-evolution with the environment. He argues, like Uhl Bien et al. (2007), that leadership in complex systems necessarily must be shared in the form of distributed intelligence. Only by way of distributed intelligence adequate assessments of external and internal change can be made and using them as bandwagons for their own system, and making use of positive feedback and the potentials of dissipative self-organization.

Hereafter, we analyse two cases that illustrate the interrelation between system state and implementation problems. In one case, which we can characterize as relatively closed from its environment, we observe an abundance of negative feedback loops which cause many problems of indecisiveness and non-progress. In the other case, which is much more open to external influences (and thus to opportunities) positive feedback loops caused a transition of land use.

9.4 Case descriptions

In this section, we present two case studies (conducted between 2006 and 2009) in which attempts have been made to generate a climate adaptation strategy. In the case of Groot Mijdrecht Noord a spatial reallocation of functions was necessary due to the need for retention capacity and the slow settling of the ground in the polders of this area. The dominant agricultural function had, according to climate change experts, to be replaced by nature development and water retention. In the case of Perkpolder, located alongside the Scheldt Estuary, the sea dikes had to be enforced, and more space for the estuary had to be realized, in order to enhance its capacity to dissipate tidal energy.

While in the case of Perkpolder a vital coalition of private, societal and public actors was able to realize an appealing plan with advantages for a broad constellation of actors within an acceptable time period, the process with regard to Groot Mijdrecht Noord was much more indecisive and time-consuming. We suppose that these differences can be explained by analysing the way in which the governance systems in these cases functioned.

Context Groot Mijdrecht Noord

In large parts of the Netherlands, climate adaptation mainly means increasing water retention capacity to store rainwater. This includes the peat meadow areas of the Green Heart of Holland, the green open area in-between the main cities of Western Netherlands. The soil of the Green Heart used to be built-up of thick layers of peat. Part of this has been used as fuel, leaving low polders and lakes, but a lot has been spared and is in use as agricultural area, nature reserve, or both. The area is under threat of slow urbanization; where large schemes are still controlled by the state, there are smaller local schemes and farms, even barns, are converted to mansions.

Even light agricultural use of peat soil requires lowering of the water table to below ground level, which causes oxidation of the peat and therefore soil subsidence. The last century, heavy machines required firmer soil, which has sometimes resulted in several meters subsidence. In many low lying parts, salt ground water now has started to intrude, which will seriously hamper agriculture and harm natural ecosystems. Different forms and intensities of land use have created a patchwork of water tables which become increasingly difficult and expensive to manage. Natural areas are now high-lying and must be kept wet to preserve their biodiversity, whilst the water is draining and there is a risk of local dike failure. Intensive (profitable) agriculture located in the vicinity of the nature reserves scattered around the area therefore creates problems of water management. On top of this, it is foreseen that parts of the Green Heart will have to be flooded as retention area in the future in periods of high rainfall, in particular close to cities. The chosen areas must be low-lying parts which are now used by intensive agriculture. That makes the costs of a transition in spatial function, as well as its social impact, rather high.

Groot Mijdrecht Noord

This case study further focuses on Groot Mijdrecht Noord ('Mijdrecht'). Mijdrecht is a low-lying polder of less then 10 km^2 in the Green Heart. It is surrounded by dikes and canals with higher water, and close to Amsterdam. It is mainly used for agriculture, and partly for nature. In the long term, agriculture is expected to become impossible due to continued soil subsidence, salt intrusion and groundwater bursts under pressure of the rising sea, which is several meters higher than the land. Present pumping of salt and polluted water out of the polder creates increasing problems for nature in the areas around the polder and brings high management and maintenance costs for the Water Board.

The Province, the Municipality and the Water Board agreed that radical change of land use in Mijdrecht was inevitable, sooner or later. The cooperation to realize an integral redesign of the polder was initiated by the Water Board, which was worried, as a 'do-nothing' scenario would lead to rising water management cost, bankruptcy of farmers and flood damage to property owners in Mijdrecht itself and in Amsterdam (in the absence of enough retention capacity). Several scenarios have been studied, of which the technicians consider one involving a lake for water retention to be most sustainable (http://www.grootmijdrechtnoord. nl/). However, paradoxically, landowners continue to invest in the polder; e.g.

farms are converted to mansions. The cost of a conversion of land use, which entails compensation of property owners for loss of (potential or actual) functions, is slowly rising. A binding decision about conversion depends on both sufficient government funding and political support with are at this moment both unclear and ultimately missing.

Path dependency

None of the land conversion options, as proposed by the collaborating governments, were widely supported in the Mijdrecht area. There seemed to be different sources of doubt about conversion. Farmers and inhabitants said they did not believe the scenario analysis made by the cooperating governments, and there was doubt about the actual size of financial compensation. The latter had two components: would property owners get what was promised, and would it be enough to compensate for the loss of the presently available option to convert property to a high valued mansion? Another problem was that one authority should make a formal decision (with regard to, for example, the land conversion) and therefore it would become financially liable for the effects of that decision, whilst dependent on the other government levels for co-financing. That made it risky for that specific government to take such a decision without concrete commitments of other authorities for proportional financial contributions. The financial risk was complicated by the long time span of the conversion – more than 15 years. This had to do with the financial budgeting system of the central government. The budgetary rules of the national government did not allow fixing an expenditure planning for subsidies to regional governments decades in advance. Finally, a formal plan was required because nobody in an area serving as retention area could be excluded from a change of land function. All property owners needed to participate, even those who were not willing. If the plan would be voluntary, there would remain doubts about the actual behaviour of land owners when it would be their 'turn' – they might demand higher compensation value. It was even possible that farmers would create delays because they believed the government would offer more compensation value in the future, as the prices of land near Amsterdam were expected to continue rising. Finally, the idea that thorough change was unavoidable may not have fit the existing mental frames of inhabitants, making them unwilling to weigh the risks and opportunities to their actual size. Either they might not have wanted to change their way of life as farmer, or they might have feared they would be worse off because of land use restrictions. The belief systems of inhabitants who were accustomed to deal with the water conditions in the polder in certain ways, could not be changed overnight to the opinion that conditions were too worse to continue the normal practices.

Change of the current use and development of Mijdrecht therefore depended on many factors – many layers of government must cooperate, financing should be secured for decades, and provincial authorities must approve a binding plan, whilst resistance from the area was significant. Responsible politicians hesitated to decide, since they could not oversee the political risks.

The mechanisms that explain path dependency in this case can be summarized as follows:

1. belief systems of actors (their interests in their own perception) were oriented towards conserving the existing situation,
2. policy instruments were not equipped for realizing a transition, but aimed at maintaining the existing situation;
3. the composition of the policy network led to stability and conservatism; in the general relationship between citizen and government it was not customary to believe a government when it tells you that you have a serious problem and promises you an uncertain solution; both networks were not open to each other.

Negative feedback

Ideas that a land conversion was inevitable in Mijdrecht received criticism from the vested interests in the area. As change was proposed, its justification was challenged, which led to an increasing pile of reports. A couple of patterns can be indicated as triggers or causes of negative feedback. Especially political indecisiveness mainly from the Province and the central government led to reinforcement of the lack of sense of urgency among the inhabitants and a declining willingness to cooperate.

Delays in the decision-making process easily reinforced the actual behaviour of the inhabitants of the polder who were not willing to wait with their own economic ambitions, their investment projects or private deals about house or business sale. That made the economic value of the polder only higher, and thus the resistance against change, which makes realizing a broadly supported deal even more difficult.

The inhabitants saw new knowledge which had been deemed necessary to underpin the difficult choice of land conversion, as a new opportunity to generate their own knowledge and to question the new insights and reports. They even saw it as a sign of uncertainty of politicians, and thus as proof that the decision-makers also were not convinced about the necessity of conversion.

Autopoïetic self-organization

Self-organization was apparent at the level of the socio-economy of Mijdrecht. Since land prices went up, land owners did not want to be bought out at low prices. They wanted to convert their property to higher value mansions. Once outsiders live in these mansions, they wanted urbanization to stop (open land is more valuable when it is not your property, and more pleasant), whilst the conversion plans might risk allowing some further building schemes to finance the operation. Others simply did not accept the truth as presented by the water managers, or felt they were sacrificed for the good of Amsterdam's flood protection. These interests and sentiments led to activism at the many hearings and meetings organized by the province (taking responsibility for the binding spatial plan that is required before any conversion can start). A group from the area assigned spokespersons who were in frequent contact with the planners, in developing alternative development scenarios felt back into their preceding behaviour when at a certain point they refused further cooperation and started using their direct political influence to prevent the conversion.

The conversion alliance (Water Board and Province), was aware of the countervailing power, mobilized through autopoïetic self-organization among inhabitants. Inhabitants remained against conversion despite the fact they would be better off in terms of their own criteria. This seemed to be a standard attitude toward the government, or a cultivated sentiment that the area should stay the same, despite the evidence that this is impossible under any circumstances. Any farmer trying to break away from that local culture, and supporting conversion, may fear losing his friends. This is a devil's dilemma widely described in anthropology, which comes down to a tragedy of the commons. Whilst it may be in the common interest to become more realistic, each individual has an interest to 'punish' anyone who shows a tendency toward change.

Context Perkpolder

Due to climate change and sea-level, rice a couple of dike segments in the Dutch sea dikes was no longer strong enough to safeguard the protection against floods. For these so-called 'weak links' the Dutch Water Management Authority (Rijkswaterstaat, in short: RWS) had developed an improvement program.

Alongside the Scheldt Estuary (the only remaining open sea arm in the Netherlands due to the fact that it forms the fairway to Flemish most important port – Antwerp) also some weak links were present in the sea dikes and the Zeeland department of RWS developed a specific planning to bring these pieces on the minimal required safety level. In the Netherlands that meant that the chance of a flood has to be reduced to 1 in 10,000 years.

However, alongside the Scheldt Estuary another important challenge had to be met. Due to climate change, but also due to the regular deepening of the fairway, much more sea water entered the estuary and affected not only the safety of the estuary but also its unique ecological values. Higher water levels threatened the intertidal surface areas which harboured unique estuarine flora and fauna. Therefore, the European Commission obliged that the effects of a deepening of the fairway in 1998 through dredging operations on ecosystems would be compensated by additional measures.

Against this context, the small village of Perkpolder, one of the municipalities alongside the Scheldt, got the attention of the Zeeland Department of RWS. In 1999 for the first time they proposed to the municipal government to consider the possibility of a joint effort to build new estuarial ecosystems within the current land area adjoining the Scheldt and to improve the dikes in a more landward location, giving some land back to the sea.

In first instance, the municipality was not very enthusiastic. They were busy with developing a Master Plan for this area and saw no win-win outcome with RWS. However, after two years, both the municipality and the province – who was also involved in the development of the Master plan – became convinced about the necessity to realize a powerful coalition with other stakeholders and they invited RWS to participate.

This meant the start of a constructive process which was suddenly broadened by the decision to invite private partners to present their ideas about an attractive redevelopment of the area. An intensive process of visioning and designing followed in which the various public actors together with two private actors developed concrete ideas. Part of the process was the gradual expansion of the scope of the project. Time and again the involved actors expanded their boundary judgments about the desired project scope and included new elements.

Although the intergovernmental discussion about the Collaboration Agreement was very difficult and time-consuming, the subsequent debate about the sharing of the costs and benefits was highly constructive and ended up in a concrete agreement about the implementation process. The eventual profits were shared among the province, the municipality and the two private investors.

Change events

An important change event which helps us to explain the dynamics in this case is the termination of the ferry services between Kruiningen and Perkpolder in the mid-nineties. Due to the realization of the so-called Scheldt Tunnel, the ferry service had become superfluous and the Province had terminated it. That caused an important economic decline for both villages because they missed the many forms of traffic which go with many economic activities.

Due to this termination, both the Province and the Municipality became convinced about the urgent need to invest in the area of Perkpolder. They decided to work on a Master Plan in which they outlined the redesign of the ferry plaza into a new village with recreational activities, summer houses and a golf course.

However, both actors recognized that such a huge project would be not only very expensive but also very complicated. Therefore, when RWS for the second time asked to develop a joint vision on this area both governments decided to accept this invitation.

This refers to a second change event: the decision from the European Court to oblige an extensive package of nature development projects around the Scheldt because of the deepening of the fairway and the resulting decline of the ecological situation of the estuary.

A third change event which had a positive impact upon the process was the decision of the provincial government to install a new organizational unit 'area development' specialized in supporting and assisting local and regional projects of land conversion. This new department offered the necessary knowledge and skills for the Perkpolder project to be completed.

Dissipative self-organization

Because of the desire to invest much in permanent and recreational houses, the various involved governments decided that private project developers had to join the process in order to realize an attractive and feasible proposal with a perspective on private investments.

The involvement of these private actors caused highly creative dynamics between actors with very different ways of working. The private parties proposed to hire a team of designers to develop an inspiring vision for this area. They knew that the area of Perkpolder was not very attractive for residents (because of its isolated location) and therefore they underscored the necessity of an appealing and high-quality comprehensive design.

Within the project group, a process of dissipative self-organization was clearly observed. Despite some difficulties, the project group was able to retain its internal mutual trust and to seek a mutual attractive optimum. That implied that several attempts were made to broaden the project. Ultimately, a much more substantial nature development program was included. This process of boosting and enriching the project can only be explained by the positive flow between the involved actors and their shared aim of realizing a mutual attractive proposal.

Also citizen participation enriched the debate. Young farmers – who had to leave the area – were asked to formulate proposals which fit in the area vision. That led to proposals for a vineyard and the combination of a golf course with an extensive agricultural area.

Positive feedback

The joint planning approach and the enthusiasm to realize a proposal which would be attractive for all involved actors, generated a dynamic process within the project team in which they restlessly sought to improve the vision and to work it out in a concrete plan.

There were several important sources of positive feedback within the project. The first was the positive energy within the group of involved actors. Due to the highly constructive relations they developed, they were strongly committed to the project but also to an outcome which was valuable for all involved actors.

The second source of positive feedback came from the discussion about nature restoration along the Scheldt Estuary. Rijkswaterstaat was implementing a program of nature restoration projects and was looking for suitable locations. They joined the initial attempts of the municipality to redevelop the area of Perkpolder. Later on in the process, they saw extra opportunities for nature development which were valuable for the whole project, and they realized political support to include this extra surface nature in their organizational program objectives.

A European innovation program aimed at developing innovative forms of coastal defense – Com Coast – formed the third source of positive feedback in this governance process. The program offered subsidies for developing innovative dikes (which are not damaged by waves topping the dike). Rijkswaterstaat Zeeland was looking for opportunities to implement such a dike (to realize the program objectives of Com Coast) and saw in Perkpolder a brilliant opportunity. For Perkpolder this coupling meant extra financial means to realize the entire plan and a strong stimulus to search for innovative ways of dike-enforcement.

Another source of positive feedback came from the Zeeland region in which many actors were busy with realizing a coherent development program for the whole region. Perkpolder was often mentioned as a success and an example for the other projects within this program. The national exposure that resulted from being included in this program as a 'showcase' generated extra pressure on the project team to fulfil these high expectations.

At the same time, also the Perkpolder case had some difficulties in realizing support and legitimacy. A couple of members of the Sound Board Group withdrew. Citizens criticized the plan because of their dissatisfaction with the low amount of recreational houses. Finally, there were serious problems with realizing the necessary finances. Nonetheless, these setbacks did not slow down the project.

9.5 Case comparison

The above given analysis shows that ideas from complexity can help describing governance and adaptation processes. In the Mijdrecht case, path dependency, negative feedback and conservative self-organization apparently dominated the process and adaptation was not achieved, while in the Perkpolder case, change events, positive feedback and dissipative self-organization dominated. As a result – in the period we analysed this case – the process of adaptation was relatively easy. In Table 9.1 we summarize the differences between both cases with regard to the various 'complexity' concepts. In this section we explain the differences.

Table 9.1   Differences between both cases with regard to the various 'complexity' concepts

Groot Mijdrecht Noord		Perkpolder	
Path dependency	Negative initial perceptions with regard to the proposed change (distrust), legal obligations for change, prisoners dilemma between governmental agencies	*Change events*	Termination ferry service Nature development requirements for Scheldt estuary
Negative feedback	Periodical elections, existing procedures aimed at conserving current situation, bureaucratic cautiousness, delaying participation of citizens.	*Positive feedback*	Force of attraction of plan development. Coupling with nature restoration plan. Com Coast knowledge program.
Conservative self-organization	Vested interests, existing policy agendas, gap government – citizen	*Dissipative self-organization*	Joint search towards optimization in terms of quality, goal intertwinement and added value. Constructive PPS with enthusiastic actors. Citizen participation mostly constructive and enriching

What makes Perkpolder more prepared to adapt to climate change than the Mijdrecht area? Four factors seem to explain why the governance system of Perkpolder was able to internalize the climate ambitions. Firstly, the way in which the need for adaptation was framed into a governance problem was quite different it was perceived as an economic opportunity for many, rather than as an economic threat. Secondly, the assembly of agents in the governance network that wanted to address the problem was quite different, since it included an economic alliance. Thirdly the 'natural vitality' of these agents towards changing the situation was quite different, and finally the initial conditions for adaptation where more favorable in the Perkpolder case. We will elaborate on all four explanations.

In the Perkpolder case, the transition of land use could be implemented in only a few years, with nearly all actors gaining. For the losers (farmers who have to end their business) an acceptable alternative was given. In the Mijdrecht case, the conversion would require several decades to make it affordable, and there were real sources of uncertainty for individual land owners about whether this would turn out as the government promised (all main actors agreed on that). Thus, the controversial character of the problems differs highly. The controversial character of Mijdrecht affected the willingness of actors to let go existing procedures and positions, it made them cautious to participate in a dynamic and unpredictable process. In Perkpolder, the possible gains of the area development were a strong motivation to start an uncertain process and look for unthought-of chances.

In the Perkpolder case, the governance coalition was encompassing a larger proportion of parties that needed each other for success. Its composition was also much more diverse and thus more varied, which generated more opportunities for creative links and dissipative self-organization. The involvement of private actors and an ambitious Rijkswaterstaat made this trajectory both unpredictable and enriched it with ideas about commercial business cases that made the transition credible. In the Mijdrecht case, the farmers and land owners needed to be forced to cooperate, and they did not actually cooperate with the alliance of governments and participate in the search for win-win solutions. The agenda for the transition was relatively limited: it consisted only of a zero sum game between agriculture and water management. In short, the network in Mijdrecht was less complex relative to the complexity of the governance issue, compared to Perkpolder. Acceptable solutions therefore did not emerge; solutions received no positive feedback from actors representing the land users, who were politically influential. The different amount of dissipative self-organization in both cases seems to be related to the varied composition of the governance network.

The vitality of the network of Perkpolder can be seen as a third explanation for its ability to realize its success. This had to do with the individual and collective attitude of its participations. Within the case of Perkpolder, the participating actors were risk-accepting and their mutual relations were aimed at realizing mutual gains. The involvement of private actors with strong business ambitions and the Water Management Authority with clear project objectives with regard to nature development was very helpful in putting pressure on the whole process. In the Mijdrecht case, the driving force of change was limited to the axis Water Board and Province in which especially the Province was risk-aversive. Other actors, like municipalities (e.g. Amsterdam – potentially flooded) were less supportive to make the puzzle or to communicate about urgencies of adaptation. They did not themselves feel responsible for their 'backyard'. The cooperation between water board and province itself may have been a breakthrough in dissipative self-organization with a long-term motive. However, this was still insufficient to build an alliance strong enough to go forward with the conversion. The water board even wanted to take responsibility through their financial support for more than could reasonably be asked from them. For some reason, however, the public opinion could not be mobilized by these two actors in support of a land conversion that is evidently necessary in the long term for the sake of that same public. Responsible politicians did not make the binding decision to implement a land conversion. Process managers were hired to manage this cooperation and joint interaction with citizens, but were not successful in realizing the connection with the formal political bodies. The stabilizing forces within each of the participating actors were much stronger then the adaptive forces of their collaborative effort, which was exactly opposite to the Perkpolder case.

The initial conditions in both cases were different. The attitude of citizens with respect to governmental action in Perkpolder was positive. There was a certain desire for change, due to the lagging autonomous developments of this area. Autopoïetic self-organization, even though still attractive, was not perceived as realistic and sensible. In the Mijdrecht case, a long history of bad relations between citizens and governments existed. The inhabitants of Mijdrecht were mainly highly educated 'immigrants' from Amsterdam. They were active (and successful) in defending their own interests. In Perkpolder only a minority was immigrant and their activism against the proposals was distrusted by the traditional inhabitants. In Mijdrecht the start of the project was a rather controversial proposal to implement a spatial transition which harmed existing interests seriously, while in Perkpolder the starting point was an appealing vision on a vital, profitable and attractive future for a deteriorating area.

While in the Mijdrecht case the attractiveness of the transition was only visible for the Water Board and (to a lesser extent) the Province, the transition in Perkpolder was attractive for the majority of participants. The initial attitude of many actors in Mijdrecht was against change, while in Perkpolder almost all actors were pro change. This preoccupation was reinforced by the course of events in both cases. In Mijdrecht the various doubts about the feasibility of the project reinforced the strong negative feelings of inhabitants, while in the case of Perkpolder the belief in the potentials of the project was strengthened due to its many-sided and evolving character and the growing enthusiasm of the project team. Especially the way in which a project is initially framed is strongly path-dependent and difficult to change, both positively and negatively.

9.6 Discussion and conclusion

Gradually, the possible impacts of climate change become clearer. Adaptation of spatial development is therefore assumed to be needed (Van Buuren et al., 2009). From this point of view, experts have elaborated adaptive strategies that could be successful. In the literature on climate change, the focus for success is most of the time on the content of the technical measures that should be taken: new delta dikes, flood resisting flexible barriers, resilience strategies and new large fresh water facilities needed for longer periods of drought (De Bruin et al., 2009).

In this chapter, the focus however was on the difficult implementation trajectory these adaptation measures have to go through. We have argued that these measures will have to be digested by the existing governance systems. This governance system is not dedicated to one single value or interest and is not designed by one designer. It results from a long history of interactions and a variety of contributions. Such a governance system should be perceived as a living organism and not as an instrument that should be made suitable for climate adaptation.

There seems no choice but to develop a climate adaptation strategy that fits within the characteristics of existing governance systems, and that takes the drivers of that existing system into consideration. Relatively small interventions that are acceptable to the governance system, may function as levers smoothing the path for larger interventions. Looking for such levers, which may increase the likelihood of dissipative self-organization to emerge and multi-interest alliances to appear, is the learning process that those who seek climate adaptation should adopt to become effective. Examples of such learning processes are, for example, described by Nooteboom and Marks (2009).

Successfully managing transitions has less to do with a unilateral and internally consistent design of the climate adaptation planning scheme and a strong project organization to implement it straightforward, and much more with a fit between existing processes of self-organization and problem frames within actual governance systems. The two presented cases indicate the need to deal with governance systems as complex systems with self-organizing capacity on their own.

An important precondition for a successful adaptation strategy will be the openness and willingness of climate professionals to participate in a compounded governance process where several interests have to be satisfied. Autopoïetic behaviour focusing on vested interests and well-known ways of thinking and acting are the usual state of governance systems. Denying the power of these forces is an important explanation for failing adaptation strategies. The ability to adjust the scope of the planning project and to make use of opportunities for coupling climate issues to other spatial ambitions is crucial for the 'adaptive capacity' of a governance coalition. This capacity consists of its ability to make conscious use of feedback loops and change events.

The involved actor coalition in each case is unique and decisive for change. The willingness to change and the ability to connect the need for climate adaptation to other ambitions are important drivers for realizing a climate friendly governance system. The involved actor coalition has to possess a requisite variety to intertwine climate adaptation with the self-interest of the agents. Organizing a diversity of opportunities for creative combinations, package deals and innovation seems to become an attractive implementation strategy for climate adaptation (Van Buuren and Loorbach, 2009). Otherwise, resistance emerges and, as shown in our cases, may easily dash the adaptation strategy.

Successful adaptation strategies are based on the ability to recognize and utilize existing patterns of feedback. Enlarging the nature component in the Perkpolder case is at first sight a controversial and thus undesirable option, but later on it appeared to be an effective way of realizing more support, more quality and more funding. The same holds true for the creative ideas of other participants who joined the network, attracted by the enthusiasm of its current members.

The success of climate adaptation seems to depend – paradoxically – on the willingness to embrace the logic of the existing governance system, more than on attempts to reinvent governance in compliance with climate demands. The success depends on the compliance of climate strategies with existing strategies which are often as legitimate and as needed as climate adaptation. An adaptive planning process starts not longer with a well-defined problem definition, but is a joint search between mutual dependent agents towards a commonly defined vision on the future. The complexity of the environment in which such a planning process evolves can only be dealt with when the process itself is adaptive and resilient.

Transitions are thus not only the result of coevolving events and processes (see Van Buuren & Gerrits, 2009) but also the result of the self-organizing potential within governance coalitions. This observation is obviously against many attempts to rationalize, centralize and streamline planning processes by refining the management and organization of planning projects. However, it is crucial to develop more insight into the complexity of planning and the subsequent planning approaches we need to deal with this complexity.

Our cases are stylized narratives, and do not show the underlying battle between contrary forces of change and inertia; they only show the dominant, or prevailing force. However, there are two sides to everything, and conservative and dissipative forces are always simultaneously active. Our speculations above indicate that the success of adaptation policies is at a deeper level of analysis highly influenced by the social complexity of the adaptation challenge and the cultural dispositions in the governance networks toward cooperation and change. By itself this is no surprising conclusion, and it has been drawn before in governance sciences without using complexity theory (Koppenjan and Klijn, 2004; Schaap and Van Twist, 1997). However, where the governance approach still tries to structure and dispose complex social contexts and tries to reduce this complexity as much as possible, a complex systems perspective delivers us with a conceptual framework with which we are able to describe the erratic and unpredictable nature of governance processes. Furthermore, it enables us to formulate management prescriptions which fit into the complex character of governance and take their departure point in this complexity without trying to reduce it artificially.

References

Axelrod, R.M. and M.D. Cohen (1999) *Harnessing Complexity*, Free Press, New York.

Bruin, K. de, R.B. Dellink, A. Ruijs, L. Bolwidt, M.W. van Buuren, J. Graveland, R.S. de Groot, P.J. Kuikman, S. Reinhard, R.P. Roetter, V.C. Tassone, A. Verhagen and E.C. van Ierland (2009) 'Adapting to climate change in the Netherlands; an inventory of climate adaptation options and ranking of alternatives', *Climatic Change*, 95(1-2), pp. 23-45.

Boons, F.A.A., M.W. van Buuren and G.R. Teisman (2010) 'Governance of sustainability at Airports: Moving beyond the impasse between growth and noise', *Natural Resources Forum,* 34, pp. 303-313.

Buuren, M.W. van, P.P.J. Driessen, H.F.M.W. van Rijswick, P. Rietveld, W.G.M. Salet and G.R. Teisman (2012a) 'Towards adaptive spatial planning for climate change. Balancing between robustness and flexibility', *Journal of European Environmental & Planning Law,* 9 (forthcoming).

Buuren, M.W. van, F.A.A. Boons and G.R. Teisman (2012b) 'Collaborative problem solving in a complex governance system. Amsterdam Airport Schiphol and the challenge to break path-dependency', *Systems Research and Behavioral Science,* 29(1), pp. 116-130.

Buuren, M.W. van and L. Gerrits (2008) 'Decisions as Dynamic Equilibriums in Erratic Policy Processes', *Public Management Review,* 10(3), pp. 381-399.

Buuren, M.W. van and D. Loorbach (2009) 'Policy innovation in isolation? Conditions for policy renewal by transition arenas and pilot projects', *Public Management Review*, 11(3), pp. 375-392.

Chiva Gomez, R. (2003) 'The facilitating factors for organizational learning; bringing ideas from complex adaptive systems', *Knowledge and Process Management*, 10(2), pp. 99-114.

Cilliers, P. (1998) *Complexity and Postmodernism: Understanding Complex Systems*, Routledge, London.

Dooley, K.J. (1997) 'A complex adaptive systems model of organization change', *Nonlinear Dynamics, Psychology, and Life Sciences*, 1(1), pp. 69-97.

Duit, A. and V. Galaz (2008) 'Governance and complexity; emerging issues for governance theory', *Governance*, 21(3), pp. 311-335.

Eidelson, R.J. (1997) 'Complex adaptive systems in the behavioural and social sciences', *Review of General Psychology*, 1(1), pp. 42-71.

Folke, C., S. Carpenter, T. Elmqvist, L. Gunderson, C.S. Holling and B. Walker (2002) Resilience and sustainable development; building adaptive capacity in a world of transformation, Scientific background paper on resilience for the process of The World Summit on Sustainable Development on behalf of The Environmental Advisory Council to the Swedish Government, Stockholm.

Folke, C., T. Hahn, P. Olsson and J. Norberg (2005) 'Adaptive governance of social-ecological systems', *Annual Review or Environment and Resources*, 30, pp. 441-473.

Koppenjan, J.F.M. and E.H. Klijn (2004) *Managing Uncertainties in Networks; A Network Approach To Problem Solving And Decision Making*, Routledge, London.

Luhmann, N. (1995) *Social Systems*, Stanford University Press, Stanford (US).

Mathews, K.M., M.W. White and R.G. Long (1999) 'Why study the complexity sciences in the social sciences', *Human Relations*, 52(4), pp. 439-462.

McKelvey, B. (2008) 'Emergent strategy via complexity leadership; using complexity science and adaptive tension to build distributed intelligence', in M. Uhl-Bien and R. Marion (eds.) *Complexity Leadership*, IAP, Charlotte, PA, pp. 225-268.

Mielke, A. and T. Roubicek (2003) 'A rate-independent model for inelastic behaviour of shape-memory alloys', *Multiscale Modeling and Simulation*, 1(4), pp. 571-597.

Mickwitz, P., F. Aix, S. Beck, D. Carss, N. Ferrand, Ch. Görg, A. Jensen, P. Kivimaa, Ch. Kuhlicke, W. Kuindersma, M. Máñez, M. Melanen, S. Monni, A. B. Pedersen, H. Reinert and S. van Bommel (2009) *Climate Policy Integration, Coherence and Governance.* PEER Report No 2., Partnership for European Environmental Research, Helsinki.

Nooteboom, S. and Marks, P. (2009) 'Adaptive networks as 2nd order governance systems', *Systems Research and Behavioural Sciences*, pp 1092-7026.

Schaap, L. and Twist, M.J.W. van (1997) The dynamics of closedness in networks, in: Kickert, W.J.M., Klijn, E-H., Koppenjan, J.F.M. (eds.) *Managing Complex Networks: Strategies for the Public Sector*, Sage Publications, London.

Scharpf, F. (1997) *Games Real Actors Play: Actor-centered Institutionalism in Policy Research*, Westview Press, Boulder.

Second Delta Committee (2008) *Samen werken met water; een land dat leeft, bouwt aan zijn toekomst* [Jointly dealing with water; land that lives, builds on its future], Deltacommissie, The Hague.

Sherman, J. and R. Schultz (1998) *Open Boundaries; Creating Business Innovation Through Complexity*, Perseus Books, New York, London.

Stacey, R.D. (2003) *Strategic Management and Organisational Dynamics: The Challenge of Complexity*, Prentice Hall, Harlow.

Uhl Bien, M., R. Marion and B. McKelvey (2007) 'Complexity leadership theory; shifting knowledge from the industrial to the knowledge era', *The Leadership Quarterly*, 18(4), pp. 298-318.

Website Groot Mijdrecht Noord, http://www.grootmijdrechtnoord.nl, [accessed 02/06/2009].

Chapter 10
Beyond Blueprints?
Complexity Theory as a Prospective
Influence for Metropolitan Governance

Cathy Wilkinson[1]

What do you do as a strategic spatial urban planner working in a large metropolis when you are instructed NOT to prepare a metropolitan strategy? This directive was issued in 1998 by the late Dr John Paterson, then Secretary of the Victorian Department of Infrastructure (Australia), to the planning, policy and research units of the Department. One anecdote was of a research officer sent from the Secretary's office before getting past the title slide of their powerpoint presentation because the word 'metropolitan strategy' slipped from their tongue. Dr Paterson had made his point. A metropolitan strategy was *not* to be prepared. But what to do?

10.1 Introduction

What to do? How to act? These questions encapsulate arguably one of the distinguishing features of spatial planning and governance research and practice – the focus on doing, on action. The acknowledgement that non-linear dynamics drive structural change in complex systems (Suteanu, 2005: p. 115) challenges many assumptions that have historically framed spatial planning and governance efforts. But what does it mean to plan under conditions of non-linearity, of complexity? What can one do? How can one act? This chapter will explore what happened in one city – Melbourne, Australia – over the course of several years as public servants grappled with this dilemma.

As cities continue to expand with respect to their physical area (Angel et al., 2005), population (UN, 2008), ecological footprint (Rees, 2007) and impact on ecosystem services (MA, 2005) the potential importance of spatial planning and governance only increases. The recent revival in strategic spatial planning (Salet and Faludi, 2000) is no surprise. What is more surprising is how little attention has been given to exploring forms of spatial planning and governance that respond to the city as a complex adaptive system or as a complex human system (Portugali, 2010; Wagenaar, 2010).

---

1   Cathy Wilkinson is from the Stockholm Resilience Centre, Stockholm University.

This chapter offers a unique frame on complexity and planning as it is not limited to applying a complexity theory lens in retrospect but rather reflects on a case study where the relevance of complexity theory for planning was prospectively explored in practice over several years. It provides insight into how deliberate exploration of a complexity theory framework by planning practitioners influenced the metropolitan spatial planning process in Melbourne. Using qualitative research, it asks what were the enabling conditions and how can complexity theory usefully inform metropolitan governance. Triangulation has been used to verify findings drawing on qualitative interviews, documentary and historical analysis. As a key practitioner involved throughout, my reflections on the case study period have been drawn on as one source using auto-ethnographic methods (after Ellis, 2003).

The chapter first introduces complexity theory and outlines its relevance for spatial planning and governance. In the next section a chronological history of events is provided in some detail based on the three key phases of Victorian State Government's metropolitan planning efforts for Melbourne between 1998-2005. The case study is then analysed to identify what conditions enabled exploration of a complexity theory perspective. Key insights from the Melbourne case study are then drawn out and three ways in which complexity theory usefully informs spatial planning and governance are discussed including: providing new language and metaphors for the dynamics of change in complex systems; providing new tools and methods; and challenging modes of governance based on assumptions of predictability and controllability. Finally some brief concluding remarks are made.

Before embarking on the substance of this chapter, there is one remaining clarification to make. It is critical to note that the exploration of the relevance of complexity theory for metropolitan planning was an ongoing disjointed and informal experiment. Complexity theory was by no means the dominant framing for Melbourne's metropolitan planning but one of many influences. The fear in recounting this story it that it will appear more coherent and dominant than history's reality. It should not be read as such.

10.2 Complexity theory and its relevance for spatial planning and governance

Complexity theory is concerned with complex adaptive systems governed by non-linear causality that have 'the ability to adapt and co-evolve as they organize through time' (Urry, 2005: p. 3). Westley et al. (2006) in *Getting to Maybe* provide useful analogies for different types of systems likening a simple system to baking a cake, a complicated system to sending a rocket ship to the moon and a complex adaptive system to raising a child. Put simply, the growth and development of a city is more akin to a baby, exhibiting significant unpredictability within generally known (albeit very broad) patterns of overall development. Imagine a parent raising a child as though it was a linear system entirely subject to known specifications. That is essentially the dominant way in which the city has been approached throughout history by public policy makers seeking to 'defeat disorder' (Gleeson, 2008: p. 2658) through 'orderly and proper planning' – as a linear system that is knowable, controllable and manageable. Planners are not alone. Indeed the ontological and epistemological bases of the modernist scientific endeavour could be read as assumptions of linearity within complex systems and the capacity to measure, reproduce and predict change (Suteanu, 2005). By contrast, complexity theory challenges reductionism, teaches us that effects can have an 'irreducible tangle of causes', and is founded on the basis that the whole is always greater than the sum of the parts (Coveney and Highfield, 1995).

Complexity theory emerged as scientists across a range of disciplines recognised that detailed research on isolated parts of complex systems could reveal only limited information about the behaviour of the system as a whole. Attention to complex systems as holistic entities, influencing and being influenced by the surrounding environment, meant that meta-level patterns of change could be observed. Significantly, it was recognised that these overarching patterns were emergent, based on localised rather than globally optimal decisions by agents. In this way complexity theory challenges both the source and characteristics of order in complex systems traditionally associated with linear, incremental progression governed by globally optimised decision making. Complexity theory instead argues that adaptive strategies not dependent on rational choice or full information hold sway. The consequences of this emergence or 'self-organisation' denies prediction as in complex adaptive systems 'small inputs can lead to dramatically large consequences, and very slight differences in initial conditions produce very different outcomes' (Lewin, 1993). Observation of phase transitions where a system exponentially evolves from one state to another is a case in point – such as the sudden evolution of the Anasazi culture from a simple foraging band structure to something more complex in AD 300 (Lewin, 1993).

From an examination of this literature there are three ways in which complexity theory can usefully inform spatial planning and governance emerge – by providing new language and metaphors for the dynamics of change in complex systems; by providing new tools for analysis of complex systems; and by offering new modes of governance. Each of these will be briefly expanded on now.

10.3 Language and metaphors

The first way complexity theory informs spatial planning and governance is to provide the language and metaphors necessary to conceptualise cities as complex adaptive non-linear systems. Michael Waldrop's popular science book, *Complexity: the science at the edge of order and chaos* book was a significant influence for planning practitioners involved in the Melbourne case study. What Waldrop (1992) does so well is to demonstrate the potential relevance of the key metaphors, language and emerging scientific findings of complexity theory to a wide range of complex systems, including cities. Waldrop shows how complexity theory demands fundamentally different types of questions about systems and their evolution over time. Many scholars have since articulated these same themes. For Capra (2005: p. 36) the most important contribution of complexity theory is the provision of 'appropriate language for dealing with nonlinear systems' which in turn has provided clues to what questions we should be asking about nonlinear systems. Thrift (1999) is interested in how the powerful metaphors associated with complexity theory – 'the obligatory fractals of the Mandelbrot set, the spirals in the Beloussov-Zhabotisky reaction, the life cycle of the cellular slime mould' (1999: p. 37) – have made a decisive claim that challenges the existing dominant scientific paradigm of linearity, have travelled across disciplines and from academia to popular consumption, and have become a 'means to identify and reserve a place within convention where a scientifically detailed explanation could be developed.'

10.4 Methods and tools

The second way complexity theory informs spatial planning and governance is through insight into the particular behaviour of complex adaptive systems – particularly the nature of structural urban change and its drivers. Batty (1998: p. 1943) explains that

> for hundreds of years urban researchers have sought to explain the origins of urban growth and decline but it is increasing clear that urban theory has stalled around its central quest to explain and model the genesis of locational change. It is easy enough to describe such change, to explain in hindsight why certain locations grow and other decline, but it has been well nigh impossible to develop convincing theories which enable us to make informed predictions.

Complexity theory, through its associated methodologies including cellular automata modelling, use of genetic algorithms, computer simulation and network analysis offers urban researchers new tools for examining the nature of structural change in cities. A growing number of urban scholars have advanced this field for over a decade now and each of the key complexity theories has now been applied to urban systems. Urban research has now generated dissipative cities, synergetic cities, fractal cities, agent based cities, cellular automata cities, sandpile cities and network cities (Portugali, 2010).

The most basic finding from this body of work is the confirmation that cities exhibit patterns of behaviour associated with complex adaptive systems. Indeed, as Portugali (2008: p. 257) points out, urban systems are in fact dual self-organising systems where the parts (or agents) themselves are also complex adaptive systems with 'cognitive capabilities such as learning, thinking, decision-making and the like'. The process of applying the tools and methodologies of complexity theories to urban systems has made substantial contributions to our understanding of the limitations in our existing predictive models, even if the aspration to generate something of a complete model has proved elusive (Allen, 1997). Accordingly, urban based modelling using the tools and methods of complexity theory has generated key insights into the characteristics of structural change in complex urban systems.

10.5 Governance

The third way complexity theory informs spatial planning and governance is by challenging modes of governance based on the modernist assumptions of predictability and controllability such as 'command and control', 'predict and plan' or comprehensive rational approaches. Governing complex adaptive systems requires awareness of and attention to 'non-linear dynamics, threshold effects and limited predictability' (Duit and Galez, 2008: p. 329). This means that the outcome of policy interventions cannot be known in advance as policy effects are themselves emergent properties (Wagenaar, 2007: p. 41). This of course begs the question of what, if any, capacity is there then to steer outcomes in complex adaptive systems like cities?

Axelrod and Cohen (1999) suggest a framework for harnessing complexity in complex adaptive systems where,

> Agents, of a variety of types, use their strategies, in patterned interaction, with each other and with artefacts. Performance measures on the resulting events drive the selection of agents and/or strategies through processes of error-prone copying and recombination, thus changing the frequencies of the types within the system. (Axelrod and Cohen, 1999: p. 154)

Agents here are 'collections of properties, capabilities, identities, and action preferences that interact with other agents (Axelrod and Cohen, 1999: p. 153)' (Wagenaar, 2007: p. 41). A strategy is 'the way an agent responds to its surroundings and pursues its goals' (Axelrod and Cohen, 1999: p. 4). They identify three broad categories of action that can 'harness' or take advantage of complexity – *variation* in the diversity of types (agents or strategies) within a system, *interaction* between types across a system, and *selection* processes that lead to an increase or decrease of particular types (Axelrod and Cohen, 1999: p. 153). Recent success stories of urban governance where participatory democracy (Wagenaar, 2007) or collaborative planning processes (Innes and Boohcr, 2003) have been pursued can be understood using this framework.

Wagenaar (2007) draws significantly on Axelrod and Cohen (1999) when he uses complexity theory as the analytical frame to examine urban governance through a case study of citizen participation in disadvantaged neighbourhoods in the Netherlands. He shows that 'participatory democratic arrangements are superior to representative arrangements in dealing with system complexity'

(Wagenaar, 2007: p. 41) because they allow greater variation in and interaction across distanced administrators and elected officials on the one hand and local citizens equipped with practical, narrative knowledge on the other. He argues, 'increased interaction among a larger number of actors increases variety within a system. Increased variety in turn increases the number of potential solutions to whatever problem the system faces' (Wagenaar, 2007: p. 42).

Innes and Booher (2003) in their case study of water management in California show that the collaborative planning process (CALFED) was a way to 'establish new networks among the players in the system and increase the distribution of knowledge amongst these players' (2003: p. 36). By bringing together a diversity of stakeholders and allowing independence of these stakeholders, conditions for the collective creation of an adaptive learning system are enabled (2003: p. 40). Similar to Wagenaar (2007), this generated 'genuine innovations – not just creative ideas, but ideas that get turned into new practices and institutions' (2003: p. 49).

In both these cases it was possible to bring together stakeholders with a direct interest in the focal problem. But what does complexity theory imply for metropolitan scale planning. Informed by complexity theory, Innes and Booher (1999) make suggestions for how metropolitan development performance can be improved through 'development and use of indicators and performance measures in new ways, the use of collaborative consensus building among stakeholders who best understand the different aspects of the metropolitan system, and, finally, the creation of new forms of leadership'. They emphasise the need to focus on system performance (recalling Senge's first discipline) and collective adaptive learning[2].

The examples above discuss this importance for matters of process. The same principles can also be extended to the physical structure of the city. Allen (1997: p. 252) argues that generally '"small and diverse" will allow for adaptation and change better than the "large and monumental"'. He draws out the lesson that 'plans which encourage variety and diversity in the inhabitants of a region, in their activities, their means of transportation and in the landscape, tend to lead to creative and adaptive systems capable of generating their own development and in responding to the challenges of the economic, natural and social environment'. Accordingly, 'policies should reflect this uncertainty and always allow diversity and redundancy in the system to allow for future adaptations to the emerging reality. Maintaining diverse knowledge, multiple technologies and making plans which are seemingly sub-optimal in a strict economic sense are therefore part of the message that comes out of this work.' (Allen, 1997: p. 258)

Adaptive capacity is central to the governance of complex adaptive systems. Duit and Galaz (2008: p. 319) argue that 'the adaptive capacity of a governance system can be understood as a function of the trade-off between exploration and exploitation' and that only governance types with 'high capacities for exploration *and* exploitation … can be expected to perform well regardless of the certainty and

---

2   The importance of learning has long been recognised by planning scholars (see for example Michael 1976, Friedmann and Abonyi 1976, Friedmann 1987).

rate of change' (2008: p. 329) in complex adaptive systems. Of course this requires overcoming a well-established and persistent governance dilemma. Drawing on March (1991), Duit and Galaz explain,

> ...organizations face a fundamental tension between exploration "captured by terms such as search, variation, risk taking, experimentation, play, flexibility, discovery, innovation" and exploitation, that is "refinement, choice, production, efficiency, selection, implementation, execution." The tension arises from the fact that "adaptive systems that engage in exploration to the exclusion of exploitation are likely to find that they suffer the costs of exploration without gaining many of its benefits," and "conversely, systems that engage in exploitation to the exclusion of exploration are likely to find themselves trapped in suboptimal stable equilibria" (March 1991, 71; cf. March and Olsen 2006, 12f).

In Axelrod and Cohen's terms variety is lost and premature convergence occurs when 'exploitation quickly swamps exploration' (1999: p. 43). Conversely, without exploitation there is no opportunity for learning.

The implications of complexity theory for governance fundamentally challenges the modernist project, the legacy of which pervades so many aspects of planning practice. Clearly complexity theory raises deep challenges for metropolitan governance. How metropolitan planners engaged these challenges in the Melbourne case study will now be presented.

10.6 The Melbourne case study – a chronology of events

The practice of metropolitan planning in Melbourne has a long tradition starting with the 1929 plan for development prepared by the Metropolitan Town Planning Commission. This case study follows metropolitan planning processes in Melbourne between 1998-2005. Events during this period are presented in three phases. Most space is devoted to the first phase where exploration of the relevance of complexity theory for metropolitan planning was explicitly pursued within the Department. Key events in the following two phases are included in order to examine the subsequent impact. Of particular interest across all three phases are events that inform how the exploration of complexity theory informed metropolitan planning practice either by providing new language and metaphors for the dynamics of change in complex systems, new tools for analysis of complex systems or by offering new modes of governance. It is to these themes that this chapters returns in the 'Insights' section that follows.

Phase 1 – Exploring a complexity approach to planning

The late Dr John Paterson was the Secretary of the Victorian Department of Infrastructure between 1996-1999. Paterson had particularly strong views about the role of planners and planning per se in the evolving metropolis. Dr Paterson contributed a practice review article for Urban Policy and Research journal for a series debating the role of metropolitan strategies titled, 'Choice and Necessity in Metropolitan Planning' (Paterson, 2000). He argued that disease control drove the design or redesign of cities around the separation of water supplies from sewerage and drainage systems, in turn making 'city formation subject to the rigours of utility economics and civil engineering'; the possibility of commuter suburbs was made possible by the railways; low density suburbanisation between rail corridors was catalysed by the private motor car; and the large scale segregation of land uses was pursued by the bourgeoisie in order to 'keep their streets and neighbourhoods nice and to protect their property values' (Paterson, 2000: p. 378-9). Each of these developments had profound implications for urban development yet 'no-one planned any of these things and, indeed, no-one who mattered even anticipated them.' (Paterson 2000: p. 379). Paterson's view (2000: p. 380) was that,

> Measures which might help to alleviate the direct effects of major new forces and ameliorate their unwanted side-effects are just conceivably within the anticipatory reach of the planning and development related professions.

To this end, he identified three roles for metropolitan planning – regional income growth (through provision of world class infrastructure and flexible regulation), central supervision of local planning (to resolve regional issues), and the reading and anticipation of megatrends (2000: p. 385). On the last of these, he was scathing about the depth of knowledge of the drivers of urban change and condemned academia in particular in this respect. Without this, the chances of any planning efforts being effective were minimal.

Despite some stakeholder and political pressure to embark on a metropolitan strategy development process to replace the existing widely criticised metropolitan plan – *Living Suburbs* – he persistently resisted. Instead in the second half of 1998 Paterson initiated a 'metropolitan analysis' project with the deliberately broad purpose of improving the Department's understanding of the drivers of urban change. Further he actively supported and encouraged the type of work then being produced by the Research Unit (see for example *From Doughnut City to Café Society* which examined the underlying drivers of change for emerging urban revitalisataion of the inner city) (DOI, 1998; Reynolds and Porter, 1998).

I started work as a planner in the Policy Unit of the Department of Infrastructure (DOI) in Melbourne, Australia in early 1998. I had also been lent a few years prior Michael Waldrop's book *Complexity: The Science at the Edge of Order and Chaos* and was subsequently in the middle of a Masters of Environmental Science thesis exploring the relevance of complexity theory to metropolitan planning. Not long after started at the Department I introduced a colleague from the Research Unit to Waldrop's book and we began an informal discussion group that met weekly to discuss the possible implications of complexity theory for metropolitan planning. For both of us, complexity theory fundamentally critiqued many of the assumptions on which some of the current policy and research work was based, including the capacity to predict structural change in complex adaptive systems. By way of example, the Research Unit produced population projections for Victoria which the Policy Unit used as a basis for working with local government to plan where housing was needed to accommodate future populations. We wondered whether complexity theory had the potential to overcome potentially self-fulfilling prophesies created by a 'predict and plan' approach.

At a whole of Departmental seminar in the second half of 1998, Paterson spoke of his desire for the Metropolitan Analysis Project 'to investigate the variables that influence urban processes' and used the analogy of recent scientific research that analysed the patterns and behaviours of clouds and discovered a handful of emergent properties. It was at that point that I shared my interest and limited but growing knowledge of complexity theory as applied to urban systems with the Secretary and alerted him to the informal exploration that had already started within a small group of people from the Policy and Research Units. This immediately led to the establishment of a more formalised project (or 'Skunkworks' as it became known) tasked with exploring the potential of complexity theory to assist our understanding of the drivers of urban change. Initially involvement was based on interest and availability from Departmental officers primarily within the policy, research and modelling units.

A clear priority for the Secretary was to develop an agent based model. The Secretary considered that the 'analytical tools being used to understand urban processes (had) changed very little since the 1970s' (Paterson, 2000: p. 383) and wanted to develop best practice urban modelling capability based on methodologies emerging from the complexity sciences. Whilst he recognised that Government Department's weren't the 'ideal setting for original research, particularly towards the pure end of the spectrum' (Paterson, 2000: p. 384), that is what he initiated in order to address the gap he felt the academy had neglected.

The Secretary seconded on a full time basis a mathematics professor from an Australian University who had expertise in game theory and a computer programmer from DoI's IT section to start on the model. Visits from leading complexity academics from Charles Sturt University, Australia and the University of Cranfield, United Kingdom and dialogue with Australia's national science research institute (CSIRO) were initiated. A reading group was started with the purpose of discussing and developing a shared understanding of fundamental complexity concepts and their application to urban systems before commencing development of a model. Even at an early stage however, it was clear that two groups had emerged, the modellers and the more social scientist oriented research and policy officers. Put another way, those that 'got' advanced mathematics and those that didn't. There was one intermediatary who offered mathematics 'lessons' to help the non-mathematicians keep up with the modellers, recognising that unless people with a theoretical and practical understanding of urban processes were able to contribute, the assumptions used in the new model would be problematic and learning opportunities lost. In any case, the reading group got through only

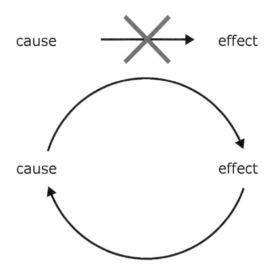

Figure 10.1   Breakthrough communicative tool used to represent non-linear dynamics of change in urban systems.

four readings before the modellers stopped attending. This fragmentation ignored the visiting University of Cranfield professor's view that it was the process of collectively re-thinking through the assumptions behind a model that was more important than any actualised model.

The lack of any formal structure for the project enhanced the divide between the modellers and the social scientists. By this stage, the purpose of the 'skunkworks' project, under the direction of the Secretary was to 'build an agent based model of Melbourne's urban system'. Generally, those with modelling skills had time formally built into their work programs to spend on the project and those without modelling skills had to find time on top of their existing work programs. At the beginning of August 1999, the Secretary decided he wanted to be able to demonstrate a working agent based model at the then Minister's August Statement. A core team was pulled full time onto making this happen. It was recognised that this model was inherently limited but it was seen as a start that could be improved over time. A simple 'sugarscape' simulation using an agent based model was prepared for this purpose.

One of the strongest barriers to approaching the city as a complex adaptive system experienced during this phase was the deep seated (and often unconscious) attachment to preconceptions of linear causality. It is not that the Departmental officers didn't recognise that the drivers of urban change are complex. Rather, it was as though cumulative decades of education and practice pre-determined the reduction and compartmentalisation of urban processes in order to be able to 'make sense' of something, even though the knowledge generated using these methods had so many limitations as to render it meaningless at worst, self-fulfilling at best – the use of demographic projections as a policy tool being a case in point. The first breakthrough in this respect came in the form of a simple diagram that reframed cause and effect relationships as non-linear (see Figure 10.1 below). This diagram became symbolic of the new approach to the background research for the Metropolitan Strategy and ended up in a presentation of preliminary findings to the Secretary. It was used by the Manager of the Research Unit to explain that the key drivers of urban change are complex and continuing emerging from the result of many local level interactions. Therefore a major task is to put together a picture or story of change at any one point in time. In many respects this diagram became a communicative tool symbolising a resistance against over-simplification of complex problems.

Phase 2 – Preparing a new metropolitan strategy

The new labour government for the State of Victoria was somewhat unexpectedly elected at the end of 1999 following nearly 10 years in opposition. The Labour Party's policy platform included the commitment to prepare a new metropolitan strategy. Three years later this would be released as *Melbourne 2030*. But in 1999, at the end of the market-orientated 1990s during which strategic planning capacity became victim to a decade long reaction against the perceived market limitations of comprehensive spatial planning, and following the Metropolitan Analysis projects under Patterson and the explicit resistance to preparing a metropolitan strategy, this was a significant change of direction. In early 2000, Professor Lyndsay Neilson was appointed as the new Departmental Secretary and work began on the metropolitan strategy. At this point the 'skunkworks' project came to an end. However it had several tangible influences on *Melbourne 2030*, most obviously the attention given to 'adaptability' in the development of the strategy.

'Adaptability' was included in *Melbourne 2030* as one of the seven guiding principles alongside six other more traditional principles including: sustainability, innovation, inclusiveness, equity, leadership and partnership. The strategy states,

> Adaptability: People can and must take into account past trends and indications of future directions. The Government is determined to plan for change and to be adaptable when faced with the unexpected. (DOI, 2002: p. 29)

The importance of designing in adaptability to change within the urban system became increasingly important over the course of the development of *Melbourne 2030*. There were several events in particular that challenged the assumed security of essential services that brought to the fore the need for a city capable of adapting to changes including: extreme and persistent hot weather during the summer of 1999/2000 that exposed the fragility of Victoria's electricity supply; continuation of drought over much of south eastern Australia resulting in dam levels continuing to decrease and serious water supply issues needing to be addressed; and the emerging climate change threat questioning the State's continued access to cheap sources of energy (coal) and degree of economic dependency on primary production and the manufacturing industry. Each of these events brought into question the adaptive capacity of Melbourne's urban structure, form and function. Post-war Melbourne, which makes up a clear majority of the geographic footprint of the city, is predominantly low density and car dependent. A more adaptable urban structure in these locations was resolved as one with a greater diversity of densities, a denser network of activity centres and much better network of public transport connections beyond the inner suburbs and across town between the radial rail network.[3]

Significant attention was also given to the meta-conditions needed for sustained implementation of the strategy over time. Widespread public ownership of the strategy and a diverse range of implementation mechanisms were two such conditions. Some of the efforts to generate broad ownership are described here,

> In formulating *Melbourne 2030*, it was acknowledged that implementation of such a complex development plan would involve many players within and beyond the state government, its institutions and agencies, and many activities beyond the state's formal planning system of legislation and regulation. This is why the state government put *Melbourne 2030* through extensive consultation within and beyond government and then made sure its approval was undertaken by the whole government. *Melbourne 2030* has been adopted by Cabinet as government policy, binding on all state government ministers, departments and agencies that have responsibility to pursue its policies. This has been done deliberately to instil a strong awareness that any such plan or strategy has significance within the overarching frameworks of governance for the city, irrespective of the means by which it is implemented. (Niven and Wilkinson, 2005: p. 216)

The Secretary, Lyndsay Neilson, had a long standing interest in the good governance of cities and advocated the need for a diverse range of implementation mechanisms including policy, legislation/regulation, fiscal, financial, institutional, asset management, knowledge management and advocacy (Neilson, 2002, Niven and Wilkinson, 2005: p. 217). There was a general awareness that change in cities is constant and the ability to harness the diversity of forces needed to shift urban systems towards more sustainable ends is not something that can be controlled. Implementation approaches must be diverse and go beyond traditional statutory planning with its zoning controls. One way to enable this is to enrol several of the implementation mechanisms listed above. So for example, *Melbourne 2030* includes a wide range of implementation mechanisms for Direction 2 (Better management of metropolitan growth) including policy statements, legislative change (Urban Growth Boundary legislation), institutional changes

---

3   Note this was also the preferred urban structure based on the other six principles and following extensive public consultation.

(establishment of Growth Areas Authority), financial support (public transport improvements), knowledge management (Urban Development Program) and advocacy (*Melbourne 2030* Implementation award). Furthermore *Melbourne 2030* recognises that implementation needs to be reviewed regularly and built in a regular 5 year review (the first of which has now been completed). Indeed instead of being relegated to the final paragraphs of the strategy, 'Better planning decisions, careful management' is included as the final Direction.

Phase 3 – Responding to unintended consequences post-release

Melbourne 2030 was released in October 2002 by the Premier of the State of Victoria at the Melbourne Museum. The launch was highly successful with almost unanimous support for the strategy from a broad range of stakeholders including peak bodies, academics and the media. *Melbourne 2030* was released as a final policy document and comment was invited on the five year implementation program that included the 226 initiatives in the strategy itself and the accompanying draft sectoral implementation plans (eg. housing, activity centres, green wedges, urban growth boundary, transport). Following a public submission phase the implementation program was finalised. Implementation was coordinated by the Strategy Development Division within the Department of Sustainability and Environment (DSE) but responsibility for the 226 initiatives was spread across the whole of government (albeit the majority remained the direct responsibility of DSE). An annual report monitoring progress of the 226 initiatives that were part of the implementation program was provided to Government.

For nearly twelve months following release of *Melbourne 2030* a significant amount of time and effort was spent giving presentations on the strategy and discussing implementation implications with a wide range of interest groups. In parallel, the work of commencing implementation began in earnest. *Melbourne 2030* contained an extensive implementation program. The officers of the Strategy Development Division were quite reasonably under increasing pressure to demonstrate progress on the 226 initiatives and accompanying implementation plans. This required a 'heads down doing' focus. As a result the capacity for ongoing strategising diminished, leaving less strategic capacity to deal with unintended consequences or continue engaging with stakeholders at a whole of strategy level.

A subsequent (re)clarification of the Strategy Development Division's implementation priorities in early 2005 and the identification of a handful of leverage points was invaluable to prioritising the work of the Division and shifting the gaze up. 'Alignment of infrastructure investment' with the priorities of *Melbourne 2030* was identified as one of three leveragable strategies. This subsequently led to successful efforts to change the criteria used by the Department of Treasury and Finance to assess consistency of proposed Departmental capital projects with Government policy. This initiative had not been identified in *Melbourne 2030* but was obviously, with hindsight, essential to successful implementation.

Finally, one subtle but important challenge to the complexity theory influenced thinking behind *Melbourne 2030* that emerged post-release was the use of the term 'blueprint' as the most common descriptor of the strategy by the media. Throughout the strategy development and particularly during the final drafting of *Melbourne 2030* the core project team worked to consistently resist conceptualisation and description of the metropolitan strategy as a 'blueprint', in the document itself and in the associated press releases. The certainty implied by this descriptor was appealing yet misrepresented entirely the intent and reality of a strategy's capacity to influence urban processes. With one exception this descriptor was avoided in text based documents. However, in the TV, radio and print media in particular, *Melbourne 2030* became the most commonly described as *Melbourne's* 'blueprint'.

The next section will reflect on some of the enabling conditions that made this unique exploration of a prospective complexity approach to metropolitan planning and governance possible. It uses complexity theory retrospectively as a frame of analysis.

10.7 Enabling conditions

Dr Paterson's interest and capacity as Secretary to direct priorities and resources was the key catalyst that facilitated conditions for the exploration of the relevance of complexity theory for metropolitan planning and governance. He publicly questioned the robustness of the scientific knowledge base on which metropolitan planning decisions were made, in particular the predictive capacity of the Department's land-use transport model and the degree to which 'planners' could influence the urban system. Accordingly he shifted the focus of the Department's work to improving understanding of the drivers of urban change and exploring development of an agent-based model of urban processes. Paterson sought a potentially radically different way of doing metropolitan planning. He resisted pressure to channel the 'drivers of change' project towards a metropolitan strategy per se and instead emphasised the need to improve and share knowledge of the drivers of structural urban change as a basis for more informed strategic interventions. In this respect he challenged interested public servants to grapple with the implications of acknowledging the city as a complex adaptive system where structural change is the result of emergent non-linear processes. Furthermore he did this at a time when the urban complexity research agenda was only just beginning to emerge.

Dr Paterson's initiative to encourage such a long exploration space in the public service was rare due to the vulnerabilities of uncertain returns, long lead times and detachment from action and decision arenas that exploration requires (March, 1991: p. 73). In some respects this can be interpreted as a deliberate strategy to avoid premature convergence (re-vergence) on a traditional comprehensive style plan. Variability is needed for a complex adaptive system to evolve and premature convergence occurs when needed variety is lost too quickly (Axelrod and Cohen,

1999: p. 44). By explicitly rejecting/delaying preparation of a metropolitan strategy Paterson actively created an 'exploratory' phase that lasted around a year. His hope was that this exploration space would be the catalyst for both an improved understanding of the drivers of urban change and development of a new agent-based model that would ultimately be able to replace the Department's existing land use-transport model.

Whilst this exploration space was a critical enabling condition, it was not sufficient as for an adaptive system to successfully adapt there needs to be a fruitful combination of both exploration and exploitation (Axelrod and Cohen, 1999). The trade-off between exploration and exploitation in organisations is well established (March, 1991) as is the difficulty of achieving an appropriate balance between the two in the governance of complex adaptive systems (Duit and Galez, 2008).

One of the actions Axelrod and Cohen (1999: p. 156) suggest to harness complexity is to 'link processes that generate extreme variation to processes that select with few mistakes in the attribution of credit'. This link was virtually absent during the first phase of Melbourne's metropolitan planning. The outputs generated in the exploration space Paterson had enabled were insufficiently connected via a 'hierachy of control' to the testbed of everyday metropolitan planning practice. It is only when bottom up organisation is channelled via a hierarchy of control that evolution thrives – information must flow in both directions (Waldrop, 1992: p. 292, cited in Wagenaar, 2007: p. 44). Paterson delayed action in terms of deliberate development of a complexity informed urban governance approach in recognition that the Department's existing basis for such an approach was ill-founded on narrow linear assumptions. As a result, the opportunity to translate into practice aspects of a new complexity based approach to metropolitan planning and test its validity and implications was lost.

The extended exploration phase did however enable the development of a new understanding of the drivers of urban change as non-linear amongst a small group of Departmental officers. To a small degree this created a 'network of reciprocal interaction' (Axelrod and Cohen, 1999: p. 156). The translation of knowledge from the first phase into the second phase was possible because many of these officers became members of the core project team. And thus, inadvertently, a small group of Departmental officers came forward into this phase of metropolitan planning replete with different questions about the city informed by complexity thinking, different communicative artefacts regarding the nature of structural change, a critical mass of peer support and a new Secretary keen to get on with a metropolitan strategy.

One of the most distinctive meta-characteristics of the second phase of metropolitan planning in Melbourne was the shift away from *exploration* of new approaches to understanding processes of urban change to *exploitation* in the form of production of a widely familiar artefact of urban planning and governance - a comprehensive spatial plan. This became the test-bed for the project team to experiment with an applied complexity approach to urban governance. It was in many ways an incomplete and unsophisticated experimentation but one that made some progress (primarily with respect to the introduction and use of the concept of 'adaptability'). The bureaucratic, consultative and political processes through which the draft metropolitan strategy were tested provided a link of sorts between 'processes that generate extreme variation (with) processes that select with few mistakes in the attribution of credit' (Axelrod and Cohen, 1999: p. 156). In this way, the familiar artefact of a metropolitan strategy evolved towards a more complexity informed approach, most notably through the inclusion of 'adaptability' as a principle.

10.8 Reflections on three ways complexity theory can inform metropolitan planning

The focus of this section is on what the Melbourne case study reveals about the three ways in which complexity theory can potentially inform metropolitan planning – by providing new language and metaphors for the dynamics of change in complex systems; by providing new tools and methods for complex systems; and by challenging established modes of governance based on assumptions of predictability and controllability.

Language and metaphors

The literature argues that complexity theory is significant as it provides 'appropriate language for dealing with nonlinear systems' (Capra, 2005: p. 36) and its associated metaphors have 'travelled across disciplines and from academia to popular consumption' (Thrift, 1999: p. 37). In the case study we see complexity theory serving this function.

Popular science texts, in particular Waldrop (1999), provided an accessible entry point for the Secretary, research officers, policy officers and modellers alike to contemplate the implications of complexity theory for urban systems. It was the mention of the emergent properties of clouds by Dr Paterson in a Department seminar that was the catalyst for the informal group of junior public servants to make contact, which in turn quickly led to the formalisation of the 'skunkworks' project. Without a recognisable language and metaphors these pivotal early connections may never have been made.

Complexity theory provided a useful starting point for public servants to challenge key assumptions such as predictability and controllability. Both the junior public servants grappling with the prediction paradox inherent in generating demographic projections to inform housing policy and Dr Paterson with his scathing critique of existing land use-transport models and understanding of the fundamental drivers of urban change, saw much potential in complexity theory.

However, whilst the language and metaphors of complexity theory provided an entry point, this case study shows that working through in detail the implications of complexity theory for metropolitan planning research, policy and practice was time consuming and confronting. Attempts to collectively translate even basic complexity theory concepts such as non-linear change were a struggle, even where it intuitively made sense. It took enormous effort and time to generate useful simplifications to capture new understanding. The communicative breakthrough to capture the new conceptualisation of the characteristics of dynamic change in complex adaptive systems was a case in point (see Figure 10.1).

Basic assumptions of complexity theory such as non-linear change, phase transitions and emergence posed fundamental challenges to the deep seated but often unconscious epistemology and ontology embedded in planners conceptualisations of the city and their practice. Awareness of the limitations of the exiting land use-transport model, knowledge of the drivers of change and potential self-fulfilling prophesy of the use of demographic projections for policy purposes gave useful encouragement to look to complexity theory for insights. However, even where complexity theory informed small initiatives such as the inclusion of 'adaptability' as a principle, the deeper implications of this were not appreciated. By way of example, once *Melbourne 2030* was in the public domain, the media used 'blueprint' as the most common descriptor. It seems that the weight of past practice, professional education and considerable sunk investment in technologies and public understanding of the established planning and development system was an ever-present weight hampering the attempted exploration of new approaches. These are examples of the different threads Wagenaar and Cook (2003: p. 143) describe when they talk about attempts 'to unravel the tightly woven modernist fabric'.

In Melbourne, the language and metaphors of complexity theory provided a useful basis for challenging many tenets of a rational comprehensive approach. However, by the end of the case study period it seems that changes of Government, Secretary and senior staff along with changing priorities and agendas rendered the exploration substantially inconsequential and left minimal explicit institutional legacies within the Department. In many respects it is no surprise that, in spite of leadership from the Secretary, institutional rigidity to change was strong. However, what this case study provides so well is a glimpse of the scale of effort required to challenge the modernist assumptions on which planning as an enterprise is based – of how tightly woven and so resistant to change those assumptions actually are.

Tools and methods

Complexity theory methodologies such as cellular automata modelling and use of genetic algorithms offer the potential to create simulations of aspects of urban systems that can reveal new insights into the dynamics of urban change. The power of the canonical experiments (such as flocking birds and the Mandelbrot set) to visually represent real life systems and the successful identification of key variables was particularly enticing for Dr Paterson in the first phase of the case study. With a background in land use-transport modelling, a sharp awareness of its limitations and an explicit desire to improve the Department's capacity in this respect, it is no surprise he was interested in exploring the potential of such modelling methodologies for urban systems. Where complexity scholars spoke of key variables, Dr Paterson called for a greater understanding of the key drivers of change in urban systems. Given his position, he was able to devote resources to this and prioritised creation of an agent-based model. He hoped this could ultimately replace the Department's land use-transport model. At a time when only limited academic effort had been devoted to this, such a hope was, to say the least, ambitious. This raises two key questions. First, what should be the purpose of such modelling efforts and secondly, what sort of institutional arrangement can best support such efforts.

Philosopher of science and colleague of Prigogine, Isabella Stengers, argues that complexity models should 'be first appreciated as enlightening abstractions, precious new tools for thinking.' (Stengers and Lissack, 2004: p. 97) rather than a 'universal source of answers'. She emphasises the critical importance of producing new kinds of conscious awaress and the contribution exploration of new tools, such as the various complexity models, can make.

> Tools modify the ones who use them. To learn how to use a tool is to enter into a new relation with reality, both an aesthetic and practical new relation. I would say that those new tools put the ones who use them in a very interesting new practical position with regards to what they address. Indeed the problem is no longer simply how to explain; it includes the problem of what is to be explained. What are the good questions? What is the relevant way to address a pattern? (Stengers and Lissack, 2004: p. 98)

In the case study a clear tension is evident between the desire to use the process to explore new questions and develop new conceptualisations and understandings of the dynamics of urban changes and the desire to produce a new model. The critical importance of the process and the deep learning opportunities it provides was emphasised during the process by the visiting University of Cranfield professor. However this did not stop fragmentation of the project into two streams, generally comprising the modellers on the one hand and the research and policy officers on the other. This fragmentation was exacerbated by an inability to communicate across disciplinary divides and differential resource allocation. The modellers were the only ones with time formally allocated reflecting the priority of the Secretary to finalise an agent-based model. A very basic sugar-scape model was prepared but as soon as Dr Paterson left in the wake of a change of Government, most modellers returned to business as usual and the existing land-use transport model lived on.

The process of developing an agent-based model using tools associated with complexity theory began in very small ways to stimulate new imagination and new insights about the nature of the dynamics of structural urban change in Melbourne. In this respect the tools and methods of complexity acted as a sort of boundary object (after Star and Griesemer, 1989). However, the potential was not realised in this case. This can be accounted for in part by the institutional inertia mentioned earlier, but also in part by the arguably premature nature of this exploration. At the time of the case study pure research applying complexity theory to the planning field was still in its infancy[4] and the location of the project within a Government Department, in spite of Paterson's commitment to deliberate exploration, eventually compromised the project. That said, the degree of practical involvement of researchers, policy officers and modellers achieved would have been unlikely should the project have been located elsewhere. It was precisely the tensions that emerged between the groups that held the potential (substantially unrealised in this case) for deeper learning and real breakthroughs. This raises an interesting paradox. The case shows the many ways in which pursuit of such an advanced research agenda within a Government Department is problematic. However it also demonstrates that to pursue such a research agenda outside of it defeats the very purpose of enabling paradigm-shifting learning opportunities for practitioners arguably best placed to work through the inherent tensions.

Governance

Complexity theory alerts us to the limitations of governance approaches based on assumptions of predictably and controllability in systems that are complex and adaptive. Scholars exploring the implications of this for urban governance in general and planning in particular emphasise the importance of diversity and adaptability in the urban structure, form and function (Allen, 1997), the paradox of prediction in complex adaptive systems (Portugali, 2008), the advantage of participatory democracy and collaborative planning processes (Innes and Booher, 2003; Wagenaar, 2007), and attention to overall system performance and collective adaptive learning (Innes and Booher, 1999)[5]. In this case study, the exploration of complexity theory by practitioners generated similar insights and subsequent attempts to influence metropolitan planning practice in this direction, albeit without the benefit of being informed by any of the publications above.

The paradox of prediction

Basic components of metropolitan scale strategic planning include how to set policy to manage future population and economic change and associated housing and transport needs. In Melbourne population projections have been used to inform housing and transport policy decisions. At the beginning of this case study, public servants from both the research and policy units of the Department grappled with the potentially self-fulfilling effect such projections can have. As complexity theory was explored as an epistemological and ontological foundation

---

4   It were scholars as Waldrop (1992), Lewin (1993), Allen (1997) and Batty (1994, 1998) influencing the participants at the outset of the case study in 1999 and complexity modelling applied to urban systems was only at an early stage.

5   Obviously complexity theory is not the only conceptual framework that leads to similar priorities.

for approaching urban governance, the profound implications of non-linearity in complex adaptive systems were exposed.

Portugali (2008: p. 256) identifies several fundamental properties of prediction in complex systems as follows,

> First, the non-linearities that typify cities imply that one cannot establish predictive cause–effect relationships between some of the variables. Second, many of the triggers for change in complex systems have the nature of mutations (Allen, 1997). As such, they are unpredictable, not because of lack of data, but because of their very nature. Third, unlike closed systems, in complex systems, the observer, with his/her actions and predictions, is part of the system – a point made by Jantsch (1981) more than two decades ago and largely ignored since then. In such a situation, predictions are essentially feed-forward loops in the system, important factors that affect the system and its future evolution with some interesting implications that include self-fulfilling and self-falsifying or self-defeating predictions noted above.

It comes as no surprise then that population projections since the very first strategic plan for Melbourne in 1929 have been proved inaccurate by history. Even the projections used as a basis for *Melbourne 2030* (released in 2002) were substantially revised in light of the 2006 census. It also comes as no surprise then that within the first exploratory phase of the case study only tentative progress was made to unpack the implications Portugali's paradox of prediction has for metropolitan planning. The use of scenarios and foresighting techniques as alternative or parallel inputs to strategic planning has only relatively recently been given attention in the planning literature (see for example Albrechts, 2004, 2005 and Hillier, 2007).

Healey (2006: p. 25) reminds us that 'Friedmann (1987) argued that the whole enterprise of planning was about the relations of knowledge to action' and that for Sandercock (2003: p. 73) '"there's nothing more political than epistemological struggles', struggles over meaning and which knowledge counts in governance processes." (Healey 2006: p. 26). What we see in the case study is just how much effort is required to question the established ontological and epistemological basis of planning which is many ways in Melbourne was substantially embedded in a legacy of rational comprehensive planning, or a 'predict and plan' approach.

Participatory democracy and collaborative planning processes

By resisting preparation of a metropolitan strategy and instead focusing Departmental effort on developing a better understanding of the drivers of change Dr Paterson created a unique opportunity for exploration of the relevance of complexity theory to metropolitan planning and governance. This approach placed significant faith in the capacity to obtain such knowledge and apply it – a capacity that has been substantially challenged in the planning literature. What it denied however, was the opportunity for a participative process of generating a metropolitan strategy with broad stakeholder ownership. This was the intent of the *Melbourne 2030* strategy development process undertaken in phase two of the case study. By stage three of the case study however, we see the capacity and effort for community engagement at the strategic level reduced after the initial release of *Melbourne 2030* and an understandable shift of focus to implementation.

Wagenaar (2007: p. 17) argues that participative and deliberative models of governance are so much more effective in complex adaptive (human) systems because they 'increase interaction within systems and thereby system diversity and creativity'. He explains,

> By giving citizens genuine influence in local governance, we effectively change both the architecture of and the interaction patterns in the neighbourhood system. Giving citizens influence effectively changes the conceptual space of the system—the institutional and procedural categories that influence the proximity of actors in a system. Proximity expresses the probability that the agents in a system will interact. And interaction is essential for stimulating diversity and variety; both are conditions for generating creative solutions to problems. (2007:41-42)

Collaborative planning approaches (after Healey, 2006a) are in many respects consistent with a complexity theory approach because they encourage feedback and interaction in complex (human) systems. What this case study reveals is the real governance challenge at the metropolitan scale of sustaining a participative or deliberative model of governance throughout an ongoing process. It also raises the question of how initiatives to explore new ways of understanding the urban system can be pursued in a participative manner.

Adaptability and dealing with unintended consequences

Innes and Booher (1999) argue that a complexity perspective encourages attention to collective adaptive learning in order to respond to the inevitable unintended consequences of policy. If as Wagenaar (2007: p. 41) argues 'policy effects are emergent properties', then the period immediately following release of a metropolitan strategy should provide a rich ground for observing and responding to the emergent properties of a new policy. In this case study, the governance implications of this were only appreciated by the public servants in hindsight.

The release of *Melbourne 2030* was a significant intervention in a complex adaptive system. The immediate post-release period was important as a period for acknowledging unintended consequences and adapting implementation efforts accordingly towards desired trajectories. Indeed, 'adaptability' was included as a principle in *Melbourne 2030* in recognition that planners cannot know with certainty the consequence of a policy intervention. The inclusion of 'adaptability' as a principle was significant because it represented an explicit shift in public policy towards acknowledgement of the inherent uncertainties, of urban policy problems. This had the potential to stimulate conditions for harnessing complexity by allowing for the possibility of a different type of dialogue and action – a mode with room for failure, ongoing adaptation to unexpected changes or unintended consequences, the time for genuine co-evolution of bottom up solutions to meta-scale problems and spaces for more interaction amongst stakeholders. The irony during the third phase of the case study is that at precisely the time when adaptability and openness to continued uncertainty was particularly important, the act of releasing *Melbourne 2030* brought intense, multi-directional pressure to contain uncertainty which was manifested in many ways including the persistent description of *Melbourne 2030* as a 'blueprint', the internal and stakeholder pressure post-release on a heads-down approach to the prescribed implementation program including the 226 initiatives and more centralised effort to coordinate the significant implementation effort.

10.9 Conclusion

The case study presented in this chapter offers a unique perspective on a metropolitan planning process where complexity theory was explored prospectively by public servants within a State Government Department in Melbourne, Australia over a number of years. This chapter has explored the potential relevance of complexity theory to metropolitan planning by examining this case study.

Three ways in which complexity theory informs metropolitan planning were identified from the literature – by providing new language and metaphors for the dynamics of change in complex systems; by providing new tools and methods for complex systems; and by challenging established modes of governance based on assumptions of predictability and controllability. The relevance of each of these was then examined drawing insights from the case study. It was confirmed that whilst complexity theory does indeed hold this potential in these three ways, each was realised to differing extents through this case study.

The case study reveals how deeply a practical engagement with complexity theory by practitioners in an institutional setting such as a Government Department challenges the epistemological and ontological assumptions on which metropolitan planning is based. Assumptions of predictability and controllability are embedded in the education of planners, the tools and technologies of planning and the institutional culture of planning both within Government and in the public sphere. In the case study, in spite of an unprecedented opportunity to explore the relevance of complexity theory for metropolitan planning, the institutional legacy of this exploration was minimal.

The pervasiveness of the modernist project is not new to planning or urban studies. Similarly, the challenges of institutional rigidity are known. Perhaps the most significant contribution this case study makes is to demonstrate that whilst complexity theory is not a panacea for unravelling the tightly woven threads of the modernist project, it does provide a useful conceptual framework that can assist in challenging some of the assumptions on which this project is founded. The language and metaphors of complexity theory are accessible and do serve as something of a boundary object. Exploration of the tools and methods of complexity theory does invite new types of questioning. Finally, the epistemological and ontological assumptions embedded in a complexity approach to metropolitan planning establish a different basis for governance. However, even under conditions of strong leadership with extensive opportunity for exploration, the potential of complexity theory to usefully inform metropolitan planning is extremely fragile.

Finally, this chapter has demonstrated that case studies of the prospective use of complexity theory in planning practice provide a qualitatively different kind of insight to the retrospective use of complexity theory as an analytical framework. More research in this vein will make a useful contribution to the transfer of complexity theory to the planning field – a disciplinary endeavour still emerging from its infancy[6].

Acknowledgements

I would like to specially thank Hendrik Wagenaar and Libby Porter for their ongoing critical insights and feedback on early drafts of this chapter. I am grateful to Luleå University, in particular Professor Maria Viklander, the Stockholm Resilience Centre, Urban-NET and Formas for supporting the writing of this chapter. I also thank the anonymous reviewers for their useful comments.

References

Albrechts, L. (2004) Strategic (spatial) planning reexamined, *Environment and Planning B-Planning & Design*, 31(5), pp. 743-758.
Albrechts, L. (2005) Creativity as a drive for change, *Planning Theory*, 4(3), pp. 247-269.
Allen, P.M. (1997) *Cities and regions as self-organizing systems: models of complexity*, Gordon and Breach Science Publishers, Amsterdam.
Angel, S., S.C. Sheppard, and D.L. Civco (2005) *The dynamics of global urban expansion*, Department of Transport and Urban Development, The World Bank, Washington, DC.
Axelrod, R. and M.D. Cohen (1999) *Harnessing complexity: Organizational implications of a scientific frontier*, Free Press, New York.
Batty, M. (1998) Urban evolution on the desktop: simulation with the use of extended cellular automata, *Environment and Planning A*, 30, pp. 1943-1967.

---

6   After Chettiparamb (2005).

Batty, M. and P. Longley (1994) *Fractal Cities*, Academic Press, London.

Capra, F. (2005) Complexity and life, *Theory, Culture and Society*, 22 (5), pp. 33-44.

Chettiparabamb, A. (2006) Metaphors in Complexity Theory and Planning, *Planning Theory*, 5 (71), pp. 71-91.

Coveny, P. and R. Highfield (1995) *Frontiers of complexity – The Search for Order in a Chaotic World*, Faber and Faber, London.

Department of Infrastructure (DOI) (1998) *From Doughnut City to Café Society*, Victorian Government, Melbourne.

Department of Infrastructure (DOI) (2002) *Melbourne 2030 - planning for sustainable growth*, Victorian Government, Melbourne.

Duit, A. and V. Galaz (2008) Governance and Complexity - Emerging Issues for Governance Theory, *Governance: An International Journal of Policy, Administration, and Institutions*, 21 (3), pp. 311-335.

Ellis, C. (2003) *The Ethnographic I: A Methodological Novel about Autoethnography*, AltaMira Press, Walnut Creek.

Gleeson, B. (2008) Critical commentary: waking from the dream: An australian perspective on urban resilience, *Urban Studies*, 45 (13), pp. 2653-2668.

Friedmann, J. (1987) *Planning in the public domain; From knowledge to action*, Princeton University Press, Princeton.

Friedmann, J. and Abonyi, G. (1976) Social learning: a new model for policy research, *Environment and Planning A*, 8 December, pp. 927-940.

Healey, P. (2006). *Urban complexity and spatial strategies: towards a relational planning for our times*, Routledge, London.

Healey, P. (2006a). *Collaborative planning: Shaping places in fragmented societies*, Palgrave Macmillian, New York.

Hillier, J. (2007) *Stretching beyond the horizon: A multiplanar theory of spatial planning and governance*, Ashgate, Aldershot (UK).

Innes, J. and Booher, D.E. (1999) Metropolitan development as a complex system: A New Approach to Sustainability, *Economic Development Quarterly*, 13, pp. 141-156.

Innes, J.E. and D.E. Booher (2003) Collaborative policymaking: governance through dialogue, in: M. Hajer and H. Wagenaar (Eds.) *Deliberative policy analysis: understanding governance in the network society*, Cambridge University Press, Cambridge, pp. 33-59.

Lewin, R. (1993) *Complexity: life at the edge of chaos*, Collier Books, New York.

March, J.G. (1991) Exploration and Exploitation in organizational learning, *Organizational Science*, 2 (1), pp.71-87.

Michael, D. (1976) *On learning to plan – and planning to learn*, Jossey-Bass Publishers, San Fransisco.

MA (Millenium Assessment) (2005). *Ecosystems and human well-being: Synthesis*, Island Press, Washinton, DC.

Neilson, L. (2002) Instruments of governance in urban management, *Australian Planner*, 39 (2), pp. 97-102.

Niven, S. and C. Wilkinson (2005) Reinventing Melbourne, in: E. Charlesworth (Ed.) *Cityedge: case studies in contemporary urbanism*, Architectural Press, Oxford.

Paterson, J. (2000) Choice and Necessity in Metropolitan Planning, *Urban Policy and Research*, 18 (3), pp. 377-386.

Portugali, J. (1999) *Self-organization and the City*, Springer, Heidelberg (D).

Portugali, J. (2008) Learning from paradoxes about prediction and planning in self-organizing cities, *Planning Theory*, 7 (3), pp. 248-262.

Portugali, J. (2010) 'Statis is data: toward a complexity theory of resilient cities', Presentation at the 8th AESOP Planning and Complexity Workshop – 'Resilient Cities', Stockholm Resilience Centre, February 26-27.

Rees, W.E. (2007) Deluding ourselves, *Alternatives Journal*, 33 (2-3), pp. 45-46.

Millenium Assessment (2005) *Ecosystems and Human Well-being: Synthesis*, Island Press, Washington, DC.

Reynolds, J. and Porter, L. (1998) Melbourne's inner city revival, *Urban Policy and Research*, 16 (1), pp. 63-68.

Salet, W. and A. Faludi (eds.) (2000) *The revival of strategic spatial planning*, Royal Netherlands Academy of Arts and Sciences, Amsterdam.

Sandercock, L. (2003) *Cosmopolis II: mongrel cities in the 21st century*, Continuum, London.

Star, S.L. & Griesemer, J.R. (1989) Institutional Ecology, Translations and Boundary Objects: Amateurs and Professionals in Berkeley's Museum of Vertebrate Zoology, 1907-39, *Social Studies of Science* 19 (4): pp. 387-420.

Stengers, I. (2004) The challenge of complexity: Unfolding the ethics of science. In memoriam Ilya Prigogine, *E:CO*, 6 (1-2): pp. 92-9

Suteanu, C. (2005) Complexity, science and the public: The geography of a new interpretation, *Theory, Culture and Society*, 22 (5), pp. 113-140.

Thrift, N. (1999) The place of complexity, *Theory, Culture and Society*, 16 (3), pp. 31-69.

UN (2008) *Urban Population, Development and the Environment*, United Nations Population Division, New York.

Urry, J. (2005) The complexity turn, *Theory, Culture and Society*, 22 (5), pp.1-14.

Wagenaar, H. (2007) Governance, complexity, and democratic participation: How citizens and public officials harness the complexities of neighborhood decline, *The American Review of Public Administration*, 37 (17), pp. 17-50.

Wagenaar, H. (2010) Enacting Complexity: Resilience, Urban Governance and Pragmatism, Presentation at the 8th AESOP Planning and Complexity Workshop – 'Resilient Cities', Stockholm Resilience Centre, February 26-27, 2010.

Wagenaar, H. and Cook, N. (2003) Understanding policy practices: action, dialectic and deliberation in policy analysis, in: M. Hajer and H. Wagenaar *Deliberative policy analysis – understanding governance in the network society*, Cambridge University Press, Cambridge.

Waldrop, M. (1992) *Complexity – the emerging science at the edge of order and chaos*, Penguin Books, London.
Westley, F., B. Zimmerman, and M.Q. Patton (2006) *Getting to maybe: how the world is changed,* Vintage, Toronto.

Chapter 11

Considering Complex Systems: The Implications of the Complexity Frame of Reference for Planning

David Byrne[1]

The point I am making here is that we need a new basis for knowledge, and my argument is that the complexity frame of reference provides us with that, and we need a process of social action which is transformative – a most important word – and which can accommodate complex knowledge process in the enactment of the future, which is another way of saying in planning and then implementing on the basis of that planning.

11.1 Introduction

The starting point for any discussion of the implications of the complexity frame of reference for planning has to be the stipulation that planning in general is a process that is concerned with shaping the future trajectories of complex systems. That is a relatively straightforward statement but is has a lot of content. It indicates that the socio-ecological systems[2] are indeed complex, that they have trajectories i.e. pathways to the future, and that purposive human action can shape the nature of those trajectories.[3] The first two propositions are not contentious but the third is. Friedrich Von Hayek in his prize lecture on being awarded the Swedish Riksbank prize in Economic Sciences (1974) gave a first rate account of the general complexity frame of reference but considered that the nature of complex systems was such that:

> ... in the social field the erroneous belief that the exercise of some power is likely to have beneficial consequences is likely to lead to a new power to coerce

---

1   David Byrne is Professor in the School of Applied Social Sciences at the Durham University.

2   The economic here is firmly subsumed within the social.

3   Note that this implies that social complexity has an added dimension which takes it beyond the frame of autopoiesis. Social systems sometimes self organize – crowds for example, but mostly organization reflects purposive action.

other men being conferred on some authority. Even if such power is not in itself bad, its exercise is likely to lead to impede the function of those spontaneous ordering forces by which, without understanding them, man is largely assisted in the pursuit of his aims. We are only beginning to understand on how subtle a communication system the functioning of an advanced industrial society is based – a communication system which we call the market and which turns out to be a more efficient mechanism for digesting dispersed information than any that man has deliberately designed.' (1974 REF)

In 2010 with market failures resonating around the world we are plainly at the end of an era in which a bastardized but essentially accurate version of Von Hayek's message that markets are good and planning of any kind is bad, dominated the intellectual framework of governance. Neo-liberalism is on its last legs and with luck will have expired by the time this essay is published. That said Von Hayek as always had a point. If we are going to plan we are going to have to plan on the basis of valid knowledge claims. Planning in general, and spatial land use planning in particular (remembering that control over land use has been the most important planning power in democratic systems since the mid twentieth century), have in the past worked with a mechanistic understanding of the nature of the socio-economic systems they sought to shape.[4] Whether there was relatively strong planning as in the UK from the outbreak of the Second World War until the mid 1970s, or much weaker planning systems subordinated to market interests[5] which was the status of UK planning from the early 1980s until the present, planning processes have relied upon a set of knowledge claims which are linear and scientistic. There was a failure to recognize the significance of non-linearity, the need for a much more organic frame of reference, and the need to get beyond models of social process which derive from Newtonian mechanics.

That sets the question which we must address here. Is it possible to formulate an approach to understanding nested and intersecting (two further terms which will require some subsequent elaboration) complex systems which will provide us (and who 'us' are also requires very careful consideration) with a knowledge basis on which we can develop a planning process which in some sort of dialectical

---

4   The shift in terminology from socio-ecological to socio-economic in this historical reflection is quite deliberate. We should be thinking and acting in relation to socio-ecological systems with the economic subsumed as a sub-set of the social. We used to think, and all too often still think and even worse act, in terms of economic systems with the social seen as a byproduct of economic development and the ecological at best receiving little more than lip service.

5   In reality we had little in the way of free market operation, particularly in urban systems. Instead private sector development interests have dominated often very coercive governance of urban systems which have operated behind a covering rhetoric of marketforces. The vile pathfinder schemes in Northern English cities illustrate this very well (Allen, 2008).

synthesis will do better than either the thesis of mechanistic planning or the anti-thesis of reliance on market processes alone? We had better be able to answer YES to that because if one thing is clear in a context of both socio-economic and ecological crisis at the beginning of the twenty-first century, if we can't do this then bad things are going to happen.

Let me return to two quotations which I have deployed before in framing an earlier preliminary consideration of these issues. First consider Unger specifying the nature of the knowledge problem:

> ... a practice of social and historical explanation, sensitive to structure but aware of contingency, is not yet at hand. We must build it as we go along, by reconstructing the available tools of social science and social theory. Its absence denies us a credible account of how transformation happens. (2000: 24)

and then Friedmann arguing for a revival of a theory of transactive planning, that is to say reminding us that some thirty years ago he argued that:

> ... a new way of thinking about planning was needed that would emphasize the relationship between knowledge and action ... These ideas ... shifted the discourses of planning away from planning as an *instrument of control* to one of *innovation and action*. (2003: 8)

and asserting that this is still true today.

11.2 Some terminology and definitions

It is not appropriate to reiterate yet again all the elements of a complex frame of reference but some general elements in that frame should be specified before proceeding further. First, let us specify what is meant by the term 'complex system'. Let us say in summary that complex systems are systems with emergent properties. In other words we cannot generate an understanding of the nature of the system and its past, present, and potential future trajectories (the plural is deliberate) by an analytical process in which we reduce the system conceptually to its elements and model it in terms of those elements. Note that word trajectory – systems move through the state space which defines the possible character of that system with characteristics in terms of the system's traces[6] which have different values at different time points. What interests us is if this trajectory stays much the same, albeit with some variation in attribute values, or if it changes in some radical fashion which transforms the character of the systems whilst maintaining its integrity as a system. That is to say does the system maintain a trajectory in its

---

6   See Byrne, 2002 for a discussion of the distinction between trace and measured value on a variable here.

present attractor in state space or does it undergo a metamorphosis. One additional useful specification is that such systems operate in terms of auto-eco-organization (see Smith and Jenks, 2006). In other words they self organize but do so in relation to the whole of their environment which operates to condition the character of the organization which emerges from self organization in context. That context is provided by other systems, most of which are also complex.

It is important to recognize that systems are intersected and nesting, that boundaries, as Cilliers (2001) indicates, are all of separators, connectors, and transmitters, and that there is no hierarchy of influence in relation to direction of causation among systems. That systems are nested does not mean that those 'higher' in the set are necessarily determinant in relation to those contained within them. Container may have a causal influence on contained. Contained may have a causal influence on container. There may be a reflexive relationship with causal influences running in both directions. In relation to social systems the last case is by far the most common. This point is extremely important because it is a rejection of the simplistic forms of discussion of globalization which have dominated social thought for most of the last two decades. The work of Castells and particularly his great trilogy examining *The Information Age: Economy, Society and Culture* (1996; 1997; 1998) is perhaps the best representative of that tradition in which, in crude summary, the global system contained all else and forces emerging from global networks – and particularly the global financial networks which were the embodiment of 'the mother of all accumulations' – were the key drivers of social development and change.[7] On the contrary we have to recognize that we are dealing here with co-evolution (see Gerrits, 2008) of all the systems of relevance to us.

The implications of this in relation to planning are that plans at any spatial level below the global are in fact constitutive of the global system itself to just as much a degree as that global system is constitutive of these other spatial levels. Relationships are always recursive. So acts of governance, and in particular planning, at local, regional, national and trans-national block (e.g. the European Union) levels all serve to constitute the global. It is as it is because of them just as they, recursively, are as they are because of it. Let us be clear here. 'Anti-planning' neo-liberal assertions of market dominance which have informed planning processes of all kinds, but particularly urban spatial planning, have operated locally to create a global reality which is now imploding all around us with a new set of block, national, regional, local, neighbourhood, household, and individual consequences. The reference to the levels of household and individual serves to remind us that people's own individual acts also matter here. As Smith has reminded us:

---

7   It is perhaps a little cruel, but nonetheless thoroughly enjoyable, to reflect on how important nation states and political actors have turned out to be in resolving the crisis engendered by the globalized stupidity of the real actors in those financial networks, contrary to all the guff peddled about their irrelevance by social scientists functioning to a considerable degree as the ideologues of those social interests.

... the accumulation strategies of capitalist logics, structures and actors, to which many urban analysts devote so much attention, are not the sole, or at times even the most important agencies in the constitution of urban life. As important, if not more so, has been the impact of ordinary women and men – the consciousness, intentionality, everyday practices and collective action – on the social construction of urban life. (2001: 6)

Let us note that Smith also mentions collective action – to that theme we will return. The issue of the nature of boundaries also requires some elaboration. Cilliers specifies the nature of boundaries for us in ontological terms:

Boundaries [of complex systems] are simultaneously a function of the activity of the system itself, and a product of the strategy of description involved. In other words, we frame the system by describing it in a certain way (for a certain purpose) but we are constrained in where the frame can be drawn. The boundary of the system is therefore neither a function of our description, nor is it a purely natural thing. (Cilliers, 2001: 141)

A key point here is that our framings are 'for a certain purpose'. Reality shapes what we deal with but so does our purpose in dealing with it. Let us be clear here. When we engage in planning we are dealing with open complex systems, in contradistinction to closed systems – a distinction which also matters in relation to our frame of understanding in that we are dealing with 'general complexity' rather than 'restricted complexity' to which issue we shall turn in a moment. Here Cilliers turns to Zeleny (1996) who specifies the nature of boundaries in open systems very well and appropriately reconciles the apparent contradiction between the idea of openness and the idea of boundary:

All social systems, and thus all living systems, create, maintain and degrade their own boundaries. These boundaries do not separate but intimately connect the system with its environment. They do not have to be just physical or topological, but are primarily functional, behavioural, and communicational. They are not "perimeters" but functional constitutive components of a given system. (1996: 133)

Cilliers develops this point by challenging the notion that boundaries are somehow placed so as to separate. Rather we have to recognize that sub-systems can be parts of multiple other systems, that there are multiple interconnections, that we might even have to think of systems as consisting of boundaries alone. In summary: 'Everything is always interacting and interfacing with others and with the environment; the notions of "inside" and "outside" are never simple and uncontested.' (2001: 142) Indeed we might consider that given Cilliers' ontological specification of complex systems as both real *and* constructed, as made by us but made out of something rather than being mere reifications and moreover made by us for a purpose, then not only are boundaries contestable, they are constructed. It is precisely that construction which is itself contestable. This is of the greatest importance for any planning exercise since the specification of the system or systems which are being planned for constitutes the boundaries and this necessarily implies that there will be the potential for political and interest group conflicts in this process.

We have to be careful here about the idea of 'spatial' in relation to boundaries. Planning in governance is usually about planning within a spatial range. This is evident with land use planning but units of governance are usually defined in relation to territorial coverage. So planning a health system for example is an exercise which relates to the form and delivery of services within a specific area. However, that spatial boundary does not bound off the system being planned. So elements of the regional, national and global all have significance. For example potential global patterns of transmission of disease matter for local health systems. However, this is not just a matter of 'health and its domain'. So global economic changes with consequent impacts on employment, incomes, food prices etc. all have potential implications for a local health system. At the same time the health system cannot be planned in isolation from for example local social care systems, transport systems, and community organization. Of course limits have to be set in any planning exercise but the setting of those limits must be explicit, transparent and open to continuous argument and revision. Moreover, there should be some very careful attention to the nature of reality in this process. Realities can and should be contested. A pertinent example is provided by the majority and minority reports of the Redcliffe Maud Commission on the reorganization of local government in England and Wales (Cmnd 4040, 1969). The majority of the commission worked with a notion of local governance systems which derived from existing administrative structures. Derek Senior in his dissenting minority report argued that the contemporary social and economic reality required a definition of governance systems which focused on real 'city regions' with a very different set of spatial boundaries.[8] This is particularly clear example of an important dispute in political administration which was about setting the working boundaries of complex systems for planning purposes.

Next in this discussion of concepts and terminology, let us take up the issue of restricted and general complexity. These terms are due to Maurin (2006) but correspond to the terms 'simplistic complexity' and 'complex complexity' as these are deployed by Gerrits:

> Simplistic Complexity is essentially complexity within closed systems, with the emergence of structures and processes depending entirely on the (fixed) variables within the system. Such systems display complex behaviours but are deemed simplistic because the roots of this complexity always remain within the

---

8   Correctly as we now generally recognize. English local governance is still a complete mess in consequence of the failure to follow Senior's recommendations.

closed system. This means that the dynamics are confined by the variables that define the system. ....

   In social reality, the number and nature of the variables defining an emerging structure or process is not fixed but rather changeable. Complex adaptive systems are considered to be open and constantly exchanging energy with other systems and with such systems, the constituent variables do not define its borders. ... What constitutes and limits a system is relative to the agents' and observer's locality, which corresponds with the arguments on agency and boundary judgements ... and as such is connected ad infinitum to other representations of systems. (2008: 20-21)

So when we say we are dealing with open complex systems we are dealing with systems which in general cannot be represented by models derived from rules in something like game theory. In other words the emergence in such systems is not reducible to something less than the system itself. To say this is not to dismiss modeling, and in particular not to dismiss simulation as a sometimes useful tool in representing systems. Rather it is to say be careful and recognize the very definite limits to the use of tools which embody a restricted version of complexity in dealing with open complex systems. That said of course, even those tools, recognizing as they do the reality of emergence, are much more isomorphic with complex reality than the linear modeling tools which have dominated science since Newton and statistical modeling for about a century.

   This leads us into a necessary discussion of the tools of social science which might inform processes of planning in relation to complex systems. As Cilliers (2001) reminds us we are in something of a bind here. We cannot model complex or general complexity in a complete fashion with anything less complex than the fully described system itself – the map of the country is the country with every dynamic process in full swing. At the same time we have to make models so the key thing is the acknowledgement of the limitations of those models. However, in planning there is something else to consider. We are not just representing reality, we are engaged in shaping its future form. Of course that shaping is path dependent, we essentially and necessarily start from here, but we go forward to make what will be. Adam's work (see for example 2004) is of very considerable value in helping us to think about the implications of this. As she says: 'The creation of the future is what makes us human.' (2004: 298) but:

... we have as yet no obvious equivalent aids to extend ourselves into the future, to surface latent processes, uncover potential outcomes and access the "virtual real". There is thus much work to be done in this field if the gap between ability to act and inability to know is to be narrowed. (2004: 314)

This is much what Unger said in the quotation above. Well – maybe thinking in the complex frame of reference is a way forward for us here.

This is not the place to present a full account of the tools of social science which might be deployed in relation to these issues but some things can be identified as helpful. Essentially all useful tools in one way or another are narratives by which is meant not just text based narratives derived from documents and reflecting the past but also all other means of representing the past including data series and images and narratives which project into the future. Human beings can imagine futures and act to achieve them. The traditional form of 'future narrative' is projection on the basis of linear modeling, probably the least useful, and frequently dangerously useless, approach to this problem. However, simulation, with its limitations recognized; personal and collective narratives of expectation and desire; comparative narratives which deploy all of the techniques of looking at the similar to find out the role of differences[9] in creating difference now so that we might create difference in the future, all of these provide us with narratives which might guide our actions in the planning process. The key word there is actions – acts – things which we do. Let us now turn to how we might think about that action when we try to shape the futures of complex social systems.

11.3 Transformative planning: acting on complex systems

Ambrose Bierce in his notorious and wonderful *Devil's Dictionary* (1911) defined 'plan' thus:

PLAN, v. Bother about the best method of achieving an accidental result.

He also and relevantly for the following discussion defined the word 'consult':

CONSULT, v.i. To seek another's disapproval of a course already decided on.

(See http://www.alcyone.com/max/lit/devils/c.html)

A degree of cynicism is always appropriate when considering processes of political administration. However, we generally do not agree with Bierce that things just happen. Rather we want to have some set of processes by which we decide on a future state we want to achieve and then set in train actions which will lead to that state being realized. Geddes description of the appropriate method in urban planning being to survey – see what is already, plan – decide on objectives, and implement – engage in action to achieve those objectives, adds in the element of establishing current conditions and thereby addressing the substance of path dependency. As 'planning' became established simultaneously as a profession and

---

9   Ragin's (2000) tool of Qualitative Comparative Analysis is particularly useful here.

as an academic field[10] it, in common with applied social science in general, tended to turn to positivist frames of understanding and linear and mechanistic models of urban process, despite the radical organicism of Geddes who has the best claim to be the founder of modern urban planning. In plain English planners made assertions to the effect that if we do this, then that will happen and it will happen because we have a scientific understanding of how things work. The basis of their knowledge claims was mechanistic and linear although they were addressing the development of a complex system. Jane Jacobs' classic *The Death and Life of Great American Cities* (1961) explicitly informed by her participation in the foundational collective development of complexity theory, the Macy Seminars, rejected this absolutely and demonstrated the negative impact of trying to shape a complex system in this way.

Jacobs' critique of planning addressed issues of understanding the nature of cities as systems but was also concerned with competing interests in urban systems. That is to say it addressed the issue of conflict. This second theme has characterized most of the interesting social scientific examinations of planning processes, and in particular processes of urban regeneration, ever since. From Gans (1962) consideration of the impact of planning on Boston's Italian Americans through to contemporary discussions of Pathfinder schemes in Northern English cities (see Allen, 2008) critics have often, and almost invariably correctly, identified planning and related processes as having a negative impact on the lives of working class and other subordinate social groups. What is interesting here is that urban planning was in origin understood as a radical process and those who have attacked it as interfering with the supposedly superior rationales of market forces have often identified it as such. Here the term 'evangelistic bureaucrat' coined by Davies (1972) is useful. Planners asserted that they were acting rationally and scientifically but were understood by many of those affected by their decisions to be both ignorant of real social contexts and to be serving elite interests.

The political justification for interventionist planning in democracies has always been that plans are subject to democratic scrutiny and that ultimate decisions are taken by elected representatives. We have of course to address the real nature of democratic process in what in slightly different ways Crouch (2000) and Nelson (1995) have identified as 'post-democratic' systems. By this they mean not that the formal processes of representative democracy, including in particular multi-party competition for elected office, have been eliminated. Rather in effect it does not make much difference if tweedle dum or tweedle dee or even tweedle dother gets elected. The political programmes enacted and decisions taken will be essentially the same and both will prioritize the interests of business elites. This is a perfectly reasonable representation particularly of Anglo-American politics since the early 1980s but things may be changing in the US at least in

---

10   Field is a better term than discipline since planning draws on a variety of disciplines which have distinctive theoretical and methodological programmes in addressing substantive issues of understanding and practice.

consequence of the current crisis. The reality of planning and particularly of inner urban regeneration (particularly in the UK) has been that since the since the early 1980s the interests of urban speculation and finance capital accumulation – Castells' mother of all accumulations – have been allowed to dominate all planning process. The consequences over that period have been a progressive and massive deindustrialization of formerly industrial working class cities and a recasting of those cities towards a post-industrial status. In Marx's very useful expression we have seen a transformation of quantity into quality – a phase shift.

However, as Marx and Schumpeter always reminded us, capitalism is a crisis prone system. In other words it is a complex system subject to sudden radical transformations from which it emerges recast but stronger (Schumpeter's creative destruction) or even collapses (Marx's anticipation) and is transformed into something else – for Marx socialism or barbarism. Let us agree something now. We are currently in the grips of a crisis which demonstrates that global capitalism is a complex system and is at a phase shift point. The origins of that crisis actually lie in the secondary circuit of accumulation as identified by Lefebvre (1970) and in the way in which efforts to extend that circuit so that it drew in the poorer US urban residents as sources of revenue created toxic debt in the form of sub-prime mortgages which was multiplied as derivatives and has brought the world banking system crashing down around our ears. Let us also remember that this extension of debt was used to 'buy off' the social discontent which might have resulted from the stagnation of real wages and massive increases in inequality particularly in the US and the UK. The reality is that much of that debt in the US came from poor people refinancing their houses, often to pay for health care for which they either lacked insurance or were inadequately insured. We have a path dependency to cope with, context matters, and this is the current context.

All this said we also have to recognize that planning processes informed by explicitly social democratic and redistributionist ideals and enacted by more or less radical local governments based on representative democracy were in the 1960s responsible for massive 'planning disasters' (Hall, 1980) and considerable popular resentment. It was this that led to the Skeffington report in 1969 which was intended to develop a system for public participation in relation to planning processes. Skeffington interestingly used a language of complexity in presenting its rationale:

Life ... is becoming more and more complex, and one cannot leave all the problems to one's representatives. They need some help in reaching the right decision and opportunity should be provided for discussions with all those involved. ... Planning is a prime example of the need for this participation for it affects everyone. ... This becomes all the more vital when the demands of a complex society occasion massive changes; changes which in some areas may completely alter the character of a town, a neighbourhood or a rural area. The pace, intensity and scale of change will inevitable bring bewilderment and frustration if people affected think it is to be imposed without respect for their views. (Skeffington Report, 1969: 3)

Bruton and Nicholson comment that this quotation suggests that: '... public participation in planning was introduced in part as a response to the complex and "wicked" nature of planning problems and the need to take account of contingent factors in dealing with those problems.' (1987: 162) The term 'wicked issues' is very widely employed in contemporary discussions of policy and practices. The expression is usually considered as having originated with Rittel and Webber (1973) and has been defined thus:

> Wicked issues are those that seem to defy solution, or where seemingly sound interventions turn out to have unexpected consequences and results. Solutions that worked in one place fail when imposed on others. Ideas that remedy one problem can create a new set of circumstances, often with unintended consequences that then need resolution. (Hargadon and Plsek, 2004: 2)

It is apparent from the description that wicked issues arise in complex systems with complex processes of causation in operation. This means that conventional approaches to resolution which depend upon the development of universally applicable rules and procedures will not work. However, the political wickedness of these issues is by no means merely a technical matter or rather by no means just a matter of the problems of administering complex socio-political systems in a technical mode. Conventional organization theory emphasizes the issue of multiple stakeholders i.e. without the jargon conflicting interests, and there is a complexity-related discussion in the planning literature exemplified by Innes and Booher (1999) which discusses the processes necessary to achieve consensus in relation to the resolution of the issues which arise when development processes are understood as occurring within complex systems. We have to remember that it may well be, particularly in a context of crisis, that some differences of interest are utterly irreconcilable and that the supposed establishment of consensus is only too often a cover for the fixing of matters on the terms of the dominant group or groups.

At one level Skeffington's desire for public participation was motivated by the view that there were information deficits in relation to the taking of planning decisions. It was necessary to have a better knowledge base and participation was more effective in yielding that knowledge base than the traditional channels of democratic representation, particularly in mass democracies. This was not to challenge the right of elected representatives to take decisions but it did imply that neither they nor the planners had enough information to take those decisions properly and participation was a way of redressing that deficit. However, Skeffington went further:

> Participation involves doing as well as talking and there will only be full
> participation when the public are able to take an active part throughout the plan
> making process. (Skeffington Report, 1969: 1)

That implies some participation in the actual decision making process. However, in the UK in particular developments in governance have moved in quite the opposite direction. There has been legislative restriction in relation to the capacity of the public to object to major planning proposals and much of local governance, and particularly the governance of urban regeneration, has been take away from representative democratic local government and handed over to appointed bodies beginning with the Urban Development Corporations of the 1980s. Even worse much of this activity is now in the hands of public private partnerships and the introduction of a commercial element has been used to deny public accountability on the grounds of commercial confidentiality. Of course all this is in a state of meltdown in the current crisis since the virtually complete drying up of private funding and the collapse of the housing market has brought all these quasi commercial (although always massively reliant on public subsidy) activities to a grinding halt.[11]

Is there another way? Well there are some examples, mostly from the democratic global south, which suggest that alternatives do exist which allow for at least a greater degree of genuine participation in governance in general and planning processes in particular. The general perspective informing these developments is often derived from the work of Paolo Freire and employs in different ways, and with differing degrees of adherence to his own radical engagement, a vocabulary of dialogue, participatory research, and empowerment. Far too often this language is used in a context where as Amin puts it:

> ... those responsible for community action will become agents for the
> domestication of local politics, charged to deliver a consensual and responsible
> citizenry that performs the regeneration expectations of ruling elites. (2005: 620)

However, rhetoric not withstanding there have been real efforts to do things differently. The classic technique is that of participatory budgeting, with budgeting understood as underpinning all aspects of managing the governance of complex urban systems. Novy and Leubolt (2005) give an account of the operations of this system in Porto Alegre under an administration run by the Workers Party, one of the founders of which was Freire himself. It has to be noted that the Workers Party (PT) lost control of Porto Alegre in 2004 and that nationally in Brazil under President Lula it has governed in accordance with neo-liberal prescriptions. That said the actual mechanisms of engagement *and* surrender of real power from central administration to local participatory procedures in Porto Alegre represent

---

11   For a discussion of the history of urban regeneration in the UK see Imrie and Raco (2003)

one of the few examples of real participatory democracy in practice on the metropolitan scale. To return both to the question of 'who are us?' and the issue of collective action, these mechanisms offered some real power to the dispossessed as 'us' and allowed collectivities of action to emerge in relation to real issues. However, conflict remained. The Workers Party has lost control over many Brazilian metropolises because the middle classes have, correctly, felt squeezed between the accommodations it has made with elites and global capitalism on the one hand, and its efforts to do something for the Brazilian poor on the other.

The record of radical action in relation to planning complex urban systems in the neo-liberal era has not been encouraging. Former radicals in power have almost invariably accommodated to what they have understood to be the inexorable logic of globalization i.e. to determination of the range of possible actions by the power of global finance capitalism. In other words if we think in terms of nested and intersecting complex systems, then the environment of all city regions, indeed of all planning processes in governance, has just been radically transformed. There has been a phase shift at that level, induced by the internal contradictions of global finance capitalism and that complex system's intersections with everyday life and local urban systems in housing markets. Crisis does mean opportunity. There is a much greater scope for action, not least because the ideological hegemony of TINA – there is no alternative to neo-liberalism – is a busted flush if ever there was one. Indeed the complete collapse of the financial basis of neo-liberal market oriented urban regeneration, engendered by the simultaneous and profoundly inter-connected crises both in obtaining finance and in consumer purchasing of the products of those markets in housing and all aspects of retail, means that something different must be done.

This is where action matters. In complex systems which include human action as part of the control parameter set, and in social systems human action can be the key control parameter although always within context – people make history but not in circumstances of their own choosing – then it is never a matter of what will happen but rather of what will be made to happen. Planning is a key process in this in every sense in which that term can be deployed in relation to governance. AND there is a great necessity. Urban systems in what is now predominantly an urban world, and rural systems as well of course, are all facing a profound ecological crisis in the form of global warming. This itself is the product of human action through industrialization. As the great grandson and grandson of coal miners I recognize the background to that exactly. The issues facing planning are not merely those of achieving a more egalitarian and democratic form of social order. This seems to be on the agenda again in a way it has not been since the immediate aftermath of the Second World War. We also have to think about ensuring some sort of survival of human civilization on this planet.

11.4 Final comments

So let me conclude this chapter with some specification of the issues in relation to the future trajectory of human society in general which planners must address in any effort to manage the future trajectory of the set of complex systems within which any developed form of human social organization might be possible. It is of course possible to list these as a set of bullet points but that kind of linear presentation itself misrepresents the reality with which we – all of us in democratic societies – have to contend in any planning process. A Venn diagram is a better, if not entirely adequate, mode here and that is what Figure 11.1 is – an effort at defining the complex systems with which planning must engage in this context of ecological and economic crisis.

Figure 11.1 shows that everything is contained within the global socio-eco-system – Gaia in Lovelock's terms but with the significance of human actions recognized for the system. Hence, the addition of socio to eco. The global human socio-cultural-economic system impacts on that overall system but also contains the global financial system and local socio-eco-spatial systems, both of which impact on each other *and* on the socio-cultural land socio-economic systems. Everything is nested and global finance and local socio-eco-spatial systems have a high degree of intersection. This means that actions at every possible level matter for all other levels.

This gives us a complexity take on sustainability. In other words sustainability cannot be achieved by actions in relation to any single system. The traditional negative feedback tools of control are simply not enough to shape the future trajectories of these systems taken together. They may certainly be part of any policy process but we have to do more than try to stabilize these systems by keeping them bringing them back to their recent apparent equilibria. Rather we have to envisage a radical but desirable transformation of the systems and engage in the appropriate actions which might achieve that transformation as opposed to others which exist in the possibility space for their interwoven futures.

That means that we have to have narratives of those futures. The narrative of ecological and social sustainability probably requires a reduction in global consumption coupled with a radical redistribution of that consumption. That may seem a pipe dream but the actual collapse of financial accumulation and debt-based personal consumption in the 'West' does offer the possibility of this alternative. The harsh reality that real incomes have not increased for almost three decades and consumption has been fuelled by a mixture of debt and the cheapness of imported goods has already had consequences. The most obvious of this has been demographic. The failure of almost all developed nations to actually reproduce their own populations from births to their own citizens is really an extraordinary development and to a considerable extent has been a prefiguring indicator of profound system change. This alone has required mass immigration to sustain labour forces across what used to be called the 'advanced industrial countries'. Couple this with the extra-ordinary degree of urbanization of the global South

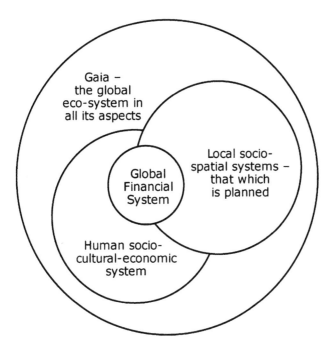

Figure 11.1   Defining complex systems with which planning must engage in the context of ecological and economic crisis

which has operated along a continuum from the relatively ordered globalization of the new Chinese industrial cities through the intermediate state of Indian cities which combine industrial growth with extreme displaced poverty to the displaced poverty of the cities of failed states like the Congo and we see the character of global problems for planning processes.

In this context the development of effective democratic forms of planning both in the old democracies of Europe, North America and Australasia and in the enormous newer democracies of the global south – Brazil, India, South Africa for example – is of enormous significance. It is worth noting that in undemocratic but nonetheless more and more citizen right based China, the same issues are emerging in the same way. So this chapter ends with a demand for not sustainability as that is traditionally understood i.e. in complex terms as the restoration of existing equilibria, but for a carefully and collectively imagined transformation towards a desirable sustainable future.

References

Adam, B. (2004) Memory of Futures, *Kronoscope*, 4(2), pp. 297-315.
Allen, C. (2008) *Housing Market Renewal and Social Class*, Routledge, London.

Amin A. (2005) *Local Community on Trial,* Economy and Society, 34(4), pp. 612-633.

Bruton, M. and Nicholson, D. (1987) *Local Planning in Practice,* Hutchinson, London.

Castells, M. (1996) *The Rise of the Network Society,* Blackwell, Oxford.

Castells, M. (1997) *The Power of Identity,* Blackwell, Oxford.

Castells, M. (1998) *End of Millennium,* Blackwell, Oxford.

Cilliers, P. (2001) Boundaries, Hierarchies and Networks in Complex Systems, *International Journal of Innovation Management,* 5(2), pp. 135-147.

Crouch, C. (2000) *Coping with Postdemocracy,* Fabian Society, London.

Davies, J.G. (1972) *The Evangelistic Bureaucrat,* Tavistock, London.

Gans, H. (1962) *The Urban Villagers,* Free Press of Glencoe, New York.

Gerrits, L. (2008) *The Gentle Art of Coevolution,* Erasmus University, Rotterdam.

Hall, P. (1980) *Great Planning Disasters,* University of California Press, Berkeley, Los Angeles, London.

Hargadon, J. and Plsek, P. (2004) Complexity and Health Workforce, JLI Working Paper 6-2.

Imrie, R. and Raco, M. (eds) (2003) *New Labour, Community and Urban Policy,* Policy Press, Bristol.

Innes, J.E. and Booher, D.E. (1999) Metropolitan Development as Complex System, *Economic Development Quarterly,* 13(2), pp. 141-56.

Jacobs, J. (1961) *The Death and Life of Great American Cities,* Jonathan Cape, London.

Khalil, E.L. and Boulding, K.E. (eds) (1996) *Evolution, Order and Complexity,* Routledge, London.

Lefebvre, H. (2003 [1970]) *The Urban Revolution,* University of Minnesota Press, Minneapolis.

Maurin, E. (2006) 'Restricted Complexity, Ge.neral Complexity' at: http://cogprints.org/5217/1/Morin.pdf

Nelson, J.I. (1995) *Post-Industrial Capitalism,* Sage, London.

Novy, A. and Leubolt, B. (2005) *Participatory budgeting in Porto Alegre: Social innovation and the dialectical relationship of state and civil society,* Urban Studies, 42(11), pp. 2023-2036.

Ragin, C. (2000) *Fuzzy Set Social Science,* University of Chicago Press, Chicago.

Rittel, H. and Webber, M. (1973) Dilemmas in a General Theory of Planning, *Policy Sciences,* 4, pp. 155-159.

Skeffington Report (1969) *People and Plannng: Report of the Committee on Public Participation in Planning,* HMSO, London.

Smith, J. and Jenks, C. (2006) *Qualitative Complexity,* Routledge, London.

Smith, M.P. (2001) *Transnational Urbanism: Locating Globalization,* Blackwell, Malden.

Zeleny, M. (1996) On the Social Nature of Autopoietic Systems, in: E.L. Khalil and K.E. Boulding (eds) (1996) *Evolution, Order and Complexity,* Routledge, London, pp. 122-143.

PART III
Assemblage and a Relational
Attitude to Planning

Chapter 12

A Different View of Relational Complexity. Imagining Places through the Deleuzean Social Cartography

Valeria Monno[1]

This chapter discusses the concept of relational complexity as a crucial interpretative framework enabling relational/collaborative planning to produce alternative spatial and governance imaginations. The chapter begins by describing the relational planning code, specifically its point of view on agents, time and space, knowledge and the 'proper' processes through which managing the multiple relationships shaping places in order to discover new ways to live together in a city or neighbourhood. Then, it contrasts the relational complexity perspective with a Deleuzian understanding of the multiple dynamics shaping places in order to explore its potentialities in freeing creative energies by avoiding the reproduction of existing oppression and marginalization. Such exploration is carried out by mapping the social cartography of one of the many governance processes inspired by the relational complexity which, despite being considered a success, failed at imagining alternative urban developments and reproduced existing exclusions. Finally, besides highlighting some crucial weaknesses underlying the relational perspective, the chapter suggests that a Deleuzean understanding of complexity could help planning to learn from contextual and dynamic features of an unknown complexity and experiment with forms of knowing and acting, learning and imagining, taking into account the many injustices and power games emerging in the making of the city.

12.1 Planning entrapped imaginations

In urban planning, imagination has always played a relevant role as tangible representations of a desired perfect future. At the beginning, urban planners' imaginations were translated into a utopian urban form embedding values and techniques to be used to modernize the unjust geographies of cities. Post-modernist critiques have shown the illusiveness of utopian physical images since

---

1   Valeria Monno (PhD) is Assistant Professor in Urban and Regional Planning at the Polytechnic of Bari (Italy).

they unavoidably impose and fix specific space and social order (Rodwin, 1981; Harvey, 1996) thus reproducing existing injustices. As David Harvey (1996: 284) suggests: "to produce one dominant cartographic image out of all this multiplicity" [in cities] is a power-laden act of domination. It is to force a singular discursive representational exercise upon multiple cartographies, to suppress difference and to establish a homogeneity of representation."

By the 1990s, as a result of the inadequacy of physical planning in managing the postmodern fragmented city, urban imagination had been reconceived as a democratic, plural process with fairly strong links to spatial constructions. It could be termed "utopia in becoming" (Sandercock, 1998); this substituted the modernist physical image with a political progressive project which realized itself in its making. "From this perspective any emancipatory politics calls for a living Utopianism of process as opposed to the dead Utopianism of spatialized urban form" (Harvey, 1996: 436).

By combining a relational understanding of the complex dynamics shaping the quality of places (Massey, 1994; 2005; Amin and Thrift, 2002) with the ideal of collaborative strategy-making developing through governance processes (Healey, 1997; 2006), the relational planning approach (Healey, 2007; Albrechts, 2008) seemed to provide planners with a robust theory of planning as a living utopianism of process. In a fragmented society, a planning approach with an appreciation of "relational complexity" shaping places would enable planning to democratically deal with multiple time-spaces, diverse stakeholders and their manifold perspectives in order to produce spatial and governance imaginations able to reduce oppressions and exclusions.

In fact, within a relational complexity perspective a place-particular social and physical geography is seen as a double creation (Healey, 2006). On the one hand, in a fragmented society, places are anything but "meeting places", nodes of a social life which is made out of entities, micro and macro contingent and institutionalized whose dialectical relationships shape and develop at many different spatial scales and timescales through asymmetric, power-filled, fluid and changeable social networks and flows (Amin, 2009). A place, rather than being an area with boundaries around, is a node, a "meeting place" of changeable and fluid networks and flows in a specific moment and thus characterized by a specific power geometry (Massey, 1994; 2005).

On the other hand, a relational complexity perspective conceives places as consciously produced by collective action. When we deal with complexity in the social and human domain we cannot escape the moment of choice (Heylighen et al., 2006: 15). After all, "complexity means being forced to select; being forced to select means contingency; and contingency means risk" (Luhmann, 1995: 25). Thus, places can be understood as part of a selective effort of collective imagination aimed at reshaping the qualities of places.

Changing the quality of a place implies developing a politics which encounters the actors who populate the multiple networks that any place is embroiled in; this is in order to transform their relationships and related unjust power geometries though a strategy making activity. In a network society, imagining a different place quality with an appreciation of relational complexity is not a matter of producing a physical design. It is about combining an appreciation of the open, dynamic, multiple and emergent nature of social relations with some degree of stabilizing force (Healey, 2006). For this purpose, a collaborative mode of governance has to be developed in order to recognize the complex interrelations between place qualities and multiple space-time relational dynamics and allow the transformation of well-established, unjust power geometries.

Collaborative/deliberative governance processes offer egalitarian arenas (Fung, 2005) in which to manage the relational complexity and associated tensions between One and multiple. Multiple stories, trajectories and geometries of power which shape places can be intercepted in them, reproduced as discursive struggles, and changed through persuasive argumentations. Arguing in collaborative arenas always generates a profound change in knowledge frameworks and their underlying cultural conceptions, systems of understanding and meaning (Healey, 2004; Schön and Rein, 1994).

Strategy-making is a crucial activity in balancing the emergent nature of social relationships with some degree of stabilizing force. It is a highly selective activity aimed at focusing on the distinctive histories and geographies of the relational dynamics of a particular place and identifying just those issues requiring collective attention (Healey, 2006: 542). It aims to mobilize and then filter only those concepts of spatial organization (strategic frames) having sufficient allocative, authoritative and imaginative force to shape both the materialities and identities of particular places and the networks which transect and give value to them (Healey, 2006: 527). The collaborative articulation and filtering of the multiple imaginations transecting a place in a shared vision push actors to reframe their knowledge frameworks, cultural conceptions, systems of understanding and meaning.

Table 12.1   The code of the relational planning approach

Relational complexity	Actors Networks and webs	Inclusion	Mobilizing	Filtering	Balance

Thus, a relational strategy-making activity not only captures a place relational complexity, but also changes established and dynamic relations among actors and the relationships between the actors and places. It does so by forcing actors, each involved with his/her own horizons and spatial imaginations, to collaboratively pay attention to place qualities and imagine, create, shape, nurture and sustain them. Strategy-making and change are indeed inescapably linked (Davoudi and Strange, 2009). The inclusive and consensual feature of the process prevents the strategy from remaining a mere utopia. In this way, "'permanences' are created in the dynamic relational dialectics of urban life" (Healey, 2002: 519).

However, contrary to all expectations, the relational planning perspective seems in practice to reproduce the well-established physicalist urban imagination exclusions and oppressions rather than freeing transformative creative energies (Healey, 2006; 2009). Faced with this evidence, relational planners have started to wonder "if the collaborative enterprise is an "impossible venture", destined to drop back into just the kind of oppressive and exclusionary practices for which past planning endeavours have been so much criticized" (Healey, 2006: 526) They wonder how it could be possible to think of new prospects for developing spatial and governance imaginations which are based on a different way of seeing the relational complexity in order to arrive at a kind of perspective synthesis or which to base collective action. The challenge is to push the concept of 'relational complexity' further (Healey, 2006).

In fact, as Hillier argues (2007: 36), such a concept "whilst recognizing the interconnections of people and place, of activities and territories remains a nodal network view, in which the network itself becomes an actor; a view in which a place is a product. [...] In the face of the dynamic social complexity the relational approach provides a conceptualization of spatial planning as provider of strategic frames of reference within which a balance can be struck between what can be fixed and what can be left to emerge."

In what follows, this chapter takes up the challenge to push the relational complexity concept further. Yet, contrary to the usual criticisms it does not debate this issue by focusing on the limits of deliberative democracy (Flyvbjerg, 1998; Mouffe, 2005; Purcell, 2009; Swyngedouw, 2008). Analogously, it does not try to reflect on it from a procedural point of view. In this chapter which questions relational complexity, pushing it further implies challenging it by adopting other and different conceptualizations of social complexity. The Deleuzean way of thinking and commitment to conceptualizing the possibilities that life holds open for us outside of any dualism (Deleuze and Parnet, 1977: vii) is the theoretical background on which basis the chapter challenges the concept of relational complexity as a proper way of interpreting and thus managing the quality of places in practice.

12.2 A Deleuzian understanding of the relationality of places

> What distinguishes the map from the tracing is that it is entirely oriented toward an experimentation in contact with the real. The map does not reproduce an unconscious closed in upon itself; it constructs the unconscious.... The map is open and connectable in all of its dimensions; it is detachable, reversible, susceptible to constant modification....
>
> A map has multiple entryways, as opposed to the tracing, which always comes back "to the same." (Deleuze and Guattari, 1987. 3-25).

Reading Deleuze as a planner, despite his obscure and esoteric language articulated around key concepts which defy any systematized knowledge, can be a fascinating challenge since it deals with a question which is at the base of any planning endeavour: "how might we live differently in a city or neighbourhood?"

In a world that holds banality as a virtue and originality a disease, Deleuze's engagement with the question "how might one live?" challenges us to think about what other possibilities life holds open for us and how we might think about things in ways that would open up new areas of life (May 2005: 3).

For him, thinking about the possibilities that life holds open for us implied thinking the unthinkable (Deleuze and Parnet, 1996): thinking out of the codes to create a constellation of concepts functioning as a toolbox and enabling the encounter and experimentation of new possibilities of living together. However, Deleuze never said how one should live, nor did he explain which is the best way to get from here to there. In fact Deleuze always fought against "words of order" or codes which discipline thought and transform it into a new order.

He does not provide us either with a political program or normative rules (Patton, 2007). Instead his theory of creation rather than of discovery (May, 2005) offers us a conceptual cartography oriented not so much at explaining the true nature of things, but to knowing reality through its dynamics and not within the framework of dominant codes.

Difference seen as a process of variation of tension, time redefined as non-linear but evolving through becomings or turning points which shape a rhizomatic (nonarborescent or nonhierarchical) space, the individual redefined as multiplicity and the multiplicity of thought intended as a qualitative rather than quantitative heterogeneity were some of the pillars at the basis of a search oriented at reinterpreting social dynamics and change.

In Deleuze's engagement with Guattari's thinking, a constellation of concepts were created to inquire into the dynamics of multitude – or as Parent (Deleuze and Parnet, 1996) defines it 'an active pluralism'- out of any dualism one/many individual/collective resistance/dominion. Multitude, multiplicity, assemblage and becoming are some of the concepts on which this chapter focuses on.

The concept of "multitude was created precisely in order to escape the abstract opposition between the multiple and the one, to escape dialectics, to succeed in conceiving the multiple in the pure state, to cease treating it as a numerical fragment of a lost Unity or Totality or as the organic element of a Unity or Totality yet to come, and instead distinguish between different types of multiplicity" (Deleuze and Guattari, 1987: 32).

In fact from their point of view a multiplicity is not definable as a determinate substance or subject or as the form which determines it or the processes and the functions it fulfils. "A multiplicity has neither subject nor object, only determinations, magnitudes, and dimensions that cannot increase in number without the multiplicity changing in nature (the laws of combination therefore increase in number as the multiplicity grows)" (Deleuze and Guattari, 1987: 8). "An assemblage is precisely this increase in the dimensions of a multiplicity that necessarily changes in nature as it expands its connections" (Deleuze and Guattari, 1987: 8).

Specifically an assemblage is a multiplicity which is made up of many heterogeneous human and non-human agents which establishes liaisons, relations between them. It links a material content (passions, actions, bodies) and enunciations (laws, plans, statements) in a nonlinear relation (Deleuze and Guattari, 1987). A multiplicity evolves through extensive relations which modulate its movement and rest, speed and slowness, and intensive relations which represent an agent capacity to affect and be affected since any agent is a "degree of power" (a capacity to affect) (Deleuze and Guattari, 1987). The first kind of relations maintains the multiplicity in existence as the same thing. The second type of relations, instead, produces changes and transformations.

Thus, within an assemblage "it is never filiations which are important, but alliances, alloys; these are not successions, lines of descent, but contagions, epidemics, the wind" (Deleuze and Parnet, 1977: 69). The reciprocal movement among forces which operate inside and between different assemblages determine their being molar/disciplining or molecular/(out of the established order). There is no single central governing power in an assemblage, nor an equally-distributed power, but rather there is power acting as a field of forces or as plurality in transformation (McFarlane, 2009).

From Deleuze and Guattari's perspective, an assemblage can be molecular (transformative) or molar (disciplining) depending on the kinds of prevailing line/force tracing it. In fact, "the 'line', as opposed to the 'point' is a dynamic element. A line does not go from a point to another, but passes between the points, ceaselessly bifurcating and diverging" (Deleuze and Parnet, 1977: vii). The line is a true becoming, a turning point between the past and future, always silently working. As such, a line belongs to geography since it signifies orientation, direction, entry and exit. In an assemblage the molar lines trace out a disciplining order, the molecular ones instead operate by fracturing the disciplined order. Finally, a line of flight represents the transgression which opens up to a new order. A line of flight is a true becoming-other, it is a force which changes the relationships between the molar and molecular. The multitude evolves as an interplay between these two assemblages and through becomings (turning points) and events which break down and change the force between minor and molar in a rhizomatic way.

It is only by mapping the interplay of the lines that we are that social complexity can be understood. For this purpose, Deleuze localizes the map, the cartography of the social in the middle of things (rhizoma) since the interplay among lines there can generate new possibilities of living together (Fuglsang, Sorensen, 2006). For him, mapping "is not a matter of searching for an origin, but of evaluating displacements. Every map is a redistribution of impasses and breakthroughs, of thresholds and enclosures, which necessarily go from bottom to top" (Deleuze 1997: 61). As Gatens maintains (2000: 64) in Deleuze and Guattari's conception, a map "is the expression of a shifting ground between alternatives rather than the representation of a true reality." In other words, mapping is "no longer an unconscious of commemoration but one of mobilization" (Deleuze 1997: 61).

Deleuze's cartographic approach enriches the geography of tracing lines by including within it "the space of possibility, what could be, as a crucial dimension of what is or what was. It brings crossroads – places where other choices might be made, other paths taken – out of the shadow of deterministic analytics. It brings alternatives within closer reach" (Bihel and Locke, 2010: 323). The geography is a means of "wresting history from itself in order to discover becomings that do not belong to history even if they fall back into it" (Deleuze and Guattari, 1987: 96 cited in Armstrong, 2002: 47). If the present is what we are, Deleuze and Guattari explain, then "the actual is not what we are but, rather, what we become, what we are in the process of becoming [...] our becoming-other" (Deleuze and Guattari, 1994: 112).

As a shifting ground between alternatives, the cartography of the social opens up the possibility to an unusual voyage into the exploration of the quality of places in relation to governance processes and the production of alternative urban and spatial imaginations. Instead of focusing on the quality of places as a node crossed by a set of actors and relationships, it redefines places as maps located in the middle of an evolving cartography (Table 12.2) in which the actors become assemblages or composite development which exchange agents, ideas, knowledge, practices, materials and resources. Here, actors' relationships are replaced by the interplay among forces and lines and the agency does not belong to each member of the assemblage, but to the groupings themselves: the milieu, or specific arrangement of things, through which forces and trajectories inhere and transform (Bennett, 2005; McFairlane, 2009).

Table 12.2   Differences between the relational and social cartography

Complexity	Relational / places as node Focus on actors and flows an	Assemblage / places as assemblage Focus on movement and lines
Actors	*Autonomous agents – Mental states*	*Components – potentials*
Space	*Structured – relational flows*	*Rhizomatic – unstructured movement*
Dynamic	*Cooperation – conflict Inclusion – exclusion*	*mix molar- molecular- lines of flights*

Complexity	Relational / places as node Focus on actors and flows an	Assemblage / places as assemblage Focus on movement and lines
Relations	*(PERSUASIVE) Discursive – Argumentation*	*(AFFECTIVE) Interplay among and Intensive (material) – extensive (expressive)*
Change	*Linear time – Equilibrium*	*Becoming – Events*
Know-ledge	*Asset – beyond what is known Convergence/selectivity*	*Change of learning – knowing beyond what is taken to be the known*
Power	*Concentred and diffused*	*Diffusing and concentring*

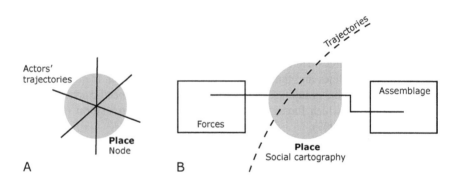

Figure 12.1   A) Place as a node B) Place as a map

Thus, at the risk of trivializing the Deleuzean thinking, in the following paragraphs I use the social cartography to analyse one the many governance processes which by following the relational complexity perspective excluded alternative spatial and governance imagination. The map – meaning the social cartography of a place – is indented as a tool to interrogate and challenge in practice the presumed suitability of the concept of relational complexity to interpret the quality of places and its associated planning code as a proper way of imagining different, more just and democratic urban developments.

12.3 A different view of the production of urban imaginations: the social cartography of Enziteto

The episode which I am going to narrate occurred in Bari, a quite wealthy and modern medium-sized city in Southern Italy, between 2004 and 2006. During this time a relational style of governance in urban policy-making was emerging to carry out what at the time was defined as the "Barese Spring" or the Apulian "Gentle Revolution". Both these slogans indicated a diffused need and desire to change a top-down style of urban policy-making into a more collaborative and inclusive way of governance inspired by values of social, economic and environmental justice. This relational and inclusive governance model had gained a prominent position in Italy since, on the one hand, it made visible citizens' claims giving them a "formal" place in decision-making processes and, on the other hand, emphasized a conception of public administration as collective actor and impartial enabler of social mobilization, coordinator of different actions and efficient financing machine of formal policies and programme processes (Governa, Saccomanno, 2004).

During that period, for the first time in this city, several women living in a deprived neighbourhood called "Enziteto" overtly challenged the logic of the top-down and entrepreneurial local city making. These women transformed their participation in TSEO (Territorial System for Equal Opportunities), an EU-Equal Initiative funded project aimed at including them in the labour market, into a political action challenging power relationships producing Enziteto as one of the several urban ghettos necessary to the opulent development of the city. Enziteto, which up to that point had been seen as an amorphous place, turned into being an unusual coalescing of forces that produced something like a bottleneck, a point of fusion, or a moment of joy.

Although the "Enziteto Women" (EW) were taken as one of the symbols of 'Barese Spring' and the Apulian 'Gentle Revolution' by the two left wing coalitions, their spatial and urban imaginations never punctured the process of reimagining the city. As soon as the reformist change was stabilized this group of women was forgotten and thrown away in the garbage can called failure.

The story of Enziteto during the period 2004-2006 is a critical reflection on my active involvement in the EW group as a researcher and sometime as an activist. It draws on my work diary in which were noted working notes reporting my own reflections on these women's ongoing action; protocols of interviews which I carried out at different times with the aim of tracing the evolution of these women's way of thinking and acting, and accounts of my participant observation of informal and formal meetings with public officials. It is also based on different official CD-ROMs and other documents which were produced by these women to testify their actions to the EU-Equal Initiative, occasional documentaries made by these women to document their active engagement in changing the Enziteto everyday life, and local newspaper articles and TV shows reporting or debating the Enziteto case during those two years.

Following Table 12.2, I describe the governance process through the social cartography of Enziteto. This is localized within the interplay of two assemblages shaping this neighbourhood evolution: namely the women and governance. Each assemblage is populated by different metamorphic agents kept together by specific and changing microphysics of knowledge/power which define its content and expression. The map evolves through three trajectories of thinking and action of varying length, shape and duration: the women's line of flight, women within governance, and governance without women. Each trajectory evolution is described by focusing on:

- Transformations of its components (actors, technologies and typologies of social action);
- Use of different typologies of relationships (extensive/intensive);
- Interplay among forces which operate inside and between different assemblages (molar-control over individuals and collective space; molecular-transformation; lines of flight- radical change);
- Interplay between creative energies and different ways of knowing and imagining.

The passage (becoming) from one trajectory to another signals a change in the quality of an assemblage in terms of agents, microphysics of knowledge/power, intensive and extensive reciprocal relationships.

12.4 Trajectories: powers and desires

A crack in the silence: the Women's lines of flights

The TSEO project started in 2002 in Enziteto. At its conception only a few women living in the neighbourhood joined it. It was seen as another futile promise of getting a job. But in less than one year the women's participation in the daily TSEO afternoon meetings increased quickly and TSEO was transformed into a multiform space of action aimed at challenging and undoing what Ranciere (2004) calls "the partition of the sensible": the distribution of places and roles, and the systems of procedures for legitimizing this distribution.

On the one hand, the daily TSEO meetings represented a public space in which for the first time these women could publicly tell their stories marked by violence, loneliness and oppression and collectively try to (re)make sense of their lives. Here, these powerless women could create acts, language, and symbols countering and destabilizing the unwritten rules which produced their everyday oppression and therefore search for alternative ways of dealing with their everyday problems.

On the other hand, these women's daily spontaneous trips to the TSEO meetings was lived as a performative act of rebellion which traced out the socio-political silence permeating everyday life in Enziteto and arrested "the system inertia"

(Drexler, 2007). Their moving bodies transformed the silence into a spontaneous action which disordered the established power geometries and showed that another world was possible. Their meetings and movements asked: Whose city is it? What counts as social justice in our city? What about our right to have a decent living environment? What can be done to change Enziteto?

Other forms of symbolic collective action were organized and the inertia of that desolate place was replaced by street parties and feasts, some of them carried out in front of the local criminal bosses' houses, despite the fact that the local criminality had threatened the EW. The EW also produced plays and movies to publically represent their everyday lives and participated in seminars and conferences in order to narrate their suffering and desire to change the whole city. The passive participation of a small group of women in a participative project had been changed into an affective political space of action calling for a radical redefinition of the practices of distribution of injustice at the urban level.

Between 2004 and 2005 the Municipal and Regional Governments' electoral campaigns intersected the Enziteto Women's flights. The two competing left-wing coalitions took the Enziteto Women as the symbol of their commitment to democratic change. As the leader of the left wing coalition competing for the Regional Government electoral campaign affirmed: "There are no exogenous solutions to regenerating a deprived neighbourhood," only citizens like "EW with their brave stories can lead us to salvation" (TV talk show, Il Graffio, April 2005). The alliance among the EW and the two left-wing coalitions had initiated an era of a more just urban and regional development based on participatory governance which made credible the dream of starting the "Barese Spring" and the regional "Gentle Revolution".

A new hope to connect women's flights with a desire for governance had been created.

Women within governance. Encountering imagination

During the Municipal and Regional Governments' electoral campaigns, the EW's involvement in the new participatory governance meant participating in the construction of more democratic and just imaginations on urban development. The two left-wing coalitions both formally and informally asked the EW to construct, on the one hand, a new alliance among citizens, local planners and intellectuals interested in sketching participative urban developments and, on the other hand, a networked alliance among the left-wing coalition competing for the Regional Government and groups of active citizens living in the most deprived neighbourhoods of the five provinces of the Apulia Region.

Although planners, intellectuals and politicians conceived the women's participation as an occasion to transform their "creative activities" into rational and understandable ideas to be negotiated within governance processes, the EW transformed the two experiments into something else.

The former aimed at producing a participative rehabilitation plan and a regeneration scenario for Enziteto. From being a usual exercise of listening to local needs and knowledge the EW's participation in the rehabilitation plan became an active "walking and asking" of women, citizens, students and researchers throughout the neighbourhood which aimed at rewriting the story of that place as a contested space. Instead of considering knowledge as a sort of passive asset which is supposed to be crystallized in some people or place and waiting to be reawakened, represented and reorganized, it was considered as an active resource which could be contingently made and remade, manipulated and changed through the active transformation of a place. Besides indicating different rehabilitation actions the plan constructed a way of conceiving participation as the emergence of a new political subject within the established order challenging the places and roles assigned to people.

Analogously, since the scenario-building experiments appeared to the women as abstract exercises with no connection with their everyday lives, it was converted into an effort aimed at elaborating an alternative conception of what a democratic future urban development should be. Against the "tyranny" of participatory tools (Khotary, 2001) and the selective search for shared strategic frames, the EW opposed a concept of urban future as path (Figure 12.1) connecting and developing in the middle of a plurality of activities which transgress physical boundaries, dominant visions of the world and well-established ways of collective action.

For these women the ability of imagining another world could not be detached from the space of political action which was flourishing around and because of them. It could be said, by paraphrasing Gouldner (1970: 491), that the space of action represented a sort of necessary middle ground which allows those who wanted to change their praxes to move beyond the categories which have defined them and be able to imagine a life at the same time lived and not yet lived. In fact, acting, "making experience in this space by acting in the present with a critical memory" (Personal interview) gave these women a chance to experience new ways of linking reality and possibility and to reinterpret their experience through the re- and de-construction of their knowledge in a way which made them able to face practical problems by challenging and changing relations and power geometries which shaped their lives.

The "network" experiment evoked the possibility of breaking the social and physical boundaries which entrapped these women in Enziteto. However, the network idea as connector of nodes gave these women the impression that it was anything but an empty signifier. Despite repositioning Enziteto in other flows and webs of relationships, the kind of nodes and connections and the network purpose needed to be spelled out. By reflecting on their activities, the EW rethought the network as an open text whose entry points would be different social change perspectives. In fact, during the EW's group activities at least two different conceptions of social change had already emerged.

Some women were strongly convinced that "even an individual human being can change the world" (personal interview). Others felt that "stories count only if they converge in some form of social organization" (Personal interview). Rather than being alternative solutions and opting for one of them, these two conceptions had represented options of action allowing differences and boundaries among values and norms to be deconstructed, re-imagined and acted upon. Having defined their project the women started travelling in order to build the network.

The hope to construct a shared imagination started to be shackled by the EW's critical engagement.

Governance without women. Balancing between emergence and hegemony

At the beginning of 2006, when the EW's flights had invaded the city as an alternative politics of place, the two left-wing coalitions which had won the Municipal and Regional Governments' electoral campaign defined new rules of governance in order to stabilize the change. Strategic plans and urban regeneration programs would enact the gentle revolution in urban planning.

This required disciplining and scaling out once and for all the creative role played by the EW to one of the many activist groups or actors having specific/ local claims. Yet, the EW did not see themselves as actors acting on the basis of rational and calculative political behaviour, or as an emerging social movement which systematically faced oppressive forces. They just wanted to be considered as citizens equal to other citizens of Bari and be free to act as autonomous political subjects in order to reach this goal. The two left-wing coalitions which had always controlled the EW's transgressive actions through formal and informal communication, started to delegitimize the EW's work and restrict their field of action to a social, care-oriented commitment.

The rehabilitation plan regeneration scenarios were quickly dismissed and forgotten by the Municipal Government. Similarly, the EW's perspective on the networks soon clashed with the hegemonic reformist project of the Regional Government. As soon as the five periphery networks began to materialize, different regional councillors explained to these women that the regeneration of five peripheries was "a profoundly unjust initiative, since it privileged a few" and that "a deprived neighbourhood should be conceptualized as a mental state rather than a material one, which ought to be changed by each individual living in an urban periphery."

The governance rules fractured the group. A few women accepted the rules of governance thinking in order to exert a stronger influence on decision-making processes. However, their involvement never achieved any significant results. Others, although desiring to collaborate with public institutions, decided not to exchange their autonomy and their own way of connecting, thinking and acting with a promise of inclusion in a confusing world of argumentations and vague promises. Accepting involvement in governance processes would implicitly erase the transformative and political dimension of their action. They chose to become 'minoritian' meaning the ability to preserve their potential to transform affects beliefs and political sensibilities. Another group came back home with a feeling of profound distrust in public institutions.

As a result, the EW was excluded from governance processes as the value of the revolution that had been initiated was not recognized. When the TSEO project ended and its meeting point was closed, these women were forgotten by local governments and thrown in the garbage can called failure. Nowadays Enziteto has some of its public building rehabilitated, its street' names evoke joy, hope and freedom. Many regeneration programmes have improved life in many other deprived neighbourhoods. However everyday life in Enziteto is much worse than before despite the proliferation of formal and informal governance processes aimed at producing more democratic and just spatial and governance imaginations.

12.5 The silence of the relational complexity

> The end of the common world has come when it is seen only under one aspect and is permitted to present itself in only one perspective. (Arendt, 1958: 57)

The Deleuzean analysis of the EW story highlights some crucial weaknesses underlying the concept of relational complexity. In what follows I focus only on those which are directly connected to the construction of new spatial and governance imaginations.

Where is geography? Actors vs political subjects

Although the local governments tried to include the women as an "actor" inhabiting one of the many webs and networks transecting a place, they never did see these women's activities as geographies of resistance and change. In the attempt to manage the relational complexity, by following Deleuze and Guattuari, it could be said that the governance assemblage looked at the history of Enziteto but missed its geography.

In the case of Enziteto such a geography was inseparable from the women's moving bodies and their affective and symbolic actions which showed and undid the distribution of places and roles, and the systems of procedures for legitimizing this distribution. Even if for a while, the Enziteto geography was inseparable by the transgressive, unstructured movement of transformation of the EW from a group of women into a political subject.

The relational perspective is blind to performative meanings. By being so focused on individual agents as social fragments claiming to be listened to and included in governance processes, it is unable to see "how space and place are implicated in the hows and whys of power in ways that do not just reproduce familiar assumptions about power being a resource that is held or transmitted – or the newer assumption that power is imminently everywhere. (Painter, in press cited in Chaturvedi and Painter: 391).

In the end, the relational perspective is again a way of seeing the world "at a distance", without people, in which the future of place is determined by larger, powerful, invisible structures (Friedmann, 2010). Its focus on the individual agency (Amin and Thrift, 2002) prevents the relational approach from seeing how diverse actors come and stick together in the face of huge risks and uncertainties; what kind of mechanisms bind actors together and what kind of problems such mechanisms introduce for achieving political goals; how actors learn from and innovate upon their activities; how collective action can become a powerful and cohesive driver of political change (Nicholls, 2009).

Furthermore, as Anderson (2008) notes, beyond 'relations' there are many forms of 'elation' such as encounter, belonging, etc. which a relational perspective cannot easily intercept. At the same time, the relations of non-connection are not properly considered. These kinds of relationships are instead relevant to understanding trends such as the durability of particular places or spaces or the disclosing of alternative space times that flicker out of existence or those space times that never came to be realized.

The omission within the relational approach of an appreciation of forces/lines which constitute social complexity, facilitates and reproduces a conception of places as something abstract whose materiality can only be physically or discursively conceived. Instead, people, individually and collectively, can make a difference not only by joining closed discursive arenas, but by tracing the established order shaping places in everyday life.

Table 12.3   Enziteto as a map: the evolution of the trajectories

Trajectories	Dynamics Forces/Lines	Action	Movement
Women's flights	*Transgressive*	*Performative Spontaneous*	*Affective* *Challenging the partition of sensible*
Women within Governance	*Molecural Minoritarian*	*Experimental Cooperative*	*Transformative Reshaping boundaries*
Governance without Women	*Molar Hegemonic Assimilation*	*Communicative*	*Stabilising operative closure*

Where is imagination? Technological dis-junctions vs creative con-junctions

The erasure of the EW's reconceptualization of participatory planning and governance tools from governance processes raises another crucial problem that concerns the adequacy of a conceptualization of places as a double creation in creating alternative spatial and governance imaginations and its focus on selectivity. Once a place is deprived from the geographies of resistance and change it is easier to interpret emergent, spontaneous ways of making the city in terms of a disturbing disorder in need of being regulated by some regime of rules. Creative energies might enrich collective imaginative efforts as long as they are transformed into a positive factor of creativity and adaptation.

Thinking of the quality of place as a double creation should facilitate managing the disorder in the city by balancing emerging and stabilizing forces. Unless creative emergent, spontaneous collective imaginations enclosed in networks and flows of social relations are mobilized and filtered through specific regime of rules, tools and technologies of government, they risk paralysing or threatening the efficacy of democratic decision-making processes. Governance and spatial imaginations enclosed in and growing up in urban democratic politic are deemed, if they want to make a difference, to chose whether to be disciplined or forgotten. Otherwise these will remain nothing more than creative energies having little influence on the processes of production of the city.

The EW's reconceptualization of participatory planning tools into a "walking and asking" activity, the redefinition of the regeneration scenarios as "a path", and the replacement of the network with a text, present the conceptualization of places as a double creation as having a central problem: the technologization of experience and the consequent self-censoring of imagination. These women's continuous critical engagement and manipulation of participatory planning tools and modes of governance show that governance and planning technologies are not dead tools, but active agents disciplining the relationships between knowing and acting, imagining and learning.

Specifically, mobilization and filtering technologies displace a subject from the action to the decision space. Such a displacement entraps the collective imagination and learning into an a-social space which first removes the knowing subject from its location thus producing 'unlocatable, and so irresponsible, knowledge claims' (Haraway 1991: 191) and next regulates it by means of a monodimensional negotiative logic.

On the one hand, mobilization and filtering processes reduce knowledge and experience to passive assets, and jeopardized knowing and learning processes in a sporadic sequence of "occasions" of reframing and selection with no connection to the ways in which we live and know the city. On the other hand, by redesigning the boundaries between experience and action, these technologies interrupt the "path" connecting imagination to learning.

Similarly, instead of freeing spatial and governance imaginations as a way of acting and critically reflecting on the future to change power geometries shaping

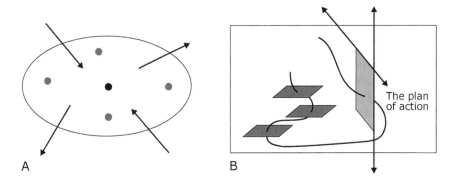

Figure 12.2   Different gathering logic A) relational B) assemblage

places, the selective search of strategic frames calms the impulse of transgression and transforms it into a search of solutions that have no connection with dwelling, this last intended as a practical coping action, which is also rooted in non-deliberate modus operandi (Monno, 2008). By erasing experience and action, mobilization and filtering processes censor alternative ways of linking, knowing and acting, imagining and learning that have the capacity to force a profound revision of the categories of the real and therefore what is possible.

Through selective strategy-making activities creative energies can be approached in terms of order/disorder and accepted/dismissed as appropriate/inappropriate, necessary/unnecessary in relation to the urgency to make "choices" as to what can be imagined. Yet, if the emergence of disorder can undermine the process of decision-making impossible to take or fragile, its erasure or suppression is an equal threat to democratization. This is because disruption is often a strategy in expanding the field of public address and an important element in broader struggles to expand and reorder the democratic public (Staehely, 2009).

Complexity or just a cybernetic order? Distribution vs Equity

Despite attempting to democratically manage the interplay between order/disorder, emergent/intentional, the relational appreciation of complexity remains entrapped within a systemic, cybernetic vision of the complexity of social relations. Complexity remains a black-box evolving through communicative relationships among fragmented autonomous agents, regulated by a negotiative logic whose democracy and 'justice' are downgraded to a set of variables of control such as inclusion/exclusion, conflict/consensus, agreement/disagreements (Figure 12.2). As a result, the relational perspective is always at risk of translating the modernist zoning into a zoning of discourse and interest and distributive advantages.

Yet the EW's refusal to join the governance assemblage and their reconceptualization of network as text highlight that once the complexity of social relations shaping the quality of places is equalled to a black-box, democracy and justice, exclusions and oppressions lose their spatiality, concreteness and urgency leaving room for more troubling issues of negotiations.

Their refusal to join the governance assemblage showed that what counts in a governance process is not only who is included or excluded within a predefined order, but also why and on what presuppositions. As Dikeç (2005: 177) explains inclusion/exclusion make sense only if they are correlated at the rules shaping the "partition of sensible" (Ranciere, 2004). In other words, the democratic theme precisely is not the inclusion of the excluded; it is the posture of the redefinition of the whole (Dikeç, 2005: 177).

In the end everything in politics turns on the distribution of spaces and things. If the EW had accepted their inclusion in formal governance processes they would have abandon the concept and practice of the common space within which inclusion/exclusion make sense only if they are correlated at the rules shaping the "partition of sensible" and thus contested in order to question the dominant distribution of spaces and things.

These women's refusal was intended to provoke the comparison among the aggregative/distributive logic underlying the governance style of urban policy-making with one opened to challenging an existing order (Figure 12.2). In the first case the borders between political and apolitical behaviours are already established. By operating in an inside/outside logic what counts as justice consists of being inside of the process, being a recognizable subject having a role and place in the process to negotiate distributive advantages. In the second case what matters is the construction of an open space of action. Here, having-equity is replaced by doing-equality (May, 2009). Equality is not made up of power relationships; it is made up of relationships between worlds.

For example, within an in/out dualistic perspective, the power of minorities is measured by 'their capacity to enter into and make themselves felt within the majority system' (Deleuze and Guattari, 1987: 471). Self-exclusion, however worrying, is usually not considered as relevant or more easily judged as a form of apolitical behaviour. And in fact, the EW's refusal to participate in governance processes was easily dismissed and forgotten as a form of inability to join the successful reformist project. Instead the women's self-exclusion from the governance assemblage was a political action aimed at blurring predefined boundaries between the political and the apolitical.

In the second case "political" is the space for the arrangement of public encounter of heterogeneous groups and individuals (Swyngedouw, 2008). In this case the power of minorities "is not measured by their capacity to enter into and make themselves felt within the majority system" (Deleuze and Guattari, 1987: 471). They carry the potential to transform the affects, beliefs and political sensibilities of a population in ways that amount to the advent of a new people (Patton, 2007). By their very nature, processes of minoritarian-becoming will always exceed or escape from the confines of any given majority (Patton, 2010: 193).

12.6 Pushing the relational complexity further

In this Chapter I have questioned the concept of relational complexity as a crucial interpretative framework which prevents planning from imagining more just spatial and governance imaginations. The comparison of this concept with a Deleuzean understanding of multiple dynamics shaping places has revealed crucial pitfalls underlying the relational complexity which constraint the transformative, imaginative potential of the relational/collaborative planning code and re-produce existing exclusions and marginalization.

Constraining factors are a methodological individualism focused on actors' interactions in the absence of a theoretical reflection of collective action which obscures place and people geographies; it focuses on decision-making processes which, by displacing knowing subjects in technological and abstract argumentative spaces, erases the experience and censors ways of connecting knowing and action, imagination and learning based on a logic transformative of people-place; a cybernetic approach towards the interplay between order/disorder, emergent/intentional which reduces inclusion and justice to variables of control of a cybernetic complexity.

At the same time, such factors "create a habitus" which, on the one hand, "gives the sensation of freedom through a diversity of imaginative and interpretative choices, but nevertheless suggests a structure that limits the imaginative and interpretative choices of our imaginations" and, on the other hand, "results in the negation of the social as a political and epistemological category and in the legitimation of dominant ideological narratives around the nature of reality" (Weiner, 2009: 150).

If seen from a Deleuzean perspective, pushing the relational complexity further in order to develop spatial and governance imagination and discourses that have the capacity to initiate a shift necessarily implies opening up the relational complexity black-box perspective and changing its associated planning code. This, in turn, as Morin suggests (1992), means coming back to consider complexity as a problem rather than a solution and making planning part of the problem which it aims to resolve: planning technologies are neither dead tools nor just disciplining government technologies, but rather active agents (Latour, 1999).

The Deleuzean perspective can help planning to take into account such an option and, specifically, to develop forms of planning able not only to manage the change but also to consider it as a location of possible new normative orientations. The cartography of the social offers the opportunity to "see", "hear", "feel" and "read" the multiple dynamics which shape places within their own context: the lived-in, struggling spaces within which small cracks as well as existing orders have their own strategic imaginations. Instead of tracing the contextual and dynamic features of an unknown complexity, an attitude of seeing, hearing, feeling the evolving social cartography of places can enable the relational approach not only to look for what is possible but also to question the categories of the real through new ways of connecting experience and action, learning and imagination.

Table 12.4   A comparison between EW ideas and the code of the relational planning approach

Relational planning	Encountering Actors/network	Including	Mobilizing	Filtering	Balancing
EW Planning code	*Encountering social cartographies*	*Texturing/ interweaving trajectories*		*Discovering Connections between Experience and Action*	
			Constructing spaces of action autonomous/ coping with crucial practical problems	*Learning and imagination*	*Equity Moving, reorienting the field of forces*
		Developing paths through projects and actions		*Tracing/ Constructing geographies of resistance and action*	

Instead of taking relational complexity as the "solution" to reconnect planning to places, a Deleuzean cartographical perspective could enable planners to learn how to reconnect planning to place in practice by directly facing three challenges: taking into account the exclusion of alternative ways of imagining the city in terms of transformation of field of forces; recognizing political subjects and alternative imaginations as emerging from the interplay of different assemblages; reconsidering the production of imagination as evolving through multiple actions implying a form of gathering through generative critique and not only a selective logic.

The EW case suggests that reconsidering places as evolving interplay among assemblages of volatile trajectories and hybrid and changing agents could enable planning to open up and enter the social complexity black-box, learn to interpret the disorder rather than control it and experiment with forms of planning in practice which do not obscure the evolving geography of resistance and change and their embedded imaginations, such as the EW idea of path and text, but which discovers new codes of planning (Table 12.4).

However, this Chapter does not invoke the assemblage as another proper way of seeing, hearing, feeling and reading the complexity shaping places. If planning cannot escape the violence that it exercises any time it assumes certain intentionalities concerning a specific spatial imagination (Swyngedouw, 2008), it can try to coexist together with the 'other' -the urban democratic politics- by means of a critical engagement with its own assumptions, by learning to challenge its own "word of order". What an assemblage perspective could do is enable the relational/collaborative planning to see how it could become more just and robust by revealing its theoretical weaknesses as well as instrumental manipulations and above all opening up its code to a profound revision of the categories of the real and therefore what is possible (Monno and Khakee, 2011).

A Deleuzean cartography is only a way to 'slow-down' the anxiety of the hegemonic dream of planning and favour the development of "functions as strategies of complexity reduction while avoiding the trap of homogenization" (Van Wezemael, 2008: 180) so that planning could continue asking how we might live together differently in a city or neighbourhood by taking into account the many injustices and power games emerging in the making of the city.

References

Amin, A. and Thrift, N. (2002) *Cities: Reimagining the Urban*, Polity Press, Sage.

Amin, A. (2009) Relational thinking, *Doreen Massey: Space, Place and Politics* http://www.sciencelive.org/component/option,com_mediadb/task,view/idstr, Open-podcast-feeds_doreen_massey_rss2_xml/Itemid, p. 97.

Anderson, B. (2008) Doreen Massey For Space (2005). In: Hubbard P., Valentine G. and Kitchin R., *Key Texts in Human Geography*, Sage, London, pp. 227-235.

Arendt, H. (1958) *The Human Condition*, Chicago: University of Chicago Press.

Armstrong, A. (2002) Agency reconfigured: Narrative continuities and connective transformations, *Contretemps*, 3, pp. 42-53.

Biehl, J. and Locke, P. (2010) Deleuze and the anthropology of becoming, *Current Anthropology*, 51(3), pp. 317- 351.

Bennett, J. (2005) The agency of assemblages and the North American blackout, *Public Culture*, 17(3), pp. 445-465.

Chaturvedi, S. Painter, J. (2007) Whose world, whose order? Spatiality, geopolitics and the limits of the world order concept, *Cooperation and Conflict*, 42(4), pp. 375–395.

Davoudi, S. and Strange, I. (eds) (2009) *Conceptions of Space and Place in Strategic. Spatial Planning.* Routledge, London.

Deleuze, G. and Guattari, F. (1987) *A Thousand Plateaus: Capitalism and Schizophrenia*, U. of Minnesota Press, Minneapolis.

Deleuze, G. and Parnet, C. (1977) *Dialogues*, Flammarion, Paris.

Deleuze, G. and Guattari, F. (1994) *What is Philosophy?*, Verso, London.

Deleuze, G. (1997) *Essays Critical and Clinical*, University of Minnesota Press, Minneapolis.

Dikeç, M. (2005) Space, politics, and the political, *Environment and Planning D*, 23(2), pp. 171-188.

Drexler, J.M. (2007) Politics improper: Iris Marion Young, Hannah Arendt, and the power of performativity, *Hypatia*, 22(4), pp. 1-15.

Flyvbjerg, B. (1998) *Rationality and Power: Democracy in Practice*, University of Chicago Press, Chicago.

Forester, J. (1989) *Planning in the Face of Power*, University of California, Berkley.

Friedmann, J. (2010) Place and place-making in cities: A global perspective, *Planning Theory and Practice*, 11(2), pp. 149-165.

Fuglsang, M., Sorensen, B.M. (eds.) (2006) *Deleuze and the Social*, Edinburgh University Press, Edinburgh.

Fung, A. (2005) Deliberation before the revolution: Toward an ethics of deliberative democracy in an unjust world, *Political Theory*, 33(2), pp. 397-419.

Gatens, M. (2000) Feminism as "password": Re-thinking the "possible" with Spinoza and Deleuze, *Hypatia*, 15(2), pp 59-75.

Gouldner, A., (1970) The coming crisis of Western sociology, Basic Books, New York.

Haraway, D. (1991) Simians, *Cyborgs and Women: The Reinvention of Nature*, Routledge, London.

Harvey, D. (1996) Justice, *Nature and the Geography of Difference*, Blackwell, Oxford.

Healey, P. (1997) *Collaborative Planning: Shaping Places in Fragmented Societies*, Macmillan, London.

Healey, P. (2002) Planning in relational space time: Responding to new Urban realities. In: Bridge G. and Watson S. (eds) *A Companion to the City*, Blackwell, Oxford, pp. 518-528.

Healey, P. (2006) Relational complexity and the imaginative power of strategic spatial planning, *European Planning Studies*, 14(4), pp. 525-546.

Healey, P. (2007) *Urban Complexity and Spatial Strategies: Towards a Relational Planning for Our Times*, Routledge, London and New York.

Heylighen, F., CIlliers, P., Gershenson, C. (2006) *Complexity and Philosophy*, http://en.scientificcommons.org/24878833.

Hillier, J. (2007) *Stretching Beyond the Horizon A Multiplanar Theory of Spatial Planning and Governance*, Ashgate, Aldershot.

Kothari, U. (2001) Power, knowledge and social control in participatory development. In: B. Cooke and U. Kothari (eds.) *Participation: The New Tyranny?*, Zed Books, London, pp. 139-152.

Latour, B. (1999) Morality and technology: the end of the means, http://www.bruno-latour.fr/articles/article/080-en.html.

Luhmann, N. (1995) *Social Systems*, Stanford University Press, Stanford.

Massey, D. (1994) *Space, Place, and Gender*, University of Minnesota Press, Minneapolis.

Massey, D. (2005) *For Space*, Sage, London.

May, T. (2005) *Gilles Deleuze: An Introduction*, Cambridge University Press, Cambridge.

May, T. (2008) *The Political Thought of Jacques Rancière: Creating Equality*, Pennsylvania State University Press, University Park.

McFarlane, C. (2007) Translocal assemblages: Space power and social movements, *Geoforum*, 40(4), pp. 561-567.

Monno, V. and Khakee, A. (2011) More of the same or just right and robust? Evaluating participatory planning. In: Hull, A., Alexander, E and Khakee, A. (eds) *Planning Evaluation*, Routledge, London.

Morin, E. (1992) From the concept of system to the paradigm of complexity, *Journal of Social and Evolutionary Systems*, 15(4), pp. 371-385.

Mouffe, C. (2005) *On The Political, Thinking in Action*, Routledge, London.

Nicholls, W. (2009) Place, networks, space: theorising the geographies of social movements, *Trans Inst Br Geogr*, 34(1), pp. 178–193.

Patton, P. (2007) Political normativity and poststructuralism: The case of Gilles Deleuze, *Vortrag ins Institutscolloquium des Philosophischen*, Institutsder Freien Universität, Berlin, November.

Patton, P. (2010) *Deleuzian Concepts: Philosophy, Colonization, Politics*, Stanford University Press, Stanford.

Purcell, M. (2009), Resisting neoliberalization: Communicative planning or counter-hegemonic movements?, *Planning Theory*, 8(2), pp. 140-165.

Ranciere, J. (1999) *Disagreement: Politics and Philosophy*, University of Minnesota Press, Minneapolis.

Ranciere, J. (2004) *The Politics of Aesthetics: The Distribution of the Sensible*, Continuum, London and New York.

Rodwin, F.L. (1981) *Cities and City Planning*, Plenum Press, New York.

Sandercock, L. (1998) *Towards Cosmopolis, Planning for Multicultural Cities*, John Wiley & Sons, New York.

Staeheli, L.A. (2009) Political geography: democracy and the disorderly public, *Progress in Human Geography*, 34(1), pp. 67-78.

Swyngedouw, E. (2008) The multiple and the one. In: Van den Brouck J., Moulaert F. and Oosterlynck S. (eds) *Empowering the Planning Fields*, Acco, Leuven, pp. 135-141.

Van Wezemael, J. (2008), The contribution of assemblage theory and minor politics for democratic network governance, *Planning Theory*, 7(2), pp. 165-185.

Weiner, E.J. (2009) Time is on our side: Rewriting the space of imagination, *Situations: Project of the Radical Imagination*, 30(1), pp. 127-150.

Chapter 13

On the Emergence of Agency in Participatory Strategic Planning

Jean Hillier and Joris E. Van Wezemael[1]

In our chapter we build on the often-elided distinction between assemblage or ensemble and *agencement* in an empirical case of participatory strategic planning in the North-East of England, in which multiple relational 'strategies' (conscious and non-conscious) were mobilized and performed. Our tracing of community involvement strategies shows that alleged 'front-loading' in regeneration planning – aiming to make planning policy-making more democratic and to empower local people by starting from what people know and really want or desire – largely failed. The network of actants involved in the strategic planning process remained a set of assemblages. Citizens, in particular, did not achieve strategic agency/*agencement*. We outline key Deleuzoguattarian terms used in the chapter, including assemblage, *agencement* and territoriality. We explain the multiple nuances of the French verb, *expérimenter*, in English translated variously as to interpret, experience or experiment. We ask how might relations between actants gather sufficient force intensities to generate strategic agency/*agencement* and eventuate change rather than simply remain as assemblages.

13.1 Introduction

Theorizations and practices of strategic spatial planning policy making and implementation have increasingly emphasized the agency of civil society in an engagement of (but not always 'with') people as 'active consumer-participant[s] in knowledge production' (Leadbeater and Miller, 2004, cited in Hinchliffe et al., 2005: 2). Civic or citizen engagement and participatory deliberation, if appropriately empathetic, egalitarian, open-minded and reason-centred (Delli Carpini et al., 2004), theoretically produce a range of positive democratic outcomes, including increasingly more active citizens (Barber, 1984), increased tolerance and empathy with the Other (Gutmann and Thompson, 1996), increased understanding

1   Jean Hillier is Professor and Associate Dean in the School of Global Studies, Social Science and Planning at the RMIT University, Melbourne. Joris E. Van Wezemael is Professor at the Socio-spatial complexity lab of the University of Freiburg; and Pensimo Management Ltd,, Switzerland.

of citizens' own needs and preferences (Chambers, 1996) and resolution of deep conflicts in democratic decisions which are 'informed, enlightened and authentic' (Gastil, 2000: 25).

Lejano (2006) highlights the importance of participatory policy-making activities being coherent not only with governance structures, but with places and with actants' everyday lives. This would suggest that policies should be fashioned and instituted in a place, using resources of that place. Lejano suggests, however, that sometimes the policy 'landscape' has to be reworked or manipulated to make the new policy work. Citizen engagement in such instances may be more akin to Arnstein's (1969) rungs of manipulation, therapy and informing (nonparticipation and tokenism) at the bottom of her ladder of citizen participation in which citizen agency is highly restricted.

In this chapter we propose a reading of citizen participation based on baroque complexity (Kwa, 2002) – 'looking down' (Law, 2004) – and Deleuzoguattarian geophilosophy. We suggest how researchers and practitioners might work more effectively with the disorderly real rather than ordered networks through an awareness of rhizomic connections, of multiplicities and how they might interconnect, and of potential becomings or actualizations, and what the pragmatics of dealing with all these might be (see Wise, 2006: 177).

We critically analyse an empirical case of citizen participation in the development of a local strategic Area Action Plan (AAP) from Newcastle-upon-Tyne in North-East England. As Deleuze and Guattari (1987: 250) advise, 'Case by case, we can tell whether the line is consistent, in other words, whether the heterogeneities [of actants] effectively function in a multiplicity of symbiosis, whether the multiplicities are effectively transformed through the becoming of a passage', or whether elements perform predominantly independently or even biotrophically.

We build on the often-elided distinction (Phillips, 2006) between *assemblage* or *ensemble* and *agencement* to demonstrate the failure of democratic policy-making – or 'front-loading' of citizen participation – in our empirical study of inner urban regeneration planning. The generation of strategic agency is vital to the transformation of an assemblage into an *agencement*. In our case, *agencement* did not emerge. Our tracing indicates that the strategic planning practitioners involved interpreted rather than experienced and/or experimented with community desires.

Our questions include:

• How have the networks evolved? What underlying mentalities, perceptions and assumptions exist and develop, with what impacts on performance?
• How do the particular networks perform citizen participation? Do they perform as assemblage/s or as *agencement*?
• Can we identify what transforms an assemblage into an *agencement*? What is it that generates strategic agency?
• What challenges and opportunities can be discerned both theoretically and practically?

We analyse how a planning project, as a particular moment in an ongoing/evolving set of relations, generates a range of subject positions and attempts to co-ordinate them into a single plan. We decentre land as the 'object' of the plan to concentrate on the performance of the 'fractional relations' (Law, 2002: 9) between elements or entities to examine how 'singular' subjects and objects are constructed.

We outline key Deleuzoguattarian terms used in the chapter, including assemblage, *agencement* and interpretation/experience/experimentation. We ask how might relations between actants gather sufficient force intensities to generate *agencement* and eventuate change, rather than simply remain as assemblages.

13.2 From assemblage to *agencement*

We outline a theoretical framework which conceptualizes the relational complexities, multiplicities and contingencies entangled in citizen participation processes. As such, we connect with a relational (rather than a Euclidean) concept of the production of place in which urban areas are viewed no longer as objectively identifiable, integrated economic and social systems, but rather as spaces of complex multiple social relations; each having their own space-time dynamics and spatial reach.

In such a view, a place is not a given. Rather, what is at stake is the manner in which it is produced and maintained by the connection of physical and mental, relational networks, and how it is performative. Therefore, a place can no longer be seen as a distinct, unitary physical entity. It is materially experienced as a significant but relatively fluid conjunction of multiple networks. The connections of those networks can be investigated in order to grasp not just their momentary fixity (represented, for instance, in a local Area Plan), but also their performativity, either as assemblage or *agencement*.

Spatial planning can be regarded as the art (or science) of spatial manipulation – the manipulation of the actualization of difference. Planning is a mediator between multiple representations of the 'good' in the continuous process of space-becoming or spacing. Thus the phenomena with which planning struggles have become 'less about territorial boundaries and states and more about connection and flow' (Law and Urry, 2003: 10).

Emphasizing connectivity, our view of the world is rhizomic (Deleuze and Guattari, 1987). The fabric of the rhizome is conjunction: 'and'. Planning officers *and* local residents *and* politicians, 'and, and, and' (Deleuze and Parnet, 2002: 9). Deleuze and Guattari (1987: 21) characterize a rhizome as connecting points to other points, bringing into play different and heterogeneous regimes of signs, composed of directions in motion, with neither a beginning nor an end, but always a middle: 'always incomplete, always in the midst of being formed' (Deleuze, 1997: 1). A rhizome is constructed by the interplay of the multiple relations which constitute its complex entity.

In order to investigate rhizomes associated with our case example, we do not ask what a thing *is* (its 'essence'), but *what it can do* (Deleuze and Guattari, 1987: 40) and *how it changes* (Patton, 2006: 27). What an entity can do refers to how it can connect/relate both materially and expressively (for instance, through language); what processes of power it performs. How it changes refers to the way connections are maintained, cut, (re-)established; whether strategic agency is actualized.

We refer to the Deleuzoguattarian conceptualization of striated space. Striated spaces are regulated, ordered and closed; spaces 'inhabited by subjects with supposed free will, but bound together by a compromise with power' (Bonta, 2001: 2). Striated spaces are classified, regulated and managed in networks which perform realignment of economic, political and socio-cultural elements (Hillier, 2007). Striated space tends to be associated with the state: 'one of the fundamental tasks of the State is to striate the space' (Deleuze and Guattari, 1987: 479). Striating space attempts to inscribe some form of stability or fixity into flux, to draw lines and situate 'locales', such as the Newcastle regeneration area, within universal co-ordinate systems, such as central government policy frames and planning legislation. Uncertainties, unpredictabilities and possibilities of variation must be codified and neutralized. As Deleuze and Guattari (1987: 494) explain, striated space is dominated by 'the requirements of long-distance vision: constancy of orientation' and 'constitution of a central perspective'. The result is a space of sites rather than of places.

Deleuze and Guattari use the term 'territory' in a metaphorical sense to depict sites of political engagement, their lines of power, practices and institutions (O'Neill and McGuirk, 2005: 285). Territorialization is a form of action on, or capture of, individual or social forces which seeks to limit or constrain their possibilities for action. It involves 'the creation of meaning in social space through the forging of coded connections and distinctions' (Brown and Lunt, 2002: 17) into some form of uniformity or consistency, such as regulations, land use development plans and so on; Deleuzoguattarian striations.

John Phillips (2006) points out that the traditional translation of Deleuze and Guattari's term *agencement* by the English term 'assemblage' is 'not a good approximation' (Phillips, 2006: 108, Van Wezemael, 2008). As Phillips indicates, there is a world of difference between the terms. Deleuze and Guattari only rarely use the French term *assemblage*, for which 'assemblage' would be the literal translation. *Assemblage* would be used to refer to, for example, disparate elements which are assembled together (such as a loose growing network of friendly neighbours and a city council). Deleuze and Guattari tend to use the words *ensemble* or *association* rather than assemblage to indicate *non-directional groups of actors*.

The term *agencement* implies agency and strategy. Deleuze (1988 [1970]) appears to have developed the notion of *agencement* from his work on Spinoza's idea of the common notion; the 'having in common' becoming a 'third body' in an event. *Agencement* thus implies an agency and immanence which assemblage does not. An *agencement*, therefore, is more than simply an assemblage. It is a process of 'agencing' (Bogue, 2007: 145-146) – an active bringing-into-existence of its own agency. In the concept of *agencement* the constituent elements intersect, fold together and transform themselves and each other (such as a 'neighbourhood' with a clear sense of itself as a political actor when local politicians propose changes in neighbourhood policing). They create and unmake territories, opening up and/or closing off possible lines of flight.

In asking 'what makes an assemblage into an *agencement*', one would investigate the relations between the entities or elements in the collective: 'in a multiplicity, what counts are not the terms or the elements, but what there is "between", the between, a set of relations which are not separable from each other' (Deleuze and Parnet, 1987: viii). Moreover, *agencements* are 'passional' compositions of desire (Deleuze and Guattari, 1987: 399). The rationality of an *agencement* does not exist without the desires which constitute it and the passions (affects) which it brings into play (Deleuze and Guattari, 1987: 399).

An *agencement* achieves vitality through its relations, but as Buchanan (2000: 120) notes, 'it also has its illnesses'. The most potent 'illness' is that of stratification. Deleuzean strata are the actualized 'striated' regulations or orderings of elements which result from processes of organizing, sorting and consolidation (Deleuze and Guattari, 1987). Over-stratification or regulation stultifies and inhibits transformation: '[w]hen positioning of any kind comes a determining first, movement comes a problematic second' (Massumi, 2002: 3).

The assemblage/*agencement*-related issues we address in our case example include:

1. What time-space realities interrelate in the (participatory) place-making?
2. What entry-points are relevant in the rhizomic processes of participation?
3. What forms of communication are associated with different agent/actant networks? What realities does this constitute?
4. What connectivities are produced? How do they relate to the generation (or not) of agencement? How does this relate to institutionalized formal planning processes?

13.3 On interpretosis and experimentation

Michel Foucault used the term *interpréter* in a specific sense; a process which involves the deployment of power. Interpretation is an evaluative and stratifying relation of force in which the interpreter is an intermediary. Foucault, then, was concerned about the power of the interpreter as intermediary, but also about the tendency for interpretation to become self-referential in that it reifies both the text and the author-principle in the figure of the interpreter and installs a central anchor-point – the authoritative interpretation – which performs as 'truth'. Such an interpretive perspective essentially involves an often unquestioned evaluative standpoint and what Foucault (2000: 310) terms 'a priori parcelling' into outcomes in which 'the work does not itself speak, but something always speaks through it' (Lambert, 2006: 14).

Deleuze and Guattari (1987: 114) claim that 'the interpretive priest, the seer, is one of the despot-god's bureaucrats' who suffers from the 'disease' of 'interpretosis', an obsessive-compulsive deciphering and categorization of hidden meaning. Whilst such categorization may confer a certain stability and order to the analysis, categories are always reductionist and limited, bounded by the socio-cultural realm to which the interpretation belongs.

We refer to Deleuze and Guattari's dicta of: 'Experiment, never interpret' (Deleuze and Parnet, 2002: 48) ['Expérimentez, n'interprétez jamais' (1977: 60)] and 'Experiment, don't signify and interpret' (Deleuze and Guattari, 1987: 139). In French, this injunction reads as 'expérimentez au lieu de signifier et d'interpréter!' (1980: 173). However, the French verb *expérimenter* signifies *both* to know from experience *and* to experiment. The noun is *expérience,* signifying both experience and experiment, defined in *Le Robert Micro* (Rey and Morvan, 2006: 524) as 'a broadening or enrichment of knowledge' (our translation).

Deleuze and Guattari (1987: 138) suggest that we 'combat the mechanisms of interpretation' through experiencing and experimentation *with* rather than interpretation *of* texts. Experiencing entails performing an encounter between the text, the speaker and the force relations in which they are entangled: an exploration of the relations and conditions of possibility between different elements.

We aim to uncover rhizomic connections, conjunctions and disjunctions between discursivities and materialities, their flows and blockages, the institutional and other structures which affect them. As Connolly (2006: 72) describes, 'it is through creative movement back and forth among experience, reflection on it, experimental observation, reflexive awareness of such experimentation, and the cautious application of specific techniques … that the most promising and dangerous possibilities emerge'.

Spatial planners often stratify as an organizing principle for discussion. There can be several 'stages' of stratification in strategic spatial planning processes. For instance, pre-public consultation, different categories or types of people may be 'identified', called into being and framed by planners; during consultation, stratification may occur geographically, by technique and so on; and stratification may also occur in the rationalization of the outputs from consultation. (See Hillier and Van Wezemael, 2008, for a detailed example of stratification processes in spatial planning.) The key to creative spatial planning practice thus lies in the power to allow group identities to establish which are not informed by some spatio-temporal subjugation to institutional power, but which afford groups the freedom to deterritorialize dominant discourses and practices to provoke a *space of possibility*; a space to experiment; a space of *agencement*.

Power operates through stratification in which social strata (often regarded by planning actants as 'us' and 'them') are created by processes of subjectification/ subjectivation and signification, underlain by a process of organization. Subjectification positions the subject through grammar, 'through the way in which it orders and positions its speakers and sets out their choices for them – they may enter into these forced, conjugated choices or be silent' (Thanem and Linstead, 2006: 46). Deleuze and Guattari (1987: 75-85; 119-134) argue that subjectification depends on language and discourse as expression.

Chains of signification invoke normative interpretations of subjectivity. The use of 'plannerspeak' – such as jargon-replete reference to statutory process – serves to order activities and command compliance. Organization performs through segmentation; the 'compartmentalization of human existence, and by extension of space ... rigidified in the modern State' (Bonta and Protevi, 2004: 139). Segmentation is binary (an either/or of us/them, is/is not, has/has not), circular (in concentric rings of 'myness' (Bonta and Protevi, 2004: 140) from home to neighbourhood to city and so on) and linear (in time and space). It is achieved through creating functions for spaces and times; coding land uses in performances of molar segmentation which process molecular energies (including local residents' desires), ordering them and draining them of power of variation. Organization, moreover, imposes chronological timescales: 'the time of the creation of possibles must be curtailed and fenced in with rigorous established procedures and deadlines' (Lazzarato, 2006: 176). As Thanem and Linstead (2006: 48) write, 'for Deleuze, organization is about order, order is about power.'

Issues which we address in our case example include:

- How do planners cope with the multiplicity and heterogeneity of truths? How do planners cope with potential new lines of change?
- Which unforeseen connections are cut back/shattered in order to (temporarily) stabilize a future project?
- How do the present and the absent relate? Are there virtual voices of those experiencing the place in the future? What role do planners play in advocating the absent?
- What knowledge/skills unfold in the participation arena? What strategies evolve and could evolve in practice? How might these relate to the formal goals of planning (system) and to community politics?

13.4 'Front-loading' spatial planning in north-east England

Our methods for data retrieval and analysis include participatory observation (one of us worked with the urban renewal team for several months), text analysis (which included the chronological reading of all available documents on the riverside development produced since 1999), field observation (at community meetings and the like), additional interviews with people who appeared to occupy powerful positions in social networks. After a first round of analysis we organized a focus group meeting where we confronted the planners with preliminary findings in order to trigger additional debate. For reasons of ethical research practice, we have anonymized respondents and removed identifiers from texts cited.

In this section we trace the practices and strategies of citizen participation in preparation of an Area Action Plan (AAP) and trace the connections that do or do not generate spaces of possibilities for *agencement* to emerge. This Plan aims at bringing about major changes in a former heavy industrial riverside area of Newcastle. The AAP will have the status of the City Council's statutory plan for future planning decisions in the area.

Strategic planning processes were initiated due to official perceptions that the riverside area was suffering from socio-economic problems that required a drastic initiative to break vicious cycles of (population, social, economic and infrastructural) decline. The key objectives of plans produced since 1999 have been to stem population decline and attract new people to the area, thus sustaining the community: 'a challenge for this Master Plan, and those who will implement it, to break this cycle of decline, to put [the area] back on the map, and to raise the profile of the place to one of real choice where people want to live, work and spend their leisure time' (LD, 2004b: 17). Plan goals include a reduction in low-demand property, increased community cohesion, and better use of green spaces (NCC, 2002: 9).

However, the framing of the process seems conscious of relational assemblages and generation of a place as it relates the evolution of the riverside area to many issues that lie both within and beyond the perimeter of the Area Action Plan. Furthermore, the intervention into the physical texture of the space clearly does not bring about the change that is hoped for. Ideally, we argue that interventions should allow all participants/actants to experience the place from many perspectives, to experience the relations between perspectives and between actants, and to experiment with stirring up striated relations (that generated a negative lock-in) to trigger the energy that may be set free when people, places, discourses and desires are connected and related anew. Thus, the space-time framing of the process is strategic and although it can be viewed as a 'given' in a certain way –it nevertheless leaves space for a pre-individual field of becoming. How do the particular networks perform citizen participation? Do they perform as assemblage or as *agencement*?

In official documents the population of the area is striated in the sense that it is given an identity and it is subjected into 'one' community. Officials describe the community as 'respectable working class' (LD, 2004c: 51). The so called evidence-based analysis (LD, 2004c), the first step in the well-defined formal planning procedure, states that '[t]he housing, population and services in the area are now in a state that is fundamentally unstable: and unsustainable beyond the short term' (LD, 2004c: 137). Trend extrapolation and evidence from this analysis make it clear that regeneration must stretch well beyond just 'patching-up' the existing situation (LD, 2004c). The report states that without radical action, the population will continue to fall; more and more dwellings on more and more estates will fail to let; yet more demolitions will take out blocks and units, leaving increasing gaps in the fabric; community services will dwindle and close; and dereliction will worsen the image and stigma of the area even further (LD, 2004c)

The regeneration of this riverside area is viewed as a tough and challenging task. The official process of regeneration commenced in 1999 and was still ongoing in 2009. The process comprises distinct phases of citizen participation which differ in terms of their major goals and 'degrees of freedom' of possibility spaces offered, but also with respect to planners' underlying mentalities, perceptions and assumptions:

1. An initial phase of capacity building during the city-wide Going for Growth regeneration initiative (1999-2002)
2. A phase of master planning, producing a set of visions for the area (January 2002-November 2004)
3. A phase of compulsory consultation on the 'Options' (September/October 2005)
4. A phase which aims at working with the community in implementation of the chosen strategy (2009).

We focus discussion on phases 2 and 3, since they aimed at more extensive citizen participation.

Table 13.1   Overview of selected participatory events

Timeframe	Project	Stated goal / achievement in Planning process	Outcome
1999 – January 2002	*Going for Growth*	'Capacity building'.	The „Network" was formed in a process of capacity building in order to support and bring together community groups who would be most affected by the *Going for Growth* plans. They have been involved in the procurement process to select a development partner for the area and engaged in work to develop an initial master plan and community consultation process.
June 2002	Residential week-end	Establish strong working relation between the preferred partner and the Network.	Strong working relation.

Timeframe	Project	Stated goal / achievement in Planning process	Outcome
September 2002	Round I Community events	Open event. Community asked to give comment on "What is good about X that they wouldn't want to lose" and "What needs to be improved in X to make it a better place to live".	Low attendance: 115 people in 5 meetings.
November 2002	Round II Community events	Discuss emerging ideas and the development framework plan.	Very low attendance.
November 2002	Discussions in Specific Areas	Discussion of impacts of local development plan prior to the development of options.	Strengthening local concerns about demolition of housing.
March 2003	Round III Community involvement	Discuss emerging thinking for initial master plan. Exhibition material shows material for initial master plan, particularly outline of early action areas.	Very mixed feedback. Attitude of community hard to tell! Hardly a view on the vision for the AAP-area. Commitment to establish working groups which concentrate on early action areas.
September – October 2005	Consultation on Preferred Options Report	Wider range of consultation techniques used. Includes ,outreach sessions' and the focus groups.	Option 3, 'Major Impact' chosen.

Two basic conditions for community involvement assumed that:

- the process must aim at participation of a *heterogeneous community* in the development of draft plans in a 'community approach', and
- it must develop a number of *visions for the development of the whole area* and not for 'isolated' sites. (drawn from LD and NCC texts)

Both the potential of heterogeneity, as well as that of developing integrated visions, open up toward a space that could allow the emergence of an *agencement*. However, the way that particular citizen participation projects were carried out indicate that the planners' *interpreted* the riverside area as a space of given sites, populated by one community, rather than *experienced* the different realities and desires of the various inhabitants and potential inhabitants, and the differential spacing connectivities of the area. Such interpretation performs striation and fixes the place as a given. It disallows experience and experimentation. This ex-ante striation pre-establishes a compromise with power both on the side of the planners and some 'representatives' of 'the' community.

Although the target is given, the actualization of a limited set of 'solutions' from the multiplicity of potential options should be developed jointly in a process of 'front-loaded' regeneration planning (NCC, 2002: 9). As we demonstrate, however, in our example 'front-loading' tended to become the rhetorical/discursive representation of 'top-loading'. Although discursively signified as front-loaded, engaged participants, local citizens were organized into particular segmented, linear, time-slots for 'consultation', the outcomes of which were then interpreted accordingly. The dominant power of the regeneration team to organize a heavily-striated plan-making process prevented experimentation and the emergence of local capacities or *agencement*. In what follows we will trace the process of participatory planning and map out the potential (or otherwise) for *agencement* to emerge.

13.5 Fields of relevance: 'the community' or multiple 'communities'?

As our theoretical approach makes clear, place emerges from the actions of multiple networks or assemblages. People with postal addresses within a particular geographical area do not automatically constitute one or *the* 'community'. They may not know each other and may have little in common besides a NE postal signifier. Furthermore, since the multiple networks often exceed the physical area of the place, relevant voices may not be found exclusively within the area. Since the regeneration process aims at transforming the area – that is, it interferes with the generative processes that produce both people and place – it is crucial to understand how they are both subjectified and signified in this instance, and how these subjectifications and significations affect potential transformation of assemblages into *agencements*.

The stated purpose of community participation in development of the AAP was described as being to:

- help build crucial relationships between different community groups in order to produce an inclusive development plan;
- involve the community in decision-making and in reviewing the content of development plans and to produce transparency so that everybody involved knows when he/she is engaged in the project;

- report on the involvement and how engagement has influenced the decisions made (LD, 2004a).

The so called 'major regeneration partner' made a commitment to 'close working with local communities' (LD, 2004a: 4) in the master planning process and beyond. According to the consultant, this should ensure that the plan is 'robust and has the broad support of the community and reflects the community's hopes and aspirations for the future' (LD, 2004a: 4). However, as our analysis will show, there is a significant gap between the rhetoric of empowerment that allegedly permits strategic agency to unfold and new trajectories to emerge, on the one hand, and the stratification of the voices into narrowly framed and manageable forms of citizen participation that discipline people, leaving power relations unchallenged, eroding sites of resistance and disabling strategic agency. The ex-ante framing of the process undermines the potentials of connections between elements in the assemblage to pick up speed and intensity and develop *agencement*.

From the start of the master planning process in early 2002 the Council's preferred regeneration partners established close collaboration with the 'Community Network', which was referred to as 'The Network'. The planners use The Network – an assemblage of local residents – as the (only) entry point for experience in the processes of participation. The Network consists of members of locally active resident associations and community groups, who are signified and subjectified as 'representatives'. It emerged and was stabilized around one specific attractor: there had been common concern about the extensive demolition plans of the *Going for Growth* initiative which brought resident groups together in order to have a stronger, united voice around the protection of people's homes from demolition. Network representatives – mostly elderly long-term residents – exemplify what planners interpret as the 'given' *core population* (LD, 2004b). The Network demonstrates a liberal-representational assemblage: representatives are formally elected (at very poorly attended meetings) so they theoretically speak for the people and represent them (at least they were interpreted in this way by the planners). The planner's entry-point made impossible the emergence of group identities not already subjugated to given sites and identities (or institutional power).

The relational place was clearly performed as an assemblage with a given identity, a given community, and pre-established relations of specific groups to specific places. The population is thus interpreted and homogenized due to the chosen procedures of civic engagement which organize the process, its significations and subjectifications. The way the assemblages evolved made it very unlikely that strategic agency might develop in the sense of the *becoming of a third body* on the basis of relating the yet unrelated and opening up a possibility space for group identities beyond subjugation. We describe the assumptions of planners as acts of interpretation, reproducing their underlying mentalities and perceptions. As planners in our focus group explained, they do not believe in a 'holy grail of community involvement'. The project involved a mere assembling of the given as interpreted, rather than an experience of and experimentation with people and groups that were not heard. Places and issues were not related. The joint process was striated into a mechanism of formal-organizational procedures, which reproduced the planner's self-image, their relation to state-power (via their control over statutory processes) all of which rendered experimentation impossible in the area as a political field.

The planners clearly fuelled processes of striation as they reinforce the given as performed along their lines of interpretation, and a virtual lack of experimentation hampered (new) dynamic relations from evolving. We can illustrate this as follows through reference to a series of texts and utterances.

Planners had little intention of performing 'inclusivity' or permitting other actants to generate strategic agency. Their discursive reference to producing an 'inclusive' plan by involving the community in decision making stabilized their own role as the experts under the planning legislation. They territorialized the process, since 'we know what is realistically deliverable, we give people a window to work within' (FG). Another team member commented, 'we steer them to our predetermined choice' (FG). Residents clearly are subjectified as people to whom both process and outcome needed to be 'sold' (FG).

The limitations of civic engagement are apparent from the stratification of the Network as 'the community' with a signified capacity that builds solely on the basis of the concern about the future of particular estates, and the selection of particular resident-based groups as the only entry point to the community. Whereas the review of consultation feedback rates and attendance at community events (LD, 2004a, 2004b) simply states that about 90% of the population should be considered as 'highly apathetic' in terms of engagement with the regeneration process, we suggest that this mentality has been performed and amplified significantly by framing and performing the public participation process as required information-gathering.

There is no concept of multiple community/ies as being more-than-one coherent entity, but less-than-many separate entities. A concept of the connection of heterogeneous relational assemblages or networks would have opened up a more dynamic perspective on the absent; especially the area's people-to-come (Deleuze, 1997). The relational topology between the planners' attitudes and assumptions towards the inhabitants of the regeneration area thus cannot accommodate the opportunity to nudge the process away from stable states and pre-given issues in the sense of disparate elements that are merely assembled. Moving to a possibility space where the degrees of freedom are higher, where community identities and subjectivities are unstable and not yet defined, and where alternative potential states can be actualized would open up towards the potential transformation of the community assemblage into *agencement*. Think of potentially agonistic relations between the experiences, hopes and aspirations of the present community/ies and potential new residents which can be mapped only in forms of experimentation beyond interpretative re-inforcing of both already-actualized relations and the planner's 'expert' role. The same can be argued if we shift our attention to conceptions of space. The planners' approach illustrates the mentality of space as a container or as a space of sites: the community interpreted as a closed network of people living within pre-designated boundaries rather than a relational network that gives rise to generative processes which eventually generate (spatially unbounded) places.

The stratification of the population into a given community can also be illustrated in the many reports of the master planning process. 'The community' is mostly addressed in the singular. This enacts a mentality of a homogeneous population with a given, fixed and stable identity. In community-participation events (see table above) no analysis of participants (by age, gender, ethnicity or neighbourhood) was made. And where different groups are mentioned, the planners connect or merge them in order to produce an 'inclusive plan'; a very different interpretation of 'inclusive' to that which we believe was intended.

Imposing 'preferred options'

Residents were absent from processes of objective-setting. In the whole succession of phases of civic engagement, subjectivation of the residents by those with power to set the objectives was a constant. Organization is about order, order is about power; the planners, as expert professionals, used their organizing power to frame the civic engagement process largely according to habit, to suit their own desires, and eventually to prevent an uncontrollable emergence of strategic agency (or as we would call it: *agencement*). The first step in this stratification strategy is a binary segmentation between professional experts versus the lay people which is performed into a powerful self-reinforcing identity-projection in the sense of 'us versus them'.

The multiple communities of the Newcastle regeneration area were thus 'consulted' in a heavily striated space, rather than supported to develop capacities, become fully-engaged in the plan-making network and/or to achieve strategic agency. Clearly planners perceived themselves as approaching plan-making 'differently' to the area's residents. In a central perspective that performs organization local residents were perceived as 'not singing from the same hymn sheet' (FG). They were rendered irrelevant, impossible, and repressed. Since 'some people won't engage' and have 'entrenched views' which are 'out of touch with reality' (FG), the planners saw the 'need to sell them the wider product' (FG). Communication thus tended to be one-way, *from* planning officers who regarded their task as being to get 'this person on that street [to] understand what we're trying to communicate to them' (FG). Thus, it is no surprise that the 'options' for the mandatory 'Preferred Options Report' were technically produced in the planning office and include alternatives which are out of scope with regard to the established objectives for regeneration of the wider area. Thus the 'options' were not 'preferred' since they could not be linked to alternative 'visions' for the area derived from citizen participation.

All three Options offered for consultation reflect more or less of the same. The area's 'problems' have been organized in such a way that only certain 'solutions' or actions are likely to occur (Shields, 1996). The regeneration team planners, however, were unrepentant about what Habermas (1970) would term their systematic distortion of communication. In our attempt to trace underlying rationales and mentalities behind such actions, focus group participants discussed the questions 'how honest should we be? Should we have explained to people what the Major option entailed?' (FG) and agreed that honesty would not have been the best policy in this instance for reasons including a belief that:

> the Minor impacts won't do the job, so it was unacceptable, even if it had been chosen;
> the Minor option wasn't an option;
> If the Minor option had been chosen, there would be no program (FG).

The regeneration team used its professional expertise to determine the technically-best outcome for the AAP area. Both their reluctance to experiment and allow for the emergence of strategic agency which they would not control, and their performing a demarcation line between experts (with their 'true' knowledge) and lay people (with their 'entrenched views') added to their obvious goal to stay in their comfort zone and thus also 'in control'. The jargon-replete talk about participation is a resource for the pursuit of exactly this aim. Planners used their statutory power to organize the Options in favour of a particular outcome. They used techniques of qualculation to represent and justify the Options, retaining tight control over territorialization of the spaces involved. Our case example clearly supports Fung's (2006: 69) claim that 'many (perhaps most) public policies and decisions are determined not through aggregation or deliberation but rather through the *technical expertise* of officials whose training and professional specialization suits them to solving particular problems' (emphasis in original).

A liminal space for experimentation

The so called outreach session phase of the citizen participation followed (too) late in the planning process. Its aim was to engage 'hard-to-reach' groups. There are several issues that make this particularly important to our argument. First, the sessions were run by external consultants who did not share the interpreted 'image' (given identity) of the riverside area population. Second, the 'hard-to-reach groups are by definition different from 'The Network'. This implies a vision of another population, which is not (yet) known and certainly not re-presented. Thirdly, since The Network is stabilized around estate-focused issues, the outreach sessions had to choose different entry-points. They therefore perform citizen participation in a different way: The consultants performed a different summoning up of 'community' and created a different individuation of community relations by means of rupturing the hitherto purely non-relational geographical and residential focus represented by the limited Network.

Four sessions, run by planning consultants, were held with young people, three with older people, two with young parents, two with asylum seekers and one with community centre users. It appears that the outreach sessions generated the richest accounts or experiences and the highest degree of potentialities or experimentation in the process. The process spans a field of multiple becomings. The outreach sessions demonstrate that civic engagement can be an experimental, creative process rather than a method to 'rubber-stamp' or obtain agreement for predetermined representations.

The outreach groups referred to many issues relating to specific local areas, but also to the regeneration area as a whole and beyond to the wider city. Thus the connectivities of people (such as around age-related issues) create a relational entity other than the geographical residential allegiance as imposed by the planners. The groups in the outreach sessions demonstrate an ability to address issues from multiple angles and to move well beyond the (often self-centred) interest in how exactly a neighbourhood could be changed. They embraced issues that went 'far beyond the needs of their particular group, reflecting a concern about all aspects of the area and all sections of the community' (Consultants, 2005: 36). They recognized and accepted that different and often agonizing visions and virtualities can and do exist simultaneously. The outreach sessions illustrate that the planners' decision, in 2002, to work primarily with resident groups organized the entire civic engagement process around an assemblage of specific and pre-given sub-areas instead of along multiple relational assemblages of interests, problems and issues. The future morphogenesis of the area as a multiplicity of places to become was never problematized

It would appear from our investigations that collaborative processes of civic engagement, such as the outreach sessions, can generate capacity to produce different visions (virtuals) and to lead to the emergence of possibility space that provide a 'place' for *agencement* to emerge. The consequence for strategic planning can be the actualization of potentially different outcomes to those produced through consultation processes as in our regeneration case.

Unfortunately, little happened as a result of the outreach sessions as the planners did not pay particular attention to the information gathered. However, our tracing of connections and the mapping out of their potentials indicates that in the outreach sessions the consultants triggered the release of energy that allows group identities to establish way beyond a subjugation to institutional power, and thus a given compromise with power.

13.6 Conclusions

We developed our analysis in this chapter from the differentiation of the terms assemblage and *agencement*, which helped us to discern networks and situations in which elements things are merely assembled, from networks and situations where strategic agency may evolve. Tracing planning action in the phases of master planning and statutory consultation on the 'Options' in our case study, highlights the 'illness' of stratification as well as the overlooked potential for *agencement* (outreach sessions). The conception of interpretation/experience/

experimentation was especially helpful for analysis of how processes were framed, when and where they were striated and under which conditions they released – or were prevented from releasing – creative energy which may or may not lead to emergence of potentially beneficial *agencement*. Our case example highlights and illustrates that citizen engagement in strategic spatial planning performs in agonistic (if not antagonistic) tension between nationally territorialized, (post) bureaucratic programs and rationalized projects (such as front-loading), central and local political direction and the desires of the subjects of government (local residents) themselves.

We should like planning practice to pay attention to the connectivity of human and non-human networks (Van Wezemael, 2010) and especially to the ways in which different realities of time and space interrelate – or clash. It is in this perspective that planning may be called the art of 'bringing into line the significance of the irretrievable, indeterminate, and excessive qualities of everyday life with an immanent, creative and pragmatic project for future social explication' (Thrift and Dewsbury, 2000: 428). Planning practice is a performative (Dewsbury, 2000) shaping of time-space: 'every move … is an untimely moment redistributing what has gone before while opening up what may yet come' (Deleuze, 1991: 96). It is a form of pragmatism in action in which 'policy plugs into production, and production into policy' (Wise, 2006: 191; 2002: 230). Less interpretive, more experiential and more experimental approaches to citizen participation processes would, however, be bureaucratically and politically unsettling and 'risky', for, as Wise (2006: 191) explains, they would 'not only apprehend the probability of "opportunities that are unforeseen", but simultaneously anticipate the movements of the city and accept that policy outcomes are experimental and unpredictable'.

We argue the need for such 'risks' as they are intrinsically related to experimentation. Experimentation may imply significant risks for the planner as in facilitating the connectivities between elements in assemblages, planners cede much of their control. They cannot predict with certainty what might take place. We imply the significance of a trajectory or direction (perhaps towards sustainable regeneration as in our case example) whilst simultaneously affirming the complex multiplicity of potential paths which might be followed.

We argue that planners might usefully perform as Deleuzean 'intercessors' (Deleuze, 1995). For Deleuze, intercession involves a 'going between' in the production of 'creative interference' (Bogue, 2007: 13) as in disturbance of sound waves on a radio. Deleuze stresses that there is no necessity of actants fully understanding each other for the creative process of intercession to take place. Rather, they 'falsify' (1995: 126) each other's ideas, interpreting and understanding them in their own way. Intercession, then, is 'a form of positive dissonance, made possible through an openness to interferences that disturb one's regular harmonic vibrations' (Bogue, 2007: 14). Intercession is important in the generation of *agencement*. As such it is a passage resonant with the thinking of

Walter Benjamin's *Passagenwerk*[2] (1982) which connects the dissimilar to obtain new understandings.[3]

It takes little to move to the notion of space as passage: a space of change, of flow, of potentiality and constraint. Space as precipitated by the relationality between elements, where relationality resembles an 'impolite conversation' (Stephen Loo, pers. comm. June 2007); a sense of the dynamic which comes out of disparity. We argue that spatial planning practice then should be concerned with creative encounters of disparate entities; with experimentation rather than interpretation.

We conclude by suggesting that if citizens are to become empowered (perform strategic agency) in their engagement with processes of strategic spatial planning, public officials need to think differently, to 'step outside what's been thought before … [to] venture outside what's familiar and reassuring … to invent new concepts for unknown lands' (Deleuze, 1995: 103), to experiment and to allow possibilities for something new to emerge.

References

Arnstein, S. (1969) 'The ladder of citizen participation', *Journal of the Institute of American Planners*, 35(4), pp. 216-224.

Barber, B. (1984) *Strong Democracy*, University of California Press, Berkeley, CA.

Benjamin, W. (1982) *Das Passagen-Werk*, (2 vols), (ed. Tiedemann R.), Suhrkamp Verlag, Frankfurt-am-Main.

Bogue, R. (2007) *Deleuze's Way: Essays in Transverse Ethics and Aesthetics*, Ashgate, Aldershot.

Bonta, M. (2001) 'Toward a cultural geography of complex spaces'. Paper presented at SE Division AAG meeting, Lexington KY. http://ntweb.deltastate. edu/mbonta/Deleuze.html [accessed 27/08/2004].

Bonta, M. and Protevi, J. (2004) *Deleuze and Geophilosophy: A Guide and Glossary*, Edinburgh University Press, Edinburgh.

Brown, S. and Lunt, P. (2002) 'A genealogy of the social identity tradition: Deleuze and Guattari and social psychology', *British Journal of Social Psychology*, 41, pp. 1-23.

---

2   Although the nuances of Benjamin's *Passagenwerk* remain in Europe, the translation to 'Arcade' in English loses the concept of transience, movement and instability completely.

3   The notion of 'passage' is plural. In French, a *passeur* may be a mountain guide, a ferryperson, or a cross-border smuggler; *passant* refers to transience or arbitrariness. As a noun, it refers to a wayfarer, which also resonates strongly with the Deleuzoguattarian nomad. In all of these relational terms, it is the line (or passage) rather than the point which is important.

Buchanan, I. (2000) *Deleuzism: a Metacommentary*, Duke University Press, Durham, NC.

Chambers, S. (1996) *Reasonable Democracy*, Cornell University Press, Ithaca, NY.

Connolly, W.E. (2006) 'Experience or experiment', *Daedalus*, 135(3), pp. 67-75. http://lion.chadwyck.co.uk/searchFulltext.do?id=R03847927 [accessed 21/04/2008].

'Consultants' (2005) *'Consultation Feedback Report'*, http://www.newcastle.gov. uk/ [accessed 10.02.2007].

Deleuze, G. (1988) [1970] *Spinoza: practical philosophy*, (trans. Hurley, R.), City Light Books, San Francisco.

Deleuze, G. (1991) [1960] *Bergsonism*, (trans. Tomlinson, H. and Habberjam, B.), Zone Books, New York.

Deleuze, G. (1995) [1990] *Negotiations 1972-1990*, (trans. Joughin, M.), Columbia University Press, New York.

Deleuze, G. (1997) [1993] *Essays Critical and Clinical* (trans Smith, D.W. and Greco, M.) University of Minnesota Press, Minneapolis, MN.

Deleuze, G. and Guattari, F. (1987) [1980] *A Thousand Plateaus: Capitalism and Schizophrenia*, (trans. Massumi B.), Athlone Press, London.

Deleuze, G. and Parnet, C. (1987) [1977] *Dialogues*, (trans. Tomlinson, H. and Habberjam B.), Athlone Press, London.

Deleuze, G. and Parnet, C. (2002) [1977] *Dialogues II*, (trans. Tomlinson H. and Habberjam B.), Continuum, London.

Delli Carpini, M., Cook, F. and Jacobs, L. (2004) 'Public deliberation, discursive participation and citizen engagement: a review of the empirical literature', *Annual Review of Political Science*, 7, pp. 315-344.

Dewsbury, J.D. (2000) 'Performativity and the event: enacting a philosophy of difference', *Environment and Planning D, Society & Space*, 18, pp. 473-496.

Foucault, M. (2000) [1968] 'On the archaeology of the sciences: response to the epistemology circle', in Faubion, J. (ed) *Michel Foucault: Aesthetics*, Essential Works of Foucault 1954-1984, Vol. 2, Penguin, Harmondsworth, pp. 297-333.

Fung, A. (2006) 'Varieties of participation in complex governance', *Public Administration Review*, Special Issue, pp. 66-75.

Gastil, J. (2000) *By Popular Demand*, University of California Press, Berkeley, CA.

Gutmann, A. and Thompson, D. (1996) *Democracy and Disagreement*, Harvard University Press, Cambridge, MA.

Habermas, J. (1970) 'On systematically distorted communication', *Inquiry*, 13, pp. 205-218.

Hillier, J. (2007) *Stretching Beyond the Horizon: A Multiplanar Theory of Spatial Planning and Governance*, Ashgate, Aldershot.

Hillier, J. and Van Wezemael, J. (2008) '"Empty, swept and garnished": the Public Finance Initiative case of Throckley Middle School', *Space and Polity*, 12(2), pp. 157-181.

Hinchliffe, S., Kearnes, M., Degen, M. and Whatmore, S. (2005) 'Ecologies and economics of action – sustainability, calculations and other things, http://www. open.ac.uk /socialsciences/habitable_cities/habitable_citiessubset/habitable_ citiesinfopops/ecologies.pdf [accessed August 2006].

Kwa, C. (2002) 'Romantic and Baroque conceptions of complex wholes in the sciences', in Law, J. and Mol, A. (eds) *Complexities: Social Studies of Knowledge Practices*, Duke University Press, Durham, NC, pp. 23-52.

Lambert, G. (2006) *Who's Afraid of Deleuze and Guattari?* Continuum, London.

Law, J. (2002) 'On hidden heterogeneities: complexity, formalism, and aircraft design', in Law, J. and Mol, A. (eds) *Complexities*, Duke University Press, Durham, NC, pp. 116-141.

Law, J. (2004) 'And if the global were small and noncoherent? Method, complexity and the baroque', *Environment and Planning D, Society & Space, 22*, pp. 13-26.

Law, J. and Urry, J. (2003) [2002] 'Enacting the social', Centre for Science Studies, Lancaster University. http://www.comp.lancs.ac.uk/sociology/papers/ Law-Urry-Enacting-the-Social.pdf [accessed 31/05/2004].

Lazzarato, M. (2006) 'The concepts of life and living in the societies of control', in Fuglsang, M. and Sørensen, B. (eds) *Deleuze Connections*. Edinburgh University Press, Edinburgh, pp. 171-190.

LD (2004a) *Statement of Community Involvement,* http://www.newcastle.gov.uk/ [accessed 10/02/2007].

LD (2004b) '*Master Plan'*, http://www.newcastle.gov.uk/ [accessed 10/02/2007].

LD (2004c) *'Change'*, http://www.newcastle.gov.uk/ [accessed 10/02/2007].

Leadbeater, C. and Miller, P. (2004) *The Pro-Am Revolution – How Enthusiasts are Changing our Economy and Society*, Demos, London.

Lejano, R. (2006) *Frameworks for Policy Analysis: Merging Text and Context*, Routledge, London.

Massumi, B. (2002) *Parables for the Virtual: Movement, Affect, Sensation*, Duke University Press, Durham, NC.

Newcastle City Council (NCC) (2002) *'City Sub-regional Plan'*, http://www. newcastle.gov.uk [accessed 08/02/2007].

O'Neill, P. and McGuirk, P. (2005) 'Reterritorialisation of economies and institutions: the rise of the Sydney Basin economy', *Space and Polity*, 9(3), pp. 283-305.

Patton, P. (2006) 'Order, Exteriority and Flat Multiplicities in the Social', in Fuglsang, M. and Sørensen, B.(eds) *Deleuze and the Social.* Edinburgh University Press, Edinburgh: 21-38.

Phillips, J. (2006) 'Agencement/assemblage', *Theory, Culture, Society*, 23(2-3), pp. 108-109.

Rey, A. and Morvan, D. (2006) *Le Robert micro*, Le Robert, Paris.

Shields, R. (1996) 'A guide to urban representation and what to do about it: alternative traditions of urban theory', in King, A. (ed) *Re-Presenting the City*. New York University Press, New York: 227-252.

Thanem, T. and Linstead, S. (2006) 'The trembling organisation: order, change and the philosophy of the virtual', in Fuglsang, M. and Sørensen, B. (eds) *Deleuze Connections*. Edinburgh University Press, Edinburgh: 39-57.

Thrift, N. and Dewsbury, J.D. (2000) 'Dead geographies – and how to make them live', *Environment and Planning D, Society & Space*, 18, pp. 411-432.

Van Wezemael, J. (2008) 'The Contribution of Assemblage Theory and Minor Politics for Democratic Network Governance'. *Planning Theory*, 7(2), pp. 165-185.

Van Wezemael, J. (2010) 'Modulation of Singularities – a Complexity Approach to Planning Competitions', in Hillier, J. and Healey, P. (eds.) *Conceptual Challenges for Planning Theory*. Ashgate, Aldershot.

Wise, P. (2002) 'Cultural policy and multiplicities', *International Journal of Cultural Policy*, 8(2), pp. 221-231.

Wise, P. (2006) 'Australia's Gold Coast: a city producing itself', in Lindner, C. (ed) *Urban Space and Cityscapes*, Routledge, London, pp. 177-191.

Chapter 14
Population Thinking in Architecture

Peter Trummer[1]

The assumptions of population thinking are diametrically opposed to those of the typologist. The populationist stresses the uniqueness of everything in the organic world. What is true for the human species, that no two individual are alike, is equally true for all other species of animals and plants... all organisms and organic phenomena are composed of unique features and can be described collectively only in statistical terms. Individuals, or any kind of organic entities, form populations of which we can determine the arithmetic mean and the statistics of variation. Averages are merely statistical abstractions, only the individuals which the population is opposed have reality. The ultimate conclusions of the population thinker and of the typologist are precisely the opposite. For the typologist, the type (eidos) is real and the variation an illusion, while for the populationist the type (average) is an abstraction and only the variation is real. No ways of looking at nature could be more different. (Mayr, 1963: 4)

If we were to replace the essences as the explanation of the identity of material objects and natural kinds we need to specify the way in which multiplicities relate to the physical processes which generate those material objects and kinds. (DeLanda, 2002: 13)

14.1 Introduction

The shift from typological thinking to population thinking is perhaps the greatest conceptual revolution to have taken place in biology. When the evolutionary biologist Ernst Mayr wrote the above words in 1963, he could not have possibly imagined that the question of types would soon fuel a key polemic in the discipline of architecture as well. Indeed, the concept of types once lay so deeply rooted at the heart of architecture's disciplinary knowledge that it seemed unthinkable to even question it. As Rafael Moneo keenly observed in a 1978 issue of *Opposition*, "To raise the question of typology in architecture is to raise a question of the nature of the architectural work itself. To answer it means, for each generation, a redefinition of the essence of architecture and an explanation of all its attendant problems." (Moneo, 1978)

---

1   Peter Trummer is Professor and Head of the Institute of Urban Design and Urban Planning at the University of Innsbruck.

Several contemporary architects appear to have taken up Moneo's challenge to engage the question of types. As a result, we are now witnessing the rebirth of the typological debate two decades after it first emerged. FOA's Alejandro Zaera-Polo and Farshid Moussavi wrote an entire book on the topic of Phylogeneses, and the Architectural Association in London also recently published a book on typological formations specifically on renewable building types in the city. (Lee and Jacoby, 2007) But perhaps the most visible proof of typology's return in architecture is the CCTV building in Beijing by OMA's Rem Koolhaas. Its prominent use of the arch – one of the most enduring architectural archetypes – for the Chinese State Television headquarters reminds me a bit of Oswald Mathias Ungers' Hochhaus Messetor, the entrance to Frankfurt's Fair-Area. At a 1982 meeting with American architects in Charlottesville, to which he was invited by Philip Johnson, Ungers defended his typological approach by arguing that the use of archetypes was a critical question not so much for theoreticians but first and foremost for practicing architects who regularly deal with big business. (Cepl and Ungers, 2007) So perhaps the increased emphasis today on the relationship between architecture and commerce has also contributed to reviving the debate on typologies.

In any case, Moneo was certainly correct when he encouraged architects to address the question of types in order to redefine the very essence of their discipline. But I would like to go even further by raising the question of types in order to then replace it with a different one: that of populations. Instead of asking how we could interpret the idea of typological thinking in architecture today, I would like to speculate what the re-origination of population thinking – in stark opposition to typological thinking – could mean for the discipline of architecture and especially for its design practice.

It is difficult to over-emphasize how diametrically opposed two ways of seeing the world truly are. In fact, they are so far removed that our task of moving from one to the other is not always easy. Here I would like to introduce Gilles Deleuze's idea of the *multiplicity* as an alternative idea to the essentialism of types. For this purpose, I will use Manuel DeLanda's outline of Deleuze's argument from his book *Intensive Science and Virtual Philosophy*. After discussing a few of DeLanda's examples, I will particularly focus on the idea of population thinking as one form of multiplicity. Finally, I will conclude this chapter by speculating on what the re-origination of population thinking could mean for the discipline of architecture and how it could change our urban design practice.

What I wish to demonstrate here is that architectural thinking is always, in one way or another, affected by a much wider production of knowledge. My intention is not to prove that architecture literally applies or copies knowledge from other disciplines. Rather, it is to show how ideas from other disciplines become productively and justifiably originated in architecture. We must not forget that all knowledge and all ideas emerge from the same pool of genes, as biologist would say, or out of the same matter, as a physicist would argue. As such, this chapter can be described as a trans-disciplinary investigation into how the concept of population thinking could become re-originated in architecture and what effect this would have on our design practices.

14.2 Multiplicity versus essentialism

In his book *Intensive Science and Virtual Philosophy*, Manuel DeLanda gives us a powerful clue to understanding the difference between these two ways of seeing reality. The first way is that of Essentialism, based on typological thinking, and the other way is that of Multiplicities, based on the morphogenetic processes that form our material world. DeLanda states that the key philosophical concept at the heart of typological thinking consists of the notion of *essences*. The "essence of a thing is that which explains its identity, that is, those fundamentals traits without which an object would not be what it is. If such an essence is shared by many objects, then possession of a common essence would also explain the fact that these objects *resemble* each other and, indeed, they from a distinct *natural kind* of things." (DeLanda, 2002: 9)

In opposition to this way of looking at the reality of physical objects, DeLanda introduces the Deleuzian concept of "multiplicity." Contrary to typological thinking, whereby an object is defined by an essence to which it bears a resemblance, DeLanda defines the Deleuzian concept of multiplicity as following: "A Species is not defined by its essential traits but rather by the morphogenetic process that give rise to it [   ] While an essentialist account of species is basically static, a morphogenetic account is inherently dynamic. And while an essentialist account may rely on factors that transcend the realm of matter and energy (eternal archetypes, for instance) a morphogenetic account gets rid of all transcendent factors using exclusively form-generating resources which are immanent to the material world." (DeLanda, 2009: 9) So for Deleuze, all material reality is based on orderings that do not transcend the here-and-now. He even goes as far as to apply the idea of multiplicities and its morphogenetic processes to all material realities – not just inanimate ones, but animate ones as well. In Deleuze's eyes, all "ideas are multiplicities: every idea is a multiplicity or a variety." (Deleuze, 1997: 182) The consequence of this thought can be best demonstrated when it comes to defining a group of things or objects. A morphogenetic process contends that a "[m]ultiplicity must not designate a combination of the many and the one, but rather an organization belonging to the many as such, which has no need whatsoever of unity in order to form a system." (Deleuze, 1997: 182) This means that in opposition to typological thought, in which all members of a species resemble, to a greater or lesser degree, their single founding type, a multiplicity is based on the accumulated effects produced by the individual members of the species – each one acting in relationship to the others. It is from this viewpoint that we must apprehend Deleuzian ontology, since he states in his book *Difference and Repetition* that "everything is a multiplicity in so far as it incarnates an idea...

instead of the enormous opposition between the one and the many, there is only the variety of multiplicities – or in other words, difference." (8)

Perhaps we can now grasp more clearly what DeLanda truly meant in the quote at the beginning of this essay. He was postulating that when we replace typological thought as way to explain and understand material objects, we need to specify the way in which a multiplicity relates to the physical processes which lie behind these material objects. In his book *Intensive Sciences and Virtual Philosophy*, DeLanda touches on a series of examples that define the idea of multiplicities in various disciplines – such as Riemann's idea of multiplicity, the idea of group theory in geometry, examples from the realm of physics, and the idea of population thinking in biology.

In this chapter I will briefly discuss some of these examples, and I will also try to formulate how such a morphogenetic approach can be re-originated within architectural and urban practices. I want to be clear that by re-origination I do not mean the literal application of the idea of multiplicities, or merely using this idea as a metaphor. Instead I will try to follow DeLanda's thoughts in order to specify how a morphogenetic approach could help us understand the genesis of forms within our discipline.

The reason why we must stress the difference between the idea of the "one" and the idea of the "many" is that the former was long (and largely still is) the only accepted theory for explaining the genesis of architectural forms. The most influential and recurring example of this typological thought was first defined by Quatremère de Quincy around the end of the 18th century and the beginning of the 19th century. This concept structures the relationship between the one and the many around the key distinction between the *type*, which consists of the pure and unaltered idea of an object, and the *replica*, which is an application of this type. This definition of type, which is based on the notion of essences, suggests that every architectural design or urban plan is nothing more than an iteration of some eternal essence called the idea or type. Indeed, the distinction between the Type and the Replica formed the backbone of Aldo Rossi's argument in *Architecture and the City*, which has dominated architectural theory in urban design practices for almost 50 years. The intention of this essay is to offer a critique – or better, an alternative – to this prevailing disciplinary knowledge.

14.3 Typological thinking in architecture

I would like to begin with one particular moment in history in which typological thinking actually proved relevant to the argument of this essay. This moment was that of the post-war research projects on the morphological structure of Italian cities undertaken by Saverio Muratori and his student Gianfranco Caniggia (Caniggia, 1998). Both men were researching the specific processes that lie behind the material organizations of architectural objects and which give rise to the shape of the city fabric. The reason why I find these two practitioners so interesting is that even though they remained trapped within a conventional idea of types as defined above, they had nonetheless begun to look at the city's morphogenetic processes. My guess is that perhaps they simply did not know how to describe their conclusions in other ways than through the concept of 'types' and 'replicas.' In spite of this major shortcoming, I nevertheless believe that the idea of population thinking was first originated in architecture and urbanism at this precise moment in history.

Type and Replica

Quatremère de Quincy's intention was to help architecture reconstruct its link with the past. For him, this link had to remain constant throughout time. We must remember that it was during this period that the national state, industrialization, and capitalism all emerged. It was the same moment in which rational thought was instated as the sole justified form of knowledge. Amongst this particular context, Quatremère desired to expose the link between an architectural object and its socio-cultural relevance – or in other words, between the object and its meaning. He wanted to present architecture as a coherent system, and in order to do so he constructed a theory of the originating principles from which architecture is born. (Lavin, 1992: 86) Quatremère's approach to the idea of types, as Sylvia Lavin states so clearly in her book on him, was to radicalize it by secularizing its meaning. By eliminating Platonist ideas from the notion of type, Quatremère eliminated the long-standing assumption that types were created by God. Therefore types could now be seen no longer as links to the realm of the sacred, but rather as links that connect us back to profane history and its valuable 'origins.' Type thus identified an abstract continuity that could be traced throughout the architectural production of man over the ages.

In Quatremère de Quincy's eyes, the evolution from primitive hut to advanced construction closely parallels that of a primitive society towards a civilized nation state. (Lavin, 1992: 89) He basically equated society to an architectural work and vice versa. Quatremère thus laid the foundation for seeing architecture as a mode of representation. He scrupulously distinguished between the notion of the type and that of the replica. Type "is the result not of nature but of an inspired idea and is an act of self-conscious creation," which is then applied in the form of the replica – in other words, as a variation on the original idea. (Lavin, 1992: 96)

Muratori and Caniggia engaged the question of types partly because the Modern functionalist planning of the 1920 and 1930s had so completely failed. In contrast to the ignorance of Modernist city planning, which disregarded the evolution of the city and its citizens, Muratori tried to explain the formal and structural continuity of traditional cities. In his "Studi per una operante storia Urbana di Venezia," he suggested that the city fabric is composed of many continuities at different scales. What Muratori did in Venice, and which Gianfranco Caniggia later continued, was to unravel the urban fabric over time. They would redraw the material organization of the city in order to identify each housing unit and its specific characteristics.

"If we see that two or more houses have similar characteristics, we label them together and say that these two houses belong to the same 'building type.' [...] If I retrieve the elements that I recognize as being similar in a unitary definition, I obtain a statistically derived 'building type:' in other words, I see numerous buildings existing of two dwelling stories placed on the top of a ground floor, with two windows per story and with a large door, and a small door on the ground floor." (Caniggia and Maffei, 2001: 51)

This methodology clearly led them to identify these features for which they could find the underlying "house concept," or what they called the "mental map." (Caniggia and Maffei, 2001: 52) Muratori identified this mental map – which is the product of spontaneous consciousness – as the underlying principle for the city's specific layout. This spontaneous or collective consciousness came to serve as their definition of type. So in order to understand the diversity of individual housing units, or namely a species of objects, they would define the specificities of the statistical average of them all. But it is perplexing that Caniggia and Muratori remained so vested in Quatremère de Quincy's idea of the type-replica system, because several aspects of their research demonstrate striking similarities with our current understanding of multiplicities. One of these is their definition for typological processes, and another is their idea on individuation.

For Caniggia and Muratori, the typological process consists of the progressive differentiation of building types within a same cultural area. "14th century builders build their houses according to type and house concept at the time, 15th century builders build their houses according to the concept and type in force during their area." (Caniggia and Maffei, 2001: 54) The change which is undergone by the house concept, which now depends on the time period as well as the influence of what is built nearby, results in the individuation of each building through the typological process.

In this sense, their work presents strong analogies with species concepts borrowed from the realm of biology. The urban fabric of the city is seen here as an organism unfolding from many smaller cells, which are comprised of the individual buildings. "Caniggia tries to demonstrate that building is an organism that is integral to the whole human being-body, mind and spirit. This has formidable implications for the future understanding of buildings. If, for example, building processes govern buildings, the main question for building and design theory is less one of ethics defining right and wrong, a central theme in urban design theory, than one of interaction between genetic contents and environments, and of random selection." (Caniggia and Maffei, 2001: 21)

Thanks to its visionary take on the city as a "biological" process, and not merely in a metaphorical way, the work of Caniggia and his colleagues consists of an attempt to re-originate population thinking within architecture. But one can only wonder why they found it necessary to describe their analyses in such worn-out typological terms. Their approach considered the individual variations as real, but it failed to push the implications of this insight. Because the variations on the ground were still reduced to statistical abstractions, and not seen as powerful and productive forces in themselves, Caniggia and Muratori remained trapped in a typological approach instead of thinking in terms of populations of multiplicities. Caniggia and Muratori wanted to find the essential features that give rise to the individuation of the buildings, rather than *identifying the morphogenetic process that defines the species as a population.* It is clear that the biological ideas of the Transformationists possess some striking resemblances to their idea of spontaneous consciousness as the driving force for evolutionary change in buildings, even though I have no idea if Murattori or Caniggia were aware of them. In any case, it is certainly true that Muratori and Caniggia defined the variations of building types as a process of differentiation due to the environmental forces of a particular period. Spontaneous consciousness defined the form of building which was to be made; it was inherited by all builders and shared within a same spatial and temporary zone.

In this manner their work is situated in direct opposition to that of Modernist city planning, since they understood type not as an abstract concept but rather as an element which characterizes the organization of the actual city as an organism. This organism was itself defined by the accumulation of individual housing cells.

14.4 Population thinking

Ernst Mayr introduced the biological idea of population thinking in response to Charles Darwin's *On the Origin of Species by Means of Natural Selection, or the Preservation of Favoured Races in the Struggle for Life.* When Mayr writes that "the assumptions of population thinking are diametrically opposed to those of the typologist," he means that "for the typologist, the type (eidos) is real and the variation an illusion, while for the populationist the type (average) is an abstraction and only the variation is real." Through these words, he effectively replaced one species concept by another. A species concept is a conceptual tool that we use to create a class or a family of similar things, all of which are grouped under a common name. Since it emerged in biology, the term "species" is usually applied to describe living organisms; but it also has been used to describe inanimate objects in the world of physics and even to describe human artifacts.

Population thinking quickly became the only accepted species concept within biology, following on the heels of the universal acceptance of Darwin's theory of evolution. Two aspects of population thinking are tremendously relevant for the intentions of the present argument. The first is how a group of objects or individuals is defined differently by the typologist or the populationist as a form of species. The second and perhaps the more important aspect is how the differences among individuals are explained in terms of morphogenesis.

Two kinds of typological thinking emerged in biology in order to describe the genesis of individuals. One is called transmutationism and the other it called transformationism. (Mayr, 2002: 83) Both of these schools are based on a typological approach, but each one has a slightly different explanation for how types change throughout history. The transmutationist believed, as Mayr tells us, that change could only occur by the birth of new types. "Since a type (essence) cannot evolve gradually (types are considered to be constant), a new type can originate only through an instantaneous 'mutation' or 'saltation' of existing types, which thereby give rise to a new class or type." (Mayr, 2002: 85). Supporters of this idea, according to Mayr, see the world as full of discontinuities.

While the transmutationists rejected any form of gradual transformation, the transformationists, on the other hand, believed fully in the implications of evolution and they invented the concept of gradual evolution (Mayr, 2002: 87). The discipline of Biology further distinguishes between two forms of transformationism. The difference between these two sub-categories lies in how they see what influences gradual change within a species. One movement of transformationism "postulated that types (essences) are steadily improvements of types or essences by intrinsic drives, and that evolution was believed to take place not by the origin of new types, but by the transformation of existing types." (Mayr, 2002: 89) This view became known in biology as finalism, and it sees all transformations as impelled by an inevitable drift towards perfection. This notion brings should bring to mind our previous thoughts on Quatremère de Quincy, who interpreted the evolution from primitive huts to advanced construction as analogous to the evolution of primitive society towards advanced forms of civilization. The second group of transformationalists was comprised of followers of Lamarck. Unlike the finalists, these scholars saw evolution as resulting from gradual changes that originated from the animals themselves through their constant efforts better adapt to their environment. In this manner, the environment would directly influence the animals' genetic material via their reactions to it. (Mayr, 2002: 88) Many of us are indeed familiar with the famous Lamarckian example of giraffes who, as they stretch their necks to reach the highest tree branches, would hypothetically pass on this information onto the next generation such that the latter benefit from even longer necks.

But in the end, all of these theories are typological ones that continue to believe in transcendental essences, and which classify species according to their morphological resemblances. The populationist, on the other hand, identifies a species by its morphogenetic process, the process through which the individual differences come about. And this is why population thinking is so radically different from typological thinking. It not only replaces typological thinking, but it even goes as far as erasing its roots.

For a populationist, "[a] species is a group of interbreeding natural populations that are reproductively isolated from other such groups." Firstly, "it is a protected gene pool, whereby an individual is merely a temporary vessel holding a small portion of the contents of a gene pool for a short period of time." Secondly, "[t]he species is also an ecological unit that, regardless of the individual composing it, interacts as a unit with other species with which it shares the environment." And thirdly, "the members of a species constitute a reproductive community." (Mayr, 1963: 21) In order to better understand what population thinking is or how it distinguishes itself from other species concepts, we must first look at the way in which it defines the relationship between the individual and its larger species. It does this by constructing a peculiar link between two kinds of *differences*. One kind of difference consists of those between individuals, each of which is of course different from all the others. The second is comprised of the differences between species. But the key paradox here is that is that first form of difference is what allows the second form of difference to exist. For without its diversity of individuals, the whole species would be gone. And this is why this concept is named population thinking: there needs to be a critical mass of different individuals in order to create a gene pool that can be considered as a group.

In this way, the notion of populations hints at Deleuze's definition of multiplicity. It does not define itself through the relationship between the one and the many, but rather through the interaction between the many and the many. Differences are not merely idiosyncratic takes on a common theme, but rather they exist in their own right. Populations are comprised of pure variation, and it is the variation that lies at the source of their organization – not some abstract, transcendental motif.

In order to originate population thinking in architecture, we must first understand how biology explains the morphogenetic process of this species concept. This process can be clearly explained thanks to Mendel's identification of 'genotype' and 'phenotype.' The terminological distinction between the phenotype and the genotype is based on the idea that the "genetic material itself is the genome or Genotype, which controls the production of the body of an organism and all of its attributes, the Phenotype This Phenotype is the result of the interaction of the Genotype with the environment during development. The variation of the Phenotype produced by a given Genotype under different environmental conditions is called its norms of reaction." (Mayr, 2002: 98) Mayr gives us a simple example of this key distinction by describing how "a given plant may grow to be larger and more luxurious under favourable conditions of fertilizing and watering than without these environmental factors. Leaves of the water buttercup (Ranunculus flabellaris) produced under the water are feathery and very different from the broadened leaves on the branches above water." (Mayr, 2002: 99). Thus it is the Phenotype that is exposed to natural selection, and never the Genotype. This crucial distinction between a mortal, disposable body which is nothing more than a mere transmitter, and its immortal chain of hereditary instructions is precisely what revolutionized biology. (Goodwin, 1994: 27)

So then what does the scientific-sounding term 'morphogenetic process' truly mean? It consists of how something changes over time under the influence of external forces as well as its own internal forces. For mankind and other vertebrates, the study of the morphogenetic process occurs mainly in the field of embryology. This research looks at the development of an organism's embryo as it matures, changes, and eventually unfolds "differentiated tissues and organs". (DeLanda, 2002: 16). This unfolding is called "progressive differentiation". (DeLanda, 2002: 17) It is precisely this notion of studying how a form emerges which can be applied not just to biology but to all things. The morphogenetic process is in no way constrained to only biology, but can rather be seen as a transdisciplinary concept.

14.5 Its re-origination in architecture

Research dealing with the dynamical potential of interacting systems – like that of population thinking – took place not just in biology but also in the disciplines of economics, sociology, physics, and politics. Even in the discipline of geography, thinking along the terms of population dynamics was decisive for the work of the Chicago School of Burgess, Park, and McKensie (1925), in their study of human ecologies in Chicago. And let us not forget the work of Walter Christaller, for whom the formation of densities in cities emerged as the accumulation of individual behavior based on economic forces.

But despite the differences between these disciplines, all of these examples share the fact that they overthrew the *Hylomorphic Model* of thinking about the relationship between Matter and Form within Western culture. (Deleuze and Guattari, 1987) The term "hylomorph" indicates an preconceived idea that is used to design things, such as a table. It is derived from the word *hyle*, meaning wood, and *morph*, meaning form. So when we design a table by means of the hylomorphic model, we take a form (*morph*) – the image of the table we would like to design – and we press it into the wood (*hyle*) – the material out of which the image needs to come alive. The effect is a copy, or a representation, of what we imagined the table should look like.

Indeed, the hylomorphic model denies the interrelationship between *form* (ideas) on the one hand and *hyle* (matter) on the other (Gilbert, 1964). "The critique of the hylomorphic schema, which sees matter as a homogenous and form as fixed, *is based on the existence* [...] *of a zone of medium and intermediary dimension*, of energetic and molecular dimensions" (Deleuze and Guattari, 1987: 409) between them. This zone can be referred to as a morphogenetic space, in which both substance (hyle) and ideas (form) are in a dynamic relationship. Deleuze called this dynamic condition the *machinic phylum*. (Deleuze and Guattari, 1987: 409)

In his article "The Machinic Phylum," Manuel DeLanda unfolds this philosophical concept and examines its significance in what he calls "the emergence of novelty," where matter is seen as an active material with "morphogenetic capabilities" to generate different structures through the constraints of its material properties. To demonstrate what he means by this, let us take an example that he uses in this article. In the realm of physics, DeLanda explains, "a population of interacting physical entities, such as molecules, can be constrained energetically to force it to display organized collective behaviour." (DeLanda, 1997) The example that is often used to illustrate this behaviour is the formation of soap bubbles. The molecules of the soap collectively attempt to minimize the tension of the surface. Each soap bubble differs according to the way in which the molecules organized themselves in their search for the most minimal surface tension. Another example which DeLanda describes is the formation of crystals. "If you hold a crystal, made out of carbon, it could take the shape of a diamond with its beautifully regular tetrahedral form. But it could be graphite, whose hexagonal sheets sheer off as it is rubbed over paper." (Goodwin, 1994). Therefore DeLanda demonstrates how one substance can occur in many different forms.

Both of these examples show that when processes of progressive differentiation are embedded within a Machinic Phylum, they begin to adapt to its physicality through the interrelationship between metrical and non-metrical properties. The metrical properties of the soap bubble or the crystals are defined by the non-metrical properties of the minimal surface tension (in the case of the soap) or the by minimized bonding energy (in the case of the crystals). As DeLanda explains, all of this occurs through the collective behaviour of a population of molecules without any need for a predefined schema to guide them from overhead. (DeLanda, 1997)

The point I want to make here is that the potential re-origination of population thinking in architecture lies precisely within the differentiation of metrical properties combined with non-metrical properties. When it comes to the built environment, the metrical properties consist of lengths, heights, surfaces, and volumes (also called extensive properties) (Deleuze, 1997: 223) and the non-metrical properties consist of temperature, pressure, tension, and capacities (also called intensive properties) (Deleuze, 1997: 223).

Now what does this mean for the genesis of architectural forms? Let us take a look at Jorn Utzon's Sydney Opera House. Below the entrance to the delivery zone, Utzon built a structural frame of repetitive beams. These repetitive beams look at first glance like a strangely curved surface, as if they were an aesthetically-driven creation with no particular purpose or constraints. But upon closer inspection we see that Utzon had developed a kind of geometrical transformation (Fromonot and Thompson, 1998), or better, a metrical system, by which the curvature of the beams is defined according to the position of a point moving along a diagonal line. In one stage, the section of the beams takes on the form of a square, while in another it becomes a T-shape. What drives the diversity of the beams' sectional shapes is the structural force distribution, or as we can now call it, the intensive property of the space. So the form of the beam is differentiated through the relationship between the metrical constrains of its plywood framework and the non-metrical distribution of forces from its structural diagram.

We can even examine a whole group of buildings from a similar point of view. Let us take, for example, a Chinese courtyard house. If I were a typologist, I would define the features that characterize its identity through its essences. Thus I would define the courtyard house as a solid with a void in the middle which comprises the courtyard. But if we look at all the existing variations of Chinese courtyard houses, we see that each of these houses form completely different organizations. Houses in the north of China are organized as individual housing units arranged within a framed landscape, while houses in the south of China take on the organization of a compact block with vertical masses of different sizes. What drives their morphogenetic process and determines these variations?

Each of the houses can be described as a material organization that is actualized by three kinds of external forces: the structural, the climatic and the socio-economic. First, their specific layout and its metrical constraints are dictated by the capabilities of local manufacturing processes. Second, it is immediately clear that the climate plays a strong role in the houses' forms. Depending on where it is located, each house works either as a heating or cooling machine. The sun penetration in the north is facilitated in order to heat up the spaces. Therefore the layout of freestanding houses within a landscape allows them to perform as heat islands. But in the south, the whole construction works like a cooling machine. Both of its courtyards – one of which is smaller than the other – generate a certain amount of air circulation thanks to the pressure differences caused by the different temperatures of the skylights. And third, the internal organization of the circulation responds to the social distribution of the family structure. Through its various dimensions and depths, the circulation structures various kinds of intimacies. (Trummer, 2006/2007) Thus the materialization of each house is embedded within the structural performance of this complex framework. In this sense, we could define the Chinese courtyard houses as a population of material organizations, each differentiated by the performance of the structural system (with its metrical properties) as well as its ecological and sociological forces (with their non-metrical properties).

How can we generate such morphogenetic potential within the discipline of urbanism? The research that I have undertaken in the last couple of years has looked at the cities of Madrid, Shanghai, Phoenix Arizona and Mexico City. It focused particularly on areas where the growth of the city meets the ecology of the raw landscape.

In the case of Phoenix, Arizona, the matter to be urbanized is the Sonoran Desert. As the world's wettest desert, it is the expression of its specific ecology (itself formed by the relationship between consolidated and unconsolidated rock), its extreme differences in topography, its seasonal floods, and the unusual flora which all determine its network of "washes." However, the forces of modern planning – a culture that only knows how to subdivide land in order produce the maximum number of similar plots – are pressing into the raw desert, erasing its distinctive ecology, and creating a tabula rasa condition. This process works along the lines of the hylomorphic model described above, since the typical idea of a neighbourhood is literally pressed into the material substance of the desert.

To appreciate the morphogenetic potential of the desert, we must first think of it as an active matter. This means that it is not enough to understand its natural ecology, but moreover we must also understand how it can be an active participant in the forces that govern urbanization. Its intensive properties, like the surface tension that gives shape to soap bubbles, or like the minimized bonding energy that forms crystals, must be clearly understood. Only then might the desert be seen as an active matter that could enable the actualization of various forms of urban layouts.

The two intensive properties that drove the research projects are the heat radiation of the soil and the economic value of the Sonoran Desert. Both of these territorial conditions are non-metrical properties; in other words, they can only be understood as a field in which every point is gradually different from its neighbouring one. This results in a multiplicity condition where every location in the desert landscape affects the location next to it. Each of the properties we looked at is generated by specific territorial conditions: the density of the vegetation (in the case of heat radiation) or the manifold objectives that determine the economic value, such as topography, accessibility, vegetation density, water retention and noise pollution. Thus, if the rules of subdivision are applied to this activated matter, then the specific territorial conditions generate a differentiated field of housing units – a population – that differ in terms of degrees (in sizes and property values) while also differing in terms of kind (in their internal organizations). The projects (Trummer, 2007/2008) looked at the specific territorial condition of the desert and what its territorial properties could mean for the production of large-scale urban projects. Whether the desert is read as an economical problem in terms of property value or as a environmental problem by means of its radiation (heat island effect), in each case it generates a differentiated field of housing units that offers a much larger diversity of houses than even that of the metropolitan region.

As such, the accumulation of housing units defines a multiplicity whereby each of the individual houses belongs to a species; all were born through the morphogenetic processes that their environment allowed them to unfold.

14.6 Conclusion

In this chapter, I have tried to argue how population thinking can be re-originated in architecture. I have done this by demonstrating that population thinking performs as a multiplicity, which redefines the relationship between the one and many as an organization of the many as such. I have further tried to outline what this means for our understanding of forms, namely the potential to produce novelty through the constraints of the metrical and non-metrical properties of spaces. This allowed me to show what such ideas could mean for our understanding of architectural forms and its resulting buildings. The approach that I described here is based on the understanding of a morphogenetic process which allows us to imagine the new. It can therefore act in as a radical alternative to our prevailing way of understanding the genesis of architectural forms, and it can do so in opposition to predefined typologies which purportedly comprise timeless and transcendent categories.

The aim of this thesis is to give the discipline of architecture the theoretical framework to project new forms of realities embedded within our existing regimes of urbanization. In this sense, I want to demonstrate that we have the ability to actualize completely new worlds even within our current form of capitalism.

References

Caniggia, G., G.L. Maffei (2001) *Interpreting Basic Building-Architectural Composition and Building Typology*, Alinea, Firence (I).

Cataldi, G. (1998) Designing in stage: theory and design in the typological concept of the Italian school of Saverio Muratori, in: A. Petruccioli (ed.) *Typological Processes and Design Theory*, AKPIA, Harvard University and MIT, Cambridge (US), pp. 35-54.

Cepl, J., O.M. Ungers (2007) Eine Intellektuelle Biographie [An Intellectual Biography], Verlag der Buchhandlung Walther König, Köln, p. 430.

DeLanda, M. (1997) The machinic phylum, in, *TechnoMorphica*, V2_Publisher, Amsterdam, Taken from the V2-Archive: http://framework.v2.nl/archive/archive/ node/text/.xslt/nodenr-70071.

DeLanda, M. (2002) *Intensive Science and Virtual Philosophy*, Continuum, New York.

Deleuze, G. (1997) *Difference and Repetition*, The Athlone Press, London.

Deleuze, G. and F. Guattari (1987) *A Thousand Plateaus – Capitalism and Schizophrenia*, Continuum, New York and The Athlone Press, London.

Fromonot, F., Ch. Thompson (1998) *Jørn Utzon – The Sydney Opera House*, Electra/Gingko Press, Corte Madera.

Goodwin, B. (1994) *How the Leopard Changed its Spots*, Phoenix Giants, London.

Lavin, S. (1992) *Quatremère de Quincy – and the invention of a modern Language of Architecture*, The MIT Press, Cambridge (US) and London.

Lee, Ch. and Jacoby, S. (eds.) (2007) Typological Formations – Renewable Building Types and the City, AA Agendas 5, AA Publication, London.

Mayr, E. (1963) *Populations, Species and Evolution*, Harvard University Press, Cambridge and London.

Mayr, E. (2002) *What Evolution is*, Phoenix, London.

Moneo, R. (1978) On Typology, *OPPOSITIONS*, 13, Summer, the MIT Press, pp. 22-45.

Park, R., E.W. Burgess and R.D. McKenzie (1925) *The City*. University of Chicago Press, Chicago.

Simondon, G. (1964) *Simondon and the Physico-Biological Genesis of the Individual*, Chapter One: "Form and Matter, Section I—Foundations of the Hylemorphic Model: Technology of the Capture of Form". Original in French: *L'individu et sa genèse physicobiologique*. Presses Universitaires de France, Paris, pp. 27-39.

Trummer, P. (ed.) (2006/2007) *Associative Design*, Synthetic Vernacular, Shanghai and Berlage Institute, Rotterdam.

Trummer, P. (2007/2008) *Associative Design*, Urban Ecologies, Phoenix and Berlage Institute, Rotterdam.

Chapter 15

Coevolving Adaptive and Power Networks: Collective Leadership for Effective Planning

Sibout Nooteboom and Jurian Edelenbos[1]

Spatial problems in a globalizing world with a growing population, and a more 'space-intensive' and fast economy, become increasingly complex and dynamic (Castells, 2000). Public and private organizations try to deal with these problems by organizing interests and by implementing policies. The complexity of the organizational and policy 'structure' (i.e. the governance system) should, according to the 'law of requisite variety' (Ashby, 1956, 1964), match the complexity of the spatial, economic and physical system. To be effective, a governance system should reflect external diversity (cf. Ashby, 1964; see also Van Wezemael, this volume). Thus, a more effective way to handle diversity in the environment is to create diversity in the governance system itself that reflects the diversity in the spatial, economic and physical system while adding something specific to it. In this way a fruitful coevolution between governance system and spatial system is created that facilitates innovation (cf. Edelenbos et al., 2008; see also Gerrits and Teisman, this volume). Governance structure should not only be refined, but dynamic as well, as the world constantly changes.

15.1 Introduction

However, organizations and their policies have a natural tendency to be inert (Teisman, 2005). Reform is a slow process, with a lot of political fuss driven by short-term, and small-scale interests. In this chapter, we develop ideas about how governance systems sometimes succeed in forming a higher-order structure that guides reform in the interest of longer-term, larger-scale interests. This process is driven by personal leadership of those who are not only motivated by their short-term material interests. In such a way, leadership may become an 'integrative influence' (Panzar et al., 2007). Such networks of leaders, influencing tomorrow's social structure or the 'fine unofficial structure' within the 'rough official structure', may be called adaptive networks, because they emerge from the official

---

1   Sibout Nooteboom, Associate Professor, and Jurian Edelenbos, Professor, are from the Department of Public Administration, Erasmus University, Rotterdam. Nooteboom is also associated with the Dutch Ministry of Internal Affairs.

– but inert – governance system to help it adapt to changing circumstances. They operate in the context or 'shadow' of these formal decision-making processes. The hypothesis is that these adaptive networks may become self-standing systems that co-evolve with the governance system (which again co-evolves with the spatial system). They are separate from the official governance system because they are not motivated by 'official' organizational short-term interests, whilst being aware that they depend on opportunities in the formal networks, and that their members have mixed motives – i.e. operate in both systems. These opportunities may often be limited to the willingness of official leaders to communicate in a different way with their supporter groups about long-term issues – allowing for the integrative influence of adaptive networks (i.e. less populist striving for personal short-term success by advocating partial approaches). These official leaders depend on the feedback they receive from their supporters in order to make a next step (Surowiecki, 2004). Adaptive networks are an ideal type, opposing 'power networks'. In adaptive networks creative breakthroughs in inert or even deadlocked policy issues are developed, whereas in power networks negotiation and politics take place that often sustain the deadlocked situation. Literature on complexity leadership and complex adaptive systems often stress the relevance of interplay between the power and adaptive networks (Uhl-Bien et al., 2007). In this chapter we explore this assumption by using different theoretical thoughts on complexity theory and theory on public management and governance.

Our socio-economic development is neither the result of the blueprint of one great leader, nor is it totally out of control. Globalization, with its spatial implications, may be a force stronger than us, but we may still try to create a more desirable form of it. It is about the alignment or coevolution between adaptive and power networks. Plans as persuasive documents and planning as the process of preparing such documents and enforcing their intended outcome are in this view the result of a battle between interests (i.e. power network) that may or may not lead to effective plans, of which the outcomes may or may not be appreciated in hindsight. There is often agreement about the need to correct undesirable 'autonomous' developments, but not about the precise *way* of correction. Still, plans may be useful tools of communication about one's intentions, remaining aware that these may only co-exist and co-evolve with, not control, the intentions of others. Plans may fulfil an invaluable role in that co-evolution of intentions. We hypothesize that the interplay between adaptive networks and power networks consciously influence that co-evolution between ideas, issues and interests. Adaptive networks are oriented to goal orientation on the long term, whereas power networks are focused on reaching short term goals (Nooteboom, 2006).

Aligning intentions

What matters is the degree in which a society is able to develop 'aligned intentions': to agree about desirable futures and ways of influencing the future, which interests should have priority, and how interests that profit less are compensated for their loss if that is required for fairness or acceptability. This may be less a desire of fairness however than one out of necessity, since in Western democracies those who think they do not profit enough have many ways to delay government plans. Under such complex conditions, agreement in society only exists to a small degree. Whilst the basic rules of society are not broken, spatial plans that imply considerable corrections of the status quo development often either remain ineffective or do not emerge from the process in the first place.

Game theory, incrementalism, and levers

Scharpf (1997) indicates that the relatively complex planning problems of society need to be solved through a game he termed 'complex problem solving'. In Scharpf's view this game is unlikely to solve complex problems, since representatives from opposing interest groups, having political influence or representing parts of government itself, need to negotiate about short-term outcomes of a planning process, whilst a short-term solution that solves all problems is not at hand. At best, a way of influencing development may be found that in the long term would reduce some of the problem. Lindblom's incrementalism (1956, 1979) makes similar inferences. Incremental changes may be produced as political outcomes, but they may also be 'clever' in the sense that they have indirect effects on development, which could lead to a build-up of social and economic tension and desirable breakthroughs at later stages. High levies on oil consumption, for example, may prove critical in stimulating a breakthrough to sustainable energy. This is known as punctuated equilibrium (Mulder and Van den Bergh, 1999). Systems are seen to go through periods in which everything is seemingly at ease and other periods of severe fluctuation (Baumgartner and Jones, 1993; Mulder and Van den Bergh, 1999). The reversal into periods of fast change is not necessarily caused by one particular event, although events can function as the final trigger, but is seen to be the result of a build-up of system pressure. Such pressure can increase whilst the system appears to be in a rather stable state until a certain threshold is reached. After that, swift changes take place that cause the transition from one state to the other. A phenomenon or condition occurring far away in time and space may have a delayed reaction on the subsystem, thus making it difficult to pinpoint the cause of every effect (Stacey, 2003; Flood, 1999; Senge, 1990).

Systematic communication about the importance of a species, a nature reserve or a problem like climate change may actually build-up support for measures even if these create economic cost on the short term. Plans and official policies may reinforce such communication. Initiatives to make social connections between opposing groups may enable a search process for mutually acceptable solutions. All such kinds of interventions may seem small at first, but actually have the effect of a lever, according to Peter Senge's (1990) systems thinking. This is coined in complexity theory as non-linearity. Sharpf (1998) indicates that looking for such levers requires trust, interest in each other's wider perspectives and motives.

15.2 Looking for levers for alignment

The idea of levers for a desirable future in the light of complex spatial problems leads to the following questions, to which we return in the conclusion:

1. how can one 'know' what a desirable future is from the perspective of a large social system
2. how can one who 'knows' what a desirable future is, identify incremental (and therefore acceptable) interventions that actually may contribute to desirable breakthroughs in development
3. how can this person actually achieve such interventions in a world where power is shared and that is dominated by contrasting short-term interests.

These questions are unanswerable if one is looking for an objective view from any given complex normative perspective. *The key point we make is that this should not be tried, but instead a researcher might assess the degree to which such normative perspectives are 'linked' in a social system, and the extent to which conduct in the system is led by that complex and dynamic perspective, even where the short term mind frames still dominate the policy process.* Those covering a wide range of subsystems and linking their perceptions and acting jointly, may also be expected to be able to form a relatively accurate joint perception of the system and opportunities to put levers in place that have the best chance of contributing to a future that will be appreciated. However, this is difficult to observe. Individuals may present themselves differently than they really are, hiding their true agenda and contributing to false joint agendas. They may look for power and control as a goal in itself. This might in particular happen if they are only driven by the need to produce short-term successes in the negotiation about official decisions.

Our key assumption and epistemic strategy is that observing this process, and assessing the interconnectivity of a social system, becomes possible if policy makers start to jointly and consciously separate the games they play according to system levels or in other words, according to short and long term. If they do that, we hypothesize that social networks of interacting individuals emerge at a different 'level', putting the interactions at the level they emerge from at the heart of their process. They create images of images, and use these meta-images to adapt their behaviour at primary level. That is why Nooteboom (2006) has termed them 'adaptive networks'.

To make these points, the following questions are answered hereafter:

• Which theories are available describing 'levels' of social systems?
• How do these theories relate to 'networks' – i.e. relatively stable patterns of interaction?
• How can these be observed and applied in a case study?
• What does this mean for planners?

We focus on the governance system and within it we distinguish the individual, the adaptive and the governance systems level, emerging from and operating on the economic–spatial systems. We contend that this boundary judgement (i.e. separating these three levels as units of thinking / analysis) actually can make a social system more capable of influencing its own future.

15.3 Which theories describe 'levels' of social systems?

W. Ross Ashby's *Principles of the self-organizing system* (1962) sets the stage for self-organization of embedded (ordered) systems, evolving to increasing complexity. Ashby indicates that one system level may be stable enough for embedded systems to emerge in isolated parts (i.e. agents have more frequent internal interaction than external interaction). His thinking has been applied to a range of systems, like neural networks, galaxies or atoms. Since 1973, system theories have defined levels as 'holons': nested part-whole units of analysis (Koestler, 1973). The idea of holons has been widely adopted in the social sciences by authors like Stacey (2003), Axelrod and Cohen (1999) and Ostrom (2005). A holon emerges from its constituent parts (which are lower-level holons), but the whole is more than the sum of parts and displays its own characteristics and laws. Its behaviour at its own level can be studied without knowledge of its parts, although its behaviour can only be explained as a result of self-organization from its component system levels. For example, biological systems emerge from the level of genes, and whereas ecosystems can be described without knowledge of genes, behaviour of composing species largely depends on them (e.g. Dawkins, 1976).

In public management, action arenas (Ostrom, 2005) or policy networks (e.g. Teisman, 1995) are often seen as such holons, composed of individuals who represent organizational interests. In branches of sociology and communication theory, networks are actually seen as caused by a clash between 'discourses' (Hajer, 2003), 'codes' (Shannon, 1948; Luhmann, 1995; Leydesdorff, 2010), 'organizing themes' (Stacey, 2003) or 'memes' (a hypothesized social analogue of genes; Dawkins, 1976). Organizations and individuals are then seen as the carriers of ideas that are holons themselves as ideas cannot be separated from the social systems that carry them, and which direct human behaviour as much as reversibly.

These memes are reproduced under institutional pressure and path dependency. This is known under the name of *conceptual replication* (Toulmin, 1972; Campbell, 1987; Hull, 1988). These chunks or threads of information cannot reproduce by themselves, however; they need hosts. During interaction and exchange of opinion the chunks of information jump from one actor to another (De Jong and Edelenbos, 2007). Those involved generally experience this as 'progressive insight' or 'learning'. Actors absorb new concepts and mutate existing ones to enable them to incorporate their fresh insights. During the course of the interactions a selection process takes place between the various concepts used in the interaction process. Some of them are replicated to brains ('living memory') much more frequently and are more commonly found in official reports and working documents ('external memory'); others gradually fall into disuse because they are forgotten, become less popular or attractive, or are no longer deemed appropriate to the situation in which they are supposed to be used. Important factor here is the extent to which actors' perceptions of one another differ: people are less likely to adopt one another's concepts indiscriminately if their frames, conceptual frameworks and perceptions differ substantially (Sabatier and Jenkins, 1993).

According to Hajer (2003), the discourses that meet in policy arenas are 'feeding' on the emotions people experience in their daily practices. These emotions, like angriness about traffic jams or about whale hunting, are transformed in social systems to ways of reasoning about desirable policies – i.e. discourses (discourses feed on emotions). Discourses channel themselves through self-organization through to policy arenas (networks), where governments, public actors and pressure groups interact. These are driven by several 'memes', some of which keep the 'peace' (e.g. knowledge about democratic stability or power balances), like the Dutch 'polder culture', and this 'peace' may create a platform with room for conflict, which again forms the basis for emerging decisions, partly reflecting the status quo, and partly the result of an incremental learning process. Ways of conflict resolution may also be deeply cultural 'memes'.

A major question is, to which extent does this learning process *respond* to changes in the economic and physical system, and to which extent is it capable of *influencing* it. Some authors to that end distinguish order levels of governance. Spangenberg (2007) relates first-order governance to hierarchical command and control, and second order as a level that emerges to correct the failure of first-order governance. Kooiman (2003) considers solving problems and creating opportunities for actors in society to be first-order governance, building governing institutions as second-order governance, and building values and principles as a third order. Pahl-Wostl (2007) presents the following multi-level governance structure: active negotiation and learning platforms; actor networks where many are more passive; and the governance regime of the larger societal system.

We prefer, in agreement with Spangenberg, to see order levels as emerging from each other through transitions in behaviour of their constituent basic agents which are humans – much like the ideas of Maslov (1943) and Graves (Beck and Cowan, 1996), who claim individuals may fulfil certain level of needs and then reach a next level. Such motives may be shared in groups. A transition to a next order is defined by a switch to additional behaviour that itself does not fit in the continuing circular causality of the previously existing order level, but may seek to influence it and may stabilize. In terms of governance, a policy maker may try to achieve his official targets in a negotiation process, but at the same time he may interact with opponents to do that in such a way that satisfies the mutual long-term interest as well (see also Stacey, 2003). This requires 'integrative leadership' (Panzar et al., 2007) and metacapability (Hazy, 2007). It requires that leaders play a dual management strategy (Edelenbos et al., 2008): one focusing on control and order (short term), and another focusing on letting go and dynamics (long term). On the short, term leadership distributes organizational resources towards exploitation, on the long term, towards exploration (March, 1999).

The time and energy a policy maker spends on that search process is only rewarded in the long term through its effects on the larger system of which both players form part. This behaviour is altruistic in the sense that the actor does not aim to maximize his short-term returns in the more basic level. However, the individual, driven by these higher-order memes (Beck and Cowan, 1996), is programmed to maximize his longer-term returns, like altruistic behaviour of animals always can be explained as selfish behaviour of their genes (Dawkins, 1976). Both memes and genes need first to survive on the short term before they can survive at the long term. 'Terms' in complex social systems may also be defined as scales – as higher scale equals higher-order holon-level, the higher the first level to which two agents belong, the larger their social distance. Each next scale-time level depends on the capacity of agents to make resources available for the next level.

Social structure therefore, according to these theories, has several embedded levels. Every description of these levels, however, may be a gross simplification of reality. On the other hand agents develop their own, necessarily simplified, perceptions of reality – which includes their perception of the social structure they belong to and interact with, and how that coevolves with the physical system (e.g. Gerrits, 2008). If this perception guides their conduct, social systems are most fundamentally the product of self-construction, and, as implied above, social systems, holons and memes are all the same thing, and agents can observe only a small part of that social reality, while a lot may also be tacit knowledge, or totally subconscious (e.g. Stacey, 2003). And interpretations may easily be wrong.

15.4 How do these theories relate to 'networks'?

Policy networks may be defined as relatively stable patterns of interaction between social systems or agents (which may be individuals). The deeply theoretical notions about levels of governance above are met by several more practical ideas about the behaviour of policy networks. We name a few hereafter, and hope the reader will see how this links with the idea of different systems levels, where a higher-order level co-evolves with a previously existing lower-order level, and crosses power-related boundaries within or between large organizations, and therefore parts of a governance system.

Communities of Practice (Wenger, 1998)

Wenger (1998) defines Communities of Practice as groups of people who share a concern for something they do and learn how to do it better as they interact regularly. Three characteristics are crucial: it has an identity defined by a shared domain of interest; membership therefore implies a commitment to this identity. They value their collective competence and learn from each other, even though few people outside the group may value or even recognize their expertise. Members engage in joint activities and discussions, help each other, and share information, but not necessarily work together on a daily basis. They share a repertoire of resources: experiences, stories, tools, ways of addressing recurring problems. This takes time and sustained interaction; i.e. it is an investment

> Communities of practice are everywhere; [...] when it is given a name and brought into focus, it becomes a perspective that can help us understand our world better. In particular, it allows us to see past more obvious formal structures such as organizations, classrooms, or nations, and perceive the structures defined by engagement in practice and the informal learning that comes with it. [...] the very characteristics that make communities of practice a good fit for stewarding knowledge – utonomy, practitioner-orientation, informality, crossing boundaries – are also characteristics that make them a challenge for traditional hierarchical organizations. How this challenge is going to affect these organizations remains to be seen. (Wenger, 1998: 247).

Learning organizations (Senge, 1990)

Senge has popularized the idea of a lever, which may be discovered through systems thinking. In this view, individuals and organizations become able to re-create themselves proactively. Thus, for a 'learning organization it is not enough to survive. '"Survival learning" or what is more often termed "adaptive learning" is necessary. But for a learning organization, "adaptive learning" must be joined by "generative learning", learning that enhances our capacity to create' (Senge, 1990). This requires, among others, team learning. So, such teams can be seen as networks that are crucial to organizational learning. (See also http://www.infed.org/thinkers/senge.htm)

Shadow themes brought forward by informal social structures (Stacey, 1993; 2003)

Stacey (1993; 2003) describes how in organizations there are legitimate themes, which may be talked about in the open, and shadow themes that are only discussed between people who trust each other. He claims that shadow conversations are driven by ideology. Acting in public may create tensions because the real motives remain concealed for those not trusted. In the shadow of the formal organization, informal organizations carry shadow themes. The deeper themes that drive shadow conversations are often subconscious, and behaviour is rationalized. This includes behaviour that keeps boundaries between networks in place. These processes always operate in any organization, and relate to the reproduction and potential transformation of power relations. Stacey argues that some level of consciousness about informal processes is needed to be able to change power relations – if that were needed for some larger interest. Subconscious themes in his eyes may break through the surface if informal interactions intentionally try to do so, after which trust may develop and elements of change can emerge to formal interactions, in public. He points to the importance of diversity in shadow themes and informal groups, which should be fostered as a goal by itself, since it is a requisite for transformation. (This looks a lot like the Law of Requisite Variety, which Ashby has proposed for general systems theory.) The distinction between 'legitimate' and 'shadow' is important because the tension between the two is a potential source of diversity. Shadow communications shape, and are shaped by, power relations. New forms of conversation may emerge, which is tantamount to shifts in power relations. Anxiety, which may be caused by an overemphasis on performance according to 'official' criteria, triggers defensive routines, and suppresses free conversation about shadow themes. Culture and psychology, which, like power relations, are part of the social structure, are therefore determinants of adaptive organizations. Anxious, inert organizations only change if they are forced by circumstances and something new can grow on the debris, unless shadow groups are capable of turning the culture around before it is too late. This is why leadership is needed to start a process of self-organization that cannot be created top down.

Structural Tension (Fritz, 1989)

Fritz (1989) was one of the first to write about how one may become aware of tensions to 'attract' creative ideas that cannot be known in advance or planned, but that resolve the tension. Groups and individuals may feel the tension between what is now separately desired and what is jointly desired for the longer term. Nooteboom (2006) describes how tensions in Parliament, driven by the interests of private groups and non-governmental organizations, trickle down to the level of individual policy makers who find opportunities for social change that fit the tension. He also describes how this leads to a resonance of communications that create tensions in a larger social network, leading to the emergence of increasingly integrative forces, fostering a diversity of creative ideas. Nooteboom (2007) indicates how in spatial development tensions may be managed through instruments like Environmental Impact Assessment that create interdependency between developers and affected interests. The tension between status quo development and a desirable future is made tangible in the present and may influence development. In short, Fritz's idea of cultivating rather than ignoring tension may be the essence of what it is to think at a higher-order level

Adaptive networks (Nooteboom, 2006)

Nooteboom (2006) has described how influential informal networks (termed adaptive networks) have emerged and explicitly looked for sustainable development of a large societal system like the transport and energy system. Since in this system public and private organizations and political pressure groups are in a deadlock, creative solutions are difficult to create, but adaptive networks influenced the official leadership of these organizations to communicate in a different way with their supporter groups. Change managers in this adaptive network used phrases like 'wisdom of the crowd' and 'co-evolution between social subsystems'. By developing across borders between contrasting organizations they were able to merge their knowledge and create a joint long-term perception of sustainable transport. From this perception they were able to influence their respective leaders (taking part in the adaptive network but less intensively), who communicated more congruent ideas with their stakeholder groups. Since the group included parties that often were enemies in public debate, like the oil industry and environmental groups, personal relationships and trust needed to be developed. As feedback returned from the official organizations, in several steps official platforms could be erected where parties talked about interventions for sustainable transport. In the shadow of these platforms, exerting structural tension, new informal groups emerged looking explicitly for possible breakthroughs behind the scenes. However, as soon as ideas were safe enough, they were communicated as ideas for middle-term desires in the platform, where the government participated and could develop their part of interventions for change. Thus, there was co-evolution between parts of society, and between official structure and unofficial structure, and these two were both necessary – stagnation in either duality would have caused overall stagnation. A most striking feature was that many policy makers crossing societal gaps 'consciously' self-organized into highly dynamic adaptive networks, which developed their own rules about interaction and trust. As soon as the system started to transform, they moved to another structural tension.

Recent authors of adaptive governance

Several authors write about the governance of social-spatial or social-ecological systems, and like Nooteboom (2006) they are often concerned with sustainable development and environmental issues. For example, Folke et al. (2005) write about 'bridging organizations' (much like Nooteboom's platforms) that seem to lower the cost of collaboration and conflict resolution. Holling et al. (2006) refer to shadow networks in the context of social-ecological systems. Pelling et al. (2007) refer to shadow spaces for adaptive capacity in relation to climate change. Pahl-Wostl (2007), relating to adaptive water management, refers to the importance of informal networks, and indicates that this should become integral part of the management regime. Edelenbos (2010) speaks of 'complexity sensitiveness' in which formal governments institutions adjust to vision forming and idea creation in informal institutions. Adaptive governance is then about developing boundary spanning activities in which existing boundaries are crossed or made porous (Williams, 2007). However, how can one be sure that newly emerging networks, in their informal stages, are actually of a higher order than other networks in the governance system; i.e. purely bridging?

15.5 How can boundary spanning be observed and applied in a case study?

Observing 'higher-orderedness' of networks

Clearly, the idea of layers within governance networks is not new. In particular theories about social learning processes refer to informal, shadow or adaptive groups or networks. They emerge from formal networks which are the context for the official processes, which are again the context of informal networks and processes. The idea of adaptive networks adds that informal groups, emerging from a governance system, are alive if they have an identity that aims to influence the formal structure and be influenced by it, and is 'fed' by 'higher order motives'. These higher order motives may be at odds with 'lower order motives', and adaptive networks deliberately use the tension between both levels in a creative way. If the adaptive group thinks it has successfully influenced the governance system it emerges from, it is motivated to continue its existence, it has its own 'metabolism', and therefore in biological terms it is a living organism (see also Ashby (1962) who already used such a metaphor). However, any organism develops a tendency to become a goal by itself competing with other organisms; in this case competing for the attention and time of policy makers, like any lower-order network. How can higher-orderedness then be observed empirically?

The structure and process of a governance system are relatively easily observed by review of (policy) documents and public statements of policy makers, and by regular interviews with influential policy makers. However, it is less easy to observe adaptive networks. These groups obviously have their local views which easily might be partial, one-sided and wrong about effective action for a desirable future. The future they desire might not be the future others desire. It is not knowable if unconnected learning groups with different views about desirable futures might be able to learn from each other and develop a joint view of a desirable future. So, how then can we answer the original three questions about planning of this chapter, where even the first one creates difficulties? Different scientists will give different answers, since they use different methods. Also scientists interpret what they observe through a mental frame, which in the case of scientists is called a method. Ever since Descartes, who only wanted to rely on his own senses, scientific method is something mysterious, with currently a major difference between positivists (who believe there are knowable facts) and constructivists (who believe every fact is a socially constructed meme).

Method in second-order (social) cybernetics

So, in terms of Schon and Rhein (1994), scientists could use some 'frame reflection'. This chapter is not the place for such reflection, but moving back to systems theory, we would like to refer to the 'frame' of second order cybernetics. Cybernetics is the study of communication and control (e.g. Ashby, 1956; Wiener, 1961). First order or engineering cybernetics studies circular causality in physical systems, with the aim of observing, understanding and controlling these systems. Second order or biological cybernetics includes the role of the observer, who is studied as a part of the system (Foerster, 1995; Maturana and Varela, 1998). A key feature is the circularity of reciprocity. The brain constructs images of first order reality as a second order reality. In social cybernetics, the observer is a social participant of the system. Ideas are supposed to be accepted if they serve the observer's purposes as a social participant; these purposes themselves are also socially constructed and perhaps driven by biological needs. On the other hand, the link between biological need fulfilment and constructed realities is often unclear. Consequently, through transformation of conceptual systems, society may change (Umpelby, 2006).

The point is, all this is also valid for scientists who try to observe the early stages of emerging new ideas, shadow themes as Stacey (2003) indicates; a scientist like any participant can only observe what occurs in his own direct environment, and what happens outside is a matter of indirect interpretation. When new conceptual systems emerge it is for those who 'carry' them not knowable if they will break through, and as soon as new conceptual systems break through so others can also see them, it is difficult for these others to identify where they really have originated. They will only see the official leaders uttering innovative ideas, but inspired by whom? A scientist observing hypothesized adaptive networks only will see what really happens behind the scenes if he is trusted and therefore a member of the network. What he can do to 'validate' the 'truth' of their reasoning is to assess the amount of connectivity they reach: does a group 'merge' perceptions originating in far corners of a large social system? Do they actually bridge subsystems that are poorly connected in the 'official' governance system?

'Trust' as key variable

Nooteboom (2006) describes how an adaptive network bridged the environmental movement and the transport sector, and the public sector with the private sector, by explicitly building up trust across these gaps, looking for common ground and giving each other room for competition in the policy process at another level, whilst also reflecting on the windows of opportunity at other levels (Kingdon, 1995), looking smaller interventions for the common benefit. They gave each other more information about opportunities and internal dynamics of the (otherwise competing) subsystem, because there was trust that this would not be misused.

The importance of trust as an important precondition for letting go short term oriented self-interest, is underlined in different strands of literature. Trust enables actors to assume an open and vulnerable position, since they expect others to refrain from opportunistic behaviour (Deakin and Michie, 1997; Deakin and Wilkinson, 1998). The actor trusts that the partner will take his or her interests into account in the interaction (Nooteboom, 2002; Rousseau et al., 1998).

In risky situations, trust is a precondition for undertaking any action (Gambetta, 1988a; 1988b; Lane and Bachmann, 1998), and lack of all trust will paralyse. The assumption in most of the literature on trust is that actors will refrain from action (and cooperation) if trust is absent. Think of the frozen deer syndrome: a deer in car headlights chooses death by collision over jumping into the dark. Action requires a conscious choice and trust that the alternative will be better. Trust facilitates, solidifies and enhances performance of cooperation (Edelenbos and Klijn, 2008). In trustworthy situations, actors are prepared to look for solutions that go beyond short term self-interests toward common and long term interests, because one can trust that the other will do the same. This process has potential positive effect on the short term as well. Actors may give favours with no immediate return (Ring and Van de Ven, 1992), and forced to do something potentially harmful to the other they may apologize in advance, knowing that the relationship can buffer such behaviour.

The jump sideways in the dark by a dear in headlights can be seen as a creative act. In fact, trust is often seen as key factor in innovation processes (Nooteboom, 2002; Zand, 1972; Ring and Van de Ven, 1994). Learning and discovering new things requires knowledge exchange and intensive interaction. Nooteboom (1998) mentions the example of small companies that maintain a network of contacts with other organizations, thus acquiring the necessary specific knowledge they do not have themselves. Trust plays an important role in facilitating interaction (Edelenbos and Klijn, 2008).

Observing trust through action research

Therefore, Nooteboom (2006) indicates, through trust, sensitive inside-information could be shared in the networks he studied, and it became easier to match opportunities in their different subsystems. It is important that the researcher operates as a kind of 'an accepted insider' in the networks and subsystems. The researcher conducts 'learning evaluation through action research' (Edelenbos and Van Buuren, 2007). Research is a process that is characterized by defining time and again the practical circumstances and by, time and again, developing ideas and insight in interaction with these practical circumstances (Greenwood and Levin, 1988, 75-76). The researcher is closely involved in the process of policy-making and in a way even a part of it. The evaluator does not relate to his environment in an impersonal manner. In uncertain and unique situations, for which standard solutions are not available, he needs to contribute to this policy context where he is part of the policy practice in a reflexive way. The researcher is in constant interaction with the actors he is observing and evaluating.

In this way researchers are able to identify shifts in communication by official leaders with their larger supporter groups as incremental steps toward change. They used the feedback from these supporters to build up support for next steps in a wide communication and learning process. The fact that these people all were influential in their own subsystem (which they had to prove to each other) and the fact that they had to bridge the perceptions of their different stakeholder groups may be taken as indications that this adaptive group actually was helping a large governance system to change with a view to a widely shared common interest. As a group they never made themselves known in the governance system – they were linked to power but not driven by some interest of the group to remain 'alive'. As the tensions they fed upon were either resolved or proved irresolvable, they moved on to other tensions and the network's composition co-evolved with their identity. One basis of trust in this case was that members of the adaptive network did not personally take the credit in the governance system for breaking ideas, which was verified by interviews in the social environment. Breaking ideas could have emerged in other networks as well.

The scientist has only to convince his peers that opponents from the governance system develop mutual trust and verify their new ideas in the governance system before creating direct interventions about use of official power and resources. This openness distinguishes it from a backroom looking for personal power or career. This enables the observer to verify indirectly the motive of participants, and identify the network as 'higher-order', enabling it to become alive and use the tension with the lower-order level as a self-standing creative force. All the substantial aspects (the merged perceptions, the observed windows of opportunity, the successes defined as emerging ideas as incremental step toward a common goal) remain inter-subjective assessments by the adaptive network, which the scientist has difficulty verifying. And, of course, there is always the possibility that trust may not sustain and the group was collectively wrong.

15.6 What does this mean for planners?

Planners should argue why their proposals are in the 'public interest'. However, as argued above, the public interest is a social construct that may or may not be widely shared. From the normative point of view that plans should be in a wide interest, planners should therefore look for widely shared definitions of the public interest. The original questions can now be answered as follows.

How can one 'know' what a desirable future is from the perspective of a large social system

The answer is, the chance of finding an adequate description of a desirable future is increased by developing trust. Investing in relationships offers the opportunity to merge real perceptions without hidden agendas. It requires the willingness and skill of frame reflection and explicit acceptance to invest on a personal basis, i.e. not driven by desire of success in terms of the *existing* frames in the own hierarchical organization. This attitude, displayed from several sides, can be a basis of trust and learning on a common basis. The lessons learned include shared perceptions of desirable futures, which form the 'identity' of this group. If the adaptive group spans a large social system, its identity will be abstract and the future it desires only achievable on a long term. Yet, these may be used to influence official planning processes, which create, as mentioned above, a platform for interactions in the official governance arena.

How can one who 'knows' what a desirable future is, identify incremental (and therefore acceptable) interventions that actually may contribute to desirable breakthroughs in development

Once trust and common ideas about the future emerge in a higher-order interaction, the tension with the present situation of the governance system, which is not heading in a desirable direction, may be sensed and used as a source of inspiration. Since planners who are member of adaptive groups are also influential members of the governance system, they can see the internal dynamics of the subsystems they belong too, and therefore they are able to identify the interventions official leaders may be willing to make. In the case of really sensitive political situations this would limit to reducing hostile and polarizing language. From there, tensions in the governance system may be identified in public debate, as well as possible (initially very wide) avenues of change in a common interest. In that way, official leaders from different subsystems generate an adaptive tension, inviting their policy makers to develop proposals that release some of the tension they have created.

How can this person actually achieve such interventions in a world where power is shared and that is dominated by contrasting short-term interest

The question is, how can a planner inspired by adaptive tensions become influential so that official leaders are willing to listen and take the risk of being the first uttering innovative ideas that might be received badly by supporters, or by opponents. The answer is that these planners should be able to make this risk acceptable for their official leaders and even turn the risk into an opportunity. A 'narrative' is required explaining the adaptive tensions, the windows of opportunity, the possible matches, and anticipated responses to innovative utterances. Different official leaders may be strong in position, or they may feel threatened. Thus, planners should be intensely aware of the position of their political leaders whom they should follow in the official world, whilst continuously inviting them for dialogue about the analysis that has been produced in adaptive networks. They should be aware of the importance of the unofficial world and the fact that it both may seize power through conspiracy as it is necessary to produce proactive social change. They should become reflexive practitioner and constantly assess the real motives for informal interactions.

Complex systems leadership

The considerations above make clear where the title of this chapter comes from: proactive governance depends on the existence of adaptive networks, and these depend on self-organization of planners who look for the 'public interest'. Adaptive networks are therefore the expression of collective leadership. Nonetheless, adaptive networks and the amount of connectivity they generate remain difficult to observe. Fragmented adaptive networks are everywhere, but do they actually connect large social systems through direct or indirect personal relationships? Or are they more aimed at partial, short-term or even individual interests without consideration of larger systems? Existing theories indicate that leadership in complex systems must be a shared leadership (e.g. Panzar et al., 2007). This shared leadership has a focus on the coevolutionary relationship between the short and long term. The long term discussion, which is often hidden undercurrent in governance systems (Nooteboom, 2006), is fed by the short term. The short term goals developed and implemented in the visible policy arenas, are influenced, by the longer term undercurrent which is invisible for outsiders. Leaders with meta-capabilities and competences are needed to operate in such coevolving perspective (Hazy, 2007; Uhl-Bien, 2007) in which an orientation on creating trustworthy relationships and cooperation is present.

References

Ashby, W.R. (1956) *An Introduction to Cybernetics*, Chapman & Hall, London.
Ashby, W.R. (1962) *Principles of the Self-Organizing System*. Classical Papers – Principles of the self-organizing system. E:CO Special Double Issue Vol. 6 Nos. 1-2, 2004, pp. 102-126, Originally published as Ashby, W.R. (1962). "Principles of the self-organizing system," in: H. Von Foerster and G.W. Zopf, Jr. (eds.) Principles of Self-Organization – Transactions of the University of Illinois Symposium, Pergamon Press, London, pp. 255-278.
Axelrod, R. and M.D. Cohen (1999) *Harnessing Complexity. Organizational Implications of a Scientific Frontier*, New York, The Free Press.
Baumgartner, F.R. and B.D. Jones (1993) *Agendas and Instability in American Politics*, The University of Chicago Press, Chicago.
Beck, D.E. and C. Cowan (1996) *Spiral Dynamics: Mastering Values, Leadership and Change*, Blackwell, Cambridge.
Brandenburger A. and B. Nalebuff (1996) *Co-Opetition: A Revolution Mindset That Combines Competition and Cooperation*, Doubleday Business, New York.
Castells, M. (2000, first edition 1996) *The Rise of the Network Society: Economy, Society and Culture*, Blackwell, Cambridge.
Dawkins, R. (1976) *The Selfish Gene*, Oxford University Press, Oxford.
De Jong, M. and J. Edelenbos (2007) An Insider's Look into Policy Transfer in Trans-national Expert Networks, *European Planning Studies*, 15(5), pp. 687-706.

Edelenbos, J. and E.H. Klijn (2007) Trust in Complex Decision-Making Networks: A Theoretical and Empirical Exploration, *Administration and Society*, 39(1), pp. 25-50.

Edelenbos, J., L. Gerrits and M. van Gils (2008) The Coevolutionary Relation Between Dutch Mainport Policies and the Development of the Seaport Rotterdam, *Emergence: Co-Evolution*, 10(2), pp. 48-59.

Edelenbos, J. (2010) *Water as Connective Current. On Water Governance and the Importance of Dynamic Water Management*, Boom/Lemma, The Hague.

Flood, R.L. (1999) *Rethinking the Fifth Discipline: Learning Within the Unknowable*, Routledge, London.

Foerster, H. v. (1995) *The Cybernetics of Cybernetics*, FutureSystems Inc, Minneapolis.

Folke F., T. Hahn, P. Olsson and J. Norberg (2005) Adaptive governance of social-ecological Systems, *Annu. Rev. Environ. Resour*, 30, pp. 441–73.

Fritz, R. (1989) *Path of Least Resistance: Learning to Become the Creative Force in Your Own Life*, Ballantine Books, New York.

Gerrits, L.M. (2008) *The Gentle Art of Coevolution: A Complexity Theory Perspective on Decision Making over Estuaries in Germany, Belgium and The Netherlands*. http://hdl.handle.net/1765/11152.

Hajer, M. (2003) Coalitions, Practices, and Meaning in Environmental Politics – from Acid Rain to BSE, in: Howarth, D. and J. Torfing (eds.) *Discourse Theory in European Politics*, Palgrave Macmillan, Basingstoke, pp. 297-315.

Hazy, J.K. (2007) Leadership or Luck: The System Dynamics of Intel's Shift to Microprocessors in the 1970s and 1980s, in: Uhl-Bien, M. and R. Marion (eds.) *Complexity Leadership. Conceptual Foundations*, Information Age Publishing, Charlotte, pp. 347-378.

Kingdon, J.W. (1995 [1984]) *Agendas, Alternatives and Public Policies*, HarperCollins College Publishers, New York.

Kooiman, J. (2003) *Governing as Governance*, Sage Publications, Thousand Oaks.

Leydesdorff, L. (2010) Luhmann Reconsidered: Steps Towards an Empirical Research Program in the Sociology of Communication?, in: Grant, C. (ed.) *Beyond Universal Pragmatics: Essays in the Philosophy of Communication*, Peter Lang, Oxford, pp. 149-173.

Lindblom, C.E. (1959) The Science of Muddling Through, *Public Administration Review*, 19, pp. 79-88.

Lindblom, C.E. (1979) Still Muddling, Not Yet Through, *Public Administration Review*, 39, pp. 517-525.

Luhmann, N. (1995) *Social Systems*, Stanford University Press, Stanford.

March, J.G. (1999) *The Pursuit of Organizational Intelligence*, Blackwell Publishers Ltd, Oxford.

Maslov, A. (1943) A Theory of Human Motivation, *Psychological Review*, 50, pp. 370-396.

Maturana, H. and F. Varela (1998) *The Tree of Knowledge*, Shambhala Press, Boston.

Morgan, G. (1997) *Images of Organization*, Sage, Thousand Oaks.

Mulder, P. and J.C.J.M. v.d. Bergh (1999) Evolutionary Economic Theories of Sustainable Development, *Growth and Change*, 32(4), pp. 110-134.

Nooteboom, B, (1998) *Management van Partnerships* [management of partnerships], Academic Service, Schoonhoven.

Nooteboom, S. (2006) *Adaptive Networks: The Governance for Sustainable Development*, Eburon, Delft.

Nooteboom, S. (2007) Impact Assessment Procedures and Complexity Theories, *EIA Review*, 27, pp. 645-665.

Olsson, P., L.H. Gunderson, S.R. Carpenter, P. Ryan, L. Lebel, C. Folke, and C.S. Holling (2006) Shooting the Rapids: Navigating Transitions to Adaptive Governance of Social-ecological Systems, *Ecology and Society*, 11(1), p. 18, [online] URL: http://www. ecologyandsociety.org/vol11/iss1/art18/.

Ostrom, E. (2005) *Understanding Institutional Diversity*, Princeton University Press, Princeton.

Pahl-Wostl, C. (2007) Requirements for Adaptive Water Management, In: Pahl-Wostl, C., Kabat, P., and Möltgen (eds) *Adaptive and Integrated Water Management: Coping with Complexity and Uncertainty*, Springer Verlag, Berlin, pp. 1-22.

Panzar, C., J.J. Hazy, and B. McKelvey (2007) The Paradox of Complex Organizations: Leadership as Integrative Influence, in: J.K Hazy, J.A. Goldstein and B.B. Lichtenstein (eds.) *Complex Systems Leadership Theory, New Perspectives from Complexity Science on Social and Organizational Effectiveness*, Volume 1, ISCE Publishing, Mansfield, pp. 305-325.

Pelling, M., C. High, J. Dearing and D. Smith (2007) Shadow Spaces for Social Learning: A Relational Understanding of Adaptive Capacity to Climate Change within Organizations, *Environment and Planning A*. Advance Online Publication.

Ring, P.A. and Van de Ven, A. (1994) Developmental Processes of Cooperative Interorganizational Relationships, *Academy of Management Review*, 19, pp. 90-118.

Sabatier, P. and H.C. Jenkins-Smith (1993) *An Advocacy Coalition Approach*, Westview Press, Boulder.

Scharpf, F.W. (1997) *Games Real Actors Play: Actor-centered Institutionalism in Policy Research*, Westview Press, Boulder.

Schon, D.A (1983) *The Reflective Practitioner: How Professionals Think in Action*, Basic Books, New York.

Schon, D.A. and M. Rein (1994) *Frame Reflection: Toward the Resolution of Intractable Policy Controversies*, Basic Books, New York.

Senge, P.M. (1990) *The Fifth Discipline: The Art and Practice of the Learning Organization*, Currency Doubleday, New York.

Shannon, C.E. (1948) A Mathematical Theory of Communication, *Bell System Technical Journal*, 27, pp. 379-423 and 623-356.

Coevolving Adaptive and Power Networks   365

Spangenberg, J.H. (2007) Second Order Governance: Learning Processes to Identify Indicators, *Corporate Social Responsibility and Environmental Management*, 15(3), pp. 125-185.

Stacey, R. (2003 [1993]) *Strategic Mangement and Organisational Dynamics. The Challenge of Complexity*, Prentice Hall, Upper Saddle River.

Surowiecki, J. (2004) *The Wisdom of Crowds: Why the Many Are Smarter than the Few and How Collective Wisdom Shapes Business, Economies, Societies, and Nations*, Doubleday, New York.

Teisman, G.R. (2005) *Public Management on the Edge of Chaos and Order; about Leadership and Organizing in Complexity* (in Dutch), Academic Service, The Hague.

Uhl-Bien, M., Marion, R. and McKelvey, B. (2007) Complexity Leadership Theory: Shifting Leadership From the Industrial to the Knowledge Era. *The Leadership Quaterly*, 18, pp. 298-318.

Umpelby, S.A. (2006) Fundamentals and History of Cybernetics 1: A tutorial presented, World Multi-Conference on Systemics, Cybernetics and Informatics, Orlando.

Wenger, E. (1998) *Communities of Practice: Learning, Meaning, and Identity.* Cambridge University Press, Cambridge.

Wiener, N. (1961) *Cybernetics*, MIT Press, New York.

Williams, P. (2002) The Competent Boundary Spanner. *Public Administration*, 80(1), pp. 103-124.

Zand, D.E. (1972) Trust and Managerial Problem Solving, *Administrative Science Quarterly*, 17(2), pp. 229-39.

PART IV
Simulating in between the Real and the Ideal

Chapter 16

The Metaverse as Lab to Experiment with Problems of Organized Complexity

Oswald Devisch[1]

In 1948 Warren Weaver, later accredited with being one of the founding fathers of complexity theory, introduced the notion 'Problems of Organized Complexity', referring to complex problems displaying essential features of organization, and proclaimed simulations as the tool to tackle these problems. Since Weaver's proclamation, (computer) simulations have indeed been explored, also within the field of planning, to operate in – in the case of planning – complex physical settings. Such explorations typically start off as theoretical experiments, but seldom make it to the planning practice.

In 2007, in their Metaverse Roadmap, Smart, Cascio and Paffendorf proclaim that electronic computing (including simulations) is increasingly becoming an indispensable part of our everyday life, to the degree that it is no longer always clear what is real and what is virtual (i.e. computed).

So, whereas planners only seem to hesitantly adopt electronic computing in their practice, they increasingly do so, without resistance, in their daily life. This ambiguous attitude is taken as the point of origin to, on the one hand, reassess Weaver's proclamation – now that electronic computing seems to be everywhere, does it help answering problems of organized complexity? – and to, on the other hand, explore how electronic computing can help planners and urban designers addressing complex physical settings? To answer both questions we first introduce the Metaverse Roadmap, to then define three avenues along which electronic computing can be employed by planners, to finally illustrate one avenue in more detail and return to Weaver.

16.1 Introduction

In 'Science and Complexity' Warren Weaver (1948) tries to get a view of 'the function of science'. To get this view he proposes to run through the history of science. Up to the 19th century, Weaver writes, science mainly addressed so-called 'Problems of Simplicity' – problems with a limited number of variables.

---

1   Oswald Devisch is Professor at the Department of Architecture and Arts, PHL University College, Diepenbeek, Belgium.

In tackling such problems, science brought us the telephone, the radio, the automobile, and the airplane. From 1900 onwards, Weaver continues, science started to look at problems involving very large numbers of variables. The then developed techniques of probability theory and statistical mechanics revealed that though each individual variable behaves erratic (or disorganized), the system as a whole possesses 'certain orderly and analysable average properties', making Weaver label these problems 'Problems of Disorganized Complexity'. He gives as examples the motion of the atoms or stars, and the laws of thermodynamics. At this point Weaver ends his historic overview, be it that he is not satisfied, remarking that a whole range of problems neither involve two (or three or four), nor a large amount of variables, and for that matter cannot be addressed with simple equations nor with statistics. Weaver therefore comes up with a third category of problems: one where the number of variables lies somewhere in between two and a lot. The most important characteristic of this category, he continues, is however not this number, but the fact that these problems 'show the essential feature of organization', granting them the title of 'Problems of Organized Complexity'. Think of economic markets, the reproduction of living creatures, and social group behaviour. At the moment of Weaver's writing, no methodologies existed that could help answering this type of problems, making Weaver conclude that the search for such methodologies would be the function of science in the coming years. Weaver saw two developments that could hint at such a methodology: the use of electronic computing and multi-disciplinary (or mixed team) research.

More than half a century later, Johnson (2002) considers Weaver's text to be the founding text of complexity theory, 'the point at which the study of complex systems began to think of itself as a unified field' (pp. 46). Johnson continues stating that the first real breakthrough in this field came from within urban planning, with Jane Jacobs referring in her book 'The Death and Life of Great American Cities' to cities as 'problems of organized complexity'. A credo that has been repeated ever since, with scholars (e.g. Batty, 2005; Portugali, 2000) illustrating how principles of self-organization and emergence return in urban processes such as traffic congestion, pedestrian crowding, gentrification, and segregation. In their attempt to tackle these problems, planners have – Weaver in mind – indeed been relying on, among others, electronic computing, implemented as spatial interaction models, discrete choice models, and – more recently – microsimulation models. For an overview, see Timmermans (2003). Despite the evolution towards ever more complex and realistic models, the adoption rate within the planning practice remains low (Lee, 1994).

16.2 Metaverse roadmap

In their 'cross-industry public foresight project', Smart, Cascio and Paffendorf (2007) introduce the term metaverse, referring to 'the convergence of virtually-enhanced physical reality and physically persistent virtual space' (p. 4). What they in fact argue is that electronic computations, specified as 3D-webtools and -objects, are being embedded in nearly every aspect of our environment, as such becoming 'persistent features of our lives'. They claim that the metaverse will 'shape the development of many technological realms' (p. 4), giving examples such as rapid prototyping in the field of manufacturing, real-time world modelling in the area of logistics and transportation, and virtual experimentation labs in the domain of artificial intelligence. In an attempt to foresee how these developments might evolve in both the near as the long future, Smart et al. invited 'distinguished industry leaders, technologists, analysts, and creatives' to come up with a Metaverse Roadmap, four scenarios – Mirror Worlds, Virtual Worlds, Augmented Reality, and Lifelogging – all illustrating how electronic computing indeed is part of the everyday life of a lot of people and how it will increasingly do so in the future.

At the time Weaver introduced us to Problems of Organized Complexity, electronic computing was still in its infancy. Judging from Smart et al.'s foresight project, electronic computing is – 60 years later – radically changing the way we live, work and play, to the point where the distinction between what is real and what is computed is no longer always that clear. To some, this blurring implies no less than the collapse of geography (Ondrejka in Hudson-Smith, Milton, Dearden and Batty, 2007). One could indeed question the concept of a nation state in a time where one can be with anyone, everywhere at any time. The dawn of the metaverse makes it the right moment to reassess Weaver's statement that electronic computing holds the key to answer Problems of Organized Complexity. In other words, how can the four metaverse scenarios be employed to understand and manage complex systems, and more specific, complex physical environments?

As mentioned earlier, planners do already rely on electronic computation, e.g. to assess their intervention intentions. As we will argue, this type of computation could be classified under the metaverse 'mirror worlds'-scenario. The question we would like to address is what planners can learn from the other three scenarios. In search of an answer, we will first introduce all four metaverse-scenarios and illustrate each one with examples potentially relevant to planning. Secondly we will propose three avenues towards adopting these scenarios – and electronic computation in general – in planning. We will argue that though each of these avenues does address problems of organized complexity, they do this in a significantly different fashion. To make this argument we will rely on the concepts of emergence and adaptation. Finally we will follow one of the three avenues, and make suggestions as to how the metaverse scenarios can be combined into instruments that can enhance our understanding of complex physical environments.

Interesting to note finally is that the metaverse is not the only concept that s being used to reason about the blending of real and computed worlds. Joseph ²ine,[2] for instance, uses the term 'multiverse' to refer to no less than eight parallel universes (instead of the two of the metaverse, namely the real versus the virtual

---

2   Joseph Pine during a presentation at the fourth Mobile Monday Amsterdam meeting: http://www.mobilemonday.nl/.

universe), illustrating how electronic computation fundamentally changed our conceptions of time, space and matter.

16.3 Four metaverse scenarios illustrated

In their exploration as to how virtualization might impact our physical world, the authors of the Metaverse Roadmap propose four scenarios: mirror worlds, virtual worlds, augmented reality, and lifelogging, structured along – what the authors refer to as – two 'key continua', with one continuum ranging from augmentation to simulation, and the other from intimate to external (see Smart et al. 2007). The idea behind these continua is that the selection of four scenarios is by no means exhaustive. In our search for what planners can learn from recent developments within electronic computation, the proposed metaverse scenarios will suffice though. The continua will therefore not be considered. For the same reason, the selection of examples is limited to those (potentially) relevant to planning.

The most simple scenario to introduce is the Mirror World scenario (MW). The underlying idea is that one can employ electronic computing to develop digital reflections of the physical world: electronically computed copies of our surroundings, complete with buildings and streets, but also with the weather, traffic, and the whereabouts of people, all continuously updated in real-time. The best known attempt of developing such a MW is Google Earth,[3] a free, web-based, open-standards digital map of Earth. Google Earth not only allows users to zoom in on all corners of Earth's surface, but also stimulates them to upload information: personal information, but also information of general interest such as the location of services, train timetables, and the weather. Google Earth allows importing content from other user-generated-content websites such as Wikipedia (for text), Panoramio (for images), Youtube (for movies), and GigaPan (for panoramas), turning it into an ever-expanding information source, slowly turning into a true mirror world.

For the purpose of our search, a distinction can be made between two categories of MWs: namely MWs serving as databases and MWs serving as social environments. Google Earth obviously belongs to the first category. A MW belonging to the second category is Twinity.[4] Twinity is a 3D virtual copy of (parts of) our physical world, detailed up to the level of individual buildings. The idea is that inhabitants of this MW buy virtual property (representing physical property) furnish it, and inhabit it. According to the developers, this act of furnishing should form the basis of social interaction. A similar example is Twitter,[5] where a real world-map and your real-time position on this map form the starting point of a conversation with members of your social network.

---

3   http://earth.google.com/.
4   http://www.twinity.com/.
5   http://twitter.com/.

MW serving as social environments could also be argued to fall under virtual worlds. Virtual Worlds (VW) differ from MWs in that they involve modelling alternate realities, rather than the world around us. In their Roadmap, Smart et al. make a distinction between VW-based multiplayer games and VW-based social environments. VW-based multiplayer games are defined as being goal oriented with social interaction used as a tool for task completion. Our search in mind, we will only consider a particular type of games, namely strategy games, where winning the game is not so much a matter of collaboration but of skill. The archetype of a strategy game is chess. Crucial is that there is more than one way to play and win the game. In order to get better, the player will have to learn the rules of the game. VW-based multiplayer strategy games can range from war-games, to economic simulations, to city-building games. A popular exponent of this last category is SimCity.[6] SimCity is predominantly a single-player game: taking up the role of a mayor, the player has to either build a new city from scratch, or has to manage an existing city through a natural disaster, a nuclear power plant meltdown, etc. To achieve this he can develop residences, set local tax rates, construct a power grid, provide transportation systems and so on. What is particularly relevant to our search for planning tools is the multiplayer online version of SimCity, in which a city can be shared online by passing it from mayor to mayor, for a limited period of time. That is, you borrow a city, see where it is up to, push its development in a direction of your choosing, and then leave it when your term expires. Daniel Lobo (2005: 16) proposes an alternative version where the players work together, managing the city as a team, rather than competing as rival mayors. 'This development [...] would open new ways to explore conceptual city scenarios that, with the right framework, could start at SimCity helping us to understand urban environments better.'

VW-based social environments differ from (strategy) games in that the aim is not necessarily to win or even to play, but rather to socialize. Computed social environments really function more as large-scale online communities using elements of gaming in the service of a larger goal of developing a community (Book, 2004). Second Life[7] is currently one of the most popular social VWs. Second Life differs from other VWs, such as role-playing games like World of Warcraft, in that it is completely reliant on player-generated content. A resident of Second Life is known as an avatar, which is a three-dimensional figure visible to the player. Each avatar can construct objects, ranging from shoes, to buildings, to even whole islands. These objects then form the setting for the meeting of other residents, settings often without any reference to the physical world. Pierce (2006) describes, for instance, how the closing of the computer game 'URU: Ages Beyond Myst' made a group of ex-URU players immigrate into Second Life, where they reconstructed their old gaming-environment, gradually developing new artefacts and modes of interaction, as such creating a society parallel to the

---

6   http://simcitysocieties.ea.com/.
7   http://secondlife.com/.

one they are a physical part of. A more common phenomenon though is that the generated content partly mirrors the physical world and partly doesn't: take for instance the reconstruction of real world symbolic places – such as Amsterdam, Dublin, Barcelona- or buildings –such as the Eiffel Tower and Sydney Opera House,[8] serving as settings for social encounters. Another phenomenon is that real world social networks have a digital counterpart, be it that all members play a different role than in real life.

In Augmented Reality (AR), the opposite occurs, as virtuality is being adopted into the physical world (rather than reality being (partly) turned virtual). Basically augmenting reality implies adding intelligence to real life objects relying on electronic computing. The simplest form of added intelligence is information: one can, for instance, specify where an object comes from, how it is made, what it consists of. Equipped with the correct technology, eventual buyers can then access this information. A highly popular application is urban annotation, a practice where people can link messages (text, images or video) to geographical locations. A pioneering urban annotation project is Urban Tapestries.[9] Urban Tapestries employs urban annotation to stimulate people and communities of people to publicly 'author' the environment around them. By associating stories with places, relationships are drawn between places, ready for others to explore. Urban Tapestries should, according to the authors, result in an 'anthropology of ourselves', organically built up collective memories that 'trace and embellish different kinds of relationships across places, time and communities' (Lane, 2008: 5).

A more complex form of added intelligence is autonomous decision-making: objects are upgraded so that they can sense their environment and react or even anticipate to what they sense – all following pre-defined algorithms. An often coined concept here is 'Intelligent Environments' referring to spaces equipped with invisible technology, allowing users to seamlessly interact with objects in these spaces. The ambition of the Aware Home Research Initiative,[10] for instance, is to create a home environment that is aware of its occupants whereabouts and activities, and is able to act upon this awareness. The fact that AR applications sense individual users and react differently to each user makes that each of these users may have a different experience of the same physical location. AR applications even allow users to coordinate these experiences making Smart et al. (2006) ponder that people might start using AR to hide those aspects of an environment they considered unpleasant, 'choosing to see only "Potemkin Villages", an informational façade catering to their pre-existing biases and desires' (p. 13).

The last scenario, Lifelogging (LL), is quite similar to Augmented Reality, in that intelligence is added to objects, be it that here it is the object itself that adds the intelligence by continuously logging its internal state. LL in fact equips an object with a memory. Smart et al. (2007) point out that not only objects (object

---

8   For a more complete overview see: http://www.kzero.co.uk/blog/.
9   http://urbantapestries.net/.
10   http://awarehome.imtc.gatech.edu/.

lifelogs) but also people (user lifelogs) can be equipped with such a memory. To Van Kranenburg (2008) this implies that we no longer only possess a physical body, but also a so-called 'data body', which, like our physical body, can be read by others. Popular examples of object LL are GPS trackers (global positioning system trackers). The most advanced ones not only track or log the route you follow, but also the temperature around you, your speed, your altitude, your blood pressure, and so on. All these data can then, at the end of your trip, be visualized with, for instance, Google Earth. A more complex form of LL are objects (or people) that not only log their internal state, but also the state of the environment around them. Think for instance of digital traffic camera's streaming real-time road congestion information to a server. These cameras could then be programmed to evaluate this information and autonomously adjust the maximum speed on that particular road. But then we are in the AR scenario.

Though the four scenarios might still seem limited to the realm of tech-geeks, the examples do indicate that a lot of us indeed live in both a physical and a computed world – a computed world that can take on many forms. What the examples also illustrate is that the metaverse does have an impact on spatial planning, an impact that will only increase, potentially generating – as the authors of the Metaverse Roadmap suggest – new planning instruments: 'In the longer-term time horizon, given a sufficiently robust model of the real world, complete with abundant live data sources and preferences and values maps of the inhabitants, mirror worlds will eventually come to offer a powerful method of testing plans through data mining and simulation' (p. 11). But before we continue exploring this potential, let us first try to find out how the above scenarios could be employed in the planning process.

16.4 Weaver and planners in the metaverse

In a paper on visualization in spatial modeling Batty, Steadman and Xie (2004) define four distinct purposes of visualization: education, exploration, explanation, and engagement. Batty et al. (2004) nevertheless stress that each visualization typically serves multiple purposes, 'often with one purpose dominating'. With education, the authors refer to visualizations designed for the prime purpose of getting the message over of how a model actually works. Visualizations thus that 'enable an understanding which would not be possible without pictorial help' (p. 9). With exploration, the authors refer to visualizations designed to help investigating (rather than simply explaining) how a model works. The more complicated a simulation, the authors argue, the more likely that exploration is required to test the limits of the model, and to enable researchers to be sensitized to the impacts of their scientific decisions. With explanation, the authors refer to visualizations to confirm or falsify some theory which is embodied within the model. Central here, the authors write, is the visualization of patterns in both input and output. With engagement, finally, the authors refer to visualizations developed to engage non-modelling experts into using, but also into assembling, the model.

To structure our search for how planners can employ electronic computing (rather than visualization only) to tackle complex physical environments, we chose to redefine the four purposes of Batty et al. (2004) to three, so called, avenues: informing (cf. education and exploration), managing (cf. engagement) and experimenting (cf. explanation). Informing refers to employing electronic computing to communicate about (complex) spatial processes. Communication only goes one-way: the developer specifies the information, which the user can then explore, but not alter. Managing refers to employing electronic computing to complete a (spatial) intervention. Intervening typically involves experts from a variety of fields, all relying on their own background nevertheless having to cooperate. In this case, communication goes two ways: users can both explore and add information (related to their expertise). To structure the communication, users have to follow a strict protocol, not only limiting the type of information that can be added, but also the moment it can be added. Experimenting, finally, refers to employing electronic computing to deal with unknown (aspects of) spatial processes. Again, communication goes two ways, but there is no protocol. The user can, at all times, intervene, trying out assumptions to, in an ad-hoc fashion, gain an understanding of the spatial process being simulated.

We argue that all three avenues do address Weaver's Problems of Organized Complexity, be it in two fundamentally different ways. To illustrate this difference, let us look at how the key-concepts of complex systems, namely emergence and adaptation, are implemented. The first and the second avenue, informing and managing, presuppose – at least from the developer side – some prior knowledge of the spatial processes being addressed. In the case of informing, for instance, it is precisely this knowledge that is being communicated to the user. To guarantee a successful communication, the electronic computation should therefore always generate the same outcome. In the case of managing, this knowledge concerns not so much the outcome of the computation, but rather the process. During the computation, the experts involved may continuously add new information, impacting the final outcome, but not the process itself. What both informing and managing thus have in common is that prior knowledge is scripted into the computation, in the form of assumptions or rules. So, though electronic computing pursuing informing and managing may display principles of emergence – in that the final outcome is generated and not programmed – one may argue that this emergence is in fact false – in that this outcome is – at least to some extent – predictable. The same argument can be made concerning adaptability – in the case of managing, the computations do adapt to new inputs from user-experts – but this adaptability too is deterministic in that the process is predefined. So, though electronic computations belonging to this category are indeed able to address Weaver's Problems of Organized Complexity, they are only able to address those Problems the developer is already familiar with.

The third avenue, experimenting, on the contrary does not presuppose pre-knowledge. The addressed spatial processes are typically new for both the developer and the user. In an attempt to try and understand these processes, users should be able to intervene in autonomously running computations, not only changing the input but also the computation process itself, and assess the reactions to these interventions. Computations belonging to this category not only display the true characteristics of emergence, but also of adaptation, in that no prior knowledge is scripted in the computations making the outcome at all times unpredictable.

An example will clarify this difference. Take for instance the (spatial) process of pedestrian dynamics. Shiode and Torrens (2008) are developing a fully immersive simulation of crowd behaviour relying on 'geographic automata'. Not the behaviour of the group is modelled, but the behaviour of single pedestrians. In letting these pedestrians interact with each other and with the environment, the group behaviour emerges – in this case crowding. This project belongs to our first category of electronic computations: it does simulate emergent behaviour on the level of the group, but is deterministic on the level of individual pedestrians (apart maybe from an error component). An individual pedestrian will, for instance, never try out actions it is not programmed to follow.

The Mobile Landscapes project, developed at the Senseable City Lab (Ratti, Pulselli, Williams and Frenchman, 2006), also researches pedestrian dynamics, not by modelling the behaviour of individual pedestrians, but by monitoring their real-time behaviour. In their Milan case-study, they mapped the cell-phone usage at different times of the day. Upon analysing the collected data, the researchers were able to reconstruct the intensity of urban activities and their evolution through time and space. Their visualizations not only show recurring daily patterns, but also discrete activities such as a football match or a concert. This project belongs to our second category of electronic computations: though it is in fact just a real-time visualization of an urban process, it does allow experimenting with this process as we will illustrate later.

The majority of electronic computing projects currently being developed within spatial planning only follow two out of the three listed avenues – informing and managing – and are, at least partially, deterministic, as such belonging to the first category. Recent examples of such projects are the Regionmaker,[11] Kaisersrot,[12] and CommunityViz.[13] One may argue that these projects do allow experimenting, for instance running what-if scenarios, but this experimenting is only possible within the 'game-rules'. Like a strategy game, one plays the game till the underlying rules are reconstructed, to then exchange it for a new game.

Recall that the metaverse scenarios in principle encompass all possible electronic computing applications, including those currently being used and developed within spatial planning. The metaverse scenarios can therefore obviously be employed to inform about and manage spatial processes. Virtual Worlds, for instance, claim to serve three goals: gaming, education and socializing (De Nood and Attema, 2007), corresponding with the two first avenues. But what about

---

11   http://www.mvrdv.nl/.
12   http://www.kaisersrot.com/.
13   http://www.communityviz.com/.

the third avenue: experimenting with unknown spatial processes. We argue that the metaverse scenarios indeed allow for experimenting, and that this is exactly here that the metaverse scenarios can contribute to spatial planning and – echoing Weaver – that science can contribute to planning. To support this argument we will now list a number of concrete projects and suggestions for projects illustrating how all this could be accomplished.

16.5 The metaverse as lab

Though the four metaverse scenarios do hint at a number of promising avenues for adopting electronic computing within planning, the most exciting developments occur where two or more of these scenarios overlap. The following examples will illustrate this point. Regarding the choice of examples, the only selection criterion is that they should allow for experimenting with complex physical settings (our third avenue).

A first category of examples can be categorized under the terms embedded sensing or urban sensing (Cuff, Hansen and Kang, 2008). What they have in common is the observation that the number of objects and people that possesses sensors (or computing devices) is that large and that the data these sensors collect is that accessible, that these objects and people become a potential source of information through which one can monitor the state of the environment these objects and people reside in.

A first example illustrating this potential is the TomTom[14] Map Update service, guaranteeing drivers, relying on TomTom navigation software, fully updated maps. TomTom's Map Share technology allows individual drivers to make small corrections on the maps they are using and upload these corrections to the TomTom community, as such generating maps perfectly mirroring the actual traffic situation. A second example is the project 'Tracing the visitors eye' (Girardin, Fiore, Blat and Ratti, 2007). This time, pictures uploaded to Flickr[15], a community sourced site, serve as source of information, and more precisely pictures taken within a period of two years in the Province of Florence, Italy. What the authors observed is that, according to these pictures, the travel behaviour of American tourists differs completely from Italians, and this without doing any observations at the spot.

Urban sensing requires that planners reeducate themselves as data-miners, scanning the omnipresent data streams for patterns. In a podcast by Francica and Schutzberg (2008), urban sensing has been referred to as 'geographic information collection following the principle of least effort', where people go about doing their daily things, while at the same time providing, for instance planners, with valuable data. They give the example of people mapping the presence of WIFI spots, while driving their daily routes. Similarly one could imagine detailed

---

14   http://www.tomtom.com.
15   http://www.flickr.com.

mappings of aspects such as pollution, congestion, crowding, or even complete urban, navigable, 3D environments (Snavely, Garg, Seitz and Szeliski, 2008). In any case, urban sensing holds the promise for planners to gain access to information which they, so far, did not have access to: because it either belonged to the private realm, or because it was simply not considered interesting.

Girardin (2008) points at the role software plays within the process of data-mining. What will shape cities, he states, are not so much the data but the software that process these data. Interpretation is still up to the planner. What will therefore be important in the future, he continues, is 'how the abundant data streams can provide new abilities to model and simulate very complex urban systems in real-time'. Mirror Worlds thus, being continuously updated relying on lifelogging.

In their WikiCity project, Calabrese, Kloeckl and Ratti (2007) take the concept of urban sensing a step further by confronting individual 'sensing' citizens with visualizations (projected on urban screens) of the data streams they produce as a collective. So, rather than only generating real-time maps of urban dynamics, Calabrese et al. (2007) employ these maps to steer these dynamics by making individual citizens aware of, and possibly reconsider, their active role in these dynamics. WikiCity could still be considered a Mirror World, but this time combined with the augmented reality scenario, instead of the lifelogging scenario as is the case with urban sensing. Again, projects like WikiCity stimulate experimenting with complex physical settings visualizing the real-time impact of interventions on (spatial) behaviour.

A third category of examples are those effectuating the – earlier mentioned – prognosis by the authors of the Metaverse Roadmap envisioning mirror worlds as testing environments for assessing urban plans 'through data mining and simulation' (Smart et al., 2007). Hudson-Smith, Milton, Dearden and Batty (2007) speak in this regard of virtual mirror worlds, a merging of virtual and mirror worlds, hinting at the integration of Second Life and Google Earth, dubbed Second Earth.

At the Centre for Advanced Spatial Analysis (CASA) researchers are experimenting with distributing geographical information via Second Life. Their Virtual London application (a 3D visualization of London), for instance, can be consulted in Second Life. Their aim is not to simply disclose (geographical) information, but to frame this information by visualizing it among information plotted at other scales, with other graphic styles, or even related to other geographical locations. According to the researchers (Hudson-Smith et al., 2007) switching between scales, styles and locations should then stimulate debate, resulting in more precise information.

A second way of using virtual mirror worlds, besides disclosing and debating geographical information, is in organizing small scale experiments in collaborative planning. Key is the dependence of virtual worlds, like Second Life, on user-generated content, turning these worlds into a continuing experiment in participatory culture (Jenkins, 2007). Residents of the borough of Queens, NY, for instance, were invited in Second Life to communally design their new neighbourhood's park (Pfaffendorf, 2006). Another example is Studio Wikitecture, a group of likeminded 'interested in exploring the application of an open-source paradigm to the design and production of both real and virtual architecture and urban planning' (Chase, Schultz and Brouchoud, 2008). To this end, Wikitecture developed its own 'inworld interface' in Second Life to, very much like a conventional wiki, keep track of and vote on each other's designs. They invite everyone to use this interface and take part in their ongoing design projects, stressing that 'you don't need any experience in architecture, engineering, or anything really, to participate'. Architecture as a communal project thus. And as the Studio proudly announces, their approach is being appreciated as they won the third price in an international design competition[16].

Summarizing, as with Urban Sensing and the WikiCity project, virtual mirror worlds allow for experimenting, not by analysing real time urban processes but by observing virtual behaviour in real world spaces. The establishing of a separate scientific field, cyberethnography (Teli, Pisanu and Hakken, 2007), devoted to the study of online groups in relation to their off-line situations, only confirms the relevance of this scenario.

A last category of examples also resolves around virtual worlds, but plants these firmly in the physical world. For the purpose of our search these examples can be referred to as serious ubiquitous urban games. Ubiquitous games are games that take place in our everyday surroundings, but that rely on locative and media technology to augment these surroundings and objects in these surroundings with invisible and networked computing functionality (McGonigal, 2006). Serious games are games that can (also) be employed for non-entertainment purposes. One example is the Games Atelier[17] developed by the Waag Society, a mobile education platform geared towards kids in second grade. The kids not only play the game, but also develop the game concept, invent tasks, rewards and punishments, and link all this to actual locations. The underlying idea is that the Games Atelier stimulates fantasy and curiosity and increases the social skills of the players. For an overview of serious ubiquitous games see McGonigal (2006) and von Borries, Walz and Böttger (2007).

In terms of the metaverse scenarios, ubiquitous games (UG) are in fact a blending of virtual worlds and augmented reality, projecting a virtual world on top of the real world. In contrast to the previous category of virtual mirror worlds, UG allow planners to experiment in the actual world, with actual people, rather than discussing simulations of the virtual world with virtual people. One could for instance imagine employing UG to visualize invisible information on site, such as how a particular building used to look, or what is being done within that building. But also more abstract information such as the amount of electromagnetic activity, the degree of air pollution, or even building regulations. Such visualizations could generate an awareness of the complexity or value of a particular location, possible resulting in a more respectful attitude towards these locations. Besides visualizing

---

16   http://www.openarchitecturenetwork.org/challenge/asia/.
17   http://www.waag.org/project/gamesatelier.

invisible information, one could also imagine UG being employed to visualize possible futures, again on the spot, for instance of how a location might look after an intervention. These possible futures could then be discussed and even adjusted on the spot, collaboratively with future users.

This scenario is not even that farfetched as mainstream software starts to appear allowing even layman to make their own UG. Companies like Semapedia[18] and Tikitag,[19] for instance, provide the hardware to make your own tags, and thus to link your stories to any physical object you want, ready for others to read. Or, Mediascapes,[20] a free-of-charge application running on mobile devices with a GPS functionality, that allows you to invent your own game with your own characters, tasks and rewards, linked to real world places. When a player passes one of these places, a part of your story appears on his/her mobile device. Again, it only takes a small step to use this application to collaboratively generate alternative spatial environments.

Summarizing, UG allow for experimenting, not so much by providing real-time visualizations of actual urban environments, or by making citizens aware of their (spatial) behavior, but by allowing real-time planning of actual urban environments, be it that the impact remains only virtual.

16.6 Conclusion

In 1948 Weaver proclaimed electronic computing as the answer to Problems of Organized Complexity. More than half a century later, the authors of the Metaverse Roadmap (Smart et al., 2007) illustrate that electronic computing is being embedded in nearly every aspect of our environment, growing into an indispensible part of our everyday life. This omnipresence of electronic computing is here taken as an excuse to reassess Weaver's proclamation, and to explore how electronic computing can help planners and urban designers to answer Spatial Problems of Organized Complexity.

We argued that electronic computing can assist planners and urban designers along three avenues: by supporting informing, managing, and/or experimenting. We furthermore argued that the most exciting developments seem to take place along the third avenue, experimenting, since it is only recently that technology allows to truly capture 'complex' phenomena like emergence and adaptation; phenomena that are indispensable while running (behavioral) experiments in spatial settings. Two of those developments are real-time interactive mapping of spatial processes, and collaborative planning on site.

According to the authors of the Metaverse Roadmap (2007: 4), 'the convergence of virtually-enhanced physical reality and physically persistent

---

18   http://www.semapedia.org/.
19   http://www.tikitag.com/.
20   http://www.mscapers.com/.

virtual space' will only increase. So it is safe to say that Weaver's proclamation still holds, be it that the implementation of this proclamation is certainly richer than he could ever have imagined.

References

Batty, M., P. Steadman and Y. Xie (2004) Visualization in Spatial Modeling. CASA Working Paper Series, 79, UCL, London.

Batty, M. (2005) *Cities and Complexity: Understanding Cities with Cellular Automata, Agent-Based Models, and Fractals*, MIT Press, Boston.

Book, B. (2004) 'Moving Beyond the Game: Social Virtual Worlds', Paper presented at the State of Play 2 Conference, New York, 6-8 October.

Calabrese, F., K. Kloeckl and C. Ratti (2007) 'WikiCity: Real-Time Location-Sensitive Tools for the City', 10th International Conference on Computers in Urban Planning and Urban Management, 11-13 July, Foz de Iguacu, Parana.

Chase, S., R. Schultz and J. Brouchoud (2008) 'Gather 'round the Wiki-Tree: Virtual Worlds as an Open Platform for Architectural Collaboration'. The 26th Education and research in Computer Aided Architectural Design in Europe Conference, September 17-19, Antwerp.

Cuff, D., M. Hansen and J. Kang (2008) 'Urban Sensing: Out of the Woods', *Communications of the ACM*, 51(3), pp. 24-33.

De Nood, D. and J. Attema (2007) 'Residents in Analyse: de Feiten over Second Life na de Hype [Residents under therapy: the Facts of Second Life after the Hype]', EPN Rapport, http://www.secondlife.nl/images/inventory/761344793d9d8b773490e2060 65d69af.pdf (accessed August 12, 2008).

Devisch, O. (2008) 'Should Planners Start Playing Computer Games? Arguments from SimCity and Second Life', *Planning Theory & Practice*, 9(2), pp. 209-226.

Francica, J. and A. Schutzberg (2008) Podcast: You are a Sensor http://www.directionsmag.com/article.php?article_id=2818&trv=1 (Posted on July 15, 2008, Accessed August 12, 2008).

Girardin, F., F.D. Fiore, J. Blat and C. Ratti (2007) 'Understanding of tourist dynamics from explicitly disclosed location information', Presented at: The 4th International Symposium on LBS & TeleCartography, November 8-10, Hong Kong Polytechnic University, PR China.

Girardin, F. (2008) 'Real-time Cities', MIT SENSEable City Lab round table report, April 14th, MIT, Cambridge.

Greenfield, A. (2006) *Everyware: The Dawning Age of Ubiquitous Computing (Voices That Matter*, New Riders Publishing, Berkeley.

Johnson, S. (2002) *Emergence: The Connected Lives of Ants, Brains, Cities, and Software*, Scribner, New York.

Hill, D. (2008) 'The Street as Platform', http://www.cityofsound.com/blog/2008/02/the-street-as-p.html (accessed August 12, 2008).

Hudson-Smith, A., R. Milton, J. Dearden and M. Batty (2007) 'Virtual Cities: Digital Mirrors into a Recursive World', CASA Working Paper Series, 125, UCL, London.

Hudson-Smith, A. and A. Crooks (2008) 'The Renaissance of Geographic Information: Neogeography, Gaming and Second Life', CASA Working Paper Series, 142, UCL, London.

Lane, G. (2008) 'Social Tapestries: public authoring and civil society', http://diffusion.org.uk/?p=572, (accessed August 12, 2008).

Lee, D.B. (1994) 'Retrospective on Large-Scale Urban Models', *Journal of the American Planning Association*, 60(1), pp. 35-40.

McGonigal, J. (2006) 'This Might Be a Game: Ubiquitous Play and Performance at the Turn of the Twenty-First Century', PhD thesis, University of California, Berkeley (US).

Pearce, C. (2006) 'Productive Play: Game Culture From the Bottom Up', *Games and Culture*, 1(1), pp. 17-24.

Pfaffendorf, J. (2006) '3D Wiki for Landing Lights Park', http://nyls.blogs.com/demoisland/2006/01/3d_wiki_for_lan.html, (accessed August 12, 2008).

Portugali, J. (2000) *Self-Organisation and the City*, Springer-Verlag, Berlin, Heidelberg.

Ratti, C., Pulselli, R.M., Williams, S., and Frenchman, D. (2006) 'Mobile Landscapes: using location data from cell phones for urban analysis', *Environment and Planning B: Planning and Design*, 33(5), pp. 27-748.

Shiode, N. and Torrens, P. M. (2008). 'Comparing the growth dynamics of real and virtual cities', in: Hornsby, K. and Yuan, M., (Eds.) *Understanding Dynamics of Geographic Domains*, CRC Press, Boca Raton.

Smart, J., J. Cascio and J. Paffendorf, (2007) 'Metaverse Roadmap Overview', http://www.metaverseroadmap.org/MetaverseRoadmapOverview.pdf (accessed August 12, 2008).

Snavely, N., Garg, R., S. M. Seitz, and R. Szeliski (2008) 'Finding Paths through the World's Photos', ACM Transactions on Graphics, SIGGRAPH 2008.

Teli, M., F. Pisanu and D. Hakken (2007) 'The Internet as a Library-of-People: For a Cyberethnography of Online Groups', *Forum: Qualitative Social Research*, 8(3), Art. 33.

Timmermans, H.J.P. (2003) 'The Saga of Integrated Land Use-Transport Modeling: How Many More Dreams Before we Wake Up?', In: *Proceedings of the 10th International Conference on Travel Behaviour*, August 10-15, Lucerne.

Van Kranenburg, R. (2008) 'The Internet of Things: A Critique of Ambient Technology and the All-Seeing Network of RFID', Network Notebooks 02, Institute of Network Cultures, Amsterdam.

Von Borries, F., S.P. Walz and M. Böttger (eds.) (2007) *Space Time Play, Computer Games, Architecture and Urbanism: the Next Level*, Birkhäuser, Basel.

Weaver, W. (1948) 'Science and Complexity', *American Scientist*, 36, pp. 536-541.

Chapter 17

The Use of Agent-Based Modeling for Studying the Social and Physical Environment of Cities

Andrew Crooks[1]

The agent-based modeling (ABM) paradigm provides a mechanism for understanding the effects of interactions of individuals and through such interactions emergent structures develop, both in the social and physical environment of cities. This chapter explores how through the use of ABM, and its linkage with complexity theory, allows one to create agent-based models for the studying cities from the bottom-up. Specifically the chapter focuses on segregation and land-use change. Furthermore, it will highlight the growing interest between geographical information systems (GIS) and ABM. This linkage is allowing modellers to create spatially explicit agent-based models, thus relating agents to actual geographical places. This approach allows one to explore the link between socio-economic geography of the city and its built physical form, and can support decision-making regarding interventions within the social and physical environment.

17.1 Introduction

Cities play a critical role in our lives, providing habitats for more than half the world's population. The United Nations expects that over half (3.3 billion people) of the world's population will be located in urban areas by 2008 (United Nations, 2007) and this proportion is predicted to increase to over 75 percent by the year 2100. However, understanding such systems is not at all an easy task as they are composed of many parts which are dynamic, rapidly evolving, undergoing continual growth, change, decline and restructuring usually simultaneously (White and Engelen, 1993). Such change is a result of the interaction of large numbers of discrete actors interacting within space. This heterogeneous nature of cities makes it difficult to generalize localized problems from that of city-wide problems. Although our understanding of cities has increased throughout

---

1   Andrew Crooks is Assistant Professor in the Department of Computational Social Science. Krasnow Institute for Advanced Study, George Mason University, Fairfax, Virginia (US).

the twentieth century, incorporating ideas and theories from a diverse range of subjects including economics, geography, history, philosophy, mathematics and more recently computer science, it is now very clear that there are intrinsic difficulties in applying such understanding to policy analysis and decision making.

As Wilson (2000) writes, such understanding of cities represents '…one of the major scientific challenges of our time'. Human behaviour cannot be understood or predicted in the same way as in the sciences such as in the physical or chemical world. To understand urban problems such as sprawl, congestion, segregation, crime, migration and housing markets, researchers have recently focused on a bottom-up approach to urban systems, specifically researching the reasoning on which individual decisions are made. One such approach is agent-based modelling (ABM) which allows one to simulate the individual actions of diverse agents, measuring the resulting system behaviour and outcomes over time. This modelling approach provides an important medium for the study and management of urban systems affected by countless factors including economic, social, and environmental which are notoriously difficult to simulate (Torrens, 2000).

The remainder of the chapter will provide a general overview of why there is a need for agent-based models for studying cities, how it links to how we believe cities operate through ideas of complexity theory, review and discuss a range of applications where agent-based models have been developed specifically focusing on urban phenomena at the individual level linking it to complexity theory where appropriate, and how such models lead to more aggregate structures developing in the social and physical environment. The chapter will conclude with challenges modellers face when using agent-based models to study cities, and identify future avenues of research especially in relation to decision making.

17.2 Why the growth of agent-based models for cities?

The growth of ABM coincides with how our views and thinking about urban systems has changed. Rather than adopting a reductionist view of systems, whereby the modeller makes the assumption that cities operate from the top-down and results are filtered to the individual components of the system (see Torrens, 2004), people are now adopting a reassembly approach to the system (O'Sullivan, 2004). This change follows the realisation that, planning and public policy do not always work in a top-down manner; aggregate conditions develop from the bottom-up, from the interaction of a large number of elements at a local scale (Pickles, 1995). Thus there is a move towards individualistic, bottom-up explanations of urban form and behaviour which links to what we know about complex systems. Such an approach is ABM, however, before discussing the advantages of ABM and how this relates to our understanding of cities, a brief examination of complexity science is first needed.

An exact definition of complexity is hard to pin down; as it has different meanings to different people. However, Manson's (2001; 2007) taxonomy helps to clarify the broad subject area by classifying complexity research into three broad categories: algorithmic (i.e. the complexity of a system lies in the difficulty faced in describing system characteristics), deterministic (i.e. unpredictable dynamic behaviour of relatively simple deterministic systems, where unpredictable refers to the sensitivity of outcomes based on initial conditions) and aggregate complexity (i.e. the study of phenomena characterized by interactions among many distinct components). These categories refer to aspects of phenomena that are not mutually exclusive and while these three major divisions allow a more coherent understanding of complexity theory, but these are not the only possible classifications (see for a debate: Reitsma, 2003; Manson, 2003).

Nonetheless, the main characteristics of complex systems – self-organization, emergence, non-linearity, feedback and path dependence – provide a new way of thinking about cities and new tools for solving problems faced by cities. Emergent phenomena are characterized by stable macroscopic patterns arising from local interaction of individual entities (Epstein and Axtell, 1996). A small number of rules or laws, applied at a local level and among many entities, are capable of generating complex global phenomena: collective behaviours, extensive spatial patterns, hierarchies etc. are manifested in such a way that the actions of the parts do not simply sum to the activity of the whole. Thus, emergent phenomena can exhibit properties that are decoupled (i.e. logically independent) from the properties of the system's parts. For example, a traffic jam often forms in the opposing lane to a traffic accident, a consequence of 'rubber-necking'. Studying the behaviour of collections of entities focuses attention on relationships between entities (O'Sullivan, 2004) because before change is noticed at the aggregate level, it has already taken place at the micro-level. Characteristics of emergent phenomena make them difficult to understand and predict, particularly as emergent outcomes can be counterintuitive (Epstein, 1999). Furthermore, the importance of history/path dependence make models based on such notions very sensitive to initial conditions and to small variations in interaction rules (Couclelis, 2002). Using such models for prediction can therefore be challenging. Despite this, complexity theory has brought awareness of the subtle, diverse, and interconnected facets common to many phenomena, and continues to contribute many powerful concepts, modelling approaches and techniques especially in relation to agent-based models (see below).

The use of complexity theory has numerous advantages with regard to our understanding and interpretation of cities. Cities happen to be problems of organized complexity they present situations in which half a dozen quantities are all varying simultaneously and in subtly interconnected ways (Jacobs, 1961). Change is only noticeable when different patterns become discernable, but before change at the macro-level can be seen, it is taking place at many micro-levels (subsystems) simultaneously, all of which interact separately, together forming a complex web of interactions (Holland, 1995). Understanding such systems from the 'bottom-up' is crucial with regard to urban planning (Batty, 1995). Urban geography provides many examples of self-organization and emergence; for example, it is the local-scale interactive behaviour (commuting, moving) of many individual objects (vehicles, people) from which structured and ordered patterns emerge in the aggregate, such as peak-hour traffic congestion (Nagel et al., 1997) and the large-scale spatial clustering of socioeconomic groups by residence (Schelling, 1971). In urban economies, large-scale economies of agglomeration and dispersion have long been understood to operate from local-scale interactive dynamics (Krugman, 1996). Additionally, cities exhibit several signatures, characteristic of complexity, including fractal dimensionality and self-similarity across scales, self organisation, and emergence (see Batty and Longley, 1994; Allen, 1997; Portugali, 2000).

In summary, complexity science offers a new way of thinking about cities, especially when combined with ABM, and provides us with new tools to explore and analyse urban systems from the 'bottom-up'. In a sense, agent-based models can be thought of as miniature laboratories where the key attributes and behaviour of agents, and the environment in which they are housed, can be altered and the repercussions observed over the course of multiple simulation runs, thus providing a tool to 'think with' and therefore supporting decision making.

But what is meant by ABM? While there is no universal agreement on a precise definition of the term 'agent, definitions tend to agree on more points than they disagree (Macal and North, 2005). Agent characteristics are difficult to extract from the literature in a consistent and concise manner, because they are applied differently within disciplines (Castle and Crooks, 2006). Furthermore, the agent-based concept is a mindset more than a technology, where a system is described from the perspective of its constituent parts (Bonabeau, 2002). The concept of an agent is meant to be a tool for analysing a system, not an absolute classification where entities can be defined as agents or non-agents (Russell and Norvig, 2003). A detailed discussion about the definition and characteristics of agents is beyond the scope of this chapter and readers are referred to writings of Wooldridge and Jennings (1995), Torrens (2004), Macal and North (2005), and Castle and Crooks (2006), for further discussions.

However, there are several key features of agents which make them attractive to studying cities and as a tool for complexity science in general. First is their ability to model multiple autonomous units (i.e. governed without the influence of centralized control), situated within a model or simulation environment. Animate (mobile) agents can be considered as agents who move about the systems, such as pedestrians. In contrast, inanimate (immobile) agents such as land parcels do not move but can change state. Secondly, ABM allows for the representation of a heterogeneous population therefore the notion of a mean individual is redundant, a common assumption of past urban models (Torrens, 2000). Agents permit the development of autonomous individuals. For example, an agent representing a human could have attributes such as age, sex, job etc. Groups of agents can exist, but they are spawned from the bottom-up, and are thus amalgamations of similar autonomous individuals. Such heterogeneity allows for the specification of agents with varying degrees of rationality (see Axelrod, 2007). This offers advantages over approaches that assume perfectly rational individuals, if they consider individuals at all. Thirdly, agents are active because they exert independent influence in a simulation. These autonomous units are capable of processing information and exchanging this information with other agents in order to make independent decisions. A relationship between agents is specified, linking agents to other agents and/or other entities within a system. Relationships may be specified in a variety of ways, from simply reactive (i.e. agents only perform actions when triggered to do so by some external stimulus) to goal-directed (i.e. seeking a particular goal). Furthermore, agents can also be designed to be adaptive, producing Complex Adaptive Systems (CAS; Holland, 1995). Agents can be designed to alter their state depending on their current state, permitting agents to adapt with a form of memory or learning.

The ability of agent-based models to describe the behaviour and interactions of a system additionally allows for system dynamics to be directly incorporated into the model. This represents a movement away from the static nature of earlier styles of urban modelling which was one of their major failings (see Batty, 1976). However, while time in agent-based models is still discrete, i.e. it still moves in 'snapshots, the time steps may be small enough to approximate real time dynamics. Additionally, it is apparent that different processes occur in space and over different time scales (Liu and Andersson, 2004). For example, the location of residents and businesses is affected by long term processes, such as economic cycles and transport projects, and short term events in the form of daily commuting or hourly social interactions. Agent-based models can incorporate these different scale time processes into a single simulation by using a variety of automata clocks designed to mimic the temporal attributes of the specific urban process under study (Torrens, 2003), thus allowing the modeller to realistically simulate urban development (O'Sullivan, 2001). The choice of time in terms of both an event-scheduling approach and a temporal resolution can have important consequences for the behaviour of the model (see Brown et al., 2005b for a more detailed discussion). In relation to urban dynamics, the ability to model different aspects of time is highly appealing. It is not just different temporal periods that can be incorporated within an agent-based model but different spatial scales can also be included. This flexibility is extremely important as it is the phenomena of interest which drives the scale to be used, not the modelling methodology. For example, from the micro movement of pedestrians within a building during an evacuation (e.g. Castle, 2007), to the movement of cars on a street network (e.g. Nagel et al., 1999), to the study of urban growth (e.g. Brown et al., 2005a). Additionally, as ABM allows for the representation of individual objects, it is therefore possible to combine these objects to represent phenomena at different scales within the same model. This means agent-based models can be useful tools for studying the effects of processes that operate at multiple scales and organizational levels (Brown, 2006). Furthermore, ABM incorporates many of the advances made in urban modelling such as dynamics, detail, usability, spatial flexibility and realism (see Torrens, 2000; 2001).

17.3 Example applications of agent-based models for cities

In many, cases ABM is a 'natural' method for describing and simulating a system composed of real-world entities, especially when using object-orientated principles (see Castle and Crooks, 2006; Torrens, 2001). The agent-based approach is more akin to reality than other modelling approaches, rendering ABM inherently suited to simulating people and objects in realistic ways. Agent-based simulations provide an opportunity to represent and test social theories which cannot easily be described using mathematical formula (Axelrod, 1997). Agent-based models often map more naturally to the structure of the problem than equation-based models (Parunak et al., 1998) by specifying simple behavioural and transition rules attached to well defined entities, therefore providing a medium for the infusion of any geographic theory or methodology into the model. Furthermore, by modelling the behaviour of individual entities interacting, the agent-based approach enables users to study the aggregate properties of the system from the bottom-up. For these reasons ABM is increasingly being used as a tool to study a diverse range of phenomena. From archaeological reconstruction of ancient civilizations (Axtell et al., 2002); size-frequency distributions for traffic jams (Nagel and Rasmussen, 1994); spatial patterns of unemployment (Topa, 2001), to name but a few. The remainder of this section explores a range of applications from the micro to the macro and demonstrates how ABM can be used to study a range of problems within cities with a particular emphasis on the social and physical environments. But before describing such models a caveat is needed, that it is impractical to comprehensively and thoroughly review the full range of ABM applications and provide adequate descriptions of each model within this chapter. Within this section we therefore only explore a small number of models, chosen to demonstrate that the interaction of individual agents lead to the emergence of more aggregate patterns.

Despite the advantages of ABM as a tool for simulation, ABM has only recently started to be adopted in urban systems research. Thomas Schelling is credited with developing the first social agent-based model in which agents represent people, and agent interactions represent a socially relevant process. Schelling's (1971) model demonstrated that stark geographical segregated patterns can emerge from migratory movements among two culturally distinct, but relatively tolerant, types of household via mild discriminatory choices by individuals. (Schelling-type models and models inspired by it will be further explored below). Yet ABM did not begin to feature prominently in the geographical literature until the mid-1990s, when Epstein and Axtell (1996) extended the notion of modelling people to growing entire artificial societies. The goal was to understand the emergence of patterns, trends, or other characteristics observable in a society and its geography. Epstein and Axtell's Sugarscape model demonstrated that agents could emerge with a variety of characteristics and behaviours suggestive of a rudimentary society (e.g. in terms of patterns of death, disease, trade, health, culture, conflict, war, etc)

17.4 Residential segregation

We start our exploration with 'segregation'. Interest in such phenomena arises because people get separated along different lines and in different ways. There is segregation by sex, age, income, language, colour, taste, comparative advantage, and accidents of historical location. Some segregation is organised; some is economically determined; some results from specialised communication systems; and some results from the interplay of individual choices that discriminate and is seen in many cities. It is worth noting that it is not just residential groups that segregate, for segregation takes many other forms. Types of land-use, for example, residential, commercial, agricultural, are segregated in space. Types of businesses and industries are often segregated in clusters that indicate how they relate to one another. Interest in simple models such as Schelling's model for explaining such complex phenomena arise because while patterns of segregation are all too clear when one travels around any urban area. For example, there are clear clusters of economic groups and residential groups based on ethnicity or social class. One might think that individuals must have strong preferences for these racially or economically homogeneous neighbourhoods to emerge. However, this is not the case. Empirical evidence suggests that individuals do not have strong racial preferences, but have rather mild preferences (see Clark, 1991; Antonovics et al., 2003). Furthermore, to find clear examples of the segregation process taking place is difficult, because it only becomes noticeable when it is clearly underway, and by then a detailed chronology becomes impossible to reconstruct (Batty et al., 2004). So while it is possible to quantify the degree of segregation within neighbourhoods (e.g. Reardon and O'Sullivan, 2004), it tells us little about the behaviour that leads to, or that leads away, from particular outcomes. To understand this behaviour, we have to examine how individual choice leads to these outcomes, a process that can be explored through the use of ABM.

Schelling's model is excellent because it distils the key features enabling us to understand how segregation might arise. The model does not presume to tell us about the entire workings of the social and economic world, but focuses on the task at hand, namely to explain why weak individual preferences are consistent with strong and persistent patterns of segregation. The rules within the Schelling model are simple, simply stated all agents want to be located in areas where a certain percentage of their neighbours are like themselves. However, these simple rules give rise to complex and unanticipated behaviour in the system. This key feature of the model arises because the decisions of any one individual can impact in unexpected and unanticipated ways upon the decisions of others. A group of individuals can be perfectly happy in a neighbourhood. Unexpectedly, an agent arrives to fill an empty space. The newcomer may tip the balance – 'residential tipping' – so the agents who were previously content now decide to move. In turn, their moves may disrupt settled neighbourhoods elsewhere, and so the effects percolate through the system. No single individual intends this to happen or even necessarily desires this overall outcome, but local interactions between them produce global segregation.

What is important about this model and with many other agent-based models is that one cannot predict the precise outcome of a particular simulation, as the model is sensitive to initial conditions and interaction rules. When the model starts, we possess all the information that exists about it, for we know exactly how each individual behaves. At any stage of the simulation, we know exactly what has happened. Yet we cannot predict the exact outcome of any particular solution to the simulation. However, we know broadly that at each outcome, the agents will separate into distinct neighbourhoods surrounded by their own type and during the simulation neighbourhoods will change. This has important implications with respect to policy decision making. Since we cannot predict it, we cannot control it, even though we have full and complete information (Ormerod, 2005).

Unknowingly, Schelling was one of the pioneers in the field of ABM (Schelling, 2006). He emphasised the value of starting with rules of behaviour for individuals and using simulations to discover the implications for large scale outcomes. His model highlights how peoples' actions may be influenced by others who act in a given way and how changes in individual behaviour alter the makeup of the population. Thus individuals' actions are both a response to some population statistic and contribute to that statistic. Schelling's model has generated important insights regarding how micro-level residential choice behaviour can produce complex aggregate-level patterns of ethnic residential segregation. Additionally, it has continued to inspire theory and research into the segregation phenomena. For example, Bruch and Mare (2005) compared Schelling's model with stated preference data on residential choice for various race-ethnic groups (e.g. Asians, Hispanics, whites and blacks) within American cities. The preference data showed that most people were unwilling to live in neighbourhoods in which their own race-ethnic group is the minority. However, Schelling's work has also received criticism; for example, Massey and Denton (1993) correctly point out that the 'residential-tipping' point model is not sufficient in itself as an explanation of segregation for many reasons. They comment that while it accurately captures the dynamic effects of prejudice, it accepts as a given the existence of racial discrimination. But what really matters is that individuals have preferences for both place and people. The remainder of this section will briefly explore some of the ABM applications which extend or are inspired by Schelling's original model.

Others have extended the Schelling model to incorporate other factors into their models, such as the inclusion of preferences for neighbourhood status and housing quality, and differing levels of socio-economic inequality within and between ethnic populations (see Fossett and Senft, 2004). Bruch (2006) explored the relationship between race and income, and how both interact to produce and maintain segregated neighbourhoods within Los Angeles. Within the model, agents were given a race and an income, and the model examined the probability of an agent moving into a neighbourhood of a given racial and economic composition. Crooks (2008) explores adding new agents and removing old agents from an existing population and how such change altered existing neighbourhood patterns. This phenomenon can be considered as the effect of immigration, or aging and the death of populations in urban areas.

Researchers from Tel Aviv University have been particularly active in the field of ABM, segregation and residential dynamics. They have investigated residential dynamics using agent-based models from abstract systems to real-world examples (see Benenson, 1998; Benenson et al., 2002; Omer, 2005). Benenson (1998) explored how a theoretical city evolved when agents have both economic and cultural preferences. Omer (2005) extended the Schelling model to include a further hierarchical level; that is, the agents' ethnic identities are organised in a two-level hierarchy where each agent belongs to an ethnic group and a subgroup. For example, the British Asian community is multi-differentiated in terms of nationality, country of origin, religion, caste, class and language. Extending the Schelling model to include additional hierarchical level allows for further research dealing with the role of ethnic preferences on residential choice.

Of special interest is the study of fine scale residential segregation using individual census records and GIS data for representing streets and buildings (see Benenson and Omer, 2003). Benenson *et al.* (2002) have used this kind of detailed dataset to simulate ethnic residential dynamics between 1955-1995 in the Yaffo area of Tel Aviv. The model itself consists of two interacting layers, one layer representing mobile agents comprised of three cultural groups that of Jews, Arab Muslims, and Arab Christians, located on a physical environment layer representing streets and buildings. Each house is converted into a Voronoi polygon rather than using a regular cell space model (e.g. Fossett and Senft, 2004). The agents' residential behaviour within the model is affected by the ethnic composition of the neighbourhood defined using Voronoi polygons. A neighbour is a Voronoi polygon that has a common boundary and features such as roads act as barriers between these neighbourhoods.

Many of the models so far discussed, use cells to represent the agents environment. Within such cell space models neighbourhoods are often based on 'Moore' neighbourhood or 'von Neumann' neighbourhood or variations of these (Batty, 2005b). However, neighbourhoods mean different things to different people. Some may perceive a neighbourhood as houses that are directly attached to their home (e.g. Benenson et al., 2002), while others may consider a street, or a collection of streets as their neighbourhood. A number of authors have demonstrated that neighbourhood sizes impact on the pattern of segregation (see for example, Laurie and Jaggi, 2003; O'Sullivan et al., 2003) but few take into account the impact of physical and spatial barriers (notable exceptions include Benenson et al., 2002; Crooks, 2008). This is crucial for studying residential patterns within cities. For example, areas within cities are bounded by features such as highways, railway lines, rivers, lakes, and parks which can act as boundaries between residential groups (e.g. Rabin, 1987). Such divisions may promote numerous forms of separation such as residential segregation or influence urban form, yet are often overlooked in aggregate zonal analysis (Talen, 2003) and in

ABM. Crooks (2008) explored the effect that such features have on the outcome of a Schelling type model and demonstrated how such features can be incorporated into this type of model.

The examples presented in this section can be viewed as a continuum between abstract demonstrations to real-world applications. Each one brings something new to the basic insights Schelling first presented. There are those that apply the Schelling model to empirical data (e.g. Bruch and Mare, 2005), those that explore the effect of differing neighborhood sizes (e.g. O'Sullivan et al., 2003) or shapes (e.g. Benenson et al., 2002) or how through adding new agents and removing old agents from an existing population, altered existing neighbourhood patterns (e.g. Crooks, 2008), those that extend the Schelling model to incorporate subgroups (e.g. Omer, 2005) which has the potential to allow the model to be applied to different ethnic or socio-economic groups that makeup a city or region if so desired. Others introduce and explore other determinants of segregation such as income and housing quality (e.g. Fossett and Senft, 2004).

17.5 Residential location

Moving away from segregation, the chapter explores more generally location choice within cities, and how agent-based models can be used to study such phenomena. Such interest arises as new and more established inhabitants and businesses within urban areas are faced with the fundamental decision of 'where to locate?'. This choice of location results from complex interrelationships between individual actions constrained by many social, political and economic factors. For example, for a resident, location is a trade-off between price of dwelling, type of residence and its location, both in terms of neighbourhood and in relation to place of work, all of which vary depending on age, sex, marital status and income.

There are various models and modelling techniques pertaining to the development of cities and regions (see Wilson, 2000), but one model that lies at the heart of urban economic theory is the trade-off between a consumer's demand to minimize distance travelled to various activities and a desire to capture as much living space as possible. This theory was first formally articulated by Alonso (1964) and can been seen as extending the work of von Thünen (1826). Alonso's model assumed that in the monocentric industrial cities, residents arranged their locations around the central business district (CBD) according to this trade-off between distance (travel cost) and space. As with Schelling's model, the model is simple, it abstracts key elements of the system to explain how land-use within a city is organised. The model illustrates that the structure of preferences and the market for various land-uses appears to lead to wealthy groups being able to capture more space at the edge of the city than the poorer groups who are confined to the inner areas around the CBD. However, the model does not explore dynamics *per se*, it simply assumes that the pattern of land-use is the result of a equilibrium based formula and leaves one to wonder how and why changes might occur.

By shifting our attention to ABM allows us to explore the evolution of land-use in urban areas from the interaction of many individuals rather than just providing a static snapshot. This approach is appealing as it has the potential to provide a detailed description and explanation of the evolution of urban spatial structure at differing scales. Additionally, this approach to modelling urban systems provides an improvement over past generations of models as it provides the flexibility which permits the consideration of many more factors. For example, in both the Alonso and von Thünen models, features of the landscape such as rivers and roads are often ignored, so that distance to the centre is the underlying determinant of land-use change. Additionally, Alonso's model fails to explain the complexity of the spatial and temporal patterns of urban growth (see Anas et al., 1998 for a discussion). For example, it assumes all employment is centrally located, and it fails to take into account the distinctive nature of buildings and their use which are not easily changed, thus displaying a strong degree of inertia. Furthermore, the use of agent-based models allows us to model both imperfect competition and limited knowledge (see Tesfatsion and Judd, 2006) and how the decisions and actions of agents can be influenced by past locational decisions (path dependence). The resulting land-use patterns reflect the actions of many individuals, all competing for the same area, and interacting over space and time.

There are numerous agent-based models examining land-use and land-use change and it is not the intention to reiterate these (see Parker, 2005). However, there are relatively few that examine the work of Alonso and von Thünen explicitly (e.g. Kii and Doi, 2005; Sasaki and Box, 2003 respectively). For example, Kii and Doi (2005) model two types of households and commercial firms with two different incomes. Within the model, agents are land-consuming entities, one agent can occupy one cell which is determined by which agent can pay the highest value. This competition between individual agents for the same space within the urban setting over time results in land-use patterns similar to ideas postulated by Alonso (1964). Sasaki and Box (2003) used von Thünen's model to demonstrate how a collection of autonomous individuals operating in a cellular space environment can contribute to the formation of an optimal land-use pattern as described by von Thünen by applying theories of positive feedback and lock-in. Hammam *et al.* (2004) have extended the Sasaki and Box (2003) model to include irregular cells representing farmers and these cells have the ability to change shape, growing or shrinking depending on competition for land. Such an approach has much potential as land parcels in urban areas change shape over time, for example, through changes in function or activity. Additionally, Parker and Meretsky (2004) used the von Thünen model as the basis of an agent-based model to explore conflicts arising between urban and agricultural land-uses which affect the value of particular land-uses. The common thread between the land-use models above is how urban form and function develops through the competition of agents. Furthermore, such models highlight how the ideas, concepts and techniques pertaining to 'classical' urban theory and modelling can be combined using ABM, thereby adding dynamics to such models and showing how urban structures emerge from the bottom-up therefore providing a blended modelling approach (North and Macal, 2007).

17.6 Abstract to 'real' world applications: linking GIS and ABM

Many of the models presented above represent space abstractly. However, there is a growing interest in the integration of GIS and ABM through coupling and embedding (see Castle and Crooks, 2006; Brown et al., 2005b; Parker, 2005; Benenson and Torrens, 2004; Gimblett, 2002; for reviews and applications). For agent-based modellers, this integration provides the ability to have agents that are related to actual geographic locations. This is of crucial importance with regard to urban modelling, as everything within a city or region is connected to a place. Furthermore, it allows modellers to think about how objects or agents and their aggregations, interact and change in space and time (Batty, 2005a). For GIS users, it provides the ability to model the emergence of phenomena through individual interactions of features on a GIS over time and space (Najlis and North, 2004). While the integration of ABM and GIS is clearly possible, allowing for a finer grain of urban models, there is no guarantee that by moving to a finer grain, the robustness of the aggregated results will be improved (Lee, 1994). For example, when going from total population to household types to individuals, there is no level at which behaviour (such as location choice) is better known. However, the creation of agent-based models allows one to build tools/models to explore such behaviour and how this manifests itself in aggregate form. A brief review of spatially explicit agent-based models will now follow.

ABM is increasingly being used as a tool for the spatial simulation of a wide variety of urban phenomena (some of which have been discussed above) including: urban housing dynamics (e.g. Benenson et al., 2002); urban growth (e.g. Xie et al., 2005), segregation (e.g. Crooks, 2008); residential and business location (e.g. Torrens, 2006; Barros, 2004) and gentrification (e.g. Torrens and Nara, 2007). Brown et al. (2005a) examine residential location with respect to land-use change at the urban-rural fringe. Focusing on how individual decision-making drives land-use decisions, such a modelling approach allows users formulate and test alternative policies and interventions that could reduce environmental costs and enhance environmental benefits. A similar model has also been developed by Yin and Muller (2007), who examine land-use-land-cover change at the urban-rural fringe incorporating households decision making in terms of preferences for accessibility, amenities, and scenic views. Additionally, Bossomaier *et al.* (2007) have developed an agent-based model to study house price evolution in Bathurst, Australia, which focuses on vendor/buyer behaviour. The agent's decisions of where to locate is affected by spatial attributes of actual land-parcels including distance from amenities such as parks, area, elevation, orientation and environmental factors such as flood risk. These spatial factors combined with an agent's perceptions about the economy, new developments such as factories and roads, along with social trends in the desirability of house ownership and property investment then influence how buyers and sellers modify the price relative to the neighbourhood.

The ability to model and explore how agents move around their environment has allowed the study of micro-scale phenomena such as pedestrian models, which explore how agents move around their environment. Useful examples of spatially explicit models include: the simulation of pedestrians in the urban centres (e.g. Haklay et al., 2001), the examination of crowd congestion (e.g. Batty et al., 2003), emergency evacuation of buildings (e.g. Castle, 2007), or terrorist attacks within the built environment (Mysore et al., 2006). In such models one can explore how the built environment impacts on movement of pedestrians, for example. Furthermore, these models demonstrate how micro interactions with many individuals lead to emergent patterns such as crowds. The ABM paradigm is also commonly used to simulate traffic movement (e.g. Barrett *et al.*, 2001), and attempts have also been made to couple traffic models to different models. For example, Thorp *et al.* (2006) evaluated different evacuation options for residents in a wildfire event in Santa Fe, by combining a traffic model to a fire model, and using several geographical datasets (e.g. digital elevation model, tree canopy data, road networks, and houses).

17.7 Discussion

The models presented in this chapter demonstrate the ability to move beyond a reductionist (or top-down) approach for studying systems. Instead of dissecting models into logically justified components, the focus lies on multiple interactions among simple basic units which correspond to physically existing entities such as people. This generative (or bottom-up) approach allows us to explore how a small number of rules or laws, applied at a local level and among many entities, are capable of generating complex global phenomena at different temporal resolutions – collective behaviours, extensive spatial patterns, hierarchies – manifested in such a way that the actions of the parts do not simply sum to the activity of the whole. The richness of the system therefore lies in the way in which interactions between individual entities and their environment generate adaptations over time. Not withstanding this, the examples also demonstrate how agent-based models provide a suitable means for exploring many aspects of urban phenomena, how human beings change their environment, and how they are affected by it. Such change occurs at the physical, social and economic level, a result of complex interactions between many different individual entities (Liu et al., 2007).

Many of the ABM applications currently utilizing geospatial data do so using a cellular space representation of reality. A regular cellular space is populated with agents that can migrate between cells (e.g. Portugali, 2000). Such models show the importance of considering mobility between cells when exploring the processes of segregation and immigration. Often, it is assumed that agents' movement behaviour depends on the properties of neighbouring cells and neighbours. This approach can be related to the supply of data in raster data formats, the computational power needed to compute complex geometries, and the lack of tools necessary to create agents operating in vector space. While agent-based models created using the cellular partition of space have provided valuable insights into urban phenomena, especially as they can capture geographic detail, they miss geometric detail. This area is critical to good applications but is barely touched upon in the literature (Batty, 2005b) with a few exceptions, (e.g. Benenson et al., 2002; Crooks, 2008). The ability to represent the world as a series of points, lines and polygons allows the inclusion of geometry into the modelling process, therefore allowing for different sizes of features such as houses, roads and so on to be portrayed. Furthermore, this allows the use of land parcel datasets that are extensive and fine scale. However before exploring this, it needs to be stressed that vector representation is not necessarily more appropriate for modelling than raster representation. For example, Landis (2001) changed from vector-based polygons to raster-based grid cells in his Californian Urban Futures models to simplify computation. Additionally, Benenson *et al.* (2005) comment that while vector GIS can represent urban objects in spatially explicit models, for theoretical models the points of a regular grid usually suffice. However, researchers have started using irregular spaces (e.g. Semboloni, 2000), and discovered that many models are sensitive to variations in the structure and size of neighbourhoods between locations in the grid (e.g. O'Sullivan, 2001). This is a topic that the author believes needs further investigation.

For example, many research topics in urban geography and planning explore interactions between spatial socio-economic processes and the built environment. Research into gentrification and social segregation for example, is closely linked to individuals buying and selling of buildings through the property market and urban form. Despite these links, direct measurement and analysis of the built environment is seldom employed in urban geography or ABM applications. The reasons for this omission are that the complexity of urban form data creates difficulties in compiling and analysing datasets; and that the aggregate methodologies used in geographical research do not integrate easily with the fine scale nature of urban form data.

Often the complexity of the built environment is minimized within many agent-based models. For example, buildings are represented as squares or agents movement being restricted to discrete cells. Never-the-less there is a growing interest in linking these geographical and geometrical approaches to provide an improved understanding of cities (Batty, 2007). Over the last decade there has been a continuing development of geographic information technologies and the emergence of rich fine scale digital data sources (Longley, 2003) such as Ordnance Surveys (OS) MasterMap® in the United Kingdom. These new detailed datasets have enhanced spatial and non-spatial information, which provides opportunities to model and analyse cities that were unimaginable in the past. These datasets are sufficiently intensive to analyse detailed patterns and morphologies but also sufficiently extensive to enable patterns to be generalized to entire metropolitan areas. It is now possible to link the aggregate socio-economic approach that forms the basis of geographical analysis to the geometric built environment approach that is employed in local urban planning. Batty (2007) has termed this process 'Geography and Geometry', the merging of iconic and symbolic urban models, and it opens up many possibilities for research. Such combined datasets will allow key indicators of urban form and structure – such as density, mix of uses and accessibility – to be measured and analysed. Fine scale relationships between urban form, function and accessibility can be explored to provide an evidence base for research topics such as urban form and sustainability research, the housing property market, regeneration and gentrification, land-use change and neighbourhood definition (Galster, 2001) and act as a foundation for the creation and initialization of geospatial agent-based models for urban simulations which consider geometrical relationships directly in the simulation process.

For instance in the United Kingdom, there is a database on land parcels (e.g. building footprints) and associated land-uses (OS MasterMap Address Layer 2®), and road segment data (OS MasterMap Integrated Transport Network™ Layer). Current GIS are capable of encoding these datasets into the foundations of a simulation along with providing methods for relating these objects based on their proximity, intersection, adjacency or visibility to each other. However, one major stumbling block in relation to ABM, and modelling more generally, is that there is potentially too much detail when studying an entire city instead of a small area, the problem can become too computationally intensive for the current generation of computers. This problem can be overcome by considering the level of abstraction needed to examine the phenomena of interest and the purpose of the model, for example, is 'all the detail needed?' (see Crooks et al., 2008). Alternatively a series of smaller models could be created to examine specific aspects of the system. There is also a lack of personal data both for the present and the past. For example, in the UK, the smallest measure of individual data from the census is the output area which contains approximately 125 households, notwithstanding access to personal data (see Benenson et al., 2002). One potential solution is to synthetically generate the population through microsimulation techniques (e.g. Birkin et al., 2006).

17.8 Conclusion

Complexity now dominates our thinking about cities and this has changed our modelling approach. What becomes clear is that the processes at the core of urban modelling occur in space and change over time. We therefore need a different style of modelling coupled with new tools for studying urban systems (see Torrens, 2001). This has led our attention to shift from the aggregate to disaggregate, to that of modelling individuals with individual characteristics located in space whose behaviour has to be described over time. The applications reviewed in this chapter demonstrate how through the interaction of individual entities more complex aggregate structures develop. Examples include the economic distribution of land-uses or segregated neighbourhoods. The models range from explanatory models used to explore theory and generate hypotheses about urban change, to descriptive models concerned with making predictions, to how systems might evolve. Many consider the ABM paradigm as an electronic laboratory to test ideas and theory of urban change, to help understand and potentially predict future events, through analysis and experimentation in a controlled computer environment. This ability to test, refine and create numerous variations of models allows us create many models to explain the same phenomena based on the individual. However, one needs to balance the complexities of such models from insights gained from them in order to aid decision making. Perhaps one of the challenges arising from this is the need for ways of comparing such models. Attempts at devising ontologies and protocols for model comparison are being made, such as the ODD (overview, design concepts, details) protocol proposed by Grimm *et al.* (2006) might be one solution.

The growing interest in the integration of ABM and GIS was also discussed. Such integration allows agent-based models to be spatially explicit and capture model processes in both in time and space. However, this new generation of models is largely experimental in their development, and in many instances have not been applied in practice to the same extent as 'traditional' techniques, especially those of spatial interaction models. There is a need to move from explanatory models to more applied models and empirically based models (Parker et al., 2003) if the ABM paradigm is to prove useful for policy makers. Additionally, when modelling urban systems it is argued that there needs to be consideration of the role of the built environment (geometry) in the simulation process. There are several challenges ABM faces ranging across the spectrum of theory to practice, hypothesis to application (see Crooks et al., 2008). Validation schemes are a classic example of this. One reason for this is simply a function of the degree to which micro-geography of urban systems is still largely unknown in many situations. Nevertheless, this style of modelling provides a tool for testing the impact of changes such as land use type or transportation in dense metropolitan areas. This approach is less focused on predicting the right future, but more on understanding and exploring the system. It focuses on its behaviour and prediction of possible outcomes based on informed speculation incorporating individuals and dynamics. To this extent agent-based models may potentially assist policy makers in the same way as planning support systems do (see Brail and Klosterman, 2001). This is consistent with the notion that cities, and the societies they are part of, are intrinsically complex and inherently unpredictable (Batty, 2008). It is therefore virtually impossible to make meaningful predictions for such systems, or at least predictions that would form the basis of medium or long term policy-making (Batty, 2001). These models focus on the way local actions generate global outcomes, where system properties emerge from the bottom-up. This is in contrast to past generations of large scale urban models, which were economically driven, and focused on urban growth and transport infrastructure investment. This new style of modelling focuses on other issues which affect cities, specifically inequalities between the rich and poor, segregation along ethnic lines, redevelopment and so on. Such a move potentially offers a greater understanding of urban areas, to model future scenarios for cities, and prepare for challenges such as land-use, population, housing and employment change.

References

Allen, P.M. (1997) Cities and Regions as Self-Organizing Systems: Models of Complexity, Gordon and Breach Science Publishers, Amsterdam.

Alonso, W. (1964) Location and Land Use: Toward a General Theory of Land Rent, Harvard University Press, Cambridge.

Anas, A., Arnott, R. and Small, K.A. (1998) Urban Spatial Structure, *Journal of Economic Literature*, 36(3), pp. 1426-1464.

Antonovics, K., Arcidiacono, P. and Walsh, R. (2003) Games and Discrimination: Lessons From the Weakest Link, Department of Economics, University of California at San Diego, Working Paper Series 2003-03, San Diego (US), Available at http://www.econ.ucsd.edu/papers/files/2003-03.pdf.

Axelrod, R. (1997), *The Complexity of Cooperation: Agent-Based Models of Competition and Collaboration*, Princeton University Press, Princeton.

Axelrod, R. (2007) Simulation in the Social Sciences, in Rennard, J.P. (ed.) *Handbook of Research on Nature Inspired Computing for Economy and Management*, Idea Group, Hershey, pp. 90-100.

Axtell, R., Epstein, J.M., Dean, J.S., Gumerman, G.J., Swedlund, A.C., Harburger, J., Chakravarty, S., Hammond, R., Parker, J. and Parker, M. (2002) Population Growth and Collapse in a Multiagent Model of the Kayenta Anasazi in Long House Valley, Proceedings of the National Academy of Sciences of the United States of America (PNAS), 99(3), pp. 7275-7279.

Barros, J. (2004) Urban Growth in Latin American Cities: Exploring Urban Dynamics through Agent-Based Simulation, Ph.D. Thesis, University College London, London.

Batty, M. (1976) *Urban Modelling: Algorithms, Calibrations, Predictions*, Cambridge University Press, Cambridge.

Batty, M. (1995) Cities and Complexity: Implications for Modelling Sustainability, in Brotchie, J., Batty, M., Blakely, E., Hall, P. and Newton, P. (eds.), *Cities in Competition. Productive and Sustainable Cities for the 21st Century*, Longman, Melbourne, Australia, pp. 469-486.

Batty, M. (2001) Models in Planning: Technological Imperatives and Changing Roles, *International Journal of Applied Earth Observation and Geoinformation*, 3(3), pp. 252-266.

Batty, M. (2005a) Approaches to Modelling in GIS: Spatial Representation and Temporal Dynamics, in Maguire, D.J., Batty, M. and Goodchild, M.F. (eds.), *GIS, Spatial Analysis and Modelling*, ESRI Press, Redlands, pp. 41-61.

Batty, M. (2005b) *Cities and Complexity: Understanding Cities with Cellular Automata, Agent-Based Models, and Fractals*, The MIT Press, Cambridge.

Batty, M. (2007) Model Cities, *Town Planning Review*, 78(2), pp. 125-178.

Batty, M. (2008) Fifty Years of Urban Modelling: Macro-Statics to Micro-Dynamics, in Albeverio, S., Andrey, D., Giordano, P. and Vancheri, A. (eds.), *The Dynamics of Complex Urban Systems: An Interdisciplinary Approach*, Springer Physica-Verlag, New York, pp. 1-20.

Batty, M., Barros, J. and Alves, S., Jr. (2004), Cities: Continuity, Transformation and Emergence, Centre for Advanced Spatial Analysis (University College London): Working Paper 72, London.

Batty, M., Desyllas, J. and Duxbury, E. (2003) Safety in Numbers? Modelling Crowds and Designing Control for the Notting Hill Carnival, *Urban Studies*, 40(8), pp. 1573-1590.

Batty, M. and Longley, P.A. (1994), *Fractal Cities: A Geometry of Form and Functions*, Academic Press, London.

Benenson, I. (1998) Multi-Agent Simulations of Residential Dynamics in a City, *Computers, Environment and Urban Systems*, 22(1), pp. 25-42.

Benenson, I., Aronovich, S. and Noam, S. (2005) Let's Talk Objects: Generic Methodology for Urban High-Resolution Simulation, *Computers, Environment and Urban Systems*, 29(4), pp. 425-453.

Benenson, I. and Omer, I. (2003) High-Resolution Census Data: Simple Ways to Make Them Useful, *Data Science Journal (Spatial Data Usability Special Section)*, 2, pp. 117-127.

Benenson, I., Omer, I. and Hatna, E. (2002) Entity-Based Modelling of Urban Residential Dynamics: The Case of Yaffo, Tel Aviv, *Environment and Planning B*, 29(4), pp. 491-512.

Benenson, I. and Torrens, P.M. (2004), *Geosimulation: Automata-Based Modelling of Urban Phenomena*, John Wiley & Sons, London.

Birkin, M., Turner, A. and Wu, B. (2006) A Synthetic Demographic Model of the UK Population: Methods, Progress and Problems, Proceedings of the 2nd International Conference on e-Social Science, Manchester, England, Available at http://www.ncess.ac.uk/events/conference/2006/.

Bonabeau, E. (2002) Agent-Based Modelling: Methods and Techniques for Simulating Human Systems, *Proceedings of the National Academy of Sciences of the United States of America (PNAS)*, 99(3), pp. 7280-7287.

Bossomaier, T., Amri, S. and Thompson, J. (2007) Agent-Based Modelling of House Price Evolution, Proceedings of the 2007 IEEE Symposium on Artificial Life (CI-ALife 2007), Honolulu, pp. 463-467.

Brail, R.K. and Klosterman, R.E. (2001), *Planning Support Systems: Integrating Geographic Information Systems, Models and Visualisation Tools*, ESRI Press Redlands.

Brown, D.G. (2006) Agent-Based Models, in Geist, H. (ed.) *The Earth's Changing Land: An Encyclopaedia of Land-Use and Land-Cover Change*, Greenwood Publishing Group, Westport, pp. 7-13.

Brown, D.G., Page, S.E., Riolo, R., Zellner, M. and Rand, W. (2005a) Path Dependence and the Validation of Agent-Based Spatial Models of Land Use, *International Journal of Geographical Information Science*, 19(2), pp. 153–174.

Brown, D.G., Riolo, R., Robinson, D.T., North, M.J. and Rand, W. (2005b) Spatial Process and Data Models: Toward Integration of Agent-Based Models and GIS, *Journal of Geographical Systems*, 7(1), pp. 25-47.

Bruch, E. (2006) Residential Mobility, Income Inequality, and Race/Ethnic Segregation in Los Angeles, Population Association of America (PAA) 2006 Annual Meeting Program, Los Angeles, CA, Available at http://paa2006. princeton.edu/ download.aspx?submissionId=60143.

Bruch, E. and Mare, R.D. (2005), Neighbourhood Choice and Neighbourhood Change, California Centre for Population Research University of California – Los Angeles, Los Angeles, CA, Available at http://www.stat.ucla.edu/~bruch/ NCNC.pdf.

Castle, C.J.E. (2007), Agent-Based Modelling of Pedestrian Evacuation: A Study of London's King's Cross Underground Station, PhD Thesis, University College London, London.

Castle, C.J.E. and Crooks, A.T. (2006), Principles and Concepts of Agent-Based Modelling for Developing Geospatial Simulations, Centre for Advanced Spatial Analysis, Working Paper 110, University College London, London.

Clark, W.A.V. (1991) Residential Preferences and Neighbourhood Racial Segregation: A Test of the Schelling Segregation Model, *Demography*, 28(1), pp. 1-19.

Couclelis, H. (2002) Modelling Frameworks, Paradigms, and Approaches, in Clarke, K.C., Parks, B.E. and Crane, M.P. (eds.), *Geographic Information Systems and Environmental Modelling*, Prentice Hall, London, pp. 36–50.

Crooks, A.T. (2008), Constructing and Implementing an Agent-Based Model of Residential Segregation through Vector GIS, Centre for Advanced Spatial Analysis (University College London): Working Paper 133, London.

Crooks, A.T., Castle, C.J.E. and Batty, M. (2008) Key Challenges in Agent-Based Modelling for Geo-spatial Simulation, *Computers, Environment and Urban Systems*, 32(6), pp. 417-430.

Epstein, J.M. (1999) Agent-Based Computational Models and Generative Social Science, *Complexity*, 4(5), pp. 41-60.

Epstein, J.M. and Axtell, R. (1996), *Growing Artificial Societies: Social Science from the Bottom Up*, MIT Press, Cambridge (US).

Fossett, M. and Senft, R. (2004) SIMSEG and Generative Models: A Typology of Model-Generated Segregation Patterns, in Macal, C.M., Sallach, D. and North, M.J. (eds.), *Proceedings of the Agent 2004 Conference on Social Dynamics: Interaction, Reflexivity and Emergence*, Chicago, IL, pp. 39-78, Available at http://www.agent2005.anl.gov/Agent2004.pdf.

Galster, G. (2001) On the Nature of Neighbourhood, *Urban Studies*, 38(12), pp. 2111-2124.

Gimblett, H.R. (2002), *Integrating Geographic Information Systems and Agent-Based Modelling Techniques for Simulating Social and Ecological Processes*, Oxford University Press, Oxford.

Grimm, V., Berger, U. et al. (2006) A Standard Protocol for Describing Individual-Based and Agent-Based Models, *Ecological Modelling*, 198(1-2), pp. 115-126.

Haklay, M., O'Sullivan, D., Thurstain-Goodwin, M. and Schelhorn, T. (2001) "So Go Downtown": Simulating Pedestrian Movement in Town Centres, *Environment and Planning B*, 28(3), pp. 343-359.

Hammam, Y., Moore, A., Whigham, P. and Freeman, C. (2004) Irregular Vector-Agent Based Simulation for Land-Use Modelling, The 16th Annual Colloquium of the Spatial Information Research Centre, University of Otago, Dunedin, New Zealand.

Holland, J.H. (1995), *Hidden Order: How Adaptation Builds Complexity*, Addison-Wesley, Reading (US).

Jacobs, J. (1961), *The Death and Life of Great American Cities*, Vintage Books, New York.

Kii, M. and Doi, K. (2005) Multiagent Land-Use and Transport Model for Policy Evaluation of a Compact City, *Environment and Planning B*, 32(4), pp. 485-504.

Krugman, P.R. (1996), *The Self-Organizing Economy*, Blackwell Publishers, Oxford.

Landis, J.D. (2001) CUF, CUFII, and CURBA: A Family of Spatially Explicit Urban Growth and Land-Use Policy Simulation Models, in Brail, R.K. and Klosterman, R.E. (eds.), *Planning Support Systems: Integrating Geographic Information Systems, Models and Visualisation Tools*, ESRI Press, Redlands (US), pp. 157-200.

Laurie, A.J. and Jaggi, N.K. (2003) Role of 'Vision' in Neighbourhood Racial Segregation: A Variant of the Schelling Segregation Model, *Urban Studies*, 40(13), pp. 2687-2704.

Lee, D.B. (1994) Retrospective on Large-Scale Urban Models, *Journal of the American Planning Association*, 60(1), pp. 35-40.

Liu, J., Dietz, T. et al. (2007) Complexity of Coupled Human and Natural Systems, *Science*, 317(5844), pp. 1513-1516.

Liu, X. and Andersson, C. (2004) Assessing the Impact of Temporal Dynamics on Land-Use Change Modelling, *Computers Environment and Urban Systems*, 28(1-2), pp. 107-124.

Longley, P.A. (2003) Geographical Information Systems: Developments in Socio-Economic Data Infrastructures, *Progress in Human Geography*, 27(1), pp. 114-121.

Macal, C.M. and North, M.J. (2005) Tutorial on Agent-Based Modelling and Simulation, in Euhl, M.E., Steiger, N.M., Armstrong, F.B. and Joines, J.A. (eds.), Proceedings of the 2005 Winter Simulation Conference, Orlando, pp. 2-15.

Manson, S.M. (2001) Simplifying Complexity: A Review of Complexity Theory, *Geoforum*, 32(3), pp. 405-414.

Manson, S.M. (2003) Epistemological Possibilities and Imperatives of Complexity Research: A Reply to Reitsma, *Geoforum*, 34(1), pp. 17-20.

Manson, S.M. (2007) Challenges to Evaluating Models of Geographic Complexity, *Environment and Planning B*, 34(2), pp. 245-260.

Massey, D.S. and Denton, N.A. (1993), *American Apartheid Segregation and the Making of the Underclass*, Harvard University Press, Cambridge.

Mysore, V., Narzisi, G. and Mishra, B. (2006) Agent Modelling of a Sarin Attack in Manhattan, in Jennings, N.R., Tambe, M., Ishida, T. and Ramchurn, S.D. (eds.), *First International Workshop on Agent Technology for Disaster Management*, Future University, Hakodate, Japan.

Nagel, K., Beckman, R.J. and Barrett, C.L. (1999), TRANSIMS for Urban Planning, Los Alamos National Laboratory, Los Alamos, NM, Available at http://citeseer.ist.psu.edu/cache/papers/cs/7513/http:zSzzSztransims.tsasa. lanl.govzSzPS_FileszSz98-4389.pdf/nagel99transims.pdf.

Nagel, K. and Rasmussen, S. (1994) Traffic at the Edge of Chaos, in Brooks, R. (ed.) *Artificial Life IV*, MIT Press, Cambridge, pp. 222-236.

Nagel, K., Rasmussen, S. and Barrett, C.L. (1997) Network Traffic as a Self-Organized Critical Phenomenon, in Schweitzer, F. (ed.) *Self-organization of Complex Structures: from Individual to Collective Dynamics*, Gordon and Breach Science Publishers, Amsterdam, pp. 579-592.

Najlis, R. and North, M.J. (2004) Repast for GIS, in Macal, C.M., Sallach, D. and North, M.J. (eds.), Proceedings of the Agent 2004 Conference on Social Dynamics: Interaction, Reflexivity and Emergence, Chicago, IL, pp. 255-260, Available at http://www.agent2005.anl.gov/Agent2004.pdf.

North, M.J. and Macal, C.M. (2007), *Managing Business Complexity: Discovering Strategic Solutions with Agent-Based Modelling and Simulation*, Oxford University Press, New York.

O'Sullivan, D. (2001) *Exploring Spatial Process Dynamics using Irregular Cellular Automaton Models, Geographical Analysis*, 33(1), pp. 1-18.

O'Sullivan, D. (2004) Complexity Science and Human Geography, *Transactions of the Institute of British Geographers*, 29(3), pp. 282-295.

O'Sullivan, D., MacGill, J. and Yu, C. (2003) Agent-Based Residential Segregation: A Hierarchically Structured Spatial Model, in Macal, C.M., North, M.J. and Sallach, D. (eds.), Proceedings of Agent 2003 Conference on Challenges in Social Simulation, The University of Chicago, IL, pp. 493-507, Available at http://www.agent2004.anl.gov/Agent2003.pdf.

Omer, I. (2005) How Ethnicity Influences Residential Distributions: an Agent-Based Simulation, *Environment and Planning B*, 32(5), pp. 657-672.

Ormerod, P. (2005), *Why Most Things Fail: Evolution, Extinction and Economics*, Faber and Faber, London.

Parker, D.C. (2005) Integration of Geographic Information Systems and Agent-Based Models of Land Use: Challenges and Prospects, in Maguire, D.J., Batty,

M. and Goodchild, M.F. (eds.), GIS, Spatial Analysis and Modelling, ESRI Press, Redlands, pp. 403-422.

Parker, D.C., Manson, S.M., Janssen, M.A., Hoffmann, M.J. and Deadman, P. (2003) Multi-Agent Systems for the Simulation of Land-Use and Land-Cover Change: A Review, *Annals of the Association of American Geographers*, 93(2), pp. 314-337.

Parker, D.C. and Meretsky, V. (2004) Measuring Pattern Outcomes in an Agent-Based Model of Edge-Effect Externalities Using Spatial Metrics, *Agriculture, Ecosystems and Environment*, 101(2-3), pp. 233-250.

Parunak, H.V.D., Savit, R. and Riolo, R.L. (1998) Agent-Based Modelling vs. Equation-Based Modelling: A Case Study and Users' Guide, Proceedings of Multi-Agent Systems and Agent-Based Simulation (MABS'98), Paris, pp. 10-25, Available at http://www.newvectors.net/staff/parunakv/mabs98.pdf.

Pickles, J. (1995), *Ground Truth: The Social Implications of Geographic Information Systems*, Guilford Press, New York.

Portugali, J. (2000), *Self-Organization and the City*, Springer-Verlag, London.

Rabin, Y. (1987) The Roots of Segregation in the Eighties: The Role of Local Government Actions, in Tobin, G.A. (ed.) *Divided Neighbourhoods: Changing Patterns of Racial Segregation*, Sage Publications, London, pp. 208-226.

Reardon, S.F. and O'Sullivan, D. (2004) Measures of Spatial Segregation, *Sociological Methodology*, 34(1), pp. 121-162.

Reitsma, F. (2003) A Response to Simplifying Complexity, *Geoforum*, 34(1), pp. 13-16.

Russell, S. and Norvig, P. (2003), *Artificial Intelligence: A Modern Approach*, Prentice Hall, Upper Saddle River.

Sasaki, Y. and Box, P. (2003) Agent-Based Verification of von Thünen's Location Theory, *Journal of Artificial Societies and Social Simulation*, 6(2), Available at http://jasss.soc.surrey.ac.uk/6/2/9.html.

Schelling, T.C. (1971) Dynamic Models of Segregation, *Journal of Mathematical Sociology*, 1(1), pp. 143-186.

Schelling, T.C. (2006) Some Fun, Thirty-Five Years Ago, in Tesfatsion, L. and Judd, K.L. (eds.), *Handbook of Computational Economics: Agent-Based Computational Economics*, North-Holland Publishing, Amsterdam, pp. 1639-1644.

Semboloni, F. (2000) The Growth of an Urban Cluster into a Dynamic, Self-Modifying Spatial Pattern, *Environment and Planning B*, 27(4), pp. 549-564.

Talen, E. (2003) Measuring Urbanism: Issues in Smart Growth Research, *Journal of Urban Design*, 8(3), pp. 195-215.

Tesfatsion, L. and Judd, K.L. (2006), *Handbook of Computational Economics: Agent-Based Computational Economics Volume 2*, North-Holland Publishing, Amsterdam.

Thorp, J., Guerin, S., Wimberly, F., Rossbach, M., Densmore, O., Agar, M. and Roberts, D. (2006) Agent-Based Modelling of Wildfire Evacuation, in Sallach, D., Macal, C.M. and North, M.J. (eds.), Proceedings of the Agent 2006

Conference on Social Agents: Results and Prospects, University of Chicago and Argonne National Laboratory, Chicago, IL, Available at http://agent2007. anl.gov/2006procpdf/ Agent_2006.pdf.

Thünen, J.H., von. (1826), Der Isolierte Staat in Beziehung auf Landwirtschaft und Nationalokonomie [The Isolated State in relation to Planning and Macro Economics], Gustav Fisher, Stuttgart (G).

Topa, G. (2001) Social Interactions, Local Spillovers and Unemployment, *Review of Economic Studies*, 68(2), pp. 261-295.

Torrens, P.M. (2000), How Land-Use-Transportation Models Work, Centre for Advanced Spatial Analysis (University College London): Working Paper 20, London.

Torrens, P.M. (2001), Can Geocomputation Save Urban Simulation? Throw Some Agents into the Mixture, Simmer, and Wait, Centre for Advanced Spatial Analysis (University College London): Working Paper 32, London.

Torrens, P.M. (2003) Automata-Based Models of Urban Systems, in Longley, P.A. and Batty, M. (eds.), *Advanced Spatial Analysis: The CASA Book of GIS*, ESRI Press, Redlands, pp. 61-81.

Torrens, P.M. (2004), Simulating Sprawl: A Dynamic Entity-Based Approach to Modelling North American Suburban Sprawl Using Cellular Automata and Multi-Agent Systems, Ph.D. Thesis, University College London, London.

Torrens, P.M. (2006) Simulating Sprawl, *Annals of the Association of American Geographers*, 96(2), pp. 248-275.

Torrens, P.M. and Nara, A. (2007) Modelling Gentrification Dynamics: A Hybrid Approach, Computers, *Environment and Urban Systems*, 31(3), pp. 337-361.

United Nations (2007), State of World Population 2007: Unleashing the Potential of Urban Growth, United Nations Population Fund, New York, Available at http://www.unfpa.org/swp/2007/presskit/pdf/sowp2007_eng.pdf.

White, R. and Engelen, G. (1993) Cellular Automata and Fractal Urban Form: A Cellular Modelling Approach to the Evolution of Urban Land Use Patterns, *Environment and Planning A*, 25(8), pp. 1175-1199.

Wilson, A.G. (2000), *Complex Spatial Systems: The Modelling Foundations of Urban and Regional Analysis*, Pearson Education, Harlow.

Wooldridge, M. and Jennings, N.R. (1995) Intelligent Agents: Theory and Practice, *Knowledge Engineering Review*, 10(2), pp. 115-152.

Xie, Y., Batty, M. and Zhao, K. (2005), Simulating Emergent Urban Form: Desakota in China, Centre for Advanced Spatial Analysis (University College London): Working Paper 95, London.

Yin, L. and Muller, B. (2007) Residential Location and the Biophysical Environment: Exurban Development Agents in a Heterogeneous Landscape, *Environment and Planning B*, 34(2), pp. 279-295.

Chapter 18
Building Mega-Models for Megacities

Paul M. Torrens[1]

Urban simulations are an important toolkit for theorizing about cities, testing ideas and hypotheses, and evaluating plans and policies. As a field of research, urban modelling is at an important stage in its development. The pace of urbanization and city growth, and the ever-increasing rate of adaptation of urban phenomena, have, to some extent, accelerated beyond the abilities of previous generations of modelling methodology to remain practically relevant and diagnostically useful. These challenges are particularly significant for urban models tasked with representing the dynamics of the world's megacities, which manifest among the most complicated and complex human-environmental systems. A next-generation of urban modelling is perhaps needed to conceptualize the dynamics of the world's megacities, which are, in many instances, growing in number, size, and influence at unprecedented rates.

18.1 Introduction

The rationale for studying urban systems and phenomena is varied and compelling. Urban activities are among the most significant of the Earth's land-uses. Cities host vast amounts of the world's built and technical infrastructure, they are seats of innovation and creativity, they have served among the most important engines of land cover change through history, and they are significant sources of anthropogenic contributions to the Earth's climate systems. Cities also serve as hubs of human activity: they provide the ambient human infrastructure for much of the world's social, economic, and cultural systems, as well as providing the substrate that houses the majority of the world's population. Urban systems are still growing in extent and volume throughout the world. In many areas, the pace of urban expansion is actually accelerating, sometimes strikingly so. This is particularly true in the world's megacities: unified urban agglomerations with populations of at least ten million inhabitants. It is here, in megacities, that the greatest engines of the world's urban activity – and all of its associated problems and promise – are to be found.

---

1   Paul Torrens is Associate Professor, Geosimulation Research Laboratory, Department of Geographical Sciences, University of Maryland, College Park.

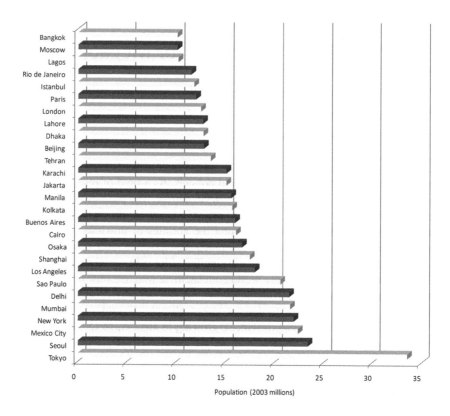

Figure 18.1   The world's 27 megacities

In the last 30 years, the number of megacities in the world has increased from three to 20 (Figure 18.1). The United States, for example, hosts three megacities: New York, Los Angeles, and the burgeoning Chicago megacity (Figure 18.2). The geography of this mega-urbanization is uneven. Most megacities in the developed world are projected to reach a level of stasis in their growth, growing at slower rates as their populations saturate their urban environment and the dominant role that they play in their constituent national systems – and globally – locks-in, at least for the time being. Growth in the Los Angeles-Long Beach-Santa Ana megacity is forecast to expand by only 6.5% (+0.8 million, to 13.1 million total) between 2005 and 2015, while that of Tokyo is set to appreciate by <1% (+0.3 million, to 35.5 million total) over the same time-frame (Moore and Gardner 2007). No net growth is projected for the Osaka-Kobe megacity over that period (its population is set to remain steadfast at 11.3 million in total) (Moore and Gardner, 2007). Meanwhile, megacities in the developing world are forecast to accelerate in their growth: Lagos megacity is projected to expand by 48%, adding 5.2 million people (to 16.1 million total) between 2005 and 2015, Dhaka is estimated to grow by 35% (+4.4 million, to 16.8 million total), Karachi by 31% (+3.6 million, to 15.2 million

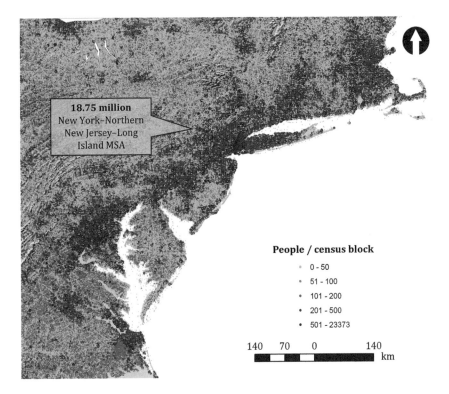

Figure 18.2(a)   The New York megacity

total), Jakarta by 27% (+3.6 million, to 16.8 million total), and Kolkata (Calcutta) by 19% (+2.7 million, to 17 million total) over the same time period (Moore and Gardner, 2007).

Understanding how and why megacities form in diverse locations, at varying times, and how they develop over diverse time-scales are important goals for science across disciplines and interests. Indeed, megacities hold the answers to many "big science" questions that remain to be answered (see, for example, the special issue of *Science* magazine on "cities" (American Association for the Advancement of Science, 2008; http://www.sciencemag.org/cities/video/). As megacities grow and consolidate with massive tangible footprints and huge populations, so also will their influence on the world's physical, natural, social, and technical systems expand and intensify. The pace of their emergence, development, and growth has, to a certain extent, outpaced our ability – as scientists – to keep track of their driving mechanics. Appreciating and understanding the future evolution of megacities is critical in explaining the futures of the world's demography, economic markets, climate variability, innovation, and in postulating about many other factors.

Exploring these issues is largely intractable without the use of computer models. Yet, the traditional cadre of simulation methodology that we have at our disposal is

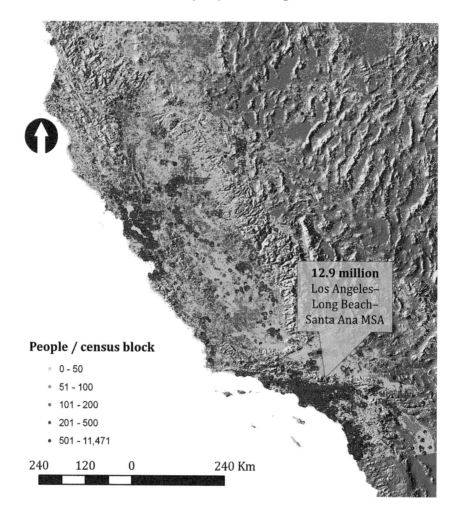

People / census block

·   0 - 50

·   51 - 100

·   101 - 200

·   201 - 500

·   501 - 11,471

240   120   0   240 Km

Figure 18.2(b)   The Los Angeles megacity

largely inadequate for examining the complexity of megacities in any serious fashion and serves to limit the range of questions that scientists can pose in simulation.

Mega-models are not commonly developed for megacities, although their potential usefulness as planning and decision support systems, and as synthetic laboratories for trying-out ideas, hypothesizing about possible urban futures, and testing what-if scenarios has, perhaps, never been greater. In this chapter, I will take a look at why robust mega-urban models do not feature more prominently in the scientific record and I will focus, in particular, on the limitations that have prevented their proliferation, as well as the promising avenues of academic and applied inquiry that might move the state-of-the-art in directions that might accelerate the pace of innovation in urban simulation and its applied use.

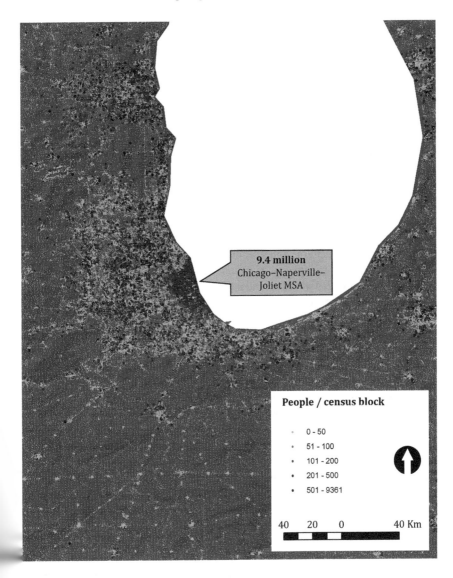

Figure 18.2(c)   The burgeoning Chicago megacity

18.2 Massive, unwieldy megacities

Megacities are extraordinarily large and cumbrous phenomena. Their enormous size and complicated details veil many of their attributes to inquiry. These massive urban behemoths are complex mega-systems (if we consider their role in a world ecology of billions of people, we can perhaps consider them as giga-systems) composed of many interacting parts, each intertwined through a bewildering array of non-linear and dynamic phenomena that scale up and down and weave throughout the fabric of the past, present, and future. In the case of these huge urban agglomerations, the orders of magnitude in scaling from the individual to the system are many times greater than one would usually encounter in urban studies. The number of state descriptors and linkages required to explain the functioning of megacities are also substantially greater, as are the potential trajectories for the system's state-space (land-use, land cover, zoning, etc.) over time. Pinpointing the emergence of novel patterns and phenomena in megacity evolution is an arduous task considering the cacophony of actions and interactions within the megacity that must be scrutinized in order to identify such innovation.

Megacities are highly variable. Some, such as London, Tokyo, and New York, are long-standing global cities (Sassen, 1991) that have dominated atop the world's urban hierarchy for hundreds of years. In other cases, megacity emergence is a relatively recent phenomenon. The developing Guangzhou megacity in China, for example, had a population of just 2.7 million thirty years ago; by 2015 it is expected to reach 10.4 million (Moore and Gardner, 2007). Although it is now home to 11 million people, the Lagos megacity in Nigeria had a population of 1.9 million thirty years ago (Moore and Gardner, 2007). Traditionally, megacities have grown in developed countries with relatively advanced economies: France, Japan, South Korea, the United Kingdom, and the United States, but more recently, megacities have emerged in developing countries (Bangladesh, Egypt, Indonesia, Nigeria, Pakistan, the Philippines) and newly-industrializing nations (Brazil, China, India, Mexico, Thailand, Turkey). Moreover, the rate of emergence and expansion of city-systems in non-traditional host countries is growing. Economic output and the quality of life in these diverse megacities vary considerably: the Gross Domestic Product of Bangladesh is $73.7 billion and the average life expectancy is 63/63 (male/female), while GDP in the United States is 186 times greater, at $13.8 trillion and the average life expectancy is 75/80 (male/female) (using GDP figures from the International Monetary Fund, 2007 and life expectancy averages from the World Health Organization, 2007).

Experimenting with such mammoth and rapidly adapting systems in any sort of tangible fashion on the ground is, understandably, prohibitively difficult. In these instances, we may turn to simulations as an alternative (or ancillary) medium for exploring the processes and phenomena that drive megacity dynamics. Simulations can serve as an artificial laboratory for experimenting and theorizing about their present conditions, as well as their past and future trajectories.

There are, however, fundamental challenges in representing megacity systems in simulation. Traditional toolkits and methods for modelling cities and city-systems are limited in their ability to treat the complexities that drive urbanization on a mega-level. Those toolkits largely dictate the sets of questions that can be posed in simulation, constrained within the limitations of the specific assumptions that they make, rather than being flexible in handling multiply-interacting city systems across a variety of scales (Batty and Torrens, 2005).

18.3 Simulations, simulacra and the synthetic city

A plethora of models exist for simulating urban *sub-systems* at macro-scales (e.g., inter-regional migration (McHugh and Gober, 1992), scaling and allometry in global city-size distributions (Batty, 2008), and the geography of national urban agglomeration economies (Fujita et al., 2001; Krugman, 1996), as well as characterizing sub-systems at meso-scales (e.g., intra-urban traffic flow (Nagel and Schreckenberg, 1992), formation of urban heat islands (Brazel et al., 2000), and urban epidemic dynamics (Eubank et al., 2004), and micro-scales (e.g., pedestrian activity along city streets (Haklay et al., 2001), vehicle parking behaviour (Benenson et al., 2006), and emergency evacuation behaviour (Nara and Torrens, 2007). Such sub-systems are found in megacities, but sub-system models do not address megacities as entities in their own right and seldom consider the dynamics of these systems as special cases in megacity contexts. Global climate models, for example, often treat cities as a simple binary classification – urban or not urban – in accounting for land cover in the boundary-layer of the Earth's climate systems.

Much of the innovation in city simulators has been achieved in building models of urban-scale traffic systems, at the level of individual drivers, their decisions, actions, and interactions, propagated up-scale and down-scale between the city and the road (Barrett et al., 1999; Torrens, 2005). Sophisticated models of property markets and residential formation at the geography of interacting households and communities have also been built (Benenson et al., 2002; O'Sullivan, 2002; Torrens and Nara, 2007). In these instances, the path from individual agent to larger-scale system (and back again), and all of the complex interactions that take place in between can be relatively easily identified and expressed algorithmically, within spatial, temporal, and system confines, largely because there are long traditions of social science, behavioural, and economic research into these sub-systems, and data for calibrating and verifying models against ground-truth are often available at these scales. These remain, however, limited cases and they explain only one of many (isolated) components that drive the development and day-to-day functioning of megacities.

In an ideal situation, we could couple many sub-system models together to generate a *mega-model* that explains the intricate inner-workings of megacities at the detail of its constituent components. This is insufferably difficult to achieve in practice because individual models are often developed for independent purposes, with purpose-specific data models, methodological approaches, spatial resolutions, constraining assumptions, system closures, time-scales, and so on. Nevertheless, some researchers have made attempts to develop such mega-models, thereby proving the concept of the mega-model and its potential promise.

Some urban mega-models are developed from a systems engineering perspective, coupling the information flow between diverse sub-system models as "stocks and flows" models that determine the elasticity in intra-system relationships (Forrester, 1969). These are not strictly integrated models, but capture massive urban systems at a synoptic scale nonetheless, and explain the relative exchange of materials and goods on an intra-urban level.

The closest analog to the ideal of a mega-model is the large-scale urban model, most commonly developed for operational use by metropolitan planning organizations in estimating the ability of the city to provide future urban services. Generally, large-scale urban models are designed to couple land-use and transport simulations, with occasional connections to air quality models or air quality analysis through their predictions of aggregate vehicle emissions to the boundary-layer atmosphere. Previous generations of these models were developed as coupled land-use and transportation simulators, in which a land-use model generated trips that are subsequently simulated over large-geography urban systems as traffic flows; the DRAM/EMPAL model (the Disaggregated Residential Allocation Model and the Employment Allocation Model) was a widely-deployed example of such a trip-generator, focusing on the push and pull factors that anchored trips in the urban system (Putman, 1983). These models were often built on microsimulation (Clarke, 1996) and regional science (Isard, 1975) methodologies, which for the most part used relatively simple heuristics (often based on physics of spatial interactions (Fotheringham and O'Kelly, 1989) and parametric statistics for estimating discrete choices for activity types and locations (Louviere et al., 2000) to extrapolate future values from coarse-resolution socioeconomic data-sets. Large-scale urban models have been applied in evaluating planning and policy alternatives in many megacities, with mixed usefulness (Batty, 1994). In traditional form, large-scale models tend to treat urban dynamics in a crude, abstract fashion, and although they may be loose-coupled to environmental models in some cases (Wegener, 1994a), they largely fail to treat the full range of sub-systems that account for megacity formation and adaptation in sufficient detail to be maximally useful for robust experimentation *in silico* (to use a term I have borrowed from Steven Levy (1992)).

More recently, a next generation of large-scale urban models has been developed as planning support systems, which more closely approach the ideal of an integrated, intricate model of an entire city-system. Detail has been added to these systems, in large part, by developing a slew of sub-models that handle demographics, lifecycle transition, migration patterns, a diversity of modes of transportation, land-use change, and property markets. Two planning support systems stand out in particular – the California Urban Futures models (Landis, 2001), and UrbanSim (Waddell, 2002). Urbanism, in particular, is relatively widely used in operational city planning. It was initially developed as an urban economic model, designed to estimate the future trajectories of urban land markets, but several efforts are underway to extend the model by integrating it with ancillary activity, travel, and traffic models, as well as models of urban natural environments, and the lifecycle of resource use in constructing large city-systems (Li et al., 2007).

A parallel thread of model development has been carried out in the sustainability sciences, focused predominantly on modelling the role of human-environment interactions upon land-use and land cover change. The sustainability science community has benefitted greatly from increasing availability of remotely-sensed data at finer-grained resolutions and covering longitudinal periods of time. Many of these models are focused on large city-systems, with an emphasis on the extension of expanding cities into the urban-rural interface through suburban sprawl, edge city formation, and exurban development (Parker et al., 2003).

Many model-developers have turned to complexity studies in search of methodology for treating the complexities inherent in large city-systems. Most have been built around automata (cellular automata, agent-based models, individual-based models, multi-agent systems, geographic automata) (Benenson and Torrens, 2004), following the success of such tools in generating signature complexities in the Artificial Life community, economics, mathematical sciences, ecology, computer science, and physics (Wolfram, 2002). These bottom-up approaches, representing city-systems at the scale of individual actors and their activities, are perhaps the most intricate urban mega-models. Development work at Sandia National Labs' National Infrastructure Simulation and Analysis Center (NISAC) in New Mexico in the United States is perhaps the exemplar of these approaches. Using a shared simulation architecture, NISAC is working to develop bottom-up agent-based and graph-based models of diverse but integrated socio-technical systems (public health, utility infrastructures, network infrastructures, vehicle traffic flow, and the economy) for whole cities and the entire United States (Eidson and Ehlen, 2005).

18.4 The challenges of developing megacity models

A number of constraints have slowed progress in developing and applying more robust models of megacities. Perhaps the greatest challenge in building more useful models of megacities as artificial laboratories is the sheer size and complexity of the urban systems that they encapsulate. To a certain extent, abstract models that at least represent megacities in a proxy fashion should be sufficiently useful as experimental toolkits, but other challenges remain in advancing beyond proxies.

The constituent drivers of megacities remain largely unknown in social science, behavioural science, and even in the design and engineering sciences. Megacities are organic, bottom-up, dynamic, and adaptive systems that do not readily make sense microscopically, synoptically, or from vistas in between. The science of modelling megacities is being developed at the same time that theories are being forwarded, evaluated, accepted, rejected, and modified. Concurrently, megacities are growing, adapting, accelerating, and reaching relative equilibrium in different places and contexts. There is a need for a simulation methodology that can flexibly keep step with these developments on the ground and in our theoretical discussions. Most urban models are unrealistic representations of the systems that they simulate and this does not help to advance the state-of-the-art. Algorithmically, urban models generally retain an overarching focus on simple rule-of-thumb heuristics from urban studies (grow on the edge of the urban mass, don't build on steep slopes, fill-in interstitial urban sites if they are surrounded by sufficient development, and so on (Clarke et al., 1997). In other cases the models are largely data-driven: their algorithms focus on spatially distributing the data that is fed to them; these models are generally only as good as the data that they are fed and little reliance can be placed upon their future extrapolations. They are, as the cliché goes, "tools to think with" (Negroponte, 1995) rather than serving as decision support systems. Consequently, few models make it out of sheltered laboratory settings to engage with theory or to be used on the ground in informing decisions.

In other fields (climatology, cosmology, macroeconomics, for example), standard models have been in place for many decades and these serve as a foundation for innovation in their respective scientific communities. There is no (robust) standard model for cities or megacities, largely because each city is rather unique in its composite patterns and processes in a much more variable way than (imaginatively) comparable structures in climatology, cosmology, and macroeconomics might be considered. Invariably, then, model-builders must start anew in constructing new tools and this slows the pace of innovation. Building a common platform for urban simulation, one that treats some of the more generic components of city-systems, may help to ease this constraint.

Sophistication in urban simulation is almost always closely allied to the availability of data, and the plentitude of data at high spatial and temporal resolutions, covering a multitude of urban sub-systems. With the exception of remotely-sensed imagery relating to land-cover, such data are often in short supply, particularly at the micro-scale (Torrens, 2006). Recent developments in cyberinfrastructure for automated sensing and data collection over distributed sensor webs suggest that issues of data availability may be resolved in the near future, but sufficiently complete data-sets will most likely be in short supply perpetually for many urban sub-systems, particularly those relating to human decision-making. These data are simply too difficult to collect over megacities or to infer, even using cell-phone records or patterns of vehicle or currency mobility, for example (although attempts to do so have been made (Brockman et al., 2006; González et al., 2008).

For systems in which data may be available, they are often required in massive volumes to feed ravenously data-hungry urban simulations. Similarly, the data that complex simulations output often spill-out in volumes that are many times greater in size than the resources that are initially input. Sophisticated dataware

are therefore needed to visualize inputs and outputs in a scientific fashion and to mine data for knowledge discovery and generation. There has been a fantastic amount of innovation in visualizing complex information, in the development of information systems for handling massive data-sets, and in crafting intelligent routines for knowledge discovery, data-mining, and reality-mining of large data reservoirs. With few examples (Batty et al., 2001), much of this innovation has not yet been introduced to urban simulation, particularly as a decision support system.

Issues of calibrating, validating, and verifying complex urban simulations often compound these problems. Because megacities are such large and unwieldy phenomena, garnering ground truth for the purposes of model-fitting is a very difficult task. Models are therefore often built blindly, as proofs-of-concept, or are built from theory, which is almost always anecdotal, qualitative, and even normative in nature. Building robust models on such a permeable foundation is quite a difficult undertaking. Improving data resources and related dataware may help to resolve such issues, but complicating factors remain as grand challenges, particularly in treating uncertainty and stochasticity in the interface between models, data, and "truth".

Large-scale urban models, if simulated with any serious degree of fidelity to the mega-systems that they are tasked in representing, are usually massive software engineering projects that require considerable computing resources. To some degree, principles of encapsulation, abstraction, clustering, scheduling, and distributed processing from high-performance computing may be used to great advantage in urban simulation and already are, for example, in traffic modelling (Nagel and Rickert, 2001), where road segments may be neatly parsed and passed between processing units on parallel systems. Considering megacities more comprehensively, however, involves treating massively dynamic and interacting agents and agencies with many-to-many relationships that scale-up, scale-down, and act and interact with complex and fluid feedback contingencies. Such processes and phenomena are not as easily and discretely packaged as computable packets.

18.5 Pushing the state-of-the-art beyond current research difficulties

It is, perhaps, readily apparent to the reader that the number of constraints upon advancing large-geography and large-scale (at small resolution) urban modelling are many. Progress is being made, however, in overcoming the problems that I have detailed.

The most promising development has come in the form of research into flexible future methodologies for urban simulation that will allow models to be constructed with a greater level of realism and at improved spatial and temporal resolutions. The most encouraging advances have come from the adaptation of older technologies, based around automata and information processing, and their modification for use in building models of cities from the bottom-up, popularly referred to as geosimulation (Benenson and Torrens, 2004). Modelling tools developed under these approaches have a number of advantages in representing cities. Automata are universal computers and can process any data and compute any algorithm that is input to them; they are therefore flexible in their ability to be configured to represent the myriad of entities and processes that constitute massively unwieldy megacities. Specifying how each of these components should be designed and allowed to interact, however, is a huge undertaking (Torrens and O'Sullivan, 2001).

Almost concurrently, research into the complex signatures and properties of urban systems has grown in popularity (and focus). Advances are slowly being made in understanding the mechanisms that determine how cities function as complex adaptive systems (Batty, 2005). To the extent that deterministic laws can be considered as describing those mechanisms, plausible theories of what they might be, how they might work, and how they may interconnect are being postulated and examined, particularly as regards the scaling and allometry of urban systems under conditions of self-organization (Batty, 2008; Batty and Longley, 1994; Bettencourt et al., 2007; Gabaix, 1999; Portugali, 2000; Portugali, 2006; Rozenfeld et al., 2008; Zipf, 1949).

Efforts are being made to remedy data shortages through artificial generation of realistic-enough data through statistical manipulation of group information. Originally pioneered as micro-analysis (Orcutt et al., 1976; Orcutt et al., 1961), much of the recent work in this area has been carried out in the field of microsimulation (Ballas et al., 2005; Clarke, 1996). Microsimulation involves statistical down-scaling of coarse-resolution (often zonal) data, generally recorded for census-taking units such as enumeration districts, blocks, blockgroups, traffic analysis zones, tracts, and so forth, to micro-level, perhaps even at the scale of individual households. Similar schemes are employed in the derivation of synthetic data populations for agent-based models, for example, as used in the TRANSIMS traffic model (TRansportation ANalysis SIMulation System) developed at Los Alamos National Laboratory in the United States (Bush, 2001). Nevertheless, these approaches suffer from well-known difficulties posed by ecological fallacy and modifiable areal unit problems (Openshaw, 1983), and likely always will.

While no standard urban model exists, the Federal Highway Administration in the United States has launched an initiative to foster its development (among other goals): the Travel Model Improvement Program (http://tmip.fhwa.dot. gov/). Earlier collaborative efforts to benchmark and consolidate large-scale urban models in Australia, Germany, the Netherlands, Japan, Sweden, the United Kingdom, and the United States, established in 1981 and run until 1991 under the International Study Group on Land-Use Transport Interaction (ISGLUTI) Program, have continued in a similar fashion to the Travel Model Improvement Program in the United States, but with greater emphasis being placed on modeling land-use activity and change (Wegener, 1994b). That scheme was succeeded by the SPARTACUS (System for Planning and Research in Towns and Cities for Urban Sustainability) project, applied to Europe and supported by the European Union's Fourth Framework for Research and Technology Development from

1996 to 1998 (Wegener, 2000). SPARTACUS focused on modeling land-use and transportation, in addition to modelling related environmental impacts in the form of air pollution, noise pollution, and resource consumption; social impacts in the context of health, equity, and accessibility to opportunities; and economic effects of urbanization. The PROPOLIS (Planning and Research of Policies for Land Use and Transport for Increasing Urban Sustainability) Project, organized under the European Union's Fifth Framework, continued this work further, running from 2000 to 2002 (Lautso et al., 2004). Under PROPOLIS, integrated urban models were applied at city-level to test cases in Bilbao, Brussels, Dortmund, Helsinki, Naples, Swindon, and Vicenza.

18.6 Conclusions

The relationship between urban modelling and megacities is circular. Megacities are ungainly entities and they do not lend themselves to an ease of observation or understanding. Their massively complex nature prohibits tractability in modelling their patterns, processes, pasts, and potential futures. Nevertheless, models are needed in assisting researchers, planners, policy-makers, urban managers, and citizens to study the inner-workings of mega-cities, *because* urban complexity veils megacities to inquiry by tangible means.

Despite the awkward relationship between models of megacities and their real-world counterparts on the ground, there is an urgent need for advancing the science of urban simulation to the level that it can begin to serve as a robust and flexible laboratory for experimenting with ideas and theories that might better explain why megacities form where and when they do, how they work, how they adapt, and what their future trajectories might be. The argument for using simulation as an artificial laboratory for formulating and testing plans and policies to guide future urban sustainability is equally compelling.

The barriers to pushing the state-of-the-art in developing mega-models for megacities are numerous, but they are not insurmountable. Significant progress in understanding the bewildering complexity of such behemoth systems has been made, researchers are beginning to distill that understanding to methodology that can support a next generation of mega-models, and the first signs of this science filtering into practice on the ground are beginning to show. This seems like a really good time to jump on the bandwagon and join in.

Acknowledgements

This material is based upon work supported by the National Science Foundation under Grant Nos. 1002519 and 0643322.

References

American Association for the Advancement of Science (2008) Special issue: Cities. *Science*, 319 (5864).

Ballas, D., G.P. Clarke, D. Dorling, H. Eyre, B. Thomas and D. Rossiter (2005) SimBritain: a spatial microsimulation approach to population dynamics, *Population, Space and Place*, 11, pp. 13-34.

Barrett, C.L., R.J. Beckman, K.P. Berkbigler, K.R. Bisset, B.W. Bush, S. Eubank, J.M. Hurford, G. Konjevod, D.A. Kubicek, M.V. Marathe, J.D. Morgeson, M. Rickert, P.R. Romero, L.L. Smith, M.P. Speckman, P.L. Speckman, P.E. Stretz, G.L. Thayer, and M.D. Williams (1999) TRANSIMS (TRansportation ANalysis SIMulation System). Volume 0: Overview, Los Alamos National Laboratory, Los Alamos.

Batty, M. (1994) A chronicle of scientific planning: the Anglo-American modeling experience, *Journal of the American Planning Association*, 60 (1), pp. 7-16.

Batty, M. (2005) *Cities and Complexity: Understanding Cities with Cellular Automata, Agent-Based Models, and Fractals*, The MIT Press, Cambridge.

Batty, M. (2008) The size, scale, and shape of cities, *Science*, 319 (5864), pp. 769-771.

Batty, M., D. Chapman, S. Evans, M. Haklay, S. Kueppers, N. Shiode, A. Smith, and P.M. Torrens (2001) Visualizing the city: communicating urban design to planners and decision-makers, In: R.K. Brail and R.E. Klosterman (eds) *Planning Support Systems in Practice: Integrating Geographic Information Systems, Models, and Visualization Tools*, ESRI Press and Center for Urban Policy Research Press. Redlands and New Brunswick, pp. 405-443.

Batty, M., and P. Longley (1994) *Fractal Cities*, Academic Press, London.

Batty, M., and P.M. Torrens (2005) Modeling and prediction in a complex world, *Futures*, 37 (7), pp. 745-766.

Benenson, I., S. Birfur and V. Kharbash (2006) Geographic Automata Systems and the OBEUS software for their implementation, In: J. Portugali (ed.) *Complex Artificial Environments*, Springer, Berlin, pp. 137-153.

Benenson, I., I. Omer, and E. Hatna (2002) Entity-based modeling of urban residential dynamics: the case of Yaffo, Tel Aviv, *Environment and Planning B: Planning and Design*, 29, pp. 491-512.

Benenson, I., and P.M. Torrens (2004) *Geosimulation: Automata-Based Modeling of Urban Phenomena*, John Wiley & Sons, London.

Bettencourt, L., J. Lobo, D. Helbing, C. Kühnert, and G. West (2007) Growth, innovation, scaling and the pace of life in cities, *Proceedings of the National Academy of Sciences*, 104 (17), pp. 7301-7306.

Brazel, A., N. Selover, R. Vose, and G. Heisler (2000) The tale of two climates – Baltimore and Phoenix urban LTER sites, *Climate Research*, 15, pp. 123-135.

Brockman, D., L. Hufnagel, and T. Geisel (2006) The scaling laws of human travel, *Nature*, 439, pp. 462-465.

Bush, B.W. (2001) Portland Synthetic Population, Los Alamos National Laboratory, Los Alamos.

Clarke, G.P. (ed.) (1996) *Microsimulation for Urban and Regional Policy Analysis*, *European Research in Regional Science*, 6, Pion, London.

Clarke, K.C., S. Hoppen, and L. Gaydos (1997) A self-modifying cellular automaton model of historical urbanization in the San Francisco Bay area, *Environment and Planning B*, 24, pp. 247-261.

Eidson, E.D. and M.A. Ehlen (2005) NISAC Agent-Based Laboratory for Economics (N-ABLE): Overview of agent and simulation architectures, In *SAND2005-0263*, Sandia National Labs, Albuquerque (US).

Eubank, S., H. Guclu, A. Kumar, M.V. Marathe, A. Srinivasan, Z. Toroczkai and N. Wang (2004) Modelling disease outbreaks in realistic urban social networks, *Nature*, 429 (6988), pp. 180-184.

Forrester, J. (1969) *Urban Dynamics*, The MIT Press. Cambridge.

Fotheringham, A.S. and M.E. O'Kelly (1989) *Spatial Interaction Models: Formulations and Applications*, Studies in Operational Regional Science, Kluwer Academic Publishers, Dordrecht.

Fujita, M., P. Krugman, and A.J. Venables (2001) *The Spatial Economy: Cities, Regions, and International Trade*, The MIT Press, Cambridge.

Gabaix, X. 1999. Zipf's law for cities: an explanation, *Quarterly Journal of Economics*, 114, pp. 739-767.

González, M.C., C.A. Hidalgo, and A.L. Barabási (2008) Understanding individual human mobility patterns, *Nature*, 453 (7196), pp. 779-782.

Haklay, M., D. O'Sullivan, M. Thurstain-Goodwin and T. Schelhorn (2001) "So go downtown": simulating pedestrian movement in town centres. *Environment and Planning B*, 28 (3), pp. 343-359.

Isard, W. (1975) *Introduction to Regional Science*, Prentice-Hall, Englewood Cliffs.

Krugman, P. (1996) *The Self-Organizing Economy*, Blackwell, Malden.

Landis, J. (2001) CUF, CUF II, and CURBA: a family of spatially explicit urban growth and land-use policy simulation models. In: R.K. Brail and R.E. Klosterman (eds.) *Planning Support Systems: Integrating Geogrphic Information Systems, Models, and Visualization Tools*, ESRI Press, Redlands, pp. 157-200.

Lautso, K., K. Spiekermann, M. Wegener, I. Sheppard, P. Steadman, A. Martino, R. Domingo, and S. Gayda (2004) PROPOLIS: Planning and Research of Policies for Land Use and Transport for Increasing Urban Sustainability, LT Consultants, Helsinki.

Levy, S. (1992) *Artificial Life: The Quest for a New Creation*, Second ed., Penguin Books, London.

Li, K., Z. Peng, J. Crittenden, S. Guhathakurta, A. Sawhney, H. Fernando, P. McCartney, N. Grimm, H. Joshi, G. Konjevod, Y. Choi, S. Winter, D. Gerrity, R. Kahhat, Y. Chen, B. Allenby, and P.M. Torrens (2007) Development of a framework for quantifying the environmental impacts of urban development and construction practices. *Environmental Science and Technology*, 41 (14), pp. 5130-5136.

Louviere, J.J., D.A. Hensher, and J.D. Swatt (2000) *Stated Choice Methods: Analysis and Application*, Cambridge University Press, Cambridge.

McHugh, K., and P. Gober (1992) Short-term dynamics of the U.S. interstate migration system, 1980-1988. *Growth and Change*, 23 (4), pp. 428-445.

Moore, S.K., and A. Gardner (2007) Megacities by the numbers, *IEEE Spectrum*, June, pp. 24-25.

Nagel, K., and M. Rickert (2001) Parallel implementation of the TRANSIMS micro-simulation, *Parallel Computing*, 27 (12), pp. 1611-1639.

Nagel, K., and M. Schreckenberg (1992) A cellular automaton model for freeway traffic. *Journal de Physique I*, 2 (12), pp. 2221-2229.

Nara, A., and P.M. Torrens (2007) Spatial and temporal analysis of pedestrian egress behavior and efficiency. In: H. Samet, C. Shahabi and M. Schneider (eds.) *Association of Computing Machinery (ACM) Advances in Geographic Information Systems*, Association of Computing Machinery, New York, pp. 284-287.

Negroponte, N. (1995) *Being Digital*, Coronet, London.

O'Sullivan, D. (2002) Toward micro-scale spatial modeling of gentrification, *Journal of Geographical Systems*, 4 (3), pp. 251-274.

Openshaw, S. (1983) *The Modifiable Areal Unit Problem*, CATMOG 38, GeoBooks, Norwich.

Orcutt, G., S. Caldwell, and R. Wertheimer (1976) *Policy Exploration through Microanalytic Simulation*, The Urban Institute, Washington, D.C.

Orcutt, G., M. Greenberger, J. Korbel, and A. Rivlin (1961) *Microanalysis of Socioeconomic Systems: a Simulation Study*, Harper & Row, New York.

Parker, D.C., S.M. Manson, M.A. Janssen, M.J. Hoffmann, and P. Deadman (2003) Multi-Agent System models for the simulation of land-use and land-cover change: a review, *Annals of the Association of American Geographers*, 93 (2), pp. 314-337.

Portugali, J. (2000) *Self-Organization and the City*, Springer-Verlag, Berlin.

Portugali, J. (ed.) (2006) *Complex Artificial Environments*, Springer-Verlag, Berlin.

Putman, S.H. (1983) *Integrated Urban Models*, Pion, London.

Rozenfeld, H.D., D. Rybski, J.S. Andrade Jr., M. Batty, H.E. Stanley and H.A. Makse (2008) Laws of population growth, *Proceedings of the National Academy of Sciences*, 105 (48), pp. 18702-18707.

Sassen, S. (1991) *The Global City: New York, London, Tokyo*, Princeton University Press, Princeton.

Torrens, P.M. (2005) Geosimulation approaches to traffic modeling. In: P. Stopher, K. Button, K. Haynes and D. Hensher (eds.) *Transport Geography and Spatial Systems*, Pergamon, London, pp. 549-565.

Torrens, P.M. (2006) Remote sensing as dataware for human settlement simulation, In: M. Ridd and J.D. Hipple (eds.) *Remote Sensing of Human Settlements*,

American Society of Photogrammetry and Remote Sensing, Bethesda, pp. 693-699.

Torrens, P.M., and A. Nara (2007) Modeling gentrification dynamics: A hybrid appraoch, *Computers, Environment and Urban Systems*, 31 (3), pp. 337-361.

Torrens, P.M., and D. O'Sullivan. 2001. Cellular automata and urban simulation: where do we go from here? *Environment and Planning B*, 28 (2), pp. 163-168.

Waddell, P.A. (2002) Urbansim: modeling urban development for land use, transportation and environmental planning, *Journal of the American Planning Association*, 68 (3), pp. 297-314.

Wegener, M. (1994a) Operational urban models: state of the art, *Journal of the American Planning Association*, 60, pp. 17-29.

Wegener, M. (1994b) Urban/regional models and planning cultures: lessons from cross-national modelling project, *Environment and Planning B*, 21 (5), pp. 629-641.

Wegener, M. (2000) A new ISGLUTI: the SPARTACUS and PROPOLIS Projects. Paper read at Second Oregon Symposium on Integrated Land Use and Transport Models, at Portland (US).

Wolfram, S. (2002) *A New Kind of Science*, Wolfram Media Inc., Champaign.

Zipf, G. (1949) *Human Behavior and the Principle of Last Effort*, Addison-Wesley, Cambridge.

Index

For Product Safety Concerns and Information please contact our
EU representative GPSR@taylorandfrancis.com Taylor & Francis
Verlag GmbH, Kaufingerstraße 24, 80331 München, Germany